PSYCHOTHERAPY WITH SEX-ABUSE VICTIMS:
TRUE, FALSE, AND HYSTERICAL

PSYCHOTHERAPY WITH SEX-ABUSE VICTIMS:
TRUE, FALSE, AND HYSTERICAL

Richard A. Gardner, M.D.

Clinical Professor of Child Psychiatry
Columbia University
College of Physicians and Surgeons

Creative Therapeutics, Inc.
155 County Road, Cresskill, New Jersey 07626-0317

© 1996 by Creative Therapeutics, Inc.

All rights reserved.
No part of this book may be reproduced in any form
or by any means without permission in writing from the publisher.

Library of Congress Cataloging-in-Publication Data

Gardner, Richard A.
    Psychotherapy with sex-abuse victims : true, false, and hysterical
/ Richard A. Gardner.
      p.   cm.
   Includes bibliographical references and index.
   ISBN 0-933812-41-8 (alk. paper)
    1. Sexually abused children. 2. Child sexual abuse–
–Investigation. 3. False memory syndrome. I. Title.
   [DNLM: 1. Child Abuse, Sexual. 2. Child Reactive Disorders–
–psychology. 3. Psychotherapy—methods. 4. Interview,
Psychological—methods.   WA 320 G228p 1996]
RJ507.S49G37   1996
618.92'858223—dc20
DNLM/DLC
for Library of Congress   95-47817
                                                                                  CIP

PRINTED IN THE UNITED STATES OF AMERICA
10 9 8 7 6 5 4 3 2 1

Don't stand there, do something!
> *Traditional advice to helpers*

Don't do something, stand there!
> *Advice given to author and fellow medical students to emphasize the importance of making a diagnosis before embarking upon a treatment program*

Other Books by Richard A. Gardner, M.D.

The Boys and Girls Book About Divorce
Therapeutic Communication with Children:
The Mutual Storytelling Technique
Dr. Gardner's Stories About the Real World, Volume I
Dr. Gardner's Stories About the Real World, Volume II
Dr. Gardner's Fairy Tales for Today's Children
Understanding Children: A Parents Guide to Child Rearing
MBD: The Family Book About Minimal Brain Dysfunction
Psychotherapeutic Approaches to the Resistant Child
Psychotherapy with Children of Divorce
Dr. Gardner's Modern Fairy Tales
The Parents Book About Divorce
The Boys and Girls Book About One-Parent Families
The Objective Diagnosis of Minimal Brain Dysfunction
Dorothy and the Lizard of Oz
Dr. Gardner's Fables for Our Times
The Boys and Girls Book About Stepfamilies
Family Evaluation in Child Custody Litigation
Separation Anxiety Disorder: Psychodynamics and Psychotherapy
Child Custody Litigation: A Guide for Parents
  and Mental Health Professionals
The Psychotherapeutic Techniques of Richard A. Gardner
Hyperactivity, The So-Called Attention-Deficit Disorder,
  and the Group of MBD Syndromes
The Parental Alienation Syndrome and the Differentiation
  Between Fabricated and Genuine Child Sex Abuse
Psychotherapy with Adolescents
Family Evaluation in Child Custody Mediation, Arbitration,
  and Litigation
The Girls and Boys Book About Good and Bad Behavior
Sex Abuse Hysteria: Salem Witch Trials Revisited
The Parents Book About Divorce—Second Edition
The Psychotherapeutic Techniques of Richard A. Gardner—Revised
The Parental Alienation Syndrome: A Guide
  for Mental Health and Legal Professionals
Self-Esteem Problems of Children: Psychodynamics
  and Psychotherapy
Conduct Disorders of Childhood: Psychodynamics and Psychotherapy
Protocols for the Sex-Abuse Evaluation
Psychotherapy with Children Alleging Sexual Abuse
Testifying in Court: A Guide for Mental Health Professionals
Psychogenic Learning Disabilities: Psychodynamics
  and Psychotherapy
Dream Analysis in Psychotherapy

CONTENTS

	ACKNOWLEDGMENTS	xv
	INTRODUCTION	xvii
1	**A THEORY ABOUT THE VARIETY OF HUMAN SEXUAL BEHAVIOR**	1
	INTRODUCTION	1
	GENDER DIFFERENCES IN MATING PATTERNS	2
	DAWKINS'S THEORY OF GENE SURVIVAL AND TRANSMISSION	7
	THE APPLICATION OF DAWKINS'S THEORY TO HUMAN SEXUAL VARIETY	12
	Introduction	12
	The Paraphilias of *DSM-IV*	17
	Further Comments on the Paraphilias	30
	Sexual Dysfunctions	31
	SHOULD HOMOSEXUALITY BE LISTED AMONG THE PARAPHILIAS?	31
	THE CAUSES OF MALE PEDOPHILIA	37
	Social and Cultural Factors	37
	The Imprinting Factor	40
	Identification with the Aggressor	43
	The Domination Factor	44
	Passivity and Impaired Self-Assertion	44
	Similarities Between Children and Females	45
	Compensation for Feelings of Emotional Deprivation	46
	Narcissism	47

	Masochistic Factors	49
	Recent Social and Cultural Factors Operative in the United States	49
	Concluding Comments on Pedophilia	50
	CONCLUDING COMMENTS	50
2	**THE EMBEDMENT-IN-THE-BRAIN-CIRCUITRY PHENOMENON (EBCP)**	55
	INTRODUCTION	55
	IMPRINTING	57
	Imprinting in Lower Animals	57
	The Question of Imprinting in Human Beings	58
	"PSYCHOPATHOLOGY OF EVERYDAY LIFE"	60
	THE POSTTRAUMATIC STRESS DISORDER	64
	DISSOCIATION	65
	OBSESSIVE-COMPULSIVE DISORDER	67
	SEXUAL FANTASIES AND PROCLIVITIES	70
	One's "First True Love"	71
	Homosexuality	72
	Pedophilia	73
	Residua of Childhood Sexual Experiences in Adult Sexual Life	76
	False Sex-Abuse Accusers	78
	THERAPEUTIC IMPLICATIONS	79
3	**TREATMENT OF CHILDREN WHO HAVE ACTUALLY BEEN SEXUALLY ABUSED**	83
	INTRODUCTION	83
	SOME COMMENTS ABOUT THERAPISTS WHO TREAT SEXUALLY ABUSED CHILDREN	86
	THE CLINICAL PICTURE OF THE SEXUALLY ABUSED CHILD	90
	Introduction	90
	The So-Called Child Sex-Abuse Syndrome	90
	The Sexual Abuse Accommodation Syndrome	91
	Some of the Symptoms *Sometimes* Seen in Sexually Abused Children	92
	Symptoms Unrelated to the Posttraumatic Stress Disorder	94
	PRELIMINARY CONSIDERATIONS REGARDING THE TREATMENT OF SEXUALLY ABUSED CHILDREN	95
	The Child May Not Need Treatment	95
	Psychotherapeutic Work with the Whole Family	96
	Meaningful Protection from Further Sexual Abuse	97

Group Therapeutic Experiences	98
The Effects of Litigation on the Child's Treatment	99
TECHNICAL ASPECTS OF THE TREATMENT OF SEXUALLY ABUSED CHILDREN	**100**
Introduction	100
The Home Videocassette Recorder	101
Desensitization Play	101
PSYCHOTHERAPEUTIC APPROACHES TO SOME OF THE COMMON SYMPTOMS OF SEXUALLY ABUSED CHILDREN	**102**
Hypersexualization	102
Regression	105
Guilt	106
Self-Esteem Problems	111
Loss of Trust	113
Anger Problems	114
Depression	117
Fears, Tension, Anxiety, and Derivative Symptoms	119
Confusion	122
School Problems	124
Pathological Compliance	126
Pseudomaturity	128
Problems in the Relationship with the Father	130
Problems in the Relationship with the Mother	132
Retraction (Recantation)	133
TREATMENT OF THE MOTHER	**135**
Dealing with the Mother's Hysteria	135
Discouraging Litigation	135
Group Therapy	136
Improving the Mother-Child Relationship	136
Dealing with Passivity and Inadequacy	140
Dealing with Sexual Problems	142
TREATMENT OF THE FATHER	**144**
Introduction	144
Group Therapy	146
Improving the Father-Child Relationship	147
Enhancing Self-Esteem	149
Dealing with Guilt (or Lack of It)	151
Dealing with Isolation	153
Dealing with the Exaggerated Need to Control and/or Dominate	154
Dealing with the Excessively Moralistic Pedophile	156
Dealing with Impulsivity	157

Dealing with Homosexuality	158
Dealing with Substance Abuse	160
Counseling with the Mother and Father Together	162
Progesterone Acetate	163
CLINICAL EXAMPLES	164
The Girl and the Bus Driver	164
The Boy and the Pediatrician	168
The Boy and the Virgins	172
The Girl at the Wedding	176
Sex Abuse and Parental Neglect	192

4 PROGRAMMING NONABUSED CHILDREN TO BELIEVE THEY WERE SEXUALLY ABUSED — 211

INTRODUCTION	211
CHILDREN'S MEMORY AND SUGGESTIBILITY	213
Introduction	213
Studies on Children's Memory and Suggestibility	214
PSYCHODYNAMIC FACTORS OPERATIVE IN CHILDREN'S FALSE ACCUSATIONS OF SEX ABUSE	227
Introduction	227
Ingratiation to Adult Authorities	227
The Keeping-up-with-the-Joneses Phenomenon	228
Enhanced Attention and Notoriety	230
Release of Hostility	231
Infectiousness of Emotions	233
Reactions to Normal Childhood Sexuality	233
Psychodynamic Factors Conducive to the Development of a Parental Alienation Syndrome	238
Shame over Recanting	243
Concluding Comments	244
WHO ARE THESE PEOPLE?	245
WHAT DO THEY DO?	247
"Children Never Lie"	247
The Blank-Screen Principle	248
Leading Stimuli, Leading Gestures, and Leading Questions	248
Early Interview Maneuvers	273
Ascertaining Whether the Child Can Differentiate Between the Truth and a Lie	276
"The Truth" as Code-Term for Sex Abuse	279
Repeating-the-Same-Question Technique	280
Belief in the Preposterous	281

Rationalizing as Credible the Incredible	283
Selective Ignoring of the Impossible	284
The Utilization of the Yes/No Question	285
The So-called Indicators of Sex Abuse	287
"The Sex-Abuse Syndrome"	295
The Child Sexual Abuse Accommodation Syndrome	295
Conditioning Techniques	302
The So-called Disclosure	303
More Direct Coercive Techniques	304
The "Inappropriate-Affect" Maneuver	305
The "Dissociation" Maneuver	307
Rehearsal	311
The Use of In-Vogue Jargon	312
Involvement with Parents, the Accused, and the Accuser	313
WHY DO THESE PEOPLE FUNCTION IN THIS WAY?	316
Impaired Educational Background	316
The Education of Validators	324
The "Holier-than-Thou" Phenomenon	326
The Erosion of Values	328
Sex-Abuse Victims as Validators	330
The Sexually Inhibited	333
Sadists	333
Paranoids	334
Overzealous Feminists	335
The Hypocrites	335
The Young and/or Naive	336
Monetary Gain	337
Other Personality Factors	338
CONCLUDING COMMENTS	340
5 WHAT DOES A PROGRAMMED CHILD LOOK LIKE?	**343**
INTRODUCTION	343
OTHER FOLLOW-UP STUDIES	346
LEGAL PROCESS/"THERAPY" TRAUMA	347
FACTORS THAT COMMONLY CONTRIBUTE TO AND INTENSIFY LEGAL PROCESS/"THERAPY" TRAUMA	349
Removal of the Child and/or Alleged Abuser	349
The Systematic Erosion and Destruction of the Parent-Child Bond	350
"Empowering" Techniques	350
Courtroom Interrogations	351

	COMMON SYMPTOMS CHARACTERISTICALLY SEEN IN PROGRAMMED CHILDREN	352
	Impaired Reality Testing	353
	Fears	355
	Antisocial Behavior and Psychopathy	357
	Interest in "Mysteries"	360
	The Inculcation of Sexual Psychopathology	361
	The Creation of "Professional Victims"	362
6	**TREATMENT WITH NONABUSED CHILDREN PROGRAMMED TO BELIEVE THEY WERE SEXUALLY ABUSED**	**365**
	BEFORE THE TREATMENT CAN BEGIN...	365
	REMOVAL OF THE CHILD FROM TREATMENT WITH AN OVERZEALOUS THERAPIST	365
	CESSATION OF LITIGATION	366
	SERIOUS CONSIDERATION OF THE NO-TREATMENT OPTION	368
	THE CRUCIAL ROLE OF THERAPY WITH ALL FAMILY MEMBERS	370
	INDIVIDUAL WORK WITH THE CHILD	370
	The Importance of the Blank-Screen Approach	370
	Dealing with Cognitive Distortions	371
	Dealing with Emotional Problems	376
	DEALING WITH THE FALSELY ACCUSING MOTHER	380
	DEALING WITH THE FALSELY ACCUSED FATHER	382
	FAMILY WORK	383
	CLINICAL EXAMPLE	384
7	**CHILD SEX ABUSE AND HYSTERIA 1890s (AUSTRIA)/1990s (U.S.)**	**419**
	HYSTERIA AS A HISTORICAL PHENOMENON	421
	Group and Mass Hysteria	421
	Individual Hysteria	427
	MY CONCEPT OF HYSTERIA	429
	Introduction	429
	Manifestations and Psychodynamics	430
	Concluding Comments on My Concept of Hysteria	438

8	**TREATMENT OF CHILDREN WITH SEX-ABUSE HYSTERIA**	**439**
	INTRODUCTION	439
	HYSTERICAL REACTIONS TO ISOLATED, SUPERFICIAL SEXUAL OVERTURES	440
	HYSTERICAL REACTIONS TO NORMAL SEXUAL URGES	454
	EPILOGUE: WHERE DO WE GO FROM HERE?	**507**
	REFERENCES	**511**
	AUTHOR INDEX	**525**
	SUBJECT INDEX	**529**

ACKNOWLEDGMENTS

I deeply appreciate the dedication of my assistants, Donna La Tourette, Carol Gibbon, and Linda Gould for typing the manuscript of this book in its various renditions. I am especially grateful to Donna La Tourette for her additional contributions to its production. I am also indebted to Danny Angel for his invaluable contributions to the book's production. I am grateful to Muriel Jorgensen for her diligence in copyediting the manuscript. She provided useful suggestions and, at the same time, exhibited respect for my wishes regarding style and format. I am grateful to Susan Cox for her diligence in the proofreading of the page proofs.

Most importantly, I wish to express my gratitude to the hundreds of parents and children involved in sex-abuse accusations from whom I have learned most of what is contained in this book. Some of the children were indeed victims of bona fide sexual abuse. Others were programmed to promulgate false accusations of sex abuse. These children were victims of another kind—victims of those who promulgated in them the belief that they were abused when they were not. Some of the adults who were accused were indeed bona fide perpetrators. Others were falsely accused, and they too can justifiably be considered victims—victims of those who falsely accused them of crimes they did not commit. Some of the accusers did indeed have good reason to believe that their children were sexually abused. Others, unfortunately, were promulgating false accusations. In some situations the false accusation was a conscious and deliberate fabrication. In other situations it was a delusion. Some accusations began as a fabrication and then progressed to become a delusion. In most cases, whether the accusation was true or false, the accusers were influenced, to varying degrees, by overzealous and/or incompetent sex-abuse "experts," so ubiquitous in recent years is the sex-abuse hysteria that we have been witnessing since the early 1980s. Many of these accusers, then, were also victims—victims of the zealots/incompetents. But even these "experts" have made a contribution to this book because my reviews of their audiotapes, videotapes, and reports have provided me with invaluable information for this book's preparation and my understanding of hysteria.

INTRODUCTION

From the late 1950s, when I began my psychiatric training, to the early 1980s, I occasionally saw patients who had been sexually abused. I saw children whose sexual abuse occurred in the context of physical and emotional abuse. There was not one case in which there was any doubt in my mind that the allegations were valid. I saw women who had been raped. I also saw women who had been sexually abused as children, most often by close family members. Typically, these women's attempts to disclose the abuse were met with denial and even punitive reactions by other family members. Interestingly, I found that the residual effects on many of these women ranged from no residual symptoms at all to psychosis, and all points in between. I saw men who had been sexually abused as children. Again, the effects of these childhood abuses in later life ranged from none at all to psychosis, and all points in between. All of these patients had credible stories, and even today I do not believe that any one of them ever provided me with a false description of what had taken place.

I use the word *false* here to refer to any sex-abuse allegation that has no basis in reality. False allegations range from those that are conscious fabrications to those that are delusional. Actually, there is a continuum from the fabrication to the delusion. Furthermore, what may begin as a fabrication may end up as a delusion, especially if the accusing party (whether alleged child victim or adult accuser) is convinced by overzealous examiners (especially "validators") that abuse took place when there is absolutely no evidence for such.

In the early 1980s I began witnessing a new phenomenon, namely, false sex-abuse accusations in the context of child-custody disputes. Such accusations were particularly attractive to an angry parent because they served as an effective vengeance and/or exclusionary maneuver. During that period, when I brought this observation to the attention of mental health professionals, I was met with outcries of rage and derision. "Children never lie when they make accusations of sex abuse." I was angrily told that I should "believe the children." I was also warned that public statements of this kind were dangerous because my comments would be used by defense attorneys to exonerate known and well-documented sex-abuse perpetrators. My response was this:

> I am 100 percent convinced that *some* of these accusations are false. I am not denying that bona fide sex abuse is widespread and an ancient tradition. What I am saying is that *some* of these accusations are false and that we are seeing more of them in association with the burgeoning child-custody disputes. Rather than deny this reality, we have to develop criteria for differentiating between true and false sex-abuse accusations. It is only in this way that we will be able to deal properly with those who have indeed sexually abused children and to protect those who have been falsely accused. Obviously, this is an extremely important area to which we should devote ourselves.

During the next few years, in spite of significant antagonism, I continued to devote my efforts to the development of differentiating criteria.

In the mid-1980s I began getting invitations to do evaluations in the context of nursery school and day-care center sex-abuse accusations. At first, I refused such invitations because of my insistence that I be allowed to see all three parties, namely, the accuser, the accused, and the alleged child victims. Although strict adherence to this position worked well in civil cases, especially divorce disputes, it was practically impossible to achieve this goal in criminal cases (down which track the nursery school cases were going). Accordingly, after reading and learning about what I considered to be terrible miscarriages of justice—with the incarceration of individuals whom I considered to be innocent—I decided to take a less stringent position and agreed to involve myself in such cases. However, I still made every attempt to evaluate all three parties. In addition, I made no promises beforehand that I would serve as an advocate of the inviting party, but only agreed to do so if, after interviewing available parties and reviewing documents, I concluded that I could do so with conviction. In most cases, this could be accomplished in a few hours. In some cases it took longer, and in one case it was not until after 40 hours of interviewing and reviewing materials that I came to the conclusion that I could support the position of the inviting party.

I was surprised to find (although in retrospect I should not have been) that, with rare exception, the same criteria that proved useful in custody cases were also applicable (with minor alterations) to the nursery school situation. What was originally surprising became less so when I came to appreciate that the very same "validators" were involved, and they were using the same misguided techniques for "validation." One of the differences between the two situations, i.e., the divorce and nursery school situation, related to the hysteria element. Hysteria increases the likelihood of cross-fertilization, in which one child's scenario—via transmission through parents, therapists, validators, police investigators, and so on—is likely to end up in another child's sex-abuse accusation. My earlier experiences with differentiating between true and false sex-abuse accusations resulted in the publication in 1987 of my book, *The Parental Alienation Syndrome and the Differentiation Between Fabricated and Genuine Child Sex Abuse*.

In the early 1990s I became involved with situations in which adult women were accusing their fathers of having sexually abused them in childhood, especially early childhood. The experiences I had in the divorce and nursery school situations proved useful for developing criteria for differentiating between true and false accusations in this category. Furthermore, the things I learned from these women (some of whom were genuinely abused as children) provided me with information useful in the refinement of my differentiating criteria for children. Also, during recent years I have become involved with increasing frequency in other categories of child sexual abuse, e.g., abuse by clergymen, scoutmasters, school bus drivers, teachers, tutors, babysitters, and caretakers in hospitals and residential treatment centers. Again, some of these were true and some of these were clearly false. A common phenomenon was one in which the alleged perpetrator had indeed sexually abused one or more children and then others, who had never been abused, joined the bona fide accusers in order to reap the benefits of the lawsuits against the perpetrator. I refer to this as the *belated jumping-on-the-bandwagon phenomenon*, the primary purpose of which is the acquisition of money. The evaluation of these people, as well, provided me with important data for the development of my differentiating criteria.

Throughout the years, most of the sex-abuse cases in which I was involved were in the context of lawsuits. Such involvement necessitated my providing testimony in courtrooms. This was an extremely valuable experience, especially because it required me to be as objective as possible with regard to my differentiating criteria. The fields of psychiatry and psychology are generally viewed as among the least objective of all the scientific disciplines (and justifiably so). Presenting one's findings at a case conference in a hospital or clinic setting is very different from making presentations on the witness stand, especially under cross-examination by a dubious and even hostile attorney. It is in this setting that it behooves the evaluator to be extremely stringent with regard to differentiating fact from fantasy. These courtroom experiences were extremely valuable in the development of my differentiating criteria. My 1992 book, *True and False Accusations of Child Sex Abuse*, represented the culmination of my efforts to develop differentiating criteria up to that point. The book also included material on the treatment of both categories of victims, those who were truly abused and those who were programmed to believe they were abused when they were not.

My 1995 volume, *Protocols for the Sex-Abuse Evaluation*, represents an expansion of my differentiating criteria in what is an ever-growing field. This book is an elaboration of the therapeutic material in the 1992 volume. It includes as well material on a third category of children, those who have not been abused, and have not been programmed to believe they were abused, but have been deleteriously affected by the sex-abuse hysteria that we have been witnessing since the early 1980s. This book, then, should well be viewed as a companion volume to the *Protocols* book (especially because both are spinoffs and elaborations of the 1992 volume). However, the reader does well to view the *Protocols* book as Volume I and this book as Volume II in that it is necessary to properly differentiate between true and false sex-abuse accusations before one even considers embarking upon a treatment program.

INTRODUCTION xxi

We in medicine reflexively follow the principle that diagnosis must precede treatment. Unfortunately, many mental health professionals involved in sex-abuse cases, both at the evaluative and therapeutic levels, do not strictly adhere to this important principle. Those who embark upon "treatment" of sexually abused children, often by court order, without questioning for one second the validity of the diagnosis, are causing significant psychological damage to countless children. This book, then, is *only* for those who have made a proper diagnosis.

The book begins with the presentation of my views on the variety of human sexual behavior. Particular emphasis is given to the paraphilias, of which pedophilia is an example. I then present, for the first time in print, the concept that I refer to as the *embedment-in-the-brain-circuitry phenomenon (EBCP)*. I am not claiming to be describing anything really new here; I am only claiming that this concept has not been given the attention it deserves by mental health professionals. An understanding of this concept is extremely important if one is to treat the kinds of psychopathology that may result from sexual abuse, especially in situations where the diagnosis of posttraumatic stress disorder is warranted.

Next, I focus on the techniques I have found useful for the treatment of children who have actually been sexually abused. I not only utilize traditional approaches here but describe as well some of my own that I have developed since I entered the field of psychiatry in the late 1950s. I then describe in detail the processes by which nonabused children can be programmed to believe that they were abused. Such programming is per se a form of child abuse, especially because the sexual element is central to such programming. The brainwashing experience shares with bona fide sex abuse the risk of the child's subsequently developing sexual problems in adolescence and even later in adult life. In the next chapter I describe what a programmed child looks like. Again, my vast experience in lawsuits has provided me with the data to make some important statements about such children. I then describe the treatment of programmed children, with particular emphasis on the risks of the misuse of therapy, a misuse that may actually entrench the child's belief that abuses occurred when there were none.

There is no question that, since the early 1980s, we have been witnessing a wave of sex-abuse hysteria that can justifiably be considered an epidemic. In the course of this hysteria I have learned much about the psychodynamics of hysteria at every level: individual, group, and mass. The manifestations and psychodynamics of hysteria that I describe here go beyond the relatively narrow explanations provided by Sigmund Freud a century ago. A chapter is devoted to these observations, with some data on "early returns" from follow-up studies of children subjected to the hysteria.

Last, I focus on the treatment of children suffering with sex-abuse hysteria. Some of the children in this category have not really been molested, but overtures have convinced them and their families that they were. Other children in this category have had normal sexual thoughts and feelings that, in an atmosphere of hysteria, have come to be labeled pathological manifestations. Accordingly, they may consider themselves loathsome and perverted for entertaining sexual thoughts and feelings that are entirely within the normal range.

As has always been true in my previous publications, the focus is on direct techniques based on psychodynamic understanding of the processes underlying the patient's disorder. Furthermore, clinical vignettes (often verbatim) are provided in order that the reader can learn exactly what I do and why I have utilized a particular therapeutic maneuver.

# ONE

A THEORY ABOUT THE VARIETY OF HUMAN SEXUAL BEHAVIOR

Be fruitful and multiply and fill the earth. . . .

Genesis 1:28

I have found the missing link between the higher ape and civilized man: It is we.

Konrad Lorenz

The lion is generally considered to be king of the beasts. This is not true. Human beings are more properly designated king of the beasts.

Richard A. Gardner

Man becomes civilized when his animal impulses are tamed, subdued, and transcended by his social nature.

Abba Eban

INTRODUCTION

I have never felt completely comfortable with the terms *natural* and *unnatural* when they apply to human sexual behavior. In a sense, one could say that any form of sexual behavior that can be exhibited by a human being must be considered natural in that it is part of the human repertoire. Generally, the term *unnatural* has been applied to those variations that have been considered unacceptable to a particular social group. In a somewhat grandiose fashion, each society considers natural (in compliance with God's [or nature's] purposes) those particular forms of sexual behavior that are widely practiced and accepted and deems unnatural (at variance with nature's [or God's] purposes) those forms of sexual behavior that are atypical and/or by social convention "wrong," "bad," "disgusting," etc. Sometimes sexual behavior that does not lead directly to procreation has been subsumed under the unnatural rubric. As I hope to demonstrate, even those forms of sexual behavior that do not lead immediately to procreation may still serve nature's purposes and thereby do not warrant being excluded from the list of the so-called natural forms of human sexual behavior.

GENDER DIFFERENCES IN MATING PATTERNS

In order to appreciate fully the theory I propose, it is important first for the reader to understand my concept of the origins of gender differences in mating patterns. I believe that there is genetic programming for women to be more passive, coy, and seductive, and for men to be more assertive and aggressive in the courtship process. Although social influences certainly play a role in such patterns, I believe that the genetic factors are the more important. I recognize that this is an unpopular thing to say at a time when male/female egalitarianism is very much in vogue, yet I believe that I have good arguments to support my position. No one can deny that up until the 20th century men were primarily the hunters and fighters (protectors and warriors). Women, in contrast, were primarily the child rearers. I am making no judgments here regarding whether this was good or bad or right or wrong, only that it was the reality of the world up until the 20th century for the vast majority of people. Of course, there were and still are occasional societies in which this principle did not hold, but these exceptions do not in any way detract from the validity of my generalization. (There is always an island in the South Pacific that will demonstrate any point—in support or in refutation.)

It is reasonable to state that those men who were genetically strong in the hunting/fighting functions were more likely to survive than those who were not. Those who were weaker in these functions were less likely to have food for survival and/or the capacity to protect themselves from their enemies. Consequently, their genes were not as likely to have been passed down to subsequent generations. Also, those who were weak in these areas were less likely to attract women, in that women tend (then and now) to consider as desirable mates men who exhibit a high capacity for providing food, clothing, and shelter for themselves and their children and high capability for protecting the potential family from enemies. This is another reason why the genes of men who were weaker in these areas were less likely to survive in the genetic pool. Similarly, women who were stronger in the child-rearing realm were more likely to be viewed by men as desirable mates and their genes, as well, were more likely to be passed down to their progeny. The greater aggressiveness of the male was not, I believe, simply confined to hunting and warring; it was also utilized in the service of mating. More aggressive men, then, were more likely to be successful in acquiring mates. And so we have another factor favoring the selective survival of more aggressive men.

Youngsters today of both sexes carry within them these genetic programs. Although we human beings are less beholden to our instinctual drives than are lower animals, we are still affected by them. A bird, for example, during the mating season, may have no choice other than to go through the mating ritual of its species. We humans have procreative urges, but we are not required to mate in any particular season, nor are we compelled to follow rigid mating patterns of behavior. However, this does not preclude our being programmed for such mating patterns with the resultant pressure for their expression.

There is another factor operative in what I believe to be gender differences in mating patterns. This relates more directly to reproductive capacity. It is a principle of Darwin's theory of natural selection and survival of the fittest that each species generally produces far more offspring than can possibly survive. Those particular forms that are most adaptable to the environment in which they have been born are more likely to survive and perpetuate the species. Those that are less adaptable to the particular environment will generally die off. This is the central element in the Darwinian theory. If one examines this further, one finds that there are two factors operative here: *quantity* and *quality*.

With regard to *quantity*, the number of offspring produced is far greater than can possibly survive in a particular environment. With regard to *quality*, the quality or type of offspring that is most adaptable to the specific environment is most likely to survive. Accordingly, one must consider both quantity control and quality control. Furthermore, with regard to quantity, the general thrust is for an organism to produce as many offspring as possible, i.e., the greatest quantity possible—most often far more than can possibly survive. With regard to quality, the general thrust is to select, narrow down, and restrict survival to those forms that will adapt best to and survive in a particular environment. The two processes of control, then, are antagonistic. The quantity control factors work toward the survival of the greatest number of offspring. The quality control factors operate to reduce and/or limit the number of offspring that will survive. Those forms that ultimately survive represent a balance of these two antagonistic forces.

In many forms of life, one of the sexes is specifically designated to provide quantity and the other quality. Often, it is not difficult to determine which sex is primarily involved in which function. This is certainly the case for the human being. Men are clearly the ones involved in producing the greatest quantity of offspring, whereas women are the quality controllers. If one were to simply view human beings as baby factories, whose main purpose is to perpetuate the species (a not absurd view), and if one were to ask which sex is more likely to produce a high quantity of offspring, it is clearly the male. If a man were to devote his whole life to the procreative process, it is reasonable that he could father one to two babies a day, providing, of course, he was provided with women who were in the fertile stages of their menstrual cycles. Accordingly, the male is reasonably capable of fathering 500 babies a year. We know that we could start using males for this purpose at about the age of 13 or 14, but we do not know the upper age at which such utilization would no longer be possible. There are men in their 90s who have viable sperm. But let us, more practically, end the male's fecund period at 75, because most men do not live beyond that age, and older men are less likely to father 500 babies a year. Accordingly, it is reasonable to say that the average male has a fecund period of 60 years. Fathering 500 babies a year for 60 years would enable a man to father 30,000 babies. (I am not addressing myself here to practicality, only to the issue of maximum possible reproductive capacity if one were to make use of men and women for this purpose.) In contrast, if a woman were to devote her fecund life to being a baby factory, she could reasonably reproduce one child a year from age 13 to about 56 (the oldest "proven" age at which a woman has been demonstrated to give birth). This will give her approximately 40 to 45 babies. Accordingly, it is reasonable to conclude that the male is very much the one capable of producing the greatest quantity of offspring.

What I have said thus far relates purely to biological capacity. The next question relates to the actual behavior of each of the sexes regarding the procreative process. The *potential* for being a reproductive factory is there, but in practice individuals generally have other things to do with their lives besides fornicating and propagating. And probably the most important of these other functions is child rearing. If no concern is given to the protection of the young, then babies will not survive and there would be no point to devoting one's life solely to manufacturing them. This brings us to quality control, the second step necessary for species survival. It is here that women have played the more formidable role. In order to carry out this function, it behooved women to be more circumspect with regard to mate selection. Those who were so were more likely to be chosen as mates and more likely to pass their stronger child-rearing genes down to their offspring.

Men, I believe, have been programmed to crave sex indiscriminately with large numbers of women, i.e., to impregnate as many women as possible. From the roving bands of men in perpetual heat, a woman must select the man who is most likely to remain around after impregnation and serve the role of food gatherer and protector. In order to realize this important goal, women do best to be less impulsive with regard to gratifying indiscriminately their sexual urges—in order that they assess more objectively a potential father of their children. Women who were slower in sexual arousal were more likely to be judicious in mate selection and, therefore, more likely to survive. They were more likely to select men who would provide food, clothing, shelter, and protection. Accordingly, I believe that the *average* (I did not say all) present-day woman is slower in sexual arousal than the average man. Once aroused, however, a woman is more likely to attempt to maintain an ongoing relationship with her mate. In contrast, the average (I did not say all) present-day man is quicker in sexual arousal than the average woman. Once gratified, he is less likely to be desirous of maintaining the relationship. I believe that most women would confirm this statement in that the most common complaint single women have is that men are less interested in "commitment" (the in-vogue word for this phenomenon) than women are.

The old saying is applicable here: "Men are looking for girls, and girls are looking for husbands." Men are on the prowl. They are not only out hunting for prey to kill and eat, but hunting for female prey to serve as sexual companions. I believe that if one were able to create a printout of the average adult male's sexual thoughts throughout the course of the day, they would be formidable, especially printouts associated with day-to-day experiences in which the individual is not fully preoccupied with work. I believe that one would find that sexual thoughts would be associated with a large percentage of the man's encounters with females from the teen period and upward. These would involve some kind of sexual encounter. Secretaries, stewardesses, nurses, receptionists, waitresses, and the wide variety of other women that men inevitably encounter in the course of their day become stimuli for such sexual fantasies. Some confirmation of this "fantasy" of mine is to be found in Shanor's study (1978) in which he found that men between ages 12 and 40 think of sex an average of six times per hour. But the distribution over age ranges is not even. Between ages 12 and 19 the frequency is *20 times per hour* (approximately once every three minutes). Things slow down somewhat after that, so that between ages 30 and 39 it is four times an hour.

In short, most men are extremely promiscuous (if not physically, at least psychologically). The main difference between those to whom this label is applied and those to whom it is not relates to the degree to which the man overtly tries to gain gratification for these urges. From the roving bands of men in heat, the woman must reject the large majority or else she will find herself impregnated by a man who has already gone on to the next cave or condo. She is much more concerned with relationships. I believe that this phenomenon is one of the factors involved in women having greater orgastic capacity than men. Although the woman is more likely to need caressing and tender overtures to be aroused, once aroused she is more likely to remain aroused longer. The male reaches his orgasm and immediately goes into a refractory period ("zonks out," falls asleep). The majority of women have the potential for multiple orgasms. This, I believe, serves the purpose of enhancing procreative capacity. Her multiple orgasmic capacity enables her to "hang in there longer" and ensure that the male who is slow to ejaculation is likely to be sustained in his interest and involvement.

Last, I believe that what I have said here is one explanation for the fact that men are generally more likely to be sexually excited by visual stimuli, whereas women are more likely to respond to tactile stimuli. The roving bands of men spot their prey at a distance and can get excited merely at the sight of a woman. This is in part a derivative of their hunting functions and it also serves to enlarge the potential population of sexual partners. This phenomenon also serves to explain the fact that it is the men who stand around peering lasciviously at women, whereas it is far less common for women to do this as obviously and exhibitionistically as men. Many years ago there was a popular song entitled, "Standing on the Corner, Watching the Girls Go By." And it was not women who were standing on the corner, but men! Women, in contrast, need caressing, tenderness, and reassurance that the man will remain around for supplying food and protection for herself and her children. This is one of the reasons why men are more likely than women to be sexually aroused by visual pornographic material.

DAWKINS'S THEORY OF GENE SURVIVAL AND TRANSMISSION

I wish to emphasize that the theory proposed below may very well have been thought of previously by others. Although I have not either read about or heard about it from others, it rests heavily on one proposed by Dawkins (1976). In fact, one might consider my theory an extension of Dawkins's applied specifically to the various forms of human sexual behavior. This theory, as is true of Dawkins's, rests heavily on Darwinian theory—especially the concepts of natural selection and the survival of the fittest. My theory, like Darwin's and Dawkins's, does not address itself to such ultimate questions as those related to the forces (entities, God, etc.) that created these principles and might very well be involved in their implementation. It does not concern itself with how atoms and molecules got to be here, nor does it concern itself with the origin of the principles that govern their interactions, both simple and complex. Rather, it concerns itself with the implementation of these entities and principles and the physical manifestations of their interactions—from the simplest to the most complex levels, from the earliest to the most recent. Nor does it concern itself with the ultimate purpose(s) of all of this, considering the fact, for example, that all life on earth will ultimately perish and that all forms of sexual behavior—both the "natural" and the "unnatural" varieties—will no longer serve any purpose, at least on this sphere, which we call Earth.

It is well to begin at the beginning, which (as Maria in *The Sound of Music* said) is a very good place to start. This sphere, like many other celestial bodies in the universe, began with its complement of elements, among which were to be found carbon, hydrogen, oxygen, and nitrogen—the fundamental building blocks of life. Under the influence of environmental conditions (influences emanating from the sun as well as those in the intervening space), simple molecules formed by atomic union. Most important for the purposes of this discussion were water (H_2O), carbon dioxide (CO_2), methane (CH_4), and ammonia (NH_4). After exposure to ultraviolet light and electric currents (probably related to primordial lightning), more complex molecules were formed—especially amino acids, the building blocks of proteins. Scientists have been able to reproduce such transformations in a flask by subjecting the aforementioned simple molecules to ultraviolet radiation and electric currents. Laboratory simulations of the chemical conditions on Earth before the beginning of life (as we know it) have produced organic substances such as purines and pyrimidines, which are the building blocks of the genetic molecule DNA. One can readily envision, then, a primordial "soup" in which the simpler and more complex molecules floated. The main method of production (or "creation") of the more complex molecules was the exposure of the simpler ones to the environmental conditions conducive to their formation. This method of formation of complex molecules depends upon the influence of external forces and, presumably, without their presence there would be no creation of the more complex forms.

The next step was the one in which certain molecules exhibited the capacity to reproduce themselves, a process that Dawkins (and others certainly) refer to as *replication*. The method that appears to have been most successful (in fact, it appears to be the only one on Earth that we know of) was the one utilized by the DNA molecule. This molecule, made of segments that are to be found floating around in the primordial soup, reproduces itself by absorbing onto itself from the surrounding mixture those particular building blocks that correspond to those already strung on its helical (spiral) chain. The original molecule serves as a mold or template. It attracts corresponding smaller molecules from the soup, each free molecule attached to its own kind on the original model. Ultimately, this results in the formation of a clone of the original DNA molecule. In the next step the two strands separate: *Voilà*, reproduction! Each new strand then becomes a model for further replications, thus producing geometric growth in population.

If all the DNA molecules were cloned from the *original*, there would be few errors. However, with this kind of geometric progression, in which each *new* DNA molecule becomes a template for the reproduction of itself, there is a greater likelihood that "errors" or alternative forms may result, each of which may also survive. We have, then, the introduction of *variety*. Some of the forms have a greater likelihood of survival than others, depending upon the internal stability of the molecular chain.

Ultimately, the free-floating smaller molecules in the primordial soup become scarce as they are utilized ("eaten up") in the formation of the larger DNA molecules. Some sort of competition, then, arises as the DNA molecules compete with one another for the ever scarcer simpler radicals. The next step, according to Dawkins, was basically the phase of cannibalism. Because of the scarcity of free-floating smaller molecules in the primordial mixture, the DNA strands began breaking off segments of their neighbors in order to be provided with "food" for the replication process. The next step—and this was an extremely important one—was the formation by DNA molecules of protective coatings, a physical wall that served as a kind of armor that protected the DNA strand from being cannibalized by its neighbors. These entities (DNA strands, surrounded by protective shells) are basically what we are talking about when we discuss viruses. The protective shell is necessary for the survival of the internal core of DNA. Dawkins refers to this entity as a "survival machine," and this is the term he uses for all subsequent living forms, the function of which is to provide a housing for DNA molecules, especially with regard to their protection.

The next step involved the union of different types of DNA strands (which I will now call genes) to combine their efforts in the service of enhancing the likelihood of survival of the protective coating. Each could serve a different function and thereby increase the likelihood of survival over those with less complex mechanisms for adaptation in the primordial soup. We see, then, the formation of the simplest cells in which the genes are clustered together in the nucleus and the survival wall being represented by the surrounding cytoplasm and cell membrane (for animals) or cell wall (for plants). Obviously, we are describing here one-cell animals and plants. The next step in the evolution of living forms was the bringing together of individual cells into colonies. Here different parts of the colonies could perform different functions—enhancing, thereby, the chances of the DNA surviving. Those cells that were able to live together as colonies, each performing separate but unifying functions, would be at an advantage over those cells that floated about in isolation.

Dawkins then continues:

> A major branch of survival machines, now called plants, started to use sunlight directly themselves to build up complex molecules from simple ones, reenacting at much higher speed the synthetic processes of the original soup. Another branch, now known as animals, "discovered" how to exploit the chemical labors of the plants, either by eating them, or by eating other animals. Both main branches of survival machines evolved more and more ingenious tricks to increase their efficiency in their various ways of life, and new ways of life were continually being opened up. Subbranches and sub-subbranches of survival machines evolved more and more ingenious tricks to increase their efficiency in their various ways of life, and new ways of life were continually being opened up. Subbranches and sub-subbranches evolved, each one excelling in a particular special-

ized way of making a living: in the sea, on the ground, in the air, underground, up trees, inside other living bodies. This subbranching has given rise to the immense diversity of animals and plants which so impresses us today. (p. 133)

Every survival machine, then, can be viewed as a colony of DNA strands surrounded by successive layers of protective mechanisms. Its purpose, however, is not simply to protect the genes from cannibalistic destruction, but to provide mechanisms for the reproduction of the DNA strands. Here we are talking about the methods by which the particular form of life enables the DNA strands to pass down from generation to generation, each time ridding itself of the housing in which it temporarily resides and providing itself with a new and temporary survival machine. Dawkins states:

> Another aspect of the particulateness [sic] of the gene is that it does not grow senile; it is no more likely to die when it is a million years old than when it is only a hundred. It leaps from body to body down the generations, manipulating body after body in its own way and for its own ends, abandoning a succession of mortal bodies before they sink in senility and death. (p. 133)

Although the gene itself is in a constant state of equilibrium with surrounding atoms and smaller molecules available for its replication, its basic structure and appearance are always the same. It can be compared to a skyscraper that periodically and continually replaces its bricks with others provided externally. Both new bricks and old bricks are essentially immutable in that atoms do not "grow old."

Each cell has the information necessary to re-create the whole survival machine. Furthermore, it has the power to influence various parts of the survival machine, especially with regard to the protective mechanisms necessary for survival and the mechanisms necessary for reproduction, i.e., transmission of DNA replications from one temporary survival machine to the next and so on down the generations.

The millions of different kinds of plants and animals are testimony to the wide variety of survival machines that have evolved over eons. All the cells, all the tissues, all the organ systems, and all the plants and animals that incorporate DNA molecules share in common this one principle: the protection of the genes and their transmission to the next generation. The human brain is but one example of such a system. It is one of the latest and most complex examples of a part of the housing machine that serves to protect the DNA as well as enhance the likelihood that it will be transmitted to the next generation. Although designed by and in a sense controlled by DNA, it has a certain autonomy of its own in that it exerts some influence over the automatic control that genes have over the survival machine, especially with regard to the time of expression of the protective and procreative forces. For example, lower animals appear to have no choice but to perform their specific mating patterns at prescribed times and places. We have the ability to suppress somewhat these cravings, but still we are often obsessed with and sometimes even enslaved by them.

As mentioned, Dawkins's theory could be considered the inevitable extension of the Darwinian theory. The major determinant as to whether a particular survival machine will indeed perform its functions is related to the efficiency of the mechanisms devised for protecting DNA and enabling it to transmit its replications down to form the next generation of survival machines. There is selective survival of those machines that are most likely to perform these functions in a particular environment, and there is selective failure to survive (and thereby destruction of DNA) of those housings that are less capable of survival in the particular environment in which the genes find themselves.

THE APPLICATION OF DAWKINS'S THEORY TO HUMAN SEXUAL VARIETY

Introduction

There is no problem applying Dawkins's theory to adult heterosexuality. We can view the human body as the survival machine for our sperm and ova, which are basically housings for our DNA. The sexual act is the step by which DNA replications are transmitted to the next generation of housing machines (our children). All the things we do in our lives can be viewed as steps toward this end. Just about every activity of our daily lives, throughout the 24-hour cycle, can be viewed either as an attempt to protect and preserve our DNA or as a step toward its transmission. Every meal we eat, every breath we breathe, every penny we earn, every bit of work we do, can easily be considered part of this grand plan. When we sleep, we are recouping and saving up our energy for the next day's round of survival activities. Other activities, which might initially be considered exceptions to this principle, on careful inquiry may very well be found to be related.

Everything we learn has the potential to serve us in the enhancement of our capacity to survive, either immediately or remotely. Purely scientific inquiry, although initially unrelated, might ultimately find practical applications that serve human survival. What about art and music? Here again they might not initially appear to fit this scheme. However, art is used to enhance female and male attractiveness (in clothing styles and cosmetics), and the artist, in part, wants to impress the lady of his choosing. ("You must come up to my place sometime and view my etchings.") Or, the artist may wish to earn money, again in the service of providing himself (herself) with food, clothing, and shelter—which all serve in the survival of the temporary machine in which his (her) genes are housed. Music can serve similar purposes, for both musician ("She will certainly love me when she hears the music I have created") and the listener ("I love him for the music he has created"). Pleasure, like sleep, is necessary for us when we need to recoup our energies. When I try to think of examples of human endeavor that might not fit under this grand rubric, I am unable to do so. Accordingly, I will stop giving examples that support the theory and go on to a discussion of the forms of sexuality that do not initially appear to do so.

With regard to the atypical forms of sexuality, those that may not initially appear to serve the purposes of procreation, I wish to state at the outset that each of these has, I believe, a genetic and an environmental contribution. The genetic contribution may very well be the result of "gene error," the kind of error that brings about a form of atypical sexual behavior. If a mutation is not of survival value, it is not maintained for long in the genetic pool, and the housing in which it is incorporated is destroyed by natural processes (both the housing and the DNA within decompose and in many cases are "eaten by worms"). The kinds of atypical human sexuality discussed here are not in this category because the human beings who exhibit these variations have definitely survived. One does well, also, to view the combination of genetic predisposition and environmental influences as varying. Accordingly, in some individuals the genetic loading may be very high, so much so that little if any environmental contribution may be necessary for the quality to become exhibited. In others the genetic contribution may be low or even nonexistent; however, environmental (especially family) influences are so formidable that the sexual pattern becomes the primary mode of expression for that individual. One does well, also, to view these two examples as the extremes and to view all individuals who exhibit the particular sexual behavior as lying at some point in between these two extremes.

I am in full agreement with Freud's (1905) theory of the "polymorphous perversity" of the human infant. The infant will exhibit every form of sexual activity known to humanity. Each society suppresses those forms that it considers unacceptable and allows expression of those that it considers acceptable. However, residua of the unacceptable variations often press for expression and may be found in various aspects of adult sexuality, both typical and atypical. All, however, are *natural* if one is defining the word as a sexual form of behavior that exists in human beings, regardless of the particular society's attitude toward that specific mode of sexual expression.

There is good reason to believe that most, if not all, children have the capacity to reach orgasm at the time they are born. (I am not recommending that we conduct any scientific studies to prove or disprove what I have just said.) Certainly, infants in the first few months of life may rub their genitals as they lie on their abdomens, and their associated facial expressions are strongly suggestive of orgasm. There are people who claim that they cannot remember a time when they did not masturbate. And not all of these people have been sexually abused as children. Like all things in this world, there is a bell-shaped curve, and the age at which people first experienced orgasms also lies on a bell-shaped curve. Most people would date their first orgasm to the pubertal period, but there are many who can go much further back. It is reasonable to assume that there is a small fraction of the population who, without any particular external stimulation (sexual molestation or otherwise), normally experienced such high sexual urges in early infancy and found relief through masturbation. (Recently, sonograms have shown baby boys holding their penises in utero.) This, too, is "natural" and this, too, lends credibility to my belief that children are not only naturally sexual but that they may be the initiators of sexual activities. Although these overtures do not initially serve procreative purposes, they ultimately do because the child who is sexually active at an early age is more likely to be sexually active in adolescence and thereby provide his (her) DNA for the next generation of survival machines.

The common childhood game, aptly called "You-Show-Me-Yours-and-I'll-Show-You-Mine" is yet another example of childhood sexuality. Certainly curiosity plays a role in such games. Parents begin teaching children, at a very early age, that certain parts of their bodies are to be strictly covered up and not to be exposed to others. Such prohibitions, of course, engender enormous curiosity, a curiosity that can be satisfied by voyeuristic/exhibitionistic games. But the games often go beyond the visual level and frequently involve touching, even with sexual excitation and intent. We see here the influence of DNA already at work. I suspect (but I am not certain) that boys are more interested than girls in these games because of the aforementioned high visual loading to their sexual interest.

Some further examples. A common practice for little children is to play with their genitals, even to the point of orgasm. Furthermore, it is also common for little girls to smell their fingers after such play and they will often find the odors enjoyable to sniff. Commonly, they will be taught by their mothers that such a practice is unacceptable. Boys smelling their fingers after touching their genitals is less common, but it is the analogous practice. This olfactory gratification is much more highly developed in lower animals for whom scents play an important role in sexual activity. Residua of this phenomenon certainly exist in humans. We recognize it as "normal" for men to enjoy cunnilingus, a part of which pleasure comes from the olfactory stimulation that such activity provides. And women as well (again, in many segments of our society) enjoy immensely this activity. Here again, we see the residua of a childhood form of sexuality expressing itself in adult heterosexual behavior.

Moreover, orgastic pleasure may very well be the most intense known to the human being. The craving for this gratification is extremely strong and, of course, is the driving force behind the procreative process. The reduction of high sexual tensions and the craving for orgastic gratification is DNA's main method of bringing about reproductive activity and, by extension, its passage to the next generation.

Another example. All agree that infants enjoy immensely the breastfeeding experience. Mothers in our society are encouraged to express deep involvement in this practice and are permitted to speak about how psychologically and physically pleasurable breastfeeding is. However, few women will speak openly about orgasmic gratifications associated with the breastfeeding of their infants. It is more acceptable to describe breast stimulation pleasure as part of adult heterosexual activities. It is also acceptable to describe physical pleasure in association with a male partner's breastsucking as part of foreplay. I am not claiming that most women experience orgasms when breastfeeding their infants. I am only claiming that some women do, and that more probably would if they were to overcome the social inhibitions against such gratification.

Women's potential for pleasurable response to breastfeeding serves important biological purposes. It increases the likelihood that she will breastfeed her child, increasing thereby the likelihood that her progeny will survive. It increases the likelihood that she will want to breastfeed subsequent babies, either her own or those of others. It produces in general a heightened level of sexuality, keeps the sexual juices flowing (not only the milk), and increases thereby the likelihood that she will have heterosexual sexual encounters. It increases also the likelihood that she will enjoy her breasts being sucked by adult males during heterosexual encounters. Her pleasure, which is a residuum of both her own breastfeeding in her own infancy (via projective identification with her breastfeeding infant) and the pleasurable sensation provided by the sucking of her breasts, serves to enhance the man's pleasure (via her excitation). Residua of the man's breastfeeding gratifications in his own infancy also contribute to the pleasure experienced by the man when engaging in breastsucking during the heterosexual encounter. These residua, one in each of the parties, enhance the likelihood of copulation and thereby the passage of DNA to the next generation.

It is important for the reader to appreciate that I am making no value judgments on any of these sexual activities. Each society does this and our society is no exception. My purpose here is to present a valueless explanation of these activities. The reader should recognize that I, as a product of the society in which I live, have my biases, prejudices, etc., but these are irrelevant to my presentation here.

The Paraphilias of *DSM-IV*

At this point I address myself to each of the forms of atypical sexuality described in *DSM-IV* (American Psychiatric Association, 1994). These are the forms of atypical sexuality that are considered by the *DSM-IV* nomenclature committee to be manifestations of psychiatric disorder. It would be a naive reader who is not appreciative of the fact that there is not a disorder here that was not considered the norm in some other society at some time and some place. This list, therefore, represents the beliefs and even the biases of the nomenclature committee. One confirmation of this point is the fact that homosexuality was considered a bona fide disease in *DSM-II* (American Psychiatric Association, 1968) and the previous *DSM* (American Psychiatric Association, 1952) (which has no number and is now retrospectively sometimes referred to as *DSM-I*). The authors of *DSM-III* (American Psychiatric Association, 1980) took the position that if a person is homosexual and wishes to change his (her) orientation, then the individual might then be considered to be suffering with a psychiatric disorder and might thereby be justifiably treated for such. To the best of my knowledge, this is the first time in the history of medicine that patients themselves make the decision regarding whether or not they have a disease. The homosexual person, then, who was seeking treatment under *DSM-III* criteria had to "enter through the back door" to qualify for a diagnosis under this system.

In *DSM-III-R* (American Psychiatric Association, 1987) homosexuality was not even listed as a disorder per se. However, if one looked up the word in the index, there was a reference under the very last of the list of sexual disorders: "302.90 Sexual Disorder Not Otherwise Specified." Here were listed sexual disorders that were not to be found listed in any of the previous categories. Three examples were given, the third of which was: "Persistent and marked distress about one's sexual orientation." It was only here that a homosexual person— who was distressed about his (her) sexual orientation—could justifiably be considered to have a disorder. It is of interest that the just-quoted lines are the very last ones in the section on sexual disorders. One cannot even find the word *homosexuality* in the index of *DSM-IV*. However, the category "Sexual Disorder Not Otherwise Specified" is still to be found, as is the requirement that the individual experience "persistent and marked distress about sexual orientation." Accordingly, to carry the back door analogy further, the homosexual person who is entering treatment under the *DSM-IV* provisions must creep through a little trap door that is cut into the back door (the kind that a dog might use). Enough said about the vicissitudes, biases, and unreliability of *DSM-IV.*

A paraphilia is defined as a form of sexual expression that is atypical or "off the beaten track." It is a sexual activity that is found on a parallel track (thus the prefix "para" [Greek: besides]) but is still a form of lovemaking (thus the word "philia" [Greek: love]). *DSM-IV* considers the paraphilias to be "sexual disorders," which is a more recent term for "diseases." I will address myself to each of the paraphilias, in the order in which they appear in *DSM-IV,* and comment on each, especially with regard to the aforementioned theory. I will give particular attention to the issue of the "justification" for such atypical sexuality, especially with regard to the question of its function and purpose if it does not serve the immediate aims of reproduction and species survival. *DSM-IV* emphasizes that the paraphilic label is justified when the activity is the primary or one of the primary sources of sexual gratification of the individual. The label might not be justified if it exhibits itself only rarely and is a minor part of the person's sexual repertoire. The committee uses the six-month cut-off point for a duration that justifies the diagnosis but, I am certain, recognizes this as somewhat artificial.

Furthermore (and this is important), for each of the paraphilias there is included an important diagnostic proviso: "The fantasies, sexual urges, or behaviors cause clinically significant distress or impairment in social, occupational, or other important areas of functioning." Accordingly, if an individual does not suffer distress or impairment in functioning, then the presence of this form of sexuality would not be considered a manifestation of a disorder. This too presents us with problems, especially from the point of view of a therapist who may be consulted regarding treatment. These are strange kinds of disorders indeed. They are disorders if the person suffers distress or functional impairment, but not disorders if these sequelae are not present. The issue of distress presents problems for the consultant who is being asked to make a decision as to whether a disease is present. Most would agree that a person who is not distressed by homicidal thoughts is still suffering with a disease. Here again we have the problem attendant to the patients making the decision regarding whether or not a disease is present. I mention these problems because they lend confirmation to my belief that the nomenclature committee has had significant difficulties with the paraphilias, especially with regard to the question of whether they are indeed diseases (or, to use the committee's euphemism, "disorders"). Such ambivalence is relevant to my theory about the etiology and purposes of the paraphilias.

The main point I will be making with regard to each of the paraphilias is that they do, in a way, serve the purposes of species survival and are therefore part of the natural repertoire of humanity. They serve this end by their ability to enhance the general level of sexual excitation in society and thereby increase the likelihood that people will involve themselves in activities that are more directly contributory to the reproductive (and, by extension, species survival) process. I recognize that for each of the paraphilias there are a wide variety of psychodynamic mechanisms that may be operative in producing the behavior. However, it is not my purpose here to discuss these in detail. Rather, I will only discuss those psychodynamic aspects that pertain to the aforementioned theory.

Exhibitionism is defined as:

> Over a period of at least six months, recurrent intense sexual urges and sexually arousing fantasies, sexual urges, or behaviors involving the exposure of one's genitals to an unsuspecting stranger.

Although exhibitionism is primarily a male characteristic in its "raw form" (that is, as exhibited by "flashers"), it certainly does exist in women in a more subtle form. Seductive gesturing, provocative dancing (not necessarily by burlesque queens and go-go girls), and hysterical behavior generally involve some degree of exhibitionistic sexuality. Accordingly, when one considers these common forms of female exhibitionism, the behavior is much more common among women than men.

Although the flasher may wish to startle and gain a sense of power and importance, much more than arouse sexuality, there is still that element operative in this clearly sexual act. And although the exhibitionistic woman may want flattery and attention, more than sexual gratification, the activity is still a form of foreplay and may very well lead to more overt sexual activity. For both sexes the behavior is designed (at least in part) to produce sexual hormone secretions into the bloodstream of the observer and enhance thereby the likelihood of sexual activity and reproduction.

We have strict rules in our society regarding when and where one can be sexually exhibitionistic. Furthermore, exhibitionism is more acceptable in women than in men. The principle is well demonstrated by the old observation: If a woman undresses in front of a window, a man in the street looking at her may be charged with being a voyeur ("peeping Tom"). In contrast, if a man undresses in front of a window and a woman in the street looks at him, he may be charged with exhibitionism (indecent exposure). These differences in social attitude notwithstanding, exhibitionism has survival value in that it provides visual stimuli that result in the kinds of hormonal secretions that may result in procreation.

Fetishism is defined as:

> Over a period of at least six months, recurrent, intense sexually arousing fantasies, sexual urges, or behaviors involving the use of nonliving objects (e.g., female undergarments).
>
> The fetish objects are not limited to articles of female clothing used in cross-dressing (as in Transvestic Fetishism) or devices designed for the purpose of tactile genital stimulation (e.g., vibrator).

Here, too, the same principles hold. Often the object may be used in place of "the real thing" when sexual encounters with humans are not available. The fetishistic object may become the symbol of the human sexual object and bring about the same degree of excitation. Fetishism not only serves the purposes of sexual release, but also lessens the likelihood of the sexual organs "drying up." The practice thereby keeps sexual cravings alive and increases the possibility of reproduction. Even the person who may fear sexual encounters at that point, and uses the fetishistic object as a substitute, is keeping himself (herself) in the pool of sexually craving individuals and thereby increases the likelihood of species survival. Here again we see the principle that some of the fetishistic objects (such as vibrators) are borrowed from normal sexuality but are considered pathological when they are used in preference to the interpersonal type of sexual experience. I trust that the *DSM-IV* committee did not consider the use of vibrators per se to warrant the diagnosis of fetishism and recognized that their use as a "sexual aid" is "normal."

Frotteurism is defined as:

> Over a period of at least six months, recurrent, intense sexually arousing fantasies, sexual urges, or behaviors involving touching and rubbing against a nonconsenting person.

These are the people who rub up against others in subways, buses, elevators, and other crowded places. They are people who are considered to be getting their "cheap thrills" in a socially unacceptable way. Once again, men are far more likely than women to be involved in this paraphilia and, once again, they are most often the initiators. This is consistent with what I have said previously about the male being genetically programmed to play the more aggressive role in mating pattern rituals. Women, however, cannot be considered to be completely free of this disorder. As every frotteur knows, there are a certain fraction of women who will not immediately recoil and withdraw, and thereby get across the message that they have no wish to participate in this activity. In spite of "rejections" by the majority of women, there are still enough around who will go along with the secret game and thereby gratify their own frotteuristic cravings without suffering social stigma.

I once interviewed a man who was a frotteur and who claimed that approximately 25 percent of all the women against whom he rubbed his penis responded. Most allowed him to masturbate himself against them, using the motions of the moving vehicle as the cover-up for their own more active participation in the process. Some even rubbed their vulvas against him, thereby gratifying themselves as well. On a few occasions the activity ultimately resulted in their going off together for a sexual encounter. Frotteurism also serves survival purposes. It increases the general level of sexual excitation and thereby increases the likelihood of sexual reproduction.

Pedophilia is defined as:

> Over a period of at least six months, recurrent, intense sexually arousing fantasies, sexual urges, or behaviors involving sexual activity with a prepubescent child or children (generally age 13 years or younger).
> The person is at least 16 years old and at least 5 years older than the child or children in Criterion A.
> **Note:** Do not include an individual in late adolescence involved in an ongoing sexual relationship with a 12- or 13-year-old.

It is obvious that the *DSM-IV* nomenclature committee had great difficulty with this definition. The requirement that the person be "at least 16 years old" presents problems if a 15-1/2-year-old boy has a sexual experience with a five-year-old girl. Although he has satisfied the requirement that there be at least a five-year age difference between the two, he would not be considered a pedophile by this definition. In contrast, the jury before whom he is tried for this act (and for which he might get life imprisonment) might very well consider him to be a pedophile. Actually, the *DSM-IV* committee is not alone here. There is no good definition of pedophilia.

Whatever definition one uses, there are loopholes. One must make exceptions, such as the *DSM-IV* committee did. If one uses the dictionary definition, i.e., a sexual act between an adult and a child, one is immediately confronted with the problem of what constitutes an adult and what constitutes a child. Does adulthood begin at puberty, at 16, at 18, at 21? All of these ages (and others) have been used at various times by different societies (and even within the same society) as a cutoff point for the definition of adulthood. If one wants to use puberty as the point of differentiation, there are still difficulties. If a *post*pubertal 13-year-old has sex with a *pre*pubertal 11-year-old, is that pedophilia? Most would say no. If a *post*pubertal 11-year-old has a sexual activity with a *pre*pubertal 13-year-old, is the younger one then considered to have sexually molested the older? Again, we see that there is no end to the complications with any of these definitions. All of them attempt to define the parameters of unacceptability (whether psychiatric/diagnostic or legal/criminal) and all fail. Basically, the definition of a pedophile for a psychiatrist is what the nomenclature committee of the American Psychiatric Association considers to be a pedophile for that particular edition of DSM. And the definition by the legal system is not only the one recorded in the statutes of the particular state (and there is great variation), but what the jury decides is pedophilia on the basis of the evidence presented at the accused's trial.

Pertinent to my theory here is that pedophilia also serves procreative purposes. Obviously, it does not serve such purposes on the immediate level in that children cannot become pregnant, nor can they make others pregnant. However, the child who is drawn into sexual encounters at an early age is likely to become highly sexualized and crave sexual experiences during the prepubertal years. Such a "charged up child" is more likely to become sexually active after puberty and more likely, therefore, to transmit his (her) genes to his (her) progeny at an early age. (I will have more to say about pedophilia in the next chapter because of its central importance to this book.)

The younger the survival machine at the time sexual urges appear, the longer will be the span of procreative capacity, and the greater the likelihood the individual will create more survival machines in the next generation. The ideal then—from DNA's point of view—is for the child to be sexually active very early, to have a highly sexualized childhood, and begin procreating at the time of puberty. This increases the likelihood that more survival machines will be produced for the next generation.

Sexual Masochism is defined as:

> Over a period of at least six months, recurrent, intense sexually arousing fantasies, sexual urges, or behaviors involving the act (real, not simulated) of being humiliated, beaten, bound, or otherwise made to suffer.

Sexual Sadism Sexual masochism is intrinsically associated with sexual sadism. In fact, the two together are often referred to as "sadomasochism." Accordingly, I will present here the *DSM-III-R* definition of sexual sadism and then discuss both together.

> Over a period of at least six months, recurrent, intense sexually arousing fantasies, sexual urges, or behaviors involving acts (real, not simulated) in which the psychological or physical suffering (including humiliation) of the victim is sexually exciting to the person.

Clearly, sadomasochism allows gratification of hostile impulses for the sadist. The motives for the masochist are not so obvious, but from the psychological point of view the individual is gaining some kind of gratification. For some people masochism serves to alleviate their guilt over sexual expression. Punishment can assuage guilt. Some people need the punishment afterward, and some before, and some at the time of the guilt-provoking act. Masochism may relate to identification with masochistic models, the feeling that this is the best that one can get, that more benevolent relationships would not be possible, and other psychological mechanisms that are beyond my purposes here.

Sadomasochism may also serve survival value. Sexual courtship patterns in our society have often been compared to a "hunt." The man, traditionally more assertive (as mentioned, I believe there is some genetic programming here, although environmental factors are certainly operative), seeks his "prey," the woman. If successful, he may consider himself to have made a "conquest." The woman's role is generally one of passivity, coyness, and seductivity in which she lures the man to approach her and make sexual advances. (Here, again, I believe genetic factors play an important role, although environmental ones are certainly operative.) Domination enters here and, in extreme cases, rape. Accordingly, we see a continuum from the normal courting pattern of female passivity and male aggressivity to the more aggressive forms of sexual approach and domination, with a culmination in rape—the extreme example of domination. Every point on this continuum increases the likelihood that the woman will engage in a sexual act and thereby procreate.

Our society encourages women to be seductive, coy, and enticing and encourages men to be forthright, aggressive, and pursuing. The more coercive elements enter into the male's behavior, the greater the likelihood our society will condemn him. The theme of pursuit and domination, however, is widespread. Many years ago I read a survey in which women were asked about their favorite movie scene. The one that took first place was a scene from "Gone with the Wind" in which Rhett Butler, overcome with sexual passion and frustration, grabs Scarlett O'Hara, picks her up in his arms, and runs up the stairs into the house and presumably up to the bedroom. We accept this as normal, but we will not accept more coercive elements. This reflects society's repression of the animal within us: a male animal who has the potential for rape and a female animal who, by merely a small extension of permissible attitudes, may become masochistic—thereby gaining sexual pleasure from being beaten, bound, and otherwise made to suffer.

It may very well be that for some masochistic women, allowing themselves to be beaten into submission is the price they are willing to pay for gaining the gratification of receiving the sperm. When less aggressive partners are not available, partners who don't take the domination factor too far, they will accept sperm from a sadistic individual, rather than not have any sperm at all.

I wish to emphasize again that I am placing no value judgments on these behaviors at this point. Rather, I am trying to explain the purposes of certain forms of sexual behavior that are found in every society and are dealt with differently by each society, and even by the same society at different times. Their ubiquity is a testament to the fact that they are natural, i.e., they are part of the human repertoire. We should not let our revulsion and condemnation of them interfere with our ability to understand them. In fact, it is through such understanding that we will be in a better position to decide how to deal with these atypical forms, from both the psychiatric and legal points of view.

Transvestic Fetishism is defined as:

> Over a period of at least six months, in a heterosexual male, recurrent, intense sexually arousing fantasies, sexual urges, or behaviors involving cross-dressing.

The comments I have made previously about fetishism are applicable to transvestic fetishism. In this form of fetishism the objects that cause the sexual arousal are not only female clothing, but cross-dressing, a particular utilization of female clothing. As noted in the *DSM-IV* definition, these men are usually heterosexual, are sexually aroused by wearing female attire, and are thereby more likely to engage in heterosexual activities—increasing thereby the likelihood of procreation and the passage of their DNA down to the next generation.

It may come as a surprise to the reader to learn that the majority of transvestic fetishists are heterosexual. Certainly, there are homosexuals who wear female clothing as a way of attracting men for sexual purposes. However, these people are different from transvestic fetishists. Female impersonators are probably the most well known examples of transvestic fetishists. With rare exception, they are heterosexual. It is of interest that *DSM-IV* does not have a pathological category for homosexual men who cross-dress, but only for heterosexual men. This is just one of the paradoxes that is to be found in *DSM-IV*, a paradox that derives from the diagnostic problems attendant to removing homosexuality from the list of psychiatric disorders.

Voyeurism is defined as:

> Over a period of at least six months, recurrent, intense sexually arousing fantasies, sexual urges, or behaviors involving the act of observing an unsuspecting person who is naked, in the process of disrobing, or engaging in sexual activity.

Voyeurism is much more common in men than women. This is not surprising considering the fact that men are much more likely to be excited by visual stimuli than women. It is the men who stand on the street corner jeering at the women passersby. It is men who are much more likely to be sexually excited by pin-up magazines, pornographic movies, and videotapes. As mentioned, I believe this phenomenon relates to the hunter qualities that are much more apparent in males than females. Traditionally, men were the hunters and protectors. It was they who went out to kill animal prey and thereby provide food for their families. Hunting involves (and even requires) visual surveillance. And hunting animals for food is akin to hunting women for procreative purposes. Similar male attributes are involved. It is reasonable to speculate that there was a selective survival of men who were visually powerful and who were good at hunting prey for food and females for procreative purposes. We see here, then, an overlap with the domination element applicable to the understanding of sadomasochism.

DSM-IV then lists seven other paraphilias that are not only less common, but would probably be considered more pathological than the aforementioned. They all share in common, however, their capacity to enhance sexual arousal and to increase, thereby, the likelihood of heterosexual experience.

Telephone Scatologia (Obscene Telephone Call)

The man who involves himself in telephone scatologia (lewdness) is clearly trying to arouse a woman. (It is rare for women to involve themselves in this kind of activity.) Although one may claim that the man so involved is basically afraid of women (and this is probably the case), he is still getting sexually aroused by the practice, even though the arousal often culminates only in masturbation. There are occasions, I am certain, in which the woman is receptive and the overture ultimately results in heterosexual activities and therefore procreation. But even when this aim is not realized (certainly more often the case), the man is still keeping his "juices flowing" and preventing them from drying up, thereby not removing himself from the heterosexual potentially procreative scene.

Necrophilia (Corpses)

One could argue that necrophilia cannot possibly serve procreative purposes. I am in agreement that a dead woman is not going to conceive a child, but this is only half the story. Obviously, a man who must resort to having sexual intercourse with dead bodies has serious difficulties in his ability to relate well to live human beings. (Again, it is not my purpose here to discuss in detail the many possible psychological factors that are operative in each of these activities.) Yet, the necrophiliac is still keeping his juices flowing and increasing, thereby, the likelihood of heterosexual involvement with a person who is more likely to conceive. (For obvious reasons, necrophilia is almost unknown in females.)

Partialism (Exclusive Focus on Part of Body)

The factors operative here are very similar to those operative in fetishism. For reasons peculiar to that individual, a particular part of the body becomes the primary source of gratification. However, this symptom is not a strange one, considering the fact that all men (and to a lesser extent women) engage in it to a certain degree. Men's breast fetish is probably the most well-known example of this phenomenon. This preoccupation stems, in part, from the fact that the breast is the first "sex object" of the male (at least according to Freudian theory), and we live in a society in which breasts are indeed worshiped. Furthermore, we enhance the importance of these organs (which are basically bags of fatty tissue intermingled with milk ducts) by social conditioning. Covering them, under most circumstances, makes them more alluring, seductive, and therefore objects of interest. There are men who are similarly turned on by buttocks and vulvas. Interestingly, women are far less likely to exhibit this symptom. This is in part related to their being less aroused by visual stimuli and more aroused by caressing, cuddling, and activities that ensure the kind of depth relationship that will increase the likelihood that the lover will stay around after conception and provide protection for themselves and their children.

Zoophilia (Animals)

Zoophilia, which is reputed to be a traditional activity among farm boys, also provides for sexual release when other outlets are not available. It may also be attractive to those who may have fears and inhibitions regarding overtures to females, who are more unpredictable than animals regarding their sexual receptivity. Contrary to popular opinion, zoophilics do not generally have sexual intercourse with animals; rather, their main source of gratification comes from hugging, cuddling, and talking—in a manner similar to a child with a pet. The zoophilia then represents a fixation at an earlier level of psychosexual development. Although progeny are obviously not possible from such relationships, the individuals engaged in such zoophilic activities might be considered to be getting practice for more appropriate partners for the purposes of evolutionary survival.

Coprophilia (Feces)

Once again, one cannot ascribe immediate survival value to this practice. It is a derivative, however, of the polymorphous perversity of children who have to learn that touching their fecal eliminations and then putting their fingers (or feces) in their mouths is generally viewed in our society as a disgusting practice. Here, too, this enhancement of sexual stimulation increases the likelihood that the individual may turn to others and thereby contribute to the procreative process.

To the best of my knowledge, most people who are involved in coprophilic activities do not actually engage in putting feces into their mouths (although a small percentage do); rather, the activities most often involve defecating on one's "loved one." The term also refers to the partner who becomes sexually excited by being defecated upon. Coprophilia is also related to sadomasochism in that the person who enjoys this activity is often involved in a sadomasochistic act with domination/submission and hostile release ("shitting on someone").

Klismaphilia (Enemas)

Anal stimulation in itself can provide sexual pleasure. Most people enjoy the gratification of a "good bowel movement," although it is not considered proper to talk about it in most circles. Furthermore, deep anal penetration, beyond the anus, can produce stimulation of the pubococcygeal muscles, which play an active role in orgasm for both males and females. Hence, an enema can be to the anus what the vibrator is to the vagina. Association of the enema with mothers who provided them in childhood may play a role in producing this type of sexual behavior. What is important for my presentation here is the fact that this kind of stimulation may serve as a prelude to heterosexual intercourse and thereby contribute to procreative purposes.

Urophilia (Urine)

One could argue that urophilia cannot possibly serve procreative purposes. There are children who continue wetting their beds—beyond the time when they should be "trained"— because they like the warm feeling the urine gives them when first passed. Of course, when it gets cold, they change their attitude about this practice. Here, again, the most common activity is not drinking urine (but a small percentage do), but urinating on the "lover." And there are those who become sexually excited by being urinated upon. This practice is analogous to coprophilia and relates to sadomasochism. Once again, the arousal may serve as a part of foreplay and ultimately results in procreative sexual acts.

Further Comments on the Paraphilias

It would be an error for the reader to conclude here that I view the paraphilias to be primarily, if not exclusively, genetically determined biological variants. Although I believe there to be a genetic loading for the paraphilias, I also believe that environmental factors are extremely important in bringing about such behavior. In fact, I consider environmental factors to be playing a more important role in the development of the paraphilias than I do in the development of homosexuality, which, as I will describe below, I also believe warrants being listed as one of the paraphilias. I say this because of the bizarreness of many of the paraphilias, a bizarreness akin to the kinds of "craziness" that justify placement in *DSM-III-R*. Many of the paraphilias are developed in an attempt to avoid intimacy, e.g., fetishism, telephone scatologia, partialism, zoophilia, and necrophilia. Others clearly allow for the release of hostility, which may be a more important factor than the sexual act that is serving as a vehicle for such gratification, e.g., sexual sadism, coprophilia, urophilia, and klismaphilia. Others derive from severe feelings of inadequacy, e.g., voyeurism, exhibitionism, sexual sadism, and pedophilia. Obviously, the psychodynamic factors operative in each of the paraphilias are quite complex, and it goes beyond the scope of this book to discuss these in detail. Even the aforementioned outline is an oversimplification in that there is much overlap and complexity to the many psychodynamic factors operative in each of the paraphilias.

One could argue that psychodynamically determined sexual inhibitions (which may contribute to the development of paraphilias) result from psychological problems that work against the expression of the primary sexual goals of DNA. Accordingly, one could claim that the very existence of the paraphilias weakens my theory. My response is this: Each of the paraphilias may be viewed as an atypical variant, as a mutant that does not primarily serve the purposes of procreation, but that may survive anyway because it can contribute (admittedly in an inefficient way) to the primary DNA goals. Similarly, the psychological inhibitions that interfere with DNA's primary expression also work against its goals, but not completely so. The fact that some forms fail to live up to the high standards put down in the optimum configuration of genetic programming does not negate the theory. My reasoning here is similar to that which holds for the sexual dysfunctions (see below) in which there are failures of genital functioning, which may then interfere with the procreative process. The presence of these weaknesses or abnormalities does not negate the theory.

Sexual Dysfunctions

The sexual dysfunctions are essentially forms of pathology in which there is some inhibition and/or impairment in the individual's capacity to engage in heterosexual intercourse. A psychogenic component is considered to be important in bringing about such disorders, but physiological factors may also be operative, especially in the presence of physical disease. These include: impairments in sexual desire, aversion to sexuality, impairment in the ability of a man to attain or maintain an erection, a man or a woman's inability to achieve orgasm, premature ejaculation, dyspareunia (pain on sexual intercourse), and vaginismus (vaginal spasm on penile entry). Clearly, all of these difficulties interfere with the likelihood of procreation and thereby warrant being included as disorders or "diseases." Obviously, they represent a failure in the fulfillment of the individual's capacity to achieve this important goal. The presence of these disorders in no way weakens my theory that there is no biological function (all of which have survival value) that may not be compromised by some disease process.

SHOULD HOMOSEXUALITY BE LISTED AMONG THE PARAPHILIAS?

As mentioned, the last *DSM-IV* section on the sexual disorders allows for the diagnosis of homosexuality (as a sexual disorder) through the "little doggie door," a subsection of the "back door" of the sexual disorders diagnoses. I, myself, would include homosexuality as one of the paraphilias, whether or not one considers any or all of them to warrant placement in *DSM-IV.* (I recognize that I am in the minority of my colleagues when I take this position, but I believe that political factors, much more than scientific, determined its strange and somewhat confusing placement in the manual.) The argument that homosexuality is "unnatural" because it does not serve procreative purposes is not valid. It certainly is a natural variant, is within the potential of all human beings, and to the best of my knowledge has appeared in every society. Furthermore, as I will elaborate below, it also serves the procreative aims of the species, although not directly.

There are some who claim that the purpose of homosexuality is similar to that of nonreproductive variants that are to be found in many species. Worker ants would be an example. They play an important role in the survival of the ant colony but are not actively involved in the reproductive process. The argument is also proposed that homosexuals serve artistic purposes in that they are traditionally more artistically sensitive (art, literature, dance, theater, etc.). This theory never rang true for me in that these activities are very recent developments in the history of the human race and would not explain the existence of homosexuality at earlier times and the survival of genes that may very well predispose people to this type of sexual variation.

Although the homosexual genetic loading may very well have arisen as a mutation (as may have been the case for other paraphilias for which there is a high genetic loading), it has survived. There is great variation among mutations with regard to their survival capacity. Some mutants are incompatible with life and the particular form dies in utero. And there are a wide variety of diseases that are manifestations of mutations that can be lethal at any age and at any stage of life. If the mutation allows survival beyond puberty, then the individual is likely to transmit the mutant genes down to the next generation. Medical science may contribute to this process by allowing for the survival of certain mutations that in earlier centuries might not have survived to the pubertal level of development but, as the result of modern medical techniques, are doing so. This is just another example of the fact that medical progress may often be a mixed blessing.

Another theory to justify homosexuality is that it serves the purposes of population control. Although I believe that this theory has more to justify it than the one that holds that homosexuals serve artistic purposes, it also does not sit well with me. Nonreproductive variants usually serve some purpose, a purpose that is readily recognized. This does not appear to be the case for homosexuals. We are certainly witnessing a population explosion that is becoming ever more serious, and even dangerous. There is no question that we will ultimately have to provide more effective methods of population control than exist at this point. The longer we allow population to grow geometrically, the greater the weight one will have to give to this theory of the purpose of homosexuality. Perhaps at this point, when the dangers are not as grave, it is a less compelling theory. But acceptance of it must presuppose considerations (by DNA or some master planner) that go very much into the future. And this does not appear to be the way DNA works. It is very much oriented to the here-and-now for the purposes of immediate transmission to the next survival machine. Impulsivity and pleasure-of-the-moment considerations appear to be much more pertinent factors in its behavior than considerations of some remote future event. It is for these reasons, as well, that I am not significantly enthusiastic about the population-control theory of homosexuality.

Homosexual genetic programming has survived not only because we have not routinely killed all homosexuals (although certain societies have attempted to do so), but because homosexuals have not confined themselves sexually to people of their own sex, but have engaged in heterosexual activities as well. In fact, it is safe to say that the vast majority of homosexuals have had some heterosexual experiences. It is also a fact that male homosexuals are typically highly sexualized individuals, much more so than the average male heterosexual, and are well known for their "promiscuity," i.e., their strong need for frequent sex with a large number of sexual partners. Male homosexuals also will typically date the onset of their strong sexual urges to earlier periods of life than heterosexuals (Kinsey et al., 1948; Tripp, 1987). Homosexuality, then, if my theory is correct, serves the purpose of heightening the general level of sexual activity and increases the chances, thereby, that such individuals may involve themselves in heterosexual activities as well.

Homosexuality also increases the likelihood that children will become involved earlier in sexual activities, increasing thereby the likelihood of their becoming actively sexual in the postpubertal period. I am referring here to the homosexual who is also a pedophile (again, much more common in males than females). Like his heterosexual pedophilic counterpart, both contribute to the likelihood that children will become active heterosexual adults.

When I presented the above theory to a colleague of mine, Dr. Jonathan Greene, he suggested that homophobia may also have survival value. Homophobes are revolted by homosexuality and may actively attempt to constrain their behavior. In extreme cases they may even attempt to eliminate homosexuals entirely. (Adolph Hitler is a well-known example of a person who tried to do this.) One traditional explanation for homophobia given by psychoanalysts is that homophobes are basically uncomfortable with their own unconscious or dimly conscious homosexual urges. By eliminating homosexuality they protect themselves from the stimulation of their own "latent homosexual impulses." I do not deny that this may certainly be a mechanism in some (if not many) homophobic individuals. And, I do not deny that there are probably other psychological mechanisms operative in this aversion. Nor do I deny social influences that teach that homosexuality is an undesirable and even disgusting form of sexual expression. However, Greene has a good point in that homophobia has survival value in that a society cannot tolerate ubiquitous homosexuality. To do so would threaten its very survival. On a very primitive level, then, the battle between homosexuals and heterosexuals is a battle for DNA survival, even though homosexuality—in a more indirect way—does ultimately contribute to DNA survival. It is an inefficient method, however, and a society has to limit the degree to which it can tolerate inefficient methods of reproduction. And all paraphilias are inefficient when compared to the traditional heterosexual reproductive modes.

One could argue, then, that homosexuality justifiably belongs among the paraphilias. It certainly satisfies the basic requirement for such inclusion, namely, that the sexual behavior is atypical (practiced only by a minority of individuals in our society) and that it does not directly serve procreative purposes.

One could argue that all of the paraphilias (whether or not one wants to include in them homosexuality) should not be included in *DSM-*

IV because the manual is devoted primarily to diseases. Although the term *disorder* is used, insurance companies still consider these variations *diseases* or *illnesses*. Exclusion of the paraphilias might deprive paraphilic individuals of the opportunity for insurance coverage if they want treatment for them. Should we therefore consider the insurance companies to be the final arbiters with regard to whether a behavioral manifestation warrants inclusion in *DSM-IV*? *DSM-IV* deals with this question somewhat obliquely by stating that in addition to the paraphilic behavioral manifestation, the individual must experience "significant distress" over the desire to engage in the paraphilic sexual practice. This, then, brings us back to the problem of patients making the decision as to whether or not the disease in fact exists. As a physician I would like to believe that a disease exists in its own right, separate from whether the patient considers it to exist and separate from whether an insurance company decides to provide coverage.

One could argue that something must be seriously deranged in a man who would prefer to have intercourse with a dead body than with a beautiful young woman. One could argue that there must be something seriously wrong with a man who would spurn sexual intercourse with an attractive and receptive young woman and, in preference, put his penis into the anus of another man. When we say that "something is wrong" with a person who engages in certain activities, we are basically saying that the individual is suffering with a psychiatric disorder. One could argue also that the probable genetic predisposition factor, a factor related to a mutation, also argues for the paraphilias to be considered psychiatric disorders. There are other psychiatric disorders that are considered to have a genetic basis, e.g., bipolar disorder and obsessive compulsive disorder (OCD). These certainly are "natural" in that they are to be found in nature, yet they are still considered to be diseases (or, euphemistically, "disorders").

It is a strange paradox that pedophilia is included as a paraphilia, but not homosexuality. Accordingly, if an adult's primary source of sexual gratification is an individual of the same sex, the behavior is not considered to warrant inclusion among the paraphilias (or anywhere else in *DSM-IV*). However, if the adult desires sex with a child (whether of the same or opposite sex), that behavior is considered to warrant inclusion among the paraphilias. This paradox lends confirmation to my aforementioned statement that the exclusion of homosexuality from *DSM-IV* has much more to do with political than psychiatric considerations.

Another paradox derives from *DSM-IV*'s exclusion of homosexuality, namely, its considering cross-dressing among heterosexuals to be a disorder (Transvestic Fetishism) but not a disorder if the individual is homosexual. Accordingly, if a homosexual cross-dresses to entice and excite another homosexual, that is normal. If a heterosexual engages in such behavior, he (she) has a disorder. An even more important paradox is the inclusion of the Gender Identity Disorder of Childhood. There is an enormous body of research that demonstrates compellingly the high correlation between childhood gender identity disorder and homosexuality during adulthood. Some of the more well known of such studies include those of Bell and Weinberg (1978), Bell et al. (1981), Bieber et al. (1962), Green (1985, 1987), Money and Russo (1979), and Zuger (1970, 1976, 1984). Friedman (1988) provides an excellent review of these studies and states, "At present, I believe that this is the only correlation between psychopathology and homosexuality that may be taken as an established fact." We see here a strange inconsistency in *DSM-IV*. An effeminate boy would be considered by *DSM-IV* to be suffering with a disorder. Yet, when this same boy becomes an adult homosexual (a highly likely outcome), he no longer is considered to have a disorder; rather, his atypicality is viewed as a normal human variant. Again, I believe that political considerations, far more than psychiatric, have brought those who have made this decision to this inexplicable and even absurd inconsistency.

Although I could argue both ways, my preference would be that all the paraphilias (including homosexuality) be included in *DSM-IV* as paraphilias and, like bipolar depression and OCD, be considered diseases (or disorders) per se. I would exclude the proviso that the individual has to have distress in order to justify the diagnosis. The fact is that the person is not going to go into treatment if he (she) does not suffer distress, the *DSM-IV* statement notwithstanding. Atypicality, per se, has traditionally been a justification for inclusion in a list of psychiatric disturbances. There are societies in which paranoia and hallucinations are the norm. There are others in which catatonic people may be worshiped and/or considered to be invested by divine spirits. As Shakespeare's Hamlet put it: "There's nothing either good or bad, but thinking makes it so." Because atypical sexuality is "bad" in our society and because people who exhibit such behavior are going to have difficulties in our society, even though often (but not always) unjustified, we must make special provisions for dealing with them, both in the legal and psychiatric professions.

THE CAUSES OF MALE PEDOPHILIA

Social and Cultural Factors

It is extremely important that the reader appreciate that sexual activities between an adult and a child are an ancient tradition and have been found to exist to a significant degree in just about every society in history that has been studied in depth. The reader who is somewhat incredulous about what I have just said does well to read the very enlightening and well-researched article by Demause (1991), which documents the ubiquity of adult-child sexual activities in the United States, Canada, Latin America, Puerto Rico, Mexico, Scandinavia, Great Britain, Germany, Italy, India, China, Japan, Thailand, and the Middle East. His review covers the wide span of history from ancient times to the present. Demause's 41-page article has 200 footnotes, each of which cites a list of further references supporting the statements made in the main body of the article. It provides compelling evidence that sexual activities between adults and children have been a worldwide phenomenon, the main difference between cultures being the attitudes toward this universal practice.

It is of interest that of all the ancient peoples, it may very well be that the Jews were the only ones who were punitive toward pedophiles. According to Kahr (1991):

> The Hebrews of yore seem to have maintained a somewhat more progressive attitude toward pedophilia, and, according to the ancient Jews, anybody who engaged in sexual activity with a boy older than nine years of age would be stoned to death; however, those who copulated with boys *under* the age of nine received only a whipping, because the Jews did not consider boys under nine as sexual beings. (p. 201)

Early Christian proscriptions against pedophilia appear to have been derived from the earlier teachings of the Jews, and our present overreaction to pedophilia represents an exaggeration of Judeo-Christian principles and is a significant factor operative in Western society's atypicality with regard to such activities.

Kahr (1991) provides further documentation of the ubiquity of child sex abuse, in the past as well as the present, with particular focus on ancient Greece, ancient Rome, ancient Egypt, and modern Western society—especially Europe and the United States. Kahr divides Western society's attitudes toward adult-child sexuality into four stages:

>   1. The Ancient Period (comprising the times of the Greeks and the Romans). Adults seduced and violated their children in an unashamed and socially acceptable manner.
>
>   2. The Medieval Period (from the rise of Christianity through the Renaissance). Under the influence of Christianity, parents were made to feel guilty over their sexual inclinations toward their children and could not abuse them with impunity. A prominent feature during this period was the phenomenon of adults projecting their own sexual impulses onto children and assuming, thereby, that the children were the initiators of sexual activity.
>
>   3. The Early Modern Period (the 18th-early 20th centuries). The enhancement even further of guilt and shame over adult-child sexuality. Pedophilic impulses are gratified pornographically, and sub rosa.
>
>   4. The Late Modern Period (latter half of the 20th century). Progressive increase in the awareness of the ubiquity of the problem. Practically no social sanction. Abused children viewed as victims.

Konker (1992) also provides an extensive review of the literature on a wide variety of cultural attitudes toward adult-child sexuality. She provides compelling evidence for the conclusion that adult-child sexual behavior is ubiquitous and has been present in just about every society studied, both past and present. For example, she states:

> In a variety of contemporary cultures it appears that adults may affectionately sniff, kiss, blow upon, fondle, and praise the genitals of young male and female children. . . . Valued adult-child sexual contact

routinely occurs as part of initiation activities in at least twenty countries throughout the world. (p. 148)

Among contemporary indigenous groups in New Guinea there are some conscious cultural constraints on father-son incestuous relationships, but male children are traditionally sexually initiated by other adult males. Sexual sadistic practices are also widespread.

Again, in New Guinea, Konker (1992) states:

Various adults' initiation practices may include sexual insults and threats, fellatio, sodomy, urethral piercing and bloodletting, and men rubbing semen on young boys. . . . Also, at initiation, Arapesh girls may have stinging needles rubbed on their bodies and thrust up their vulvas. (p. 148)

No knowledgeable individual seriously believes that the Judaic practice of circumcision (also practiced by Muslims and, interestingly, more recently by Christians) arose from the appreciation that such a procedure would protect an individual from the acquisition of certain diseases. Even now, most recognize this as a retrospective rationalization. I am convinced that the ritual is basically sexual-sadistic and that it is close enough to the obvious sexual-sadistic rituals described in detail by Demause, Kahr, and Konker to warrant this conclusion. The act is sexual in that it involves the penis. It is sadistic in that it involves a mutilation. To this day, certain Orthodox Jews require the circumciser to suck directly the blood from the circumcised penis. I myself personally observed this ritual when I was about five or six years of age and still remember it clearly. This too is sex in that it is clearly fellatio. And this too is sadistic in that the material being sucked from the penis is blood.

Accordingly, the view that pedophilia is a sickness and a crime is a reflection of Western society's present position on this subject. I am a product of my culture and I am affected by the mores of the society in which I have grown up. I too have come to believe that sexual activity between an adult and a child is a reprehensible act. However, I do not believe that it is intrinsically so; in other societies and in other times it may not be psychologically detrimental. However, I live in my society and it is my job to help people who come my way to adjust—to a reasonable degree—to the society in which they live. I am not claiming that it is my job to make them rubber stamps of the prevailing mores of the majority, only to recognize what these mores are and to appreciate that if they are ignored the individual may be in deep trouble. The indicators listed here, then, are only applicable to our society, at this point, and are in no way presented as applicable to other societies, now and in the past.

I wish to emphasize the point that there is no such thing as "the typical personality" of the adult male pedophile. There are many kinds of individuals who engage in pedophilic behavior, and they cover a broad spectrum of personality types, with much overlap regarding personality qualities. Furthermore, it is rare to find a person who is exclusively pedophilic. Most pedophiles engage in other forms of sexual behavior, especially atypical behavior (Abel et al., 1988). Also, there are varying degrees of exclusivity, ranging from those whose sexual practices include a very high percentage of pedophilic acts and those whose pedophilia may be transient and circumstantial. And this is especially the case for female pedophiles.

Those whose pedophilia appears to be a lifelong pattern are generally referred to as "fixated pedophiles" (Groth, 1979b). These are people who generally never marry and present with a history of ongoing pedophilic acts extending back into adolescence and sometimes even earlier. At the other end of the continuum are individuals who are sometimes referred to as "regressed pedophiles" (Groth, 1979b). They are individuals who may have engaged in pedophilic behavior on one, or only a few, occasions. Often they are married and do not present with a history of significant involvement in a variety of atypical sexual behaviors. The closer the individual is to the fixated end of the continuum, the greater the likelihood the term *pedophile* would be warranted; in contrast, the closer the individual is to the regressed end of the continuum, the less the likelihood one could justifiably apply this label.

The Imprinting Factor

Early experiences play an important role in determining later patterns of behavior. This is especially the case if the early experience is an extremely powerful and gratifying one. Take for example a prepubertal child who has never experienced an orgasm, or may not have even experienced strong sexual urges. Imagine, then, this child being seduced into a relationship in which there is not only enormous flattery, and enjoyable caressing, but orgastic gratification as well. It is easy to see how a child might become "hooked" by such an experience and crave frequent gratifications of the same kind. It is easy to see also how this particular pattern may become the model for subsequent sexuality when the child grows older. As I will elaborate in Chapter Two, the pattern may become embedded in the brain circuitry and can thereby have a formidable effect on future sexual orientation. Furthermore, the older the child becomes, the more autonomy and the greater the likelihood that he (she) can be the initiator of such encounters. Even when the encounters may not be particularly gratifying, and even when there may be a fear element associated with threats regarding disclosure, the child may still become accustomed to this pattern and it may still become deeply ingrained. Even when associated with fear and pain, such early experiences may still become imprinted as the primary pattern of sexual encounter, so powerful are these early influences. When repeated, it may become the only pattern the child knows. We see here a similarity to sadomasochistic individuals who are brought up in homes in which that is the primary form of interaction between people, both in and out of the bedroom scene.

There are homosexuals who date the onset of their homosexuality to just such a childhood seduction. Years later, they may still recall it as one of the most dramatic and memorable experiences of their lives. It is easy to imagine how a youngster, who never previously had an orgasm, is not only introduced to this experience at that time, but the orgasm occurs in association with adoration and flattery unlike that ever previously received. For the youngster it may be a "mind-blowing" experience (the reader will please excuse the pun), one that may affect the future course of the child's life. And, if such seduction occurs on a few occasions, the likelihood of the youngster's going down the homosexual path may be even greater. Some of these youngsters go on to become homosexuals who confine themselves to adult relationships; others become pedophiles, their own pedophilic experience having played a role in that choice (more unconscious than conscious). There are many types of individuals who cause such imprinting in children. Sometimes the seducer is the child's father (far less often the mother), uncle, grandparent, or other relative. It may have been a babysitter, teacher, neighbor, or lover of a parent. There are pedophiles for whom the imprinting process took place in the context of their serving as juvenile prostitutes. In some cases their families were living at poverty levels and relied upon their children's proceeds from prostitution to contribute to the family's support (Reeves, 1981; Phongpaichit, 1982).

Children's normal childhood exploratory play may have a role in producing a subsequent pedophilic orientation. This is especially the case if such play becomes an ongoing pattern. The sexual object, then, becomes a child. Furthermore, if high emotional charge is associated with such activities, there is an even greater likelihood that the experiences will become embedded in the brain circuitry and contribute to the pedophilic orientation. In Chapter Two I describe a patient who attributes his pedophilic orientation to such childhood experiences. In his case, the emotional charge was intensified by his mother who, after discovering the exploratory activities, embarked upon weeks of tirades of condemnation.

It is important for the reader to appreciate that the imprinting factor is not so compelling that the child who is sexually abused will automatically and inevitably become a pedophile. Throughout Melanesia and New Guinea, childhood pedophilia is a common practice, yet most of the children involved in such activities do not become pedophiles as adults (Herdt, 1981). A dramatic example of this is to be found among the Sambia tribes of New Guinea. In that tribe, as is so true of other Melanesian societies, the ejaculate is viewed as a powerful vehicle for transmission of masculine power. It is not hard to see how it could symbolize such power, considering the ubiquity of the penis as a symbol of power, even in Western society. In the Zambian tribes boys live with their parents until the age of 8, at which time they move to a men's longhouse, where they live only in the company of males. From ages 8 to 13 they engage in fellatio with adolescent boys in order to enhance their masculinity. Then, at around the time of puberty, they switch roles and become the providers of semen to the younger boys. Then, at age 19, they marry and pedophilic practices cease entirely.

Identification with the Aggressor

The imprinting factor refers primarily to neurological imprinting that may contribute to the development of pedophilia. Here I focus on the psychological elements that complement the biological brain circuitry element. The two may operate together. Stoller (1975, 1979, 1985) considers the identification-with-the-aggressor factor to be an important one driving pedophiles to involve themselves in pedophilic behavior. Specifically, many pedophiles have had childhood experiences in which they were sexually abused—experiences that were traumatic. (As mentioned, sexual activities with children need not be traumatic for the child.) One way of dealing with this trauma is to reenact it as an adult, with another victim. In this way the individual symbolically attempts to gain mastery over a childhood sexual trauma in which the individual was helpless. By reenacting the sexual activity as an adult, the individual temporarily turns a passively endured childhood trauma into an actively controlled adult triumph (Garland and Dougher, 1990). In addition, the pedophilic act may also serve to enable the individual to gain a feeling of revenge for having been subjected to the trauma, the built-up anger vented now on the abused child. Some confirmation for this theory is provided by the fact that pedophiles often reenact in great detail the same kinds of pedophilic activities that they were subjected to as children. Of course, one could attribute this simply to learning and the modeling effect, but it does provide some confirmation for the aforementioned theory. Longo (1982) and Groth (1979a) studied incarcerated pedophiles and found that they frequently recapitulated in great detail their own childhood sexual experiences. Sometimes the identification is with an adult who has not sexually traumatized the child in the course of the pedophilic act. In such circumstances, the concept of identification with the aggressor is not applicable. Here one might refer to it as "identification with the lover" and need not invoke the aforementioned more complex mechanisms.

In addition to the more specific identification with the sexual acts, the sexually molested child may identify with the general personality characteristics of the abuser. This is almost invariably the case in situations in which the abuser is a family member because children most often identify with their parents and other significant figures with whom they live. Under such circumstances, the identification is predictable. When, however, the abuser is not a family member one is also likely to see identifications, especially when there has been an ongoing relationship. This is most commonly seen in situations in which the abuser is a scoutmaster, teacher, or clergyman. The abuser may have served as a mentor, confidant, and model over many months and even years and so it is not surprising that the child will take on this person's characteristics and behavioral patterns, both sexual and nonsexual.

The Domination Factor

I have already mentioned the importance of domination in species survival and how domination is an extension of the aggression and assertiveness that the male exhibits in the courting pattern. Children, because they are weaker than females, are more easily dominated and so are even more likely to be subdued by an aggressive male. Furthermore, in our social structure, children and females are generally viewed to be of lower status. This contributes to their attractiveness as objects for pedophiles for whom the domination factor is important. And this is one of the factors, as well, explaining why pedophilia is much more common in males than females, so much so that one could say that it is a male form of behavior. Demause (1991) states, "As an adult, the pedophile must have sex with children in order to maintain the illusion of being loved, while at the same time dominating the children as they themselves once experienced domination, repeating actively their own caretakers' sadism."

Passivity and Impaired Self-Assertion

In contrast to the kinds of aggressive and domineering behaviors described above, there are some pedophiles who exhibit the opposite kind of behavior, that is, they are passive and inhibited in their capacity to assert themselves. Ayalon (1984) describes the nonviolent type of sex-abuse perpetrator. Peters (1976) also describes sex offenders as being characteristically passive and emotionally dependent. Overholser and Beck (1986) also found many of the offenders they studied to be unassertive. Sometimes individuals in this category have intellectual impairments or serious psychiatric disturbance and are willing to engage in a wide variety of atypical and even illegal behaviors into which they are coerced by more dominant individuals (such as gang or group leaders).

Similarities Between Children and Females

Children are much more like females than males. This is not only true with regard to their appearances, but their personalities as well. Children and females have less hair than males. The skin of the child is smooth, much more like that of a female than a male (Medicus and Hopf, 1990). The behavioral patterns that women exhibit in the courting process are much more like those of the normal patterns of children than those patterns exhibited by males in the courtship process. Flirting, cuteness, coyness, and seductive smiles are all part of the average child's repertoire. Such patterns are reflected in many of the comments men make to women in lovemaking, e.g., "You're my baby," "You're my sex kitten," and "You're very cute."

Furthermore, children are more like females than males in their desire for affection, intimacy, security, and trust in their relationships (Strassmann, 1981). Moreover, the adoration that the child has for the adult is similar to that which men strive for in their relationships with women. Such adoration is much more easily acquired from a child than an adult—thus the attraction of pedophilia. Of particular importance here is the esteem-enhancement element in such adoration, and this is one of the reasons why (as described above) pedophilia is particularly attractive to men with profound feelings of low self-worth. Also related is the eroticization of the parent-child love relationship. This, too, easily derives from the aforementioned factors (D'Udine, 1990; Garland and Dougher, 1990; Money, 1990). Pedophilia, then, may be viewed (at least in part) as a natural downward extension of the male's attraction to the female. It may be viewed as a generalization of the male's sexual courting pattern beyond what our society considers proper. The love/tenderness factor may be one of the reasons why a sexual encounter between an adult and a child is not necessarily psychologically traumatic.

Compensation for Feelings of Emotional Deprivation

Pedophiles often come from homes in which they grew up emotionally deprived and, in many cases, homes in which there was significant family dysfunction. An adoring child can provide a pedophile with compensation for feelings of deprivation that may have persisted from the pedophile's childhood. And if the child involved is also the product of a home in which he (she) is suffering privation, then sexual involvement with an adoring adult may become even more attractive. Mention has been made previously of the somewhat complex psychological mechanism that may be operative here, namely, the one in which the pedophile projects himself psychologically onto the child who is the object of his ministrations and thereby satisfies vicariously his own need to be the object of intense affection. He thereby provides his projected self with the love that was not obtained during his own childhood. Furthermore, the boundaries between parental love and romantic love may become blurred. This not only contributes to the gratification provided by the projected self, but also the adoration provided the pedophile by the loving child (Eibl-Eibesfeldt, 1990).

Many authors have described this relationship between pedophilia and a family background of emotional neglect. Ayalon (1984) considers emotional neglect to be a factor in the nonviolent type of incest perpetrator. Weinberg (1962) considers emotional deprivation in childhood to have been present in most of the incest offenders he studied. Gebhard and Gagnon (1964) also found that the vast majority of incestuous fathers were products of emotionally depriving homes. Money (1990) describes indifference and neglect to be part of the family background of many pedophiles. Accordingly, there is strong support in the scientific literature for this relationship.

There is strong support in the scientific literature for this factor in the development of pedophilia. Finkelhor (1986) states that "this [sexual abuse in childhood] is one of the most consistent findings of recent research." Money (1990) also describes this phenomenon, with particular emphasis on the feelings of entrapment and dilemma that such youngsters experience. When this occurs, it may result in the eroticization of parental love (Eibl-Eibesfeldt, 1990). Longo (1982) reported that approximately half of the adolescent sex offenders he studied had been sexually molested in the prepubertal years. Becker et al. (1986) found that 23 percent of adolescent sex offenders had been the subject of pedophilic experiences. Frisbie (1969) found that 24 percent of a group of sex offenders of children reported childhood histories of sexual contact with an adult. Groth (1979a) found that 25 percent of sex offenders of children had childhood sexual experiences with adults. Condy et al. (1987) found that 37 percent of sexual offenders in his study had childhood sexual experiences with an adult at least five years older than themselves. Hanson (1991) reviewed the literature on the percentage of child molesters who themselves had been sexually abused as children. When the sample size was relatively small (less than 50), the rates of child sexual abuse varied from zero to over 60. However, as the sample sizes increased, the rates converged to between 20 and 30 percent, with an average for all studies of 28 percent.

Narcissism

The most common manifestations of narcissism are low tolerance for criticism; a grandiose sense of one's importance; exaggeration of one's achievements and talents; the feeling that one is particularly unique; preoccupation with fantasies of one's success, power, brilliance, and beauty; a sense of entitlement, especially that one is particularly deserving of favorable treatment; the craving for constant attention and admiration; and impairment in the ability to give sympathy and empathy.

The narcissism so frequently seen in pedophiles is compensatory for underlying feelings of inadequacy. Many pedophiles have few if any accomplishments to point to, accomplishments that could enhance feelings of self-worth. They commonly present with a history of poor school and work performance, unsuccessful marriages, and significant impairments in their ability to form age-appropriate friendships. They have a strong craving to be loved and will gravitate toward children because children will so predictably be adoring of an adult who treats them kindly. Children are somewhat indiscriminate in their affection for and even admiration of adults. Accordingly, they are more likely to provide pedophiles with those adoring responses that can gratify the pedophile's narcissistic needs. In addition, children are less likely to be aware of sexual inadequacies, such as impotency and premature ejaculation, which would obviously be a source of embarrassment to the narcissist who is clearly unable to handle the ego debasement associated with such inadequacies. Some pedophiles, like homosexual men, are so narcissistic that they actually masturbate looking at themselves in the mirror, using their own image as the source of sexual stimulation. Lang (1994) has also made this observation.

Many homosexuals—both those with and those without pedophilic tendencies—are extremely narcissistic. They are constantly "on stage" and are ever thinking about how they appear to others. This is one of the reasons why they may gravitate to an acting career. Their sexual attraction to other men (people who look like themselves) is yet another manifestation of this narcissism. Just as there is a segment of the heterosexual population that is pedophilic, there is a segment of the homosexual population that is pedophilic.

Leahy (1991) states, "The most common diagnosis of the child abuser is that of narcissistic personality disorder. It is thought that these individuals are seeking from their intimate encounters with children some affirmation that they are both loved and desired." Kohut (1977) also comments on the narcissism of pedophiles as a mechanism for compensating for their fragile sense of self-worth and their frequent experience of self-fragmentation. Crewdson (1988) considers the pedophile's narcissism to be a direct result of the childhood sexual abuse to which many pedophiles have been subjected. Overholser and Beck (1986) found the pedophiles they studied to be socially inept, which is yet another source of feelings of inadequacy and often a result of it. Children are somewhat indiscriminate in their affection for and even admiration of adults. Accordingly, they are more likely to provide pedophiles with those responses that can serve to compensate for the pedophile's feelings of inadequacy.

Peters (1976) found the offenders he studied to be suffering with deep feelings of inferiority and inadequacy. Medicus and Hopf (1990) state:

> Because of their small size, lack of experience, and sense of insecurity, children and adolescents of either sex do not arouse feelings of inferiority, fear, and anxiety in adult males. Thus, children and adoles-

cents can become "sexual objects" for males who in sociosexual relations with adults feel inferior or anxious. (p. 141)

Therefore, because children are so craving for affection, pedophiles may seek the affection of children, who are less likely to reject them and are more easily seduced into providing affection. In a more complex way, pedophiles may project themselves psychologically onto the children who are the objects of their affection. By observing the child's pleasure, they satisfy vicariously their own need to be provided love by an adult. In this way they are reenacting and satisfying a childhood frustration. They identify themselves with a loving adult (something they had little experience with in childhood) and identify themselves with the recipient of their affections by projecting themselves simultaneously into the position of the child to whom they are providing affection.

Masochistic Factors

Involving oneself in pedophilic behavior in a society that condemns it vehemently and punishes it terribly, often providing mandatory life sentences for a first offense, makes one wonder about the motivations of individuals who involve themselves in this form of behavior. Mention has already been made of the poor judgment often exhibited by pedophiles, as well as my belief that people of lower-than-average intelligence are probably overrepresented in the pedophilic population. I suspect, also, that a strongly masochistic trend may exist in many pedophiles. After all, the risk of discovery is very great in that children are not famous for their ability to keep secrets. The threat of severe punishment does not seem to deter many pedophiles. Silva (1990), the incarcerated physician who wrote his autobiography from jail, describes himself to have continued to involve himself in pedophilic behavior even when he was out on bail for previous offenses.

Recent Social and Cultural Factors Operative in the United States

We live in a youth-oriented society. Younger women are generally considered much more attractive and desirable than older women. One factor in pedophilia may very well be the result of the downward extension and expansion of our youth-worshiping culture. A recent contribution may very well relate to the AIDS epidemic. Since the early 1980s, when AIDS was first described, there has been a growing expansion of the disease into the adult population. Children, having less sexual experience, may be viewed as safer sexual companions. At the time I write this (mid-1995), newspapers and magazines are describing an explosion of child prostitution in Southeast Asia, the clients being primarily Europeans and Americans. In accordance with ancient traditions, these children are often sold into sexual slavery, are sold to pimps by poor families, or are picked up off the streets after having been abandoned by their families.

Perhaps the "sexual revolution" that began in the '60s is playing a role. The more permissive attitude toward all forms of sexual behavior may very well increase the prevalence of pedophilia. Perhaps the increasing psychopathy of our society in the last quarter century has played a role. Previously, people were more reluctant to indulge themselves in unacceptable and antisocial impulses; perhaps indulging in child sex abuse is yet another manifestation of the basic psychopathy that has been increasing in recent years.

Concluding Comments on Pedophilia

I am certain that other psychological factors are operative in the development of pedophilia. I have delineated here those that I consider to be the most important. The reader does well to approach each patient without preconceived notions regarding which particular factors may have been operative in bringing about the particular patient's pedophilia. When interviewing pedophiles, I routinely ask the individual his (her) theory regarding its causes. Although the patient may initially claim ignorance, I have found that persistent questioning and encouragement of "guesses" will often provide me with valuable information regarding the psychogenic factors operative in its etiology. Generally, the individual provides a response that includes one or more of the factors described here.

CONCLUDING COMMENTS

I present here a theory that attempts to bring together a wide variety of human sexual phenomena and provides a common explanation for what may initially appear to be different disorders. Although each of these types of human sexual activity has its own set of causes (both genetic and environmental), they share in common the thread that they all potentially serve the ends of procreation (directly or indirectly), and therefore specifically the transmission of DNA down to the next survival machine.

Freud (1930) in his *Civilization and Its Discontents* points out that society must suppress and repress sexuality if any constructive work is to be done. If all individuals were free to indulge themselves in any form of sexual encounter, we would have little time to involve ourselves in the constructive work necessary for the survival of society. Gibbon (1776-1788) considers widespread licentiousness to have been an important factor in the decline of the Roman Empire. The biblical story of God's destruction of the cities of Sodom and Gomorrah is certainly (at least) a metaphor for the same phenomenon. It may very well be true, as well, that intrafamilial sex, especially, had to be suppressed because of the rivalries that it engendered. Certainly most people in our society (sexual revolution notwithstanding) view sex as a special kind of relationship. This is especially true of women, who are much more oriented to the emotional-relationship element in sex. Women are much more oriented toward sexual exclusivity. The opposite side of the exclusivity coin is jealousy. A man, too, is not free from such jealous feelings, especially when another man has sexual opportunities with a woman with whom he is enamored. If it is true that such feelings are of ancient tradition and may have even existed in primitive times, then taboos against incest might have arisen in order to protect people from the devastating effects on the family of such jealous rivalries. Inhibitions have a way of spreading, often to areas that were not part of the central focus at the time of their origin, and this is what might have happened with regard to the widespread sexual inhibitions that we observe in Western society today.

I do not believe it is likely that inhibitions against incest arose from the appreciation that inbreeding may bring about the clinical expression of recessive genes and thereby produce an increase in maladaptive forms. First, I believe that this is a relatively late development in our understanding. In fact, it is probable that the relationship between sexual intercourse and pregnancy has only recently become understood, and this is especially likely to have been the case in societies in which a wide variety of sexual practices were engaged in at all ages. Furthermore, when a family is relatively free of undesirable genes, inbreeding can be beneficial in that it preserves the "purity" of the strain. I am certain that a wide variety of other factors have been involved in the development of sexual inhibitions, but it is beyond the purposes of this book to discuss them.

Mention has already been made of the fact that the paraphilias are much more common in males than females. I believe that the main reason for this difference relates to the aforementioned theory in which I consider men to be primarily involved in the quantity-control aspect of reproduction and women in the quality-control aspect. The biologically programmed "promiscuity" of men easily spreads to their being far less discriminating with regard to the receptacle in which they are willing to deposit their sperm. Accordingly, receptacles that may not immediately bring about an increase in the population may still be utilized, so pervasive and compelling are the urges. The obsessive-compulsive nature of the male sexual drive and the overrepresentation of males in the paraphilic population enhances, I believe, the credibility of my theory.

The presentation of my theory would not be complete without some discussion of masturbation. One could argue that it does not support the theory because this widespread practice serves absolutely no procreative function. In fact, it can be viewed as a "waste" of sexual urges because it does not lead to the transmission of DNA into the next generation of survival machines. I could argue even further that it defeats DNA's purposes in that it allows for a reduction in sexual drive and therefore lessens the likelihood of the immediate quest for procreation. These arguments notwithstanding, I believe that masturbation also serves DNA's purposes. It keeps the juices flowing and thereby contributes to the prevention of disuse atrophy of the reproductive apparatus. More importantly, it serves DNA survival in another way. It allows for the release and gratification of sexual tensions and cravings so that the individual may then be free to direct attention to other survival considerations such as the acquisition of food, clothing, and shelter. Without this form of release, individuals might be continually in a state of excitation and frustration and thereby not be able to provide proper attention to other activities necessary for the survival of the temporary housing machines. The genitals do not exist in isolation from the rest of the body.

They require nourishment and protection. The survival machine cannot merely focus on providing opportunities for the copulatory organs to perform their function. Rather, it must also direct itself to other necessary matters that keep the genital organs in good health, functioning properly, and protected from danger. Such activities are not likely to be accomplished effectively and efficiently if the housing machine is distracted significantly by unsatisfied sexual cravings.

As mentioned, I have been particularly careful to avoid making any judgments about these atypical forms of human behavior. I believe, however, that many societies have been unjustifiably punitive to those who exhibit these paraphilic variations and have not been giving proper respect to the genetic factors that may very well be operative. Such considerations might result in greater tolerance for those who exhibit these atypical sexual proclivities. My hope is that this theory will play a role (admittedly small) in bringing about greater sympathy and respect for those individuals who exhibit these variations of sexual behavior. Recognizing that they do play a role in species survival may contribute to some alteration of this unfortunate attitude.

It would be an error for the reader to conclude that I am condoning all of these forms of sexual behavior. I think each one must be considered in its own right with regard to the judgments that one passes on them. An important determinant of my own judgments relates to the coercive element, especially when the coerced person is weaker and/or younger. Although pedophilia may ultimately serve nature's purposes, it is still a form of exploitation of an innocent party. Sadomasochism may also serve the purposes of the survival of the human species, but it is basically a form of cruelty that we could well do without. I have mentioned that we differ from lower animals with regard to the development of the human brain, which has the capacity to suppress and repress those forces that press for indiscriminate reproduction of DNA and its passage down the generations from one survival machine to another. Also, consideration must be given to the social attitude toward a particular variation. It is a disservice to guide children along an atypical developmental track (especially when there is no evidence that their genes are propelling them along that path), because they will predictably suffer for their atypicality. I am not suggesting that we submit to every social prejudice. What I am suggesting is that we try to educate society to be less prejudiced and to be less condemning of those with paraphilias (especially those that do not cause harm to younger and/or weaker individuals).

☐ TWO

THE EMBEDMENT-IN-THE-BRAIN-CIRCUITRY PHENOMENON (EBCP)

INTRODUCTION

My primary purpose in this chapter is to focus on the phenomenon of the seemingly purposeless embedment of mental material into the brain circuitry. Although such material originally may have had some purpose, it appears to persist beyond the time when it has served some purpose. For reasons unknown to the individual, it persists indefinitely, possibly throughout life. Such cognitive material appears to have a life of its own and spins around in the brain circuitry long after it has served some function. Psychologists and psychiatrists have not given this phenomenon the attention it deserves, especially as a contributory factor in the development and perpetuation of psychopathology. This phenomenon also has important therapeutic implications.

I will refer to this process as the *Embedment-in-the-Brain-Circuitry Phenomenon* (EBCP). I use the word *mental* to refer to psychological brain processes, which are on a continuum. On one end of the continuum is purely cognitive material, with no associated emotional (affective) concomitants. An example of this would be a "pure thought" without any emotional content such as one would experience when calmly adding up a row of numbers. Of course, if the numbers represent the amount of money one has, then emotional elements may appear. At the other end of the continuum are pure emotions, with little if any associated emotional cognitive concomitants. An example of this would be a nightmare in which the individual experiences only morbid fear without any knowledge of its source. However, if some kind of cognitive material appears, such as some menacing figure, the experience could not then be viewed as "pure emotion." A panic attack in which the only experience is morbid fear would be another example. However, once cognitive elements are introduced, such as the fear that one is going to have a heart attack, then this would represent some shift (albeit small) down the continuum toward the purely cognitive end. Most mental material is likely to fall in between these two ends of the continuum.

Obviously, the newborn infant is ill equipped to survive without a significant amount of care by older individuals. Obviously, also, if the infant is to survive, it must learn techniques for survival. It must have the capacity to learn, i.e., modify behavior as a result of experience. In order to accomplish this, the infant must be able to store in memory what is learned at any particular time in order to make use of what has been learned at any future time. Learning, then, can be reasonably defined as a change in an organism's behavior as a result of experience. The younger the child, the more primitive the learning mechanisms are because of the inability of the brain substance to accommodate more complex forms of learning. However, the human brain has the capacity to learn at the very earliest levels of life. There is also a hierarchy with regard to the complexity of the learning process. An amoeba can be "taught" to avoid a noxious stimulus. This is a form of learning in that there appears to be some kind of "memory" that enables the organism to avoid repetition of exposure to a specific noxious stimulus. This is one of the simplest forms of learning, often referred to as conditioned learning. Obviously, the amoeba cannot involve itself in more complex forms of learning because it does not have brain circuitry to accomplish more complex tasks.

Each organism at the time of its "birth" has a capacity for learning, a capacity that, in higher animals, becomes more complex over time, during which the organisms can learn from experience. There must be, however, a certain potential for learning at the time of birth in order to enable the individual to survive. It cannot wait until it "grows up" and then start to use the learning mechanisms.

Another important factor here is the speed of learning. The more complex forms of cognitive learning can only occur over a long period, often many years. Our educational process is probably the best example of this phenomenon. Even conditioned learning often takes time, and the more complex the task, the longer the conditioning process.

IMPRINTING

Imprinting in Lower Animals

Ethologists use the term *imprinting* to refer to a response pattern that develops in the earliest hours of life, arises under very specific circumstances, and cannot be extinguished by subsequent experiences. This response pattern occurs during what is referred to as the *critical period* because it will not develop if the same circumstances are operative significantly before or significantly after this particular segment of time.

Some of the seminal work in this area was done by Lorenz (1937, 1950), who introduced the term *imprinting* to refer to this phenomenon. Lorenz worked primarily with greylag geese, but the principles of the imprinting process have been verified in many other species by other investigators. For example, the basic principle is well demonstrated by studies on ducklings conducted by Hess (1966). The fertilized egg of a duck is removed from the nest of the biological mother and placed in the nest of a surrogate duck. Once hatched, the duckling is allowed to remain with the surrogate mother during the first two to three days of life, during which time the duckling demonstrates various manifestations of an attachment bond with the surrogate. One of these is the tendency to follow her wherever she goes. If, after the first few days, the duckling is returned to the nest of its biological mother, it shows few if any manifestations of attachment, especially the following response. And no amount of effort on the biological mother's part to involve the duckling is successful.

If one studies this phenomenon further, one finds that there is a critical period during which this attachment response develops and that involvement with the surrogate before and after this critical period is less likely to result in the formation of an attachment bond. For mallard ducklings the critical period is from 13 to 16 hours. The imprinting response cannot be viewed as an example of a learned reflex in that it cannot be "taught" before or after the critical period, and it cannot be extinguished by traditional punishment or negative reinforcement. Furthermore, imprinting is somewhat indiscriminate in that if the surrogate is a mechanical toy, the bond will develop in association with it and the duckling will follow the mechanical toy throughout its life—no matter how many attempts are made to get it to follow the biological mother. Attempts to suppress the response by such techniques as shocking the duckling each time it touches the mechanical toy often serve instead to strengthen the response. This further demonstrates the point that this phenomenon is not to be considered an example of a learned or conditioned response. If the egg is hatched in a situation in which the newborn duckling is deprived of all contact with any kind of moving figure, animate or inanimate, for a length of time that extends beyond the critical period, then no following response at all can be evoked. Under these circumstances the duckling will not be capable of attaching itself to any caretaking figure, whether it be the biological mother or a human being. It is reasonable to assume that the capacity to form the imprinted response is genetically programmed in that each species has its own critical period for the elicitation of it. Accordingly, I consider it reasonable to refer to it as *instinctual*.

The Question of Imprinting in Human Beings

I believe that human infants exhibit a similar phenomenon during the earliest months of life. I do not believe, however, that it is so specific that one can measure accurately an exact critical period, as one can in lower animals. One of the ways in which human beings differ from lower animals is the flexibility of the instinctual response and its capacity to be modified to varying degrees by the individuals themselves and the social environment. Certain birds, for example, are compelled to perform specific ritualistic mating dances during the mating season. They have no choice but to do so. The capacity for the particular response is programmed into their genes and is elicited by certain environmental stimuli that occur at specific times of the year. Although we human beings have procreative urges that produce the desire to mate, we are not compelled to act on these instinctual responses in a reflex manner. We have a certain degree of conscious control over them, and our social environment can play a significant role in modifying these instinctive responses.

Like the duckling, the human infant forms an attachment bond with its mother or her surrogate. If the human infant is not provided tender loving care during infancy, the child may literally waste away and die. In less extreme situations—in which the caretaker simply does not provide significant affection, tenderness, cuddling, protection, and so on—the infant is not likely to form this bond and, I believe, may never form it. Like the duckling who does not develop a following response if it has been deprived of contact with moving figures for a time that extends beyond the critical period, humans who have been significantly deprived during their critical periods for imprinting will similarly be unable to form an attachment bond—regardless of how benevolent, devoted, dedicated, and loving the caretaking individual. Although I cannot specify a particular segment of time—such as one can with a duckling and other lower species—I believe that this kind of critical period exists in humans within the first few months of life. I cannot be more specific. However, the time span in humans is probably broader and more variable than that of lower animals. And, as is true of lower species, if a human infant does not form this bond during the critical period, I do not believe that *it can ever be formed*. Such individuals may very well become psychotic or psychopathic, or develop other forms of severe psychopathology. Elsewhere (Gardner, 1988b, 1994a), I have elaborated on some of these.

Of pertinence to my discussion here is the capacity of the human brain to learn quickly under certain circumstances, circumstances that involve threat to survival. As I will elaborate upon below, I believe that the human brain has the capacity for quick learning, similar to the kind of learning seen in imprinting. Although this may have survival value, the imprinted mental material may remain spinning around in the brain long after it has served its purpose.

"PSYCHOPATHOLOGY OF EVERYDAY LIFE"

To the best of my knowledge, the term *psychopathology of everyday life* was introduced by Sigmund Freud to refer to the utilization of psychoanalytic insights for explaining a variety of common forms of thinking and behaving. Whereas Freud and his followers would give attention to the psychodynamic factors (both Freudian and non-Freudian), they have not given proper attention to the EBCP as an important contributing factor to such mental and behavioral manifestations.

The EBCP is basically known to all of us. We all have mental material floating around in our brains that periodically intrudes itself into conscious awareness, material that once served some purpose and no longer does so. A common example, well known to individuals who have spent years involved in very demanding academic pursuits, is the dream of being back in school and anticipating, often with terror, a forthcoming examination for which one is ill prepared. Commonly, the dream ends with the individual waking up with a sigh of relief that it was "only a dream." I personally have such a dream once or twice a year. Many years ago, I mentioned this to a colleague and his response to me was: "Doesn't every Jewish boy who went to medical school have that dream?"

Another example from my own personal experience. I was born in 1931. In 1941 the United States formally entered World War II. (It was informally involved for at least two or three years before that.) At that time, the predictions were that the war would last seven to ten years, which meant that I myself might have to go into the military service in my late teens. The prospect of being drafted into the infantry (the most likely course as I understood it at that time) was a bleak one and my hopes were that somehow, some way, the war would end sooner—before my 18th birthday in 1949. Although I did not think about it daily, the specter of my being drafted into the infantry hovered over me during those years, epitomized by the fantasy of receiving a letter in the mail from my draft board informing me that I would now have to enter the Army. As is well known, in 1945, after dropping two atom bombs on Japan (not one but two), the Japanese prematurely surrendered.

One would think that my sigh of relief at age 14 would have resulted in the complete evaporation of my anticipation of receiving that dreaded letter from my draft board. It did not. In 1950 the Korean War began. I was then 19 and in college. Although "a perfect age" for being drafted, college students who achieved a high score on a national examination were deferred. (If there was *one* thing that Jewish boys from the Bronx High School of Science relished, it was national competitive examinations!) Not surprisingly, I achieved the required score and was deferred. (I recognize now the inequity and possibly even the immorality of that policy, but in 1950 such considerations did not enter my mind.) Yet, even after passing that exam, thoughts of receiving that letter from my draft board did not leave my mind. I am not claiming that I walked around obsessed with these concerns; I am only stating that they came to mind from time to time for no apparent reason.

In 1952, upon entrance to medical school, I signed up with "The Berry Plan" (named, I believe, after the general who originated it), a program in which I committed myself to military service following the completion of my residency (approximately eight to nine years hence). *Now*, there would be no reason for me to be concerned about any letter from my draft board. I was already formally *in* the service, only my day of entry would be in 1960. Furthermore, I was not going to serve as *Kanonenfutter* (cannon fodder) in the infantry; rather, I was going to be a doctor and an officer. Yet, I still had occasional thoughts about receiving a letter from the draft board.

From 1960 to 1962 I served as a psychiatrist at the primary U.S. Army hospital in Frankfurt-am-Main, Germany. When I left the service at age 31, I learned that under the "doctor draft," the program under which I was serving, my military obligation would last until *age 52*! There was no imminent danger of my being drafted again. I was merely being put on notice that people who were deferred for medical training had that obligation. I was reassured, again, that because I had already served I would be very low priority for reinduction. Yet thoughts of receiving that letter from the draft board would occasionally enter my mind, perhaps once a month or so. Again, I was not plagued by them, nor have I ever been.

Most people do not dance with glee when reaching the age of 52. To me, obviously, it was a special event in that now the Army could no longer "get me." The fantasy then turned to one like this: The postman comes and gives me this special delivery certified letter. I open it up. It's from the draft board, informing me that I have been drafted.

"Ha, ha! I have already served," say I as I wave my honorable discharge papers under the nose of some guy in the draft board. "You can't have me now! Besides, I'm over 52. Here's my birth certificate to prove it!" As I write this, I am 64. Yet, I still have occasional thoughts of receiving that letter from the draft board. Although I know intellectually that they are not drafting 64-year-old men (in fact, they are not drafting anyone at this point), I still have occasional thoughts of that letter coming.

Obviously, such thoughts serve no useful purpose. I believe that this experience—spanning a half-century—demonstrates well the EBCP. Furthermore, my very writing now about this occasional fantasy embeds the material even more deeply into my brain circuitry. The idea that talking (or writing) about it gets it out of my system is not valid for this phenomenon. In fact, it may not be valid for any phenomenon. Rather, talking about it does just the opposite, namely, it embeds it even more deeply into the brain circuitry. One could argue that psychodynamic factors are operative in my periodic recollections, factors that are fueling their perpetuation. I cannot deny this, especially because it is impossible to disprove entirely any speculation regarding psychodynamic processes. It is also not possible to prove them valid. For myself, with regard to these recollections, I do not believe that psychodynamic factors are playing an important role, if any role at all. I believe that the EBCP explanation is the more likely one.

Another example: About 25 years ago, while writing one of my earlier articles, I asked an editor about the proper placement of commas before and after "e.g." She told me that the preferred procedure, in most situations, is to put commas on either side. For some strange reason, when writing or dictating an e.g., I automatically think of her telling me to put commas on either side. I really do not need that extra thought. It serves no useful purpose. I got her message and utilized it. One could argue that this too has some psychological meaning, perhaps that I was interested in her, for purposes far beyond learning the placement of commas, and that recalling her in association with the comma instructions also provides me with a mental image of her. Well, she was 25 years older than I. One could argue then that she was a mother figure for me. I cannot deny any of these explanations. And even if one or both of these psychodynamic explanations are operative, I do not believe that they provide for the full explanation as to why I have hooked her in with my recollection of the punctuation principle. Of course, the learning-by-association principle is operative here, but also, I believe, is the EBCP.

Traumatic experiences are very likely to result in the EBCP. Take divorce as an example. A couple is married X number of years and has Y number of children. They then go through a very painful child-custody dispute, which lasts three years. Their funds are depleted and they both end up "basket cases," *both* the "winner" and the "loser." Five years later both are remarried, allegedly happily. They each have new spouses with whom they have good relationships, nothing like the old ones. Yet, unwelcome and painful thoughts related to their earlier divorce experiences still spin around in their brains. I do not believe that any amount of psychotherapy is going to reduce such recollections. In fact, such therapy might even increase the frequency of such thoughts because of the inevitable muckraking that is involved in the therapeutic process. Moreover, the "deeper," more prolonged, and more extensive the psychotherapy, the greater the likelihood these recollections will increase in frequency. I do not deny the potential benefits of such treatment; I focus here only on its inevitable untoward effects.

The EBCP is probably the best explanation for the universal observation that we learn best from our own experiences, especially painful ones. The wise men of the ages have passed down to us advice derived from their experiences. Their hope is that their descendents will learn from their mistakes and avail themselves of the wisdom they derived from their own experiences, often painful. The great works of philosophy and literature, especially the Bible, are testament to this legacy. Yet, most of us learn little from these sages. Rather, we learn most from the experiences that we have had, especially those that were painful. I am not saying that we do not repeat our mistakes; I am only saying that we are less likely to repeat them if we have suffered pain in association with them. An experience associated with high levels of emotion is more likely to become deeply embedded in the brain circuitry. In addition to the higher embedding potential of an emotionally charged experience is the fact that a highly emotional experience is likely to be repeated more than one that is more neutral or that is free of emotions, and this too increases the likelihood that it will become entrenched into the psychic structure.

The analogy with the formation of a river may be applicable here. A river may begin as a small, narrow stream of water, perhaps only a few feet wide. As this little stream flows, it pulls earth, pebbles, and small rocks along with it and gradually forms a crevice. As this deepens and widens, a stream gradually develops. As the stream progressively deepens and widens, it may ultimately warrant the term *rivulet*, then *river*. Other streams may enter into it, causing ever more widening and deepening. The same phenomenon, I believe, takes place in the brain—but, obviously, at far more complex levels.

THE POSTTRAUMATIC STRESS DISORDER

The Posttraumatic Stress Disorder (PTSD) provides an excellent example of the EBCP. In order to justify the diagnosis, according to *DSM-IV*:

> A. The person has been exposed to a traumatic event in which both of the following were present:
> (1) the person experienced, witnessed, or was confronted with an event or events that involved actual or threatened death or serious injury, or a threat to the physical integrity of self or others
> (2) the person's response involved intense fear, helplessness, or horror.

In order to make the diagnosis, a multiplicity of symptoms must be present for at least one month and cause significant clinical distress or impairment. *Some* of the symptoms commonly seen are:

> Recurrent and intrusive distressing recollections of the event, including images, thoughts, or perceptions... recurrent distressing dreams of the event... acting or feeling as if the traumatic event were recurring (includes a sense of reliving the experience, illusions, hallucinations, and dissociative flashback episodes... intense psychological distress at exposure to internal or external cues that symbolize or resemble an aspect of the traumatic event... physiological reactivity on exposure to internal or external cues that symbolize or resemble an aspect of the traumatic event

... efforts to avoid thoughts, feelings, or conversations associated with the trauma ... hypervigilance ... exaggerated startle response.

The PTSD may be the only disorder in *DSM-IV* in which the symptoms may play a role in the therapeutic process. The trauma has resulted in a flooding of stimuli into the brain circuitry. One could argue that their remaining there serves important purposes. One would be to desensitize the person to the psychologically traumatic effects of the trauma. It is as if each time the person reexperiences the event, it becomes a little more tolerable. It is reasonable to view the PTSD, then, as nature's form of systematic desensitization. Furthermore, one could argue that PTSD symptoms may be useful for introducing coping mechanisms (especially fight or flight) that could be useful for helping the patient avoid recurrence of the same traumatic experience. When a trauma is so severe that a PTSD develops, the flooding of stimuli into the brain is so rapid that ECBP occurs very quickly. Furthermore, it is highly likely that the processes of systematic desensitization and EBCP, although therapeutic, also lessen the likelihood that the individual will be able to forget the traumatic experience. At the same time that the patient is deriving the benefits of the desensitization process, he (she) is entrenching the mental material ever more deeply into the brain circuitry via the EBCP. The benefits of the EBCP are that the individual is less likely to forget the coping mechanisms (fight or flight) that might be useful for preventing a recurrence. But there is a price to be paid for this deepening of memory, namely, the inability to forget. The more one remembers, the less capacity to forget. The more one desensitizes, the more EBCP, and the less capacity to forget about the experience. An analogy can be made here to taking a potent drug with a powerful, untoward side effect. It appears to be the psychological price that the patient pays for the curative process. There are implications here for the therapeutic process, especially a therapeutic process that encourages the person to think about the trauma.

DISSOCIATION

Most people who suffer with PTSD have fairly clear memories of the major events associated with their trauma. There are some individuals, however, who dissociate the trauma, and this is especially likely to occur when the trauma is very severe, e.g., military combat, earthquakes, tornadoes, floods, rape, and attempted murder. There is a massive flooding of stimuli into the brain circuitry. The unity of consciousness is disrupted. There is a disintegration of consciousness and certain segments of the personality may operate autonomously. Continuity and consistency of thoughts are disconnected from one another. Identity confusion and identity alteration may occur. There is a loss of sense of the passage of time. The person may experience perceptual distortions, illusions, or feelings that the surrounding world is strange or unreal (derealization). Sometimes there is complete amnesia for the event (psychogenic amnesia) or the individual enters into an altered state of consciousness in the context of which complex behaviors are exhibited that are subsequently unknown to the patient (psychogenic fugue). The phenomenon may be associated with psychic numbing, which also serves to protect the individual from full appreciation of the trauma. (The reader interested in a more detailed description of the dissociative phenomena does well to refer to Steinberg's contribution [1993]). Dissociation is well compared to the overloaded computer that short circuits and stops functioning because it cannot deal with the massive amount of information being poured in.

In chronic abuse this pattern may become deeply entrenched to the point where the process becomes automatic: each time the person is abused, he (she) automatically dissociates and thereby protects himself (herself) from the pain of the experience. The result may be (in a small percentage of cases) no conscious recall of the traumatic events.

Such dissociative episodes may then occur in situations in which the person is reminded of the abuse by cues that are similar to those that existed at the time of the original abuse. It is as if the traumatic experience and its derivative dissociative states, not in conscious awareness, are very much embedded in the brain circuitry. Exposure to a similar situation triggers some dim and possibly unconscious recollection of these events, a recollection that may be associated with powerful emotional concomitants similar to those experienced at the time of the original trauma. Such triggers then produce the disorganization of thinking typical of dissociation. Under such circumstances, there are likely to be other manifestations of dissociation in which the person may be amnesic for certain time blocks during which events that transpired are totally obliterated from the person's memory but have been clearly observed by others. This is not simply a matter of forgetting certain events, which all people do, but there is total obliteration of conscious memory of such events and confusion when confronted by observers of the individual's involvement in such events.

Dissociation is very controversial at this point, even regarding whether or not it actually exists. This is especially the case with regard to the multiple personality disorder (more recently renamed in *DSM-IV* the dissociative identity disorder). I myself consider it quite rare, far less common than the PTSD (the far more likely reaction to trauma). Overzealous examiners often frivolously apply the concept of dissociation to even the most transient episodes of inattentiveness and "spacing out." This may be done in circumstances in which there was absolutely no evidence for bona fide dissociation at the time of the original alleged abuse. This is most commonly done by examiners who want to justify sexual abuse as the trauma when the patient does not have any conscious recollection of having been so traumatized. In the course of "therapy" for such dissociated traumas and residual effects, the patient cannot only be led to believe that she was sexually traumatized, but the belief becomes deeply embedded in the brain circuitry to the point where it becomes a fixed delusion (Gardner, 1992a, 1994a, 1995a).

OBSESSIVE-COMPULSIVE DISORDER

Obsessive-Compulsive Disorder (OCD) provides another good example of the ECBP. Throughout most of this century, primarily under the influence of psychoanalytic teaching, OCD was generally considered to be a purely psychological disorder. More recently, the pendulum has shifted significantly toward the organic etiological explanation. This biological explanation has been given significant support by the findings that certain drugs such as Anafranil (clomipramine) and Prozac (fluoxetine) often bring about alleviation of OCD symptoms. However, when patients discontinue such medications, symptoms usually return.

Traditionally, patients with OCD suffer with obsessions (repeated thoughts) and compulsions (the repeated need to enact certain behaviors). Obsessive preoccupations are intrusive and inappropriate and cause marked tension or distress. Compulsive acts are often referred to as *rituals* and appear to be meaningless or serve no useful purpose; yet the individual is almost powerless to prevent himself (herself) from performing them. Although a particular individual may suffer more with obsessions or compulsions, generally there is a combination.

Typical obsessions are: repeated fear that food and dishes are contaminated with disease-engendering agents, obsessive desires to shout obscenities in public situations, and repeated and undesirable sexual imagery that is unacceptable to the individual. Common repetitive behaviors seen in the compulsions include: handwashing, putting things in specific order, repeated checking (lights on or off, TV on or off), and counting rituals (the goal of which is to prevent or reduce anxiety).

There may very well be a genetic loading or predisposition to the development of the OCD. However, I believe that the *original* OCD symptoms (which usually appear in childhood) generally served some psychological purpose. Then, after they have become deeply entrenched in the brain circuitry, they continue circulating there and may have "a life of their own" when they no longer serve any purpose. For example, the OCD symptoms may have originated in childhood as a mechanism for magically reducing guilt over hostility. Then, after this guilt-assuaging mechanism has been used for many months and years, it continues to spin around in the brain circuitry even though the person has matured enough to recognize that such magical ways of assuaging guilt are not really necessary. The person may have progressed to a more mature level with regard to comfort with socially unacceptable hostile thoughts and feelings, but may still be plagued by the earlier guilt-reducing mechanisms that "just don't seem to go away." The OCD symptoms thereby become ego-alien, yet the person is helpless to put the thoughts out of his (her) mind or stop himself (herself) from acting out the OCD compulsions.

This explanation for the OCD is well demonstrated by Tom, age 45, who told me in his first interview that he suffered with OCD from the age of about seven or eight. I told Tom of my belief that although OCD might have a constitutional/biological basis, I still consider environmental factors to be contributory, especially at the time of the origin of the symptoms. Accordingly, because I could do nothing about the biological factors, the only help I could possibly provide him was to address ourselves to the environmental. I then explored with Tom what might have been the environmental factors that could have contributed to the development of his OCD. As a result of such inquiry, I learned that as long as Tom could remember, his mother was continually warning him not to upset his father and especially not to express anger toward him. She told Tom that if he did engage in such behavior, his father might die of a heart attack. Throughout the course of Tom's childhood, his father was perfectly healthy and there was never any real medical reason for his mother's concerns. Tom recalled, as early as age four, developing a ritual in which he would touch a table four times, with the belief that this procedure would protect his father from dying of a heart attack. In the course of my inquiry, Tom gained insight into the fact that this ritual served as a magical protection against the fulfillment of hostile wishes that he inwardly harbored toward his father. He came to appreciate that he was taught to feel very guilty about the normal hostility that all people feel in all relationships and that this ritual protected him from his fantasized consequences of anger expression.

Another one of Tom's mother's favorite themes was to say to Tom, "Don't make me choose between you and your father, because I'll always choose him." Tom had never asked his mother to make this choice; in fact, the notion never even entered his mind until the time his mother introduced it. In the course of our discussion, Tom came to appreciate that this message also engendered in him great hostility, which he felt guilty about expressing.

Two weeks after this interview, Tom claimed that he was enjoying a significant alleviation of his OCD and attributed it to the insights he had gained in his session. He complimented me on my expertise and thanked me profusely for the help I had provided him. I am not easily flattered by such professions of cure and have always been somewhat suspicious of them. This was especially the case because such preoccupations had been entrenched in Tom's brain circuitry for almost forty years. I told Tom that I was pleased that our conversation had such good results, but that it was difficult for me to believe that after all these years his symptoms would completely evaporate. Furthermore, even if they had, there was no question that Tom's anger-inhibition problem still persisted and was not simply confined to the OCD symptoms, but manifested itself in other areas. I told him, what was already obvious, that even though his mother was no longer alive, his father was old and senile, and the anger-inhibiting messages that his mother was communicating at that time should no longer be operative; yet, residua of that anger inhibition were still present in his life. I pointed out to him how this problem was causing difficulties in his relationships with his wife and son. This suggested strongly that his mother's dictates were still floating around in his brain via the EBCP. Thus, my dubiety about his "cure."

As therapy progressed, it became increasingly clear that the primary cause was the EBCP situation that prevailed at that time. I advised him that until he was more comfortable expressing his resentment in other areas, it was likely that there would be an exacerbation of the OCD. And this is what came to pass. When there was a return of symptoms, I prescribed Prozac, which proved somewhat efficacious. We also worked on his anger-inhibition problem. It became increasingly clear to me that he was no longer the guilt-ridden person that he was at age five, but that his mother's dictates were still entrenched in his mind via the EBCP. He became less beholden to them and could more easily ignore them. But therapy was not successful in obliterating these thoughts from his mind. He just felt less of a need to obey them. Prozac helped, I believe, because it interferes with the transmission in the brain circuitry of the unacceptable psychological material that manifests itself symptomologically as the OCD.

SEXUAL FANTASIES AND PROCLIVITIES

All of us have a repertoire of personal sexual fantasies and proclivities. Usually, these are the accumulated result of our earlier sexual experiences, some often dating back to early childhood. It may very well be that the variety of such preferred sexual fantasies and activities is so great that no two people are identical. The EBCP is very much operative here in that sexual experiences that are repeated and/or associated with very high emotional tone are more likely to be embedded in the brain circuitry. I am not addressing myself here to whether or not one puts the label of psychopathology on any of these sexual fantasies or activities; I am only addressing myself to the way the EBCP plays a role in determining one's preferred sexual fantasies and activities.

One's "First True Love"

The adolescent's first romantic encounter serves well as a good example of the EBCP. Romantic, loving feelings can be extremely powerful. In many cases they can be an obsession and become the all-consuming preoccupation of the youngster (and even older people). When such feelings are associated with the first sexual experiences, especially the first orgastic experiences, the emotional impact can be profound. Under such circumstances, even a relatively short experience can become deeply embedded in the psychic structure. This first encounter is likely to become a model for all subsequent amorous encounters. Often, the loved person is idealized, and the obvious deficiencies of the individual are completely ignored. This idealized relationship then becomes the model for all subsequent relationships, sometimes with disastrous results throughout the course of the individual's life. Whereas in adolescence the individual's cognitive immaturity enables the person "in love" to harbor obvious distortions of reality, residua of this illogicality may blur reason throughout the course of one's life. The individual seeks to find a substitute for the original loved one, a substitute that will bring about the same state of elation. This too may require a "willing suspension of disbelief." The delusional world so created may ultimately bring about an enormous amount of grief for both parties. (Of course, many other factors are operative in the romantic love phenomenon, and I have discussed these elsewhere [Gardner, 1991b,c; 1992c]). Here I focus on the EBCP as an important element. It is a partial explanation for people who, throughout life, involve themselves in what are obviously improper and even destructive relationships in association with which they create delusions about each other that are in direct contradiction to what is the reality of the situation.

Less dramatically, EBCP plays an important role in the choice of one's sexual partners. It is not surprising that most people tend to gravitate toward partners from their own ethnic background. This, in part, relates to the fact that one's first love relationship is with one's parents, who then become the models for their substitutes, the subsequent lovers in one's life. If a boy has a good relationship with his mother, she will become the model for the girls he will gravitate toward, his adolescent professions of rejection and even scorn of his mother notwithstanding. And the same principle holds for girls with regard to their relationships with their fathers and his subsequent substitutes. What I am saying here has absolutely nothing to do with the existence (or lack of existence) of the Oedipus complex. I am addressing myself here only to the EBCP as an important determinant of these choices. It determines the qualities that one is going to be attracted to because these are qualities that were associated with high emotional charge in early childhood and were frequently introduced into the brain circuitry via the fact that the parenting figures are the main ones the child encounters in the early years of life. The principle is epitomized by the old song, "I Want a Girl Just Like the Girl Who Married Dear Old Dad." (Referring to this phenomenon as "oedipal" does not, I believe, provide additional information—especially if one studiously separates fact from fantasy.)

Homosexuality

Although homosexuality may certainly have a genetic/biological substratum, environmental factors may also be operative in bringing about this sexual orientation. I focus here on the EBCP as a factor operative in the development of homosexuality of *some* individuals.

Fred, a 12-year-old boy, was, by all known criteria, moving down the heterosexual track. He had already expressed some interest in girls and had already had heterosexual fantasies. Fred's life pattern, then, had been typically heterosexual. He had engaged in the rough-and-tumble play in earlier years, play that is one of the most important predictors of whether a youngster is going to go down the heterosexual or homosexual track (Green, 1985, 1987). Fred's involvements in competitive sports was typically age-appropriate and heterosexual, and he had good heterosexual models in his father, teachers, and male relatives. At age 12, before he had ever experienced an orgasm, Fred was sexually seduced by a homosexual male. However, the seduction was not an isolated rape; rather, it was the culmination of an ongoing seductive (often referred to as "grooming") process by a scoutmaster. During the two years prior to the seduction, Fred had deeply admired this man, who had been his confidant and had bestowed upon him continual praise and admiration. In the course of the sexual encounters, Fred not only experienced his first orgasms but was provided with "love" and "affection" at such a high rate of intensity that, from Fred's point of view, he had never experienced pleasures compared to those that he enjoyed with his scoutmaster. Fred became obsessed with this man, who in turn was obsessed with him. The man became his "first love" and Fred believed at that time that this experience was not only the greatest he had ever had, but that nothing in the future would ever be able to compare with it. After six months, the man lost interest, rejected the boy, and then moved on to another "lover." The boy continued to move along the homosexual track and, as an adult, continued to believe that had he not had this experience at age 12, he probably would have become heterosexual.

Some, but certainly not all, boys who have this experience shift from the heterosexual to the homosexual track. This is especially the case in situations in which the pursuit of heterosexual partners frequently results in rejection, the most common outcome in early adolescence. Homosexual overtures, however, are far less likely to be spurned, especially when young boys are involved. This kind of an experience, not uncommon among men who ultimately become homosexual, can be explained readily by the EBCP. I am not denying a possible (and even probable) genetic/biological predisposition for many homosexuals. I am only describing here *another* route to that pattern, a route for which the basic genetic substratum may very well have been heterosexual, but the EBCP superimposed itself onto that foundation and brought about a pattern of homosexual orientation.

Pedophilia

Pedophilia may very well have a genetic substratum, but I believe also that environmental factors are likely to play a role in whether an individual will select pedophilia as the primary mode of sexual orientation. Here I focus on the EBCP as a factor that may be operative in bringing about pedophilia.

I once interviewed a 42-year-old man, Glen, who told me that he was a pedophile and that he has always been a pedophile. He said that he had never acted out on his pedophilic impulses because of his fear of disclosure, social stigmatization, and even imprisonment. Glen had never married and he gratified his pedophilic impulses by masturbation, especially in association with child pornographic materials. I asked him the traditional question I ask all patients who have atypical sexual orientations, namely, what *their* theory is regarding how they got that way. Glen believed that his sexual orientation would have been typically heterosexual if not for a certain experience he had when he was five years old. He and two girls his age were in the woods behind his house playing the exploratory game, "You Show Me Yours and I'll Show You Mine." However, it had not reached the point of genital exposure; rather, the two girls pulled up their dresses and showed him their panties. And he pulled down his pants and showed them his underpants. In the course of the third such encounter, the children were discovered by Glen's mother, a strongly religious woman who immediately broke out into a tirade of rage against all three children and then sent the two little girls home. She called the girls' mothers, informed them of what had occurred, and all mothers agreed to place upon the children stringent restrictions. During the next few weeks, Glen's mother was obsessed with what she had seen. Her rage outbursts to Glen were ongoing and often lasted an hour or two. She constantly invoked religious proscriptions against such behavior, exhorted Glen on how sinful he and the other children had been, and repeatedly made him promise that he would never do such a terrible thing again. Glen said to me, "Her shit-fits lasted at least three weeks and she never let up."

During the ensuing years, with a certain amount of fascination, he intermittently thought about his experiences with the two girls. At the age of 14 he first experienced very strong sexual urges and began to masturbate. However, when he compared notes with his friends, he found that he was not particularly interested in utilizing pinup magazines in that he did not find himself particularly attracted to adult women, especially those who were fully developed. And this was true also with regard to girls in his class, who he also came to learn were common sources of masturbatory stimuli for his boyfriends. Rather, he found himself on occasion thinking sensuously about those girls who were less well developed physically. His most stimulating masturbatory fantasy, however, was the two little girls in their panties, with whom he had his first "sexual" encounter at age five. Although when masturbating he tried strongly to think about the pinup girls in the magazines and the girls in his class, it just "didn't work" for him. At 15 he tried dating a few classmates in the hope that he might overcome his problem. Again, this just "didn't work," even though he chose the youngest looking and the least well developed girls. Finally, by 16, he gave up entirely the attempt to become a normal heterosexual boy and resigned himself to the fact that he was a pedophile, even though he did not use that term at the time.

I believe that the most likely explanation for Glen's pedophilia relates to the EBCP. Had his mother responded in the more common and healthier way, he might not have developed along the pedophilic track. One might even say that he might not have been fixated at the pedophilic level. Had his mother, with compassion, understanding, and benevolence, told the children that this behavior was not acceptable and that when they were older, they would be freer to engage themselves in such behavior, he might not have become a pedophile. I believe it was the mother's three weeks of "shit-fits" that was the primary (if not exclusive) determinant of Glen's pedophilia. The mother "never let up" and, in the course of her harangues, deeply entrenched into her son's brain circuitry the fantasies and thoughts of the sexual encounters with the girls. Each time she screamed at him, he could not but think about these encounters. As mentioned, high emotional tone is an important determinant as to whether psychic material is embedded into the brain circuitry, and such high emotional tone is more likely to be associated with trauma. The trauma in this case was Glen's mother. She converted a normal childhood encounter into a sexual trauma. If she had just mildly reprimanded Glen and then exercised reasonable precautions, the imagery might not have been entrenched so deeply, if at all, into his brain circuitry. The powerful emotions that then became associated with these encounters, emotions that the mother engendered, played a role in the entrenchment process. In addition, her harangues repeatedly brought the imagery of these encounters into mental awareness and, by extension, embedded them more deeply into Glen's brain circuitry. I often thought it would be of interest to find out how many pedophiles had experiences of this kind in early childhood in that it might be a possible explanation for *some* with this orientation.

Residua of Childhood Sexual Experiences in Adult Sexual Life

Women who have been sexually abused in childhood will sometimes incorporate (consciously or unconsciously) residua of their early sexual experiences into their adult sexual fantasies and activities. Sometimes these are unwanted elements, but they persist nevertheless. For example, a woman who stared at a design on the wallpaper to distract herself from her childhood sexual encounters with her stepfather may find that she needs such stimuli in order to become sexually aroused. One man once told me that while he was dating his wife, she told him that she had been sexually abused by her father during childhood. Specifically, from age 7 through 11, he had come into her room at night for sexual encounters. In the early years, there was fondling and masturbation. But starting at age 9, she was having sexual intercourse with him.

Subsequently, when my patient and his fiancée became more intimate, she somewhat apologetically asked him if he would enact a particular ritual as part of their foreplay. Specifically, she asked him to enter the bedroom from the hall and, while approaching the bed, to first take off his pajama bottoms and then his pajama top. All this was to be done while walking toward the bed. Then, while she was lying on her left side, she wanted him to lie behind her on his left side as well. She somewhat ashamedly told him that this was exactly what her father did prior to having sex with her and that she needed a lover to perform this particular ritual if she was to become sexually aroused. She wished that she did not need these preliminary steps, but hoped that he would understand. I do not believe that this is an isolated example. Just as desired early sexual activities become incorporated into brain circuitry, so do the undesired. Both may be associated with strong emotions, thereby increasing the likelihood of embedment in the brain circuitry. Both are likely to be thought about frequently, thereby also increasing the likelihood of embedment in the brain circuitry. Although intellectually undesired, such residua may become necessary for sexual arousal. This need for adult reenactment of a childhood sexual trauma provides an excellent example of the EBCP.

Carl, at the age of 14, was seduced into believing that anal intercourse with his minister was an important prelude to his subsequent sexual encounters with girls and that these experiences would make him more successful in such pursuits. He engaged in these homosexual activities over an 18-month period, at the end of which time the minister was jailed. In the years following, visual images of his sexual experiences with his abuser intruded themselves into his traditionally heterosexual masturbatory fantasies—in spite of his attempts to exclude them. We see here an excellent example of the EBCP. The sexual experiences were associated with a high level of emotion and became repeatedly embedded in Carl's brain circuitry, so much so that he could not exclude them from his masturbatory fantasies, in spite of his very strong desire that they would "just evaporate."

At 18, while having sexual intercourse with his first girlfriend, she asked him not to thrust so vigorously because he was causing her pain. In spite of his intellectual recognition that her request was reasonable, he felt compelled to thrust even more vigorously, causing her severe pain and bleeding. Afterward, he realized that her comments were identical to those he himself had made to his minister when he was being anally penetrated. Specifically, when he told his minister that the anal penetration was hurting him, the minister ignored him and merely continued thrusting. We see here not only an excellent example of the way in which residua of earlier sexual experiences become incorporated into future sexual fantasies and activities, but also the identification-with-the-aggressor phenomenon so often seen in those who have been sexually abused. The EBCP provides a viable explanation for such incorporation and identification.

Hindman (1991) describes this phenomenon of subsequent incorporation of the childhood experiences as a common sequela among those who have been severely traumatized in the course of their abuse. He states of these patients:

> Sexual responsiveness during the sexual abuse scenarios did not seem to dissolve or discontinue in adulthood. What seems to be a tragic effect of the most severely traumatized patient is that because of their sexual

responsiveness, many patients manifested signs of continual arousal toward either the perpetrator or to the kinds of activities taking place during the sexual abuse. It seems to be an especially traumatic combination for the horrors of abuse and sexual arousal to be remembered.

We see then that not only pleasant but unpleasant sexual experiences can be incorporated into the brain circuitry. Apparently, the cognitive element is not the most important determinant as to whether such material will be incorporated into the psychic structure; rather, it is the degree to which the cognitive material is associated with high emotional charge and the frequency with which the thoughts and feelings are repeated. High pleasure (such as was the situation for Fred, the 12-year-old boy who became homosexual) and intense pain (as it was for Carl, the 14-year-old boy abused by his minister) both have the potential for deep embedment in the brain circuitry.

False Sex-Abuse Accusers

The EBCP can also shed light on the experience some women have when they make an accusation of sex abuse when there is little if any evidence for such. The accusation may begin with a suspicion that may have absolutely no basis in reality. The suspicion exists only in the mind of the accuser, and there is no evidence that the child has been abused and no evidence that the accused party has pedophilic tendencies. The suspicion may have been planted in an era of sex-abuse hysteria, when such suspicions are widespread (Gardner, 1991a). Next, the mother brings the child to an "expert," who, with anatomical dolls and leading questions, elicits from the child some comments that are then considered confirmatory of sexual abuse. The expert, then, is required to report this "abuse" to the proper investigatory authorities, including a child protection service and often the police. Once "gangbusters" descend upon this child, there is a high likelihood that he (she) will spin off ever more elaborate descriptions of the alleged sexual abuses. In the course of all this, lawyers may then be brought in for civil and/or criminal lawsuits. Over the next few years (a not uncommon duration), the mother's suspicion becomes a preoccupation, then a hysterical manifestation that spreads to others, and finally a delusion in which there is the fixed belief that the abuse occurred. The delusion here is supported by the overzealous experts and "validators" who convince the mother that her decision was valid. Most often, it is supported by a coterie of friends, relatives, and other "enablers." If she is in a group of mothers of abused children, the belief may be even more deeply entrenched.

An element operative in the development of this induced delusion is the ECBP. The more the notion of sex abuse spins around in the mother's brain, the more deeply it becomes entrenched in the brain circuitry, and the more likely it is to become a fixed belief. The child too may develop the same delusion, especially after years of "therapy," the purpose of which is to encourage ongoing hostility toward the alleged perpetrator (hitting dolls, drawing pictures of him in jail, etc.) and extracting ever more details about the abuses. Ultimately, a folie-à-deux is produced in which both the mother and the child have developed a delusion that may persist throughout life, so powerful is the ECBP.

My experience has been that women who have gone down the track to developing such delusions are incurable in that by that point there is absolutely no insight into the process that has taken place. Their children, however, may be put into treatment. These children have also been abused by the promulgator as well as the therapist and legal health professionals who may have entrenched their delusion. In subsequent chapters I will focus on the importance of the therapist's appreciating the EBCP when treating these children, those who have been sexually abused, and those who have been swept up in the sex-abuse hysteria of our times.

THERAPEUTIC IMPLICATIONS

The therapeutic implications of the EBCP are formidable. If I am correct, then psychotherapeutic attempts to change the behaviors generated from EBCP material may be very difficult, if not impossible. Courts routinely order psychotherapy for sexual offenders, and there are those who present themselves as providing such treatment. I am basically dubious about the efficacy of treatment for sex offenders. The older the individual, the longer the particular pattern has been spinning around in the person's brain and the less the likelihood of its being changed by a psychotherapeutic technique. Even aversive behavioral techniques are not likely to be efficacious in that they cannot introduce in a short time frame stimuli that are going to effectively compete with those that have been spinning around and entrenching themselves in the person's brain circuitry for many years.

In mid-century, Kinsey was very critical of those psychotherapists (especially psychoanalysts) who claimed that they could "cure" homosexuality with psychodynamic and psychoanalytic techniques. The story goes (and I do not have this firsthand) that Kinsey informally spread the word that he would like to see *one* exclusively homosexual person who had been successfully converted to heterosexuality by psychotherapeutic techniques. For many years, no one stepped forward. The story goes that, while off on a lecture tour, the phone rang in his hotel room. The caller announced to Kinsey that *he* was the person whom Kinsey had been looking for, that he had been a homosexual and had been "cured" by psychodynamic psychoanalysis. The man was ready to come to Kinsey's hotel and meet him there at the earliest possible mutual convenience. Right then was not too soon. Kinsey, so the story goes, told the man that before he came to the hotel, he would like to ask him *one* question. The man agreed and this was the alleged interchange:

> *Kinsey*: What do you think about when you masturbate?
> *Caller*: Well, I still think about men.
> *Kinsey*: Don't waste your time coming here. You're not the person I'm looking for.

Increasingly, in recent years, child abuse by clergymen has been brought to the attention of the public. A common response on the part of the churches so accused is that these clergymen are going into "treatment." Some of them are in their 50s, 60s, and even older. Perhaps some of these spokespeople do indeed believe that these clergymen are going to be cured. Others, I suspect, know very well that this is generally impossible and that they are merely perpetrating a fraud upon the public. In either case, it is improper and even deceptive to promulgate the notion that treatment can change the sexual orientation of an adult. The chance of changing an adult homosexual to an adult heterosexual is the same as changing an adult heterosexual to an adult homosexual. And attempts to change a pedophile into a person whose sexual interests will be exclusively toward adults is also likely to prove futile.

The ECBP also has important relevance for the treatment of patients who have been traumatized. The therapy of such patients must be embarked upon cautiously, with full appreciation of the natural desensitization process. The therapist should not muckrake and dredge up recollections of the trauma in compliance with some therapeutic principle that to do so is salutary. This is especially the case if the therapist subscribes to the notion that it is first important to "get everything out before the 'healing' process can begin." Rather, the therapist should respect the normal desensitization process and its concomitant reduction in the frequency with which the individual thinks about the trauma. The muckraking process may do the individual more harm than good in that it can have the effect of more deeply entrenching thoughts about the trauma, thereby perpetuating the patient's preoccupation with it. And this is what happens in "survivor groups" and those who may involve themselves in political-action groups related to their trauma. Whatever benefits they may derive from these activities, a heavy price is paid with regard to the more deepening entrenchment of the traumatic thoughts and feelings in the patient's brain circuitry.

This point is well demonstrated by an old Laurel and Hardy movie. As I recall it, Oliver Hardy falls deeply in love with a young woman, a woman who has absolutely no interest in him and repeatedly spurns his overtures. The more he is rebuffed, the more deeply "in love" he falls and the more obsessed he is with this woman. Finally, the two decide to join the French Foreign Legion in an attempt to remove Oliver from this woman and thereby help him forget her. And so they join the Legion and go off to the North African desert. Soon thereafter Stan asks Oliver, "Well, did you forget her?" Immediately, Oliver angrily responds, "Stop asking me that. The more you ask me that, the harder it will be to forget her!" Predictably, Stan continues to ask Oliver whether he has forgotten her, and, more predictably, Oliver goes into zany fits of frustration and rage during which he beseeches Stan to stop asking this question and threatens terrible retaliations if he continues to do so. Therapists who work with PTSD patients and other disorders in which the EBCP is operative do well to keep this vignette in mind.

☐ THREE

TREATMENT OF CHILDREN WHO HAVE ACTUALLY BEEN SEXUALLY ABUSED

INTRODUCTION

One should not even begin thinking about the treatment of a child who has allegedly been sexually abused until one is certain that the child has indeed been sexually abused. The use of such terms as "possibly," "symptoms consistent with sex abuse," and "probably" implies a level of certainty that is inadequate for the purposes of treating a child for sex abuse. To treat under such circumstances is to risk involving oneself in the kind of sham therapy described in detail in Chapter Four. The crucial question, then, is *how* certain a therapist must be before embarking on a treatment program for such children. The answer: a very high degree of certainty. I am not stating that the only patients who should be treated are those whom the therapist himself (herself) has observed in an act of sexual abuse. Rather, I am only saying that the therapist should be convinced that the child has been abused before embarking on the treatment. Such conviction is best obtained if the therapist has conducted the evaluation and has personally come to the conclusion that the abuse has indeed taken place. Such an evaluation, as mentioned so many times previously, should include the allegedly abused child, the accuser (most often the mother), and the alleged perpetrator (whenever possible). Therapists who have not conducted the initial evaluation themselves do well to consider the credentials and credibility of previous evaluators who have come to the conclusion that the child was sexually abused. If the previous evaluator has conducted the type of examination utilized by the kinds of "validators" described in Chapter Four, then it is crucial that the therapist do a follow-up evaluation. Such an evaluation should include not only a careful review of previous reports and examinations, but an update examination conducted oneself in accordance with the guidelines described in *Protocols for the Sex-Abuse Evaluation* (Gardner, 1995a).

It is important, when conducting such preliminary examinations (whether they be the child's first evaluation or a pretreatment follow-up), that the therapist consider other sources of the presenting symptoms, sources unrelated to sexual abuse. The child's symptoms may be the result of legal-process trauma associated with the series of interviews to which the child has been previously subjected. As described previously (Gardner, 1995a), there is no "Sex Abuse Syndrome" or typical picture of the child who has been sexually abused. The symptoms range from none at all to psychosis and all points in between. Some of the more common symptoms seen in children who are sexually abused may also be seen in children who have been subjected to legal-process trauma, e.g., nightmares, sexual excitation, high levels of anxiety, and bedwetting. In such cases, a sensitive way of ascertaining whether the symptoms were the result of sexual abuse or legal-process trauma is to determine when they began. Those symptoms that began during the time frame of exposure to the alleged perpetrator are more likely to be direct derivatives of the sex abuse. Those symptoms that began after disclosure are more likely to be the result of legal-process trauma. Or the symptoms may be the result of the so-called treatment that the child has received, treatment of the type described in Chapter Four. If the child has been embroiled in a child-custody dispute, then one must consider the possibility that the symptoms derive from that exposure and embroilment rather than the alleged sex abuse. Elsewhere (Gardner, 1976, 1986) I have described in detail the symptoms commonly exhibited by such children.

Most judges are very quick to order treatment for children who have allegedly been sexually abused, no matter how minuscule the evidence and no matter how improbable the likelihood that the child was indeed abused. They do this in part because of some deep conviction for the efficacy of psychotherapy, a conviction that I do not share. Furthermore, judges often do this to "cover" themselves and thereby protect themselves from criticism that they did not do everything possible to protect the child. Such referrals reflect profound ignorance about the psychotherapeutic process. The idea that someone can treat the child for a disorder that may not be present is absurd. Unfortunately, my experience has been that the vast majority of therapists are willing to take on such referrals, especially in clinic settings where an arrangement has been made for the clinic to provide therapeutic services for all court referrals. But even in the private-practice setting there are many therapists who reflexively accept such referrals. This is a misguided and even dangerous practice and can result in the kinds of problems described in Chapter Four. There are many therapists who naively believe that they have no choice but to accept a court referral. They do not seem to appreciate that we are not living in a totalitarian state and that we cannot be court ordered to treat anyone whom we do not wish to engage in therapy. The judge can do absolutely nothing at all to a therapist who refuses to accept a child into treatment. Therapists who fear that such refusal will cut off a supply of future referrals are prostituting themselves. However, they are not simply acting reprehensibly; they are bringing about psychiatric disturbances in those nonabused children whom they are treating because the judges decided that the sex abuse took place.

In this chapter I focus primarily on the treatment of children whose sex abuse has taken place in the intrafamilial setting. In most such cases the accuser is the mother, and the accused is the father or stepfather. I will not make a sharp differentiation between those sex abusers who are married to the mothers and those who are not. The marital status of the parents is often of little relevance to the child. What is relevant is whether the abuser is likely to continue abusing the child and what can be done (if anything) to salvage a relationship that has been compromised by the sexual abuse. Accordingly, I will be dealing with situations in which the therapist has access to the abuser. Of course, there are many children who have been sexually abused by strangers. Obviously, under those circumstances, it is extremely unlikely that the therapist will have any involvement with the abuser. However, many of the therapeutic techniques described in this chapter are still applicable. Accordingly, these techniques (with minimal modifications) should prove useful in the treatment of children who were not abused in the home, but were abused elsewhere, e.g., in school settings and by strangers. Because the accuser is most often the mother, I will, for simplicity of presentation, refer to the accuser as the mother and the accused as the father. However, I recognize that there are certainly families (admittedly a small percentage) in which the abuser is the mother and the accuser is the father.

SOME COMMENTS ABOUT THERAPISTS WHO TREAT SEXUALLY ABUSED CHILDREN

I recognize that there are many highly skilled and sensitive therapists who are treating sexually abused children. I recognize, as well, that there are many therapists who take a sober attitude regarding the treatment of these children and have the same concerns as I regarding their treatment, especially with regard to my caveats about the treatment of children who are not genuinely abused. I recognize that there are many well-qualified and well-credentialed individuals who are not in the categories I am describing below. These are not the people about whom the public needs to be warned. It is about the unqualified "therapists" and the fanatics that the public should be aware.

We are living at a time when there are tens of thousands of people (and perhaps more) who are treating children who have allegedly been sexually abused. It is impossible to know exactly how many individuals are engaged in such therapy because many of them have no formal credentials for providing this treatment. Accordingly, they are not listed as members of any of the traditional organizations of therapists. In addition, even within those disciplines that are recognized and accredited to provide such treatment, it is very difficult to determine how many of these individuals are actually treating such children. It is reasonable to say, however, that there are many people who are providing such "therapy" who have no formal training recognized by any formal discipline. Accordingly, many of these people are charlatans, and/or psychopaths, and/or incompetent. And even in the traditional professions in which the training of therapists is in some way monitored, there is still a significant percentage of people in the charlatan/psychopath/incompetent category. Treatment of sexually abused children is very much a growth industry in these times of sex-abuse hysteria (Gardner, 1991a). Under these circumstances there *appears* to be a burgeoning need for such therapists, which predictably will result in the appearance of individuals who will be happy to provide such services. It is almost as if they sprout out of the ground, stream out from hidden places, or just somehow spring into existence—ready and willing to treat the ever-growing mass of sexually abused children that we are led to believe are in dire need of such services.

Like all fields, child sex abuse has its share of individuals who enter for psychopathological purposes, and my own field of psychiatry is no exception to this phenomenon. When I was in medical school, in the early 1950s, the general consensus was that the craziest people went into psychiatry. Unfortunately, this was often a valid observation. I remember in college making the observation that some of the paranoid types gravitated toward law. And this, too, was a valid observation. Now to the field of child sex abuse. There are women who were sexually abused themselves who gravitate toward this field. For some of these women the choice may be a healthy one, and their child patients may enjoy enormous benefit from the personal experiences of these women. They have "been there" themselves, and they know what it's all about. They may be able to bring to these children a degree of sympathy, empathy, and sensitivity not possessed by others who have not been subjected to such experiences. There are other sexually abused women, however, who have not resolved the problems that derived from their experiences, especially problems related to ongoing resentment toward men. They are attracted to the field because it allows them to gratify vicariously their ongoing pent-up hostilities toward men. They ever wave the banner that "children never lie" and, when serving as evaluators (or "validators"), no man is innocent. When serving as "therapists," the therapy is focused on a continual campaign of denigration of the child's father—both symbolically and actually.

The feminist movement, as well, includes a wide variety of women on a continuum from the healthiest and most reasonable to the most fanatic. Some of those in the fanatic group also gravitate toward the child sex-abuse field because it provides them with the wonderful opportunity to vent rage on all men. What better way to wreak vengeance on men than to be party to a process that can incarcerate them almost instantaneously after extracting a few choice words from a child, with the assistance of anatomically correct dolls and leading questions. What better way to wreak vengeance on men than to systematically program a child—over weeks, months, and even years—to believe that the father is a despicable individual and deserves the most vile and sadistic treatment.

Therapists who assume that a sexual encounter between an adult and a child will necessarily cause the child to suffer with severe psychiatric disturbances are going to be compromised in the treatment of these children. The therapist must appreciate that there are many children who have had such encounters who do *not* suffer untoward reactions. We adults, in our society, would consider them to have been abused. However, as mentioned previously (especially Chapter One), there have been and still are many societies in which such encounters are not viewed as heinous crimes or terrible sins and the children who involve themselves with adults in this way do not suffer psychiatric disturbances. Therapists who do not accept this possibility are going to produce in their patients psychiatric disturbances that would not have otherwise arisen.

Many sexually abused children exhibit high levels of sexual excitation. They have been brought prematurely into adult levels of sexual arousal that may continue even after the cessation of the sexual stimulation. (My experience has been that sometimes such excitation dies down and sometimes it does not.) Because of such children's cognitive immaturity, impulsivity, and lack of good judgment, they may make sexual overtures to the therapist in a variety of ways. The child may attempt to rub his (her) genitals against the therapist or try to touch or fondle the therapist in a sexual manner. Therapists who become unduly upset or even sexually excited by such overtures may be compromised in their treatment of these children. I will discuss below the therapeutic recommendation of masturbation in reducing the excitation of sexually abused children. The therapist who has the conviction for such a recommendation may thereby protect himself (herself) from uncomfortable reactions attendant to such overtures.

To the best of my knowledge, all 50 states now have laws requiring the reporting of child sex abuse. It is not my purpose here to discuss the pros and cons of such laws. I will focus here on the effects of such reporting on the therapeutic process. Such reporting, however justified, will inevitably compromise the child's therapy. Competent child therapists recognize the importance of the therapist doing everything possible to have a good relationship with both of the child's parents, regardless of their marital status and regardless of the kinds of behavior (sometimes alienating) they may manifest. If the child is caught in the middle of a tug of war between the therapist and a parent, the parent is likely to win and the therapist is likely to lose. But the tug of war in itself compromises the treatment. A parent who harbors formidable hostility toward the therapist is likely to compromise significantly the child's treatment. And "blowing the whistle" on an abusing parent to outside authorities (such as a child protection service and/or the police), authorities who might very well place that parent in jail, is likely to engender enormous rage in that parent.

Accordingly, individuals who have been the initial reporters of the abuse to outside authorities should not be the ones who embark upon the treatment. I cannot emphasize this point strongly enough. If, after the reporting has been made by someone else, the evaluator becomes the therapist, then there need be no problems regarding the alienating of a parent by such reporting. But things are not that simple. If the accuser, the accused, and the child all agree that the abuse took place, then the evaluator can indeed serve as therapist. If, however, the accused denies that the abuse took place and the evaluator is convinced that it did, then the therapy will be compromised by the accused's position. The accused will view the therapist as someone who is trying to extract the truth from him, and this cannot but compromise his relationship with the therapist and, by extension, the therapist's relationship with the child.

THE CLINICAL PICTURE OF THE SEXUALLY ABUSED CHILD

Introduction

First, I wish to emphasize that there is no *typical* clinical picture of the sexually abused child. There are many children who have sexual encounters with adults who do not suffer at all any untoward reactions. Children who have not been traumatized are not going to reveal symptoms and so may not warrant any treatment at all.

But even those children who have experienced sexual encounters with adults, and who have reacted negatively to the experience, do not present any typical clinical picture. Rather, they present with a wide variety of symptoms that do not lend themselves well to being placed under any particular rubric. Accordingly, therapists do well to appreciate this variety and try to avoid pigeonholing the child or trying to determine whether the child fits into some particular diagnostic category. The therapist does well to view the symptomatic reactions to lie along a continuum from no symptoms at all to chronic psychosis, and all points in between.

The So-Called Child Sex-Abuse Syndrome

On a number of occasions, especially in legal documents associated with court cases in which sex abuse is alleged, one comes across the term *the child sex-abuse syndrome*. The implication here is that there is indeed a particular syndrome that is diagnostic of children who are sexually abused. Typically, the syndrome includes nightmares, bedwetting, mood changes, fears, withdrawal, depression, and a long list of other behavioral manifestations (both normal and abnormal) to the point where practically every disorder found in *DSM-IV* would be included. As mentioned, there is no such syndrome and the quest for such is futile.

From the legal point of view, an attempt is being made to verify the abuse by the invocation of this mythical syndrome. It is basically the attempt to enhance the examiner's credibility by using the "scientific" nomenclature of medicine. Although there is no such syndrome to be found in any authoritative medical or psychiatric text, examiners who use this term hope to gain greater credibility in the courtroom. From the evaluator's point of view it may be used to verify that the child was indeed abused. And from the therapist's point of view, its existence may be considered a justification for embarking on treatment. I often like to use the analogy here to the "battered-woman syndrome." There is no such entity as a battered-woman syndrome. There is a wide variety of reactions that women have to such maltreatment, so wide a variety that the reactions do not lend themselves to such categorization. It is no surprise, then, that *DSM-IV* has no category even closely related to the so-called sex-abuse syndrome or battered-woman syndrome.

The Sexual Abuse Accommodation Syndrome

Elsewhere (Gardner, 1992a) I have discussed Summit's (1983) "sexual abuse accommodation syndrome," especially with regard to its use by "validators" as a diagnostic instrument. As mentioned, it was designed to describe phenomenologically the sequence of reactions some children have after they have been sexually abused. In addition to its misapplication as a diagnostic instrument, it even has drawbacks as a description of children's reactions to bona fide sexual abuse. At the time when Summit published his article, it was indeed the case that mothers and child protection services were likely to be disbelieving, and such disbelief played a role in producing the symptomatic sequence Summit describes. Such incredulity is no longer common. In fact, just the opposite is true, namely, people are too willing to accept as valid the most preposterous and frivolous sex-abuse allegations. Without the disbelief contribution, the symptomatic series described by Summit is less likely to occur. Furthermore, the series of reactions that Summit describes is applicable to children who are abused in the intrafamilial situation, especially by fathers and stepfathers. So "trapped," they are more likely to exhibit the kinds of symptomatic accommodations that result from their entrapment. Accordingly, the reaction pattern is less likely to be seen in nursery schools, day-care centers, and situations in which the abuse is perpetrated by a stranger. Moreover, Summit's patients were generally school-aged children. Many sex-abuse accusations today are made by younger children, especially in nursery schools and day-care centers. It may very well be that, even in Summit's time, the reactions of these younger children might have been different. Accordingly, we see yet another reason why Summit's symptoms are not applicable to a sex-abuse evaluation. In short, evaluators of sexually abused children, even children who were abused in the intrafamilial situation, are not as likely to find the same symptoms Summit saw a decade ago.

Some of the Symptoms *Sometimes* Seen in Sexually Abused Children

The reader will note that I have emphasized the words *some* and *sometimes* in the above heading in order to emphasize the point that the symptoms described below are not universally seen, nor are they *typical* of children who are sexually abused. They are common, however, in children who have been traumatized by repeated sexual abuse. This is especially the case if the child has been programmed to believe that a heinous crime has been perpetrated. Under these circumstances, the child may exhibit symptoms related to the natural desensitization process that takes place following a trauma.

Natural Desensitization This desensitization process involves repetition of the trauma, both verbally and emotionally. The individual is preoccupied with thoughts and feelings about the trauma, so much so that it may become an obsession. Every opportunity is taken to talk about the experience(s). And even in one's dreams they may be replayed. The purpose here is primarily desensitization. It is as if each time the person relives the experience it becomes a little more bearable. One can say that this phenomenon is an excellent example of nature's treatment process: behavior modification.

Posttraumatic Stress Disorder (PTSD) (*DSM-IV* 309.81) As mentioned, there is no category in *DSM-IV* that specifically delineates the symptomatic reactions a child will have to sexual abuse. The category that is most often used for such children is the PTSD. These are a series of reactions that individuals may manifest following exposure to an unusual trauma, and sex abuse is one such trauma. I present here the main criteria that are pertinent to the sexually abused child. I will comment on each criterion, especially with regard to its application and misapplication.

(1) Recurrent recollections of the trauma, both verbally and in play. The play recollections may be represented symbolically because of the child's guilt and/or embarrassment over direct revelation. The recollections may not be verbalized if the child has been threatened with dire consequences if a disclosure is made.

(2) Recurrent dreams of the sexual events. All children dream and all children have nightmares. It is important to differentiate between the predictable and inevitable nightmares that all children have and nightmares that are particularly related to sex abuse. A common error made by overzealous evaluators is to assume that all nightmares are manifestations of sex abuse. This may lead to a faulty conclusion of sex abuse and even incarceration of innocent individuals. For a dream or nightmare to be considered a manifestation of the PTSD, it must have very specific symbols that are definitely recognizable as related to sexual encounters. Such dreams are sometimes referred to as "trauma specific." This is no place for analytic speculations and projections by the evaluator.

(3) Reliving of the experience. This manifestation is related to #1. There are not only recollections and emotional reactions, but actual hallucinatory experiences in which the individual actually believes that the events are taking place. My experience has been that this is a very rare phenomenon in sexual abuse, although one may see it commonly after combat traumas and severe traumas such as earthquakes, hurricanes, and fires.

(4) Intense psychological distress associated with exposure to events that symbolize or resemble the trauma. The child may generalize from the accused and become fearful of all men. Or the child may become unduly anxious when entering bedrooms, the bedroom having been the site of the sexual abuse.

(5) Withdrawal to avoid thoughts, feelings, or activities that remind the child of the trauma. Sexually abused children may withdraw in gen-

eral in order to protect themselves from exposures that remind them of their sexual encounters. Accordingly, a sexually abused girl may not only be fearful of all men, but may withdraw and isolate herself in order to protect herself from any encounters with them.

(6) Manifestations of a high tension level. The tensions and anxieties attendant to the abuse may result in other symptoms that are derivatives of high tension level. These include irritability, difficulty concentrating, and sleeplessness. The sleeplessness may also relate to a fear of going into the bedroom lest the sexual encounter be repeated.

(7) Hypervigilance and exaggerated startle response. Continually concerned with a repetition of the abuse, the child may become hypervigilant and may react with an exaggerated startle response to minor discomforting stimuli.

The PTSD has become the "rubber-stamp" diagnosis for children who have been alleged to have been sexually abused. One reason for this is that it is the only diagnosis in *DSM-IV* that can be used for "validation." Stating that the child exhibits symptoms of the PTSD lends a note of scientific credibility to the conclusion that the child under consideration was indeed sexually molested. The diagnosis, then, is similar in this regard to Summit's sexual-abuse accommodation syndrome. Accordingly, the PTSD has become a favorite diagnosis for zealous evaluators, who will utilize every possible maneuver to justify their preconceived conclusion that the child was sexually abused. In many such cases I myself saw few if any symptoms of the PTSD. What was clear was that the examiner exaggerated occasional and fleeting thoughts and feelings to a level warranting this diagnosis. In some cases I was convinced that the evaluator was fabricating signs and/or symptoms and even deluding himself (herself), so great was the need to fit the child's symptoms into the procrustean bed of the PTSD.

Symptoms Unrelated to the Posttraumatic Stress Disorder

Elsewhere (Gardner, 1995a) I have presented a series of other symptoms that one may see in children who have been sexually abused, symptoms not manifestations of the PTSD. It is unfortunate that many evaluators ignore these because of their rigid and reflexive gravitation toward the PTSD. Their need to provide the PTSD diagnosis, which they believe adds credibility to the conclusion that the child was sexually abused, lessens the likelihood that they will utilize the criteria that are more likely to differentiate between true and false sex abuse. In this chapter I describe the treatment of some of the more common symptoms of sexually abused children, e.g., guilt, loss of trust, anger, depression, and school difficulties—not only those symptoms to be found under the PTSD rubric.

PRELIMINARY CONSIDERATIONS REGARDING THE TREATMENT OF SEXUALLY ABUSED CHILDREN

The Child May Not Need Treatment

It is *extremely* important for therapists to appreciate that the child who has been genuinely abused may *not* need psychotherapeutic intervention. This statement may come as a surprise to many, but I believe that this option has not been given the attention it deserves. First, for some children there has been no actual trauma, there are no symptoms, and so treatment is not necessary. For others, there may have been trauma, but this doesn't mean that psychotherapeutic intervention is necessary. I have mentioned already that the PTSD is nature's natural form of systematic desensitization. In fact, the PTSD is the only disorder listed in *DSM-IV* in which the symptoms are part of the curative process. Each time the child relives the trauma, he (she) becomes a little better accommodated to it. All of us have had the experience of being traumatized, and all of us have had the experience of dealing with it by a mild form of PTSD. A good example would be involvement in an automobile accident. Immediately following the experience, one becomes preoccupied with the event, talks incessantly about it to friends and relatives, and may even dream about the experience during the following days and even weeks. However, for most people, over time, the preoccupations diminish—often to a point where they may be entirely forgotten. A similar process occurs when we mourn after the death of a loved one. We must have the greatest respect for nature's desensitization process and not artificially prolong it by the kind of "muckraking" that may take place in the psychotherapeutic situation. We want to facilitate the desensitization process, not artificially prolong it.

On the one hand, we certainly want early evaluation and intervention—if warranted. On the other hand, we don't want to make the person worse. What should we do then? How do we know whether intervention is necessary? I find quite useful in this regard an inquiry into *other* areas of the child's functioning—areas not directly related to sexual abuse—in order to ascertain whether the child is exhibiting symptoms unrelated to the sexual abuse. Accordingly, I inquire into school functioning, relationships with peers, and home functioning. I try to determine whether other *DSM-IV* diagnoses might be applicable. I try to determine whether any of the symptomatic manifestations are to be found in the list of indicators described in my book, *Protocols for the Sex-Abuse Evaluation* (Gardner, 1995a). If none of these additional symptoms is present, then I am less likely to provide treatment. In short, if there are no symptoms that I consider to be derived from the sex abuse, and there are no other symptoms unrelated to sex abuse, then I will not treat. I make the assumption that the sex abuse was not traumatic or, if it was, the child has dealt with the trauma by a natural desensitization process. In short, if there are no symptoms, I will not treat because I have no symptoms to serve as targets for my treatment. This refusal to treat does not preclude, however, providing advice, recommendations, and periodic follow-ups.

Psychotherapeutic Work with the *Whole* Family

I believe that the optimum therapeutic approach is the one in which *one* therapist works with the whole family: the mother, the father, and the sexually abused child. This statement, I suspect, will surprise and even startle some readers. The notion of the same therapist working with a child and the "despicable pervert" who perpetrated this heinous crime on this innocent child victim is unthinkable to some therapists. As I will emphasize below, therapists do well to be very cautious about bringing about a situation in which they promulgate alienation of a child from a parent, even the parent who has sexually abused the child. Of the more than five billion people on earth, the child has only two biological parents and that is all that nature (or God) is going to assign that child. If a parent wishes healthy involvement with a child, sex-abuse history notwithstanding, that parent should at least be given the opportunity—when safe—to effect such a relationship. The best way to accomplish this goal is for the same therapist to be involved with all three parties, both individually and in joint interview.

Courts commonly assign each of the parties his (her) own separate therapist. Ostensibly, this "covers the ground" and everyone is being taken care of. The judge has discharged his (her) duty in what is seemingly an effective and thorough manner. Little consideration is given to the inevitable divisiveness of such a therapeutic approach. I am not referring here simply to the divisive effect of this approach on intact families (sex abuse notwithstanding); I hold the same position for separating and divorced families. Even though separated or divorced, both parents are still parents and both should be involved in the child's life, and treatment is one segment of the child's life.

Meaningful Protection from Further Sexual Abuse

No matter how skilled the therapist, and no matter how knowledgeable, treatment is going to be seriously compromised if the child is not first protected from further abuse. No matter how productive the sessions, if the child returns to an environment in which there is an ongoing danger of repetition of the abuse, the therapist's attempts are likely to prove futile. Accordingly, the therapist must make an attempt to assess the degree of danger and assist in the implementation of whatever measures may be necessary to provide the child with protection. In some cases this is not possible while the offender and the child are living in the same home. My experience has been that courts and child protection services tend to be overzealous and overcautious with regard to removing people from homes when there has been an allegation of sex abuse. Commonly, either the father or the child is precipitously removed from the home, often with only minimal evidence that sexual abuse has taken place. Often little consideration is given to the devastating effects of these maneuvers on family stability. These individuals (who wield great power) often work on the principle: "If there is any risk of sexual abuse, no matter how small, no matter how remote, we must zealously protect the child from the perpetrator, and the breakup of the family unit is a small price to pay when one compares the detrimental effects of such disruption with the devastating effects of further abuse." And this position is often taken even when the evidence is minuscule. It is taken in order to "be on the safe side."

Competent evaluators make some attempt to assess the degree of danger, especially with regard to the likelihood of recurrence. Many pedophiles are indeed compulsive, and separation from the child is a reasonable measure to take. Other perpetrators, however, are not that compelled to act out on their impulses, especially after their behavior has been brought to the attention of child protection services and legal and judicial authorities. Sometimes the therapy will be possible under circumstances in which all three are still living together. In other situations, it may be necessary for the perpetrator to leave the home, with the child visiting with him under reasonable surveillance. I believe it is preferable that such visits take place in a home situation rather than in the more sterile environment of a community facility, the visits taking place under the surveillance of community personnel such as social workers and probation workers.

In situations in which the offender is so compulsive, punitive, and abusive that permanent removal is warranted, the child does well to form a relationship with a father surrogate. Under such circumstances the therapist might try to encourage deeper involvement with male relatives such as uncles and grandfathers.

Group Therapeutic Experiences

Group therapy can also be useful as an adjunct to the individual and family therapeutic programs. This is especially useful for children ages 10 and above. (My experiences have not been good with group therapy with younger children. They are much too rambunctious and there is much too much horseplay.) Many sexually abused children consider themselves to be unique with regard to their experience. This contributes to feelings of self-loathing. Having the experience that there are other children who have been similarly abused generally helps them to feel less loathsome. Although I generally prefer heterogeneous groups over homogeneous groups (Gardner, 1988b), this is probably one situation in which homogeneous groups are indicated. Group therapy can also help sexually abused children work through other problems. However, it is crucial that the therapist not pressure family members into focusing on the sex abuse. To do so risks the embedment of the thoughts and feelings into the brain circuitry as described in Chapter Two. Furthermore, such focus can deprive the family members of the opportunity to work out the derivative problems as well as problems unrelated to the sexual abuse.

The Effects of Litigation on the Child's Treatment

At the outset, the therapist should do everything possible to discourage continuation of litigation. The likelihood that the therapy will be successful—while litigation still continues—is very small. When the litigation involves a child-custody dispute, it will inevitably contribute to the development, prolongation, and/or intensification of the child's psychopathology. Therapists who believe that their efforts can successfully counterbalance the negative effects of such litigation are being unrealistic and even grandiose. The litigation also has the effect of "muckraking," bringing up the old material, and thereby working against the evolution of the natural desensitization process. It is likely to embed psychopathological reactions into the brain circuitry and thereby intensify them.

Litigation may add additional traumas in association with the child's being interviewed by psychologists, psychiatrists, lawyers, and judges. In many cases it involves the child's giving direct testimony in the courtroom (and this is especially true of older children), and this too can be psychologically traumatic. If the accused is on trial for the sex abuse, and a decision is going to be made regarding the penalty, this will also have profound effects upon the treatment. The tensions and anxieties associated with such trials are enormous, and these inevitably filter down to the child. The guilt that such a trial engenders in the accusing child is generally enormous, and the fear of retaliation and/or retribution by the abuser may be formidable. Although therapists are often quite impotent regarding their ability to affect the speed (or more accurately, slowness) with which these proceedings progress (or more accurately, creep), they should still make every attempt (through the parents, lawyers, and courts) to emphasize the importance of rapid decisions and resolutions.

Under these circumstances I will often say to parents something along these lines: "It is important for you to know that as long as the lawsuits continue, the likelihood of my helping your child is reduced significantly. There is no law requiring you to continue with your child-custody dispute. There is no law requiring you to promulgate lawsuits against those whom you believe sexually abused your child. I am not saying that such lawsuits are always without merit, and they sometimes even have social benefit. However, you should know the price being paid by your child by your voluntary involvement in them." As mentioned elsewhere (Gardner, 1992b), I refer to this as "the-ball-is-in-your-court" principle.

TECHNICAL ASPECTS OF THE TREATMENT OF SEXUALLY ABUSED CHILDREN

Introduction

In this section, I focus on psychotherapeutic approaches to some of the more common symptoms exhibited by sexually abused children. I will not elaborate in detail on the specific technical maneuvers I utilize; rather, I will present general principles and approaches that should prove useful in the alleviation of selected common symptoms. However, at the end of this chapter I will provide some illustrative clinical examples that will enable the reader to learn exactly how I implement my methods. The reader who is interested in further details about my specific techniques may wish to refer to my full-length text on this subject (Gardner, 1992b).

The Home Videocassette Recorder

Elsewhere (Gardner, 1992b) I describe the utilization of the home videocassette recorder in child psychotherapy. The instrument can be an extremely valuable therapeutic adjunct. It can be particularly useful in the treatment of the sexually abused child because of its capacity to provide reiteration of psychotherapeutic messages. The sexually abused child needs desensitization and, as mentioned, one of the ways such children provide themselves with such desensitization is by repeatedly thinking about their trauma. Because of this benefit, some children who have been sexually abused will repeatedly request to view the videotape. Of course, other benefits are being derived simultaneously, e.g., an opportunity to hear once again my therapeutic messages that recommend specific coping mechanisms and protective maneuvers. Furthermore, the reexposure has the effect of reentrenching the relationship with the therapist and this, of course, is crucial if the child is to have a meaningful psychotherapeutic experience.

Desensitization Play

I have already mentioned desensitization as an important factor in the self-curative process following trauma. Children are likely to incorporate the desensitization process into their play. The symbols and other metaphors thereby created allow the desensitization process to proceed in a manner that lessens guilt and anxiety, because the child does not recognize consciously that the play is actually portraying his (her) own experiences. This process should be respected and the therapist does well *not* to try to bring into conscious awareness the material so produced. Therapists with a strong commitment to the psychoanalytic concept—people who believe in a strict application of Freud's dictum: "Where there is unconscious, there shall conscious be"—are likely to try to help the child gain conscious insight into the underlying meaning of these symbols. Although a psychoanalyst myself, I believe that there are situations in which such an approach can produce unnecessary guilt and anxiety and compromise, thereby, the psychotherapeutic process. And this is one of the situations in which such an approach is likely to bring about this untoward and unnecessary result.

However, it is not the purpose of therapy simply to catalyze and facilitate the expression of such desensitization material. Rather, the therapist should be listening carefully to its content and be trying to use the material so produced as a point of departure for responding therapeutic interchanges. These may be provided at the symbolic level (for younger children this is preferable) or by direct discussion (for those children who are less needful of the symbolic disguise). Commonly, sexually abused children will introduce themes in which they are fleeing the perpetrator. The perpetrator may not be consciously recognized as such or symbolized as some fearsome creature who, by the nature of his acts, is a clear representation of the abuser. Following such scenarios, the therapist does well to introduce alternative coping mechanisms such as vigilance, calling for help, avoiding situations in which the abuse might recur, and reassurance that the abuser will not be in a situation that will allow him to repeat the abuse. The therapist does well to substitute appropriate and reasonable adaptive mechanisms for inappropriate ones (such as being protected by a superhero). The child (especially boys) may introduce unreasonable macho-type fighting mechanisms as an attempt to cope (such as throwing the perpetrator out the window), and these too must be substituted (preferably symbolically) with more reasonable modes of adaptation.

PSYCHOTHERAPEUTIC APPROACHES TO SOME OF THE COMMON SYMPTOMS OF SEXUALLY ABUSED CHILDREN

Hypersexualization

Some children who have been sexually abused are prematurely brought up to adult levels of sexual excitation. Even when the abuse discontinues, they may continue to have strong sexual urges, urges far stronger than other children their age. Obviously, I am talking here about the children whose sexual activities involved physical gratifications, especially to the point of orgasm. I am not talking here about those children whose sexual encounters have been primarily, if not exclusively, painful. Parents can be advised that the level of high sexual excitation may very well decrease by itself as time passes; however, they should also be informed that for some children this may not be the case. I generally advise parents of hypersexualized children to try to distract them into involvement in other areas such as games, sports, and schoolwork. However, as adults well know, these sublimatory activities have their limits and may not be completely successful in channeling off sexual urges.

Many of the children in this category are obsessed with desires to engage in sex play with peers. I generally advise parents to respond to these requests along these lines: "I know what you want to do, and what you want to do is not bad. It's not wrong. It's not a sin. It's not a crime. It's not something they'll put you in jail for. However, it's not allowed. You'll get into a lot of trouble if you do that. Janey's (Billy's) mother and father will get very upset if you do that. When you're older, and you have a girlfriend (boyfriend) and you love one another very much, and if the two of you want to do things like that together, that's your private business and most people think it's okay. Now why don't we just play a game, take a walk, etc...."

One problem with the aforementioned approach is that the child may respond with questions such as "*Why* can't I play those games with Janey (Billy)?" and "Why do their parents get angry about those games?" The best answer I have for these questions (and I am not claiming that it is a perfect one) is that in our Western society such practices are considered improper and even sinful. Some societies are neutral to these practices among children, and there are even societies that encourage such activity among children. Many books and doctoral theses have been written to explain the reasons for these cultural differences. And all the answers, I am certain, are not yet in. Such discussions may enable adults to spend some very interesting hours, but they are beyond the comprehension of the children I am talking about here. Accordingly, the best answer is "It's not allowed." However, parents who feel the need might add, "When you're older you'll be able to understand better why it's not allowed." The parent who feels the need to give the child the *real* reasons is not likely to be successful in imparting this information because it is generally far beyond the level of comprehension of younger children.

When these more conservative measures do not work, I will then discuss with the parent the question of encouraging the child to

104 TREATMENT OF SEXUALLY ABUSED CHILDREN

masturbate. Some parents are quite receptive to this consideration and others "flip out." Few are neutral on the subject. For those who are unreceptive, I try to emphasize the value of this practice as an important contribution to civilized society. Because of masturbation, no one needs to tolerate ongoing sexual frustration and no one needs to get involved in the enormous amount of trouble that individuals with unsatisfied sexual cravings can bring upon themselves. For the parent who is receptive to considering this valuable psychotherapeutic outlet, I recommend comments along these lines: "I'm just not going to let you go around touching people's private parts. That's not permitted. If you still feel that you want to do those things, I suggest you go into the bedroom or bathroom, or some other private place, and rub or touch yourself. You can touch your *own* private parts. If you do that for a while you may get rid of those strong feelings. That's a perfectly fine thing to do, but it's private. It's not the kind of thing people do in public." Again, for the precocious child who might ask, "*Why* is it not proper to do these things in public places," I have the same answers provided above for why Billy and Janey can't fondle each other's genitals. Unless the children who ask these questions are going to move to one of those places that anthropologists have written libraries about, the child is going to have to resign himself (herself) to the constraints and inhibitions of Western civilization.

One could argue that encouraging masturbation is tantamount to encouraging an activity that may predictably contribute to the perpetuation of the high level of sexual excitation. One could argue that the prepubertal child does better to go back to a low level of sexual excitation and can wait until puberty to deal with the masturbatory outlet at that time. I am in full agreement that this would probably be the preferable course and that the recommendation may very well contribute to a maintenance of the high level. However, the reader should note that I introduce this option only *after* others (the more conservative ones) prove futile. The negative effects on the child of walking around in a constant state of "horniness"—especially excitation that is not permitted release and gratification—are worse, I believe, than the negative effects of the maintenance of the higher level of sexual excitation, excitation that may result from masturbation. Like most problems and dilemmas in life, things cannot simply be reduced to one good solution and one bad solution. Rather, like most things in life, there are many good solutions and many bad solutions. Here we have to choose which is the less detrimental of two bad solutions.

Regression

Children who have been sexually abused often exhibit regressive symptoms. These include thumbsucking, bedwetting, soiling, baby talk, desire to suck a bottle, enjoyment of the fetal position, excessive demand for cuddling, etc. Sometimes these regressive symptoms reflect a failure to progress along the developmental track. Sometimes they reflect a regression from higher levels of functioning. In either case, they represent an attempt to remain fixated at lower levels of psychological functioning as a form of protection from traumas associated with more advanced levels. Obviously, it is unlikely that the child is going to progress along the developmental track as long as there is a danger of the repetition of the abuse—thus the importance of this danger being removed or a low-risk danger reassuringly clarified at the outset of the treatment.

Children who are progressing along the developmental track in the course of their treatment may periodically still exhibit the desire to regress to the earlier levels. Parents should be encouraged to allow such regressive indulgence for short periods but, at the same time, firmly advise the child that such indulgence will be short-lived. To indulge it on an ongoing basis is to contribute to its perpetuation. And the therapist, as well, may choose to provide such indulgences—on occasion, and for short periods—in the course of the treatment. Children who are significantly deprived (emotionally and physically) prior to the trauma may have a greater need for such regressive gratifications. Those children who have been subjected to coercion and domination in a family in which all members have been dominated by an overbearing father may also have an inordinate need for regressive satisfactions. An example of such extra indulgence—for those children who therapeutically warrant this—would be allowing the child to sit on the therapist's lap while rocking him (her), allowing occasional use of a pacifier or thumbsucking, and providing more than the usual and age-appropriate level of cuddling.

Guilt

The word *guilt* is used in many ways, so much so that it may cause confusion. When a judge declares that the accused person is guilty of having committed a crime, he (she) is talking about an entirely different phenomenon than the guilt a psychiatrist refers to when he (she) states that the patient feels guilty. In the former situation, the word *guilt* is being used to refer to the court's conclusion that the individual has indeed perpetrated an illegal act. In the latter case the word refers to an inner feeling of lower self-worth associated with certain thoughts, feelings, and actions. But even the psychiatrist's use of the word is not that clear-cut and there are many different forms of guilt, each of which requires its own definition. (Below, I will provide specific examples of these different types of psychological guilt.) It probably would have been better if our language developed in such a direction that different words were used for these disparate phenomena. This is the general definition of guilt that I use when referring to psychological processes: *Guilt is the feeling of low self-worth that an individual experiences after entertaining thoughts, experiencing feelings, or committing acts that the person has been taught are wrong or bad by significant figures in early childhood.* In addition (and this is not an intrinsic part of the definition), there is a high likelihood of some anticipation of punishment or rejection if others learn about the unacceptable thoughts, feelings, or behavior.

At this point I discuss the different forms of psychological guilt, with particular focus on their role in symptom formation and treatment of sexually abused children.

Guilt About the Effects of the Divulgence on the Offender Many children have been warned and even threatened that divulgence of the sexual activities will have dire consequences for the child and/or the perpetrator and other family members, and when the child divulges the abuse, these predictions are likely to prove valid. Whereas originally the consequences were purely theoretical, and possibly not even appreciated by the child, now they become a reality. And the reality may be that the home is descended upon by police, detectives, prosecutors, and a parade of people from child protection services. This may be followed by a courtroom trial and even incarceration of the perpetrator. These events cannot but produce enormous guilt in the child. The abuser may then make comments to the child along these lines: "You see, you didn't keep our 'secret.' You told everyone what's happened, and now look at the terrible things they're doing to me." And this may only serve to increase even further the child's guilt. The perpetrator is essentially saying that the child is a terrible person for having disclosed what was going on. And such a message directs itself to the core of the child's guilt mechanism.

Therapists do well to impress upon such children that they have been the innocent victims of the perpetrator's behavior, that the fault lies within the offender, and that it was the abuser who committed the crime—not the child. This approach is most likely to be successful when the child has not been the initiator (the usual case). There are, however, children who do initiate the sexual encounter with an adult. Sometimes this is part of normal childhood curiosity and the lack of appreciation that certain parts of other people's bodies are private and not to be touched or investigated. Sometimes a child has been brought to higher levels of sexual excitation by a third party (child or adult) and then carries over the sexual excitation to the party who then becomes the offender. In either case, the therapist does well to try to impress upon the child that even here it was basically not his (her) fault. Rather, attempts should be made to get across the message that when adults are so approached, it behooves *them* to refuse to involve themselves in such activities. One also does well to communicate to the child that the court will not consider the child's initiation to be a reason for the adult's exoneration.

Guilt About Participation in the Sexual Act(s) At first, the child may not have realized that the sexual behavior is considered bad or wrong in our society. When children come to appreciate how reprehensible adult-child sexual acts are considered in our society, they may blame themselves for having engaged in the sinful and/or criminal act(s). And this will especially be the case if the child has enjoyed the activities. There is a whole continuum that must be considered here: from those children who were coerced and who gained no pleasure (and might even be considered to have been raped) to those who enjoyed immensely (with orgastic response) the sexual activities. The former children are less likely to feel this type of guilt; the latter are much more likely to experience such guilt. Children who enjoyed the sexual activities must be helped to appreciate that it was the abuser who committed the antisocial act(s).

The child may feel guilt over the *pleasure* enjoyed in the experience. If the child comes from a very religious family, a family in which pleasurable activities are somehow considered sinful, then this form of guilt is likely to be present. The examiner must try to get across the message that sex can be an enormously pleasurable activity and there is nothing intrinsically wrong with a person who enjoys it. However, there are the *wrong times* and the *wrong places* to enjoy sex with another person, and there are the *wrong people* with whom one can gain the pleasures of these gratifications. In our society, we generally consider it wrong for children to have sexual activities with adults, but we do not consider it wrong for children to have sexual pleasures by stimulating themselves. Obviously, we are once again dealing here with the question of values. As mentioned, rather than get into the philosophical, psychological, and anthropological factors operative here, I think one does well to basically subscribe to Western society's Judeo-Christian ethic regarding these matters.

Older children may be helped to appreciate that sexual encounters between an adult and a child are not universally considered to be reprehensible acts. The child might be told about other societies in which such behavior was and is considered normal. The child might be helped to appreciate the wisdom of Shakespeare's Hamlet, who said, "Nothing's either good or bad, but thinking makes it so." In such discussions the child has to be helped to appreciate that we have in our society an exaggeratedly punitive and moralistic attitude about adult-child sexual encounters. It would be an error for the reader to conclude here that I am condoning sexual encounters between an adult and a child. I believe that it is still a form of exploitation, but not one that should be dealt with as punitively as it is in our society. For example, in most states the punishment for a first-offense murder is less than a first-offense sexual abuse.

Guilt as a Component of the Self-Denigration Aspect of Depression One psychodynamic factor operative in some forms of depression is repressed rage. The depressed feelings are derivatives of the bottled-up anger that the individual feels too inhibited to express.

Sometimes the individual can express such rage, but not direct it toward those who are the sources of the anger. Rather, the person may fear that such expression will result in terrible consequences to himself (herself). Accordingly, the anger may be redirected toward the depressed individual himself (herself). This "retroflexed" rage may manifest itself in self-derogatory comments, e.g., "What a stupid idiot I am" and "What a loathsome, vile worm I am." For sexually abused children the anger may result from the feelings of being exploited and betrayed. Or it may result from the punishments inflicted upon the child for the divulgence.

This form of guilt is treated by helping the child become more comfortable with the expression of anger. One must help the child appreciate that such anger is inevitable and that the guilty feelings are inappropriate. However, one does not want to encourage wanton and unbridled expressions of anger. One wants to channel it constructively and encourage its expression in humane and civilized ways.

Guilt About Having Been Selected or Preferred Over Siblings
In some families, one child is selected for sexual encounters. In others one or more of the siblings may be involved as well. There are situations in which each of the children is led to believe that he (she) is someone special and is the only one to have been selected for such encounters and gratifications. This communicates to the child that he (she) is superior to the others and deserves special attention. At the same time, it communicates the message that attention is being withdrawn from siblings. The sense of exclusivity may produce fear of jealous reprisals by the nonfavored siblings. The anticipated rejections and sense of alienation may produce feelings of self-loathing. The guilt here, derived from this feeling of self-worth, is associated with the belief that one has engaged in reprehensible activities, activities that will bring about the scorn of significant others (in this case the child's siblings). Such a child is essentially saying to himself (herself), "What a terrible person I am for having engaged in these behaviors for which they are all criticizing me." The therapist does well to impress upon such children the notion that it was not their fault for having been so selected. The child may have been selected because he (she) is the oldest, or the only girl, the only boy, or some other selection criterion having nothing to do with the intrinsic worth of the youngster.

Guilt as a Mechanism for Controlling the Uncontrollable Some children develop the delusion that the sexual encounters were their fault. And this may be seen in situations in which there was absolutely no initiation by the child (the usual case). By considering the abuse to be under the child's own control, the child can then presumably start it and stop it at his (her) will. This belief thereby puts power into the child's hands. It transforms impotency into potency. The notion "It's my fault" implies control. The mechanism is similar to that used by children whose parents are divorcing. Such a child might say, "Daddy, I know you're leaving because I was bad. I promise I'll never be bad again. I'll be good. I'll never hit my sister. I'll turn off the television when you tell me to. Then you won't have to leave." We use the term *guilt* here because of the child's use of the words, "It's my fault." However, it is a poorly selected phrase because we are basically talking here about a delusion of control over the uncontrollable. Elsewhere (Gardner, 1969a, 1970) I have discussed this type of guilt in greater detail.

The therapeutic approach here is to help such children differentiate between things children can control and things they cannot. One can discuss in detail various examples of experiences in the two categories. For example, the child can be helped to name things that he (she) *can* control, such as when to watch television, when to do homework, and whether or not one hits a sibling. The child can be helped to then name things that he (she) cannot control, such things as thunder, lightning, where one's parents choose to live, and whether or not one's parents get a divorce. Being compelled or seduced into sexual activities is generally an activity over which children, especially younger ones, may have little if any control. I am not saying that the child should be convinced that he (she) can have no control over such acts, only that one may have little control. The child should be helped to place sexual abuse in the category of activities over which one may have little if any control. However, the older the child, the greater the likelihood the child will have some control. This delusion of control may also be reduced by helping the child develop realistic coping mechanisms, which can reduce the need for fantasy control. Providing the child with reasonable "weapons" (e.g., calling out, threatening to report the abuser, and running away) lessens the need to provide delusional forms of protection, one example of which is the form of guilt being discussed here.

Concluding Comments on Guilt Obviously, values play an important role in guilt. As mentioned, we learn from significant individuals in our society the things about which we should feel guilty and those things about which we need not feel guilty. The therapeutic approaches to the alleviation of such guilt involves an imposition of the therapist's values on the patient. But this is no different from any other kind of psychotherapeutic encounter, which, the therapist's disavowals notwithstanding, inevitably involves some attempt on the therapist's part to impose his (her) values on the patient. As I have described in detail elsewhere (Gardner, 1992b), the imposition of the therapist's values on the patient is an inevitable part of the psychotherapeutic process. Accordingly, one does well to explore guilt and value issues in depth with the child's parents and to enlist their aid and support in communicating these messages. As I am sure the reader can appreciate, this may not be easy. The father, as the offender, may be unreceptive to some of these messages. And the mother, too, may be unreceptive to some of the guilt-assuaging recommendations because of her anger toward her husband and her desire for retribution (commonly the case).

Self-Esteem Problems

Some children who have been sexually molested suffer with what is sometimes referred to as the "damaged-goods syndrome." Such children feel that their genitals have been damaged, sometimes irreparably. In some cases there is reality to this belief, because there has indeed been physical damage to the genitals. However, even when there has been some physical damage, in most cases it is not permanent. Other children have not sustained any genital damage at all, but feel this way nevertheless. Such feelings, in part, relate to society's attitude toward adult-child sexual encounters. We have selected the genitals as a special part of the body and have given enormous charge to experiences centering on that particular area. These are the "private parts." These are the parts that the child learns strictly to cover very early in life. These are the areas that if touched, played with, or otherwise manipulated by certain people may result in many years of incarceration for the initiating participant. It is easy to see how such input can contribute to the child's developing a damaged-goods syndrome, and this cannot but contribute to feelings of low self-worth. The child's body image (which is an intrinsic part of self-worth) is compromised by the feeling that one of the most important parts of the body has been harmed.

Such children need reassurances that the genitals have not been permanently damaged (most often the case). If there has been some damage—e.g., from abrasions and inflammation—these are generally transient, and these children should be reassured that with proper medical care their genitals will return to the normal state. It is more difficult to help the child who has sustained permanent damage and/or scars. The child has to be helped to appreciate that only *one* part of the body has been changed, and generally this is not in a way that should interfere at all with functioning in life. These and other distortions about the implications of the damage have to be corrected in the course of the psychotherapeutic process.

Many sexually abused children feel betrayed, impotent, and helpless. And such feelings cannot but contribute to a lowered sense of self-worth. The protection from such exploitation must come from two sources: external and internal. The child must be given reassurances that external authorities (such as the therapist, the other parent, and people involved in the child protection and legal systems) will be vigilant enough to provide protection. However, such reassurances are not likely to assuage fears completely, in that 24-hour vigils are not possible and in many cases the perpetrator may still have access, even though illegally so. Such reassurances, then, must be real, practical, and reasonably predictable. False and empty reassurances are not likely to work and will compromise the child's trust in the reassuring person. If this person is a therapist, meaningful treatment may no longer be possible, even though the two may still meet with one another. When these reassurances are real and practical, the child will feel more protected, there will be fewer feelings of impotence and helplessness, and this can compensate somewhat for the child's lowered feelings of self-worth.

In addition, the child must be helped to learn reasonable methods of self-protection. Impressing upon such children their right to say no, to scream out, to run for help, and to otherwise assert themselves can be useful. However, examiners do well to appreciate that such "empowerment" is of limited value considering the age and size differences between the adult perpetrator and child victim. Much attention is given to this aspect of such children's therapy these days; I believe that it is overrated with regard to its therapeutic efficacy. If the lessons in self-assertion are expanded to nonsexual realms as well, there is a greater likelihood that the sex-abuse protective "empowerment" lessons will be successful.

As mentioned in the section on guilt, a central element in guilt is a feeling of low self-worth. If guilt is present, then it will inevitably reduce the child's feelings of self-worth. Accordingly, it behooves examiners to ascertain exactly which type or types of guilt they are dealing with in order to address themselves properly to the lowered-self-esteem aspect of the child's guilt problem. And the examiner does well to follow the therapeutic guidelines recommended in that section.

Self-esteem is a fundamental problem for most people in treatment, and there are many factors that may contribute to a lowered sense of self-worth. Elsewhere (Gardner, 1992b) I have discussed self-esteem problems in great detail. Examiners do well to ascertain which of the many factors that can reduce self-esteem are operative in the particular child they are treating. It is only by delineating these factors that one is in a position to start alleviating them. Last, enhancement of self-esteem may be viewed as a general antidote to a wide variety of psychogenic symptoms, those associated as well as those unassociated with sex abuse.

Loss of Trust

Exploitation by the abuser causes distrust. There may not have been distrust originally, prior to the time the child learned about the significance of the sexual encounters, but there is likely to be distrust once the child reaches the point of such appreciation. The child may then complain about the abuse to her (his) mother. If the mother, in response, refuses to believe what the child is saying or, more overtly, calls the child a liar, then there is likely to be even further distrust. If the mother then continues to permit the abuse by her denial mechanisms or failure to interfere, then a further sense of distrust is engendered. If, when confronted, the abuser then denies the abuse and calls the child a liar, further distrust is generated. And such distrust may be generalized to other individuals, especially those of the same sex as the abuser.

The development of a trusting relationship with the therapist may play a role in reducing the child's general feeling of distrust. Accordingly, male therapists are preferable if the abuser was a male, even though the child may initially be fearful of a male therapist. Any therapist—male or female—who believes that helping the child cope with sex abuse involves engendering a state of ongoing animosity toward the abuser is not going to help the child reduce distrust. Rather, it only entrenches the notions that the father is a dangerous person and that untrustworthiness is one of his many defects. Many examiners consider it an important part of the therapy of sexually abused children to encourage the expression of hostility toward the perpetrator. In most cases this is a therapeutic error. The aspect of this misguided approach that I wish to focus on here relates to the child's sense of distrust. Such an approach will inevitably increase the child's feelings of distrust rather than reduce them. The therapist must also work with the mother and reduce any elements in her reactions to the abuse that may have engendered distrust. The father, too, must not only be open and honest about the abuse, but other issues as well. Both parents have to develop a different reputation regarding honesty and trustworthiness, and this cannot occur quickly; rather, it can only occur over a long time, a period in which the child gradually develops increasing trust. Reputations are not changed overnight; rather, they only change after multiple corrective experiences over time.

Anger Problems

The child may not be angry about the abuse prior to learning about its social implications. Afterward, however, when the child comes to appreciate the exploitation, there may be anger. If the mother and/or father denies the abuse, then there may be anger associated with the frustration engendered in the child by such denials. And such anger is even further intensified if the child is called a liar. Or, the child may be blamed for initiating the abuse and this, too, cannot but cause resentment when the child knows that he (she) was not the initiator (the situation in most cases). There are, of course, other possible sources of anger for abused children. The abuse may be only one part of a larger program of emotional and physical abuse, and such abuses inevitably cause significant anger.

The anger may be acted out directly; more commonly, it is suppressed or repressed. Children who have been sexually abused in the home situation have much to be angry about, especially if there has been a coercive element associated with the abuse and they recognize the degree to which they have been exploited (Caffaro-Rouget et al., 1989; Livingston et al., 1993). Because of their fear of the perpetrator, abused children are not capable of expressing their resentments directly to him. Accordingly, they may act out their anger elsewhere. If, in addition, their mothers or other potential protectors refuse to hear their complaints, the pent-up anger becomes even greater. And this may be acted out outside the home, especially in school and in the neighborhood.

Under such circumstances the anger may contribute to the formation of a wide variety of symptoms, e.g., psychosomatic complaints, depression, compulsions, phobias, and other forms of psychopathology. Therapists who work on the principle that the best way to treat such suppressed and repressed anger is to facilitate its release are taking an oversimplified approach to the treatment of such problems and are not likely to be successful. It is the belief of such therapists that the main purpose of treatment is to facilitate the cathartic release of pent-up hostility. They will often provide such children with punching bags, boxing gloves, large stand-up inflatable dolls that bounce back when struck, and other toys that facilitate anger release. The more the child screams, yells, rants, and curses, the greater they believe to be the therapeutic benefit. I sometimes refer to this as "diarrhea therapy." Of course, getting in touch with one's angry feelings is a good *first step*, and releasing the pent-up anger is also useful. However, what one must do is to use the anger constructively in such a way that there is a reduction or removal of the stimuli that are causing the anger to be generated in the first place. And this is best done in the early phases of anger generation—when the anger has not reached uncontrollable proportions and when the anger can be focused directly on the noxious stimuli. It is then that therapeutic benefit is most likely to take place. There is little therapeutic benefit to be gained when an individual has been charged up to levels of rage and fury.

I often use the analogy here of a tea kettle on a stove. The flames represent the noxious stimuli that are generating anger, and the boiling water symbolizes the hostility being engendered by the noxious stimuli. Let us consider a person with an anger-inhibition problem who is using repressed anger to fuel the formation of a wide variety of symptoms. Such a person could be symbolized by a cork or plug being placed in the spout of the tea kettle, thereby inhibiting the release of the anger. Therapists who consider it their role merely to help the patient remove the cork are being simplistic, as the analogy clearly shows. The removal of the cork has not in any way served to extinguish the flames, the cause of the boiling rage. Rather (to carry the analogy further), therapists should not only help the patient remove the cork, but connect a rubber tube to the spout, a tube that is then directed toward the flames that are causing the water to boil. The boiling water will then be used to extinguish the flames, flames that are generating the boiling in the first place. This is true treatment, and this is the course that is most likely to prove effective.

There are some children who, rather than inhibiting expression of their anger, act it out. Such children need a strengthening and an intensification of their guilt mechanisms. One of the reasons why they act out their anger is that they do not have enough internal inhibitory mechanisms to suppress and repress it. Guilt and shame are two such mechanisms. There are some therapists who believe that it is antitherapeutic to increase a patient's guilt and/or shame. I am in disagreement. Some people need less guilt, and some people need more. In fact, I think there are more people who do not have enough guilt than there are people who have too much. Each patient has to be evaluated with regard to whether more or less is needed, and the therapeutic approach should be planned accordingly. Some children *need* to feel more ashamed of themselves, and it is the role of the therapist to engender such shame. Some people need a "guilt trip," and to deprive them of such is to contribute to the perpetuation of their psychopathology. Therapists who engage in the aforementioned type of "diarrhea therapy" are likely to perpetuate and even intensify such acting out, much to the detriment of the children and their families (even the abuser).

Last, there are some children who need guilt intensification in some areas and guilt alleviation in others. (Things are generally much more complex than they may initially appear.) Again, it behooves the therapist to tailor the therapy in such a way that guilt is encouraged or discouraged, depending upon the particular behavior. Elsewhere (Gardner, 1988b, 1994a) I have discussed in great detail my approaches to children with antisocial problems.

Depression

I recognize that in recent years most psychiatrists view depression to be primarily a biological phenomenon, and they do not give much credibility to theories that involve psychodynamic components. Although I do not deny that depression may have a biological substrate, I believe that for most patients who are depressed, the psychological and environmental factors are paramount. I am not talking here about bipolar depression, which probably has a high genetic loading; rather, I am referring here to the wide variety of other types of depression with which psychiatrists must frequently deal. Children who are sexually abused may be depressed, and they often have much to be depressed about. They are captive, they are subjugated, and they are often maltreated in a wide variety of other ways. These are enough environmental indignities to depress anyone. To the degree that the therapist can change the environmental situation, to that degree will he (she) contribute to the alleviation of such children's depression.

Children who have been frequently abused, over time, are likely to become depressed, especially if they have been abused frequently over time and especially if there have been terrible threats made regarding disclosure of their sexual experiences (Kempe and Kempe, 1978; Livingston et al., 1993; Nakashima and Zakins, 1977). The main manifestations of the depression may be depressive affect, loss of appetite, listlessness, loss of enjoyment in play, impaired school curiosity and motivation, poor appetite, and difficulty sleeping. The depression may often be associated with suicidal thoughts, especially if the child is significantly guilty about the sexual experiences and/or if the child feels trapped in a situation in which the child cannot escape from being abused. The depression may be related to the feelings of betrayal engendered not only by the offender, but by the passivity and/or failure of others (often the mother) to protect the child and prevent a repetition of the abuse. Depression may be related to pent-up resentment that is not allowed expression, lest the perpetrator carry through with the threats of retaliation.

If the sexual activities have been associated with terrible threats regarding disclosure, then there is an even greater likelihood that the child will become depressed—living as he (she) does in a world of constant fear of retribution. There may also be a sense of hopelessness, especially in situations where the child feels helpless to do anything about the ongoing exploitation and about adults who might very well protect the child but refuse to do so, either by denial or overt refusal to interfere.

One factor that may contribute to a sexually abused child's depression is pent-up resentment that is not allowed expression. The "retroflexed rage" so engendered sometimes contributes to depression. Such self-flagellatory comments as "I hate myself" and "I'm stupid" are the hallmarks of self-deprecation and provide confirmation that the retroflexed-rage element is operative in that particular child's depression.

Sometimes a depression becomes so severe that a child exhibits suicidal tendencies. This is much more likely to be the case when the abuse has occurred in the home situation and the child feels trapped. One must then assess the degree of suicidal risk, and in some cases hospitalization may be necessary. Elsewhere (Gardner, 1988b) I have discussed in detail the criteria I use to determine the depth of suicidal risk.

Obviously, the longer the child remains in the captive state, the longer the child is not protected from the exploitation, the less the likelihood of alleviating the child's depression. Accordingly, antidepressant medication is going to be of little value for such children. As long as they remain in the depression-engendering situation, they will be depressed. Antidepressants might certainly provide a little "lift" under such circumstances, and they might even play a role in reducing suicidal risk. However, at best, such medications should be viewed as adjunctive in these cases, and the primary thrust of the treatment should be to take whatever steps necessary to provide the child with a safe situation. Sometimes this can be accomplished with the child still living with the perpetrator, but this is not likely to be the case in those situations in which the abuse has reached the point where the child has become depressed. Of course, the therapist must make inquiries regarding the particular things about which the child is depressed and try to effect environmental changes that may reduce the depression. If the retroflexed-rage element is present, then one must help the child feel less guilty about the expression of anger.

Another factor that may contribute to a sexually abused child's depression is the loss of the father—if he has been removed from the home. Even when the father is an abuser, the child might still want him to live in the home. The child may be locked in in a somewhat masochistic way with the abusing father, and this is a very common pattern. It sometimes comes as a surprise to people who administer shelters and residential treatment centers that children run away in order to return to homes in which they will predictably be subjected to further abuses. There are children whose abuse has not been significantly traumatic and who consider the advantages of a relationship with the father (the sexual encounters notwithstanding) to outweigh its disadvantages. Community authorities, however, reflexively break up families without giving enough attention to the arguments supporting maintenance of the family structure, the abuse notwithstanding. Accordingly, whether it is the child who is removed from the home or the abusing father who is removed from the home, the child may feel depressed about the loss of the relationship—even though there has been abuse. Even when the family unit was unstable, it may be preferable to no family unit at all or to the surrogate family unit in which the child now finds himself (herself). Once again, to the degree that the therapist can help bring about a stable family (either the original family unit or the substitute one), to that degree will this element in the child's depression be reduced. Elsewhere (Gardner, 1994b) I have discussed my approaches to adolescents who are depressed, especially those who are suicidal.

Fears, Tension, Anxiety, and Derivative Symptoms

Children who have been subjected to frequent episodes of sexual abuse may become chronically fearful and tense. They often present with an expression of "frozen watchfulness" (Goodwin, 1987). Studies conducted by DeFrancis (1969) and Tufts' New England Medical Center (1984) conclude that generalized fear is one of the most common reactions to childhood sexual abuse. These children may not only exhibit fear of people of the same sex as the perpetrator (more often than not, men) but fear of situations similar to those in which the abuse occurred: bedrooms, bathrooms, showers, washrooms, etc. This fear, especially prominent in younger children who are more helpless, relates to their feelings of impotence about being subjected to the sexual abuses. Older children may be fearful primarily of the consequences if they were to disclose any hints of what they have been subjected to. They may fear that they will be murdered, beaten, or abandoned, or that significant individuals in their lives will be subjected to similar consequences. They may fear breakup of the family if they reveal the molestation. Such fears may result in a chronic state of timidity that is observed by friends, relatives, teachers, neighbors, etc. Over the years many examiners have described the high levels of tension and anxiety in sexually abused children, including Browning and Boatman (1977), Gomes-Schwartz et al. (1985), and Kempe and Kempe (1978).

Psychosomatic complaints are common manifestations of fears and tension. Whereas in some people fears and tensions do not have physical concomitants, in others they do. Accordingly, one might see gastrointestinal complaints (such as diarrhea and vomiting), breathing difficulties, palpitations, musculoskeletal problems, headaches, etc. Another derivative complaint would be insomnia. The child has difficulty falling asleep, not only because of the tensions associated with the abuse but, in many cases, because the child fears that the abuser will come into the bedroom and perpetrate further molestations. Ongoing tensions may contribute to the chronic state of hypervigilance and increased arousal that is one of the important manifestations of the PTSD. This results in the "frozen watchfulness" described by Goodwin (1987).

The fears may also be related to the anticipated consequences of divulgence, especially if the child has been threatened with murder, beatings, suicide, abandonment, etc. There may be fears related to the breakup of the family, sometimes actually the case. Of course, I am describing here the extreme examples, but knowledge of them puts the therapist in a better position to detect the less extreme manifestations.

Obviously, the first step toward reducing such fears is to do everything possible to protect the child from further molestation. Without providing this security the therapist is not likely to be helpful. Providing the child with statements about safety and protection are certainly useful, but such reassurances are not likely to work quickly—especially for children who have been subjected to chronic sexual abuse. It is only over time, during which such children have experiences that confirm that they will not be subjected further to the abuses, that these fears are likely to lessen. Having ongoing intimate experiences with a therapist who does not exploit the child sexually, although alone with the child on many occasions, can also contribute to a reduction of such symptoms.

The child's fears may be intensified by environmental attitudes regarding the significance of the sexual acts and their consequences. As mentioned repeatedly, we live in a society that reacts in an exaggerated fashion to child sex abuse, and this is especially obvious when we consider the punishments meted out to sex abusers compared to the punishments given to people who perpetrate other crimes, even murder. Living in such a world, the child is likely to be exposed to these exaggerated reactions. Accordingly, the therapist does well to identify and explore the child's specific fears and anticipations and do everything possible to correct distortions and provide other therapeutic experiences that can potentially lessen such fears. For example, a girl may fear that no boy will ever want to date her and no man will ever want to marry her. The child has to be helped to appreciate that child sex abuse is a common occurrence and that this is not generally a reason why a man does not marry a woman.

One of the unfortunate consequences of child sex abuse is the youngster's growing up fearing and loathing sex in general. It is one of the sources of sexual inhibition in many adolescent and adult women. Accordingly, it behooves the therapist to communicate to the child that the sexual act, in the context of a loving and tender relationship, can be one of the most beautiful and gratifying human experiences. Obviously, the older the youngster, the more meaningful such comments will be. One of the criticisms I have of the so-called "therapy" that is frequently provided such children is the repeated communication of the notion that sex is invariably disgusting and painful. Although this might not be directly stated in such treatment, the exclusion of any positive comments about sex easily leads the child to conclude that it is a despicable act per se, regardless of the circumstances.

Confusion

Children who have been sexually abused often become very confused, especially after the divulgence. At first, they may have thought that the sexual act was an enjoyable experience, and this is especially the case if they were continually praised and complimented in the course of the sexual encounters. Now they learn that they have been involved in a despicable act that is considered by society to be a heinous crime. This cannot but cause confusion. After the divulgence, the abuser may vehemently deny that the sexual activities took place; but the child knows with certainty that they did. However, children are suggestible, and many perpetrators have strong psychopathic tendencies. Over time, with continual denials by the perpetrator, the child may become quite confused regarding whether or not the sexual activities did indeed occur. Sometimes the perpetrator will claim that the child was the initiator when this was not the case. This too can contribute to confusion.

Confusion is further produced by reassurances provided by parents and therapists that the abuser is the one who is at fault, and the child is not. Here we have a situation in which two people are involved in the *same* activity, yet only one is considered to be at fault, the other an innocent victim. One may go to jail, and the other does not. This seems to be a unique example of a situation where one of the collaborators in a crime is considered guilty and the other innocent. This cannot but be confusing to the child, especially if both enjoyed the experience. Accordingly, therapists should appreciate that such reassurances are a mixed blessing. On the one hand, they help the child feel less guilty; on the other hand, they may produce confusion.

As mentioned, therapists should help sexually abused children appreciate that sex is not necessarily an exploitative act and a despicable crime. Rather, under certain circumstances, it can be one of the most gratifying of all human experiences. If the child's sexual experiences were painful, it may be particularly difficult to get this message across. Attempts to do so may cause confusion as one tries to impart to the child the notion that sex can be tender, loving, and pleasurable—aspects that are not within the realm of the child's experiences. It may be difficult, if not impossible, for the child to appreciate these alternative kinds of sexual activities, and attempts to do so may cause confusion. However, if the child's experiences were pleasurable, then the comments will also cause confusion. Here, the child has engaged in a pleasurable act with the abuser, an act that was physically and psychologically pleasurable. Now the child learns that this act with a father or relative is bad, wrong, and even a crime. Yet the same act with a boyfriend, lover, or husband in a loving relationship is not in any way reprehensible, but even desirable.

Most children these days have been subjected to child sex-abuse prevention programs in which they are taught about "good touches and bad touches." Such programs inevitably produce confusion. It is okay for fathers to wash their little girls in the crotch area in association with bathing. And it is okay for fathers to wipe little girls in the crotch area in association with toilet functions. Yet, he can do this in a "good way" and he can do this in a "bad way." To ask a three- or four-year-old to make this distinction is an impossible expectation. One is asking such a child to ascertain that point on the continuum where the normal, inevitable friction associated with such activities ends and the sexual molestation degree of rubbing begins. For the vast majority of children in this age bracket, this is an impossible goal to achieve. Yet this is exactly what the instructors in such courses are asking of these children. They are being asked to make very subtle differentiations in other areas as well. When Uncle Bob or Grandpa sits three-year-old Janie on his lap, she now has to be careful that he is not touching her in a "bad" way. She has to think about whether the kiss is a "good kiss" or a "bad kiss," whether his touch is a "good touch" or a "bad touch." If she decides that what he is doing is "bad," she is taught to blow the whistle on him to everyone in sight. Uncles, grandfathers, divorced fathers, teachers, and other males who may have contact with little girls are now "running scared." It has become a dangerous world for little girls and postpubertal males. No one knows exactly how to act and this too produces confusion.

The child may have been given misinformation in the course of the abuse. For example, the abuser may have told the child that he has to "check" whether or not she has to go to the bathroom. Such checking may involve his putting his finger into her rectum or, in some cases, into the vaginal area (when the child has been properly prepared for this over time). The child may even have come to believe that putting the penis in these orifices is the way to find out whether one has to go to the bathroom. The child may have come to believe that sucking on one another's tongues is normal kissing. The child may have been taught that all little girls engage in sexual behavior with their fathers. After the abuse has been disclosed, the child is given very different messages by investigators, lawyers, and therapists. Obviously, it is the role of the therapist to correct these distortions. However, there will be inevitable confusion created in the child in the course of such cognitive rectification.

With regard to the therapeutic approaches to such confusion, it is in this area that the educational aspects of therapy are obviously the most important. All therapy, to a certain extent, involves education— especially the correction of distortions. However, the therapist must recognize the degree of cognitive immaturity of the child and the inability of the child to appreciate some of the distinctions referred to above. It may be that only with time, growth, and increasing cognitive maturity that some of these distortions will ultimately be corrected and the ensuing confusion reduced. This is one of the reasons why I do not believe in short-term psychotherapy. I am not claiming that such children need be seen two to three times a week; I am only claiming that their therapy may have to be extended over a long period. They have to develop enough cognitive maturity to understand the therapist's communications, which are designed to correct the distortions that are at the foundation of the confusion.

School Problems

School problems are a poor criterion for differentiating between true and false sex-abuse accusations. Impaired academic and social performance in school may result from a wide variety of psychological and family problems, problems having absolutely nothing to do with sex abuse. Because the school situation is one of the most sensitive indicators of a child's psychopathology, and because it is one of the earliest areas in which psychiatric difficulties may manifest themselves, impaired school performance is a very poor indicator of sex abuse (Livingston et al., 1993). Caffaro-Rouget et al. (1989) found that sexually abused children did not exhibit a higher incidence of school-related problems than nonabused children. Certainly, school problems exist in both groups. It behooves the examiner, then, to make a detailed inquiry in order to ascertain whether the child's school problems are the direct result of sexual abuse or of other causes totally unrelated to sexual abuse.

Overzealous evaluators often lose sight of this obvious point and consider any school problem to be one of the "indicators" of sex abuse. It is true, however, that the sexually abused child, especially the child who has been abused over a long period, *may* exhibit difficulties in school, both in the academic and behavioral realms. Tensions and depressed feelings may compromise academic curiosity and motivation. Children cannot be expected to concentrate in school if they are living in a constant state of terror associated with their being subjected to ongoing sexual abuse. They cannot be expected to concentrate in school if they have been terrorized by a perpetrator who threatens terrible consequences if the abuse is divulged. Children cannot be expected to concentrate in school if they dread returning to a home where they will be subjected to painful sexual experiences.

There are some children who are sexually abused who exhibit an unusual symptom regarding school. Specifically, they do everything possible to arrive at school early and try to find any excuse that will justify their staying late. They thereby distinguish themselves from the vast majority of other children who have just the opposite attitude. In such cases, the school is being used as a refuge from the home. The more such children stay out of the home, the less subjected they are to sexual abuse. In some cases these children actually run away from home and then, of course, do not come to school at all. In contrast, there are some sexually abused children who will find excuses for not going to school because of the embarrassment they suffer over their poor academic performance, i.e., academic impairment related to the aforementioned tensions, anxieties, depressed affect, and other symptoms that interfere with concentration and cooperation in school. Accordingly, we have two kinds of attitudes toward school engendered by sex abuse. Some of these children want to come early and stay late (to remove themselves from their homes) and others want to come late and leave early (to protect themselves from embarrassment caused by their academic impairments). Both situations, then, should be warning signs.

Obviously, we are once again dealing here with a situation in which therapy is going to be of little value unless the child is safe and protected from the perpetrator. It is only then that the therapist is in a position to explore other areas in which he (she) may be of help. Special tutoring may be necessary for the child to make up for the lost academic experiences. Academic motivation and curiosity may also have been compromised. To the degree that the therapist can serve as a model for these healthier attitudes toward education, to that degree may some of these attitudes "spill off" onto the child. Academic motivation and curiosity may be engendered in the child by the child's desire to emulate an academically motivated therapist and enjoy thereby the gratifications he (she) gains from such pursuits. In the course of the treatment, the therapist should do everything possible to stimulate intellectual curiosity in the child. Unfortunately, such lack of academic motivation and curiosity is seen in many, if not most, families and even in some schools. Accordingly, such children's impairments in academic motivation and curiosity go way beyond those that result from sexual abuse. Furthermore, fathers who abuse their children and/or mothers who facilitate such abuse are not likely to be the kinds of people who have a high commitment to the educational process. Accordingly, the therapist has to recognize that there may be contributory factors to the child's academic difficulties that are way beyond his (her) control. Under these circumstances only limited therapeutic goals are reasonable.

Pathological Compliance

All children, by necessity, are compliant. And the younger the child, the greater the compliance. It cannot but be otherwise. However, in the course of development children gradually achieve varying degrees of independence from their parents. And this process begins quite early. Healthy one- to two-year-olds typically insist upon feeding themselves and will intermittently grab the spoon from the feeding person. Toddlers typically run away from caretakers. However, they periodically turn around just to be sure that the caretaker is still in close range. Three-year-olds typically pass through a "no" stage in which they are negativistic to most requests by adult authorities. In this way they convince themselves of their independence. And the process continues in subsequent years. Adolescent rebellion is yet another example of this phenomenon.

Children who have been sexually abused may live in a home in which the mother and all the children are very much under the domination of the father. The family may feel that their very survival depends upon submission to the father. The sexually abused child may live in a home in which he (she) may be controlled in both body and mind. It is only through compliance that the child may be protected from the implementation of the father's threatened consequences for noncompliance. Many of these children develop a cheerful facade and inhibit themselves from expressing dissatisfaction in any situation. Identification with a compliant mother (commonly the case) may contribute to the child's pattern of compliance. And this pattern of compliance is likely to extend outside the home in areas where there is no pressure on the child to be submissive. Accordingly, in school the child may be inhibited in self-assertion. In relationships with peers, as well, the child may be passive and submissive. Obviously, these qualities interfere with academic performance and social functioning. Submissive children do not ask questions and so learn less than they might have otherwise. Submissive children do not "stand up for their rights" in social situations and so are easily taken advantage of. They are not as respected as those who are more assertive, and so they are not particularly desirable playmates for most children.

Once again, the likelihood of helping such children become more self-assertive is reduced significantly as long as the child remains under the domination of a controlling and coercive father. Even though the situation may have so changed that the likelihood of sexual abuse has been reduced significantly, the personality patterns of domination/submission are still likely to manifest themselves. If the situation is one in which the domineering father is still in the home (because of the extremely low likelihood of repeated sex abuse), it is probably more difficult to help such children with their passivity than if they were living separately. In either case, such children have to be helped to assert themselves in a wide variety of situations. The therapist who focuses primarily on messages related to sex-abuse overtures ("say no") is taking a very narrow view of this compliance problem. It is preferable to recognize that self-assertiveness spills over from one situation to another, and help in a wide variety of nonsexual areas is likely to spill over into the sexual-protection realm.

When approaching this problem, the therapist does well to focus on a specific situation in which the child exhibited inhibition in self-assertion. One should then ask such children what exactly was going through their minds at the time they inhibited themselves. Often the thoughts are appropriate ones, but they have not been verbalized; nor has there been any action taken on them. For those children who have exhibited the capacity to have responded cognitively to an appropriate degree, one does well to inquire about *why* they have not verbalized their thoughts and taken action. If the child's thoughts involve the use of profanities or other ideas that would be insulting and alienating, one has to help the child express these ideas in words that are more polite than those that entered his (her) mind. One has to find out from the child what negative feedback was expected, what terrible things she (he) anticipated would happen if such thoughts were to be expressed. Then one has to help the child verbalize these thoughts, take reasonable action on them, and have living experiences *over time* that the anticipated repercussions will not be forthcoming. For the child who is so inhibited that healthy, self-assertive thoughts do not even come to mind, the therapist has to embark on an educational program. Here the therapist has to suggest specific examples of self-assertion for the child's consideration, discuss the advantages and disadvantages, and hope that the child over time will incorporate these into his (her) psychological repertoire. Obviously, under these circumstances, help in this area is going to be slower and more prolonged. In all cases the therapist should serve as a model for self-assertion, especially against parents and others who may be trying to take advantage of him. Fee payment is a common area in which the therapist has the opportunity to demonstrate self-assertion and thereby serve as a good model for the child in this realm.

Pseudomaturity

Using a daughter as a sexual partner may expand into other areas in which she is treated like an adult, especially as a wife. Accordingly, such girls may be pressured into assuming many adult-type household tasks such as housekeeping and helping care for the other children. Sometimes the child's mother has actively fostered this role as an extension of her facilitating the child's serving as a substitute sexual partner for her husband. She may be a woman who considers sexual activities odious and uses her daughter to substitute for her and submit to sexual acts. And this may extend into the broader domestic realm in which she encourages the girl to take on other roles traditionally assumed by a wife. Both mother and father may cooperate (both overtly and covertly) in grooming the daughter into assuming additional wifely roles. Although the child may comply with these parental encouragements and demands, she certainly is not up to these tasks; beneath the facade of maturity one is likely to find a frightened child (Sgroi et al., 1982).

Once again, direct work with the child is not likely to be successful. One has to deal with both adults, as well, and focus specifically on the parental contributions to this symptom. The therapist does well to deal with the child at an age-appropriate level, neither higher nor lower. Obviously, praising the child for her pseudomaturity is antitherapeutic. The therapist does well to try to get beneath the facade and address himself (herself) to the child's underlying fears and anxieties. This approach is the first step toward helping the child gain insight into the pathological processes operative in bringing about this symptom and is the best route to bringing about an alleviation of this problem. For example, the child may be ashamed of the fact that she is not up to the tasks being expected of her. Such a child has to be helped to appreciate that this is a normal, healthy reaction and she should not feel so ashamed. She may feel guilty over the desire to refuse and may fear parental disapprobation and even punishment if she does so. She has to be helped to assert herself in such refusal and, of course, one must deal with the parental contribution in order to ensure that these efforts will prove successful. She may feel resentful over the exploitation, especially if this involves excessive housework and excessive obligations in the care of younger children. Resentments must be expressed, and the therapist must work with the parents to reduce to an age-appropriate level of involvement such utilization of the youngster in housekeeping and child-care activities.

Problems in the Relationship with the Father

As mentioned, it is important for the examiner to appreciate that the father is the only father the child will ever have. Even though the sex abuse represents a significant compromise in parenting capacity, it may still be the case that the father's bonding with the child is stronger than that of any other man on earth. There may be stepfathers, father surrogates, and other relatives who may indeed have strong bonds with the child. This does not negate the possibility (and even high probability) that the father's bonding with the child is stronger than that of any other male—past, present, and future. The examiner does well to give consideration to what I refer to as the *kidney-transplant principle*. Specifically, examiners should ask themselves this question: "If this child required a kidney transplant, who would be lining up at the hospital door to volunteer to donate one?" If the father, in spite of the deficiency of having sexually abused the child, would still be in that line, then the examiner does well to do everything possible to salvage the relationship. Obviously, the relationship is not going to be salvaged if there is still a danger of sex abuse. If this can be accomplished, i.e., the child placed in situations in which there is safety and protection, then everything should then be done to bring about an improvement in their relationship. It is unfortunate that many zealous evaluators and therapists are not appreciative of this very important fact.

In the course of such attempts toward rapprochement, it is obvious that both individual and joint interviews (both with the father and the mother, in all combinations) are warranted. It is important for the therapist to get across to the child the message that all human relationships are ambivalent and that we have "mixed feelings" about all people, even parents. There is no such thing as a parent who is perfect. There is no such thing as a person who has only qualities that we like. Everybody we know has personality characteristics that we dislike as well. The sexual exploitation has to be put on the negative list, but positives as well must be appreciated. The child must have living experiences, over time, that the abuse will not recur and that the counterbalancing positive qualities of the father are indeed present and operative. The rapprochement is not likely to be possible if the abuser denies the abuse in the face of incontrovertible evidence to the contrary. Under such circumstances I might say to the abuser:

> I have done a thorough evaluation of the sex-abuse allegation. I have interviewed in depth you, your wife, and your child. I have reviewed the pertinent evidence and I am convinced—to a very high degree of certainty—that you sexually abused your daughter. I did not see it with my own eyes, and so I cannot be 100 percent certain. But there are all the hallmarks of bona fide abuse in this situation. If you can see your way clear to admitting this, we have a point of departure for a therapy that would be designed to bring about reconciliation with your daughter and an improvement in your relationship with her. If, however, you insist upon denying this, then I see no point to my trying to effect rapprochement. I cannot conduct meaningful therapy in a situation in which a patient is lying to me, over time, about an issue that is central to the therapeutic process. And this principle is applicable to all patients, regardless of the issue about which I believe they are lying.

One of the problems here is that such an admission might subject the father to criminal action. Under such circumstances, he might protect himself from incarceration but he will compromise significantly the opportunity for meaningful rapprochement. Therapy is not for everyone. Judges, lawyers, and (unfortunately) many mental health professionals do not appreciate this obvious fact. People are ordered into therapy for problems that are basically impossible to resolve via psychotherapeutic methods, and this is one of them.

Ordering accused perpetrators into therapy is a widespread phenomenon. There are thousands of judges who do this and there are thousands of mental health professionals who have no problem accepting such individuals into treatment. Such judges have fulfilled what they consider to be their obligation, namely, to order a sick person into treatment. And the mental health professionals believe they are doing a noble thing by helping to "cure" a person with a psychiatric disorder. These people do not seem to appreciate a well-established therapeutic fact, namely, that one cannot treat a person who is lying to the therapist about a fundamental problem, and one cannot treat anyone who does not indeed have the sickness for which he (she) is ostensibly being treated.

Accordingly, whether or not the abuse occurred, such deniers are not candidates for treatment.

Problems in the Relationship with the Mother

If the mother has denied the abuse, and there is incontrovertible evidence that it took place, then the mother must be brought to the point of admitting that it occurred. In many situations, this may not be difficult. However, one must still deal with the child's resentment over the mother's having denied the abuse in the past. The child must be helped to express such resentment, but not via such techniques as banging hammers, hitting clay, or punching dolls. Rather, this kind of cathartic displacement has little value. The child must express directly to the mother the thoughts and feelings she (he) has over the mother's refusal to hear her (him) on this matter. One of the aims of such expression is to help the mother appreciate the kinds of psychological damage that can be done from such denial. This message is more likely to "sink in" if *both* the child and the therapist confront the mother. If successful in this regard, then there is less likelihood that she will deny the abuse again if there is ever a recurrence of the molestation.

One wants, also, for the mother to reach the point where she will spontaneously apologize to the child for what she has done. It is important for the therapist to appreciate that there is an enormous difference between an apology that derives from genuine inner remorse and one that is perfunctorily verbalized in order to squelch the complainant's expression of resentment. The former can be very useful therapeutically, the latter of little therapeutic value. Accordingly, the therapist who initiates the suggestion that the mother apologize is making a serious therapeutic error. To do so is to compromise significantly the likelihood that the mother's apology will be effective. People who say "I demand an apology" are naive. They are making an error. The apology that they may then be successful in obtaining (or extracting) is of little value. The recipient of the apology does not know then whether it is genuine. One does not know whether the apology would have been forthcoming if it had not been requested or demanded. Accordingly, this is clearly a situation in which the therapist does well to keep quiet and not open up his (her) mouth. If the mother herself initiates the apology, and the therapist suspects that the mother is merely going through the motions of an apology, then he (she) should point this out and get across the message that such artificial apologies just do not work. The therapist's task, then, is to help the mother reach the point where she is *genuinely* remorseful. At that point apologies (again originating within her) are more likely to be effective.

In association with the mother's denial, the child's distrust of the mother is generated. Trust is not likely to be regained in a short time. Rather, the child must have living experiences, over time, that the mother can be trusted to protect the child once again. If the mother persistently denies her role as a facilitator of the abuse, *and* the therapist has good reason to believe that she knew about it but was blinding herself psychologically, then the therapist does well to work with her in the hope that she will gain insight into what she has done. If the therapist is successful in this regard, then therapeutic work directed toward the mother's remorse and apology is possible and the child's trust may ultimately be regained. However, if the mother continues to deny her participation (when, in fact, it took place), then the likelihood of these compromises in the mother-child relationship being resolved is very small. Obviously, we have an analogy here to the father who denies being the abuser. In both cases therapy is so significantly compromised that, for all practical purposes, it will be ineffective for the resolution of these particular problems that derive from the sexual abuse.

Retraction (Recantation)

Children who have been abused may retract the accusation once they begin to appreciate the effects of the divulgence. The abuser's threats had heretofore been theoretical, and the younger the child, the less capable the ability to appreciate the consequences of the divulgence. It is extremely unlikely that most children will be able to appreciate fully the consequence of their divulgence of sexual abuse. Suddenly, as if from out of nowhere, there is a degree of commotion that may be greater than anything the child has ever experienced. Suddenly, policemen, detectives, and lawyers appear on the scene, and the child is dragged through a series of interrogations by a parade of "validators," psychologists, social workers, child protection workers, etc. There are interviews with judges, courtroom testimony, and possibly a jury trial. The father may have been taken away by the police, handcuffed, and put in jail—almost immediately. Under such circumstances it is not surprising that the child may recant in the hope of turning back the clock and undoing all that has been done. The anger at the abuser notwithstanding, the child may not have wished such devastating consequences. The child may fear that the anticipated repercussions will be realized once the abuser has the opportunity to implement them. Or the child may feel significant guilt over the consequences of the divulgence, never having realized how formidable they would be. The retraction, then, usually results from a combination of fear and guilt.

Children who fabricate a sex-abuse accusation may also recant. For them there may also be the guilt element, as they come to appreciate how terrible are the consequences of the accusation. Here there is guilt related to the knowledge that the accusation is false, *in addition* to the guilt over the consequences. Accordingly, the fabricating child will have two contributing elements to the guilt, rather than one. For both types of children, however, there must be a cognitive/maturational level reached where they can experience guilt. Accordingly, one sees little if any guilt in children under the age of three or four. I am not suggesting here that we have a sharp cutoff point. Guilt, like other complex human psychological processes, is a developmental process in which there is increasing capacity as the child grows older. The fabricating child may also have fear of retaliation. The fear here is not related to previous threats over divulgence (there were no threats made), but the fear that the accused will retaliate for the false accusation. Generally, the child who has falsely accused will be less fearful because there have been fewer (if any) threats regarding divulgence. Such fabricating children, however, may have been subjected to threats *after* their false accusation. My experience has been, however, that such threats are rare.

It is for these reasons that recanting is not a particularly good criterion for differentiating between the true and false accusation. Children in both categories will retract the accusation. In Chapter Four I will detail the practice of examiners who invoke Summit's (1983) "sexual abuse accommodation syndrome" as an instrument for confirming sex abuse. Recanting, which may be seen in many sexually abused children, is then used to justify the conclusion that the child indeed was abused. Such examiners seem not to appreciate that children who falsely accuse will also recant.

TREATMENT OF THE MOTHER

Dealing with the Mother's Hysteria

If the mother has reacted to the abuse in a hysterical fashion, or used it as an excuse for a campaign of denigration of the father, then the therapist does well to try to "sober her up." The more brouhaha she makes over the abuse, the greater the likelihood the child will react in an untoward manner. Her hysterics will increase the child's guilt, self-loathing, fears, and other untoward reactions to the abuse. She will contribute to the child's feeling that a heinous crime has been committed and will thereby lessen the likelihood of any kind of rapprochement with the father. One has to do everything possible to help her put the "crime" in proper perspective. She has to be helped to appreciate that in most societies in the history of the world, such behavior was ubiquitous, and this is still the case. One must quote to her Shakespeare's Hamlet: "There's nothing either good or bad, but thinking makes it so." The therapist need not sanction the behavior, but should try to reduce the exaggerated reaction to pedophilia that most individuals in our society have at this point.

Discouraging Litigation

If the mother is involved in litigation, she must be helped to appreciate that the longer she involves herself in lawsuits, lawyers, prosecutors, "validators," etc., the longer the child's problems will persist. She has to be helped to appreciate that such litigation will interfere with the natural desensitization process and will subject the child to a wide variety of interrogations that will inevitably be psychologically damaging. If such litigation is fueled by vengeful rage, she has to be helped to appreciate that the way she is dealing with her anger is inevitably going to be detrimental to her child.

Group Therapy

Both individual and group therapy may be useful for such mothers. Although I consider the disadvantages of homogeneous groups to outweigh the advantages, there are certain situations in which a homogeneous group may be useful. By *homogeneous*, I refer to a group in which the individuals are suffering with the same problem (such as alcoholism, obesity, etc.). In a *heterogeneous* group, each individual's primary symptoms are different, but, by dealing with the fundamental problems of life, the numbers work from a broader base and, I believe, are more likely to get to the underlying problems that are at the foundation of their difficulties (Gardner, 1992b). Furthermore, in the heterogeneous group the participants are less likely to keep specific thoughts about their presenting symptoms spinning around in their brains and thereby entrenching the psychopathological processes. This is an aspect of the psychotherapeutic process that is not given the attention it deserves. Although there are certain benefits to be derived from talking about one's symptoms, both at the manifest and latent levels, the process per se has the effect of entrenching more deeply thoughts and feelings about the symptoms and thereby perpetuating them. I am not claiming that homogeneous groups have no value; I am only claiming that they have certain limitations that are often not appreciated. With regard to mothers of sexually abused children, I believe that homogeneous groups can sometimes be useful in helping them appreciate that they are not alone and helping them reduce the aforementioned hysteria and vengeful rage that can be detrimental to all concerned. In addition to these therapeutic experiences, the mother will often require joint interviews with the father and child.

Improving the Mother-Child Relationship

It is important for the therapist to explore the area of the mother's sanctioning (consciously or unconsciously) the sexual relationship between the father and the child. Although this is common, it is not always the case and the therapist does well to determine whether such sanctioning (the more common situation) did indeed occur. If there was such sanctioning, the therapist does well to find out what the reasons were. A common reason relates to the mother's own abhorrence of sex and the use of the child as her sexual surrogate, thereby forming a replacement for herself with the father. Sometimes such abhorrence stems from the mother's having been sexually abused herself as a child. (I will comment below in greater detail on the therapeutic approaches to such a mother's sexual inhibition problem.) Relevant here is the mother's becoming increasingly aware of the mechanisms of her sanctioning—especially in situations in which she is unaware, or only dimly aware, of them. Without such awareness the steps that need to be taken to improve the mother-child relationship will be more difficult to accomplish. Furthermore, without such awareness the likelihood of the mother protecting the child in the future is also reduced. Without such awareness she is less likely to appreciate the child's sense of betrayal and thereby take steps toward reducing such feelings in the child. Without such awareness she is less likely to feel guilt, guilt that will also enhance the likelihood of rapprochement with the child. Accordingly, she will be less likely to spontaneously express her regrets and apologies over what she has done. As mentioned, apologies made without conviction are not only of no value, but they may make the situation worse.

In joint sessions in which both mother and child are present together, the therapist can focus on the mother's denial and betrayal and have each party verbalize their feelings about this situation. Obviously, the younger the child, the less likely the child is going to provide meaningful input into the joint sessions. In the course of such meetings, the mother must increase her capacity to be sensitive to the child and listen with receptivity to what the child is saying. I cannot emphasize this point strongly enough. There are tens of thousands, and possibly hundreds of thousands, of adult women who complain that when they were sexually abused as children, their mothers were unreceptive to their complaints, denied them, and threatened punishment if they were to speak further on the subject. The resultant feelings of betrayal can be lifelong. Accordingly, the therapist should do everything to reverse this insidious process at the earliest possible time. It is indeed a good example of preventive psychiatry in that, if successful, one can prevent the prolongation of a symptom that might be lifelong.

The mother and child must be encouraged to spend more time alone together in which the two of them enjoy mutual experiences. It may be that one of the reasons why the daughter turned toward the father is the impairment in the child's relationship with the mother. One should investigate into the existence of difficulties in the mother-child relationship unrelated to the sexual abuse. Resolution of these problems cannot but prove useful. Furthermore, improvement of the mother-child relationship may reduce the likelihood of the child's turning to the father for sexual affection.

As mentioned elsewhere (Gardner, 1975, 1992b), therapists do well to work closely with parents and utilize them as "assistant therapists" in the psychotherapeutic process. Accordingly, in my work with most child patients, I have the mother join me throughout the course of the session. And the younger the child, the greater the likelihood the mother will be so involved. I generally refer to this procedure as *individual child psychotherapy with parental observation and intermittent participation*. Although this may be a cumbersome label for a procedure, it states exactly the nature of the parental involvement. I do not routinely and reflexively include the mother; I only prefer to have her involvement. I still recognize that there are certain situations in which her involvement may be contraindicated, e.g., situations in which there is a symbiotic tie between the mother and child, a tie that must be attenuated if the child's symptoms are to be alleviated. For the child who has been sexually abused, such involvement may provide the mother with information useful to her in reinforcing the therapist's comments between sessions. This is especially important with regard to coping maneuvers and desensitization experiences.

If the child's abuse has involved an early introduction into adult levels of sexuality, the mother must be helped to deal with this problem. In some cases, the child returns to lower levels of sexuality after the abuse has stopped. In other cases, it may continue. For many such children, masturbation is the only reasonable outlet and should be encouraged. If the mother has some inhibitions regarding this practice, every attempt should be made to reduce them so that the child can be allowed this outlet. Of course, other methods of dealing with the sexuality can also be utilized, such as distractions, sports, and sublimatory activities. However, it should be emphasized that these substitute vehicles for release are not likely to be entirely successful, and the more direct sexual outlet must be given respect. I generally advise such mothers to make comments to the child along these lines: "If you want to rub yourself there, that's fine with me. However, that's not the kind of thing that people do in front of others. That's a private thing and it should be done in private places. Therefore, if you want to go into the bedroom or the bathroom and close the door and do that there, that's fine." For the child who is obsessed with touching or looking at other people's breasts and genitals, I advise comments along these lines: "I can understand your wanting to touch people in those private places. But that's not allowed. People get very upset with you when you try to do that. If you want to touch yourself in private places, when you're alone, that's perfectly fine with me. And when you grow up, and when you have a boyfriend (girlfriend), and the two of you love each other very much and want to do that together, that's okay with me too."

If the mother has been a contributor to the child's pseudomaturity problem, her role in bringing about this difficulty must be explored and she has to gain insight into the ways in which she has contributed. If she rationalizes such utilization of the child, by claiming that it is good for her to assume adult responsibilities and/or that she needs help in the care of the younger children, one must help her differentiate between the normal, healthy needs of the child for such mature tasks and their pathological degree. It can sometimes be difficult to find that point where the healthy becomes the pathological, but the therapist does well to attempt to do so. One certainly wants the child to feel the sense of ego enhancement that comes from assuming responsibilities, as long as they are age-appropriate aspirations and as long as the child is not being overburdened. When the exploitation elements are operative, we are then dealing with a pathological situation.

The mother also has to be helped to gain insight into the fact that encouragement of pseudomaturity may be part of a larger program of having the child become a substitute wife for the husband, a role in which the sexual aspect is only one part. In joint sessions, the child has to be helped to express to her mother her innermost thoughts and feelings regarding the assumption of this role. Perhaps the mother herself has problems in assuming adult female roles. If the therapist is successful in helping such a mother become more comfortable in the role of wife, she will have less of a need to pressure her child into assuming this role. It is important for the reader to appreciate that my use of the word *wife* should in no way be construed to imply that I am encouraging an inegalitarian situation. The husband/wife relationship can be an equal one. To encourage a relationship in which the wife's role is subservient is to perpetuate yet another kind of psychopathology.

Dealing with Passivity and Inadequacy

In some families the sexual molestation is only one part of a broader program of the father's domination over all family members. Everyone is under his subjugation in both the sexual and nonsexual realms. One manifestation of the family's passivity to the father is the mother's inability to effectively protect the children from his using them sexually. Such a mother may then serve as a model for the child's own submissiveness. Those who provide children with sex-education programs in which they teach children to "say no" do not generally give consideration to the fact that the child's passivity is not simply related to immature age and its attendant feelings of impotence and helplessness. A factor that is often operative is the child's identification with a mother who is similarly passive and inhibited in the ability to express herself. Accordingly, without work with the mother, the likelihood of success for such programs is reduced significantly.

The mother's mother (that is, the child's maternal grandmother) may have served as a model for such passivity and one cannot know how many generations of such modeling there have been. Accordingly, the therapist must have limited goals with regard to helping the mother with this personality problem. This aspect of the mother's therapeutic program may also be compromised by the fact that such assertion may be difficult, if not impossible, for the father to handle and, as a result, he may leave the marital home. His own model may have been a domineering, coercive father, and one may not know how many generations down the line this pattern has been promulgated. Domination of men over women is a deep-seated pattern in the history of the human race, and it is somewhat grandiose on the part of the therapist to believe that he (she) can alleviate such a problem with such a weak instrument as psychotherapy. However, the therapist should still try. The mother has to be helped to get in touch with her inner thoughts and feelings engendered by the father's domination. She has to be helped to assert herself and to deal with the consequences of such assertion. Joint sessions with the father may be useful. Unfortunately, many such fathers do not believe in psychotherapy and so are not available for treatment. Men who feel so insecure that they have to compensate by dominating women and children are not likely to have the ego strength to tolerate the confrontations necessary for psychotherapy to be meaningful and effective. Group therapy can also be helpful, especially groups that can provide the mother with support and advice regarding self-assertion.

Sometimes the mother's complicity in the sexual abuse of the child(ren) is not related to the father as abuser but related to other male sexual partners. These individuals may *require* the child's involvement in their sexual activities with the mother as a proviso for their continued involvement with her. They may not only threaten abandonment of her, but physical violence as well. We are dealing here, then, with group sex experiences. The mother may have initially been reluctant to involve her children in such activities, but she does so lest she lose the affection and involvement of her companion. The children may then come to enjoy the experiences because they have been prematurely brought into adult levels of sexual excitation. The therapist may reflexively try to help the mother remove herself from such a man, especially for the sake of the children. Such therapists do well to be realistic with regard to the mother's potential for a different companion (especially one who will not make the same demands) and not engender high hopes or unrealistic aspirations regarding the acquisition of a more mature, healthy, and desirable companion who might ultimately marry the mother and create a traditional nuclear family. And the same warning holds true for mothers who assert themselves against domineering husbands. Many of these mothers are deeply masochistic, and sadomasochistic relationships with men have been the family pattern as far back as one knows. The likelihood is that if such a mother were to extract herself from the sadistic man with whom she is involved, she will gravitate toward another sadist. It is almost as if she doesn't know how to relate to someone who treats her well. If such a woman does find herself with a man who is affectionate, tender, and caring, she feels like a "fish out of water." It is a strange environment for her and she does not know how to react in it. It is a world that may be entirely unknown to her. Obviously, under such circumstances, the therapist does well to have limited goals. Such masochistic mothers have to be helped to assert themselves, in both the sexual and the nonsexual realms. It is hoped that assertion in one area will "spill over" into the other.

Many of these mothers are social isolates and the social isolation has come about, in part, because the husband has tried to sequester the family from involvement in the greater world outside the home. This situation, too, contributes to feelings of inadequacy and helplessness. Such mothers have to be helped to overcome the tensions and anxieties that inhibit their movement into the mainstream of the world. She may have dependency problems, especially dependency on the husband, that have to be worked out. If such a woman becomes less dependent on her husband, she may risk alienating him. Furthermore, if she loses him, there is always the risk that she will gravitate toward another man upon whom she is dependent. This too may not easily be changed, considering that there may have been many generations in which this was the pattern for the relationship between the husband and wife.

Dealing with Sexual Problems

It is likely that the mother has sexual problems, and these must be delineated and identified. In many cases she herself was sexually molested as a child. If she has thereby become sexually inhibited and views sex as disgusting, the therapist must help her reduce such fears and guilt and reach the point of enjoying sex herself. She may never have achieved an orgasm—in spite of the fact that she was sexually molested, in spite of the fact that she had many lovers, and in spite of the fact that she is now married. The therapist, then, does well to try to help her achieve such gratification. Verbal statements about the pleasures of orgastic response are not likely to prove very useful. One has to encourage experiences, under proper situations of relaxation, which will enable her to achieve the goal of orgastic response. If she has never masturbated, one should explore her reasons why and try to convince her that there is no *good* reason why one should *never* masturbate, at any time in one's life. Vibrators can be extremely useful in this regard, and one must try to overcome any inhibition she may have with regard to their use. There are thousands (and maybe millions) of women whose first orgastic responses were enjoyed with a vibrator, and this enabled them to then go on to enjoy orgasms in other ways. (Obviously, accurate statistics on this subject would be extremely difficult to obtain.) Her own diminished guilt over masturbation will make it easier for her to encourage the practice in her daughter, if this is warranted. And her increased sexuality may lessen the need for her husband to return to their daughter for sexual gratification.

A mother who has been sexually abused as a child may have residual anger toward her molesting father or other sexual molester, and this may be interfering with her relationship with her husband. This should be explored in depth, and she should be helped to reduce such residual anger. Sometimes a "he's-more-to-be-pitied-than-scorned" attitude toward her father can be useful. Perhaps she can be helped to appreciate that in the history of the world his behavior has probably been more common than the restrained behavior of those who do not sexually abuse their children. I am not claiming here that the therapist should sanction parent-child sexuality, but rather to put it in proper perspective and help the mother appreciate that it has not been universally considered the heinous crime that it is viewed to be in Western society today. The mother has to be helped to appreciate that her experiences with her father and her child's experiences with her husband do not justify the generalization that *all* men are sexual abusers. Such a conclusion will interfere with her relationships with men in general, especially if she views them all to be dangerous perverts.

The mother has to be helped to appreciate that an ongoing campaign of vengeance against her husband is going to lessen the likelihood that their child will achieve some sort of rapprochement with him. Again, joint interviews with the husband may be useful in reducing such anger. Furthermore, attempts should be made to reduce anything the father is doing that may be contributing to the mother's anger toward him, provocative behavior that is fueling the mother's rage. This anger may be a factor contributing to her lack of sexual responsivity. If one is tense and angry with a man, one is less likely to achieve sexual gratification. Accordingly, this is a less direct, but nevertheless important, method for helping alleviate the mother's sexual problems.

TREATMENT OF THE FATHER

Introduction

First, and I cannot emphasize this point strongly enough, it is not possible to meaningfully treat a sexual offender unless he admits that he committed the offense. It is naive on the part of courts to refer to treatment a person who denies having sexually abused the child. It is naive on the judge's part to say, "If you don't go into treatment, I'll put you in jail." This makes a mockery of treatment. The therapist who goes along with this naive utilization of the therapeutic process is not serving well the court or the patient. I am reminded here of many telephone conversations I have had in recent years. They basically go along these lines:

>   *Caller*: Dr. Gardner, my name is John Doe. I'd like to go into treatment with you.
>   *Gardner*: Can you tell me something about your problems?
>   *Caller*: The judge said I have to go into treatment or else he'll put me in jail.
>   *Gardner*: What are the problems for which he has ordered treatment?
>   *Caller*: For sexual abuse of a child.
>   *Gardner*: Did you sexually abuse a child?
>   *Caller*: No, absolutely not.
>   *Gardner*: Do you have any *other* problems, other than this alleged sexual abuse?
>   *Caller*: No.
>   *Gardner*: Is there *anything* that bothers you that you think you would like to talk to a psychiatrist about?
>   *Caller*: No.
>   *Gardner*: Would you be calling me now if the judge hadn't ordered you to do so?
>   *Caller*: No.
>   *Gardner*: Let me tell you this. There are two possibilities. You *have* sexually abused this child and you're lying to me, or you *have not* sexually abused the child and you are telling me the truth. If you *have* sexually abused the child and you are lying to me, then there is absolutely no basis

for treatment because you would be lying to your psychiatrist about a central issue. Even minor lies to a psychiatrist may compromise the treatment, but a major lie—one that relates to the primary focus of the treatment—makes the treatment a sham, a mockery. Accordingly, if you have *indeed* molested this child, and are denying it to me, then I will not see you because I will not embark on a treatment program that, from the outset, is a sham.

If, however, you are telling me the truth and you *have not* indeed molested this child, then we still have no basis for treatment. What are we going to talk about? Are we going to sit here and look at one another and talk about how you didn't do that? That would be a waste of time and money. You can't have meaningful therapy for something that you didn't do.

Accordingly, it was naive on the judge's part to refer you for treatment and I will not agree to make the first appointment unless there is something you can tell me to convince me otherwise.

Caller: Are you saying then that you won't make an appointment with me?

Gardner: Yes, that is what I am saying. Unless you can give me some good reason why I should treat you under these circumstances.

Caller: Well, I guess I can't have an appointment with you. I'll have to find someone else. Can you recommend someone to me?

Gardner: No, I could not recommend any person who would be willing to treat you under such circumstances. However, I'm sure you will find someone else. And that's unfortunate. But I personally never have gone along with, and cannot see myself going along with, this kind of a mockery of the therapeutic process.

Caller (in an angry and frustrated tone): Thank you very much, Doctor, for your time.

Gardner: You're welcome!

There seems to be some kind of unwritten collusion between judges and therapists on this point. There are thousands of judges who are routinely ordering into therapy people who deny sexual molestation. They have much more respect for treatment than I. They believe they are doing their job and putting these people into "good hands." What they are really doing is perpetuating a myth about the efficacy of psychotherapy in general, especially for people who deny the problem for which they are in treatment. And they are encouraging a sea of hungry therapists (psychotherapy today is certainly a buyer's market) to "treat" people in this category.

There are situations, however, in which a father will admit that he did indeed abuse the child but will refuse therapy. Under such circumstances, a court order that the father be treated may sometimes (I repeat sometimes) prove useful. If, within a few sessions, the therapist is successful in engaging the father, then the court order may give the father a rationalization for involving himself. The father may have operated on the principle that anyone in therapy must be crazy, and he may need the court order as a rationalization for involving himself in treatment. Such a man is similar, then, to the adolescent who claims he is only in treatment because his parents are forcing him to so involve himself. If the father is in a group-therapy experience with others who have sexually abused children, then he may become more comfortable with himself, come to appreciate that he is not so unique or atypical, and then become more comfortable with the therapeutic process. In other cases, however, it is quite obvious that the therapy is going to be useless because of the continued lack of motivation for treatment. Under such circumstances, the therapist does well to discontinue the treatment and advise the court that it cannot be successful.

Group Therapy

As mentioned, I am generally much more in favor of heterogeneous group therapy than homogeneous group therapy. A heterogeneous group, by definition, consists of individuals with a wide variety of problems. A homogeneous group is one in which the individuals all have the same (or closely related) disorder(s), e.g., obesity, alcohol, drug abuse, etc. The problem with the homogeneous group is that it focuses primarily on symptomatic manifestations and thereby keeps thoughts and feelings about the presenting problem spinning around in the brain. It does not properly or frequently address itself to the underlying psychiatric difficulties (which the patient shares in common with all other human beings) that are contributing to the development of the symptom that is the focus of the group. The heterogeneous group does not have this problem. However, there are certain benefits to be derived from the homogeneous group that cannot be enjoyed by the heterogeneous group. Specifically, a pedophile may feel terribly isolated and rejected in a heterogeneous group, and there may be some justification for his feeling of alienation. He is less likely to suffer such rejection in a homogeneous group. Also, he may feel less loathsome about himself when he has direct experiences with others with the same problem. Considering the drawbacks of both situations, I believe that the ideal group for a pedophile is to be in a group in which there are both nonpedophiles and pedophiles. In this way the benefits of both can be enjoyed and the drawbacks of both types of group reduced.

Improving the Father-Child Relationship

First, one has to attempt to ascertain the degree of risk of further molestation. Obviously, there is a continuum here from little if any risk to extremely high risk, with all points in between being represented. Of course, the therapist cannot objectify this to a particular point on this continuum, but he (she) should be able to gain some information about the degree of risk. Obviously, the degree of safeguards and protections will be determined by the degree of risk. Furthermore, the degree of risk will also determine whether the child and father can remain living in the same home. As mentioned, meaningful therapy of the child is not likely to take place if there is a high risk of recurrence. Similarly, treatment of the father is not likely to be successful if he is in a highly tempting situation in which the possibility of molestation recurring is great. One does not treat alcoholics by giving them jobs as bartenders. There is an old German proverb that has applicability here: "*Die Gelegenheit macht den Dieb*" ("The opportunity makes the thief"). Accordingly, one should not set up opportunities for such molesters.

It is also important to appreciate that people who have exhibited an ongoing pattern of pedophilia are not likely to be "cured." In contrast, those for whom the pedophilic act has been an isolated experience, especially if it occurred only once or twice under certain stresses, have a much better prognosis. When the father and child do have contact, one must decide whether monitored contacts would be the only ones that are warranted at that particular point. One has to decide whether the monitoring can take place in home situations or whether it is necessary to put the two together in neutral places, such as community agencies, under the supervision of others. One has to be especially concerned about the two being together alone in a bathroom, or bedroom, or while dressing. Without the implementation of such precautions, therapy of the child is not likely to prove successful, nor is the therapy of the father likely to be effective. Even if the father does not act out the pedophilic impulses, if he is being placed in tempting situations the pedophilic impulses will become intensified and the therapy is not likely to succeed.

Joint interviews with the father and child are important if one is to successfully bring about rapprochement. What I said previously about the mother's apologizing to the child holds for the father as well. Therapists should strictly avoid recommending that the father apologize. Rather, they should hope that he will reach the point of doing so on his own. Once the therapist recommends it, one does not know whether the apology is genuine or whether it is merely an attempt to "look good" in the therapist's eyes and to comply in robot-like fashion with the therapist's recommendation. The child must have living experiences, over time, that the molestations are not going to recur. Promises and resolutions that they will not recur are of limited value only. The father's reputation for being an abuser must change, and this can only take place over time.

The child should be helped to express anger, sense of betrayal, fears, and other feelings that were probably engendered by the molestation. The father's reactions to these must be expressed, and the child's statements should be used as a point of departure for psychotherapeutic interchanges. The two must come to know one another as human beings with a wide variety of thoughts and feelings, including ambivalence toward each other. Both must be helped to be brought to the point where each can have the attitude regarding the other that "he (she) is more to be pitied than scorned." Some people have expressed surprise regarding my use of the term *pity* as a therapeutic goal. They consider *pity* to be intrinsically denigrating and antitherapeutic. I am not in agreement. One must differentiate between pity that is *benevolently* motivated and pity that is *malevolently* motivated. To say that we have pity for a person who is deformed, handicapped, or subjected to terrible human experiences (such as earthquakes, fires, concentration camps, etc.) can be benevolent. It does not necessarily mean that we are denigrating such individuals or looking down upon them. There are, however, people who will pity others as a manifestation of self-aggrandizement and the need to consider themselves superior to those who are less fortunate. Such noblesse-oblige pity is demeaning. What we want to engender in both the father and the child is a healthy sense of pity for each other's plight. The child should be able to pity the father for the curse (in our society) of having pedophilic tendencies. In other times and other places, he would be considered normal. And the father should be able to pity the child for having been a victim of his molestation, especially a victim in a society that considers his behavior a heinous crime and/or a mortal sin.

As is true for all meaningful therapy, it is preferable that much of the time *not* be spent simply focusing on the primary problem, in this case, sexual molestation. To do so may be antitherapeutic. Certainly, one must focus on the presenting problem if one is to bring about its alleviation. However, too much focus on it has negative effects. First, for children who are sexually abused, it may involve a certain amount of "muckraking," which interferes with the natural desensitization process. Also, such continual focus may have the effect of keeping the material "spinning around in the brain," when it might otherwise reduce itself. Proper attention is not given to this important negative effect of therapy. We want to help people forget about their problems. This is not going to be accomplished simply by saying, "Forget it." This is more likely to be accomplished by talking about other things that may also be therapeutically beneficial. And this should be carried out of the therapeutic situation as well, in that both father and child do well to share a wide variety of experiences that healthy fathers and children enjoy—experiences that contribute to strong bonding and healthy maturation for both.

Enhancing Self-Esteem

Most pedophiles in our society suffer with feelings of low self-esteem. They are generally viewed as pariahs and subjected to terrible scorn. It is hard to imagine pedophiles feeling good about themselves while living in such a world. Elsewhere (Gardner, 1995a) I have described the narcissism of many pedophiles, but I indicated, as well, that such narcissism is compensatory for feelings of low self-worth. Certainly, such feelings stem from factors that antedated and contributed to the development of the pedophilia. But such low self-esteem is intensified, as well, by society's reaction to such behavior.

The father has to be helped to appreciate that there is a certain amount of pedophilia in all of us and that all of us, as children, are "polymorphous perverse." If he doesn't know this already, he has to be helped to appreciate that pedophilia has been considered the norm by the vast majority of individuals in the history of the world. He has to be helped to appreciate that, even today, it is a widespread and accepted practice among literally billions of people. He has to come to appreciate that in our Western society especially, we take a very punitive and moralistic attitude toward such inclinations. However, he—like the therapist, and like others in our Western society—is a product of our culture. We are brought up in a society in which pedophilia is strongly discouraged and even condemned. The question, then, for the pedophile is why he has not come to be similarly inhibited. Often there are family-life situations that have been conducive to the development of pedophilia. (In Chapter Two I have discussed these in detail.) One must explore the particular factors that were operative in the patient's own atypical development—atypical, at least, for our society. If he himself was molested as a child, then he has to come to appreciate that this probably played a role in his own pedophilic tendencies. With regard to his feelings about himself, he has to be helped to take the attitude that he, like the child he molested, is "more to be pitied than scorned." He has had a certain amount of bad luck with regard to the early childhood experiences that were conducive to the development of his pedophilia. He has also had bad luck with regard to the place and time he was born with regard to social attitudes toward pedophilia. However, these are not reasons to condemn himself. They are not reasons to indulge the pedophilia either. Rather, although unlikely with regard to the time and place that the genetic dice fell for him and the unlucky early life experiences he had, he still must learn to control himself if he is to protect himself from the Draconian punishments meted out to those in our society who act out their pedophilic impulses. The therapist does well to explore these areas in great detail, appreciating that every patient has his/her own pattern of contributory factors.

As mentioned elsewhere (Gardner, 1992c), low self-esteem is complex and many factors contribute to it. The therapist does well to explore for these contributing factors in great detail. Everything the patient is thinking, feeling, and doing that may contribute to feelings of low self-worth must be identified and attempts made to reduce these etiological factors. Such inquiry should not simply involve areas related to the sexual molestation, but all other areas of life as well. To the degree that one is successful in raising the patient's self-esteem, to that degree one is likely to reduce the pedophilic tendencies. However, it is important to appreciate that individuals whose pedophilia is deep-seated and has been the primary sexual pattern over many years are not likely to be changed significantly by the psychotherapeutic process. They can, however, suppress the acting-out of their pedophilic drives.

Dealing with Guilt (or Lack of It)

Some pedophiles are psychopathic and have little if any guilt over their molestation of children. Others, however, feel very guilty about what they have done and the guilt in such individuals may be formidable. Of course, one does well to consider there to be a continuum, from those who are excessively guilty to those that have no guilt at all. The therapist should explore the guilt issue with the patient and ascertain at what point on this continuum the patient's guilt (or lack of it) lies.

For fathers who have little or no guilt, the therapeutic goal is to increase it. Such fathers may rationalize that pedophilia is an ancient tradition, a worldwide practice, and that there is nothing at all to be guilty about. Such fathers have to be helped to appreciate that although what they say on this point is true, this does not justify its practice in *our* society, even though our society overreacts to it. It is because our society overreacts to it that children suffer. If our society did not overreact to it, it is far less likely that children would suffer—especially if the sexual encounter has not been coercive, sadistic, or brutal (sometimes the case and sometimes not). Even if the molestation has been tender and kind, the father has to be helped to appreciate that such activities may have the effect of "locking" the child into sexualized relationships with people who are significantly older. And this can be a significant disadvantage in the dating phase of life as well as in the ability to form meaningful and stable marriages. Furthermore, if the father rationalizes the behavior with the argument "She wanted it" or "She didn't object, so she must have liked it," he has to be helped to appreciate that this is not a justifiable excuse for pedophilic behavior. Children are immature and helpless. We do not give them everything they want. We know that it is important to say no to them for their own good. Indulging a child's every whim interferes significantly with the child's ultimate adjustment in the world. Denying the child, at times, is necessary for survival in the world into which the child has been born. And denying sexual involvement with a child who invites it is a form of denial in this category.

If the father is extremely psychopathic, then the treatment may not be effective. Psychopaths are notoriously poor candidates for psychotherapeutic treatment. They have little if any guilt, no internal conflict, little if any guilt-evoking empathy for their victims, little insight into the fact they have problems, hence little if any motivation for treatment. If they are in treatment, it is usually because of some external reason; there is something to be gained for them that has nothing to do with changing themselves. For pedophiles with psychopathic tendencies, the most common reason for requesting treatment is that it has been ordered by a court, and the failure to involve oneself may result in serious consequences, even imprisonment. Accordingly, therapists do well, at the outset, to "smoke out" such specious reasons for requesting therapy.

Over the years, I have occasionally had psychopathic people come to me for treatment. Invariably there was some external motivation, unrelated to the genuine desire to change themselves, e.g., "My girlfriend says she doesn't want to go with me anymore, and will certainly never marry me, because I lie so much," "The judge ordered me to go into treatment," and "My wife said she'll divorce me unless I go into therapy." Not surprisingly, all of them have attempted (with varying degrees of success) to exploit me with regard to the payment of my fees. Accordingly, in the last few years I have taken a special approach with regard to the payment for appointments by people who I suspect from the outset are psychopathic. Before describing the procedure it is important for the reader to appreciate that I make all my appointments myself, from the first to the nth. My secretary makes none of my appointments. All new callers receive a 10- to 15-minute free interview, during which time I get an idea about the primary problems. If, during the course of this conversation, I conclude that there is strong reason to believe that the patient is a psychopath, I will make the following statement:

> My experience with people with your kind of problem is that it is best that they pay for their therapy—in cash—at the beginning of each session. My standard fee is X dollars (my standard rate at that time) per 45-minute session. A consultation for an adult is generally an hour and a half, or 2X dollars. [I say absolutely nothing else and wait for the caller's response.]

Invariably, the caller will say something along these lines: "Well, let me think about it, Doctor" or "I really don't have that kind of money." Sometimes the person will try to bargain with me and suggest we discuss the fee arrangement at the time of the consultation. Obviously, this I refuse to do. Needless to say, I have not once had the experience of such people agreeing to this program.

In contrast, fathers who have too much guilt, who are overreacting to the molestation, must be helped to appreciate that the practice is ancient and ubiquitous. They have to be helped to appreciate how strongly our society overreacts, and come to recognize that they are taking on society's attitude. Of course, it is very difficult to reduce such guilt in a world where there is such overreaction. However, this should not stop the therapist from making every attempt to put the "crime" in proper perspective. My experience has been, however, that there are many more pedophiles that have too little guilt than there are those who have too much.

Dealing with Isolation

The father may be in that category of pedophile who removes himself from society and uses his family as his own personal "harem." He may be an individual who basically fears involvement in the world and cannot relate meaningfully to others. His whole life is his family, and he uses his family members for just about all interpersonal gratifications, sexual and nonsexual. Such a pattern may be extremely difficult to modify by treatment. Going out of the home makes the father feel like "a fish out of water." Some of these individuals actually have their employment in their homes, especially in such situations as farms or home-based businesses. These individuals are less likely to be helped than those who have some experiences outside the home, especially in the workplace. Obviously, in the course of treatment, one must help these homebound individuals gain gratification in the extradomestic realm and have living experiences that such involvements can be enriching and maturing. This will lessen the need for their dependence on their family members as their sole source of human gratification. Sometimes group therapy can be useful in that it provides opportunities for intimate involvements—in a nonsexual way—with other individuals. It is here that the heterogeneous group is likely to be most valuable.

The father may have an impaired tolerance for the unpredictability and stresses of the extradomestic world, but he has to be helped to cope with its vicissitudes if he is to be successful in bringing about adaptation to and comfort with that world. For most patients therapy involves teaching coping mechanisms, i.e., teaching people how to deal better with the inevitable frustrations, disappointments, and rejections of life. Pedophiles in this category need more instruction within the therapeutic sessions regarding how to deal with the inevitable problems of life with which we are all confronted. However, this is only the "lecture" part of the course. Actual experiences in the outside "laboratory" of the world are required if these changes are to be brought about.

Dealing with the Exaggerated Need to Control and/or Dominate

The need to dominate and subjugate weaker individuals (especially women and children) is an ancient tradition. In fact, it has been the norm throughout the history of the world (with rare exception) and is very much the norm at this time, recent enlightenment and improvements notwithstanding. I suspect, as well, that there is genetic programming for men to be the more dominant and for women to be the more submissive. The more dominant men were more capable of surviving, especially in past years when the hunter-warrior role was the primary one assumed by men. But even later, when humanity moved into agricultural forms of survival, domination was still of survival value for men, especially when protecting themselves from enemies.

In contrast, women who were passive and submissive were more likely to be chosen as mates. Because docility was of selective survival value, it is probable that women are, even today, more genetically programmed to be passive. I am not placing any value judgments on this state of affairs; I am only stating what I consider to be the reality of the world. The therapist does well to give serious consideration to what I have said and to recognize that he (she) should have limited goals with regard to changing significantly the dominating propensities of pedophiles in this category. However, this does not mean that therapists should not try to bring about some reduction of the pedophile's need to dominate. Such patients have to be helped to put themselves in the position of those whom they are subjugating. They have to be helped to develop sympathy and empathy for their victims. They have to be helped to gain esteem in other areas, areas that do not involve domination. They have to be helped to delegate authority to others.

Often there has been parental modeling for domineering behavior and this, of course, will lessen the likelihood of therapeutic success. Such men have to be helped to gain insight into certain psychodynamic factors that may have been operative in bringing about the domination, factors that are idiosyncratic and separate from factors that relate to modeling with the pedophile's father and other family males. Social and cultural influences have to be clarified as well, e.g., the domination factor commonly seen in violent movies, war stories, and similar kinds of macho fare. The idiosyncratic factors, i.e., those that are particularly relevant to the individual patient's development of pedophilia, have generally been added to the family and environmental factors. Insight has to be gained into all of these, and they have to be changed in therapy to the degree possible.

When investigating the idiosyncratic factors, one should focus on low self-esteem, for which the domination may be a form of compensation. Thorough exploration of all areas in which thoughts, feelings, and behavior contribute to feelings of low self-worth should be explored. Anything that can be done to enhance self-worth should diminish the need to dominate. We see again here how low self-esteem is a central element in many forms of psychogenic psychopathology and how its alleviation can be viewed as a "universal antidote" for such difficulties (Gardner, 1992c).

Group therapy may also be useful. Here again, a heterogeneous group, especially one in which most of the people do not have domination problems, can be useful. Sometimes some of these fathers do not appreciate that domination of women is not "the way of the world" and that there are others who do not deal with women and children in this way. The domination problem may be part of generalized sadomasochism that has been a deep-seated family problem generations in the making. Under such circumstances, it is not likely to be helped to any significant degree by the psychotherapeutic process.

Dealing with the Excessively Moralistic Pedophile

It may initially appear that the term *excessively moralistic pedophile* is an oxymoron, a contradiction in terms. It would appear that pedophiles do not have *enough* morality; otherwise they would not perpetrate their heinous acts. However, there are some pedophiles who are excessively moralistic, and their moralism is a reaction formation to underlying strong sexual cravings over which they feel excessively guilty. The blanket denunciation of sexuality in all its forms serves as a cover-up and is a method of suppressing and repressing strong sexual urges that they cannot allow to emerge into conscious awareness. However, suppressive and repressive forces may weaken, and there may thereby be a breakthrough of sexual impulses into conscious awareness. And the next step, of course, is the actual physical gratification of such impulses. A clergyman, for example, who chooses a stringent religious life as a way of avoiding sexuality may find that the urges become so overpowering that they can no longer be repressed or suppressed. For that individual, the child may be viewed as the safest, most passive, and least likely to be rejecting subject for a sexual encounter. As a clergyman, he is likely to be held in high esteem and less likely to be refused. Some of the "televangelist" preachers would be in this category. Their need to warn the world about the evils and sins of sex is merely an attempt to convince themselves. People who have to proselytize, especially if they must do so to audiences of millions, are usually trying to convince themselves under the guise of convincing others. They are vicariously identifying with the subjects of their ministrations. It is as if each time they preach to others they are preaching to their projected selves. Their campaign, which attempts to obliterate sexual behavior in their constituents, serves to protect themselves from the temptations that would be engendered by the observation of sexual manifestations. If they were to be successful in obliterating sexuality from the entire world, they would presumably be protected from the temptations that they fear.

Such individuals have to be helped to become more comfortable with their sexual urges and to feel less guilty about them. We see here a good example of how the therapist's values play an important role in the psychotherapeutic process. As mentioned elsewhere (Gardner, 1992b), successful psychotherapy inevitably involves the transmission of the therapist's values to the patient. It is hoped that such transmission will be in the patient's best interests. I recognize that for some people in this category, the therapy might involve a career change. But this is not a unique situation. There are many people in therapy who decide on a career change and recognize that it is part of healthy growth and development. They come to appreciate that the career choice they made prior to treatment was injudicious and that neurotic factors contributed to it. As they become healthier, they decide to leave that career and direct their skills and talents toward healthier paths.

Dealing with Impulsivity

Impulsivity may also have a high genetic loading. I believe it is reasonable to say that men are generally more impulsive than women. Up to this century (and in many places during this century) impulsivity was of survival value for men. The impulsive man was more likely to survive as hunter and warrior than the more cautious person. The warrior who thinks, as he holds his spear, "If I kill that man, his wife and children may starve," may be exhibiting a high level of civilized sensitivity. However, during the time that he is pausing for these noble considerations, he may get a spear thrust into his chest. The "shoot first and ask questions later" motto is a valuable principle to subscribe to on the battlefield—the obvious cruelty and sadism of the dictum notwithstanding. In contrast, impulsivity was just the opposite of what most men wanted in women. Sedentary behavior, especially comfort with forethought and planning, is an important quality to have if one is to be a successful child rearer.

In addition to these genetic factors, there are certainly environmental influences that encourage impulsive behavior in men. Violence as part of the macho image is a good example. The macho man does not deliberate very long before taking action. He is "quick on the draw" and asks questions later. For the pedophile, there may be a longstanding pattern of impulsivity with regard to sexual gratification. Their urges are likely to be strong, and they demand quick release. Here again, biological loading is probably operative (we are much more like animals than we would like to believe). The impulsivity may be so great that pedophiles do not give proper consideration to the consequences of their behavior. Accordingly, one must help pedophiles "count to ten" and follow the principle: "Stop, look, think, and listen." They need significant experience with the implementation of these important principles, in both the sexual and nonsexual realms. Therapy in a heterogeneous group may be useful here in that it may provide the impulsive pedophile with the opportunity to have intimate contact with others whose healthy suppression of their impulses has been a lifelong pattern. (I am not referring here to extremely inhibited individuals, but to those who exhibit a *healthy* degree of suppression of their drives.)

Dealing with Homosexuality

In Chapter One I presented *some* of my views on homosexuality. Some pedophiles are basically homosexual, i.e., they are males who confine themselves primarily, if not exclusively, to male children as their sexual partners. They have little if any interest in having sex with female children. It is of interest to me that homosexual rights groups have distanced themselves significantly from this subgroup of homosexuals. I have yet to see a homosexual pedophile appear in the public media promulgating for gay rights. Homosexual groups know quite well that exposure of the pedophilic subgroup to the public eye will hurt their cause terribly. Homosexuals who are oriented toward peer sexual relationships have enough trouble getting public acceptance. They recognize the excessively punitive social attitudes toward pedophilia and appreciate that involvement with this subgroup will hurt their cause immeasurably.

Most therapists agree that homosexuals—especially those who are and have always been homosexual—are not likely to be treated successfully with psychotherapy. Like all things in this world, there is a continuum. There are those whose homosexuality is only a transient and isolated part of their lives, and there are those for whom homosexuality is the only sexual orientation they have ever had. Of course, there are people who are all points in between the ends of this continuum. The closer the individual is to the exclusively homosexual end of the continuum, the poorer a candidate for treatment that person is. And this is especially the case if the individual is an adult at the time of the therapy. Furthermore, there is good reason to believe that there is a biological loading for many (if not most) homosexuals and this, too, gives them a poorer prognosis with regard to changing their sexual orientation via the psychotherapeutic process.

It is important for therapists to appreciate that homosexuals run the gamut from those who are interested in young children, to those who are interested primarily in adolescents, to those who are interested primarily in peers of their own age, and, to a lesser degree, to those who are interested in older people. Heterosexuals, as well, run the same gamut of interests, the range going from primary attraction to children to primary attraction to older people. The likelihood of psychotherapy changing homosexuals to heterosexuals is as remote as the likelihood of changing heterosexuals to homosexuals. Therapists who do not believe this are likely to cause both themselves and their patients significant frustration. Accordingly, therapists do well to have very modest goals with regard to changing the homosexual pedophile's sexual orientation. And this is especially the case if the patient's pedophilia was "locked in" in childhood by having been the subject of sexual molestation himself over a long period during the formative years. Such programming makes the therapeutic prognosis for change even poorer.

Because of the relative degree of immutability of homosexual pedophilia, one's approach should be directed toward providing the child with safety and structuring the situation in such a way that there is no opportunity for acting out on the pedophilic impulses.

Dealing with Substance Abuse

Pedophilic acts commonly take place when the perpetrator is under the influence of alcohol or an addicting drug. Under such circumstances, the individual's judgment is impaired, control of impulses decrease, and the appreciation of the consequences of the behavior is reduced. I have mixed feelings about many of the treatment resources commonly utilized for the treatment of substance abuse at this time. For example, Alcoholics Anonymous (AA) is probably the favorite referral source. I cannot deny that it has certain benefits, especially with regard to helping individuals gain the support of others who have similar problems. At such meetings alcoholics feel less self-loathing and can be helped to gain some conscious control over their addiction.

One drawback of AA, in my opinion, is its reliance on higher powers to bring about change. There is a magical quality about this approach that does not appeal to me. Although the AA approach is to encourage conscious control, there is still much talk about the alcoholic's fate being in "higher hands." Accordingly, there is something contradictory about these messages, which, I am certain, lessens the likelihood that some alcoholics will exert as much conscious control as warranted. Of course, one could argue that alcoholics "need all the help they can get," both on earth and from heaven. Furthermore, there is too much emphasis on the here and now ("live from day to day"), with a corresponding deemphasis on the future. We certainly should, to some extent, live day to day. Life is short, in fact, much too short. I suspect that many people who get the most out of life are those who are exquisitely sensitive to this painful reality. However, we also must think about the future to a reasonable degree if we are to protect ourselves from future discomforts, pains, and even calamities. Another drawback of the AA approach is that it keeps brain circuits spinning with thoughts and feelings related to alcoholism and does not give proper attention to other areas of functioning, areas that should also have their circuits spinning in the brain.

Accordingly, when I do refer people to AA, I advise them of these drawbacks of the program, and I try to help them as well in my individual therapeutic sessions. It is important for therapists to appreciate that alcoholics are "notorious liars." They lie to themselves, and they lie to others. Lying is a central element in their problem and this, of course, makes it difficult to treat them therapeutically. They are also notorious rationalizers, and it is difficult to help them gain insight into their rationalizations. Many alcoholics do need a kind of rehabilitation program in which it is impossible for them to get alcohol while they are "drying out." The recidivism rate of such programs is quite high, but the programs certainly do have a place in the treatment of alcoholics. Office therapy should focus on the sources of tension and anxiety that are being relieved by the alcohol as well as other psychodynamic factors that are operative in the pathogenesis and perpetuation of the alcoholism.

It is important to appreciate that alcoholism has become part of the individual's lifestyle, similar to sadomasochism, domination/submission, and other personality patterns that may be generations in the making. The individual may not be comfortable with nonalcoholics, thus the attraction of AA. When not talking about alcohol, the person may have little to discuss. These factors have to be taken into consideration in the treatment of alcoholics, and one must do everything possible to expand their horizons and encourage involvements in a wide variety of other areas. This is one situation in which a heterogeneous group has benefits over the homogeneous group (which is what AA basically is).

With regard to drug abuse, there is much overlap with alcoholism. It too has become the lifestyle. Drug abusers, although they probably lie less often than alcoholics, are still not completely free of this particular propensity. The leaders of such groups are generally abusers themselves, with a spotty history with regard to their own "cure." They are often proselytizers and have few if any skills outside the "skill" of being a drug-abuse counselor. They therefore do not serve as good models for their "patients." There are some drug-abuse programs that discourage the patients from having contact with people who are not ex-drug abusers themselves. I consider this to be extremely poor advice. It keeps the drug-abuse circuits spinning in the brain and doesn't give non-drug-abuse brain circuits enough opportunity to develop to a proper degree.

These drawbacks notwithstanding, I still recommend such programs, but apprise patients in advance of what I consider to be their drawbacks. In my own work with the patient, I try to focus on the particular factors that were operative in bringing about and promulgating the drug abuse.

In short, to the degree that one can help the father reduce drug and/or alcohol abuse, to that degree will the therapist lessen the likelihood that the child will be sexually abused, especially if the abuse took place when the father was under the influence of the substance.

Counseling with the Mother and Father Together

Even if a divorce is going to take place because of the sex abuse, the parents should still be seen together in counseling. Therapists who hold that divorcing people should *not* be seen together are compromising significantly their psychotherapeutic efforts. The counseling can help the divorce be less traumatic. Furthermore, both are still the parents of the child and both need to cooperate and communicate in the child's best interests. Although therapy is certainly a primitive art, and although it leaves much to be desired with what it can accomplish, there is no question that joint sessions are a very effective way of improving people's cooperation and communication. The argument that the couple will only use the therapeutic session as a forum for arguing is not a reason to avoid such counseling. The arguments are the therapist's points of departure for psychotherapeutic interchanges. When there is danger of litigation, this should be strongly discouraged; the parents should be warned about the pitfalls of such a course of action, both for themselves and their children. Litigation predictably causes psychopathology for all involved parties and works against any psychotherapeutic process, whether it be for sex abuse or other problems. Elsewhere (Gardner, 1986) I have discussed these issues in greater detail.

If the parents are not separating, there is a high likelihood that there have been difficulties in their sexual relationship and that such difficulties may have been playing a role in bringing about the sexual abuse of the child. I have already discussed the kinds of sexual problems in each of the parents that can contribute to the sexual abuse of the child. The treatment of sexual problems between parents, even when there has been no sexual abuse of their children, is optimally accomplished when there is some involvement in treatment on the part of both sexual partners, even though one partner may not be the primary individual in treatment. People tend to deny, to varying degrees, their sexual problems. This is especially the case in a society (such as ours) that puts a high premium on sexual performance. The person who can be most objective about another individual's sexual functioning is the sexual partner. I am not claiming that these individuals can be completely objective, only that they have more intimate information than others. Accordingly, both partners should be seen in the counseling because of the information that each can provide about the other. In some situations, referral to a therapist particularly experienced and skilled in the treatment of sexual problems may be warranted. To the degree that the therapist can accomplish the goal of a good sex life between the parents, to that degree will he (she) lessen the likelihood of a repetition of the molestation.

In addition to focusing on the sexual problems, the therapist does well to focus on nonsexual sources of difficulties in the relationship. There may be power imbalances, especially of the domination/subjugation type. The parents may have a sadomasochistic relationship. Of course, there are many other marital problems that may be present. These create general dissension and unhappiness in the home and are likely to contribute to the need of the father to gain physical and emotional gratification from the child. Last, it is important to repeat that the treatment of the wide variety of other symptoms described thus far—symptoms in the child, the mother, and the father—is more likely to be effective if the therapist keeps in mind that joint interviews and even full-family counseling may be useful. By full-family counseling, I not only mean the child and both parents but also other children in the family, as warranted.

Progesterone Acetate

Some therapists (to the best of my knowledge they are in the minority) recommend *progesterone acetate* injections to decrease the production of testosterone and, therefore, the sexual urges of sexual offenders who repeatedly molest children. If the offender himself wishes

164 *TREATMENT OF SEXUALLY ABUSED CHILDREN*

such treatment, I would give it consideration. However, I myself would not pressure a patient into taking such injections. My main reason for this position is that progesterone is a very powerful substance and is very likely to have other effects on the human body, some that are known and some that have yet to be learned. All of us, when we take any kind of medication, no matter how many years it has been in use, are still voluntarily serving as guinea pigs for the next generation. It is for these reasons that I am very much against courts mandating such treatment, if they could. It is probably unconstitutional for a court to require such treatment, but this has not stopped some judges from ordering such therapy. It may come as a surprise to some readers that judges do many things that are unconstitutional, and this is especially seen in the realm of child sex abuse. People are handcuffed and dragged off to jail, merely on the allegation that a three-year-old girl made in the office of a "validator." And people have remained in jail for years on the basis of hearsay information provided through grapevines. The punishments meted out to sexual molesters are certainly "cruel and unusual" and clearly not consistent with the protections provided all U.S. citizens by the Eighth Amendment of the U.S. Constitution.

CLINICAL EXAMPLES

The Girl and the Bus Driver

Jane, a four-and-a-half-year-old girl, was brought for consultation because of a severe obsession with sexuality of three months' duration. The parents described normal development, sexual and otherwise. They stated that three months prior to the consultation she began to become obsessed with sex. Specifically, she would try to put her hands inside her mother's bra to feel her breasts. She would try to pick up her mother's dress in order to put her hands in her mother's crotch area. She would frequently try to zip open her father's pants in order to see his genitals and grab his penis. These were not transient and half-hearted attempts; rather, the parents literally had to physically restrain her and "fight her off" in order to protect themselves from these "sexual attacks." With her parents' friends and relatives, as well, she would attempt the same sexual encounters.

The mother belonged to a local YMCA and frequently brought the child along with her to engage in a wide variety of gymnastic and other activities. Whereas previously she had absolutely no problem with her in the locker rooms or the showers, during the three months prior to my initial consultation the situation changed drastically. She would look at other women lasciviously and, with them as well, attempt to grab and fondle their breast and genital areas. But even when restrained, Jane made the women feel uncomfortable—so salacious were her glances and staring. This behavior reached the point where the mother could no longer take her into the locker room. At social gatherings as well, the patient was a constant source of embarrassment in that no person was exempt from being prey to her sexual overtures. There were no special verbalizations other than "I want to feel your boobies," "I want to put my hand in your 'gina,'" and "I want to hold your peepee (penis)."

Naturally, when I first saw the patient I made an inquiry into the possibility that she was being sexually abused. The parents had also thought about this possibility, but claimed that they could not think of any situation in which the child might have been sexually abused. In my own inquiry, as well, I could not learn of any person who might have been a sex-abuse perpetrator, or any situation that was even suspicious of sex abuse. In fact, the parents were somewhat overprotective and had not yet put Jane in situations where she might be away from them for significant periods. She had not yet gone to day camp, nor had she had sleepover dates with friends or relatives. In fact, there wasn't a night in the child's life when she had not slept at home with both parents. From my detailed inquiry regarding undressing habits in the home, I found nothing to suggest that she was being unduly exposed to nudity or other potentially sexually provocative situations. The parents' sex life was private; they kept the door locked at night, and there had never been an occasion when Jane had any opportunity to observe parental sexual activity. She was an only child, and so there was no opportunity for sexual exposure or involvement with siblings. The parents carefully monitored her television and were certain that she had not been exposed to any R-rated movies. They did not possess sexually explicit videotapes or other sexual materials that the child might have observed or been involved with. In the initial inquiry I learned that the patient had started nursery school two months prior to the onset of her symptoms and that things there were going well. However, Jane's teacher had noticed the progressive increase in sexual comments and, not surprisingly, the teacher was also an object of Jane's sexual overtures. However, these were not so frequent and insistent that Jane created a classroom problem.

My conclusion at the end of my initial consultation was that there were two possibilities: (1) the patient was (and possibly was continuing to be) sexually molested, yet we still had to find out by whom and under what circumstances this was taking place, and (2) there was no sexual molestation, but Jane was a very early developer and sex hormones were flowing in her blood stream in much higher concentration and at a much earlier time than the vast majority of children in our society. I recommended that I see her on a weekly basis, as part of an extended evaluation, in the hope that information would be forthcoming that would give us a clue regarding what was going on.

During the first three sessions I learned absolutely nothing new that could be of assistance in my understanding of the causes of this child's hypersexualization. Jane made a number of attempts to grab my genitals and unzip my pants. Naturally, she was strictly told that this was not permitted, and Jane respected my request that she make no further attempts of this kind. The mother came into the fourth session quite upset and told me that she was quite sure that she had finally learned the cause of Jane's sexual obsessions. She related that during the preceding week Jane had once again tried to put her hand under her mother's dress. When her mother refused to allow her to do this, Jane angrily blurted out, "Nelly lets me do that to her." Immediately, everything fell into place. Nelly was the nursery school bus driver. From her gait, demeanor, and vocal intonations, the mother suspected that she might be gay. More importantly, the mother was starting to have a problem with Nelly in that she was frequently bringing Jane home late, even though the child was one of the first on the route to be dropped off. Nelly explained the lateness by claiming that she and Jane had a very good relationship and that the child asked that she be allowed to accompany Nelly throughout the course of her whole route and then leave Jane off last. On further inquiry with the child, the mother learned that it was Nelly who originated the idea of the circuitous route, a route that would enable her to bring Jane home as the last child. She also learned from Jane that prior to dropping her off, Nelly would park in an abandoned parking lot and would sexually molest the child.

The mother brought this to the attention of school authorities. Nelly reluctantly admitted that she had indeed molested Jane, and she was discharged. The mother asked my opinion regarding reporting Nelly to the police (these events took place in the late 1970s, before the reporting of such molestation was mandatory). I discouraged the mother from doing so with the argument that the child would be subjected to a series of police investigations and might possibly be involved in a criminal trial. Although such reporting might be of some benefit to society, there was no question that Jane herself would be psychologically damaged. Furthermore, I told the mother that it would make it much more difficult for me to treat Jane because such exposures would interfere with the natural desensitization process, would be likely to enhance guilt, and would have other untoward psychological effects. The mother heeded my advice, and Nelly was not reported.

From what we could learn, the child was being molested at a frequency of two to three times a week over a period of about two to three months. From what we could ascertain, the primary sexual encounters were masturbatory. Most often Jane would masturbate Nelly, but, on occasion, Nelly would fondle Jane, but not to the point of orgasm. These encounters, as best I could determine, were the causes of Jane's high level of sexual excitation. Fortunately for Jane, there was a significant diminution in her sexual preoccupations once Nelly was removed from the scene. These diminished to almost the zero level over a three-week period. During this time—as is my usual practice—I let the patient decide how much or how little she wanted to talk about her encounters with Nelly. Interestingly, she had very little to say about them. I did not believe that she had been significantly traumatized by these encounters. Although there had been a certain amount of sexual frustration that was not gratified, and although there was significant negative feedback from those toward whom she made sexual overtures, so many other things in her life were going well that these negative effects did not prove consequential.

Accordingly, I spent very little time discussing sexual matters directly. The child was told that what *Nelly* was doing was "bad" and "wrong," but that *she herself* had not done anything bad or wrong. Attempts were made to get Jane to understand that Nelly had some kind of a "problem," but I do not really believe that the child fully understood exactly what we were talking about with regard to the word *problem*. I also got across the message that when Jane is older, and that if she and a loving boyfriend and/or husband wanted to do such things with one another, and they were both approximately the same age, then there was nothing bad or wrong about that. What is bad or wrong is for an adult to do such things to a child.

Because there were no further problems, and because the patient did not verbalize anything to suggest residual difficulties, I discontinued the treatment four sessions after the mother had told me she had learned that Nelly was sexually molesting Jane. I believe that continuing the treatment beyond that point might have had the untoward effect of engendering in Jane the notion that a terrible thing had happened to her and this could contribute to feelings that she had been somehow victimized. Although she had to some extent been a victim, it was a short-lived victimization, and I did not want to have her grow up feeling that she had been "a victim!" Furthermore, Jane had no deep sense that she had been traumatized, there was little need for a desensitization process, and what little residual preoccupations she had were dissipated naturally. And I certainly was not going to make trouble for her by encouraging repetitious recall of her experiences with Nelly in order to help her "work through" this problem. Despite the fact that this is a common procedure, even in the 1970s I had serious reservations about this approach and considered it to be harmful to patients. This is a view I still hold.

The Boy and the Pediatrician

Bill was brought to me at the age of four years eleven months, with a four-month history of preoccupation with sexual matters. On a number of occasions he took out his penis and said to his mother, "Suck on it." His mother also found him putting his penis into the mouth of his sister's dolls. Bill was obsessed with the desire to pull down the panties of little girlfriends and would cry bitterly when restrained from doing so. On such occasions the mother observed him to have an erection, while crying bitterly, "I want it, I want it, I want it." The mother was certain that he was experiencing significant sexual frustration, which he somehow believed would be relieved by having the opportunity to pull down little girls' panties. When they were driving in the car together he would frequently say, "Let's go over and visit Mary," "Let's go over and see Gloria," and "Let's go over and see Joan." (These girls were Bill's classmates in nursery school or children of his mother's friends.)

During the three months prior to my initial interview, Bill began to play a particular "game" with his mother and grandparents. The child would insist that the adults who were in the home at the time (usually the mother, and sometimes one or both grandparents) all go into the bathroom with him, lock the door, stand in the bathtub, and close the shower curtains around them. They would all stand there together listening for the "bad man." Bill would periodically ask someone to peek out the door to see if the bad man was still there. It would generally take 30 to 45 minutes, during which time there was intermittent peeking, before the child was reassured that the bad man was not there. Then they would hesitantly step out of the tub and tiptoe out of the bathroom.

The mother and grandparents were certain that the child had been sexually abused and reported this to the local child protection services. In the course of my inquiry, when the mother was asked about any unusual experiences, she reported that about one month prior to the onset of symptoms the child had a very upsetting experience. Specifically, Bill was supposed to be a shepherd in his nursery school's Christmas play. (Bill's nursery school was affiliated with the church the parents attended.) Bill's parents and grandparents came to the event, and everyone was eagerly awaiting Bill's appearance. However, when Bill was to walk on the stage he saw a certain clergyman and he suddenly became panic-stricken. Bill ran off the stage and jumped into his mother's arms. There was no consoling him. He was screaming so loudly, "I want to go home, I want to go home," that the parents had no choice but to take him out of the auditorium. The parents suspected that the clergyman might have been the abuser, but they were not sure. They reported this event to the child protection services and the man was investigated. His denials were believed by some and doubted by others. The prosecutor did not consider there to be enough evidence to press charges against the minister. Accordingly, I began treatment with the belief that the child had been sexually molested, but did not know who had molested him. My hope was that in the course of the therapy I might learn something more specific that would lead us to learn who the molester might be.

I proceeded with the treatment under the assumption that the child was sexually abused. Because I believed—with a high degree of certainty—that Bill had been sexually abused, I was comfortable proceeding with the treatment without knowing exactly who the molester was. Had I significant doubt about whether molestation had occurred, I would not have embarked on the treatment program. And this is an important point. As described in Chapter Four, the so-called "treatment" of children who were not molested can cause significant psychological harm. Basically, I viewed Bill's treatment as much more an extended evaluation, during which I was trying to elicit information that might be helpful to me in understanding the circumstances of his molestation. Bill was seen once a week, during which time he preferred making up stories and creating fantasies around miniature dolls and animals. None of the human figures were naked, nor was there any particular use of materials that were explicitly sexual. A theme emerged of "someone jumping on top of someone." Comments such as these were usually associated with doll play, in which a figure or animal was assaulting another figure. I speculated that the child might be reenacting his sexual molestation, but I certainly could not be sure. In response, I provided messages in which an assaulted party would call for help from adult authorities and other more powerful figures. I also introduced the theme of running away. The coping mechanisms I introduced were not specific to sexual molestation, but related to any situation in which Bill was being overwhelmed by a dangerous and/or coercive force or greater power.

I also advised the mother about dealing with Bill's sexual cravings. She was receptive to my suggestion that she encourage him to masturbate. Accordingly, when he would have erections and cry bitterly to be allowed to pull down the panties of little girls, she would encourage him to go into the bedroom, play with himself, and do what he wanted with his penis. Both she and I recommended this approach and, to the best of our knowledge, he utilized it.

Videotapes were made of each session and, interestingly, Bill would ask to see them between sessions, sometimes two and three times. The mother found him transfixed when he watched the videotaped sessions, and he would often quote my statements. For reasons still unknown to me, the mother discontinued treatment with me after about three months and switched to another therapist. When I asked her whether she would like to discuss her reasons for the transfer, she was evasive and so I did not press the point.

About three months after the transfer, the mother called me quite excitedly. She told me that she had learned who the molester was. It turned out to have been a doctor, a pediatrician. She told me that everything came out when Bill was scheduled for a follow-up appointment with the doctor. As soon as she told Bill that she was taking him to the pediatrician, Bill went into a state of panic and began screaming that he didn't want to go back. Of course, she asked him why, and it took her about an hour to learn that he did not want to return because the pediatrician had put his penis in Bill's mouth and had made him promise that he would never tell anyone. He had threatened the child that he would put needles in his eyes if he ever told anyone about the sexual encounter. Bill told his mother that "sticky stuff" was in his mouth afterward, and that he spit it out. Bill also told his mother that the pediatrician held his head while forcing him to perform fellatio.

The mother realized, in retrospect, that the molestation took place on the day that she had brought the child for an examination, during the week prior to the onset of symptoms. About a week before the appointment, the doctor himself called her and told her that he would not be able to keep the original appointment, but he could see the child on the following Saturday. He told her that he would come to the office on that day just to see patients whom he couldn't see during the week. When she arrived at the office that Saturday, she thought it quite strange that there were no assistants there. However, she did not make any comments about that. Furthermore, the doctor did another unusual thing, namely, he walked off with the child alone, rather than having the mother accompany him (the usual procedure). While leading the child away he said, "Bill's old enough now to come with me alone." She noted also that the child was in with the doctor longer than usual, and that when Bill came out he was somewhat tense and quiet.

The mother pressed charges against the pediatrician; however, the child was very uncooperative in the course of his interviews with the prosecutor and other investigators. He became panic-stricken, hysterical, and completely uncooperative. Accordingly, the charges were dropped because of "lack of evidence."

The Boy and the Virgins

Tom, a fifteen-year-old boy, was brought to me by his mother and father (each then divorced and remarried) because his three-and-a-half-year-old half sister had told her mother that Tom had touched her "wee-wee hole." I had known the family over a period of approximately 10 years and had treated Tom from ages eight to nine because of behavior problems in school. At that time, his parents were having significant marital difficulties and there was talk of divorce. They subsequently did divorce, and each remarried. The three-and-a-half-year-old half sister was the product of the mother's second marriage. Tom was living with his mother, stepfather, and half sister. The father's new wife had four children, two daughters and two sons. The oldest, a boy, was already out of the house, and the father's new household consisted of the two girls and her brother, all teenagers.

On inquiry, I learned that Tom was very inhibited sexually. He told me that he planned to be a virgin when he got married and that he considered premarital sex "a sin." He described sexual urges, but considered masturbation to be "sick and wrong." He believed that people who engaged in this practice were "perverts." Although ashamed and guilty, he did describe two or three occasions when, while babysitting for his half sister, he spent significant time looking at her genitals and touching them. He agreed that there was a certain amount of sexual excitation associated with these activities, but he described them as much more satisfying his curiosity than satisfying sexual cravings. He denied any other sexual activities, nor did his half sister describe such.

In my interviews with the half sister, I found no evidences for significant psychological trauma. In fact, she had reported the sexual encounters in a giggling and laughing way, without any suggestion that she had been traumatized or was reacting negatively to them. Accordingly, I decided not to treat the half sister. This is in the line with the old maxim, "If it's not broken, don't fix it." There are many children who have had experiences similar or identical to this child who are given intensive "treatment," based on the assumption that such an encounter must indeed be psychologically detrimental.

I believed that it was Tom who needed the treatment, treatment for his sexual inhibition problem. My hope was that he would loosen up, become more comfortable with his sexual impulses, and not have to gratify them in this inappropriate and very dangerous way. In my sessions with him I discussed the subject of sex, how normal it is, how the urges need release, and that at his age the best releases were via involvements with girls his own age with whom he might have some kinds of mutually enjoyable sexual experiences. We also discussed masturbation as a healthy outlet, pin-up magazines, porno films, and other sexually explicit materials. I believe I was successful in reducing Tom's guilt about sex and encouraged, as well, his dating—which he did. We discussed masturbation and, with my encouragement, he began to do so using his own fantasies as well as pin-up magazine centerfolds as stimuli. We discussed in detail his involvements with girlfriends, and I was able to help him overcome his inhibitions and shyness in the dating situation. My goal here was twofold. First, I believed that his sexual inhibition problems warranted treatment in their own right, even if he had never involved himself in sexual encounters with his half sister. In addition, my hope was that reduction of his inhibitions in age-appropriate sexual activities would lessen the likelihood that he would look to his half sister as a source of sexual gratification.

I did not believe, however, that Tom's sexual involvement with his half sister was purely a sexual act and that other factors might have been operative. On exploration of these other factors, I learned that there was an anger element. Tom was angry at his mother and stepfather, especially his stepfather, who was an extremely domineering and coercive individual. At some level, he knew that the child would divulge the molestation and this would "drive my stepfather bonkers" (which it did). Accordingly, attempts were made in family interviews to reduce these sources of tension and to improve Tom's relationship with his stepfather.

The patient made videotapes of all of his sessions and routinely watched them between sessions. They provided a reiteration of my therapeutic messages and, I believe, quickened the pace of Tom's treatment. I often say that people who make videotapes of their sessions are getting two sessions for the price of one. However, this only applies if one confines oneself simply to the time element, i.e., replaying the session at no cost to the patient. Actually, much more is gained, e.g., intensification of the relationship with the therapist, entrenchment of the therapeutic messages, and the opportunity to show others (when appropriate) segments of the session as a point of departure for spinoff discussions with significant others.

In Tom's case, however, there was yet another benefit to the videotapes—a benefit that I could not have anticipated. Specifically, the molestation had ripple effects in his father's new family, which, as mentioned, consisted of Tom's new stepmother and her four children (and her three teenaged children who were still living with their mother). The stepmother, from the outset, was extremely reluctant for Tom to visit, mainly because she was jealous of the time the father spent with Tom. Her own ex-husband had abandoned her and their four children, and she was hoping to reestablish a nuclear family with Tom's father—with no interferences by Tom and any other people from her new husband's former life. Tom's father, then, was in a loyalty conflict. He felt like a rope in a tug-of-war between Tom and his wife.

When Tom's stepmother learned of the molestation, she, too, "went bonkers." Her reaction was to ban Tom from the house completely. She called him a "sex pervert" and claimed that there was a high risk that he would rape her two teenaged girls. (She insisted her daughters were virgins, and she had every intention they remain in the state of chastity until the time of their marriage. Tom had good reason to believe that these girls, ages 15 and 17, had already been "deflowered," but this is irrelevant to my already complex story.) Reassurances by Tom, Tom's father, and me that it would be unlikely that he would "gang rape" these two helpless virgins—in a setting where their older brother, mother, and father were present—proved futile. The stepmother managed to sweep the girls up in her hysteria, which reached the point that the mere mentioning of Tom's name generated in the girls severe anxiety reactions and hysterical outbursts. Interestingly, none of these three women (neither the stepmother nor her two daughters) had had much experience with Tom, so formidable were the previous exclusionary maneuvers utilized by the stepmother. The hysteria reached the point where the stepmother would not even allow the girls to have joint sessions in which

Tom, Tom's father, the two girls, and she herself were present. Even in my presence, she feared Tom would "rape" her daughters.

At the point where I felt all my therapeutic efforts were proving futile, Tom, with no suggestion on my part, offered to let the stepmother and girls select any of the videotapes of his sessions and view them. Tom believed that if they were to have the opportunity to do this, they would see that he was not the dangerous pervert they believed him to be. Interestingly, this served its purpose. The girls watched some of the tapes and came to appreciate that Tom wasn't the sex maniac they had been led to believe he was. In fact, they came to see that he was "a nice guy" and thus prevailed upon the mother to let him in the house. Although reluctant, the mother eased up on Tom and allowed him more visits to the home, even though such involvement compromised her fantasy of a new "nuclear family." I am not claiming that the whole problem of Tom's relationship with his stepmother was thereby solved; I am only claiming that the videotapes played a significant role in reducing it.

This case demonstrates well the importance of the therapist working with other individuals who are significantly involved with one's patients. I am not stating that we should automatically conduct family therapy for every patient whom we see. We should, however, try to bring in those individuals who are involved significantly with our patients, especially those individuals whose actions have a direct effect on what goes on with our patients. I am not claiming either that all of these people become officially designated as our patients. I am only claiming that we involve them in the treatment process and not concern ourselves with the exact label applied to them. In Tom's case, I was involved with two families: the mother's new family and the father's new family. Yet, these families were not seen separately. There were three or four meetings in which all four parental figures (Tom's two parents and two stepparents) were in the same room together. As mentioned elsewhere (Gardner, 1991b, 1991c), such a therapeutic program can be an extremely valuable one when parents are divorced and remarried, and I cannot recommend this approach highly enough. Tom was involved with a complex network of individuals, all of whom were interacting with one another in ways relevant to Tom's difficulties. To view Tom's molestation as simply that of a teenage boy touching the genitals of his three-and-a-half-year-old half sister is to take a very narrow, limited,

176   TREATMENT OF SEXUALLY ABUSED CHILDREN

and oversimplified view of the situation. Child protection services focus almost exclusively on the sexual act and reflexively make efforts to remove either the child or the "alleged perpetrator" from the home. Competent evaluators appreciate that the sexual act is one manifestation of a host of factors that may be operative in bringing it about. Competent therapists do everything possible to work with the network in order to bring about an alleviation of the wide variety of problems that have contributed to the abuse. This is true "protection" of the child. This is the only reasonable way to make the child "safe" from future molestations.

One last point. This family's therapy demonstrates, once again, that the treatment of children who are sexually abused should not necessarily involve direct work with the abused child. In many cases the therapist does well to do nothing. To do something with the child may do that child more harm than good. Those who reflexively "treat" are going to harm many children who would have been much better off without such "treatment." In some cases the focus should be only on the molester. In other cases, other people have to be brought in if the therapy is to be effective. And this was certainly the case in Tom's situation.

The Girl at the Wedding

I first saw Gloria when she was four-and-a-half years old. She was brought to me for consultation because two months previously she had been sexually molested by her 14-year-old cousin. He lived in Ohio and was visiting Gloria's family in New York City. Gloria had a two-year-old sister, and the cousin, Bob, babysat for the two girls on two weekend nights in the course of his one-week visit. After he left, Gloria reported to her mother that "Bob tried to put his pee-pee in my pee-pee." On further inquiry, the mother learned that on each of those two nights Bob had rubbed Gloria's vulva, kissed it, and asked her if she would let him put his penis in her vagina. The child claimed that she became frightened and refused. Bob did not then press her for further sexual activities. The mother also learned that Bob had threatened, "I'll kill you if you tell anyone." Although Gloria was initially upset by this threat, she did not believe that her cousin would kill her, and when she told her mother about these events, she was not particularly frightened. She did, however, wait until Bob had left the home before divulging these experiences.

The parents reported the molestation to Bob's parents in Ohio, who reported the matter to the local police authorities after the mother said to them, "If you don't call the local police there, I'm going to." During the subsequent two months Gloria was preoccupied with Bob's following her around the house, and reassurances that he was back in Ohio were only of limited value. She would also ask her mother to repeatedly say to a fantasized Bob, "Go away and don't come back here." The mother played out these little fantasized scenarios, and they appeared to be reassuring to the patient. Of course, we see here the kinds of coping mechanisms that abused children will often create for themselves. These are the kinds of coping mechanisms for which we should have the greatest respect, because they are indicators to us as to whether we should barge in with what we consider to be better modes of adaptation.

I subsequently saw Gloria in treatment for a period of about six weeks, with sessions once a week. Over this period I provided reinforcement of Gloria's own coping mechanisms and reassurances that her parents would never again be leaving Bob alone with her. Furthermore, I reiterated that her parents had no intentions of inviting Bob to their home in the immediate future and that she lived in New York City and Bob lived in Ohio, which was "far, far, away." Her desensitization play and preoccupation with coping mechanisms gradually diminished to a zero level over a six-week period and so I discontinued treatment. I advised the mother to call me if she noted any recurrence of these preoccupations. Furthermore, it was clear that Gloria was a healthy, stable child, living in a healthy, stable home, and she exhibited no other evidences for psychopathology. Accordingly, I found no other reason to keep Gloria in treatment. (Interestingly, the child protection services in Ohio never followed up on Bob's molestation of Gloria, nor did Gloria's family have any further information regarding whether Bob was in treatment.)

Two-and-a-half years later, when Gloria was about seven, her mother brought her back for a consultation. The main complaint at that time was lying and antisocial behavior in school. The mother informed me that there had been no reappearance of symptoms related to Gloria's sexual abuse. Early in this second round of treatment, the mother informed me that a relative in Ohio was getting married and that she, her husband, and Gloria were invited to the wedding. Bob was also going to be at the wedding, and the question was raised regarding whether Gloria should attend. The mother wanted to go to the wedding, as did Gloria, but the father was reluctant. This was discussed in a family meeting, and I myself expressed my opinion that it would be useful for Gloria to go and that all of us need extended family members. I tried to get across the point that, from everything I knew about him, Bob was not a low-life animal and that he was a human being who could be part of Gloria's family network support system, the sexual problem notwithstanding. Furthermore, we were not speaking here about Bob's babysitting again; rather, we were only talking about Bob and Gloria being together at a wedding in the presence of a couple of hundred people.

The following is a segment from a videotape made two days after Gloria attended the wedding in Ohio:

> *Therapist*: Okay, what else is happening with you?
> *Patient*: (No response.)
> *Mother* (whispers to patient): What did we do Saturday?
> *Patient*: What Saturday?
> *Mother*: Where did we go?
> *Patient*: Oh, we went to a wedding.
> *Gardner*: You went to a wedding. Okay, let's hear. Where was that wedding? I heard about that wedding.
> *Patient*: Cleveland.
> *Gardner*: In Cleveland. Okay. Let's talk about that wedding.
> *Mother* (interrupting): Who was there?
> *Patient*: Uncle John.
> *Gardner*: John, your Uncle John. Okay.
> *Patient*: I wasn't so nasty to Bob.
> *Gardner*: So you weren't nasty?
> *Patient*: Yeah.
> *Gardner*: Hhmm. Were you scared there?
> *Patient* (nodding negatively): Uh-uh.
> *Gardner*: You didn't think anything would happen to you there?

Patient (nodding positively): Uh-huh.

Gardner: And what did he. . . . Did he come over and say hello to you and things like that?

Patient: Yes.

Gardner: Uh-huh. And were you scared then?

Patient: No.

Gardner: Uh-huh. Did he try to bother you in any way?

Patient: No.

Gardner: Uh-huh. Did you have a good time there?

Patient (nodding positively): Hh-hmm.

Gardner: Was there any trouble there of any kind?

Patient: Nope!

We can see here that the patient did not suffer any untoward effects from being with Bob. This was what I had predicted. She would be provided with the living experience that she would be protected. This is far more valuable than mere verbal reassurances. The child's having actual experiences lend verification to such reassurances.

Gardner: But your dad wasn't there? Is that right? As I recall, he didn't want to go? Do you know *why* he didn't want to go? What was your understanding?

Patient: I don't know why he didn't want to go.

Gardner: Well, I recall our talking about that here last time, about his not wanting to go. Do you remember why?

Patient (nodding negatively): Uh-uh.

Gardner: Let's ask your mom.

Mother: He didn't want to go because he's still a little bit angry.

Patient: Why?

Mother: He's still upset about the past.

Patient: What past?

Gardner: What is your mother talking about when she says the past?

Patient: I don't know.

Gardner: She's talking about Bob, right? What about Bob? What's the past?

Patient: I don't know.

Gardner: You don't know or you'd rather not talk about it.

> *Patient*: I'd rather not talk about it.
> *Gardner*: Okay, because it's important. If you don't know it makes me think that maybe you don't remember, and it's very important here to be honest. Do you know that?
> *Patient*: Hh-hmm.
> *Gardner*: Honesty is the number one thing here—lying is just the opposite of what we do here. In this room it's 100 percent honest. So that if you don't want to talk about something you say, "I'd rather not discuss it." But you don't say, "I don't know," because that's a little bit of a lie, you know. It's not a *big* lie. It doesn't hurt anybody, but it's really not true. Right? Am I correct?
> *Patient*: Correct.
> *Gardner*: Okay, so we don't tell anything here that isn't 100 percent perfectly truthful. *Truth* is the key word here. All right?
> *Patient*: Hh-hmm.
> *Gardner*: Truth is the key word here. All right?

My elaboration here on the importance of telling the truth relates to the chief complaints that brought the patient back to treatment, namely, lying and other forms of antisocial behavior. I was not simply addressing myself to the relatively narrow issue of the patient telling me the truth in treatment, especially with regard to whether or not she knew the answer to my question, but expanded this principle to lying in general. In this way, I was able to get across the principle of the importance of telling the truth, without producing the embarrassment and shame that might result from talking about lying in specific areas, especially those lies that brought her back into treatment. I then turned to the mother and continued.

> *Gardner* (now talks to the mother): You see my dilemma—maybe it's a strong word—but my conflict here is this. Traumas of this kind, like many other kinds of trauma, cause a dilemma for the therapist. On the one hand, you don't want to muckrake, you don't want to keep the thing exposed when it's going to die, and be buried, and be laid to rest and lost in the past memories of the human brain. On the other hand, you don't want to leave simmering abscesses and pus pockets there that may be infecting a person's brain and life. And the question is whether going to

this wedding where Bob was, for the first time since the event, was traumatic for her. I don't know if there had been some kind of strong reaction. If she had strong reactions that would rekindle all this, I want to know about it. If she handled it well, and didn't have any strong reactions, then it tells me that things probably have been laid to rest.

Here I explained to the mother the dilemma therapists should have regarding inquiries into child sex abuse, especially when the child is asymptomatic. As mentioned, the therapist should not muckrake; however, the therapist should provide therapy when there has been failure to resolve issues relevant to the trauma. I was not simply instructing a mother here regarding my therapeutic approach but was, without mentioning it, giving her advice on how to handle Gloria with regard to her experiences with Bob and her subsequent reactions to him.

Mother: She was very positive in her reactions to him at the reception. She went over and hugged him and stayed in the same room as him. As a matter of fact, I think at one point she was sitting in the same chair together, right?

Patient: (Nods affirmatively.)

Mother: Yeah. She felt very comfortable, I felt. There were two other little girls that she was running around with. This was a reception in a home and so there were five different rooms that people were in and she set herself up for some difficulties once or twice, and I was surprised, because she let herself be the object of the person being teased.

Patient: Who?

Mother: Anyway, it was a little strange, but as far as her relationship with Bob, she did very well and I was . . .

Gardner: Okay, so you didn't see any strong reactions?

Mother: No.

Gardner: Okay, I think that was good, that you (speaking to Gloria) didn't get too upset about that. Okay.

Mother: She did put herself in a position that I thought was very strange. She had been gone about five minutes and I walked into the room. She was on the floor being sort of held down by my niece—who was the bride—and they were trying to get her to open her mouth so they could pop in a piece of candy and I don't know what precipitated that, but it was very strange. Also, when I walked into the room, there was also a stranger that I thought she was behaving rather forward to and with. And she said it was because he was a friend of the bride that she felt comfortable in teasing him and really physically coming down on him very hard. I thought she was being very aggressive with him and I thought it was inappropriate. But we discussed it and she simply said . . . I told her that's not the way to treat people and that's not the way to behave with strangers ever. And she said, "Well, he's a friend of the bride."

The mother is making reference here to some of the antisocial behavior that brought Gloria back into treatment. On the one hand, one could argue that this was normal rambunctiousness at a wedding where children are likely to get "wound up." However, Gloria was much more readily wound up than most children and would probably be one of the first to involve herself in horseplay. In this regard, she was much more like a typical seven-year-old boy than a seven-year-old girl. In fact, I considered Gloria to have some of the genetic programming that boys traditionally have, i.e., programming for rough-and-tumble play. I believe that this is a derivative of the selective survival of the warrior-hunter-protective types of men. In contrast, there was selective survival of the more sedentary, empathic types of women, women who better served child-rearing purposes. (I am not placing any values on these evolutionary developments; I am only stating the facts as I see them.)

Gardner: When your mother says physically aggressive, what was she talking about. What is she talking about now? Tell me exactly what that was.
Patient: Stranger.
Gardner: What's that?
Patient: Strangers.
Gardner: Strangers. And what were you doing. Now let's talk about being physically aggressive. Do you know what *physically aggressive* means?
Patient: What?
Gardner: You don't know. What you should have said to your mother is: "You know, I don't understand what physically aggressive means." Do you understand that? Because she thought that you knew what that meant.

Since your mother was there, why don't we have her tell us exactly what the physical aggression was. *Physical* means with your body, right? And *aggression* means—aggression means you can hurt someone. That's what aggression means. It means to fight or insult someone. Do you know what *insult* means? Or knock against them. Or be mean. Aggression can cover a lot of things. So that's what she means by physical aggression. It means that with your body you do something that bothers another person. You punch against them or you push against them.

One of the patient's problems in treatment was that she would frequently "space out" and not register what was being said to her. Such tuning out made it very difficult to engage her therapeutically, and I would often have to interrupt the conversation and define words, even the simplest words. Sometimes, even these repetitions did not register.

Mother: Or step on their toes. I think that's what you told me you started out by doing—by stepping on his toes?

Patient (nodding affirmatively): Hh-hmm.

Gardner: That would be an example.

Mother: And he was sitting in the chair.

Gardner (looking at patient): Hh-hmm. I see. So she told you to cool it, huh, on that stuff?

Patient: Hh-huh.

Gardner: Why were you doing that? Who was she singling out for this?

Mother: This was a young gentleman, maybe 19 or 20.

Gardner: Hh-hmm.

Mother: He was very friendly. He was one of the gang that was around. This was a young wedding.

Patient: His name was Sam.

Mother: His name was Sam. Okay.

Patient (spelling): S-A-M.

Mother: Okay. And he probably was very playful.

Gardner: Oh, so it was probably part of the horsing around that was going on at the wedding.

Mother: Yeah, but I just was a little disturbed that she really became

184 *TREATMENT OF SEXUALLY ABUSED CHILDREN*

overly comfortable with it and, as I said, she really came down on him rather hard because she felt it was safe territory.

Gardner: Hh-hmm.

Mother: And I don't want her to develop that.

Gardner: Okay. On the one hand, you don't want to be too uptight. You don't want to squelch too much of the childhood rambunctiousness and horseplay, which is healthy and lets out hostility in a socially acceptable way and is fun. You know, there is a teasing quality in it and it's a form of interaction. And you don't want to squelch that completely. On the other hand, you don't want to allow full abandon, you know. There's some point in between and I don't know you well enough to know where you're at on that continuum—whether you're too uptight.

Mother: No, I'm not too reserved. I'm not . . .

Gardner: You allow for that?

Mother: Yes.

Gardner: You think she was just going a little overboard?

Mother: Yeah, I do. My concern is that if anyone is going to be an exhibitionist, or if anyone is going to take things too far, I know it's going to be Gloria and I have to teach her where the limits are. And that's my major concern.

Gardner: Hh-hmm. Yeah. Okay, so I am just asking that, but it sounds like you've been taking a good middle-of-the-road position on this. If I'm wrong here, time will tell. Now, I would like to go back to your husband's not attending.

At that point, I believed that I had enough information to conclude that the mother was dealing appropriately with Gloria's rambunctiousness. Accordingly, I decided to discontinue further discussion on that point and go back to the failure of the father to attend the wedding. I believed that that was an important issue to focus on because of its implications for Gloria's attitudes toward Bob and her subsequent relationship with him. As mentioned, I believe all of us need reasonable degrees of love and affection and that we should not preclude any kind of a relationship whatsoever with an individual who may have sexually molested us. Certainly, everything should be done to protect a child from further molestation; but everything should also be done to preserve and encourage good relationships with nearest of kin.

Mother: Hh-hmm.

Gardner: What's your opinion of that?

Mother: I think he is being rigidly unforgiving and just a little too, um, just plain rigid.

Gardner: And you told him that?

Mother: No, because for a long time in our lives . . . there is just so much major tension and it has been on my mind and I was hoping that basically, religiously, that he would be able to get some messages about forgiving and letting the past go and start dealing with where time is. So I was letting this past six months go by because we are in the middle of getting into the Ten Commandments and I thought, "Boy, that's a perfect time."

Gardner: Oh, so you said nothing at this point.

Mother: No.

When the mother spoke about waiting until they came to that part of the Ten Commandments that relates to forgiving, before she would talk to her husband about his dealing with Bob, I recognized immediately that she was procrastinating. I knew that I would focus on this point soon. However, I wished to lay some foundation for that area of exploration by first pointing out the importance of maintenance of the family network and the father's support of Gloria's continuing involvement with Bob, the sexual molestation notwithstanding.

Gardner: You see, there are a couple of thoughts I have on it. One is that in a mild way it works against the therapeutic process for her in dealing with this trauma because Bob is your brother's son.

Mother: Hh-hmm.

Gardner: He's a relative. Like all relatives in this world, he has things you like and things you don't like. You feel you want to continue with your family network, their problems notwithstanding, to the degree that you want. And you want Gloria to have some involvement with her family. Clearly, the older she gets, the more she will be able to protect herself from any kind of overtures on Bob's part and his power over her will lessen. This is what I consider to be the best and healthiest route for her to take with regard to this: And that is that it doesn't mean that because he has this deficiency that you wash your hands of him for the rest of your life, that you scorn him forever, and that you treat him as a noxious, loathsome worm that you won't be in the same room with—because it robs her of some freedom, too. And it robs her of a more natural way of dealing with this problem. So I feel that, for Gloria's sake, your husband should have been there. Bob's not going to do anything at a wedding in front of the parents.

Mother: Right!

Gardner: That crazy he is not! Do you think your husband would have gone had this not happened?

Mother: I don't know. My husband, if he's tired he won't do anything for anyone. He simply pulls in for himself and he would not drive that far, that kind of a distance.

Gardner: Oh, so he wouldn't have gone anyway?

Mother: Well, it's possible.

Gardner: I see, but would you say that when he was weighing the considerations, this was a heavy consideration—tipping the balance in the negative?

Mother (nodding affirmatively): Hh-hmm.

Gardner: You see, I think that what parents *do*—I'm very big on modeling—it's one of my favorite words in this field—that what parents *do*—more than what they *say*—is what determines how a child is going to react. A good example here is a parent who smokes a cigarette. That parent is in no position to tell a teenager not to smoke.

Mother: Right.

Gardner: They can have all the charts of all the diseases and everything else. So your husband is saying, "This boy is noxious. I don't want to be in the same room with him and I will have nothing to do with him." Your husband believes that this may be a lifelong pattern of his. That's not good for Gloria in terms of continuing with hate, never forgiving, and so from a psychological point of view it's not good and, you know, it doesn't fit in with the precepts of your religious beliefs either. So it's another reason.

Mother: I completely agree.

Gardner: I feel that your statement, "I'll wait until we reach that part in our religious studies," I think was an unnecessary procrastination.

Mother: Hh-hmm.

Gardner: Do you know what I mean? If there was some more urgent precept that was broken, "Thou shall not kill" or "Thou shall not covet thy neighbor's wife," you wouldn't have waited until you reached that part. Do you know what I mean?

Mother (laughing): Right, right. (Both therapist and mother laugh together.) But I thought that having a year of talking about being forgiving and just what is set up in the commandments that—when we're his godparents—that's to me where the major issue is. We do have a responsibility for him and I feel in particular because of that we do have a responsibility. And that's where we are. And I was not willing to sit there and argue with my husband with him saying, "Absolutely no," and I'm saying, "I think you're wrong." It doesn't go anywhere. And so that's why I thought . . . it's not that important.

Gardner: Okay. I see some passivity here and some justification for yourself for not confronting him.

Mother: Hh-hmm.

Gardner: You don't have to argue. It takes two to argue. You can say, "This is my position. Let's discuss it a little bit." You don't have to have the whole day spent on harangues and big arguments; but you should let your position be known. Your saying "It's not important" is to justify your passivity.

Mother: Hh-hmm.

Gardner: Whether it's from a religious point of view or whether it's from a psychological point of view, just standing there and saying nothing, because it's a minor thing, is not going to help the situation. Minor things can often lead to major things. But my job is to select those things, even though minor, that I consider to be psychological problems.

Mother: Right.

Gardner: If somebody were to steal a penny off my desk, it would be my job to bring it to his or her attention.

Mother: Hh-hmm.

Gardner: Even if the person said, "Oh, it's only a penny. What are you worried about a penny?" it's an issue. It's a theft. So, it's a mild thing, it's a minor thing, but it's an issue. You're using religious tenets and your view that he's religious as rationalizations for nonaction. And what I'm also concerned about is this rigidity. Is this a pattern? Is this one example of a pattern of rigidity, and if it is, is this one example of your submission to rigidity without speaking up?

I asked here a very important question, namely, whether the rigidity she describes in her husband is an ongoing pattern or whether this is simply an isolated instance. It is crucial that the therapist ask questions along these lines, because focus on an isolated behavioral manifestation is rarely of any value therapeutically. All people get rigid at times, especially under stressful circumstances. There is little to work with therapeutically with such occasional, predictable forms of inappropriate or atypical behavior. One is much more interested in *patterns*. These are the areas to focus on in treatment. And I also want to know whether the mother's passivity, as well, is a pattern, or whether the incident being described here is an isolated one.

> *Mother*: I would say absolutely yes.
> *Gardner*: Yes.
> *Mother*: Absolutely.
> *Gardner*: Okay. Let's hear a couple of more examples. His rigidity, your passivity.

Once the mother states that his rigidity/her passivity problem is a pattern, I do not accept her statement immediately. I want to have further *specific examples* of the pattern in order to be sure that it is indeed the pattern she considers it to be. I cannot emphasize strongly enough that without specific examples the therapist is ill equipped to come to conclusions regarding a particular issue. Abstractions and generalizations are of little communicative value; specific examples are the richest sources of information regarding whether or not something is indeed happening.

> *Mother*: I think he said to you that he's not a person who can deal with a quick answer or a quick judgment on something most of the time. If you say to him . . .
> *Gardner* (talking to patient): Are you getting bored with this?
> *Patient*: (Nods affirmatively.)

We see here one of the drawbacks of my working together with both a child patient and a parent. When too much time is spent in a discussion with the parent, the child may very well "tune out." All therapeutic approaches have their drawbacks, and having the mother serve as "assistant therapist" is no exception to this principle. However, this drawback notwithstanding, I believe its advantages far outweigh its disadvantages.

Gardner: Okay, listen. We're going to try to make this a short discussion and we'll get to our games and talk, but this is very important. We're really talking about things that pertain to you. I know it's a little boring for you, but we'll try to make it short.

Mother: I will say, "Guess where we're gonna spend the summer? I just picked up a contact in New Mexico or we're going to live in Italy for the summer." His first answer is absolutely rejection. A flat outright no. He's not interested.

The mother's career sometimes enabled her to have the opportunity for extended work in various parts of the United States and occasionally abroad. Such assignments readily lent themselves to combinations of work and recreation. The father's business also allowed him the flexibility to join her on many of these assignments.

Gardner: Okay, and what will happen then?

Mother: And then when he has a few weeks to do his own research and to get information on the subject, then he usually totally gives the opposite answer and now New Mexico or Italy is in his bloodstream and . . .

Gardner: Okay, what do you do in this period when he's mulling over?

Mother: I try to help supply information so that he can see what's going on and get more information.

Gardner: So you do it in a way that he likes to believe it's his own decision?

Mother: It is his own decision to come.

Gardner: But you're working on him from the sidelines.

Mother: I made my decision to go.

Gardner: Yeah, but you're kind of feeding him info that will help him agree to go with you.

Mother: Yeah, I'll bring him brochures.

Gardner: Okay, so you have time to do it that way. I have no problem with that. But here you had a wedding, a one-time event with very short notice.

Mother: Very short notice, right.

Gardner: That's right, and I see your pull back. I'm just earmarking that for future reference.

Mother: Right.

Gardner: You brought up an issue, and if it's a *pattern*, I'm interested in it because we're dealing here with certain behavior patterns of Gloria's and I have to try to figure out what's going on in the family that might be affecting this pattern.

Mother: Right. Okay. That is definitely the way we work. His answers are usually a negative. His response usually on a quick decision is almost 90 percent of the time a negative response.

Gardner: And I am particularly concerned when such interactions affect Gloria directly. Can you think of any incident where it affects her directly when this happens?

Mother: Golly. You mean in front of her that she's aware of?

Gardner: Yeah.

Mother: Not that I can think of.

Gardner: Okay. I believe this may likely be playing a role in the problem of fabrication and the antisocial behavior.

Mother: Okay.

Gardner: How it does I don't know. But often these things do have some effect.

Mother: Well, I am constantly trying to avoid having confrontations with him.

Gardner: Okay.

Mother: And I am constantly making her aware of that—that you must not disturb Daddy, that we can't do this until we make amends, like clean up the mess or don't want him to get more hassled than he usually is.

Gardner: Okay, in the course of that tiptoeing around, do you in any way give messages that communicate, "Don't say things, cover up, and even lie"?

Mother: No, I simply say, "We don't want to get Daddy angry, you know, because he's going to be angry that this wasn't cleaned up."

Gardner (directed at patient): I'll ask you a question, because I know you have been a little bored here while your mother and I have been talking. Do you know what your mother was just saying? Were you listening or not? What were we just talking about?

Patient (whispers): About my daddy.

Gardner: What were we saying about your daddy?

Patient: That we don't disturb him.

Gardner: You don't disturb him. Okay, does that happen a lot, that your mother says, "Let not get him upset"?

Patient: Yes.

Gardner: Does it happen every day?

Patient: No.

Gardner: How often would you say it happens?

Patient: Hh-hmm, maybe like three days.

Gardner: Okay, let's hear from your mom. How often do you say it happens?

Mother: Often. About 50 percent of the time.

The discussion then progressed further into the mother's passivity in her relationship with her husband, and the pent-up anger that she felt over such passivity. In addition, we focused on the effects of this pattern on Gloria, especially the factor of the mother's serving as a model for such passivity. We then focused on the pent-up resentment that was thereby being engendered in Gloria, resentment that might be discharged through antisocial behavior. I will not elaborate further on this aspect of the therapy because it takes us somewhat afield from the primary purpose of this chapter, which is to focus on the treatment of child sex abuse. This segment was presented because it provides a good example of the kind of treatment one should provide such children. In this case, Gloria's treatment demonstrated my point that delving into the sex-abuse problem was not warranted because it appeared that she had worked through her initial reactions during her therapy two-and-a-half years previously. Here I was encouraging rapprochement with her cousin Bob (the sex abuser) and attempted to deal with environmental factors (here the father's reluctance for rapprochement) that might be interfering with that process.

Sex Abuse and Parental Neglect

Tina, age seven-and-a-half, was brought to the hospital by child protection services because her foster mother could no longer handle her at home. The child masturbated frequently and intermittently tried to fondle the genitals of two of the boys living in the foster home. The foster mother was able to tolerate this to some degree, but did not know that the child had been sexually abused. However, on the night before child protection was contacted, Tina took the foster mother's hand while being read a bedtime story and asked her foster mother to rub her genitals. The foster mother reacted with amazement and concern. She refused the child's request and was then told, "My mommy used to do that with me all the time. At first I told her it hurt, but then she told me that I would get used to it. And I got used to it and now I like it. Please do it." On the basis of this the child was admitted to the hospital. Although this child's hospitalization was not, in my opinion, necessary, it was not I who made the decision to admit her. It was, I believe, just one manifestation of the hysteria that we have been witnessing in the United States since the early 1980s. I am not claiming that intervention was not necessary. Nor am I claiming that Tina should have been permitted to involve herself sexually with the other foster children in the home. Nor am I claiming that the foster mother should have gratified the child's request and masturbated her. I am only saying that this was not a situation that required hospitalization.

Tina was the youngest of three children. At the time of admission her older sister was 13 and her older brother 10. Her mother, an alcoholic and drug addict, neglected the three children from birth and her father was only intermittently involved with the children. The mother was extremely promiscuous and might also have been a prostitute. On detailed inquiry there was good reason to believe that Tina and her older sister were fondled by the maternal stepgrandfather when she was three years old. Also, it is likely that there were numerous occasions when Tina was present when her mother and one of her lovers would watch pornographic videotapes. At age five one of her mother's boyfriends tongue kissed with Tina on a number of occasions. Tina also stated that this man "took off my clothes and put his hand on my wee-wee."

Finding out exactly what happened to the two girls was complicated by the fact that certain elements in their descriptions did not have credibility. For example, Tina's older sister said that one of her mother's lovers put "sticks and stones" into her vagina. Yet, the vaginal examination of the sister was normal. The selection of the term "sticks and stones" suggests the kind of borrowed scenario often seen in false accusations (Gardner, 1995a). All things considered, I concluded that both girls were sexually molested on numerous occasions and that as the result of many inquiries they began to introduce some fanciful elaborations (a not uncommon phenomenon).

At the time of the interview presented here, Tina had been in the hospital about four months and arrangements were being made for discharge to another foster home. Interestingly, the masturbation was not observed in the hospital nor was the hypersexualization. Hospital staff were making vigorous attempts to involve both the mother and the father in the treatment program—but with little success. The father refused completely to have any contact and the mother broke most of the appointments with thinly veiled rationalizations and excuses. At the time of my interview arrangements were being finalized for discharge to a new foster home that included two older boys, ages 12 and 14, and an older girl, age 10.

Joining me in the interview was the child psychiatric fellow (Dr. B.) who was treating Tina. I have often found it quite useful to interview directly the patients of the trainees I am supervising. I do this in the presence of the trainee. Prior to the segment transcribed here I obtained general information about the patient: "name, rank, and serial number" questions. In the course of that introductory inquiry (which is basically a warming up and rapport-establishing phase), an interesting and a psychodynamically significant thing happened. First, Tina identified her biological mother as Maria and her biological father as Frank. (Obviously, real names are not being used here.) When listing her siblings, she mentioned her biological sister, Sarah, and her biological brother, Ted. However, she included a third sibling, James. When Dr. B. presented this case to me, he described only two siblings: Sarah and Ted. Accordingly, I asked Tina about James and learned that James was one of the two foster children who was living in the home of Mr. and Mrs. C., her *new* foster parents. Tina had never actually met James directly; however, she did see him through the window of her room when he was visiting the hospital with his foster parents, Mr. and Mrs. C. It was on the basis of this short glimpse that she had already included him as her "brother." This to me was a statement of Tina's sense of extreme privation: she was already listing James as a brother, a child with whom she had only the most superficial relationship.

Following my collection of basic data I asked Tina what she understood to be the purpose of our interview. She responded by telling me that she did not wish to discuss with me the reasons for the interview and I did not press the point. I have not found it useful to pressure patients into talking about anything they don't wish to discuss. Any information extracted under those circumstances is so compromised by the censorship attendant to their tension and reluctance that the inquiry may not be in any way useful. Accordingly, I gave Tina a piece of paper and asked her to draw a picture:

> *Gardner*: I'm going to give you this piece of paper. Let's do it on this, this drawing pad. I want you to draw anything in the whole wide world and then tell me what you've drawn. (Turns to Dr. B.) At this point, I want a whole universe, anything in the whole wide world. I don't want her to zero in on any theme.
> *Patient*: You shouldn't look at it.
> *Gardner*: I shouldn't look at it, why not?
> *Patient*: You can look at it.

At this point, I had a choice to make. I could have conducted an inquiry of the child regarding why she did not want me to look at her picture. This might have produced some therapeutic mileage. However, the child had only been in the room a few minutes and was already comfortable. I decided that the "yield" of such an inquiry might not be worth the anxiety engendered in her by conducting it. Her response "You can look at it" lent confirmation to my belief that my question, "Why not?" was anxiety provoking. Accordingly, I let it go. As the reader will see below, there was another occasion in which Tina did not want me to look at her picture. At that time, she was more comfortable with me, and I considered an inquiry justified.

> *Gardner*: Okay, what are you drawing there? What is that?
> *Patient*: A cloud.
> *Gardner*: A cloud. Okay, finish up the drawing. What did you put in the cloud there?

Patient: I put lightning in the cloud.

Gardner: Lightning in the cloud. Okay, go ahead.

Patient: I think I need some yellow.

Gardner (to Dr. B.): You see it doesn't matter. She doesn't want to talk. You respect it. No pressure. What is pressing for expression will come out one way or another.

As mentioned, Dr. B. was a supervisee. The comments that I made to him in the course of the interview were in the service of his supervision. Under such circumstances I am studiously careful not to make any comments that might contaminate the interview by drawing the child's thoughts and feelings away from what spontaneously comes from her. This comment was made while Tina was drawing and not saying anything at that point.

Patient (pointing to her picture): Look at that.

Gardner: What is that? You tell me.

Patient: Sun.

Gardner: Sun, good. (Now turning to Dr. B.) I thought it might be that, but you never know. Sometimes you think that a child's drawing a particular thing and it's something different.

Patient (pointing to top of picture): Look at that.

Gardner: What is that?

Patient: Nighttime.

Gardner: Nighttime. Okay, that's the black sky? Okay, a cloud with lightning and it's nighttime. Is that the black sky that you're drawing there?

Patient (nodding affirmatively): Uh-huh.

Gardner: Okay. What are you doing now?

Patient: (Laughs.)

Gardner: I don't know what that is.

Patient: It's lightning.

Gardner: It's lightning?

Patient: It's in the sky.

Gardner: The lightning is in the black sky. It's black sky.

Patient: It's nighttime.

Gardner: It's nighttime, okay.

Patient: It's daytime over here.

Gardner: Oh, in one place it's nighttime and in one place it's daytime? Okay.

The reader should note that all my comments are confirmatory. They merely serve to clarify what is being drawn in the picture and assure that I do not in any way misinterpret what the child is drawing or what she is saying about her drawing. At no point do I introduce anything new. They also serve to facilitate further drawing and comments. Up to that point, the focus was primarily on the sky, the sun, and the lightning. All of these were at the top of the picture. Then Tina began drawing something in the middle of the picture, something that was not readily identifiable. It consisted of lines crossing one another.

Gardner (pointing to the newly drawn crossed lines): What's that?
Patient: It's going to be yucky.
Gardner: It's going to be yucky? What is that, that's yucky?
Patient: It's somebody dead, a-a-ah!
Gardner: Somebody's dead? Okay. Somebody is dead. Who is that person? Who is dead there? Who is the dead person?
Patient: Me.

Here we have a seven-and-a-half-year-old girl depicting herself as dead. Clearly, some powerful message was being sent here that deserved very serious attention. Unusual and atypical responses should always alert the examiner to the high probability that important material is being dealt with. And the more idiosyncratic the material, the greater the likelihood that this is the case. This is one of the important principles of psychodynamic therapy. However, when the material involves the child's depicting herself as dead, we may be dealing here with an emergency situation, one of suicidal tendencies. Dr. B. had not mentioned a suicidal risk, but this new revelation indicated that suicidal risk had to be an important part of my assessment. My experience has been that the best way to ascertain such risk is to get as much information as possible about the comment, its associated thoughts, and its sources. And this is what I planned to do here. However, I first decided to allow the child to finish her picture because of the high probability that additional material depicted therein would be of value in the assessment of the suicidal risk as well as my understanding of other problems in her life, possibly reactions to her sexual abuses.

> *Gardner*: You're dead? Okay. How come that happened? A seven-year-old girl dead. Hmmm. Very unusual. What is that you're drawing now?
> *Patient*: I'm drawing snow.
> *Gardner*: You're drawing snow. And what's that you're drawing now?
> *Patient*: It's still coming out of there.
> *Gardner*: Still coming out? That seven-year-old girl who's dead is you. What is this around her? What is that coming out?
> *Patient*: She's in a box. That's snow covering her box.
> *Gardner*: You say she's in a box?
> *Patient*: Me in a box.
> *Gardner*: You're in a box.
> *Patient*: In the ground. Sticking out of the ground.
> *Gardner*: You're *not* in the ground or you're in the ground? You're not in the ground any more, or you're still in the ground. Which is it?

It is extremely important that the examiner clarify any contradictions or confusions introduced by the child. Without such clarification the examiner is ill equipped to understand the psychodynamic meanings of the child's productions.

> *Patient*: I'm still in the ground. But my hands and feet are sticking out.
> *Resident*: Sticking out her feet and hands.
> *Gardner*: Her feet and hands are sticking out of the box?
> *Patient*: The box is in the ground.
> *Gardner*: The box is under the ground? And your feet and hands are sticking above the ground. Is that it? Do I have that right?
> *Patient*: Yeah.
> *Gardner*: The box is under the ground and your feet and hands are sticking above the ground, is that it? Okay.

Again, we see a highly idiosyncratic symbol. Tina's body is in the ground, in a box, under the earth. However, her arms and legs are sticking out. This is a strong statement of the child's craving for contact with the world even though she may feel herself dead or worthy of being dead. It is a sign of hope in a relatively hopeless situation. It is one of the bits of information that must be taken into consideration when assessing Tina's suicidal risk, a risk that must be considered when a child of this age draws such a picture.

>*Patient*: (Draws what looks like a human figure.)
>*Gardner*: What else are you drawing there? Who's that?
>*Patient*: That's my mom!
>*Gardner*: Your mother? Is that your real mom? Is that Maria?
>*Patient*: Yes. She's crying.
>*Gardner*: She's crying? Why is she crying?
>*Patient*: Because I'm big.
>*Gardner*: I see. Okay. Then what else is happening there? What's that?
>*Patient*: That's my brother and he's not happy.
>*Resident*: That's her brother and he's not happy.
>*Gardner*: That's your real brother Ted?
>*Patient*: No, this is my new brother, James, and this is my new mom.
>*Gardner*: Oh, so you're changing it. This isn't mom Maria anymore. It's your new mom, Mrs. C. And that's your new brother. You mean your new brother, James?
>*Patient*: Yes. And this is my dad.
>*Gardner*: When you say your dad, is that your real daddy, Daddy Frank?
>*Patient*: No, this is my fake dad.
>*Gardner*: What's his name?
>*Patient*: Mr. C.
>*Gardner*: Who's his wife?
>*Patient*: Mommy.
>*Gardner*: Mommy who?
>*Patient*: Mommy C.
>*Gardner*: So that's Mr. C. Mr. C. is in there?
>*Patient*: That's my other brother, James.

> *Gardner*: Your other brother? What's his name?
> *Patient*: His name is James. He's crying.
> *Gardner*: He's crying? Why is he crying?
> *Patient*: Because I'm dead.
> *Gardner*: Because you're dead. Okay. What else?

As mentioned, at the time of this session, Tina had not directly met Mr. and Mrs. C. and James. Yet, she was already incorporating them into her fantasy life. They are crying because she is dead. This is a strong statement of the profundity of this child's sense of privation. It appeared that the only way she believed she could get any kind of affection or attention from anyone is to be dead and thereby elicit a sense of loss and grief in them. Tina's life had indeed been one of continual rejection. Her natural parents neglected and abandoned her, leaving her to the care of a series of relatives and foster parents. The fantasy here involves some hope for involvement with Mr. and Mrs. C. and James, but an involvement that is clearly pathological. It is a relationship based on pity of her, emotions elicited from her grave. It appeared that this was the only kind of attention she thought she could get.

> *Patient*: Close your eyes for a minute.
> *Gardner*: Okay, *why* do you want me to close my eyes?
> *Patient*: For a minute.
> *Gardner*: *Why* do you want me to do that?
> *Patient*: Because I want to do something.
> *Gardner*: What do you want to do? Maybe I will close my eyes, but first I have to have some idea about what you want me to close my eyes for.

Were I with my grandchildren I might very well have closed my eyes under these circumstances. In that setting it would have been a normal game that one might play with a child. However, this was a professional, therapeutic situation in which it behooves the examiner to learn *why* he (she) is being asked to engage in a certain kind of behavior before automatically engaging in it. To reflexively go along with such a request might deprive the therapist of important psychodynamic information.

200   TREATMENT OF SEXUALLY ABUSED CHILDREN

>   *Patient*: (Whispers inaudibly in Dr. Gardner's ear.)
>   *Gardner*: Because you're what?
>   *Patient* (pointing to figures in the picture): Because I'm going to get out of the ground and scare these guys.
>   *Gardner*: Because you're going to scare these guys. Why do you want me to close my eyes? Why don't you want me to see it?
>   *Patient*: No.
>   *Gardner*: See. I'm very happy to play the game "Close My Eyes" but I have to know before I close my eyes *why* you want me to close my eyes. I don't just close my eyes when somebody says "close your eyes." I have to know *why*. And after I get all the reasons, then I decide whether I want to close them or not. So I have to know more about the reason.
>   *Patient*: Scare those guys.
>   *Gardner*: That you wanted to scare those guys in the picture? Okay, but why don't you want me to see it?
>   *Patient*: I didn't want to scare you.
>   *Gardner*: You don't want to scare me?
>   *Gardner*: Okay. So you don't want to scare me when you scare them. One of us has to keep his eyes open. Either Dr. B. or me. We can't both close our eyes.

At that point, I had enough of an answer to comply with Tina's request, but I did not want to have both of us keep our eyes closed. There was no telling what the child might do. It is not that I anticipated any kind of violent or destructive behavior; rather, I just wanted to be sure that one of us was observing what was happening so that we would have a better understanding of the child's behavior. I did not wish to be in a situation in which Tina was doing something that was unobserved, something that might have important psychological significance.

With regard to the actual request that I cover my eyes so that I would not be scared, I believe the request related to the intensity of Tina's desire to scare Mr. and Mrs. C. and James. Scaring people is a form of interaction that attracts the attention of the other parties. And certainly Tina was very desirous of attracting attention, so deprived was she. It was also a statement of Tina's feeling that if she were quiet she would not attract attention. By scaring people, she will predictably attract attention. There is also a possible hostile element here, in that scaring people is a normal and relatively innocuous way for children to express hostility. Tina's hostility might have been formidable, considering her belief that if I were to watch I too might be scared. Perhaps she was afraid to go too far with this normal outlet for a child's hostility. There are some who might have followed up on this, to explore further the psychodynamic factors operative in this request. I made the decision not to do so in that I wanted to allow the child to continue with the flow of her story. To investigate this psychodynamically at that point might have drawn her away from the path in which I was obtaining further information relevant to Tina's situation, especially information about the suicidal risk and the possible effects of her sexual abuse.

Patient (pointing to Dr. B.): He'll keep his eyes open.

Gardner: So you want him to keep his eyes open? I'll close my eyes now and you tell me when I can open them again. (Short time lapse) Almost finished? (More time lapses) Finished now?

Patient: No. A-a-ah!!! (Screeching sounds.)

Gardner: Okay, can I open them now?

Patient: Yeah. (Patient now pointing to new figure on the picture.) That's me. I got out of the box to scare them.

Gardner: That's you? You got out of the box to scare them? Is that what you were doing while my eyes were closed?

Patient: (Nods affirmatively.)

Gardner: Now you wanted to scare them. How did you scare them? What did you do that scared them?

Patient: I went "boo."

Gardner: You went "boo." I see. Why were they scared?

Patient: I scared them.

Gardner: Okay, then what happens after that?

Patient: I don't know.

Gardner: Oh, come on. That's a very good story you're telling here. What happens after that?

Patient: They got more happy.

Gardner: Who got more happy?

Resident: She came up and she's happier. I spit at him.

Gardner: You spit at him. Who is that?

Patient: I spit at ma.

Gardner: You spit at ma. Which mother is this, mother Maria or Mrs. C.

Patient: Mrs. C.

Gardner: You spit at Mrs. C.

Patient: At everybody.

Gardner: At everybody. Why did you do that? Why did you spit at everybody?

Patient: Because I wanted to. . . .

Gardner: Because you wanted to? Well, you know when somebody spits, it usually means that they're sad or angry or something like that. Isn't that so?

Patient: I'm happy because I got out of the box.

Gardner: You're happy because you got out of the box. Okay, so why spit?

Patient: (Patient turns over drawing, implying either that she's finished or she wants to draw another picture.)

Gardner: Before we turn over this paper, I've got some questions to ask you. Are you finished with the story?

Patient (nodding affirmatively): Yes.

Gardner: That's the whole story? It ends with spitting?

Patient (nodding affirmatively): Uh huh.

Clearly, spitting is a hostile act. This element in Tina's fantasy adds to the hostile element involved in scaring Mr. and Mrs. C. and James. The fantasy warns us that Mr. and Mrs. C. and their foster children might very well be the targets of Tina's hostility and this, of course, did not bode well for her future relationships with them. It was a "red flag" regarding what could be expected in the new home. Obviously, this was yet another area worthy of inquiry. Again, my primary purpose here was to learn more about Tina's psychodynamics, information that would then serve as a foundation for psychotherapeutic inquiry. At this point it was clear that Tina was getting restless and the aforementioned turning over the picture was one manifestation of this. She was also reaching the point of diminishing returns regarding getting more information from her.

Gardner: Okay, I have a question. You know, every story teaches us something. It has a lesson or a moral. (Patient now gets up out of her seat and walks away from the interview table.) Don't you like this game? You're doing very well at it. In fact, do you see that box over there (therapist points to the other end of the room) with prizes in it? That's a treasure chest of prizes for people who are good and cooperate.

Patient: I can see them.

Gardner: You can see them, right. But that comes at the end when you pick out a prize. But those prizes are only given to those who cooperate. So far you're doing very well.

Patient: I don't want to play this anymore.

Gardner: We can stop this in just a minute, but I have a couple of questions for you. One question is what did we learn from that story? What's the lesson from that story? What did we learn from it?

Patient: I don't know.

Gardner: Every story has a lesson. Try and think of it.

Patient: I don't know.

Gardner: You don't know? Well, try to think. Is there anything we can learn from that story? Can't think of a lesson? Shall I write down "cannot think of lesson"?

Patient: Yes.

Gardner: Shall I write that down on the chart here?

Patient: Yes.

There are some children who do not wish to have it written in their record that they could not think of a lesson to a story. There is a little fantasy here that others might see my chart and they might be embarrassed over this disclosure. Obviously, this maneuver did not work with Tina at this point.

Gardner: Yes? Okay, (writing): *Tina cannot think of a lesson*. Now I have another question for you. How did this girl die? How did you die?

Patient: Somebody cut me.

Gardner: Someone cut you. Who's someone?

Patient: A stranger.

Gardner: A stranger. Someone cut you, a stranger. And where did the person cut you, what part of your body?

Patient (pointing to her own neck): Right here.

Gardner: On the neck? And, a stranger. And that's how you died?

204 *TREATMENT OF SEXUALLY ABUSED CHILDREN*

Well, why did the stranger do that? Why would a stranger do a thing like that?

Patient: I don't know.

Gardner: Well, what could be the reasons? You can make it up in your story, you can do that. What would be the reasons? It's a made-up story, so you're not really dead. Nobody really ever cut you there, right? So it's just a made-up story. So make up why the stranger would do that.

Patient: Maybe he was mad at me.

Gardner: He was made at you? Well, what might you have done to have caused that stranger to be mad?

Patient: I don't know. Maybe I punched him.

Gardner: Maybe you punched him. So then he would kill you? Is that it? Maybe you punched him. Okay, well, why would you punch him?

Patient: I don't know.

Gardner: You don't know. You don't know why you punched him.

The reader can see here how productive can be the process of continuing to elicit ever more information from the patient. Such "brain squeezing" can provide examiners with extremely important information necessary for understanding underlying psychodynamic processes. Examiners who have little if any commitment to psychodynamically oriented therapy deprive themselves of extremely important information necessary for the understanding of a patient's symptoms. Tina's fantasy of having her neck cut is indeed a dramatic one. It was also a strong statement of Tina's belief that there are extremely malevolent people in this world who retaliate in very powerful and even lethal ways if she were to express hostility. This lent confirmation to my belief that the hostile element was involved in Tina's fantasy of scaring Mr. and Mrs. C. and James as well as spitting at them. Tina was a girl with formidable anger, anger that had been generated by the significant privations she had suffered throughout the course of her very short life. She feared powerful retaliation if she were to express her anger. My attempts to get further information about her regarding these issues were not successful.

At that point, I decided to pursue further the suicidal issue and to provide certain comments that might prove therapeutic, especially in the realm of discouraging any acting out of her suicidal fantasies. Whereas the interchange up to that point was primarily diagnostic, i.e., information gathering, following that point our interchanges were primarily therapeutic, especially in the service of discouraging the acting out of suicidal tendencies.

Gardner: Okay, tell me something. I want to ask you a question about something. You know it's a very sad thing for a girl or anybody to write a story about their being dead, and I was wondering whether you ever thought that you would like to be dead.
Patient: I don't want to do this anymore.
Gardner: You don't want to do this anymore? You don't want to talk about that?
Patient: No.
Gardner: Let me ask you one more question about that. Did you ever think of wanting to be dead yourself? Did you?
Patient: (Shakes head negatively.)
Gardner: Are you sure? Let's ask Dr. B. Did she ever talk to you about wanting to be dead?
Dr. B.: No, never.
Patient: The children in the hospital talk about it, in the groups.
Dr. B.: In some of the groups, in the group therapy sessions, she hears this from the other children.
Gardner: Oh, she hears this from some of the other children. There are other children there who want to be dead?
Patient: I said only me.

One of the drawbacks of hospitalizing a child is demonstrated here quite clearly. Children do pick up psychopathology from other children when hospitalized. People who deny this are denying reality. This does not mean that the acquired symptoms have the same depth and psychopathological significance as they do in the original child. In fact, they are less likely to be as serious but can present as symptoms nonetheless. And this is what I believe was taking place in Tina. It is not that she was free from depression and suicidal tendencies, only that a contributing factor to her suicidal thoughts was derived from the hospital group. Obviously, this contributory factor had important implications for the assessment of the degree of her suicidal risk. Considering the borrowed-scenario factor, and considering the fact that she had not mentioned suicide to Dr. B. previously, I concluded that the suicidal risk was less than I originally imagined.

Gardner: Only you? You want to be dead? Are you saying yes?
Patient: Yes.
Gardner: I want to ask you something, because this is a very important subject. Usually, if a person wants to be dead, especially a child of seven, you know, that's terrible. That's a *very* sad thing. What happened to you that you could even think about that at your age? What happened? You know if a very old person is very sick and in a lot of pain . . .
Patient: My grandma got dead in a hospital. I don't want to do this anymore.
Gardner: Do you want to draw another picture?
Patient: No.
Gardner: Okay, I just want to say one thing to you. What do you believe happens to people after they die?
Patient: They'll be sad.
Gardner: You mean after you die, are you sad? You mean do you feel sadness after you're dead?
Patient: (Unintelligible.)
Gardner: Do you feel anything after you're dead? What is your belief, your opinion?
Patient: I feel sad.
Gardner: You feel sad? Do you believe that if you die and other people are sad that you died, that that's the way of getting back at them for treating you bad? You know what I mean? You understand what I'm saying?
Patient: (Nods affirmatively.)
Gardner: Well, let me say this to you. Some people think that if you're angry at someone and you die, then they'll cry for you and love you. Because you're lying there in the grave, you feel good that they're crying. Now they'll love you. Now they'll feel bad. Have you had such ideas that after you're dead, then other people will feel bad for treating you badly? Have you ever had that idea?
Patient: (Nods affirmatively.)

Gardner: I thought you did. Well, I personally don't believe that that happens. I believe that when you're dead you don't know that they're crying, and you don't know that they feel bad because they treated you badly. That's my personal opinion. What do you think, Dr. B?

Dr. B: I agree.

Gardner: You agree. That when you're dead, you're just dead in the ground there. You can't say, "Good, now they're going to love me" or "Now they'll feel bad for what they did to me."

Gardner: Dr. B. and I both agree on that. What do you think?

Patient: I think so too.

I have found this to be a very important point when treating suicidal patients, especially youngsters. They often have the fantasy that their soul or spirit will somehow survive and enjoy watching their survivors tear their hair out, pound their chests, and otherwise wail remorsefully over how badly they treated the deceased youngster. This fantasy may be enhanced by religious teachings that emphasize the hereafter. I, like all people in this world, do not know with certainty whether there is some kind of existence after life. Although I personally am very dubious about such existence, I recognize that mine is a minority opinion. At any rate, even those who believe deeply in the existence of a hereafter are generally in agreement that a seven-year-old child should not be prematurely entering the world of the hereafter, whether it be to test this hypothesis or to remove herself from a painful and unrewarding existence. And even those who believe in the hereafter generally do not subscribe to the belief that the soul or spirit will gleefully enjoy the grief of the survivors as it hovers above the funeral site. Accordingly, dispelling this fantasy can sometimes prove useful in reducing suicidal risk. Furthermore, bringing in the assistance of another authority, Dr. B., served to enhance the clout of my messages on this issue.

At that point, it was clear to me that Tina was unreceptive to further discussion on the issue of suicide. All things considered, I did not believe that there was a genuine suicidal risk at that point, but there was good reason to believe that depression was present. I decided then to invite Tina to engage in other activities that would provide me with more information about her and could be used as points of departure for psychotherapeutic interchanges.

Gardner: Okay, now you said you wanted to draw another picture?
Patient: (Shakes head negatively.)
Gardner: You don't want to draw another picture? You don't want to do anymore of that, hm? Okay, let me ask you a question. We'll change the subject. Why don't we do this—a different kind of thing. Let's do something different here. Let's play this game. (Therapist takes *The Talking, Feeling, and Doing Game* off the shelf.) This game is called *The Talking, Feeling, and Doing Game*. Most kids like to play it.

The next 15–20 minutes were spent playing *The Talking, Feeling, and Doing Game*. Most of Tina's responses were in the normal range. None of her responses indicated that she was dealing directly with sex-abuse trauma, or even sexual problems. The one very revealing response that she gave was to the card:

"You're walking down the street and you find an envelope. Nothing is written on it. You open it up. There is a letter inside. What does the letter say?"

Tina's response was, "There is a letter from Mrs. C. It's to me. She says, 'I love you, Tina.'" I considered this response to be a strong statement about Tina's formidable feelings of emotional deprivation and her craving for human affection. She had not yet met Mrs. C., but she knew well that Mrs. C. was to be her new foster mother. Her response here indicated her deep hope that Mrs. C. would love her.

Tina's responses in the session indicated that she might engage herself in behaviors that could very well alienate Mrs. C. and other members of her family, e.g., suicidal behavior (for its attention-getting value as well as a method for testing their love of her) and expressing hostility in provocative ways (scaring them and spitting in their faces). Dr. B. was advised to encourage Tina to elaborate on all these themes in the course of his sessions with her and to help her compensate for her feelings of privation by gaining attention and affection in more constructive and less alienating ways. In addition, Dr. B. was advised to recommend to the social workers involved in Tina's case that they should stop hounding the parents to visit with Tina and to recognize that their coercive and guilt-evoking methods for bringing about commitment in the parents for involving themselves with Tina had proven futile. I suggested that he advise them to communicate to the parents where Tina and her siblings were and that social services would be receptive to facilitating visits *if and when the parents saw fit to do so.*

It is important to note that in this session, as is true of all of my sessions with patients, I do not have any preconceived notions as to what issues should be focused upon. Had Tina brought up sexual issues I certainly would have pursued them. But she did not, and so I did not rechannel her into sexual tracks. She brought me down the track of symptoms that derived from emotional deprivation and I stayed with her on that course. She brought me down the track of suicidal fantasies, and I certainly stayed with her on that course. Had she mentioned sexual abuses as contributory in the tracks she brought me down, I certainly would have explored these areas further. But she did not, and so I did not introduce them. I believe that this course is the preferable one for all abused children, whether it be sexual or otherwise. And, more generally, I believe that the more open-ended approach is the best for all children in therapy, because it is only then that the therapist will be able to determine what is *really* on the child's mind. It is my hope that the reader appreciates how a more structured approach would have deprived me of the rich information I was able to obtain by the open-ended approach utilized here with Tina. The picture of the buried girl with her hands sticking out of the ground is powerful and dramatic and is a far stronger statement of this child's situation than would have been obtained by a more structured approach.

☐ FOUR

PROGRAMMING NONABUSED CHILDREN TO BELIEVE THEY WERE SEXUALLY ABUSED

INTRODUCTION

In this chapter I focus on the techniques that are used by overzealous and often incompetent evaluators to program children to believe they were sexually abused when they were not. I will focus primarily on the improper and often naive techniques that are utilized but will also comment about these individuals themselves and what processes are operative in their zealotry and/or ineptitude. My observations and conclusions about these people are derived primarily from a detailed analysis of their reports, audiotapes, and videotapes since the early 1980s. When I say *detailed* I mean just that. In many cases I have meticulously and painstakingly analyzed videotapes, often stopping every 30 to 60 seconds, in order to comment on the technique being utilized in my court report. My best guess is that to date I have analyzed at least one thousand hours of such recordings from various parts of the United States. During this same period, I have testified in approximately 25 states. Accordingly, I bring to this critique vast experience and serious consideration.

I recognize that I am extremely critical of many (and probably most) of the people who are doing evaluations in sex-abuse cases. I appreciate that there are some (but I believe they are in the minority) who are conducting skillful evaluations that are balanced and unbiased. My experience, however, has been that the majority of those evaluators whose examinations I have had the opportunity to evaluate in depth exhibit significant deficiencies in their techniques. It is this group that I am referring to in this chapter, and it is this group that is playing a significant role in the present sex-abuse fiasco. One cannot possibly know the exact percentage of evaluators who fall into the category I am criticizing here. Furthermore, even that division is artificial in that each evaluator falls at some point along a continuum—from those who manifest most if not all of the deficiencies described here to the most competent and skilled who exhibit few if any of them. Although their percentage is not certain (and probably cannot be known), there is no question that there are enough of these inadequate and incompetent evaluators to warrant the criticisms presented here.

Some who conduct sex-abuse evaluations unashamedly refer to themselves as "validators." Those who are naive enough to apply this term to themselves are most likely performing at the levels of incompetence described in this chapter. The very fact that they are comfortable referring to themselves as validators provides strong justification for my placing them in this category. The name implies that their sole purpose is to *validate* or confirm that the abuse took place. It is the equivalent of a criminal court judge referring to himself (herself) as the "convictor" or the "incarcerator." More recently, a new "occupation" has come into vogue: "the child advocate." These individuals sanctimoniously pride themselves on the fact that they defend the rights of children (unlike the rest of us who are "unconcerned"). They, of course, hold that "children never lie about sex abuse," and they accept as valid every statement a child makes that might verify sex abuse. They also support vigorously the "rights" of their child clients to be protected from the sea of perpetrators who are ever craving to subject them to a wide variety of abuses. What I have to say here about "validators" applies to "child advocates" in that we are basically dealing with the same group.

Therapists who work with programmed children need to know the methods used in the course of their programming if they are to adequately treat them, i.e., to "deprogram" them. In this chapter, I will elaborate on these techniques. Examiners who read what I have just said here, and find themselves angry and offended, might give serious consideration to the possibility that there is validity to my criticisms and that rectification of the problem might be warranted. Those who respond to such irritation by not giving any consideration to the possibility that my criticisms are valid are likely to be depriving themselves of the opportunity to learn some useful principles and interviewing techniques.

CHILDREN'S MEMORY AND SUGGESTIBILITY

Introduction

Those who program children rely heavily on children's suggestibility and the weakness of their memory. It is important to appreciate the degree to which children are suggestible and how faulty their memories can be about experiences they have. No one can claim perfect recall and all of us forget. Furthermore, one does well to appreciate that memories do not remain unaltered over time; rather, they become restructured. The alterations are not only the result of the influences of our wishes, desire to avoid unpleasant affects, denial mechanisms, etc., but the simple erosion that takes place over time, erosion that may not be related to any particular psychological mechanisms. Events are not stored in the brain like a photograph. Rather, they may be altered in the process of storage because of inattention or psychological distortion. The storage process is not a stagnant one; rather, there is often reconstruction and restructuring. Nor should the retrieval process be viewed as simple reproduction of what is stored, but a process by which there is filtering, censorship, and the introduction of further distortions. In the process of retrieval, missing details may be filled in order to give the memory a coherence and logic that may be satisfying to the individual's sense of balance and aesthetics but may introduce further distortions. In his discussion of dreams, Freud referred to this process as "secondary elaboration," the process by which the dreamer provides the dream with a sense of continuity and organization that was not present in the actual dream material. Retrieved memories, then, are best viewed as an integration of the residual images of the stored event with subsequent desires, fears, fantasies, and attitudes toward the revelation. These subsequent embellishments may make us more comfortable, but they widen significantly the gap between the reality and our renditions of reality.

It is also important to appreciate that the human brain does not have a very effective mechanism for distinguishing between imagery derived from events that really happened and imagery related to imagination. We do not have a foolproof alerting mechanism that says to us "That image is fact" or "That image is fantasy." This might be viewed as a weakness in our memory system because it interferes with our ability to differentiate between reality and fantasy. In short, our thoughts and feelings about what we would like to believe happened often have the same status as the memory traces of what really occurred. These principles are applicable to adults and are even more applicable to children, whose mechanisms for such differentiations are even less efficient. No wonder, then, that children are so suggestible. No wonder, then, that they can be made to believe just about anything.

Studies on Children's Memory and Suggestibility

Myles-Worsley et al. (1986) studied preschool children's recollection of school events. They found that the children tended to fill in gaps in their memory by providing information from their general knowledge of school events. Brainerd and Ornstein (1991) also studied the incorporation of preexisting knowledge into verbalizations of retrieved memories. Their conclusion was, "One implication of the literature on children's knowledge is that with the passage of time, information in memory can be altered and interpreted more consistently in the light of prior knowledge. Memory, in short, may become more reconstructive and less reproductive."

All the aforementioned processes are present in adults who, presumably, we expect to be more accurate than children regarding their recollection of events. It is reasonable to view young children (under the age of four or five) to be particularly unreliable with regard to the accuracy of their recollection of events. And the longer the time gap between the actual early childhood event and the time when the child is asked to recall the event, the greater the likelihood there will be distortions. There is general agreement among those who study human memory that anyone (regardless of age) who claims recall of events prior to the age of one is probably fantasizing. Children in that age bracket do not have the cognitive ability to understand how events relate to one another, and so are not capable of storing accurate recollections of things that go on around them. Rather, their memories are much more general impressions that are highly distorted by strong emotional reactions. If this is true (and I believe it is), then the recent rash of public announcements of recollections of sex abuse prior to the age of one should be highly suspect. Most people cannot remember events before the age of four or five. It is reasonable to conclude that before that age, memories are primarily primitive pictures without significant coherence. It is also reasonable to conclude that individuals who claim accurate recollections before age four to five may very well be fantasizing, or they have come to believe what they have been told by parents and others about experiences that occurred to them during the two-to-four/five age range.

If one adds children's suggestibility, we have even further difficulty regarding the trustworthiness of children's memories. Children are ever trying to ingratiate themselves to adult authorities and will predictably alter their comments to gain such affection and/or to avoid the withdrawal of it. Although they may initially appreciate that they are altering the truth in the service of maintaining a good relationship with the interrogator, the alteration may become repeated and thereby change the initially stored impression. They are no different from adults in this regard; they are just more likely to exhibit these changes more quickly.

Memory for details is likely to be particularly faulty for events experienced during times of extreme stress. However, this does not mean that the individual loses totally the ability to recall everything about the stressful situation. But events that are recalled may be distorted. The whole body has been mobilized to deal with the danger (most often by fight or flight) and the individual's absorption in survival may preclude accurate recall of events. Under such circumstances, attention may be diverted from a wide variety of minor and, at that moment, irrelevant aspects of the event in order to focus on those elements necessary to attend to for the purposes of survival. A good example of this phenomenon is the experience of soldiers in combat who, following return from a combat zone, may note certain injuries for the first time, injuries that only then are noticed as extremely painful. Attending to the pain at the time of injury might have resulted in loss of life. Ceci (1991) describes just such a situation for the child who is a victim of sex abuse, which generally occurs "in the context of high levels of arousal; personal embarrassment; and a web of motives, threats, inducements, and suggestions that might tilt the odds one way or another that the victim will tell others what happened and tell them accurately or inaccurately." The absence of these elements in traditional laboratory studies cannot but compromise the reliability of the results. Flin (1991) also comments on the differences in the conditions of laboratory studies on memory and actual sexual-abuse events. She states, "Reporting a list of unrelated words is somewhat lacking in the emotional intensity of relating the intimate details of a sexual assault."

The examples presented above involve such a high degree of stress that the individual may actually dissociate the material. So many stimuli are entering the brain at the same time that it can be viewed as having short-circuited, thus producing amnesia, lack of memory for detail, perceptual distortions, and inability to appreciate the passage of time. When the distress is less severe and/or less acute, dissociation is not likely to occur, and the likelihood that the individual will remember the event is quite high. Stressful situations generally involve significant emotional concomitants and emotions, as mentioned, increase the likelihood that cognitive material will be embedded in the brain circuitry. This is the reason why it is highly unlikely that individuals forget completely highly traumatic experiences, especially those occurring over time.

It is important to appreciate that loss of memory is not always undesirable. In fact, as Toglia (1991) points out, it is adaptive. If we were to remember everything, it might drive us insane. This, apparently, was the situation for a patient of Luria (1968). Loftus and her colleagues have conducted many experiments that provide powerful verification for the position that the introduction of misleading postevent information competes with original information in such a way that it transforms an underlying memory and produces changes in the recollection of the event. The original memory is thereby altered, erased, or destroyed (Loftus, 1975; Loftus and Davies, 1984; Loftus et al., 1978; Loftus and Palmer, 1974; Loftus et al., 1985). In a typical experiment (original test procedure) the children first view a series of pictures depicting some event. They are then divided into two groups, those who are asked leading questions and those who are asked misleading questions about specific aspects of the original event. Last, they are tested on their memory for the originally observed details. In one variation the children view a series of slides depicting a little girl playing with a toy rabbit. Later, children in the misled group are told incorrectly that the girl had been playing with a toy dog, whereas subjects in the control group are not provided with any misinformation about the stuffed animal. In the final questioning period they are required to state whether it was a rabbit or a dog that they saw in the original pictures. Typically, the children in the misled group performed more poorly than those in the control (nonmisled group), because subjects in the misled group are more likely to report the misinformation (Zaragoza, 1991). It is important to appreciate that in these studies, although the children in the experimental (misled) group did more poorly than the control (nonmisled) group, there were still some children in the misled group who were not misled and recalled correctly the original animal. Accordingly, the introduction of misinformation does not necessarily result in memory impairment. To translate this into the realm of sexually abused children who may be providing false accusations (such as is often the case in nursery school and day-care center hysteria), there are still some children in these settings who deny they were abused, in spite of the parental and examiner coercions and introduction of misinformation.

Lindberg (1991) conducted a study in which three groups of children (third graders, sixth graders, and college students) were presented with a five-minute film about "a group of students who were taking a test." One group of subjects in each age group was told beforehand that the students in the film taking the test were a group of known cheaters. The other half were merely told that these were students taking a test. Subsequently, the students in the group that had been told that the film depicted cheaters were asked leading questions about cheating they observed in the film. In contrast, those who were not given this information beforehand were not asked misleading questions about cheating afterward. The third graders in the misled group said that 4.1 people cheated, and the college students in the misled group said that 2.52 people cheated. In contrast, both third graders and college students in the nonmisled group held that less than 2.0 people cheated. We see here yet another study confirming the effect of suggestion on children's memory. Interestingly, the youngest group remembered more of the incidental details than the oldest. Specifically, all subjects were asked to focus on the children, and no mention was made of focus on the teacher who gave the children instructions. The main recall levels for the third graders was 3.63, for the sixth graders, 3.08, and for the college students, 2.23. Accordingly, one cannot automatically state that memory improves with age and that younger subjects will remember more than older subjects for certain memory categories, in this case peripheral memory. However, these findings also confirm the well-known observation that younger children are less likely to pay attention to central issues than older children, issues they are asked to focus on by adult authorities.

Another question that must be considered when studying the relationship between memory and suggestibility is the presence of stress. Clearly, most children who are being sexually molested are being subjected to a psychological stress, and the question raised is whether their memory for the event is thereby affected. Peters (1991) studied two groups of children: one group was exposed to a fire-alarm situation while interacting with an examiner, and the other group was involved in a similar interaction, but without the fire-alarm condition. Not only did the children in the nonfire-alarm condition recall more accurately, but they were more susceptible to the influence of misleading questions. The author concludes, "Heightened arousal never increased the recognition or recall accuracy of our subjects."

Goodman (1991) provides a good review of some of the more important articles on the relationship between stress, suggestibility, and memory. The research findings are mixed, with some examiners reporting stress as having a positive effect on memory and other examiners reporting just the opposite. Goodman emphasizes the importance of studies that are designed to be ecologically valid, i.e., that attempt to reproduce the reality conditions "out there in the real world," as opposed to the laboratory. One problem with such research is the ethical one, namely, subjecting children to stress for the purposes of scientific research. Goodman also refers to her research on children's reactions to misleading questions and claims that children are particularly resistant to such questions, especially after the age of four. This has not been my experience. Furthermore, Goodman does not refer to children under the age of four, the ages of children involved in most nursery school and day-care center group-sex accusations. Also, in the divorce situation, many of the allegedly abused children are under four. My experience has been that children between three and four are the best subjects for programming a false sex-abuse accusation. Two-year-olds do not make reliable informants and five-year-olds are less readily brainwashed, although they are certainly not immune. Last, the examiners in her study do not subject the children to *repeated* misleading questions over weeks, months, and even years. Ethical researchers would not subject children to the unrelenting barrage of misleading questions to which children are frequently exposed in sex-abuse evaluations and interrogations. This is the true ecological ("real world" outside the laboratory) validity that is not taken into consideration in Goodman's studies.

Warren-Leubecker (1991) points out that studies on the relationship between stress and memory often fail to make proper differentiation between low, moderate, and high degrees of stress and that memory for events that take place under these three separate conditions might differ from one another, i.e., high degrees of stress might have different effects on memory than low degrees of stress.

Goodman and Clarke-Stewart (1991) point out the formidable difficulties in studying the effects of suggestibility on children's memories for sex abuse. The authors recognize that it is almost impossible to provide ecological validity for such studies because the examiners cannot actually observe sexual abuse taking place and then document children's memories for their experiences. Nor can the examiners actively abuse or threaten children for experimental purposes, nor can they pose as social workers or police about to remove children from their homes. Accordingly, the studies reported in this article focus on the suggestibility of nonabused children and their propensity to make false reports when nothing sexual or traumatic occurred. In their studies, such children are exposed to nonabusive events and then interviewed in ways that mimic important features of child-abuse investigations. In the first study discussed in this article, four- and seven-year-old children were asked to recall an observation made 10 to 12 days previously of a confederate playing a clown game with a child. The seven-year-olds were 93 percent accurate and the four-year-olds 83 percent accurate regarding questions about potentially abusive actions that did not take place. With regard to responses to misleading abuse questions, e.g., "He took your clothes off, didn't he?" "Did he kiss you?" no participant children and only one four-year-old bystander made a commission error. The authors conclude from this study that normal children are not suggestible with regard to misleading questions that imply sex abuse when it did not occur. The main flaw here is that the authors did not use two- and three-year-olds, the more common age range in which false sex-abuse accusations are most commonly seen. More importantly, they did not subject these children to the *barrage* of misleading questions that such children traditionally are exposed to by a *parade* of investigators over a long period.

In other studies described in this article, Goodman and Clarke-Stewart (1991) admit that a small percentage of children will indeed alter their memories in response to leading questions, but the authors come to the conclusion that because the average or *most* nonabused children resist suggestibility, children in general are not suggestible. From the point of view of the scientist, these findings may very well be useful. However, from the point of view of a person who is being falsely accused by this small percentage of suggestible children, the effects are devastating.

In another study reported in this article, children were asked four years later to recall a nonabuse interaction with an unfamiliar male confederate (subjects then seven and ten years old). Clarke-Stewart (in Goodman and Clarke-Stewart, 1991) states, "Some of the children's errors might lead to suspicion of abuse. For example, one child falsely affirmed that she had been given a bath, five children agreed to having been both hugged and kissed, and two children said 'yes' when asked if their picture had been taken in the bathtub. Nevertheless, the children were more resistant to abuse-related than to nonabuse-related suggestions." It is to be noted here that the total number of children in this study was 30: 15 seven-year-olds and 15 ten-year-olds. Accordingly, five children (17 percent) falsely claimed they had been hugged and kissed. This is typical of such studies, namely, that often as many as 20 percent of the children will give false-positive responses. Goodman is providing support here for her critics.

Goodman and Clarke-Stewart (1991) then discuss the studies of Clarke-Stewart et al. (1989). They focus here on their well-known study in which children observed a research confederate, "a janitor," either cleaning up and arranging toys (including dolls) or playing with the dolls in a rough and suggestive manner. The children were subsequently interrogated in different ways; however, misleading questions were introduced with varying degrees of pressure. The examiners were either neutral or incriminating regarding the behavior of the janitor, and in some cases they became progressively stronger and more accusatory. Goodman and Clarke-Stewart (1991) state, "Although all children who heard interrogations that were inconsistent with what they had observed eventually converted to the interrogators' view, some did so more rapidly." The authors' final summary is as follows:

> In sum, the children's interpretation of a somewhat ambiguous event was easily manipulated by an opinionated adult interviewer. In considering the implications of this research to sexual abuse investigations, however, the most important caveat to keep in mind is that the study did not involve allegations of sexual abuse but rather whether a janitor cleaned or played. Children may be more resistant to manipulation when the suggestions are about abusive acts, especially against the child himself or herself. (p. 102)

First, the statement is not valid. Some of the misleading questions were indeed of the type one sees in sex-abuse investigations. For example, the janitor did indeed look at and even clean the dolls' genital areas, and questions about this activity were asked. One of the misleading questions was, "Did he kiss the doll?" Some of the questions related to the janitor's "guilt" regarding whether he was doing his job or just "playing." And this in itself may suggest sexuality. In closing Goodman and Clarke-Stewart (1991) state, "The studies did not include the numerous interviews, examinations, and cross-examinations children often experience in actual cases. We did not imply to the children that our confederates were criminals, and we did not pose as legal authorities."

Steller (1991) is in agreement with me regarding the weaknesses of the aforementioned Goodman and Clarke-Stewart studies and supports those critical of their conclusions. He points out that in one such study, in which eight percent of the children made commission errors implying sex abuse, "This means 8% of the subjects of this condition made errors. Extrapolating this finding to forensic contexts produces an alarmingly high number of false accusations. It is reasonable to assume that the danger for analogous errors in real-life situations would be much greater than in the experimental setting."

Steller (1991) then continues:

> Goodman and Clarke-Stewart seem to have ignored their own findings in concluding that "it seems unlikely that normal children will easily yield to an interviewer's suggestion that something sexual occurred when in fact it did not." The dramatic finding was that one girl not only acquiesced to suggestions by nodding like others did, but also she "falsely claimed that the doctor had placed a stick in her rectum." The fact that the majority of children did resist overtly misleading questions is not an exciting finding; this would only be the case if one would make the assumption that all children are stupid. The finding that an erroneous allegation of extreme severity could be provoked in an experimental setting with a small sample of children is of striking importance for forensic investigations.
>
> Nobody with forensic experience would expect high frequencies of fictitious allegations of sexual abuse. In practice, the difficult detection task is to identify the false alarms, which apparently do occur to an unknown and probably low degree. According to the findings obtained by Goodman and Clarke-Stewart, they occur even under experimental conditions in which less powerful suggestive influences can be expected than under the conditions of real-life interviews conducted by parents, laypersons, and poorly trained professionals. (p. 108)

McGough (1991a) states the following about the aforementioned research of Goodman and Clarke-Stewart:

> The current legal system does little to recreate the kinds of conditions conducive to the elicitation of a reliable account by the child. In an adversarial system of justice, there are few neutral players. Given an authoritarian interviewer (police officer, criminal investigator, parent, or defense counsel), who may be consciously or subconsciously motivated to influence the child's memory; given multiple pretrial interviews; given a child's increased memory-fade over time; and given substantial inter-

vals between the observed events and testimony at trial, substantial impairment of a child's memories seems inevitable. (p. 116)

McGough (1991a) suggests, with regard to Goodman's studies:

> Both series of experiments converge to underscore the importance of the initial interview for the elicitation of an unbiased account, for the preservation of that version against later potential contamination, and perhaps to inoculate the child against predictable subsequent attempts to interfere with his or her autonomous memory. The recording of an unbiased initial interview of the child is the keystone to reform of the current processes. If a solid record were required to be made in any case involving a child witness, then no matter what pressures were thereafter brought to bear upon the child, the child and the legal system would have a benchmark against which subsequent changes could be evaluated for improper suggestiveness. (p. 117)

I am in full agreement with this recommendation. Of course, those who are staunchly convinced that "children never lie" would interpret such a nonrevealing interview to indicate that the child was too frightened and/or embarrassed to reveal all the details and that one could only expect such divulgences to take place in the context of a series of interviews with a known interviewer. This is again an example of the no-win situation in which many people accused of sex abuse find themselves.

Davies et al. (1988) compared seven- to eight-year-olds with nine- to ten-year-olds and eleven- to twelve-year-olds regarding their memory, two weeks later, about a visitor to their school, with whom each of the children had been asked to help set up equipment for a talk on road safety. Two weeks later each child was questioned about the visitor and was asked to identify the visitor's picture from a 12-picture array. When the array did not contain a picture of the visitor, children in each category made false identifications. The rate was 88 percent for the seven- to eight-year-olds and 60 percent for the older children. Once again we see the enormous effect of suggestibility on children's memory. And once again we see demonstrated that younger children are more likely to provide false information than older ones.

Dent (1991) points out that an important variable when comparing studies about the relationship between children's suggestibility and memory is the time interval between the event being recalled and the request for such recollection. Studies vary enormously on this point. Considering the universal agreement that memory fades with time, the failure to standardize this factor makes it very difficult to compare one study with another. Dent's studies also indicate that recall is greater when children are provided with specific closed-ended questions, e.g., "What color was the man's hair?" than when asked open-ended questions like, "Can you tell me what the man looked like?"

Raskin and Esplin (1991) emphasize the motivational element in the distortion of memory for events. For example, a disinterested witness to a crime is likely to have very different motivation for recollection than a person who has been the subject of the criminal act. Raskin and Esplin describe a technique for assessing credibility, namely, a technique that they refer to as *criteria-based content analysis* (CBCA) (Raskin and Steller, 1989; Raskin and Esplin, 1991). This technique is based on the work of Undeutsch (1989), who referred to the procedure as *statement reality analysis*. The technique is based on the assumption that the substantive content of a true statement will be different from that of a false (fabricated or delusional) statement. Undeutsch uses as his foundation data the statements made by tens of thousands of sexually abused children in Germany. When utilizing the method, it is important that the interviewer see the child as soon after the abuse as possible and not introduce contaminating elements in the course of the interview. When utilizing the criteria it is necessary to consider the age, experience, and cognitive ability of the witness. The examiner must be familiar with the typical kinds of statements that would be made at the various age levels. There are 19 areas of criteria related to such considerations, including the logical relationship between the components, the degree of organization, the presence of specific details, the nature of conversations, the presence of unusual details, the nature of the child's subjective mental state, changes and corrections in the description, and the similarity of the general account to that of bona fide situations.

McGough (1991b) is critical of Raskin's system because it goes against a basic tenet of the Anglo-American legal system, which is that the court and the juries are the ones who are responsible for ascertaining a witness's credibility; experts, no matter how great their expertise, are not as reliable in accomplishing this goal. McGough is reflecting here the traditional legal view. I believe that we in psychiatry and psychology have developed special techniques in recent years to enable us to assess credibility in ways superior to that of the traditional legal system, especially because we have the opportunity to interview directly—in a noncontrived setting—all three parties involved in an accusation: the accuser, the accused, and the alleged victim. I personally believe that Undeutsch, Raskin, Esplin, and others who work with CBCA are making important contributions. My only criticism is that they give too much weight to the child's statements and not enough focus on the interviews of the accuser and the accused, even though they certainly recognize the importance of such assessments.

Wells and Loftus (1991) are somewhat dubious about a scorer's capacity to properly take into consideration the different developmental levels that the examiner is required to appreciate if one is to properly assess a child's scores on the CBCA. The simple instruction that the examiner "consider" age is not, in their opinion, sufficient. Even were the examiner to use formalized standardized tests that might give some assessment of the child's developmental-cognitive level, it would still be difficult to apply these findings to the CBCA. She further criticizes the CBCA on the grounds that studies have not yet been done on its interevaluator reliability. Davies (1991) makes reference to a previous study (Davies et al., 1989), in which groups of children interacted with strangers playing the role of a public health official. A week later the children were questioned about the incident and asked to compile a composite picture of the stranger's face. One child was particularly unsure about the meeting but, after being reminded about it, proceeded to create the composite face. The investigators considered his composite to be in the average-to-poor range. They subsequently learned that this child had not been included in the previous study, but had the same name as a child who was a participant and had inadvertently been brought back a week later under the assumption that he had originally been involved in the study. We see here a good example of a child's suggestibility and the desire to ingratiate himself to adult authority.

King and Yuille (1987) conducted a study in which children in four age groups (6, 9, 11, and 16–17) were seated alone in a room when a stranger entered with plant-care equipment and tended some plants. Before leaving, the stranger noted the time, indicated that it was late, and had to leave. During the subsequent interview each child was asked, "On which arm did the man wear his watch?" In reality, the man had not worn a watch. Each child was also asked whether scissors had been used to remove a leaf. Actually, a leaf had been removed, but by hand, and scissors, which were in clear view, were not used. The younger children tended to agree with the misleading suggestions whereas the older children did not. The authors also concluded that "the less a child remembers about the event the more he can be misled, and the younger the child the less he will remember." This comment has particular relevance to sex-abuse evaluations because the child who is falsely accusing will have no actual memory of the event and so is more likely to provide "fill-ins" via misleading information provided by interrogators.

Goleman (1988) describes a study conducted by M. Lewis. In this study three-year-olds were asked to remain alone in a room and the examiner, before leaving, set up an attractive toy behind the child's back and told him (her) not to look at it while the examiner was out of the room. The children were observed through a one-way mirror. Only ten percent of the children didn't peek while the examiner was gone. Of the rest, a third admitted they had peeked, a third lied and denied that they had done so, and a third refused to say one way or the other. In short, about two-thirds of the children were deceitful, in that they either lied by omission or lied by commission. This study has less bearing on suggestibility than it has on children's susceptibility to fabrication. Saywitz (1987) states that children are apt to add material when they do not remember. Accordingly, when one asks a child for elaborations with questions such as "What else?" the child is likely to add extraneous and contradictory information.

The most comprehensive work on the subject of children's memory and suggestibility is *Jeopardy in the Courtroom* (Ceci and Bruck, 1995). Ceci has provided what I consider to be the most useful review of the literature on this subject. He includes powerful examples of children's suggestibility from many recent high-profile cases such as the McMartin case (California), the Little Rascals case (North Carolina), the Country Walk case (Florida), the Kelly Michaels case (New Jersey), and the Old Cutler case (Florida). He also includes some of his own seminal studies in this area. The book provides compelling evidence for children's suggestibility and the ways in which their recollections can be manipulated by adults.

PSYCHODYNAMIC FACTORS OPERATIVE IN CHILDREN'S FALSE ACCUSATIONS OF SEX ABUSE

Introduction

There are no "typical" psychodynamic patterns in children who provide false sex-abuse accusations. This is especially the case because there are a variety of settings in which such accusations may be seen. Here I focus on the two most common settings for such accusations, namely, the day-care center and the child custody dispute. Although there are certainly differences in the psychodynamic patterns that may operate in these two situations, there is significant overlap. In addition, factors that may be operative for older children may be less applicable to younger ones. Here I will focus on those psychological factors that are more likely to be operative in younger children, especially those between ages three and five, the most common age bracket in which one sees such false accusations. As mentioned, two-year-olds are too young to be reliable subjects for such inculcation, and children over five are less likely to distort reality. These are the children who are the most suggestible and whose memories can be "expanded" in such a way that they may predictably provide false sex-abuse accusations.

Ingratiation to Adult Authorities

Children are constantly trying to ingratiate themselves to adults, especially to adults in authority, like parents, teachers, and professionals such as physicians, lawyers, and judges. Like all of us, they want to be liked. If lying will serve this end, they are likely to do so. In divorce situations children predictably lie and say to each parent what that parent wants to hear, especially regarding criticisms of the other. This is the most common way they deal with the loyalty conflicts that emerge from divorce and especially from custody disputes. Children embroiled in a custody dispute know where their "bread is buttered." They know that when with parent A, if they express affection for parent B, they may alienate parent A. In contrast, if they join in with parent A and provide criticisms of parent B (new ammunition or more ammunition), they will ingratiate themselves to parent A. And the same procedure is used with parent B. The same principle holds when children are being interviewed by validators. They want to ingratiate themselves to them and get the "right answers." If the validator starts with the position that the sex abuse did indeed take place, the child is likely to pick this up quite early in the interview and provide just the responses that the evaluator wants to hear. This tendency of children makes it easy for evaluators to get them to say anything they want. It is almost like taking candy from a baby. Because of the child's naiveté, cognitive immaturity, and suggestibility, the job is made even easier and the child may not realize how preposterous the elicited statements and testimonials are.

The Keeping-up-with-the-Joneses Phenomenon

The examiner must appreciate that children in the nursery school setting who allege sex abuse may be doing so as a manifestation of what I refer to as the keeping-up-with-the-Joneses phenomenon. After all, if all the other kids are professing sex abuse, why be the only one who doesn't? The others claim that they were at the party where everyone got undressed. The child certainly does not want to admit that he (she) was the only one not invited to that party. The child may initially recognize that there was no such "party" but, after a series of the kinds of coercive interviews frequently conducted in sex-abuse investigations, may actually come to believe that he (she) did attend. And this is another important point. What originally may have been a fabrication or an idea introduced by another comes to be believed by the child. The fabrication then becomes a delusion. This is a common phenomenon. And these false beliefs may become so deeply entrenched that the child may accept them as valid throughout the course of life. I recall seeing one child whose class was given a presentation on sex-abuse prevention. At the end of the presentation the children were asked if anyone had ever touched them in "bad places." First, no child responded. The presenter then asked, "Are you sure?" Then, very hesitantly, one girl raised her hand and pointed to her vaginal area and whispered, "My daddy touches me there." Within a minute two other little girls imitated the exact same gesture and claimed that their daddys too had touched them "down there." All three fathers were reported to child protection services. I myself was involved in one of the cases and found absolutely no evidence that the child had ever been sexually abused.

In another case a four-year-old girl was watching a "Mr. Belvedere" television program devoted to child sex abuse. Near the end of the program Mr. Belvedere himself asked the viewers directly if they themselves had ever been touched in "bad places." He instructed those who had been subjected to such touching to inform the appropriate parent or proper authority. The parents of the child I was seeing were involved in a custody dispute. The child reported the "bad touches" to her mother, who immediately called her lawyer and the social worker whom she was seeing for therapy. Both immediately instructed her to contact child protection services. Again, by the time I saw this child, the father and the child—and even the mother—were psychological "basket cases," and I saw absolutely no evidence that this child had ever been sexually molested.

In another case two sisters, ages two and four, had spent two weeks in a shelter with their mother, who had fled from her husband because of "physical abuse." Actually, the husband had not ever touched the mother, but she was going to use the sojourn in the shelter as confirmatory evidence that her husband had indeed abused her. She was planning to leave him and anticipated that this would support her allegations in a forthcoming child custody dispute. In the shelter were many children who had indeed been sexually abused. In fact, the social worker who was assigned to the children's mother said, "Just about every child who comes here has been sexually abused. At first, they don't talk about it, but after a few days here it all comes out." Not once did it ever enter her head that the children might be picking up "stories" from others in the shelter. Not surprisingly, the two little girls I am discussing here picked up some of the ambient accusations and, not surprisingly again, the mother attempted to use these as well as ammunition in her custody dispute. What is saddest here is that the mother actually believed that her children had been sexually abused by her husband and did not appreciate the obvious fact that they were manifesting the keeping-up-with-the-Joneses phenomenon.

Enhanced Attention and Notoriety

Then there is the element of enhanced attention and even notoriety. Many of these children are surrounded by an army of people who provide them with significant attention. Mother may be listening to the child with a degree of concentration never before enjoyed by the child. She is ever walking around with pencil and paper, ready to note down what to the child may be the most meaningless and absurd comments. But soon the child picks up the particular areas that are most likely to attract attention and "stop people in their tracks." The child learns those comments that will distract the mother from other activities, like attending to other siblings or spending time with friends and neighbors. Then there are the child protection workers, the lawyers, the psychologists and psychiatrists, the prosecutors, and the judges. Neighborhood people are constantly "buzzing" about the sex-abuse scandal that took place in the child's nursery school. The children are pointed to by friends and neighbors as the ones who attend "that" nursery school that we all heard about. Many of these cases are given significant coverage by the public media. Reporters, TV announcers, and even appearances on television are possible. All this attention can be enormously gratifying to the child, who may recognize, at some level, that if nothing ever happened, then all these people would evaporate and the notoriety would come to an end.

Mappan (1980) considered the attention-getting factor to be an important one operative for the children in the Salem Witch Trials. Mappan quotes from the account given by Charles Upham (1802–1875) in his book, *Salem Witchcraft* (1867):

> At this point, if Mr. Parris [father of one of the accusing girls], the ministers, and magistrates had done their duty, the mischief might have been stopped. The girls ought to have been rebuked for their dangerous and forbidden sorceries and divinations, their meetings broken up, and all such tamperings with alleged supernaturalism and spiritualism frowned

upon. Instead of this, the neighboring ministers were summoned to meet at Mr. Parris's house to witness the extraordinary doings of the girls, and all they did was to endorse, and pray over, them. Countenance was thus given to their pretensions and the public confidence in the reality of their statements established. Magistrates from the town, church members, leading people, and people of all sorts, flocked to witness the awful power of Satan, as displayed in the tortures and contortions of the "afflicted children" who became objects of wonder, so far as their feats were regarded, and of pity in view of their agonies and convulsions. (p. 38)

Here we see how the girls, instead of being rebuked and ignored, were surrounded by an army of "ministers . . . magistrates from the town, church members, leading people, and people of all sorts." Replace these individuals with validators, psychologists, prosecutors, lawyers, friends and relatives, newspaper reporters, and television coverage and we see a repetition of the same phenomenon. In both cases the children become "objects of wonder."

Release of Hostility

All human beings must learn to deal with frustration. After all, we can only have a small fraction of all those things in life we would like to possess and so frustration is an inevitable part of the human condition. And frustration, when it persists, ultimately leads to anger. We cannot release our anger whenever and wherever we want. To do so would result in significant rejection and retaliation by significant figures around us. In early childhood we must first learn various techniques for dealing with anger, techniques that suppress, repress, and/or allow for its expression in a wide variety of ways, both healthy and pathological. A socially acceptable scapegoat provides one such mechanism of release.

In the divorce situation the child may have much to be angry about. The parent who leaves the home (usually the father) is generally viewed as an abandoner. Even though he may claim that he no longer loves the mother—but he still loves the children—from their vantage point he has abandoned the household and his reasons and justifications have little meaning for them. Their general position is, "If you really loved us you would stay. If you really loved us you would tolerate all the indignities, frustrations, and abominations you claim you are subjected to at the hands of our mother." Having little if any ability to place themselves in the position of the father, they can more comfortably subscribe to this somewhat egocentric position. There may be financial privations that engender even more anger. And when one adds to these predictable sources of hostility a parent's programming the children to view the other party as the incarnation of all the evil that ever existed in the history of the world, then even more anger is generated. And this situation, of course, leads to the development of a parental alienation syndrome (Gardner, 1992d), a disorder in which the child is programmed into a campaign of vilification and deprecation of a father. It is not difficult to see how a false sex-abuse accusation can develop under these circumstances because it predictably allows for the expression of hostility in a way that is being sanctioned by the programming parent.

In the nursery school situation the accused teachers and other day-care personnel serve as useful scapegoats for the pent-up angers of the parents and, subsequently, the children. It is almost as if most of the anger that inevitably derives from other sources is funneled into the diatribes against the alleged abusers. It is almost as if nothing other than the accused perpetrators bothers these people. What is striking in these cases is the degree of sadism that many of these children may exhibit. In many of these cases I have been impressed by what I consider to be the innate cruelty of children, a cruelty that lies just beneath the surface and is not significantly suppressed or repressed by the adult authorities who are bringing them up and educating them. These children also become used by women who harbor within themselves significant animosity toward all men. I am referring here to zealous feminists and/or women who were sexually abused as children, as well as others who, for whatever reason, harbor enormous rage toward men. They help fuel the rage that these children exhibit toward the accused. Once again, Mappan (1980) quotes Upham (1867):

> They [the accusing children] appeared as the prosecutors of every poor creature that was tried, and seemed ready to bear testimony against any one upon whom suspicion might happen to fall. It is dreadful to reflect upon the enormity of their wickedness, if they were conscious of imposture throughout. It seems to transcend the capabilities of human

crime. There is, perhaps, a slumbering element in the heart of man that sleeps forever in the bosom of the innocent and good, and requires the perpetration of a great sin to wake it into action, but which, when once aroused, impels the transgressor onward with increasing momentum, as the descending ball is accelerated in its course. It may be that crime begets an appetite for crime, which, like all other appetites, is not quieted but inflamed by gratification. (p. 37)

Infectiousness of Emotions

Then there is what I refer to as the vibrating-tuning-fork principle. This relates to the infectiousness of emotions. Emotions have a way of transmitting themselves from one individual to another, often in very rapid fashion. Walk into a room in which people are grieving for the death of a loved one. The visitor may not even know the deceased but, in a few minutes, may find himself (herself) crying or at least depressed. Comedians know well that they are far less likely to be successful with small audiences than large audiences. The large audience provides him or her with the opportunity for spreading the laughter to those who initially might not have been swept up. The same phenomenon is operative in mass hysteria (Gardner, 1991a). All of these examples operate like vibrating tuning forks: take two tuning forks of the same fixed intrinsic frequency of vibration. Strike one and hold the second (unstruck) close by. Almost immediately the second one will start to vibrate in unison with the first. Children living in a home with an enraged parent who is preoccupied with anger and who may in addition have hysterical outbursts of rage are likely to "vibrate" with such a parent and join in with similar emotions. Without knowing the exact reasons why they are so swept up, they may provide the kinds of rationalizations that result in the preposterous scenarios already described.

Reactions to Normal Childhood Sexuality

Sigmund Freud (1905) referred to children as "polymorphous perverse." I am in full agreement with Freud on this point. Children normally exhibit just about any kind of sexual behavior imaginable:

heterosexual, homosexual, bisexual, and autosexual. Infants have no problem caressing any part of anyone's body, whether it be a private part or a public part. And they have absolutely no concern for the gender of the possessor of the target part. Nor do they concern themselves with that person's sexual orientation. They will put into their mouths any object that will fit, whether it be their own or someone else's. They touch all parts of their own bodies and attempt to touch all parts of other people's bodies. In short, they touch, suck, insert, smell, and feel all of their own parts as well as of other human beings and make no particular discriminations regarding the age, sex, or relationship to them of the object of their "sexual" advances. Each society has its own list (most often quite specific) regarding which types of sexual behavior are acceptable and which are prohibited. Generally, parents provide this information in the early years of the child's life and react quite strongly when the child attempts to engage in one of the unacceptable forms of sexual behavior, that is, unacceptable in accordance with the consensus of individuals in the particular society in which the child has been born.

In our society we generally attempt to lead the child down the heterosexual track, but even here we suppress heterosexual behaviors to varying degrees up until the time of marriage and even afterward. Even in the marital bed, most subscribe to a particular "list" of behaviors that are acceptable and may exhibit strong revulsion when a spouse requests a sexual encounter that is not on the "list." But even when social suppression and repression have been successful (regarding overt behavior), residua of the early primitive polymorphous perversity persist. These suppressed impulses can be gratified in fantasy, symbolism, or vicariously by thinking about others who engage in these activities. Psychiatrists refer to those whose primary orientation is a residuum of the unacceptable and/or atypical as psychopathological or symptomatic. The man in the street will refer to these individuals as perverted. Many years ago, during my residency training, I came to this conclusion: We label as perverts those who engage in sexual behaviors that we personally find disgusting. Because their behavior disgusts us, it is probable that we are suppressing and/or repressing our own unconscious desires to engage in the very behavior we so detest.

Some examples: A three-year-old boy is playing with his penis. Many parents would hold that masturbation is a perfectly natural act but tell the child that what he is doing is a personal matter and should not be done in front of other people. The child might also be told that if he wishes to engage in that behavior, he should do so in the privacy of his own room. This is the kind of comment that many educated parents would tell their children at this time. However, even this comment communicates certain socially induced restrictions and prohibitions. The boy would not be told that it is improper in public to stick his finger in his ear, to scratch his head, or to rub his knee. It is just the genital area that requires seclusion if there is to be any kind of hand contact. Other parents might react differently. Some would do everything possible to stop the child from engaging in the activity. They might use physical restraints (quite common in the late 19th century) or threaten the boy that they will take him to the doctor and have his penis cut off. (This is what happened to Freud's famous patient, Little Hans [Freud, 1909].) The first child grows up "normal" with regard to masturbation, confining himself to doing it only in private places and not publicly. The second child might develop inhibitions in this area, and even "castration anxiety," as did Little Hans.

A little girl rubs her vulva and clitoris and then enjoys smelling the vaginal secretions on her fingers. Again, there is a wide variety of parental responses. However, in our society, even those who approve of masturbation might not approve of the olfactory sequela. Because cunnilingus is generally acceptable behavior in male/female heterosexuality (in our society at this time), it is acceptable for men to enjoy smelling these female secretions—but not women. We have a double standard here—a double standard that may contribute to a woman's feeling of disgust over the odors of her own genitals.

It is acceptable for male and female infants to enjoy sucking breasts. After the weaning period, children learn that breast sucking is only for infants. Men are allowed to engage in this "infantile" behavior as part of normal foreplay, but women who maintain a desire for such activity might be labeled as having "lesbianic tendencies"—without any connotation that this might be part of the normal female repertoire.

A three-year-old girl and her four-year-old brother are taking a shower with their father. In the course of the frolicking, each child might entertain a transient fantasy of putting the father's penis in his (her) mouth. Considering the relative heights of the three individuals, and considering the proximity of the children's mouths to the father's penis under these circumstances, it is not surprising that such a fantasy might enter each of the children's minds. It might even be expressed in the form of the children's saying laughingly, "I'm going to bite off your penis." Being so close at the time of their lives when they insert everything in sight into their mouths, it is not surprising that this fellatio fantasy is evoked in the shower. In this setting, they may both learn that this is unacceptable behavior. However, residua of these fantasies and drives may very well persist into adult life. The woman is freer to express these in a heterosexual encounter with a man (who is likely to derive great pleasure from the act). However, the boy who exhibits a continued interest in such behavior will at best be considered to have "homosexual tendencies" and may very well be considered a homosexual. Again, we see the very specific selection process and the special gender requirements for each of the sexes.

Anal functions are probably subjected to the most vigorous prohibitions. It is acceptable to say (under certain very restricted and specific circumstances) that one has had a good bowel movement and that one has enjoyed a sense of relief and pleasure. Men (especially adolescent boys) in our society are much freer to make such comments than women, but I cannot imagine that women do not enjoy the same sensations. In old-age homes, however, there appears to be gender-blind permissiveness with regard to a discussion of this topic. Anal stimulation in sexual encounters, however, is generally frowned upon and is viewed as "disgusting" and "perverted." Infants, before they have learned about these social attitudes, have no problem playing with their (or anyone else's) anus or feces—smelling, licking, and even putting such waste in their mouths.

Our attitudes toward flatus is a good example of the power of the social influence on the selective process. It is reasonable to assume that the odor of flatus is approximately the same for all individuals (within a relatively narrow range). The metabolic processes that result in the formation of these gases are quite similar in all physically healthy human beings. Yet, we generally are disgusted by the flatus of other people, but not by our own. We are generally disgusted with the sounds that other people emit when they pass gas, but we do not feel such revulsion when we ourselves create identical sounds. And this distinction (the reader will please excuse this very subtle pun) is socially learned.

My main point, for the purposes of this book, is that the *normal* child exhibits a wide variety of sexual fantasies and behaviors, many of which would be labeled as "sick" or "perverted" if exhibited by adults. I am not claiming that every child fantasizes about every type of sexual activity in the human repertoire. Each child is likely to have a "favorite" list of sexual activities that provide interest and pleasure. Those who claim that children who verbalize such fantasies or exhibit such behaviors could not have had any actual experiences in these areas have little understanding (or memory) of normal child sexuality. Those who have gone further and have considered such manifestations as "proof" that a child has been sexually abused have caused many truly innocent individuals an enormous amount of harm, even to the point of long prison sentences.

A four-year-old girl, for example, may harbor, among her collection of polymorphous perverse fantasies, thoughts about some kinds of sexual encounters with her father. Freud referred to these as oedipal fantasies. Although I am in agreement with Freud that such fantasies are quite common, I am not in agreement with him that they are at the root of most, if not all, childhood and adult psychoneurotic processes. The fantasies do not necessarily involve sexual intercourse; in fact, the younger the child, the less the likelihood she is going to envision the particular sexual act. Rather, the fantasies are a more general and primitive type involving various kinds of contact with various parts of each other's bodies. Expressing these fantasies in the last part of the 20th century may be quite dangerous. In the middle third of this century the child might be brought into deep psychoanalysis (four to five times a week, for example). In contrast, at the end of the century, the mother may call a lawyer and drag the child through a series of interrogations described in detail throughout the course of this book.

Shakespeare was right: "Lord, what fools these mortals be!" (*A Midsummer Night's Dream*). When a child expresses such a fantasy at this time in our history, everyone's ears prick up. Immediately the child senses that she has "dropped a bomb." Immediately the child senses that what she has said is "wrong" or "bad" or "dangerous." Immediately the child recognizes that she must defend herself and exonerate herself. Sometimes she is given a hint regarding how to respond by the parent who angrily inquires, "Who taught you that?" or "Where did you hear about that?" If the parents are involved in a vicious custody dispute and the child recognizes full well that the mother relishes any information critical of the father, the child is likely to blurt out, "My daddy." With lightning speed the mother calls her lawyer. If a child is going to nursery school and there is an opportunity to sue, again with lightning speed the mother calls a lawyer. If the child is found touching herself (which, in the view of some fanatic validators is only done by sexually abused children), the child may also be asked, "Who taught you that?" The idea that no one taught her *that*—and that she taught herself—is not given consideration at all. Sometimes the child will provide another universal response, "My daddy made me do it" (that is, touch herself). Sometimes the routes to the perpetrator are a little more circuitous.

Sometimes the child will point the finger at a sibling as the initiator or the coercer of the sexual activities. But there is little to be gained by an angry mother if the culprit is another child. There are none of the advantages that one can enjoy when the perpetrator is an adult. Immediately, an inquiry is conducted regarding where the *other* child learned to do these terrible things and it is not long before an appropriate "perpetrator" is identified. The notion that the child may have learned additional sexual things (beyond the aforementioned self-learned material) is not given consideration. The idea that the child may have acquired some of the sexual verbalizations from prevention programs, television programs, sex-abuse prevention books and audiotapes, and the ambient saturation with sexuality is not given consideration by such parents and the overzealous evaluators to whom they bring their children.

Psychodynamic Factors Conducive to the Development of a Parental Alienation Syndrome

Some of the aforementioned psychodynamic factors may contribute to the development of a parental alienation syndrome (Gardner, 1992d), especially release of hostility, ingratiation to adult authority, and the infectiousness of emotions. These factors were mentioned above because they may also operate in the sex-abuse hysteria situation. There are other factors that contribute to a false sex-abuse accusation in the context of a child custody dispute, factors that operate in bringing about a parental alienation syndrome but are not likely to be present in the nursery school situation. These factors contribute primarily to the development of the parental alienation syndrome, which may serve as a foundation for the sex-abuse accusation. Typically, the sex-abuse accusation comes forth at some point after the development of the syndrome, a point when less punitive and less effective exclusionary maneuvers may not have proven successful.

Maintenance of the Primary Psychological Bond In most traditional families, the child's psychological bond with the mother is stronger than that which it has with the father. Actually, the child is psychologically bonded to both parents, but there is generally a stronger bonding with the parent who was the primary caretaker in the earliest years of the child's life. In a child custody dispute, there is the threat of rupture of the primary psychological bond, especially in recent years when the court's determinations regarding parental preference are presumably sex blind, and attempts are made to bring about a 50/50 time-sharing arrangement between the parents. The child's campaign of denigration of the father, then, is an attempt to maintain the maternal tie. A sex-abuse accusation may be one of the criticisms directed at the father. The criticism may be generated from the recognition that it pleases the mother and therefore will result in a strengthening of the psychological bond with her.

Fear of Alienating the Preferred Parent In addition to the aforementioned factor—preservation of the psychological bond with the preferred parent—is the fear of alienation of the preferred parent (again, usually the mother). In the usual divorce situation, it is the father who has left the home. He has thereby created for himself the reputation of being the rejector and the abandoner. No matter how justified his leaving the home, the children will generally view him as an abandoner. Having already been abandoned by one parent, the children are not going to risk abandonment by the second. Accordingly, they fear expressing resentment to the remaining parent (usually the mother) and will automatically take her position in any conflict with the father. By joining forces with her in her campaign of vengeance and vilification of the father, they reduce the risk of her loss of affection. Again, hatching a sex-abuse scenario is likely to have a cohesive effect (admittedly in a sick way) on the relationship with the mother and thereby assuage rejection and abandonment fears.

Reaction Formation A common factor that contributes to the obsessive hatred of the father is the utilization of the reaction formation mechanism. Obsessive hatred is often a thin disguise for deep love. This is especially the case when there is absolutely no reason to justify the preoccupation with the hated person's defects. True rejection is neutrality, when there is little if any thought of the person. The opposite of love is not hate, but indifference. Each time these children think about how much they hate their fathers, they are still thinking about them. Although the visual imagery may involve hostile fantasies, their fathers are still very much on their minds. The love, however, is expressed as hate in order to assuage the guilt they would feel over overt expression of affection for their fathers, especially in their mothers' presence. This guilt is often coupled with the aforementioned fear of their mothers' rejection if such expressions of affection for their fathers were to be overtly expressed. One boy, when alone with me, stated, "I'm bad for wanting to visit with my father." This was a clear statement of guilt over his wish to visit with his father, his professions of hatred notwithstanding. This child was not born with the idea that it is bad to want to spend time with his father. Rather, he was programmed by his mother to feel guilty for having such thoughts.

A sex-abuse accusation may be added to the collection of other indignities that the father has allegedly perpetrated on the child. Previously, in the section on reactions to normal childhood sexuality, in my discussion on the sex-abuse accusation as a derivative of normal childhood sexuality, I mentioned sexual fantasies involving the father. However, I was referring here to pleasant and enjoyable fantasies. By the process of reaction formation one can turn these into unpleasant ones and thereby assuage the guilt that would be experienced if the child were to accept the fact that sexual activities are what she wants. Instead of saying, "I would love to have some sexual involvement with my father," she can say, "I hate having a sexual relationship with my father." Yet, the fantasy in both cases may be very similar if not identical. The child may not fully appreciate the significance of the terms *sexual inter-*

course and *rape*, especially the traumatic and coercive elements involved. To the child these are merely acts in which a penis is inserted into her vagina. She may not even appreciate that the attempt to do this would be extremely painful and traumatic. Accordingly, her fantasy "I want him to rape me" can be transformed, by reaction formation, to "I hate the idea of his raping me." And this may be projected out onto the father. The child is essentially saying, "It is not I who want him to rape me, it is he who wants to rape me." This too is guilt assuaging.

Identification with the Aggressor The identification-with-the-aggressor phenomenon may be operative. In identification with the aggressor, a person who is in a weak or impotent position in relation to a more overpowering, threatening individual may deal with the situation by taking on the characteristics of the stronger person. In this way the individual compensates for the feelings of insecurity and the sense of impotency attendant to being weak and vulnerable. The child whose raging mother is incessantly denigrating his father may join forces with her in an attempt to protect himself from being the target of her enormous hostility. He does this from the fear that if he were to join in with his father, he too would be the target of such violent outbursts. The mechanism is operative in the old principle, "If you can't fight 'em, join 'em." Also operative here is the "There-but-for-the-grace-of-God-go-I" mechanism. By joining the mother, the child can say to himself (herself), "If I did not do so I might be in father's position." Also operative here is the mechanism of jumping on the bandwagon of the stronger party in order to share in the joys of victory. In the course of such warfare the child uses any ammunition put into its hands by the aggressor, including a sex-abuse accusation.

Identification with an Idealized Person Related to the identification-with-the-aggressor phenomenon is the process of identification with an idealized person. In the course of the mother's deprecation, the father becomes viewed as loathsome, worthless, and an individual with few if any admirable qualities. Identification with and emulation of such a person becomes compromised. Deprived of an admirable father for identification, the child may then switch to the mother as the only person to emulate. At the same time that she denigrates the father, she is likely to whitewash herself. The identification, then, is with a perfect individual, and this is viewed as a way of attaining the state of perfection oneself. The psychological fusion that takes place here contributes to the development of the folie-à-deux relationship so commonly seen in the parental alienation syndrome. This contributes to the child's exaggerated reactions to any criticisms the father may have about the mother. Such a child operates on the principle, "I'm like her. When he criticizes her, it's the same as criticizing me." In the course of such identification, the child accepts as gospel everything the mother says, including trumped-up accusations of sex abuse.

Release of Hostility The development of a parental alienation syndrome can serve as a vehicle for the release of anger, which may have a variety of sources. It is as if it allows for the "sucking in" of a wide variety of anger-evoking experiences and allows for a sanctioned release of them, at least by the mother. If not for the presence of the parental alienation syndrome, such anger might have been suppressed, repressed, or channeled into other modes of release, both healthy and pathological. Mention has already been made of the anger engendered by the father's leaving the home, an act that is viewed as an abandonment. There may be anger at the father for the financial compromises that are most often attendant to divorce—especially a litigated divorce. When parents are swept up in their divorce and custody-dispute hostilities, they pay less attention to their children, and this produces frustration and anger in them. Not only are the children deprived of attention, but even when they are focused on, the parents have little leftover emotion for their children, so drained have they been by the divorce hostilities. There may be anger over the presence of new partners in their parents' lives. These strangers were rarely invited and, in most circumstances, are viewed as unwelcome intruders. However, the children are impotent over their presence and are most often resentful of them. There may be anger over the thwarting of reconciliation preoccupations that, as time goes on, become ever more futile—especially if new persons appear on the scene. Elsewhere (Gardner, 1976, 1979, 1986, 1991b, 1991c), I have discussed in detail these and other sources of anger for children of divorce, especially those involved in custody disputes.

Sexual Rivalry Sexual factors and sexual rivalry factors are sometimes operative in the alienation. A girl who has a seductive and romanticized relationship with her father (sometimes abetted by the father himself) may find his involvement with a new woman particularly painful. Whereas visitations may have gone somewhat smoothly prior to the father's new relationship, following the new involvement there may be a rapid deterioration in the girl's relationship with her father. Such a girl may say to her father, "You've got to choose between her and me." In such situations there may be no hope for a warm and meaningful relationship between the father's new woman friend and his daughter. Sometimes the mothers of such girls will support the animosity in that it serves well their desire for vengeance. It is not difficult to see how a sex-abuse accusation can easily arise in such a situation. The child's jealousy over the father's sexual involvement with his new woman friend may engender sexual fantasies in her, and this is especially the case in older girls.

Shame over Recanting

There are children, who, when they first allege sex abuse, have not the faintest idea about the implications and consequences of what they are professing. In their wildest dreams they never imagined the rollercoaster effect of their apparently mundane statements. They could not anticipate the avalanche that was unleashed by their seemingly innocuous comments. Some wish to recant, if only to go back to the halcyon days that existed in their lives before the "disclosure." Others may wish to recant because they recognize they have lied, and they wish to reduce the guilt attendant to such recognition. Others may wish to recant because they are ashamed, especially when they have to face the person who is suffering so terribly because of their accusations. Others may wish to recant because, although they believe they were molested, they don't believe that the "punishment fits the crime" and that the abuser should be subjected to such draconian punishments. Children in all of these categories, however, may hesitate to recant because they are ashamed to do so. The prospect of being called a liar by the horde of individuals who have jumped on the child's bandwagon is terrible to behold. The child would rather live with the painful effects associated with continual accusations than face what is considered to be the more painful prospect of standing in the center of a circle of people, all of whom are screaming "liar." And following such public humiliation, they may anticipate further punishment—unknown and possibly too horrendous to even predict with certainty.

Again, there is an uncanny similarity between the children we are seeing today and those accusing witchcraft at the Salem witch trials. On this point, once again, Mappan (1980) quotes Upham (1867):

> A fearful responsibility has been assumed, and they were irretrievably committed to their position. While they adhered to that position, their power was irresistible, and they were sure of the public sympathy and of being cherished by the public favor. If they faltered, they would be the objects of universal execration and the severest penalties of law for the wrongs already done and the falsehoods already sworn to. There was no retracing their steps; and their only safety was in continuing the excitement they had raised. New victims were constantly required to prolong the delusion, fresh fuel to keep up with the conflagration; and they went on to cry out upon others. (p. 39)

And these children fear that, if they recant, they would be "the objects of universal execration and the severest penalties of law for the wrongs already done, and the falsehoods already sworn to."

Concluding Comments

I have delineated above what I consider to be the primary psychodynamic factors operative in the child who provides a false sex-abuse accusation. It is important to appreciate that these psychodynamic factors do not operate in the child in isolation from those operative in the accuser. One does better to view the two as operating in the context of a folie-à-deux relationship. An understanding of these psychodynamic factors places the reader in a better position to utilize the criteria for differentiating between true and false sex-abuse accusations. By understanding *why* a child might be professing sex abuse enables the examiner to appreciate in greater depth the differentiating criteria and to determine whether or not a particular criterion is satisfied in borderline situations.

WHO ARE THESE PEOPLE?

There is no generally recognized training program for sex-abuse evaluators. The field is basically "open territory." Some have training in psychology, some in social work, and many in various aspects of "social service." Many are self-styled "therapists" who have absolutely no training at all, even in related disciplines. It is important for the reader to appreciate that all states have specific requirements for certification in such disciplines as psychiatry, clinical psychology, and clinical social work. States vary, however, regarding their receptivity to providing certification for family counselors, pastoral counselors, nurse practitioners, and other types of mental health professionals. I do not know of a state (and there may be one or more) that provides certification for therapists. In most states (to the best of my knowledge), anyone can hang up a shingle and say that he (she) is a therapist, and one cannot be prevented from practicing because of the failure to have certification or a license. In short, one cannot be penalized for practicing without a license if one does not have to have a license in the first place.

Some of these self-styled therapists have also crept into the sex-abuse field, where they serve not only as evaluators but as therapists. Sex abuse is a "growth industry." Until recently, they tell us, when we were not aware of how widespread the sex-abuse phenomenon was, we did not train many individuals who were qualified to conduct such evaluations and provide appropriate treatment. Now we have come to appreciate how limited are the number of people available to take on the monumental task of processing all these cases. Legislators are bombarded with requests to provide more money to train and recruit such personnel. Because of the great demand for their services and the paucity of highly qualified people, standards are lowered, requirements are ill defined, and a wide variety of obvious incompetents are conducting such evaluations and treatment.

Many of these ill-qualified and incompetent people take "courses" in which they are trained by others of questionable qualifications. What happens then is that the misinformation, ignorance, and gullibility of the teachers get passed on to their students and so on down the generations. Unfortunately, most students (happily not all) take a very passive and receptive view of their instructors. They make the assumption that the teachers must know what they are talking about or otherwise they wouldn't be in their position of authority. Walk into any classroom (even in the most prestigious colleges), and one will see an army of students writing down reflexly what their instructors are saying. The "best" students are those who regurgitate what they have been asked to memorize. Even in the best schools this process takes place. I believe that only a very small percentage of students is actually encouraged to question the authority of their instructors and to genuinely think independently and creatively. It is no surprise, then, that evaluators, who have most often had limited and even inferior educational experiences, are even more prone to accept as gospel what they are taught in these courses. Even I, who have provided expert testimony in courts on this subject, *never* received formal training (during my medical school, internship, and residency days in the 1950s) for differentiating between bona fide and fabricated sex-abuse allegations. However, I have at least had many years of training in related fields—psychiatry, psychology, child development, and medicine—which have served as a foundation for my subsequent three decades of experience in this realm.

Most sex-abuse workers operate in the context of a government agency, referred to in many states as the Child Protection Team (CPT) or Child Protection Service (CPS). Many unashamedly refer to themselves as "validators." Those who utilize this term make no secret of the fact that the vast majority (if not all) of the children they have evaluated have been sexually abused. As implied in their name, they are merely there to "validate" what everybody knows happened anyway. Otherwise, why would the child be brought forth? I am certain that a judge who referred to himself (herself) as a "convictor" would not be considered to have the neutrality that we expect of people in such positions. Yet, we say little about validators and the obvious bias implied in their very title. In their partial (I emphasize the word *partial* here) defense, many of these people have been working in settings where the vast majority of referrals relate to intrafamilial sex abuse, where the prevalence of genuine abuse is quite high. They have had little experience in vicious child-custody disputes and day-care center allegations, where the incidence is quite low. They have had little experience with making the differentiations necessary when evaluating referrals in the latter categories. Accordingly, they tend to assume that what was valid in the intrafamilial situation is valid in other situations as well. This could have been a rectifiable problem. Unfortunately, for the reasons provided throughout this book, this problem was not addressed adequately or soon enough, thereby contributing to the prevention of the mass hysteria phenomenon that we are experiencing at this time.

WHAT DO THEY DO?

Here I describe in detail the techniques that the overzealous and/or incompetent evaluators utilize in the service of programming nonabused children to believe that they were abused. Although the materials I have analyzed have been sent to me from various parts of the United States, it is amazing how similar the techniques are. Accordingly, I consider myself to be in a good position to describe in detail exactly what these examiners do. In fact, because they work so similarly—regardless of what part of the country they operate in—it is easy to make some generalizations about their techniques.

"Children Never Lie"

In order to justify and advance their prediction that the child will be found to be abused, they espouse the dictum that "children never lie" on all issues related to sex abuse. The reasoning goes that a young child, having had absolutely no exposure to or experience with sexual encounters, must be telling the truth if such an encounter is described. A related slogan is "believe the children." Even those who have had children themselves, and deal daily with the fabrications and delusions of their own children, have no problem waving these banners. In order to maintain this position they must deny the "polymorphous perversity" that Freud described almost a hundred years ago and that all parents (if they will only just look and listen) have to accept as a reality of childhood. They have to believe that the sex-abuse prevention programs to which many of their evaluees have already been exposed are in no way a contaminant to their investigatory process. They have to believe, as well, that there has been no coaching or programming (overt or covert, conscious or unconscious) by the parents who bring their children to them, even though a vicious child custody dispute may be taking place or the child is one of many parading out of a nursery school in which there is an atmosphere of mass hysteria. They have to deny, as well, the previously described ubiquity of sexual stimuli in our society.

The Blank-Screen Principle

Overzealous and biased examiners who program children to profess false accusations often ignore completely the blank-screen principle. Some have little or no appreciation for its value and may never have learned about it in their training. Some are intellectually aware of it but are so desirous of eliciting a sex-abuse accusation that they ignore the principle. The same examiner, for example, may utilize the Thematic Apperception Test (TAT) (Murray, 1936), in which there is a blank card designed to elicit blank-screen projections and, in the same closet, have anatomical dolls. (This is one of the best examples I know of psychological splitting.)

Skilled and sensitive examiners appreciate that the most valid and meaningful information is obtained in situations in which the interviewee is given full opportunity to express what is on his (her) mind. It is in this way that the examiner is in the best position to know what is "spinning around in the individual's brain." People who have been traumatized are very likely to be preoccupied with thoughts and feelings related to the trauma, thoughts and feelings that will be expressed if given the opportunity to do so without the contamination of leading questions, leading stimuli, and leading gestures. Overzealous examiners often ignore this important principle. Accordingly, one cannot then know whether the information elicited by them would have spontaneously been provided or is the result of the contaminating questions and stimuli used by those who ignore the blank-screen principle.

Leading Stimuli, Leading Gestures, and Leading Questions

Introduction During the last few years conflict has been raging over the value and place of anatomically correct dolls (more recently referred to as anatomically detailed dolls) in child sex-abuse evaluations. Studies are coming in from both camps, each claiming that the findings support its position. In the state of California the dolls are not considered to satisfy the Kelly-Frye test for admissibility, which requires that the procedure has been generally accepted as reliable in the scientific community in which it was developed. This decision was based on the weaknesses of the studies supporting their use (Gardner, 1991a; Underwager and Wakefield, 1990; Wakefield and Underwager, 1988).

Even those who are the strongest supporters of the use of the dolls generally agree that "leading questions" should be avoided as much as possible because they can produce responses in the child that may suggest sex abuse when it has not occurred. However, those who warn against the use of leading questions often use them to a significant degree in their protocols. For example, White et al. (1985) warn, "The interviewer should pose questions in a nonleading fashion." Yet, in the same protocol they list 14 questions, each of which most would consider to be highly leading, e.g., "Have you been touched on any part of your body?" "Has anyone put anything on or in any part of your body?" "Has anyone else asked you to take off your clothes?"

Boat and Everson (1988) exhibit the same disparity in their protocol regarding the caveat against using leading questions. The authors state, "Background information should therefore be used only for guiding the conversation (e.g., 'Your mommy told me you visited Uncle John last week.') and not [except in rare circumstances to be outlined later] for asking the child questions that may be leading or suggestive (e.g., 'Is Uncle John the one who hurt you?')." The authors do not appear to appreciate the fact that the statement: "Your Mommy told me you visited Uncle John last week" is very leading. Perhaps it is a little less leading than "Is Uncle John the one who hurt you?" but it is nevertheless leading in that it directs the child's attention to the visit with Uncle John the previous week, the visit during which some sexual encounter is alleged to have taken place. Furthermore, in spite of this caveat, the protocol itself includes a series of questions, each of which is highly leading [in each of the examples to be given the line (_____) represents the name the child uses for that particular body part], for example, "Has anyone touched your _____?" "Have you ever seen anybody else's _____?" "Has anyone asked you to touch their _____?" and "Has anyone taken pictures of you with your clothes off?" Most examiners, I believe, would agree that these questions are highly leading.

Obviously, we have a problem here regarding the exact definition of a leading question. Providing a definition for this term is one of the objects of this chapter. However, I will go beyond this issue and discuss the concepts of what I refer to as "leading stimuli" and "leading gestures." The introduction of these terms is important if one is to appreciate more fully what is actually occurring when examiners use anatomical dolls. In the course of my detailed analyses of videotapes in which anatomical dolls are used, I have not only noted the frequent use of leading questions but I have often observed what I refer to as *leading gestures*. Although leading questions can easily be seen on the transcripts of these interviews, the leading gestures are rarely described by the transcriber. These gestures play an important role in what is actually taking place during these interviews and, I believe, they play a role in the programming process that is occurring with the utilization of these dolls. I will also utilize the term *leading stimuli*, which refers to dolls (especially anatomical), body charts, and other instruments that can serve to contaminate the interview, especially in the direction of drawing the child into talking about sexual issues and contributing thereby to the brainwashing process.

My main purpose is to discuss in detail these three areas of importance in sex-abuse evaluation interviews: (1) leading stimuli (of which anatomical dolls represent one example), (2) leading questions, and (3) leading gestures. Defining these concepts more accurately will, it is hoped, improve communication among examiners, especially with regard to what is and what is not a leading question. It is important that the reader not view these concepts simply as yes/no phenomena, whether present or absent; rather, each is best understood as lying on a continuum from not being present at all to being utilized to a significant degree. For each of the three concepts I will demarcate four points along this continuum: not present (that is, absent), minimally present, moderately present, and maximally present. However, I wish to emphasize that these are merely guideposts for categorization. The general principle that is followed for ascertaining which level is most appropriate is the degree to which the stimulus shrinks the universe of possible responses by the interviewee. The less the shrinkage, the greater the likelihood the stimulus will fall at the "absent" end of the continuum.

And the greater the shrinkage or narrowing, the greater the likelihood the stimulus would be considered to be "maximal" in this regard.

Last, I will not make a distinction between leading questions and "suggestive questions." Although some may make a distinction between the two, I will not do so, nor will I use the term. Rather, I will use the term *leading questions* to refer to all types of questions that have the capacity to suggest an answer and utilize terminology that attempts to refine the various degrees of suggestibility within the question. Similarly, I will not make any differentiation between nonleading questions and "open-ended questions." I consider open-ended any question that does not contain within it a contaminating focus for response. My comments here will refer to the various degrees to which a question is open and will utilize terminology designed to define more specifically the degree of "open-endedness."

Leading Stimuli The stimuli that I will be focusing on here are instruments that are generally used in interviewing by mental health professionals, especially psychologists and psychiatrists. They are instruments that have been designed to elicit verbal responses by the interviewee, especially responses that reveal psychodynamic information and personality manifestations. They all involve an external visual stimulus that serves as a focus for the interviewee's verbal response. They differ from leading questions in that the stimuli in the leading-question category are entirely verbal. They differ from leading gestures in that the leading-stimuli category includes standard, well-defined materials that are easily recognized as providing visual stimuli. Leading gestures, in contrast, although visual, are an incidental form of visual stimulation that may not be directly attended to by the interviewer or the interviewee but have a profound effect on the process of the interview.

Nonleading Stimuli The ideal nonleading visual stimulus would be no stimulus at all. The psychoanalyst's blank screen for free associations would be an example. The blank card of The Thematic Apperception Test (TAT) (Murray, 1936) would also be a good example. Whereas all the other cards of the TAT depict a particular scene with a specific number of individuals, the blank card is completely blank. The universe of possible stories that the interviewee can provide is basically infinite and the external facilitating stimulus does not provide anything that could reasonably contaminate the associations and thereby "shrink" the universe of possible responses.

Minimally Leading Stimuli A good example of minimally leading stimuli are the Rorschach cards (Rorschach, 1921). These inkblots were selected because they have only limited similarity with known objects. There are some cards, however, that vaguely resemble known objects such as bats, butterflies, and "two drummers drumming." Surprisingly, these are referred to as the "popular responses" and are not particularly indicative of psychopathology. In fact, not to see these popular responses may suggest the presence of such pathology. Because most of the stimuli are not suggestive, and because the universe of possible responses has not been significantly reduced by these stimuli, I place these cards in the category of minimally leading stimuli. Another instrument in this category is The Storytelling Card Game (STCG) (Gardner, 1988a). In this psychotherapeutic game (which can also be used as a diagnostic instrument for eliciting psychodynamic material), there are 24 scene cards, 4 of which are blank. The nonblank scenes depict scenes only and do not contain any figures, human or animal. Some typical scenes are a forest, a child's bedroom, a city street, a farm. The child is asked to select one or more figurines (from an array of 15, ranging in age from infancy to old age), place them on a card, and tell a self-created story. It is almost as if the child is creating his (her) own TAT picture card. The blank card pictures used in the STCG are somewhat more contaminating than the blank card of the TAT because in the former there is an actual visual stimulus (the figurines placed on the blank card), whereas in the latter there is none. Because the children create their own pictures, the STCG pictures are less contaminating than the standard nonblank TAT cards (to be described in the next category).

The instruments used in this category have limited capacity to constrain or contaminate the universe of possible responses. They are well viewed as catalysts for projections created by the interviewee, with little potential by the external facilitating stimulus to modify significantly the interviewee's inner psychological processes.

Moderately Leading Stimuli In this category the external visual stimuli are quite specific; yet they allow for a universe of possible responses. However, because of the specificity of the external visual eliciting stimuli, the universe of possible responses is smaller than that provided by the stimuli in the previous two categories. Most of the TAT cards fall well into this category. In each of the cards one can identify easily the number of individuals depicted, the sex, and even something about the attitudes or emotions of the individuals depicted (although these tend to be somewhat vague). Some examples: Card No. 1 depicts a boy looking down at his violin, which is lying on the table in front of him. Card No. 2 depicts a schoolgirl (carrying books) behind whom is a farm scene in which an adult female, an adult male, and a horse are clearly indicated. Card No. 5 depicts an adult woman standing at a doorway looking into a room (which could be either a foyer or a living room). Card No. 17BM depicts a naked man climbing up a rope. Obviously, the TAT cards shrink the universe of possible responses much more than the stimuli in the aforementioned two categories. Yet, there is still a universe of possible responses to each of these cards.

Maximally Leading Stimuli The materials described in this category shrink significantly the universe of possible responses. They provide a highly specific stimulus that is very likely to draw the interviewee's attention directly to it. Generally, they provide stimuli that are likely to bring about strong emotional responses in the interviewee. Many of the cards in the Children's Apperception Test (CAT) (Bellak and Bellak, 1949) are in this category. Some examples: Card No. 1 depicts three chickens sitting around a table, in the center of which is a bowl of food. In the background is the adult chicken (most likely the mother). Card No. 7 depicts a tiger leaping menacingly toward a small monkey. His mouth is open. He is approximately ten times the size of the monkey. Card No. 10 depicts a bathroom scene in which there is a toilet. Sitting nearby is a mother dog spanking a baby dog.

The Children's Apperception Test-Supplement (CAT-S) (Bellak and Bellak, 1963) also contains cards that warrant placement in this category. Some examples: Card No. 5 depicts a kangaroo walking with crutches. Both his (her) left leg and tail are bandaged. Card No. 10 depicts a female cat, obviously pregnant. Because she is standing up, her abdomen is easily recognized as protuberant. TAT Card No. 8BM also warrants placement in this category. It depicts a man being operated on by two other men, one of whom is holding a knife (or scalpel). Next to him is a gun. In front of all of this is a young man looking out at the viewer. The presence of the gun, knife, and surgical operation warrant this card's being placed in the maximally leading stimulus category because it provides a much greater shrinkage of the universe of possible responses than is provided by the aforementioned TAT cards, which I considered to warrant placement in the moderately leading stimuli category.

The centerfold of many pin-up magazines warrant placement in this category. Whatever the nature of one's reactions (and I admit to a wide variety), there is no question that such a picture provides very compelling stimuli. Groth (1984) has introduced anatomical drawings that are often used in the assessment of children who are being evaluated for sexual abuse. Their purported purpose is to enable the examiner to learn exactly what terms the child uses for the various body parts. The child is presented with cards on which are depicted naked people. Both anterior and posterior views are presented. I have serious reservations about these cards. They provide maximal leading stimuli and communicate to the child that sexual issues are proper and acceptable topics to focus on. If this were indeed the only example of such stimuli used by the examiner, the cards probably wouldn't be too high a contaminant. However, when used along with anatomical dolls, leading questions, and an atmosphere in which the examiner communicates to the child that sex talk is the "name of the game in this office," they may contribute to the creation and/or promulgation of a false sex-abuse accusation. Their ostensible use for learning the names the child uses can easily be viewed as the examiner's rationalization for sexualization of the interview. The examiner could achieve the same goal by simply asking the mother, outside of the child's presence, what names the child uses for the various body parts. In this way, the examiner would gain the benefits to be derived from having this information without contaminating the interview in the sexual direction.

I consider anatomical dolls to be in this category of maximally leading stimuli. They provide highly compelling and unusual stimuli that cannot but draw the child's attention from other issues that may have been on his (her) mind. Some of these dolls have organs that are disproportionately large; others do not. But in both cases the dolls are unusual and thereby attract extra attention. They are not the kinds of dolls that the vast majority of parents (including evaluators who are parents) are likely to give their children as birthday or holiday presents. If a rambunctious teenager were to surreptitiously pencil in genitals, breasts, and pubic hair onto a set of TAT cards, the examiner would probably consider them "ruined" and be quite upset at the miscreant. Such alteration of the cards obviously makes them even more contaminating and would put them in the category of a pin-up magazine centerfold.

I wish to emphasize that my experiences with viewing the videotapes of examiners who utilize these dolls is that leading questions and leading gestures are greater contaminants than the dolls, their strong contaminating potential notwithstanding, and this is one of the reasons why many of the studies that conclude that the dolls are not contaminating are not reproducing the actual situation in which they are commonly used. Specifically, these studies are usually done under laboratory conditions in which the examiners attempt to reduce significantly the use of leading questions because of the appreciation that they have the effect of biasing a sex-abuse evaluation. A typical study involves a child being allowed to play along with the dolls. If an examiner is present, he (she) says nothing or makes a few catalytic statements. Others generally observe the child through a one-way mirror. Activities or comments that could be construed as sexual are quantified.

The main problem with these studies is that they do not accurately reproduce the conditions in the real world where examiners are literally bombarding children with leading questions in association with their use of these dolls. Those that appear to support the conclusion that the dolls are not contaminating usually include a few nonabused children who, indeed, provided responses similar to those one obtains from children who have been genuinely abused. This, of course, argues against their "safety." Of relevance here is the common finding that the majority (usually 80–95 percent) of children do not provide responses suggesting sex abuse. This figure is used to justify the conclusion that the dolls are safe. However, the same studies indicate 5–20 percent false positives, i.e., the dolls facilitating responses that are the same as those seen in children who were genuinely abused. From the point of view of an accused person, these false positives indicate that the dolls are very risky and even dangerous and could contribute to the incarceration of a person who did not sexually abuse the child being evaluated. The situation is similar, I believe, to the one in which a pharmaceutical company would propose placing on the market a drug that they claim is "only 5–20 percent lethal."

The reader who is interested in reading directly the studies that come to the aforementioned conclusions does well to refer to the articles by Gabriel (1985), White et al. (1985), Jampole and Weber (1987), Sivan et al. (1988), Glaser and Collins (1989), Clarke-Stewart et al. (1989), Thompson et al. (1991), August and Forman (1989), McIver et al. (1989), and Realmuto et al. (1990). These studies provide compelling evidence that anatomical dolls—even when used alone, without leading questions and leading gestures—play a role in bringing about and/or promulgating false sex-abuse accusations.

Bruck et al. (1995) presented anatomical dolls to two groups of three-year-old children who had received physical examinations only a few minutes previously. One group had received a genital examination and the other did not. However, those who underwent genital examinations received only superficial exams; there was no entry or penetration into body orifices. Immediately after the examination all children were presented with anatomical dolls and asked, while the examiner was pointing to the genital area, "Did the doctor touch you here?" Fifty percent of the children who did *not* receive a genital examination indicated that they *were* touched; 50 percent indicated that they were *not*. Accordingly, we see here a 50 percent error rate when the doll is used in association with a leading question and a leading gesture. Some of the children who did *not* receive a genital examination even described penetration. Some of the children were given a stethoscope and asked to demonstrate on the dolls how the doctor used it. Some indicated that he used it to examine their genitals. Although the doctor did not use a spoon in the course of the examination, when the children were presented with a spoon and asked what the doctor did with it, some of them inserted it into the genitals of the doll. If one can obtain such distortions within a few minutes of the examination, it is easy to see how the error rates would be greater if the inquiry was conducted days or weeks later (the usual case).

Saywitz et al. (1991) did a similar study on five-year-old children and found a high degree of accuracy. It is probably the case that five-year-olds are not as likely to distort as three-year-olds. However, if five-year-olds are indeed accurate then the argument for using the dolls at this age level is supported (at least for this particular study). Bruck and Ceci (1995) point out that all of the studies on anatomical dolls are conducted in relatively "pure" situations and that in actual reality leading questions typically are associated with the utilization of the dolls. And this has been my own experience, having analyzed in detail at least 1,000 hours of videotaped interviews utilizing these dolls over the last 12 years.

Ceci and Bruck (1995) provide us with the most up-to-date review of the literature on the studies of anatomical dolls and quote many studies that compellingly describe the drawbacks and risks of the dolls. Their final conclusion:

> In conclusion, we feel at this point that there has been sufficient concern raised in the literature, and enough evidence of potential misuse, without sufficiently counterbalanced evidence to the contrary, to urge that dolls not be used diagnostically, at least not with very young children. Of course, some skilled professionals will decry the loss of a valuable tool without which many children will go undiagnosed and be forced to continue living in an abusive situation. On the other hand, we have reviewed enough studies that demonstrate that *this* tool has the potential for serious misuse, including misdiagnosis, which could result in removing nonabused children from their homes, the implantation of false memories in therapy, and the imprisonment of innocent adults. Both conditions are horrific, and our goal should be to find techniques that minimize both consequences, not to support a technique that guards against one type of error at the expense of increasing the other. To do otherwise is akin to giving the cancer pill to all people, irrespective of their cancer status.

Leading Questions I use the term *leading questions* to refer to questions that engender in the mind of the listener a specific visual image that is not likely to have been produced had the question not been asked. It usually induces the formation of a visual image that may serve as a reference point for future responses and behavior. When a leading

258   *PROGRAMMING NONABUSED CHILDREN*

question is asked, the examiner cannot be sure whether the interviewee's response has been suggested by the leading question or whether it would have been provided anyway. Such "seed planting" interferes significantly with the data-collection process, the purpose of which is to ascertain whether something really happened (such as is the case in a sex-abuse evaluation). Leading questions can also contribute to the brainwashing process that can take place in the course of an evaluation. Engendering as they do fantasies of events that might not have occurred, there is the risk that the imagery that leading questions induce will come to be believed by the interviewee. Even adults often have problems remembering the original source of information or a recollection. A visual image can come to have a life of its own, especially if repeatedly suggested and brought into conscious awareness. And children, being more suggestible, are more likely to forget the source of an engendered visual image and are more likely to come to believe that the events portrayed therein actually occurred.

Consider, for example, a three-year-old girl who has never performed fellatio on her father, was never asked to do so by him, and never even entertained the notion of doing so. An examiner asks this child, "Did your father ever put his penis in your mouth?" The question engenders in the child's mind the visual image of her performing fellatio on her father. It is probable that this particular thought never previously entered her mind. The question, however, creates an image of just such an event. Her initial response may be one of denial and possibly even some revulsion. A few days later, when asked the same question (by the same or another examiner), the fellatio-with-father image is then brought into conscious awareness. However, this time she may not be able to differentiate between a recollection derived from the question asked a few days earlier and images related to an actual event. At that point she may respond with, "I think so—I'm not sure." If the examiner zealously wants the child to respond in the affirmative (a not uncommon situation, in my experience), he (she) may pursue the issue with statements such as, "Think hard," "You can tell me," "It's safe here," and "I'll make sure he won't be able to do it again." If one adds here the child's desire to ingratiate herself to the examiner, who she recognizes wants the answer to be yes, it is more likely that the child will consider the "recall" of the visual image as a manifestation of her having indeed had such an experience. It is for these reasons that leading questions can result in a sex-abuse evaluation that is much more a learning process than an exploratory one. Leading questions, then, play a role in what is often criticized as a "brainwashing" or "programming" process.

Leading questions, like leading stimuli and leading gestures, are on a hierarchy from questions that are not leading at all to those that are maximally leading. There are differentiating criteria that delineate the subcategories, but the reader does well to consider there to be a continuum, with the subcategories serving as guidelines for categorization. First, I focus primarily on the verbal communications of the evaluator (auditory stimuli), and I do not direct myself to visual environmental stimuli (including leading stimuli and leading gestures) that are usually operating simultaneously and also have an effect on the child's verbalizations.

Nonleading Questions Here, again, the psychoanalytic model can be useful. Although there have been many serious criticisms of Freudian psychoanalysis (and I agree with many of them), I do believe that the blank-screen principle is a valid one. It is the best setting for enabling the therapist to find out what is on the patient's mind, uncontaminated by comments made by the therapist. In the ideal psychoanalytic situation, the session begins without the therapist saying a word. Whether the therapist is behind the couch or face-to-face is not relevant here. What is relevant is that there is practically no direct verbal communication originating with the therapist. The patient recognizes that he (she) will be expected to start talking about the things that are coming into conscious awareness. Thus, a completely nonleading question, in its purest form, is no question at all. There are opening questions, however, that justify placement in this category. Questions like "So what's on your mind?" and "What would you like to talk about today?" still provide for a universe of possible responses. Potential contaminants provided by these questions are highly unlikely.

Young children, especially under the age of five or six (the age range in which anatomical dolls are most frequently used), do not generally respond well to such questions as "What's on your mind?" and "What would you like to talk about today?" However, after an initial

"Hello" and "Please come in" (comments that, in my experience, are genuinely nonleading), the child might be observed by the examiner to see what he (she) will do. The examiner can sit and say absolutely nothing and will sometimes be successful in getting the child to spontaneously verbalize, especially after selecting some object in the room to serve as a focus. However, once this object (often a toy) is picked up, we no longer have a blank screen. (We have, now, a category of leading stimulus.) If, however, the child starts talking spontaneously, then we do indeed have a nonleading-question type of situation. Sometimes the child's talking can be facilitated by the child's parent(s) coming in initially, especially at the beginning of the first interview. The parents' presence, obviously, makes the child more comfortable in a strange situation and increases the likelihood that the child will verbalize. However, in order to ensure that the child's verbal productions will not be contaminated by their comments and/or gestures (no matter how subtle), they must be strictly instructed to say nothing at all. If one is successful in this regard (often the case, in my experience), then one is likely to have a situation in which the child begins to talk spontaneously. Once the child is comfortable, the parent(s) can be asked to leave the room, and then one is more likely to have a setting in which spontaneous verbalizations will come forth. Last, the parents need not be brought into the second interview because of the child's previous familiarization with the examiner and his (her) procedures.

Minimally Leading Questions These are questions that narrow the universe of possible responses to a very limited degree. They are questions or openings that are rarely used as foci for the interviewee's response. An example would be a situation in which an evaluator provides the child with a wide assortment of materials (dolls, farm animals, zoo animals, drawing paper, crayons, clay, dollhouse) and simply says to the child, "You can play with anything you would like to play with here." Then, while the child is playing, the evaluator sits silently, awaiting the child's spontaneous comments and verbalized fantasies. There has been some minimal contamination here because the universe has been narrowed somewhat by virtue of the fact that the child is being asked to direct his (her) attention to the play material. However, that universe has not been narrowed significantly because there is still a large universe of possible comments the child might make while so engaged. If the child doesn't say anything, the examiner might say, "What are you thinking about while you're playing with those things?" Again, there is a large universe of possible thoughts the child might have. Here, the examiner might say, "I'd like you to tell me a story about the things you're playing with." Here, too, the universe is not significantly constricted. Children under the age of five, however, are generally not cognitively capable of providing well-organized stories—especially with a beginning, middle, and an end. However, they often will, in response to this question, provide a string of loosely connected associations. (They are likely to comply because of the aforementioned desire to ingratiate themselves to adult authority.)

The same principle is applicable in the introduction to the mutual storytelling technique (Gardner, 1968, 1971, 1992b). The introductory material provided by the therapist in the "Make-Up-a-Story Television Program" is general, nonspecific, and does not include material that has any particular "pull" toward a particular story theme. The examiner's responding story (which is therapeutically designed to include the same characters in a similar setting, but incorporates healthier modes of adaptation than those utilized by the child) does provide highly specific material. However, the response here is a therapeutic message, derived from the child's uncontaminated fantasies, and is not presented as a noncontaminated projection. (The therapeutic utilization of this game is not the purpose of this chapter. Rather, only the use of the mutual storytelling technique's story-eliciting capacity is being focused on here.)

Many (but not all) of the cards in *The Talking, Feeling, and Doing Game* (Gardner, 1973) warrant placement in this category. This board game, which was designed to elicit psychotherapeutically valuable information from children in the context of a mildly competitive board game, involves each player rolling the dice and moving a playing pawn around a curved path from start to finish. When the player's pawn lands on a white square, a Talking Card is taken, on a yellow square, a Feeling Card is taken, and on a pink square, a Doing Card is taken. When a player answers the question or responds to the instructions on the card, a reward chip is obtained. Obviously, the object of the game is not simply to earn chips and acquire a prize, but to use the cards as points of departure for psychotherapeutic interchanges between the therapist and patient. Examples of cards that warrant placement in the minimally leading questions category are: "Make up a dream," "Someone passes you a note. What does it say?" "Make believe you're looking into a crystal ball that can show anything that's happening anywhere in the whole world. What do you see?" As can be seen, there is indeed a universe of possible responses to each of these questions. Although not as large as the blank-screen universe provided by the facilitators in the category of completely nonleading questions, they are certainly close to this ideal.

Moderately Leading Questions Questions in this category narrow somewhat the universe from which the questions in the previous category draw; however, the constriction of the universe is not that great that significant idiosyncratic material cannot be obtained. Most of the cards in *The Talking, Feeling, and Doing Game* (Gardner, 1973) warrant placement in this category, for example, "If the walls of your house could talk, what would they say about your family?" "Everybody in the class was laughing at a girl. What had happened?" "A boy has something on his mind that he's afraid to tell his father. What is it that he's scared to talk about?" "Make up a lie." "What's the worst thing that ever happened to you in your whole life?" "All the girls in the class were invited to a birthday party except one. How did she feel? Why wasn't she invited?" and "Suppose two people were talking about you, and they didn't know you were listening. What do you think you would hear them saying?" These questions narrow somewhat the range of responses, but still allow for a universe of possible answers. There is a universe of possible lies that the child could possibly tell. There is a universe of possible reasons why everybody in a class would laugh at a girl. There is a universe of possible things a person could hear others saying about oneself when eavesdropping. Yet, the questions do focus somewhat on a particular area of inquiry, e.g., friendships, lying, antisocial behavior, etc.

When conducting an evaluation of children I may ask the following question: "You know, nobody is perfect. Everybody is a mixture of things you like and things you don't like. Your parents are no exception. I'd like you to tell me the things about your mother and father that you like and the things about your mother and your father that you don't like. Which one do you want to start with?" There is a universe of possible responses to this question, even though it narrows down to the assets and liabilities of the child's parents. Accordingly, they warrant placement in the category of moderately leading questions.

A verbal projective instrument designed by Kritzberg (1966) also warrants inclusion in this category. The child is asked the question, "If you had to be turned into an animal, and could choose any animal in the whole world, what animal would you choose?" After the child responds, he (she) is asked the reason for that choice. Following this, the child is asked for his (her) second and third choices and the reasons why. Then the child is asked what three animals he (she) would *not* want to be, and the reasons why. A similar series of questions could be asked about objects into which the child could be transformed and, for older children, the specific persons they would choose and not choose to be changed into if they were free to select from the whole array of humanity, living and dead, famous and not famous, real and fictional. Although there is a finite number of animals, objects, and persons (for older children) from which to choose, the number is still quite large (and the older the child, the larger the number). Although the word *universe* is not applicable here, we still do not have the kind of constriction and seed-planting that one sees in the maximally-leading-question category. Furthermore, once the animal, object, or person has been selected, the reasons for that selection allow for a much larger universe of possible responses. The second part of the question (the "why" part) provides, therefore, the more valuable information because it allows for the tapping of a larger universe of possibilities.

It is in this category that we begin to see some of the contaminating leading questions utilized by many sex-abuse evaluators. For example, the examiner might ask, "Tell me about the school you used to go to." On the surface, this seems like an innocuous enough question and would be the kind that many evaluators might ask in the course of their evaluations. However, in this particular case the examiner knows that the school the child used to attend was closed down because the directors allegedly sexually molested the children there. Taking this into consideration, and taking into consideration the fact that this was the first substantive question asked in the interview, we see how the word *universe* has no applicability here. A response that includes nonsexual events is usually of little concern to such an evaluator. And this is an important point. To the degree that the evaluator is thinking about a particular answer, to that degree the question is likely to be leading. Of course, the inclusion of this criterion makes it more difficult to assess the question on its face value regarding the degree to which it is leading, but it is not usually difficult to speculate about what's going on in the evaluator's mind when every single question is directed toward the alleged sex-abuse event, no matter how unrelated to sex they may initially appear.

I cannot emphasize this point strongly enough. The competent examiner is truly going to be open to *any* response the child provides and use that as a point of departure for further inquiry and elaboration, whether it be for evaluative or therapeutic purposes. This is the opposite of the approach utilized by most of the sex-abuse examiners whose reports I have read and/or whose videotapes I have studied and analyzed. It is clear that they start off from the position that the sex abuse is most likely to have taken place and their job is merely to fill in the details. Noncorroborative data are ignored, denials are rationalized away, and one knows then that ostensibly minimally leading questions such as "Tell me about the school you used to go to" are actually quite contaminating and warrant placement in a higher category of leading questions.

Another example is: "Tell me about your Uncle Bill." Again, one must consider this statement at two levels. Ostensibly, it may not be highly leading, although it is intrinsically leading under the best of circumstances because the focus is on one person of the 5.3 billion people on earth. However, there is still a universe of possible statements one could make about Uncle Bill. In this case, however, Uncle Bill is the alleged perpetrator. We know, also, that he has been selected from the wide assortment of the child's friends and relatives who the examiner could have chosen to focus on. We know, then, that the examiner is primarily interested in discussing the alleged sexual encounters between the child and Uncle Bill, even though the examiner may be professing a completely neutral position regarding whether sex abuse took place—the usual position of many evaluators (especially "validators"), professions of neutrality notwithstanding. Accordingly, it has a "seed-planting" effect in that the child gets the message that the examiner is interested in talking about issues related to sex abuse, a subject selected from the universe of issues that could be focused upon in the examiner's office.

Maximally Leading Questions A maximally leading question is one about which there is no doubt what the examiner is interested in discussing and/or hearing. It is one star pulled out from a million galaxies. Many are totally innocuous, e.g., "How old are you?" "What grade are you in?" and "What's your teacher's name?" These are highly selected questions, point out exactly what the examiner is looking for, and lead the child down a very specific path. Such questions may even have the fringe benefit of relaxing a child during his (her) first interview with a strange therapist. The question "What's the name of your school?" might very well be in the same category. However, if the school is the place where the alleged sex abuse took place, and if the school question is one of the first the examiner asks, then the same question now falls into the moderately leading question category (for reasons described above). If, however, the examiner asks, "Tell me exactly what your teacher, Mr. Jones, did to you after he pulled down your pants," we have a statement that warrants placement in the maximally-leading-question category. It evokes a specific image of Mr. Jones pulling down the child's pants. Mr. Jones may or may not have actually pulled down this child's pants. Once the question is asked, however, the likelihood of our knowing whether this actually happened (at least with the child as a source of information) is reduced significantly. (And this problem is compounded by examiners who see only the child and then come to a conclusion regarding whether Mr. Jones perpetrated an act of sexual abuse.)

Many of the questions in the White et al. (1985) and Boat and Everson (1988) protocols warrant placement in this category. For example, the question "Did anyone ever touch you in the wrong place?" engenders the specific fantasy of the child's being touched sexually, whether or not the child ever was. The question "Has anyone ever taken your picture?" seems innocuous enough and, one could argue, certainly does not warrant placement in the maximally-leading-question category. However, we know that the examiner who asks this question is not thinking of pictures taken at the zoo, on picnics, or at amusement centers. Rather, the examiner is thinking about child pornography, and the visual image in the examiner's mind is of an adult with a camera taking pictures of one or more naked children, possibly engaged in a wide variety of sexual activities. This is confirmed by the fact that the question is one of a series, all of which relate to sex abuse. If the child were to respond, "Oh, yes. My daddy took a lot of pictures of me when we visited Disney World," that would not be considered a satisfactory or acceptable answer. In all probability the examiner would then ask about pictures taken in other settings in the hope that a sex-abuse scenario would be described. Or, the examiner might get more specific and ask leading questions about whether the child was naked in the pictures, questions about a particular person (especially the alleged perpetrator) taking pictures, etc. Another example is: "Have you ever been without your clothes?" If the child were to say, "Of course, when my mommy gives me a bath, I don't have clothes on," the examiner is not likely to find this an acceptable answer. He (she) is likely to ask more questions about *other* people, especially the alleged perpetrator.

Many yes/no questions fall into this category. For example, "Did anyone ever touch your private places?" serves as an entree into a specific discussion about sex abuse. Whether the child says yes or no does not usually provide useful information. If the child says yes, one doesn't know whether the child is saying so in order to ingratiate himself (herself) to the evaluator or because the child really had such an experience. If the child says no, one doesn't know if the no answer relates to reality or if the child had such an experience and is too ashamed, guilt-ridden, fearful, etc., to answer in the affirmative. But less important than the significant drawbacks of the yes/no question (and lawyers have yet to learn this) is the fact that the question "plants a seed" because it induces a fantasy of a child's being touched in "private places," whether or not he (she) has had such an experience. And this is one of the ways that legal interrogations (with their frequent use of yes/no questions) program children into believing they have had such experiences when they did not.

Leading Gestures This is a most important area that has not been given proper attention by those involved in sex-abuse evaluations. Written transcripts of videotapes rarely mention the gestures of the evaluator. Only the verbalizations are usually recorded, unless something very unusual and dramatic has taken place. Audiotapes, obviously, tell us practically nothing about gestures and other body movements. Yet, throughout much of the interview, the child is looking at the evaluator and obviously is being affected by what he (she) sees. Children model themselves after adults, especially their parents and other authorities. The emulation process often involves the notion: "If I act like him (her), he (she) will like me better." The imitation factor contributes to children's learning about how to function in the adult world. There is a reflexive need on the part of children to imitate significant adults. It relates to the need to learn the acceptable patterns of behavior that will enable them to be like others and thereby fit in well with and be accepted by the group. I call it the "keeping-up-with-the-Joneses" phenomenon.

Another factor operative here is that of sanction. If the child observes the evaluator to be performing an act that might generally be considered unacceptable (for example, placing a finger in a doll's vagina or stroking a doll's penis), he (she) is more likely to repeat that act, even if aware of its unacceptability. The child often operates on the principle: "If it's okay for him (her) to do it, it's okay for me to do it also."

I divide leading gestures into four categories. Again, we are dealing here with a continuum: from nonleading gestures at the one end to maximally leading gestures at the other, and the categorization is primarily for the purpose of providing guideposts.

Nonleading Gestures Once again, we start with our old friends, the classical psychoanalysts, many of whom (but certainly not all) are experts at doing nothing. (The reader should appreciate that I myself am a trained analyst and so my criticisms of these people are not based simply on books I have read on the subject.) One of the reasons given for the psychoanalyst's sitting behind the couch is to lessen the likelihood that the patient will be affected by the psychoanalyst's facial expressions and gestures. Although I think much is lost by conducting therapy from this position, especially the human relationship (Gardner, 1988b, 1992b), these people do have a point. Although the psychoanalyst sitting behind the couch provides one of the best examples of nonleading gestures, most children who are being evaluated for sex abuse are not coming to be analyzed and most children who are in analysis do not have analysts who work from behind the couch. Nor am I recommending that sex-abuse evaluators buy couches. The evaluator, however, can indeed avoid leading gestures, gestures that provide communications that will contaminate the blank-screen interview. To ask a nonleading question without any contaminating facial expressions or gestures is easily accomplished. One can say to a child, "What would you like to do here today?" without any kind of directive movement or glances. Also, after asking nonleading introductory questions in the name-rank-and-serial-number category, the examiner just might sit, somewhat expressionless, and watch the child to see where he (she) will gravitate and wait until the child begins to speak.

Minimally Leading Gestures These gestures, like most of the gestures I discuss here, are usually associated with verbalizations that may or may not be in the same category regarding its contamination of the blank screen. If the examiner wishes to direct the child's attention to the toys, because they are likely to provide catalyzation of the expression of the child's naturally occurring fantasies, he (she) might, with an arc sweep of the hand across the toy shelves, say, "You can play with any of the toys in the room." This gesture is selective in that it strongly suggests that the child confine himself (herself) to the toys and not to other objects in the room. It restricts somewhat the universe of possible activities and statements, but it is minimally contaminating. The child still has the option to select any of the toys and if they are intrinsically of low-contamination potential, then the gesture will have served its purpose.

The examiner might take a pad of drawing paper and crayons, put them down in front of the child, and say, "I'd like you to make a drawing. Any drawing at all. Draw anything in the whole wide world that comes to mind. Then, when you finish, I'd like you to tell me about what you've drawn." This can be said while pointing to the crayons and blank sheet of paper. These gestures reinforce the verbal request and increase the likelihood that the child will provide a reasonably pure projection. The same principles hold when one is instructing a child to draw a figure for the *Draw-a-Person Test*, the *Draw-a-Family Test*, or the request that the child play with dolls, clay, fingerpaints, sand, or other traditional play therapy materials. (My assumption here is that the examiner recognizes the contaminating effects of such games as chess, Monopoly, Candy Land, etc. Unfortunately, there are many therapists who do not appreciate this obvious fact.)

Winnicott (1968) utilizes a game that he refers to as "squiggles." The therapist or the child begins by drawing with pencil on blank paper a nonrecognizable scribble ("squiggle"). The other party then pencils in additional lines and curves. Back and forth they go until the child reaches the point where he (she) recognizes some identifiable figure. Then the figure serves as a point of departure for either storytelling or other therapeutic communications. The gestures here are basically of limited contaminating potential. They contribute to the drawing of a figure of varying similarities to actual objects. However, the child is a contributor and the identification of the figure so drawn is based on what the *child* sees in it, i.e., the child's projections, rather than what the examiner considers the squiggle to look like. Because there is still a large universe of possible associations and stories to the squiggle, the game warrants categorization in the minimally-leading-gesture category.

Moderately Leading Gestures Evaluators who use anatomical dolls will commonly say to children, "Show me how he did it with the dolls." The ostensible purpose here is to facilitate the child's providing an accurate description in order to compensate for the child's immature level of verbal and cognitive communicative capacity. Another argument given for their utilization is that they help inhibited children talk about sex abuse. Although there may be some minimal justification for these arguments for the dolls being used, the encouragement of the physical enactment tends to entrench the child's belief in the events so portrayed, whether or not they actually occurred. When this direction is given, the evaluator often picks up the dolls and hands them to the child, again strengthening the power of the verbal request.

An example of a moderately leading gesture would be the examiner who says, while picking up a family of puppets, "Let's play with these hand puppets. I'll take the mother and father (places them on his [her] hands) and you take the boy and the girl and put them on your hands. Now what happens?" Under these circumstances the child is likely to start moving his (her) hands and verbalize some kind of activity while engaging the therapist's puppets in a similar activity. If it was the therapist who suggested the game, then the universe of possible associations has been significantly contaminated. But even if the child suggests the game, the game in itself has limitations imposed upon it by the physical structure of the puppets and the hands of the humans who are playing with them. Children commonly will bang the heads of the puppets, one against the other. The examiner who interprets this to

270 *PROGRAMMING NONABUSED CHILDREN*

mean that the child is angry may be stretching a point significantly. The dolls almost ask to be banged together or to engage one another in various kinds of hostile play. Accordingly, the therapist's leading gestures here bring the child down a somewhat narrow path, the path of hostile play.

Levy (1939, 1940) describes a type of child psychotherapy that he refers to as "release therapy." This method was designed to help children verbalize their thoughts and release their feelings about traumatic situations. In order to facilitate this process he structured the doll play in such a way that the child is likely to talk about a particular situation, especially a traumatic one. For example, if a child was dealing with the trauma of being in a hospital, he might walk a boy doll into a make-believe hospital room, lay the child down in a hospital bed, and ask the child to talk about what's happening to the little boy. The child who is reacting to the birth of a new sibling might be confronted with a structured doll-play situation in which the mother is breastfeeding the baby doll. The little boy doll is walked into the room, looks at the mother and baby, and the patient is asked to describe what the little boy is thinking and feeling. This game clearly involves the therapist in moderately leading gestures. Its risk is that it will pressure children into talking about issues that they may wish to repress or that they may be too anxious to discuss. It also has the drawback of "muckraking" and bringing up past traumas that have already been put to rest in a way that is not pathological.

The principle here is that the more intrusive the therapist is, the greater the likelihood of brainwashing and programming, and the greater the likelihood the therapy will produce psychological trauma. And this is what happens, I believe, with children who have never been abused and who have been "treated" for an abuse that never took place. They are made to believe that they were abused. The effects of such programming have yet to be studied in depth because these children represent what is now a new form of psychopathology (see Chapter Five).

Many evaluators are advised to ascertain, early in the first interview, the terms the child uses for the various body parts, especially the sexual ones. As mentioned, the ostensible purpose here is to enable the examiner to communicate better with the child and to understand exactly what organs are being referred to when the child mentions these in the course of the evaluation. This is traditionally accomplished by the examiners pointing to sexual parts on pictures of naked people or special dolls. Commonly, anatomical dolls are used for this purpose, although body charts (such as those of Groth [1984]) are used. Typically, the examiner first points to the various body parts on the clothed doll, e.g., while pointing to the nose the examiner asks, "What's this called?" After a few body parts are identified, the clothes come off. Usually the examiner undresses the doll or will ask the child to assist. Once the doll is naked, the examiner routinely proceeds to point to the various body parts (breasts, bellybutton, penis, vulva, buttocks, anus) and asks the child specifically to name the part pointed to.

The message being given here is that it is perfectly acceptable, proper, and even desirable to point to and even touch these organs. This is a very unique situation for the child. If a teacher were to do this, the Board of Education might unanimously vote to discharge him (her). If parents, relatives, or neighbors were to do this, they would be suspect as child abusers. It is important to appreciate that there is not only a verbal question being asked here when the examiner touches the doll's penis and asks, "What's this called?" A physical activity is being performed that basically sanctions such pointing and touching for the child. I have seen videotapes of examiners who, when asking this question, will take the penis between their thumb and forefinger and talk while manipulating it. This, too, communicates to the child that this kind of activity is acceptable to the evaluator and that if the child would like to act similarly with the doll's penis, he (she) is free to do so. This same principle operates even more poignantly when the examiner puts his (her) finger in the doll's vagina or anus and asks the question, "What's this called?" These same examiners will then consider the child's physical activities with the anatomical dolls to be an exact reenactment of their own sexual encounters.

Maximally Leading Gestures In this, the most contaminating category, the examiner uses the dolls to enact a sexual encounter that has not been enacted by the child and may not even have been described by the child. An example would be of the examiner who takes his (her) finger, inserts it into the doll's vagina, and says, "Did your grandpa put his finger in here?" The child, then, by the processes enumerated above, is likely to engage in this very same behavior with the doll, either in that session or in a subsequent session (either with the same examiner or another evaluator). This is an activity that may never have entered the child's mind previously. Talking about it provides one level of implantation of a visual image of this particular experience. Combining the verbal question with an actual physical enactment provides specific visual details that become incorporated into the mental image of the activity. This serves to enhance the likelihood of a visual image forming, an image that will be referred to in future sessions. And, if the examiner believes that what the child does with the dolls is a true reenactment of actual experiences, then a false sex-abuse accusation is likely to be supported or even created.

In one videotaped evaluation I observed, the examiner was convinced that the alleged perpetrator had taken photographs of the alleged victims of sex abuse in a nursery school. The examiner placed the naked anatomical doll on its back, pulled up the legs, and then asked the child, 'Did he take a picture of you while your legs were up like this?" When the child did not respond affirmatively, he placed the doll in the knee-chest position and asked the question again. This was repeated with other positions, many bizarre, to all of which the child responded positively. In one case I was involved in, the examiner pointed to the vagina of a picture of a naked woman and asked the child, "Did he touch you right here?" The transcript did not in any way indicate that the examiner was pointing to the vaginal area of the picture. Not surprisingly, the child not only answered in the affirmative, but the examiner used this response as evidence that the child had been sexually molested.

In one case in which I was involved, the "validator" was interviewing a two-year-old girl who, in association with parroting her four-year-old sister, claimed that her father touched her "private spot." In the course of her interview with the child, the validator undressed the male doll which she referred to as the "Jim doll." (This was at a point when the children were no longer referring to their father as "Daddy" but as "Jim" in association with the alienation from him.) While holding the doll, the examiner was stroking the penis in masturbatory fashion. As soon as her hand was dropped, the child, not surprisingly, began to imitate this motion. The examiner then asked the child, "Did you touch your daddy's wee-wee?" Not surprisingly, the child responded affirmatively. The written transcript revealed none of these maneuvers. And, on the basis of this segment of the interview, the examiner concluded that the child had masturbated her father.

On many occasions I have seen transcripts that simply indicate that the examiner is saying, "Show me on the girl doll where he put his penis." Not reported on the transcript is the examiner's pointing to and even placing his (her) finger on the vulva or even inside the doll's vagina. The child, then, takes her finger and puts it in the same orifice. It's almost like playing the game, "First you put your finger in, then I'll put my finger in." Children are the world's greatest imitators. They adhere slavishly to the dictum, "If *you're* going to do it, *I'm* going to do it too." And that's a good enough reason for a three-year-old. And in this insidious way, yet another sex-abuse accusation becomes "validated," with absolutely no evidence in the transcript of what has gone on.

Readers of transcripts are not generally aware of the significant amount of activity that is taking place with the dolls while the evaluator and child are talking. This is especially the case with regard to the dressing and undressing of the dolls. I have seen many tapes in which the child, after a short period of "sex play" with the dolls, wants to dress the dolls. Typically, the examiner will find a wide variety of excuses for discouraging the child from doing so, even to the point of physically preventing the child from putting on the doll's clothing. Obviously, the evaluator wants to prolong the period of exposure of the child to the naked dolls. And even when the child is engaged in activities with absolutely no sexual import (usually only a small fragment of these interviews are devoted to nonsexual material), the naked dolls are prominently present within the child's visual field and, obviously, serve as a reminder that they can once again be played with. Generally, it is only at the end of the session, just before it is time to leave, that the dolls are dressed. But even during the dressing phase, in which both the examiner and the child are engaged, there is visualization and touching of the sexual parts.

Early Interview Maneuvers

Typically, the child is brought to the interview by the accusing mother. It is rare for people who refer to themselves as validators to request that the father be present. On those occasions when I have had the opportunity to ask a validator why he (she) did not invite the father, common responses are, "He would deny it anyway so there's no point to my seeing him" and "My job is not to do an investigation; my job is only to interview the child in order to find out whether the child was sexually abused." Also, generally little time is spent with the mother. Usually the validator merely gets a few bits of information from her about the nature of the sex abuse but typically does not spend significant time obtaining more information, especially details of the evolution of the sex-abuse accusation, significant information about the setting in which the sex abuse allegedly occurred, and data that might relate to the mother's credibility. I have seen a number of situations in which the validator, approximately three-quarters of an hour later (by which time the child's initial "evaluation" has been completed), has written on the chart that the child was sexually abused *and* that the father sexually abused the child. In many of these cases, the validator is not even aware of the fact that the parents are involved in a highly acrimonious divorce dispute. The assumption is made, at the outset, that all one need do is interview the child and that one should be able to obtain the information necessary to "validate" the abuse. The assumption is also made that one should be able to obtain this information in the vast majority of cases from children ages two to four and that if one just perseveres long enough, the confirmatory information will ultimately be forthcoming.

My experience has been that in about half of the cases in which I have been involved, the mother has remained in the interview room with the child throughout most, if not all, of this initial interview. The justification given here is that the child would be uncomfortable alone in the room with a strange examiner. There is often little appreciation of the fact that the mother's presence serves as a serious contaminant and increases formidably the likelihood that a false accusation will be supported by the mother's presence. Often the mother helps the child "remember" what to say and the examiner appreciates her cooperation and input, with little appreciation of the educational and programming process that is transpiring.

Quite early in the interview, the validator considers it important to provide the child with some "guidelines" regarding what her purpose is. The rationale here is to help the child feel comfortable in a strange environment. Typically, the child is told that the validator's job is to help "protect" children and to help keep them "safe." Although the validator usually believes that the use of these words helps relax the child, there is little appreciation of the fact that they accomplish just the opposite. Their implication is that the child is somehow being exposed to some danger and that the validator's job is to provide protection. Such reassurances, then, only serve to entrench—at the outset—the notion that the child has indeed been subjected to some dangerous situation. Although sex abuse is not mentioned at this point, it is clear about the path down which the child is being led.

Many validators do have a short "warm-up" period (five minutes or so), the purpose of which is to help the child become more comfortable. During this period the child may be permitted to play with traditional play-therapy equipment. This initial phase may appear harmless enough and may even appear to be good therapeutic technique. However, typically, the examiner is not really concerned about the fantasies produced by the traditional equipment at this point. I have seen tapes in which very significant material has been elicited during these first few minutes, but the examiner has not appreciated the value of what is being said because he (she) has been merely going through the motions of this "warm-up" period in order to get the *real* material, which is obviously related to sex abuse. Accordingly, this material was not followed up, material that was genuinely related to what was on the child's mind at that point. Had this material been focused on, the examiner might have obtained true data that could have been useful for ascertaining whether the child had been sexually abused. So even here, where good technique is ostensibly being utilized, we already see a serious contaminant. Although some validators' examining rooms do have a traditional assortment of child play equipment, I have seen many (via videotape studies) in which the only equipment visible to the child are the anatomical dolls. Although these dolls are usually dressed, they are the *only* play equipment available to the child. Accordingly, when the child is presumably invited to engage in free play, the only equipment available is guaranteed to elicit material related to sexual issues. Some validators will, however, engage in a period of free play with standard equipment, play that is designed to relax the child and make the child more comfortable and familiar with the examiner.

Ascertaining Whether the Child Can Differentiate Between the Truth and a Lie

Early in the interview these examiners first satisfy themselves that the child can differentiate between the truth and a lie. In many states, the judge, lawyers, and all other investigators are required by statute to submit to this requirement before proceeding with the substantive issues in the interview. For example, when examining children in the three-to-five-year age level, a typical maneuver in the service of satisfying this requirement is for the examiner to point to a red object and say to the child, "This is *red*. Is that the truth or a lie?" If the child answers that the examiner is being truthful ("That's true"), the examiner may then proceed by pointing to something that is green and saying, "This is black. Is that the truth or a lie?" If the child then states that the examiner is then "lying," the examiner may then proceed to a series of other equally asinine questions in order to demonstrate that the child knows the difference between the truth and a lie.

The examples I have given here are the most common types of questions asked to ascertain whether the child knows the difference between the truth and a lie. Examiners who go through this ritual fail to appreciate that for children between the ages of two and five the word *lie* might mean "a naughty word." Between ages five and eight-and-a-half it might merely mean "something that isn't true," including a mistake (Frost, 1986). In the examples just mentioned, the child might be thinking that the examiner has made a mistake. Yet, because the child uses the words *mistake* and *lie* interchangeably, the child might say that the examiner is lying when in actuality the child believes the examiner made a mistake. McIver (1986), in a discussion of the works of Jean Piaget (*The Moral Development of Children*), refers to Piaget's position that "a lie is what an adult says it is." So much for the semantic problems inherent in this simplistic approach to the assessment of the child's credibility.

But there are other problems associated with this line of questioning. The same child is not asked the question, "Santa Claus brings you gifts at Christmas time. Is that the truth or a lie?" "The good fairy left money under your pillow after your tooth fell out. Is that the truth or a lie?" Obviously, asking any question that would be more complex—one that might result in the child's demonstrating confusion between fact and fantasy—would confront the examiner with the obvious fact that young children have great difficulty differentiating between fact and fantasies, between the truth and a lie, in a wide variety of areas. As mentioned previously, we adults are not famous for our capacity to make such differentiations either. Ignoring this obvious fact enables such examiners to proceed with the "validation." Nor do they set up situations in which the child is likely to lie, such as when accused of a transgression. Children traditionally lie under such circumstances, but to demonstrate this in the interview would, of course, raise questions about the child's veracity regarding the sexual-abuse issue.

In one sex-abuse case I was involved in, a four-and-a-half-year-old child got all the "right" answers to the simplistic truth-vs.-lie questions of the aforementioned type. The following interchange then took place:

Investigator: Good girl! And what happens to you if you tell a lie?
Child: Your nose gets bigger and bigger and bigger and bigger and bigger and bigger every time you lie!
Investigator: Like who?
Child: Like Pinocchio.
Investigator: (laughs)
Child: (laughs)

Not surprisingly, this examiner had concluded that the child knew the difference between the truth and a lie and totally ignored the implications of the child's subsequent response, namely, that her ability to differentiate between fact and fantasy did not go so far that she recognized as fantasy the nose-growing scenario in the Pinocchio story. The traditional questions select the most obvious and simplistic examples in order to "prove" that the child knows the difference. Examiners who have formulated these questions do not select questions that might truly tax the child's capacity to differentiate between fantasy and reality. It is like giving an intelligence test in which the most difficult questions are "How much is one and one?" and "What color is grass?" It is to be noted here, also, that both the child and the investigator laughed together. We see here one example of the levity that is often present in these interviews. It is often a game that can best be called, "See if you can guess the right answers." I will elaborate on this point below.

It is of interest that later in the same interview, while the child was providing allegedly corroborative details about the alleged sex abuse, she suddenly interrupted the interviewer and the following interchange took place:

> *Child*: Is my nose growing?
> *Investigator*: No. Why?
> *Child*: 'Cause.
> *Investigator*: Does that mean you're lying?
> *Child*: No.
> *Investigator*: Well, then, why would your nose be growing?
> *Child*: (laughs) I don't know, to make a joke.
> *Investigator*: Ohh . . . a joke . . . okay. Have you ever seen your daddy without his clothes on?
> *Child*: Uhh . . . sometimes.

Here, the child clearly recognized that she was lying and feared that the investigator would learn this by seeing her nose grow. The child is clearly fearful that her lying would be revealed and then protected herself from anticipated criticism for lying by claiming that she was only joking. They both laughed together about her "joke." We see here also another typical maneuver of validators, specifically, the selective inattention phenomenon. The examiner did not explore further the obvious possibility that the child was lying about the sex abuse and that her concern about her nose growing was an obvious manifestation of such concern. Rather, she and the child both laughed and then the examiner went back to her sledgehammer leading question regarding the sex abuse: "Have you ever seen your daddy without his clothes on?" Here we see another clear demonstration of the child's inability to differentiate fact from fantasy, at least with regard to the Pinocchio story. Yet this examiner concluded that the child could indeed differentiate between the truth and a lie and that she was indeed being truthful when she claimed sex abuse. Again, we see the levity of the interview, a point that I will comment on below.

What is also ignored by validators is the fact that *knowing the difference* between the truth and a lie is very different from the issue of whether the child *will actually* lie. These evaluators make the very naive assumption that because the child knows the difference between the truth and a lie, the child will not lie. The vast majority of people who commit crimes know quite well the difference between the truth and a lie; yet they still lie, especially in response to questions that might divulge their guilt. The whole inquiry regarding differentiating between the truth and a lie is a mockery, a sham, a ritual that these people go through in order to convince themselves that they are indeed getting to "the truth."

"The Truth" as Code-Term for Sex Abuse

In ancient Rome it was generally held that slaves made poor witnesses at trials because they would typically lie. Accordingly, slaves who were called upon to testify were often beaten mercilessly in order to be sure that they were telling the truth. This was the main reason why masters were generally reluctant to allow their slaves to testify—after being subjected to the aforementioned methods for "helping" them recall the truth, they were left basically useless as workers. During the Middle Ages (and beyond) it was quite common to "help" witnesses remember what the truth was by stretching their bodies on a rack, progressively turning thumb screws, and utilizing other methods of recall-engendering torture. And there are many parts of the world today in which torture is still routinely used in order to help prisoners remember "the truth." If the reader believes that such methods were used only by barbarians in the distant past, or only utilized today by sadistic psychopaths in other parts of the world, then the reader is out of touch with what is going on among mothers, validators, and children whom they are unrelentingly encouraging to tell "the truth." The methods of torture are no longer physical; they are emotional and psychological. But they are methods of torture nevertheless. And there is only one *truth* being extracted: admission of sexual abuse. Once the child is brought down the sex-abuse disclosure track, the child is unrelentingly programmed to tell "the truth."

At those times when the child describes the sexual molestation, the interrogator is satisfied and all agree that the child has been telling the truth. When, however, the child recants, does not remember, or exhibits ambivalence regarding whether the molestation did indeed occur, the child is then repeatedly coerced to tell "the truth." Denial of sexual molestation is not the truth. Only a description of molestation is "the truth." It doesn't take much time for the child to learn that the truth is merely a code term for sexual molestation. Accordingly, before interviews with validators and other interrogators, the mother intermittently (from the sidelines) reminds the child to tell "the truth." In interviews as well (mothers are often present during these interviews), the mother intermittently (from the sidelines) reminds the child to tell "the truth." And the validator knows quite well that there is only one truth. She and the mother speak the same language. They have the same shibboleth for sexual molestation. And the validator will not accept the child's negations and will only ask the child to tell "the truth." The bottom line of this whole scenario is the validator's going to court and claiming that she believes that the child was telling "the truth."

Repeating-the-Same-Question Technique

When the child does not provide the answer desired by the biased examiner, the same question will be repeated (often with greater emphasis) in the hope that the child will change his (her) response. Sometimes one such repetition will suffice; sometimes two or three are required. In any case, the child gets the message that the provided response is not the acceptable one and so an alternative is provided in the hope that this will then please the examiner. This process is not only seen in the early phases of programming but later on in the service of "cleaning up" the scenario and removing contradictory, preposterous, or other elements that would lessen the scenario's credibility.

Parents typically use this technique when they want to extract a confession from a child. A typical interchange:

Parent: Did you steal money from your brother's piggy bank?
Child: No.

Parent: I repeat! Did you steal money from your brother's piggy bank?
Child: No.
Parent: I'm going to ask you once again. I want you to tell me *the truth* now. Did you steal your brother's money?
Child: Well, I only took some of it, but he owed me money anyway.

Parents will use this principle when trying to extract a sex-abuse "disclosure" from a child. In a child-custody dispute, for example, the mother may suspect that the father molested the child during visitation. Over many months she may ask the child, at the end of each visit, detailed questions about bathing and dressing procedures in the context of which she will ask the child whether the father touched her private parts. Initially, the child denies such encounters. Ultimately, the child gets the message that a positive answer is desired. Because children are gullible, suggestible, and want to ingratiate themselves to adult authority, the child will inevitably provide an affirmative answer.

I have seen the same procedures utilized by prosecutors and other overzealous investigators in nursery school cases. Initially, the question is just repeated and denials are responded to with disbelief. Ultimately, the child gets the message and gives the desired affirmative answer. Overzealous and incompetent validators do this in the course of their therapy by asking the same question repeatedly, sometimes in the course of a single interview but often over the course of many interviews. The theory is that the child is in a phase of denial or too embarrassed to talk about the abuse, but ultimately he (she) will "disclose."

Belief in the Preposterous

No matter how preposterous the allegation, no matter how absurd, these examiners will believe them. They have no trouble believing that adult males can have sexual intercourse with two-year-old girls with no evidence of pain, bleeding, and trauma. The facts that the adult male penis cannot be accommodated by the vagina of a two-year-old and that insertion will result in the aforementioned consequences are ignored. They would believe that a child can be forced to drink urine and eat feces and yet, minutes later, be perfectly happy and friendly—without any sign or symptom of the indignities suffered only a few minutes earlier. They would believe that one person was able to undress 25 children, engage them simultaneously in a wide variety of sexual activities, and then dress them quickly in order to be picked up by their parents. And yet, not a single child left wearing the wrong sock, underwear, or other article of clothing. They believe that children can have swords inserted up their rectums with no medical evidence. They believe that children can be smeared with feces and yet be so quickly and thoroughly cleaned that not a scintilla of evidence remains to serve as a clue as to what transpired only a few minutes earlier.

They believe that children can witness the barbecuing of babies, the slaughtering of infants and animals, and their burial in cemeteries, without breathing a word of these activities for weeks and even months after exposure to these atrocities. They can believe that dozens of children can be sworn to silence without ever breathing a word to their parents about any of the tortures to which they have been subjected. They believe that children can be stabbed with scissors, knives, and other instruments in their mouths, ears, noses, vaginas, and anuses, and yet not reveal any signs of their trauma (even on medical examination) only minutes after the event. They believe that bands of men wearing masks and costumes (clowns, big bad wolf costumes, cops, firemen) can enter a school, involve the children in a wide variety of the aforementioned rituals and abuses, and then sneak out, completely unobserved by teachers, parents, and school administrators.

They believe that pedophiles are exceedingly clever and cunning in their methods, so much so that even the most experienced detectives and investigators may find no clues or remnants whatsoever of the wide variety of tortures, rituals, and abuses to which these children have been subjected. Even though no one has ever found any of the dead bodies that these children describe having been buried as a part of their abuse rituals, and even though many cemeteries have been dug up in the search for such bodies, they still believe that such sacrifices indeed took place. Many believe that hundreds of babies have been burned, stabbed, cooked, barbecued, and drowned in the service of warning children that this will happen to them if they breathe a word of their experiences to their parents. Even though not one remnant of any of the aforementioned infants has been found, the belief is still strong. It is as if the "common-sense" cells and tracks of their brains have been extirpated by a special operation.

Rationalizing as Credible the Incredible

Validators are highly skilled in their ability to utilize rationalization. This is especially the case when they are confronted with material that is absurd and ludicrous. They have devised a series of cognitive maneuvers in the service of this goal. For example, if a child states that the sexual molestation occurred in her (his) own home (something that no one on the scene believes is true), the explanation provided is that the child is fusing two different scenes and that such fusion is common among children of that age. A child may say that the molestation took place in the therapist's office, again something that no one believes is the case. A common explanation is that the child has relocated the abuse in order to place it in a "safe haven," thereby lessening the trauma. Every conceivable distortion that a child might possibly entertain can be given credibility by such rationalizations. When confronted with the fact that shoving a sword up the rectum of a child (or anyone else for that matter) would produce quick and certain death, the examiner will say, "Perhaps it was a toy sword or perhaps the perpetrator *threatened* to shove a sword up the child's rectum and the child is merely creating a fantasy that is a derivative of this threat." The greater the number of such rationalizations, and the more frequently the examiner needs to twist logic and thereby invoke one of these rationalizations, the greater the likelihood one is dealing with a false accusation. In fact, this is one of the hallmarks of the false accusation.

In one of the cases in which I was involved, many of the children claimed that the alleged perpetrator had brought the children to his own home and that he himself had called the police and was then arrested. No one really believed this and no one ever went to the trouble of asking the police whether there was any record of such a call. The therapists and investigators, however, came up with a whole series of rationalizations to justify this aspect of the scenario. Some of the explanations proffered: "He (the alleged perpetrator) dressed as a policeman and made believe that he made the call," "The children misinterpreted someone as being a policeman when he really wasn't," and "Someone else threatened that they would call the police." In the same case, one three-year-old girl claimed that the perpetrator had cut off his penis, put it on his head, and squeezed it to the point where blood dripped on the top of his head. Most of the validators (although I cannot say all) did not believe that this actually happened. Certainly, no one called in a urologist to examine the boy to see if there was any evidence for this "penisectomy" that this boy allegedly performed on himself. One of the rationalization scenarios considered was that the boy put ketchup on his head and that the child somehow considered the ketchup to be blood. (Interestingly, rationalizations were not provided for other aspects of this ludicrous scenario.)

When such rationalizations are utilized, those testifying in support of the defense do well to make comments along these lines: "Every time one utilizes this type of rationalization maneuver—a rationalization that serves to make credible the incredible—one adds to the likelihood that we are dealing here with a false accusation. The most likely things are most likely. The most likely explanation is the one that is more often related to reality. Every time one must do mental gymnastics in order to make credible the incredible, one is providing support for the argument that one is dealing with a false accusation."

Selective Ignoring of the Impossible

The aforementioned activities, although outlandish and preposterous, are still within the realm of possibility (often narrowly so). When examiners are confronted with information that even they recognize as impossible, then other psychological mechanisms must be utilized in order to maintain the delusion that the child has been sexually abused. For example, in the course of describing the abuse, the child says that her mother (the one who brought about the allegation in the first place) was present at the time when the nursery school teacher fed her "doo-doo." Because the examiner does not believe that this was the case, this bit of information will be disregarded with the excuse that "the child was tired at the time." When the child states that the abuse took place in the examiner's office, a common explanation is "That's her way of saying that she views my office as a 'safe haven' and that's why she spoke about the abuse taking place here." When confronted with inconsistencies that are mutually contradictory and would suggest that one of the versions has to be impossible, the examiner might state: "It's not my job to confront the child with inconsistencies or impossible things," or "Of course, that's impossible," or "That's just a product of his imagination. It's not even worth discussing." Sometimes nothing at all is said and when the child makes an impossible comment the examiner just goes on ignoring it as if it were never spoken.

Another way of dealing with the introduction of impossible elements into the scenario is to utilize the mechanism of splitting. Specifically, if the child states, for example, that all four grandparents were there and observed the molestation, the examiner might state, "She's confusing two events, the molestation and the family gathering." In this way the sex-abuse scenario remains "pure" and its contaminants removed.

Sometimes the examiner does not even feel the need to provide a rationalization for ignoring material that might suggest that the story is not valid. One child claimed that her nursery school teacher had picked up a car and had thrown it into a tree. The examiner unashamedly stated that, of course, this could not have happened and then went on to accept as valid all other information that supported the conclusion that sex abuse did indeed occur. This selective inattention to noncorroborating data is one of the hallmarks of these validators' interview techniques.

Another maneuver utilized by these examiners is this: "Her denial proves it's true. That's typical of these children who are sexually abused. They keep denying that it happened. That's because they were threatened with terrible consequences if they were to admit it. I've seen many such cases." Another explanation that is provided when a child denies that anything has happened is: "She's repressing it. It's been so traumatic to her that she can't talk about it. It may take months of therapy before she'll be able to admit it, even to herself. That's how powerful these repressive forces are." Obviously, there is no way for accused people to win when the child is interviewed by such validators.

The Utilization of the Yes/No Question

Competent examiners recognize the risks of the yes/no question and generally avoid it. They realize that little information is obtained from such a question. (This is something that attorneys and judges have yet to discover.) When one gets a yes or no answer, one does not know whether the interviewee is lying, telling the truth, or merely providing an answer (yes or no selected at random) to "get the examiner off his (her) back." Spontaneously verbalized sentences and paragraphs are far better sources of information. These essay-type answers are more likely to be revealing of the child's true thoughts and feelings. But these examiners do not appreciate this obvious fact. Generally, they persist in the inquiry until they get the yeses they want. Often the questions are quite confusing to the child, to the point where the child does not even understand what is being asked. In such an altered state of consciousness, the child is likely to say yes to every question in order to get the examiner to come to the end of the unrelenting series of questions. Because children are suggestible and wish to ingratiate themselves to authority, they may provide all the yes answers the examiner wishes.

The yes/no question is also used in association with the seed-planting phenomenon. On day one the examiner asks the child if she ever had a particular sexual experience—for example, whether her father put his penis in her mouth. (This is a very dangerous thing for an adult male to do to an unreceptive child [unless the child has no teeth].) The child may never have entertained such a fantasy. However, the very question has now planted the seed, and the visual image of such an encounter has now been created in the child's mind. At that point, the child who has never had such an experience will say no. During a subsequent interview, the interviewer (or another examiner) may ask the same question. This time the visual image will be brought out of memory storage and the child may be somewhat confused regarding whether such a thing actually happened. A young child may not be able to differentiate between an image that depicts something that actually happened and an image that depicts something that was suggested. In fact, we adults are not immune from such a process either. (Professional brainwashers and propagandists know well that if you tell someone a lie frequently enough, the person will believe it.) If the child then shows some confusion regarding whether such an event actually took place, the examiner is sure to hammer away at the question: "Are you sure?" "Are you sure he didn't do it?" Finally, the child says, "No, I'm not sure" and that will serve as another nail in the coffin of the accused. This is not only tragic for the falsely accused person, but it is also tragic for the child who is likely to believe for the rest of her (his) life that the event took place.

The So-called Indicators of Sex Abuse

Validators utilize an ever-growing list of "indicators" of sex abuse. These are the behavioral manifestations, which can be observed by parents, that result from sex abuse. These manifestations can be roughly divided into two categories (although there is some overlap). The first is those behaviors that most competent and knowledgeable observers would consider normal. In fact, healthy and knowledgeable parents would also consider these behaviors to be part of the normal child's repertoire. It takes a zealous validator and a gullible parent to share in the delusion that these behavioral patterns are indeed the result of sex abuse. The second category is psychological symptoms, which are listed in the manual of psychiatric disorders. Most competent evaluators recognize that these disorders have a wide variety of causes, most of which have absolutely nothing to do with sex abuse. The validators would consider most of them to result from sex abuse. Of course, this division into two categories is my own; validators have just one long list of behavioral manifestations, all of which derive from sex abuse. I will now provide a few examples from these two categories.

"Indicators" That Would Be Considered Normal by Competent Evaluators (Pathologizing Normal Behavior) Examiners who consider the behavioral manifestations in this category as signs of sex abuse must be abysmally ignorant of normal childhood development. Or, if they have received such training, they have to obliterate from memory what they have learned. Furthermore, if they themselves have children, they must deny their own observations (past or present) regarding the presence of these behaviors in their offspring. The frequency with which they are capable of ignoring what they observe is a testament to the power of the human mind to utilize selective inattention, denial, and projection. For example, one doesn't have to be a full professor of pediatrics to know that many children are still bedwetting at ages three and four. This does not prevent validators from considering bedwetting at that age to be a sign of sex abuse.

Furthermore, one does not have to be a full professor of child psychiatry to know that normal children exhibit occasional nightmares, especially in early to mid-childhood. Some of these nightmares are the direct result of frightening experiences, such as watching a "scary" movie on television or actually having a frightening experience. Such nightmares are part of the desensitization process that helps children adapt to these frightening exposures. Other nightmares arise sui generis and have complex psychological meanings that are still not completely understood (Gardner, 1988b, 1992b). Validators will typically consider nightmares to be one of the important indicators of sex abuse. Although frequent nightmares of certain types might very well be an indicator of sex abuse, these evaluators typically do not attempt to make any differentiation between normal nightmares and those that might be exhibited by sexually abused children. I have never seen a validator's report in which an inquiry has been made into the frequency and content of nightmares and the relationship between the described nightmares and the alleged abuse. Rather, the presence of a nightmare—any nightmare at all—is used as strong support for the conclusion that the child has been sexually molested. This is not the way the human mind works. If a nightmare is being used for the purposes of desensitization to a trauma (whether it be sex abuse or another kind of trauma), it is likely to serve this function soon after the abuse—even the first night following the abuse—not months or years later. Validators ignore this obvious fact in order to justify the use of the nightmare as an indicator of sex abuse. We see here yet another example of the previously described hiatus phenomenon.

Furthermore, if the nightmare is to be used as an indicator, one would think that the examiner might want to consider the *content*, especially with regard to the likelihood that it relates to sex abuse. Most validators do not seem to have any need to do this. Any nightmare, regardless of content, is used as an indicator. They can justify this with the old psychoanalytic standby that it represents a symbol for the sex abuse. The most common normal nightmare involves some malevolent entity (a point, a shadow, a monster, a bad man, a bogeyman, etc.) coming menacingly toward the child. Typically, the child wakes up just before the malevolent figure reaches the child. Invariably, evaluators consider this malevolent entity to be symbolic of the alleged sex-abuse perpetrator. Whatever the meaning of this nightmare (and my own opinion on its meaning is irrelevant at this point), they do not see the need to explain how the vast majority of nonsexually abused children will have the *same* nightmare. (The reader who is interested in my opinion of the meaning of this common nightmare might wish to refer to my publications on the meaning of children's dreams [Gardner, 1986, 1988b].) In one case in which I was involved, a three-year-old child described how the "big bad wolf" was chasing her in a dream. Predictably, the validator concluded that this dream was proof that the child had been sexually abused. This child was one of many involved in a day-care center sex-abuse "scandal." The parents actively communicated with one another regarding their children's symptoms and, not surprisingly, within a few weeks most of the other children were also reporting big-bad-wolf nightmares. Rather than consider this to be the result of the mass hysteria phenomenon, all the validators concluded that the big bad wolf represented the alleged perpetrator, an adolescent boy whom I considered to be completely innocent.

The parents are alerted to be on the lookout for any behavioral changes. Predictably, these are considered to be manifestations of sex abuse. In order to utilize this criterion, one must ignore the obvious fact that every child in the history of the world exhibits behavioral changes, often on a day-to-day basis. Normal children exhibit behavioral changes; if they did not, they would not be moving along the developmental track. The one-year-old behaves differently from the newborn infant, the two-year-old differently from the one-year-old, the three-year-old differently from the two-year-old, and so on. Development does not run an even course; rather, it moves in spurts and plateaus. Furthermore, children go ahead three steps and go back two steps, and so it goes. Children have good days and bad days (just like adults). Some of the behavioral changes that validators will consider manifestations of sex abuse are an increase in sibling rivalry, refusal to go to sleep, changing attitudes regarding foods, periods of uncooperative behavior, defiance, and exaggerated reactions to normal disciplinary measures. In one well-publicized case, the parents informed the validator that the child had developed an aversion to tuna fish. The validator quickly concluded that this was yet another proof that the child had been sexually molested. Her reasoning: The human vagina, as everyone knows, smells like fish. This child's aversion to tuna fish must relate to the fact that she had performed cunnilingus on her nursery school teacher, the alleged perpetrator. With the utilization of logic like this, it is easy to see how impotent accused individuals feel when the alleged victims are being evaluated by such sick and/or ignorant examiners.

The list of indicators that is derived from normal childhood behavior is long, and there are many other examples. I usually refer to this practice by validators as *pathologizing normal behavior*. Temper tantrums are normal, especially between the ages of two and four. In fact, it is reasonable to say that all children, at some time or another, exhibit temper tantrums. It is the normal, natural, primitive way in which children express their anger. Predictably, validators consider temper tantrums to be a manifestation of sex abuse, the child allegedly acting out the anger that was built up against the perpetrator. All siblings exhibit frequent rivalry. In fact, it is ubiquitous. The first-born is generally king (queen) of the world. The second-born now requires that the throne be shared, and worse, the time that the parents must devote to the second is greater than that which must be devoted to the first. This produces even greater rivalrous feelings. And when other children come along, there is even greater resentment over the fact that the parental involvement must be shared among all the children. I would go further and say that children who do not exhibit rivalrous feelings toward their siblings have some form of psychopathology, especially in the area of suppression and repression of their thoughts and feelings. Once again, validators ignore this reality and would consider sibling rivalry to be one of the indicators.

And now to masturbation. All normal children explore their bodies from time to time and do not differentiate between the genital area and other parts. They have to learn from others that touching oneself in that particular area is socially unacceptable, especially in public. Children usually learn by themselves that stimulation of that area can provide pleasures different from those derived from touching other areas. Although orgastic capacity is possible at birth, most young children under the age of nine or ten do not stimulate themselves to the point where they reach orgasm. Those who do may very well have been prematurely introduced into the pubital and postpubital levels of sexual arousal. Certainly, such introduction can be the result of sex abuse. But this is not the *only* reason why a younger child might masturbate to orgasm. In some children it is a tension-relieving device, especially when they grow up in homes in which there has been significant privation and/or stress. In some it can serve as an antidepressant. When a knowledgeable evaluator hears that a child is masturbating, the examiner will make detailed inquiry about the frequency, the time of onset, the circumstances under which it occurs, and whether the child masturbates to orgasm. All this information is useful in ascertaining whether the masturbation is related to sex abuse. Typically, validators do not make such inquiries. They hear the word *masturbation* and that is enough to prove that the child has been sexually molested.

Prohibition against and exaggerated reactions to masturbation have been a well-established tradition in the United States. In the late 18th century, Dr. Benjamin Rush (a signer of the Declaration of Independence and the founder of the American Psychiatric Association) warned that masturbation causes poor eyesight, epilepsy, memory loss, and pulmonary tuberculosis. He stated that women who masturbate are "feeble and of a transient nature compared to the strain of physical and moral evils which this solitary vice fixes upon the body and mind" (Michael et al., 1994).

In the late 19th century, in both the United States and England, we witnessed a period of obsessive preoccupation with and draconian condemnation of childhood masturbation. Unfortunately, physicians (who should have known better) were actively involved in this campaign of denunciation and attempts to obliterate entirely this nefarious practice. Doctors considered it to be the cause of a wide variety of illnesses, e.g., blindness, insanity, and muscle spasms. Various kinds of restraints were devised in order to prevent children from engaging in this dangerous practice. Some girls were even subjected to clitorectomies, so dangerous was the practice considered to be. Parents were given a long list of symptoms that were considered to be concomitants of masturbation. Some of the alerting signs were temper tantrums, bedwetting, sleep disturbances, appetite changes, mood fluctuations, and withdrawal. Obviously, in the hundred years since those sad times, we seem to have gone back full circle. The same list of symptoms that were indicators of masturbation are now considered to be indicators of sex abuse.

At the turn of the 19th century, the antimasturbation movement was led by J. H. Kellogg and Sylvester Graham. Kellogg claimed that his corn flakes could help people fight the masturbation urge and Graham proclaimed that his graham crackers could serve this purpose. But these men were not simply promulgating their views in the service of pushing their products; they were fanatics. Michael et al. (1994) state with regard to Graham:

> Graham, for example, wrote in his 1834 book, *A Lecture to a Young Man*, that masturbation would transform a young boy into "a confirmed and degraded idiot, whose deeply sunken and vacant, glossy eye and livid shriveled countenance, and ulcerous, toothless gums, and fetid breath, and feeble, broken voice, and emaciated and dwarfish and crooked body, and almost hairless head—covered perhaps by suppurating blisters and running sores—denote a premature old age! a blighted body—and a ruined soul!" (p. 160)

With regard to Kellogg, they state:

> Kellogg's bestselling book, *Plain Facts for Old and Young Embracing the Natural History and Hygiene of Organic Life*, published in 1888, had a similar horrifying description of the masturbator. There were thirty-nine signs of masturbation that should alert parents, Kellogg wrote, including rounded shoulders, weak backs, paleness, acne, heart palpitations, and epilepsy. The masturbating young people also could develop bashfulness, boldness, mock piety, and confusion. They might start using tobacco or biting their nails or wetting the bed.
>
> To curb masturbation, Kellogg suggested that parents bandage the child's genitals, cover them with a cage, or tie the hands. Another remedy was circumcision, "without administering an anesthetic, as the brief pain attending the operation will have a salutary effect upon the mind, especially if it be connected with the idea of punishment." Kellogg suggested that older boys have their foreskins sutured shut over the glans, to prevent an erection. His advice for parents of girls was to apply "pure carbolic acid to the clitoris." (pp. 160-161)

Legrand et al. (1989) have written a fascinating article describing the similarities between the masturbation hysteria of the late 19th century and the sex-abuse hysteria of the late 20th century, with a comparison of the lists of "indicators."

It is unfortunate that physicians have played an important role in these crazes. As I have discussed in detail elsewhere (Gardner, 1991a), it was a doctor (Dr. William Griggs of Salem) who first "diagnosed" the children in the Salem witchcraft trials as being possessed by the devil. Doctors were actively involved in the antimasturbation fanaticism of the late 19th century. And, unfortunately, there are "doctors" actively involved in the present fiasco. There are physicians who are diagnosing sex abuse in the vast majority of children they examine, utilizing criteria that are generally considered to be within the normal range (e.g., anal "winking" and hymenal tags). And there are other kinds of doctors (Ph.D. psychologists and M.D. psychiatrists) who are serving as validators and therapists and are perpetrating the abominations described throughout this book.

"Indicators" That Would Be Considered by Competent Observers to Be Symptomatic of Disorders Having Nothing to Do with Sex Abuse Here I refer to those symptoms that are to be found in the *Diagnostic and Statistical Manual of the American Psychiatric Association (DSM-IV)*. If we are to believe the validators, just about any symptom in this manual that could possibly have a psychogenic (or environmental) cause can be a manifestation of sex abuse. These would include depression, phobias, tics, obsessive-compulsive rituals, conduct disorders, antisocial behavior, hyperactivity, attention deficit disorder, headaches, gastrointestinal complaints (nausea, cramps, diarrhea), musculoskeletal complaints, etc. In short, if there is any possibility of attributing symptoms to sex abuse, the evaluator will do so. It is easier to do this when one is ignorant of the multiplicity of factors that can indeed bring about such disorders. Many validators lack this training and so have no problem with this oversimplified approach to the explanation for these symptoms.

The maneuver utilized here is to assume, often reflexly, that a psychopathological manifestation is the result of sex abuse. In order to do this, the evaluator must make the assumption that the child came from a normal, healthy home and all went well prior to the alleged sex abuse.

Typically, these examiners make little if any inquiry into the home situation. Detailed interviews of the parents are quite uncommon; rather, from the outset, the primary (and often exclusive) focus is on the child. Most often the conclusion that the child was sexually abused is made within a few minutes, with absolutely no inquiry into the family background, especially with regard to the presence of factors that might be contributory to the development of psychopathology. Many of the validators would not know how to conduct such an evaluation, so limited has been their training. Obviously, if they were to conduct such inquiries, they might learn that the origin of the symptoms has nothing to do with sex abuse but is more likely to be the result of psychopathology-engendering environmental influences.

Another common maneuver is to attribute to sex abuse the symptoms that arose directly from the series of interrogations conducted by the validators, lawyers, psychologists, psychiatrists, prosecutors, etc. A detailed history (which most of these individuals fail to take) would quickly indicate that the child's symptoms began at around the time of the interrogations, rather than at the time of the alleged sex abuse. Of course, validators would not want to believe for one moment that their allegedly sensitive and nonintrusive investigations could bring about psychopathology. I consider my own interviews to be sophisticated and to be ones in which I avoid the numerous interview pitfalls and errors described in this book. These are described in detail elsewhere (Gardner, 1995a). However, I openly admit that even my interviews may be stressful to children and might contribute to the development of psychopathology. However, in my defense, they are limited to a few interviews and I do not conduct "therapy" for sex abuse, unless I am 100 percent convinced that the abuse has indeed taken place. With regard to the stresses related to the few interviews I do conduct during evaluations, I believe that their effects are small as far as their contribution to producing long-term and even permanent psychopathology. Such stresses are a small price to pay when one considers the terrible consequences to a falsely accused person if the court (and often the jury) is not convinced that the allegation is false. We have to weigh here the trauma to the child caused by my inquiry against the psychological trauma suffered by a falsely accused person—whose life may be destroyed and who may even be incarcerated for many years.

"The Sex-Abuse Syndrome"

There are some examiners who claim that the child's symptoms are manifestations of "the sex-abuse syndrome." When asked what exactly is the sex-abuse syndrome, they will describe the particular symptoms that the child exhibits (both normal and abnormal) that are allegedly manifestations of it. As mentioned, there is no symptom that escapes being included under this rubric. The fact that *DSM-IV* does not recognize such a syndrome and the fact that it is the only syndrome in the history of psychiatry that includes *all* psychological symptoms and behavioral manifestations—both normal and abnormal—does not deter these evaluators from resorting to this meaningless statement. I sometimes have the thought, when reading the reports of such evaluators, that *DSM-IV* should have as its subtitle: "The Sex-Abuse Syndrome." It is important to note that in many states testimony based on a so-called sex-abuse syndrome is not admissible in courts of law.

The Child Sexual Abuse Accommodation Syndrome

The *child sexual abuse accommodation syndrome* (CSAAS) is a term that was introduced by Summit. His first article on this syndrome appeared in 1983. The syndrome consists of a series of reactions that children have to being sexually abused in the intrafamilial situation.

Five stages are described:

1. Secrecy
2. Helplessness
3. Entrapment and accommodation
4. Delayed, unconvincing disclosure
5. Retraction

The primary manifestations of each of these stages will first be presented. Because Summit's cases involved primarily father-daughter incest, the abuser will be referred to as the father (he) and the victim as the daughter (she).

Secrecy Typically, the child is warned by the abuser never to reveal the molestation because to do so would result in terrible consequences. The threats range from allusion to vague and nonspecific consequences to very specific ones such as "Your mother will kill you," "I'll kill your dog," and "I'll kill you." These threats may be repeated with the result that the child may become terrorized. Often, when the child attempts divulgence to others, they will respond with denial, disbelief, and warnings to the child never to mention such things. These responses tend to communicate to the child that terrible acts have been perpetrated, too terrible to talk about. They also have the effect of discouraging the child from disclosing the molestation and thereby entrenching the secrecy phase.

Helplessness Because of the disparity in size and power between the child victim and the abuser, the child feels overwhelmed and helpless. In the incestuous situation this feeling of helplessness is even more profound because the child has no escape. Children are generally easily intimidated by an adult molester, and the child's failure to find an adult advocate entrenches the sense of helplessness.

Entrapment and Accommodation It is rare for the molestation to be a one-time occurrence. Rather, more often it is repeated over months and even years. Most often the adult becomes addicted to the molestation because it is so easily accomplished. Over time, because there is no escape, the child resigns herself to the experiences as part of life's pattern.

A variety of accommodation maneuvers may then develop. Some children lessen their helplessness by developing the delusion that they themselves have been the initiators. Others become receptive and accommodating in the hope of earning the love and acceptance and avoiding the rejection of the abuser. By psychological splitting, the child denies that the abusing father is in any way "bad" and becomes convinced that he is "good." Another accommodation mechanism is a derivative of the child's being told that if she does not submit, the father will have no choice but to turn to other siblings. In this way the child comes to feel that she is acting nobly. Keeping the secret protects the mother from the devastating effects of disclosure, and this too enables the child to feel good about the maintenance of secrecy. Protecting the father from the disruption of the home, divorce, and even a jail sentence can also serve this purpose. Summit (1983) puts it well: "Maintaining a lie to keep the secret is the ultimate virtue, while telling the truth would be the greatest sin."

The rage engendered in this situation becomes internalized and contributes to the development of a wide variety of psychopathological mechanisms and, when it erupts, it is often released via a wide variety of antisocial behaviors. Males are more likely to act out their anger, whereas females are more likely to internalize it. For adolescents, drugs and alcohol may be used to deal with the painful affects attendant to the ongoing state of subjugation.

Other accommodation mechanisms are described by Summit, but to detail them would be beyond the purposes of this summary.

Delayed, Conflicted, and Unconvincing Disclosure In many cases disclosures may never be made. In most, adolescence is the earliest time of disclosure. Even in this period the mother may be disbelieving, especially because of her appreciation of the disruptive consequences to the family of her doing otherwise. Furthermore, child protective agencies, as well, may be incredulous of the child's accusations, and this too contributes to the child's sense of frustration, impotent rage, and ambivalence over disclosure.

Retraction Once the disclosure has been made, many of the predictions of the father come to be true and these contribute to retraction. Summit states:

> Her father abandons her and calls her a liar. Her mother does not believe her or decompensates into hysteria and rage. The family is fragmented, and all the children are placed in custody. The father is threatened with disgrace and imprisonment. The girl is blamed for causing the whole mess, and everyone seems to treat her like a freak. She is interrogated about all the tawdry details and encouraged to incriminate her father, yet the father remains unchallenged, remaining at home in the security of the family. She is held in custody with no apparent hope of returning home if the dependency petition is sustained.

The message from the mother is very clear, often explicit. "Why do you insist on telling those awful stories about your father? If you send him to prison, we won't be a family anymore. We'll end up on welfare with no place to stay. Is that what *you* want to do to us?"

Once again, the child bears the responsibility of either preserving or destroying the family. The role reversal continues with the "bad" choice being to tell the truth and the "good" choice being to capitulate and restore a lie for the sake of the family.

Drawbacks and Risks of Utilizing the Child Sexual Abuse Accommodation Syndrome (CSAAS) as a Diagnostic Instrument The reader does well to be reminded that Summit's article was published in 1983. Accordingly, the phenomena described therein relate to observations made 10 or more years ago. Levels 4 and 5 presuppose an incredulous mother and a disbelieving community, especially police and child protective services. This is no longer the case. In fact, the opposite is true, namely, mothers are much more likely to believe the child, and the police and child protective services err in the opposite direction and are likely to accept as valid even the most frivolous and absurd accusations.

It is also important to appreciate that Summit describes a series of reactions of children who have been sexually molested in the intrafamilial situation. Accordingly, the syndrome's application to other situations, such as nursery schools, molestation by a stranger, molestation by a babysitter, and molestation by a teacher, is inappropriate. In all of these situations the child is not living with the molester and is not as likely therefore to develop the kinds of reactions seen at those levels in which there is a sense of entrapment, especially levels 2 and 3.

This point is worthy of repetition: It is not likely that the progression of symptoms described by Summit in 1983 will be applicable to children in 1992, even those who have been molested in the intrafamilial situation. And this is especially the case for levels 2, 3, 4, and 5.

The CSAAS has enjoyed a significant amount of attention, especially via its utilization as an instrument for diagnosis, i.e., ascertaining whether a child has been sexually abused. And its use in this regard has not been confined only to allegations of sex abuse in the intrafamilial situation, but encompasses other situations as well. Nowhere in Summit's original article does he claim that it should be used for this purpose.

Furthermore, on numerous occasions (examples to be cited below) he has specifically stated that such utilization is inappropriate and goes beyond the intentions of his description. *The primary problem has been that overzealous and/or incompetent examiners have used the CSAAS as a diagnostic technique with the result that many innocent individuals have been found to be guilty of sex abuse and some have even been incarcerated.*

The *secrecy* phase has been expanded by overzealous examiners to include *denial.* Accordingly, children who have denied being sexually abused are considered to be in the secrecy phase and therefore exhibiting manifestations of sex abuse. This, of course, puts the accused in a no-win situation. If the child *admits* sexual abuse, then the allegation is considered confirmed. If the child *denies* sexual abuse, then the allegation is *still* considered confirmed by concluding that the denial is merely a manifestation of the child being in the secrecy phase of the CSAAS.

A child's sense of *helplessness* is also utilized to confirm sex abuse. Other sources of feelings of helplessness are not considered. A child, for example, exposed to and embroiled in a vicious child-custody dispute may feel like a rope in a tug-of-war. Rather than attribute such feelings of helplessness to the situation causing it, the child's helplessness is viewed as yet another manifestation of the CSAAS, and this is considered to lend support to the validity of the accusation.

The wide variety of symptoms described by Summit (only a few of which I have mentioned above), symptoms that are a derivative of the child's feelings of chronic *entrapment*, have also been utilized by overzealous examiners as confirmation of sex abuse. The causes of such symptoms are myriad and cover the wide variety of situations that could bring about psychogenic psychopathology. For example, Summit refers to the rage engendered in children during this phase. He then talks about the various symptoms that may arise depending upon whether the rage is internalized or externalized. There are hundreds of situations that can engender anger, situations that have absolutely nothing to do with sex abuse. Using such symptoms as an indicator of sex abuse is again a grievous misapplication of the CSAAS.

Ambivalent and *unconvincing disclosure* has also been misapplied. Certainly, children who have been genuinely abused may be conflicted with regard to their disclosures. However, children who are providing false accusations may also be conflicted about disclosures for various reasons. They may feel guilty and ashamed about their false accusations, especially if they are old enough to appreciate the grave consequences of their accusations. They may fear retaliation by the accused, not because they have divulged the secret of true sex abuse, but because they recognize that he has every reason to be incensed over their duplicity. Their divulgence may be unconvincing because the child is confused. The person programming the child and overzealous examiners may be trying to convince the child that the abuse did indeed take place, and the child has no recollection of such. During the process of this educational "programming" process, the child's disclosures may indeed be unconvincing and conflicted. Again, the utilization of this manifestation as a criterion for bona fide sex abuse is a grievous misapplication of the CSAAS.

Last, *retraction* may very well be seen in children who are sexually abused, especially because of their appreciation of the consequences to the accused of the divulgence. However, children who promulgate false accusations may also recant. Here, too, the recantation may stem from guilt, shame, and the appreciation of the terrible consequences to the accused of the accusation. These may not have been appreciated by the child prior to the accusation. When recantation is considered diagnostic of abuse, the accused is again placed in a no-win situation because the retraction is not considered of any consequence. The accused is deemed guilty if the child admits it, and he is considered guilty if the child denies it. There are examiners who boldly state, "The fact that the child denies it is proof that it happened." I hope the reader will believe me when I say that this is a common statement and not just one made by some fringe lunatic validators. One mother stated that her child's therapist said to her, with regard to her five-year-old son's denial, "It's not what he didn't say, but *how* he didn't say it, that proves that he was abused." (This statement provides support for those who hold that even people with low IQs can be creative.) Again, such a ludicrous position cannot but leave the accused with a sense of impotent rage.

Other Misapplications of the Child Sexual Abuse Accommodation Syndrome Mention has already been made of two areas of misapplication of the CSAAS, namely, its misuse as a diagnostic instrument and its use in sex accusations not in the intrafamilial setting. Its application in highly volatile divorce disputes has been particularly grievous because of the high incidence of false accusations in that situation. Because a sex-abuse accusation is an extremely powerful vengeance and exclusionary maneuver, such accusations have become increasingly widespread in recent years. In the nursery school situation as well, where the hysteria element is often operative, there is also good reason to believe that false accusations are widespread. In both of these situations the child is not living with the alleged perpetrator, and so an important factor in bringing about the CSAAS is not present.

Another misapplication of the CSAAS has been its use for preschool children. Summit (1991) states that the population from which he drew conclusions regarding the CSAAS were not "very young children," nor did he focus on "boy victims." Unfortunately, the CSAAS has been used as a diagnostic instrument for preschool children, and this has especially been the case in some of the more highly publicized nursery school cases such as McMartin in California, the Kelly Michaels case in New Jersey, and the Fijnje case in Florida.

Concluding Comments Regarding the Sexual Abuse Accommodation Syndrome Summit's CSAAS (1983) was not designed to serve as a diagnostic instrument. To utilize it in this way may result in innocent individuals being considered guilty of having sexually abused the alleged victim.

The symptomatic manifestations described by Summit are applicable to children abused in the intrafamilial situation and are far less likely to be applicable to children abused in other situations, such as children embroiled in child-custody disputes and children exposed to sex-abuse hysteria in nursery school situations.

The symptoms described by Summit refer to children seen prior to 1983, when child protection services, police, and parents were less alerted to the ubiquity of child sex abuse and were more likely to be disbelieving of children's disclosures. Not only is this no longer the case, but there is good reason to believe that the opposite now is true and that there are many overzealous examiners who are ready to accept as valid any allegation, no matter how frivolous and no matter how preposterous. Accordingly, the CSAAS may not even be applicable now to children whose abuse has occurred in the intrafamilial situation.

These drawbacks notwithstanding, the syndrome may have some validity as a "cause of suspicion" for an evaluator. A child who indeed has a history of such manifestations may very well have been abused, and the syndrome can serve to alert the examiner to the *possibility* of abuse. Whether or not the child does exhibit manifestations of the CSAAS, the examiner should be utilizing a much wider variety of investigative medical and psychiatric techniques in order to ascertain whether the child has indeed been sexually abused.

Conditioning Techniques

The biased examiner (one who has an investment in a disclosure of sexual abuse) is likely to provide positive reinforcement (candy, snacks, praises, and a trip to a local fast-food restaurant) for the child who provides sexual responses. Negative reinforcement (the threat of withdrawal of the aforementioned rewards) and punishment (e.g., the threat of being the only one in the group who has not provided the disclosure and thereby contributed to the socially beneficial function of putting the alleged perpetrator in jail) are commonly seen in such programming.

When one views carefully audiotapes and videotapes (especially the latter) of validators' interviews, one frequently observes significant positive reinforcement of any of the child's responses that indicate that the abuse took place and negative reinforcement and even punishment for comments that do not support the conclusion of sex abuse. Quite often the child's mother (the accuser) is in the room and the child's father (the accused) is absent and may not even know that the accusation has been made. And this is especially the case for the first interview, which may serve as a foundation for all subsequent interviews, especially with regard to what is being expected and desired by the interrogators. Some common positively reinforcing comments made after the initial disclosure are: "Very good," "That's right!" "You're doing very well!" and "You're doing a very good job!" If the child is reluctant to talk, he (she) may be told that following the interview the child will be taken to an ice cream parlor or fast-food restaurant or will be provided with some similar reward. At the end of the interview the child may be told, "There, you've said it. Don't you feel good now?" When the child doesn't get the "right" answers, the examiner may react with cold stiffness, incredulity, and repeated questions that get across the message of dissatisfaction with negative responses. McIver (1986) made the following comments about a videotaped interview of a four-and-a-half-year-old girl who was accusing a man of molesting her:

> It was clear that the child was being led to say that the defendant had touched her genital area with his hands and his mouth. The worker smiled and hugged her when she made such allegations, and was cold and non-demonstrative when she didn't.

My own experience has been that McIver's observation is typical, so much so that truly neutral questioning is rare, at least among the videotapes of the inquiries I have observed.

The So-called Disclosure

Prior to the last few years, I had no problem with the word *disclosure*. It produced no particular emotional reactions in me, and I did not react to it differently than to the vast majority of other words in the English language. However, in the last few years I find myself reacting with a combination of nausea and irritation every time I hear the word, especially when used by a validator or when I see it written in a sex-abuse evaluation. I believe that if I were hooked up to a polygraph, I would exhibit strong physiological reactions to that word, even when used in a context having nothing to do with the assessment of whether I was telling the truth. These reactions derive from its use by the vast majority of validators. They use the word *disclosure* to indicate "proof" or "validation" that the child has been sexually abused. When the child states that he (she) has been sexually abused and/or provides a description of such molestation (no matter how fragmentary), the examiner gleefully records that she has "made a disclosure." There is no neutrality here regarding whether the child's statement is truly indicative of actual sex abuse. Rather, the word *disclosure* becomes equated with confirmation that the sex abuse did indeed occur because the child described such an event. The high point of the interview has been reached. The sex abuse of the child has now been "validated." All the preliminary contaminations have proven successful. The first domino has now fallen and the rest can be expected to tumble down, one after the other, with ultimate "justice" being done to the alleged perpetrator (who is no longer the "alleged" abuser but is now merely the sex abuser). At this moment of exultation, many validators have no problem even writing down the name of the accused and stating that the sex abuse by him has been confirmed by this "disclosure."

In the nursery school and day-care center situations the problem is even worse. Here, a group of validators has been engaged to evaluate a parade of children, many of whom from the outset deny having been sexually abused. Predictably, after a series of interviews in the hands of these people, the inevitable "disclosure" is elicited (or, more accurately, coerced). Telephone calls are made, word gets around, and the message is buzzed: "Did you hear? Gloria made a 'disclosure.'" There are many innocent individuals who are rotting in jail because of such "disclosures," and I have no embarrassment describing my strong emotional reaction to the word. In fact, I would go further and say that if I were not to react strongly to this word, it would represent insensitivity on my part as a physician dedicated to the welfare of those who seek my services.

More Direct Coercive Techniques

Although all the aforementioned techniques are, in a sense, coercive, there are some maneuvers that these people utilize that are more obviously so. One is: "I know it happened and I'm going to keep you here until you tell me the truth." Other examples are: "Things like this happen to lots of kids. I know many children to whom the same thing happened. Don't worry. I'll protect you." "You can tell me. I'll make sure that he'll never do *that* again." "Now, Bobby, Jamie, Bill, Bob, etc., all told me that it happened to them. Are you going to be the only child in the whole school who is not going to tell me what happened?" The examiner here is appreciative of children's enormous need to conform and not be different from the majority. I refer to this as the "Keeping-up-with-the-Joneses" phenomenon (Gardner, 1995a). Sigston and White (1975) have studied this phenomenon in depth and provide excellent verification of its existence. It is indeed a powerful method for extracting a false sex-abuse accusation. Other examples are: "I don't believe that's the only place he touched you. I want you to tell me about the *other* places. You know there *were* other places."

The interrogator has an aura of power (a doctor, a psychologist, a policeman, a detective, etc.). Children are suggestible and are ever trying to ingratiate themselves to adult authority. The interrogator may enhance this sense of power with comments such as "I have the power to tell if you are lying" and "I know what 'the truth' is." Under such conditions of intimidation, the child is likely to provide any answer the examiner wishes the child to disclose. Powerful authorities have the power to interrogate the child until he (she) has provided the desired disclosure. It is not uncommon for such interviews to be conducted with the child alone (the authorities use their power to exclude the parents), and interviews may go on for four or five hours until the time that the child, in a state of exhaustion, provides the disclosure in order to bring about a cessation of the interview. I have listened to audiotapes in which the examiner has said, "I'm not letting you out of here until you tell me about how X played with your penis."

The physical torturing of a witness or an accused party is an ancient tradition. Inflict pain on an individual and you are likely to get a confession. These techniques are the modern-day equivalent of physical torture and, like their ancient antecedents, they also work with a high degree of predictability. Our founding fathers presumably ensured (in our Constitution) protection from such tactics for all Americans. Unfortunately, there appear to be some "loopholes" in that these torture techniques are still being utilized.

The "Inappropriate-Affect" Maneuver

American Psychiatric Glossary (Edgarton and Campbell, 1994) defines *affect* as:

> Behavior that expresses a subjectively experienced feeling state (*emotion*); affect is responsive to changing emotional states, whereas mood refers to a pervasive and sustained emotion. Common affects are euphoria, anger, and sadness.

When I was in my psychiatric residency training, in the late 1950s, *affect* was more strictly defined as the subjective (mental) aspect of an emotion, whereas the term *emotion* referred to both the mental and the physical concomitant. The physical concomitant could sometimes be observed via observation of facial expression, body movements, etc. There are typical facial expressions for fear and rage, and even lower animals exhibit similar changes in facial musculature in situations that might engender such reactions. However, we can say absolutely nothing about the internal mental state of a lower animal when the facial expression suggests fear or rage. We can make speculations, but we cannot know. With human beings we can make speculations and we can learn something about the internal mental concomitants of what the individual is telling us. But even then we cannot know with certainty, and it is a question of our belief in the credibility of the individual who describes the affect. My main point here is that affect, when used in a traditional and purer sense, is not something that another individual can know. It is only something that is known to the individual experiencing that affect.

Commonly, the word *affect* is linked with the terms *appropriate* and *inappropriate*. Psychiatrists commonly say that the individual's affect was "appropriate to ideation" or that the individual's affect was "not appropriate to ideation." This distinction is especially useful when evaluating people who are suspected of being schizophrenic, because schizophrenics typically exhibit a disassociation between affect and ideation, i.e., their affect may be inappropriate to ideation. For example, a schizophrenic may giggle upon learning about the death of a close relative.

The reader may be wondering at this point what all this has to do with the techniques used by validators. It has a lot to do with one of the techniques they use for justifying the conclusion that a child was sexually abused, especially when their conclusion is at variance with what people of common sense consider to be reasonable and highly likely. A common maneuver in such situations, especially in the courtroom, is for the validator to claim that the child's verbalizations about sexual molestation "ring true" because the affect that was associated with these verbalizations was appropriate and consistent. The validator's clinical notes only mention what the child verbalized. On occasion there may even be a notation, "The child's affect was appropriate." However, the reader must take the word of the validator that the affect was indeed appropriate, because the reader was not there to get any sense of whether this statement is true or false. Even when one has a transcript of an audiotape (or videotape), one may not know what the affect of the child was, especially whether it was appropriate or inappropriate. All one has on a transcript are the child's words. The transcript can at least provide verification of the validator's notes, but it cannot say anything about affect.

Although audiotapes can sometimes give the listener information about the child's affect, it is primarily videotapes that enable other examiners to determine whether the validator's *subjective impression* of the affect was possibly valid. My experience has been that in the vast majority of cases in which the evidence was strong for a false accusation, the videotapes indicated strongly that the child's affect was *not* appropriate to ideation, in spite of the validator's statement that such was the case. For example, the interview may have a gamelike quality, a quality not in any way suggested by the transcript. It is as if the child and interviewer are playing the game: "Can You Guess What I'm Thinking?" Such interviews are basically an educational process in which the child, by getting a series of "right" answers, learns a certain scenario that is then reproduced for the next interrogator. There is often a levity to such interviews, especially when the child gets many *right* answers. And this is especially the case when the examiner provides the kinds of positive reinforcement described above, e.g., "Good girl" or "That's right." On occasion the videotape will confirm levity suggested by the written transcript (as was the case of the previously described four-and-a-half-year-old girl who believed that her nose would grow like Pinocchio's if she lied to the investigator).

The "Dissociation" Maneuver

Related to and overlapping the inappropriate-affect maneuver is the "dissociation" maneuver. *American Psychiatric Glossary* (Edgarton and Campbell, 1994) defines dissociation as:

> The splitting off of clusters of mental contents from conscious awareness, a mechanism central to hysterical conversion and dissociative

disorders; the separation of an idea from its emotional significance and affect as seen in the inappropriate *affect* of schizophrenic patients. (p. 64)

At the time of abuse, especially when it is severely traumatic, a small percentage of children will *dissociate*. This is a phenomenon that is most often seen in situations of severe trauma, such as military combat, earthquakes, tornadoes, floods, rape, and attempted murder. There is a massive flooding of stimuli in the brain circuitry. The unity of consciousness is disrupted. There is a disintegration of consciousness and certain segments of the personality may operate autonomously. Continuity and consistency of thoughts are disconnected from one another. The sense of identity may change. There is a loss of sense of the passage of time. The person may experience perceptual distortions, illusions, feelings that the body is unreal (derealization). Sometimes there is complete amnesia for the event (psychogenic amnesia) or the individual enters into an altered state of consciousness in the context of which complex behaviors are exhibited that are unknown to the patient (psychogenic fugue). Dissociation is well compared to the overloaded computer that stops functioning because it cannot deal with the massive amount of information being poured in. This phenomenon may be associated with psychic numbing, which also serves to protect the individual from full appreciation of the trauma.

In chronic abuse this pattern may become deeply entrenched to the point where the process becomes automatic: each time the person is abused, he (she) automatically dissociates and thereby protects himself (herself) from the pain of the experience. The result may be (in a small percentage of cases) no conscious recall of the sexual events.

Such dissociative episodes may then occur in situations in which the person is reminded of the abuse by cues that are similar to those that existed at the time of the original abuse. For example, a Vietnam veteran walks past a movie house that has advertisements showing battle scenes from the movie playing therein. These, because of their similarities to the battlefield conditions in Vietnam, trigger a dissociative reaction in which his brain is flooded with flashbacks of the combat situation as well as the disorganization of thinking typical of dissociation. Under such circumstances, there are likely to be other manifestations of dissociation in which the person may be amnesic for certain time blocks during which events that transpired are totally obliterated from the person's memory; but they are events that have been clearly observed by others. This is not simply a matter of forgetting certain events, which all people do, but there is total obliteration of memory of such events and confusion when confronted by observers of the person's involvement in such events.

People who have not been traumatized and/or abused are not likely to manifest or experience bona fide dissociative phenomena. Overzealous examiners often frivolously apply the concept of dissociation to even the most transient episodes of inattentiveness and "spacing out." This may be done in circumstances when there was absolutely no evidence for bona fide dissociation at the time of the original alleged abuse.

My comments on the subject of dissociative states would not be complete without some mention of the so-called Multiple Personality Disorder, a diagnosis very much in vogue at this time. Although *DSM-IV* lists Dissociative Identity Disorder (Multiple Personality Disorder), I have not yet personally seen such a case and am extremely dubious about its existence, although I cannot be certain that it does not exist. As mentioned, one cannot prove a null hypothesis. I can, however, express my dubiety.

Many years ago, while serving as a psychiatrist in the military service, I interviewed in jail a man who had murdered another soldier in the course of a fight. Specifically, he had fired 23 rounds to the head and chest of this man. When I saw him he was clearly in an altered state of consciousness and this is basically what he had to say to me:

> *Patient*: I don't remember killing him. I have absolutely no memory of killing him. They say I killed him. . . . I must have because the bullets match my gun, which they found in the bushes. I don't remember throwing it in the bushes, but it must have been my gun because my fingerprints were on it. . . .

I do not think this man was lying. He was clearly in an altered state of consciousness and I do believe he was suffering with psychogenic amnesia. The data was dissociated because he did not want to view himself as the murderer that he actually was.

I believe that adult women who were raped might, under certain circumstances, dissociate. I believe, however, that this is rare. It is probable that some children dissociate in the course of sexual encounters with adults. I believe, also, that this is rare. Overzealous evaluators, however, are interpreting every distraction and every mild example of "spacing out" as a manifestation of dissociation. This is most commonly seen in situations where the child has not been sexually abused and the dissociation phenomenon is being brought in to give medical credibility to the evaluator's belief that the child was abused, a belief that has absolutely no basis in reality.

Dissociation, then, can be considered a stronger form of repression. Repression probably does not use up as much brain energy or as much brain-cell circuitry. When dissociation is occurring, the brain is really buzzing. Therefore, it should be differentiated from repression and placed further along the continuum of mental mechanisms that induce storage of cognitive material.

Not surprisingly, many validators have embraced the concept and have applied it to sexually abused children as part of the validation process. A common situation in which this maneuver is utilized is the one in which a child is continually subjected to an interviewer who is sledgehammering the child into describing the details of the alleged sexual encounter. If the child becomes mute, "spaced out," or otherwise uncommunicative, the validator may indicate that the child has now "dissociated." The implication here is that the interview has touched on the sex-abuse material and the child is "dissociating" this material because of the psychological pain attendant to its being allowed entrance into conscious awareness. I cannot deny that this may be a possible explanation for the observed phenomenon. However, we are most often dealing here with three- and four-year-old children, and the spacing out is generally not accompanied by any verbal statements that might provide the observer with some hint regarding exactly what is going on in the child's mind. Accordingly, one cannot state with certainty that the validator's speculation regarding what is going on is not valid. Some of the incompetents use the term dis*a*ssociation instead of dissociation. They cannot appreciate that they are not even using the correct word. There is no such word as disassociation. When one hears this term, it is a clue as to the naiveté and probable ineptitude of the user. I, personally, have never met a competent evaluator who uses this term, nor is it to be found in any of the standard references on the subject.

Overzealous evaluators who quickly invoke dissociation do not often give serious consideration to other explanations for the child's "alleged dissociative behavior." For example, one possible explanation for a child's "spacing out" relates to the fact that the child feels overwhelmed by the coercive questions and is confused by the failure to have provided the "right" answers. The child's withdrawal, then, serves to protect him (her) from further responses, responses that might again be sensed by the child as incorrect because they do not meet with the examiner's approval. It is almost as if the brain computer has broken down, so overwhelmed has it been with data. Also, there may be a fear element here that plays a role in the child's "freezing up." Not having gotten a series of "right" answers and sensing the examiner's mounting exasperation and/or impatience, the child may become afraid to provide another answer and be met once again with further negative feedback by the examiner. Freezing up protects the child from such unpleasant reactions by the evaluator. I have never yet seen a report in which the examiner has considered these alternative explanations for the child's spacing out. Rather, the examiner simply states that the child has "dissociated," and this is viewed as automatically confirmatory that the sex abuse has taken place. Elsewhere (Gardner, 1995b) I have commented further on repression, dissociation, and sex-abuse accusations.

Rehearsal

Rehearsal serves to entrench the child's scenario in the brain circuitry. This may be accomplished by introducing the anatomical dolls and body charts in practically every session, rehashing the same material, or endlessly asking for further examples of abuse. Rehearsal is part of the educational process that is central to programming.

Commonly, when a child involved in a lawsuit is scheduled for an interview in association with the litigation, the child's therapist will review the possible questions with the child and ensure that the child provides the "best" and most convincing answers. If the child is no longer in therapy, it is common for the parents to bring the child back, within a few days prior to the interview, in order to ensure that the child will provide the "correct" scenario. Children who have been genuinely abused do not need such "booster shot" interviews; they remember fairly well what happened and need no one to help them recall their experiences. In the course of such interviews the child's scenario may be "cleaned up" if it includes preposterous elements that may lessen its credibility.

Another form of rehearsal that is seen in the context of lawsuits is the parent's suggesting that the child read transcripts from previous testimony. Obviously, this maneuver is only utilized with older children and generally is not necessary when the accusation is valid.

The Use of In-Vogue Jargon

One of the clues to the programming process is the child's and/or parents' use of jargon terms that make the rounds among the validators and other overzealous examiners. These become incorporated into the child's scenarios or the parents' descriptions of the child's sexual abuses. Although such jargon may be seen in children who have been genuinely abused, my experience has been that these terms are more commonly seen when the accusation is false. Children who are denying they were abused—when a parent, therapist, or other overzealous evaluator has decided they were abused—are often considered to be "in denial." Or they may be considered to have "repressed the memory" of the abuse. They may be considered to have "dissociated" memories of the events, resulting in "amnesia." The child may claim that she (he) has been "betrayed" but does not have the faintest idea what the word means. In order for these children to "heal," they must go into intensive therapy, over a *long* period, in order to bring into conscious awareness ("retrieve") the material that has been "repressed" and/or "dissociated." If this phase of treatment is successful, the child will provide a "disclosure." On that happy day the examiner may excitedly report the success to the parents and other colleagues, especially those who may have referred the suspected "victim" to this particular therapist (who may enjoy the reputation of being particularly successful in extracting "disclosures" from children "in denial").

Perpetrators whose molestation involves only superficial indiscretions (or are on the verge of such) are often considered to have a "boundary problem." Such "therapists" often do not even consider interviewing the perpetrator, and when such an interview is suggested or requested they will respond, "There's no point speaking to him, because he'll only deny it. Frequently, such overzealous "therapists" embark immediately upon the treatment process without conducting a proper evaluation to ascertain whether the accusation is true or false.

They thereby ignore one of the most important principles of proper psychological care, namely, that diagnosis should precede treatment. Such "therapists" would not allow a physician to institute a treatment program for themselves without first conducting a proper diagnostic evaluation, but they do not see the need for such evaluations for the children who come their way. They appear to be blind to the fact that some accusations are false. Rather, they work on the principle that an accusation must be true. Some even subscribe to the dictum that "children never lie" and sanctimoniously scorn those who do not "believe the children." Some, when asked why they have not interviewed the alleged perpetrator or conducted an in-depth evaluation to ascertain whether the accusation is true or false will respond, "I'm not a detective."

In the course of the "healing process" children are taught to differentiate between "good touches" and "bad touches." In the service of such differentiation they are taught that people are not allowed to touch you in places "covered by a bathing suit." The perpetrator is generally referred to as someone who "invaded her body" or "robbed her of her childhood innocence." In the course of the "healing process" children are taught to become "empowered" by such maneuvers as calling for help and "saying no." The children are programmed to believe that they cannot "heal" until the alleged perpetrator "apologizes." If he continues to deny any molestation he may be encouraged to say to the child, "I'm sorry for what you think I did." Such advice is a clear testament to the therapeutic naiveté of such evaluators and compelling confirmation of their stupidity.

Involvement with Parents, the Accused, and the Accuser

Typically, these evaluators see little or no need to interview the accused. In fact, I have come across some who actually believe that it is illegal to interview the accused. This requires a delusional misinterpretation of the U.S. Constitution. Although the accused has the right *not* to speak to the accuser (whether in a court of law or under any other circumstances), this does not mean that the accused *cannot* speak to the accuser if he (she) wishes to. Most accused individuals (especially those who are genuinely innocent) are most eager to confront their accusers. Yet these accused individuals are often deprived of this constitutional right. There are validators who, after interviewing only the child, unashamedly write in their reports that the child was abused and *name* the accused without ever having interviewed or even spoken to him (her).

Generally, these evaluators do not even conduct detailed inquiries with the adult accuser (most often the child's mother). They take at face value her accusations and do not consider the possibility that they may be fabricated or a delusion. Rather, they do the opposite; namely, they take any shred of information that might support the conclusion and use it in the process of "validation." As mentioned, they will consider normal childhood behaviors as manifestations of sexual abuse, e.g., nightmares, bedwetting, temper tantrums, mood swings, and, of course, masturbation. The mother's report of these occurrences serves to confirm that the child was indeed abused. And the validator becomes even more convinced that the abuse took place when the child exhibits in the office what are traditionally considered to be psychopathological manifestations. Rather than look into other possible sources of such problems in family life—sources unrelated to sexual abuse—they immediately come to the conclusion that these behavioral difficulties are the direct result of the sex abuse. (As mentioned, every symptom in the diagnostic manual has been listed as a possible result of sex abuse. Accordingly, everything now fits together and the abuse is "validated.")

When questioned as to why they did not interview, or even contact, the accused, validators will provide a variety of excuses—none of which are justifiable. Some will claim that time just does not permit the kind of intensive investigation that will allow for inquiries with the accused. I cannot imagine a hospital stating publicly that time does not permit the surgeon to spend more than 30 minutes on any operation. I have been told by validators when questioned as to why they didn't contact the accused, "I'm not an investigator." This too is a rationalization. An examiner *is* an investigator. An examiner is investigating whether sex abuse took place. Another common rationalization is: "He'll lie anyway, so it's a waste of time." I suspect that this is a derivative of the "children never lie" dictum. The whole principle is: "Children never lie and accused individuals never tell the truth." And that wraps it all up. Next case!

Another argument given is: "The police don't want us to question the alleged perpetrator until after they have finished with their investigation of him." There are a number of possibilities here. One is that the police never made the request and this is simply a lie being used as a rationalization. But let us, for the sake of argument, accept as valid the statement that the police did indeed make this request. If they did, then it is inappropriate for the evaluating facility to comply with it. The ethical position for such a facility to take is that they—not the police—decide who should be interviewed and who should not and *when* the interview should take place. If the police insist on imposing their interview schedule on the facility, then the facility should consider it unethical to provide such services. I would never agree to involve myself in an evaluation in which the police are telling me when I can see an individual. I assume the police would not be telling a surgeon when he can operate, nor would any competent surgeon agree to this restriction if the police had the gall to make the request. In short, if an evaluating facility is complying with police directives, then it is compromising its evaluative procedures. There is no justification for such compliance.

Obviously, there are many ways in which interviewing the accused could be useful in such evaluations. These not only involve interviewing the accused alone, but also interviewing the accused in joint sessions with the accuser, the alleged victim, and all three together. This is the best method for "smoking out" the truth. Family therapists know this well, but these examiners seem to be oblivious to this obviously useful technique. The argument that the child might be traumatized by such a confrontation is not an excuse to preclude its utilization entirely. First, examiners should have the freedom to decide whether such joint interviews would do more good than harm. By automatically precluding involvement with the accused, this option is not utilized. Furthermore, although such confrontations may be psychologically traumatic to the child under certain circumstances, one must also consider the psychological trauma to the person falsely accused. It can result in a completely ruined life and/or years of incarceration. These rights of the accused are rarely considered by these examiners. On many occasions I have been asked to interview a child—and only the child—and then make a decision regarding whether the child has been sexually abused. I have *never* accepted such an invitation. Before involvement in the case I make every attempt to obtain a court order in which all three parties are required to participate (the accuser, the accused, and the alleged victim), individually and in any combination that I consider warranted. This does not automatically involve a joint interview with the alleged victim and the accused, but it often may. In either case, I must be given the freedom to make that decision.

WHY DO THESE PEOPLE FUNCTION IN THIS WAY?

Obviously, there is a wide variety of individuals who serve as validators. Equally obvious is the fact that for each person, there is a multiplicity of factors operative in this career choice. There are also many factors involved if one is to explain why these individuals function as they do. No one person will fit into all of the categories mentioned below; however, I am convinced that each of these explanations is applicable to at least some of the individuals who serve as validators.

Impaired Educational Background

There is no question that we are witnessing a progressive deterioration of educational standards throughout the United States. Although there are certainly areas in which things have improved in recent years, there is no question that there are more areas in which things have degenerated—so that the overall picture is much more in the direction of downhill than uphill. The erosion of standards has occurred at just about every level, from kindergarten to graduate school. No one can deny that there has been a deterioration in the public schools during the last 25 years, certainly in the large cities and probably in suburban and rural communities as well. One compelling verification of this (if one needs it) is the progressive deterioration of Scholastic Aptitude Test (SAT) scores. But the numbers here do not reflect the full story. The test has progressively become easier. Accordingly, if the test were as rigorous as it was in the past, the deterioration would become even more apparent. Here I will discuss what I consider to be some of the important factors operative in bringing about this deplorable situation, factors at the elementary, high-school, and college levels.

Elementary Schools Ours is seemingly an egalitarian educational system that assumes "all children are created equal" and all children should receive the same educational exposure. This is misguided egalitarianism. The principle blinds itself to the obvious intellectual differences that children exhibit from the time of birth. On the one hand, educators appreciate that every intelligence test has its distribution curve, from the intellectually impaired to the superior. On the other hand, our educational system in the United States does not properly accommodate these differences. I do not claim that there is no appreciation at all of these differences; I only claim that educators do not exhibit enough appreciation of these differences. Although there are special classes for learning-disabled children and technical high schools for those who are not academically inclined, the main thrust and orientation of our educational system are toward preparing youngsters to enter colleges and universities. The ideal presented is that all children should go to college and those who do not achieve this lofty goal bring shame upon themselves and their families.

Most countries have no problem accepting the fact that not all children should be on a strong academic track. Accordingly, in many countries, somewhere between the ages of nine and eleven, children are divided into three tracks. The highest track ultimately leads to the university. The lowest track ends formal, intense academic training at about age eleven or twelve and then emphasizes various trades and skills. And the middle track is somewhere between the two. Of course, if the child has been placed in the wrong track, there is still a possibility of switching. We would do well in the United States to institute such a system. It would protect many children from significant grief. To say that all people should be *treated* equally before the *law* is certainly reasonable. But to say that all are *created* equal is absurd. What is more reasonable to say, as Orwell did in *Animal Farm*, is that "some are more equal than others." Because public statements of such inegalitarianism are considered undemocratic in our society at this time, it is extremely unlikely that such changes will be introduced into our system in the foreseeable future—certainly not before the end of this century.

Many factors have contributed to school deterioration in recent years. One relates to teachers' salaries. It is unreasonable to expect that schools can attract high-quality, well-educated individuals when other careers provide much greater pay. In most municipalities garbage men make as much as, if not more than, elementary-school teachers. The public sector can generally afford to provide higher salaries than private and parochial schools; yet the public schools seem to be getting the poorest-quality teachers. The more dedicated teachers are willing to take positions for lower salaries in order to work in the more academically stimulating atmosphere of the private and/or parochial schools.

I believe there has been a general diminution in the commitment of teachers to the educational process. I am not claiming that this is true of all teachers, only that the percentage of teachers who are deeply committed to their profession has been sharply reduced in the last 15 to 20 years. One manifestation of this trend is the decreased frequency with which children are required to do homework. Giving children homework most often involves homework for the teacher. And less dedicated teachers are not willing to take on this extra responsibility. In previous years there were many more teachers who were viewed to be somewhat hard-nosed and dictatorial, yet their despotism was benevolent and years later their students were able to look back with gratitude on what they were "forced" to do. These days, "respect" for the child often involves a degree of permissiveness and indulgence that serves children ill in the course of their education. A good educational experience helps the child learn that there are times when one has to do things that may be unpleasant in order to derive future benefits. "Respecting" the child's wish not to endure such discomforts is basically not in the child's best interests. True respect for children involves the *requirement* that they do what is best for them, not the indulgence of their avoidance of reasonable responsibilities. The net result of these unfortunate trends is that children learn less during their primary and secondary school years—with the subsequent result that SAT scores have dropped significantly during the last 15 to 20 years, and many studies have demonstrated that the majority of children are abysmally ignorant of basic facts about history, geography, literature, English, and mathematics.

Another factor operative in the deterioration of the educational system has been the growth of a generation of teachers who themselves have not learned very much during their own educational processes. Often, these are teachers who went to college during the 1960s, when students' self-indulgence may have reached an all-time high. Grammar, punctuation, spelling, and foreign languages were dismissed as "irrelevant." Many other subjects that required self-discipline and hard work were also often viewed as irrelevant. Graduates of this era are now teaching our youngsters. Not only do many of these teachers serve as poor models for their students, due to their impaired commitment to the educational process, but they are compromised as well in what they can teach. I routinely ask parents to bring in my child-patients' report cards. Often I see egregious errors in grammar, punctuation, and spelling. I have had secretaries whom I have had to let go after a week or two because of their ignorance of basic English. They were not people who I felt needed time to adjust to a new job; rather, it might have taken years to get them to reach the point where they could function adequately in a standard secretarial position. They often did not even appreciate how ignorant they were. They did not even recognize that a misspelled word looked misspelled, and so they had no motivation to consult a dictionary for the correct spelling.

High School In their book *What Do Our 17-Year-Olds Know?* Ravitch and Finn (1987) report a study conducted with approximately 18,000 17-year-olds who were selected to reflect the makeup of the population as a whole regarding region, sex, race, type of school, and type of community. Some of their findings were: Thirty percent of the students did not know that Christopher Columbus reached the New World before 1750. More than 35 percent were not aware that the Watergate scandal took place after 1950. More than 30 percent believed that one consequence of the Spanish-American War was the defeat of the Spanish Armada. Approximately half of the students believed that *Nineteen Eighty-Four* dealt with the destruction of the human race in a nuclear war. Over one-third did not know that Aesop wrote fables. Over 42 percent did not know who Senator Joseph McCarthy was nor for what he became infamous. Seventy percent were unable to identify the Magna Carta. And the book goes on and on with many more examples of the abysmal ignorance of the average American teenager. These findings should not be surprising, considering the kinds of educational programs these youngsters are being provided.

Some parents bring their adolescents for treatment because of poor academic motivation. Many of these youngsters attend schools where the educational standards are low and where they are automatically moved ahead every year and then dropped off the edge of the system when they complete the twelfth grade. Some, however, are in more demanding high schools, but they still have little commitment to the educational process. Sometimes the youngster's lack of motivation is indeed related to intrafamilial and intrapsychic problems. At other times, the youngster is merely one of a stream of hundreds of thousands who are moving along an educational track that demands little and provides even less. Their teachers are uncommitted and unmotivated, watch the clock, do not give homework (homework for the student is homework for the teacher), and so do not provide models for their students—models of people who are "turned on" by learning.

College I believe that *most* (but certainly not *all*) colleges in the United States are not serving primarily as educational institutions; rather, they are serving as what I call "winter camps" that alternate with their students' summer recreational (and sometimes work) programs. Most youngsters attending colleges are not really looking for an education but for another four years of self-indulgence and prolongation of their dependent state. We have a unique disease in the United States, a disease I call *the college disease*. Millions of parents believe that it is crucial that their children attend college. They actually believe that the schools to which they are sending their children are actually serving educational purposes. When there is a demand for something, there will always be individuals who will be pleased to provide a supply of the item, especially when there is good money to be made in the business. Most college institutions in the United States are basically businesses that cater to a gullible population of parents who believe that it is *crucial* that their children (no matter how simple and/or academically unmotivated) have a college education (no matter how specious and inferior).

These institutions have their academic hierarchy, their assistant professors, associate professors, and full professors. They have their college-style buildings (especially red brick and ivy), their alumni associations, their football teams, and their fund-raising campaigns. And they even offer formal courses; the "students" take examinations, and grades are given. Yet the whole thing does not add up to what can justifiably be referred to as an education. The majority of students are not there to learn; rather they are there primarily to have a good time—

which often includes significant indulgence in sex, alcohol, and drugs. What they most often learn are some new sexual techniques, what their tolerance for alcohol is, and perhaps the use of some new drugs that they haven't tried before. They also learn how easy it is to get a college diploma. When the "students" are not engaged in these activities, they go through the motions of attending classes, but little is learned. Grade inflation fosters the delusion that they are learning something and ensures that even those with borderline intelligence will get high grades. Professors are concerned that if they give a student a grade lower than B, then the youngster will have trouble getting into graduate school and the college's reputation and popularity may thereby suffer. It is rare for someone to "flunk out." And why should they fail? Does one kick a good customer out of the store? If a customer's parents are willing to continue to pay for the services provided, it would be self-destructive of the college in this highly competitive market to cut off a predictable supply of money because of the student's failure to consume the product being offered.

I am not claiming that *all* the aforementioned criticisms apply to *all* collegiate institutions and *all* students. If I had to give a percentage of those academic institutions in the United States that fit the above description, I would say that it is in the 75–80 percent range. As mentioned, these colleges provide many of their students with gratification of pathological dependency needs. Such colleges also serve as a mechanism for transferring dependency from parents to those who administer these institutions. And thwarting college authorities (especially by antisocial behavior and refusal to study) is often a transfer of rebellion from parents to school authorities—a rebellion in which the dependency-denial element is often operative.

When I attended college, we generally went from nine A.M. to five P.M. Monday through Friday, and a half day on Saturday. Most courses met four or five times a week and laboratory courses two to three afternoons a week. It was expected that one would do four or five hours of homework a night. School began the day following Labor Day and continued right through early June. There was a one-week Christmas vacation, possibly a one-week Easter vacation, and of course national holidays. Otherwise we went to school. This is no longer the case. Even in the so-called best colleges and universities, the formal academic program is far less rigorous. Most students average two or three hours a day of classes, while professors may only have to come in five to ten hours a week and are otherwise unseen. These days, the academic year, although it may start around Labor Day, generally ends in early May. Some institutions use the Christmas and/or Easter season as an excuse for an extended holiday (two to four weeks). Others have long vacations (lasting two to four weeks) between semesters. Many need no other excuse for a long break than the season (spring or winter vacation). When I attended college, professors were on campus throughout the course of the day. Things are vastly changed. Today, it is not uncommon for professors to live at significant distances from the campus and appear only on the days they teach, and often only during the hours they teach. Otherwise, they are unavailable. Students at these institutions are being short-changed. "Educations" of this kind may cost $15,000 a year or more. Parents and students are being "ripped off."

A few years ago, a patient's mother, who taught at one of the public universities in New York City, related to me an incident that demonstrates well the deterioration of our educational systems, even at the highest level. The woman is a highly intelligent, well-trained, scholarly individual with a Ph.D. in a very demanding field. One day her chairman called her into his office and told her that he was having a problem with her, namely, that too many of her students were failing. He informed her that a 40-percent failure rate was unacceptable. She informed him that she was actually being quite generous, and that if she had graded in a more honest way about 60 percent of her students would fail. He told her that he had sat in on a couple of her classes, knew exactly what the problem was, and considered it easily rectifiable. He then went on to explain to her that she was not giving tests in the "correct" manner. What she was doing was to tell students on Friday, for example, that there would be a test on Monday covering the material in certain chapters of the textbook. This he considered "unfair" to the students. Rather, the "correct" way to give a test was to tell the students on Friday exactly what questions would be asked on Monday. Under the new system, the failure rate dropped from 40 to 20 percent, but even then she found herself being quite generous. Such procedures are a manifestation of the bastardization of the educational system. They make a farce of education and, worse, are a terrible disservice to students. The next step, of course, is merely to tell what questions will be asked and give the answers that will be expected. If one extends this further, one might as well give out (or sell) the diplomas in advance and save everybody a lot of trouble.

Things are even worse at some of the two-year colleges. Many of these institutions merely go through the motions of providing an education and are basically a sham. Students are given textbooks that are seemingly rigorous and demanding, yet in actuality the students are only required to learn a small fraction of what is presented therein. Those in charge recognize the travesty but are party to it, even at the highest levels. The net result of all this is that students are not getting a bona fide education and are thereby entering into the workplace ill equipped to handle jobs for which they are ostensibly being trained. Also they are being deprived of the feelings of accomplishment and high self-worth enjoyed by those who have acquired skills and talents through years of hard labor and dedication. The situation thereby contributes to psychopathology, because feelings of low self-worth are an important contributing factor in the development of psychogenic symptoms. In addition, such bogus education contributes to psychopathic trends (I am not saying gross psychopathy) because of the sanctions the youngsters are given for "cutting corners," taking shortcuts, and otherwise doing shabby work.

Yet, at the same time that their education is eroding, the honors that students are receiving become ever easier to acquire. When I graduated from Columbia College in 1952, my recollection is that no more than one percent graduated *summa cum laude*, perhaps another three or four percent *magna cum laude*, and perhaps another five percent *cum laude*. My recollection is that students below the top-10-percent level of the class could not hope to acquire any of these honors. In the mid-1980s I attended the Harvard College graduation of one of my children. I noted that the upper 75 percent of the class received one of these honors. In other words, a person could be in the 75th-percentile level of the class and could graduate *cum laude*. When I spoke to faculty people about this, I was informed that the school is well aware of its liberal view with regard to bestowing these honors but that it is justified because it helps graduates get into graduate school and jobs. I am dubious. Those who make these decisions are well aware that *cum laude* may very well indicate the 50th to 75th percentile of the class and will act accordingly. It serves to compromise the respect for the honor and does Harvard (and other schools who do the same) a disservice. It is one example of the intellectual and moral erosion that has taken place, even at the highest levels of education.

The Education of Validators

People who work as validators are products of this eroded educational system, at all levels, and this weakness in their educational foundation is reflected in their work. A good education, if anything, should provide individuals with "common sense." Validators, above all, lack common sense. In fact, I consider that to be the number one item on the list of their deficiencies. One has to lack common sense if one is to believe the preposterous things that they accept as valid in order to justify their conclusions. There was a time when one had to be bright in order to get into most colleges. As mentioned, this is less often the case today and there are, without question, many validators who are not particularly intelligent—even though they may have a college and/or university education. People who are less intelligent are less likely to have common sense. However, sometimes this can be rectified (to some extent) by academic work that focuses on the capacity for logical reasoning. Courses in logic, mathematics, physics, and chemistry can most likely do this (for those who are intellectually competent to handle these disciplines). In a less direct way, just about any good college course (including the arts) should involve a certain amount of logical thinking. What is clear is that many of these validators lack the basic intelligence and/or the educational exposure that might have provided them with common sense.

When I was in medical school, our professors would frequently say to us: "Remember this: The most likely things are most likely." At first, I thought the warning was both inane and unnecessary. As time went on, however, I came to appreciate the great wisdom in this seemingly absurd statement. The admonition was most often applied to situations in which a medical student would diagnose a patient as having the rare tropical disease that had just been read about the previous night. This was often done in a state of exultation associated with the pride at having made such a brilliant diagnosis. The professor, often trying to avoid putting the student down, would say something along these lines: "It looks like common viral gastroenteritis to me" or "It looks like the garden variety of bacterial pneumonia to me." The reality of the world is that the most common things *are* most common and that one does well to remember this. Validators seem to be oblivious to this ancient and obvious wisdom. Rather, they go in the opposite direction and consider as valid the most unlikely and even preposterous possibilities. One does not need a Ph.D. in advanced mathematics to recognize that the likelihood of a nursery school teacher undressing 50 three-year-old children (in order to involve them when naked in a sex orgy), and then dressing them all quickly, is not very likely to end up with every child wearing the exact same socks, shoes, underwear, dresses, pants, shirts, hats, and coats as they came in with.

Every parent knows that the best way to get a three-year-old child to say something to another person is to preface the message with: "I want to tell you a secret and I want you to promise me that you'll *never* tell anyone." This is the most predictable way to get the message into the pool of public information. Yet, these examiners believe that one can do this with a whole class of children and be confident that they will never breathe a word of their experiences to their parents or anyone else. There are three classes of people who believe that one can accomplish this goal of group secrecy by three-year-olds: (1) psychotics, (2) retardates, and (3) zealous validators. The rest of the world well appreciates that it is unreasonable to expect three-year-old children to involve themselves in conspiracies of silence, especially with regard to dramatic experiences (people dressed as clowns, monsters, etc.; engaging the children in sexual intercourse; putting swords up their rectums; feeding them feces). These examiners do not seem to appreciate that it is not very likely that one can feed feces to a group of children, make them drink their urine, and expose them to a variety of other painful and frightening indignities and yet, only minutes later, get them to skip happily out of the classroom without a speck of feces on their lips or a drop of urine on their tongues. When presented with this argument, validators claim that the children have been frightened into secrecy by threats of body mutilation, murder, etc. This too is an absurd rationalization. Let us forget, for the moment, the failure to find these mutilated bodies with which the children were threatened. The idea that the *whole* group could be frightened into silence is absurd—perhaps a few, but not *all* of them for the extended period between the alleged abuse and its divulgence. In fact, one could argue that frightened children would be even more likely to reveal quickly what they have been allegedly exposed to.

The "Holier-Than-Thou" Phenomenon

Many readers, I would guess, have seen the common bumper sticker: "I brake for animals." There is a "holier-than-thou" message being transmitted here. The implication here is that the driver of the vehicle bearing this message is a kind of individual who stops for animals and that others are less likely to do so. The message communicates to the reader in the car behind that he (she) should be ever on the alert for a sudden stop by the car ahead and that the driver in front is likely to be stopping short quite frequently. "Keep your foot close to the brakes," it says, "because you never know when you'll have to stop short. You don't have to worry about this when you follow other cars, because they're not driven by the kinds of deeply caring people who are sensitive enough to brake for animals." I have had the thought that, if I had the opportunity, I would ask such individuals if they brake for human beings. The same phenomenon is exhibited by politicians who claim proudly and sanctimoniously that they are fighting for the homeless, the elderly, the poor, and children who are abandoned. The implication is that their opponents are against these individuals.

Validators (and the aforementioned newer breed of "child advocates") often manifest this patronizing attitude. They—unlike the rest of us—are there to protect children. They—unlike the rest of us—"believe the children." The implication here is that those who do not believe the children (like the author) are somehow low-life characters who are exposing children to the sea of abusers, who are ever ready to pounce on their prey. It provides these examiners with a feeling of special importance, which likely serves to compensate for basic feelings of inadequacy. If one basically feels competent about oneself, if one basically has a strong sense of self-worth, one does not have to go around looking down one's nose at others. One does not have to go around putting up signs, waving banners, and exhorting one's superiority over others.

The same phenomenon, in a more subtle way, is exhibited by many clinicians in the mental health professions who pride themselves on their "respect" for children. They, unlike the rest of us, are *really* sensitive to children's thoughts and feelings. They, unlike the rest of us, *listen very carefully* to what children are saying and have the *deepest respect* for their wishes. In the precious atmosphere of their offices, they provide the child with "unconditional positive regard" and reflexly "respect" every thought (no matter how outlandish) and every feeling (no matter how at variance with reality) that teachers, parents, and other insensitive individuals do not provide. These same "therapists" may reflexly support the child's position in any difference he (she) may have with the parents, again in the service of respecting the child's position. When this attitude on the therapist's part is carried into a sex-abuse evaluation, it contributes to the development of false sex-abuse accusations. And, when carried over into the treatment of a child who is not sexually abused, it can contribute to the child's delusion that such an event did occur. Competent and sophisticated therapists know well that true respect for children is not complying with what they say they want but with what they really need.

I suspect that some readers (especially those whom I have criticized) would consider me to have exhibited a "holier-than-thou" attitude throughout the course of this book. I do not deny that one might easily come to this conclusion. However, in my defense, I believe that it is important to differentiate two types of criticism, namely, that which is justified and that which is unjustified. One could argue that every criticizer is exhibiting a "holier-than-thou" attitude toward the person being criticized. Whatever the criticism, no matter how constructive, it has within it the implicit message that the criticizer is superior to the person being criticized. The criticizer is basically saying that he (she) acts in a superior way, knows better, and feels it incumbent upon him (her) to communicate the corrective measures to the criticized individual so that he (she) can mend his (her) ways and be a "better person." And this holds even when the criticism is completely justified and even when the rectification of the criticized person's deficit(s) would be a boon to the world. It is important, therefore, to differentiate between criticisms that are warranted and those that are unwarranted. People who have bumper stickers saying "I brake for animals," people who wave the banner "Believe the children," and those therapists who proudly proclaim that they "respect" their child patients are in this second category. People in this category more justifiably warrant the "holier-than-thou" epithet. The important question for the reader of this book should not be whether I warrant the holier-than-thou label, but whether the criticisms I am making are valid and whether the changes that could result from their implementation are desirable.

The Erosion of Values

Most would agree that we have witnessed in the last quarter century a progressive erosion of values in the United States (and probably Western society at large). Evidence of this deterioration is to be found everywhere. Crime rates (with isolated exceptions) are ever soaring. Drug abuse is ubiquitous. Prisons in most states are overcrowded and cannot accommodate the ever-increasing flow of convicted criminals. Many are released into the street before the completion of their sentences in order to accommodate the new wave of inmates. In large cities automobile thefts, muggings, and other "minor crimes" are so commonplace that they receive little if any attention by the police, and the perpetrators rarely are meaningfully punished. Church boxes are pilfered, subway turnstiles are jumped over, garbage is strewn on streets, and human beings evacuate in public. Teachers are ever cutting corners, less homework is given, school vacations are longer, college admission (with rare exception) is easier, and handing in other students' written work is ever more common. Plagiarism among faculty people (even in the most prestigious universities) is becoming increasingly commonplace. And the probable increase in genuine child sex abuse in the intrafamilial situation is another example of this psychopathy. (The reader does well not to forget that I believe that bona fide sex abuse does indeed take place and is indeed ubiquitous and may even be on the rise.)

One of the many manifestations of this moral erosion has been the progressive insensitivity of people to one another. The Golden Rule has essentially become a quaint anachronism. It is all right for clergymen to tell children in Sunday school that they should treat one another as they themselves would like to be treated, but it is another thing to seriously implement this wisdom in the reality of the adult world. Many factors have been operative in producing this state of affairs. Parental modeling plays an important role in children's development of sympathy and empathy (which are directly related to the ability to put oneself in another person's position). The increasing popularity of day-care centers (their value and justification notwithstanding) deprives children of the kind of intimate involvement with biological parents from which values develop. No matter how dedicated the caretakers at these centers, no matter how educated they may be, they cannot provide the same kind of loving concern as a biological parent. (Elsewhere [Gardner, 1988a] I describe this in greater detail, especially with regard to a solution to this problem that would not involve condemning mothers to return to the home to merely cook and change diapers.) Violence on television and in the cinema is ubiquitous. Most often, little or nothing is portrayed about the pain suffered by the victims of such violence. In the 1960s and 1970s, during the days of the "me generation," books that emphasized the point "think of number one" often became best-sellers.

Evaluators who conclude that the vast majority (if not all) of the children they see have indeed been sexually abused are likely to have a defect in their capacity to place themselves in the positions of those who suffer from their decision. There is an element of psychopathy apparent in a person who would see a three-year-old child for a few minutes and then write a note stating that a particular individual (the father, the stepfather, a nursery school teacher, etc.) sexually abused that child. It takes a defect in the mechanisms of conscience to do such an abominable thing. One must completely ignore the effects of such a statement on the alleged perpetrator, effects that may include psychological devastation, destruction of one's lifestyle, and years of incarceration. This is what the "me generation" has wrought.

Interestingly, religious fundamentalism is most often (but certainly not always) a manifestation of moral erosion. I recognize that this statement may come as a surprise to some readers, but it is nevertheless a reality. The more the religious fundamentalist attempts to impose his (her) religious beliefs on others, the less sensitivity the religious zealot has for the person being converted. The examples are legion: Christ's crucifixion, the annihilation of the anti-church Albigensian sects in the 13th century, the Crusades, the Spanish Inquisition, the numerous religious wars in Europe between the Protestants and the Catholics, and (to skip quickly many such wars and bring us up to the present) the conflicts between the Shiite Moslems and the more moderate Islamic sects. When religious fundamentalism ignores the wishes, ideas, and feelings of other human beings, it is psychopathy masked as religiosity. It is no less a manifestation of moral erosion than the more overt examples cited above. The recent upsurge in religious fundamentalism in the United States may very well be a "backlash" to the "sexual revolution" of the 1960s and 1970s. Those in the movement who focus on sex have a convenient vehicle for their condemnation in the form of sex-abuse validation. The goal of publicly humiliating and incarcerating every "pervert" can only be reached if there is a significant defect in conscience and a suspension of the very morality that the religious proselytizers and purifiers proclaim to hold in such high esteem.

Sex-Abuse Victims as Validators

All career choices are determined by psychological factors and even psychopathological factors—and the people who choose sex-abuse work are no exception. I believe that people who have been sexually abused themselves in childhood are much more likely to enter this field than those who have not had such childhood experiences. I believe that if one were to compare the frequency of childhood sexual molestation in a thousand sex-abuse workers with three to four matched groups of workers in unrelated fields, the percentage of sex-abuse workers who were sexually molested as children would be significantly higher than the percentages in the other three or four groups. The sex-abuse field is attractive to those who were molested because it provides them with the opportunity for working through in many complex ways residual and unresolved reactions to their early traumas. I am not claiming that these factors necessarily operate at conscious levels (but they may), nor am I claiming that the processes are necessarily pathological (but they may be).

The phenomenon is no different from the factors that operate in just about any other field. To begin with my own field, many people choose medicine because they have grown up in a home with a parent who has suffered with a chronic illness. They may deal with this childhood trauma by devoting their lives to the treatment of others with that particular disorder or to the search for a cure for the parent's illness. Many choose psychiatry or psychology because they hope to gain understanding and even help for their own problems. People who frequently consider themselves to be put upon or victimized may choose law as a vehicle for protecting themselves and others from such persecutions. People who grew up in poverty may aspire to be (and even become) philanthropists; when they give to others they are basically giving to their projected selves. In all of these examples there is a range from the nonpathological to the pathological psychodynamic factors, and each person's balance lies at some point along the continuum.

Among the sex-abuse workers who have been sexually molested as children, there are many who use their career experience in healthy ways in their work—much to the benefit of abused children and their families. They have been there, they know what it's like, and they can provide a degree of sympathy and empathy not often possible for one who has never had the experience. But there are others in this group for whom pathological factors are clearly operative in their work with patients—factors that may becloud their objectivity. Some of these individuals harbor significant resentment against the original perpetrator, resentment that may not have been dealt with completely or properly. They vent their pent-up hostility on present-day offenders in a work setting that provides sanctions for such pathological release. And some of these workers operate on the principle that there will never be enough perpetrators to punish, so great is their desire to wreak vengeance on those who sexually molest children. Concluding that an alleged perpetrator is indeed innocent deprives them of their vengeful gratification. It is this subgroup of sex-abuse workers who may work with exaggerated zeal to prosecute alleged abusers and resist strongly the idea that some alleged offenders are indeed innocent. They often adhere tenaciously to the position that children *never* fabricate sex abuse. They must blind themselves to the aforementioned developments in recent years that make this notion an anachronism. Such zeal and denial have contributed significantly to the sex-abuse hysteria that we are witnessing at this time.

Furthermore, when these people "treat" sexually abused children, they can gratify vicariously the desire to treat their projected selves. They are curing themselves of the residua of their sex abuse by curing children who have been so afflicted. Again, this may be a normal, healthy mechanism for some who have been genuinely abused. However, if one has to diagnose normal children as being abused and then subject them to years of "treatment," then much psychological damage is being done and such treatment is an abomination. It can destroy children. It can provide chronic psychological trauma. Unfortunately, there are hundreds (and probably thousands) of children in the United States today who are being subjected to such "therapy."

I recognize that there will be some (especially those who work with sexually abused children) who will conclude that what I have just stated is prejudice on my part and that I have no scientific evidence to support my conclusions. I agree that I have no such studies to support my hypothesis and that my conclusions are based on my own experiences as well as the experiences of colleagues in the mental health professions (some of whom, interestingly, work in the field of sex abuse). My view of people in my own field is no less critical. There is no question that the specialty of psychiatry attracts some of the sickest medical students, and this is no doubt a factor in the reputation we have as being "crazies." This phenomenon also serves as an explanation for the fact that the suicide rate among psychiatrists is the highest of all the medical specialties. Accordingly, if I am prejudiced against sex-abuse workers, I may very well be considered to be prejudiced against people in my own field. However, one might also conclude that I am making accurate statements about both fields.

I am not at all claiming that all (or even the majority) of people involved as validators have been sexually abused as children. I am stating only that they are probably more highly represented than other groups in the population of sex-abuse workers. There are other psychological factors that may be operative. Involvement in this field provides the various kinds of sexual release described earlier in this book, e.g., vicarious gratification, reaction formation, voyeurism, etc. Many can gratify "savior syndrome" personality qualities. They devote themselves to protecting children from perverts who are to be found everywhere: among divorcing fathers, in nursery schools and day-care centers, in the streets, in parks, and in cruising cars and trucks. It's a dangerous world out there for children, with sex perverts hiding under practically every stone and lurking behind practically every tree. There is much work to be done to protect these children, and these workers have joined an army of heroes who are devoting themselves to their salvation. Is there a more noble way to spend one's life? Can there be a higher cause to which one can devote oneself?

The Sexually Inhibited

There are people who are sexually inhibited, who project out their own unacceptable sexual impulses onto others, and see sexuality everywhere. There are individuals who would like to be sexual molesters themselves, are too guilty to accept such impulses as their own, project them out onto others, and then condemn in others behavior that never occurred. What they are really condemning is their own projected fantasies; in this way they assuage their guilt. Such individuals may have minimal degrees of pedophilia (all of us have some) or they have more than the average amount. In either case, they cannot accept such impulses within themselves and must disown them. It is as if they are saying: "It is not I who wishes to involve myself sexually with children. I am too good a person to do such a terrible thing. It is they who are perpetrating these abominations, and I will do everything in my power to rid the world of such perverts." The need to do this may be so great that the condemner does not pay careful attention as to whether the individual did indeed sexually molest the child.

Sadists

Becoming a validator provides sadistic individuals with unlimited opportunities for gratification of their perversion. (Although I hesitate to use the word *perversion* for people who are homosexuals and people with other paraphilias, I have no hesitation using the word *perversion* to refer to the individuals I discuss in this section.) Sadistic individuals need others who can serve as targets for their sadism. In our society, at this time, especially in the present atmosphere of hysteria, child molesters are very much in vogue for such scapegoatism. Society has always needed its scapegoats. Obviously, in societies where adult-child sexuality is the norm, societies where pedophilia is viewed as an acceptable and even desirable form of behavior, such individuals cannot serve this purpose. Life is filled with frustrations, and frustration inevitably produces anger. People with formidable degrees of anger must find socially acceptable modalities for its discharge, and sex abusers are now being provided for the gratification of such sadists.

Paranoids

Some validators are overtly paranoid. Paranoia is much more common than is generally appreciated, especially because—in certain situations—it can have social benefit (sometimes real, sometimes fantasized). Paranoids are hypervigilant, are obsessed with any detail that might support their delusional system(s), and view as evil and/or corrupt those who would question their beliefs. And this is what we are dealing with here. What more noble cause can there be than to rid the world of sex perverts, people who perpetrate terrible abominations on innocent children. Paranoids tend to band together with others of similar persuasion and ignore or remove themselves entirely from those who would shake their delusional systems. A paranoid mother may join forces with a paranoid validator and enter into a folie-à-deux relationship. The accused father is then viewed as an enemy, as someone who is evil and corrupt, because he may provide compelling evidence that the accusation is false. Paranoids tend to espouse the satanic ritual theory of child sex abuse. The belief in a widespread conspiracy of satanic cults, through whose influences thousands of children are being sexually molested, must be a delusion. I do not doubt the existence of a small number of isolated individuals who may actually involve themselves in such rituals; what I do doubt is the alleged ubiquity of such groups, as rumor and hysteria would have us believe. Lanning (1992), who has supervised hundreds of FBI investigations into sex-abuse accusations in association with so-called satanic rituals, provides compelling support for this position. Victor (1993) has written an excellent book in which he describes the origins and development of the satanic ritual hysteria that we have been witnessing in this country in recent years.

As is well known, people who gravitate to the mental health professions (including psychiatry) often do so because of their own psychopathology. Those who believe that we in the mental health professions are necessarily psychologically healthier (whatever that means) than people in the general population are naive. Accordingly, it is reasonable to conclude that there are mental health professionals who are paranoid. Some of these people foster paranoid delusions in their patients, for example, convincing people that they were sexually molested as children and then encouraging their acting out on these delusions. This particular phenomenon is now reaching epidemic proportions. And it is being fueled by the paranoid subset of validators.

Overzealous Feminists

Although I am basically in sympathy with the aims of the feminist movement, feminists (as is true of all groups) have their share of fanatics. Some of the latter have jumped on the sex-abuse bandwagon because it provides a predictable vehicle for venting hostility toward men. These individuals also subscribe strongly (and even fanatically) to the dictum that children never lie and that any allegation of sex abuse must be true. Some of these women were subjected to cruel treatment in childhood by their fathers and other men. Some in this category have generalized from their childhood experiences and assume that all men will be equally abusive to them. Some carry with them a lifelong vendetta and have embarked upon a campaign of vengeance that will involve the destruction of every man who has the misfortune to cross their path and whom they have the opportunity to destroy. These women gravitate toward becoming validators in the same way that iron is attached to a magnet. It is the "perfect" profession for such fanatics. There is a minimum of effort, and with complete social sanction (after all, one is involved in the worthy cause of incarcerating perverts), they can humiliate, destroy, and incarcerate one man after the other in rapid succession.

The Hypocrites

And then there are the hypocrites. These are individuals who have been involved themselves in a wide variety of atypical sexual activities, and some of these people are even pedophiles. Some hypocrites are psychopathic in that they feel no guilt about sitting in judgment over others who have engaged in far less pedophilia than they, or who have engaged in no pedophilia at all. These people are indeed the true "perverts." They are drawn into the field of sex-abuse evaluations because it provides them with a socially acceptable vehicle for the gratification of their pedophilic impulses. I am not claiming that many of these people have actually engaged in pedophilic behavior; I am only claiming that psychologically they are pedophiles because of their obsession with such activities, and they get vicarious gratification of their pedophilic impulses by their involvement in this area. These people are similar to many of the individuals who gravitate toward professional ethics committees, where they sit in judgment of their colleagues.

In 1991 we saw an excellent example of this in the senatorial hearings regarding the appointment of Clarence Thomas to the Supreme Court of the United States. Sitting in judgment of Mr. Thomas was Senator Edward Kennedy, a man with an international reputation as a womanizer, a man whose girlfriend drowned at Chappaquiddick in association with an extramarital tryst. And I am convinced, as well, that most of the other individuals on that committee who were sitting in judgment of Mr. Thomas had engaged in various forms of sexual harassment far worse than he and that their sexual peccadilloes may very well have exceeded his. The committee's collective hypocrisy reached its height when they feigned horror when Professor Anita Hill (the woman who accused Justice Thomas of sexual harassment) reluctantly and dramatically revealed that the name of the protagonist of the pornographic videotape she was invited to view was "Long Dong Silver" (a name to which they responded with a "oh-goodness-gracious-me" reaction). Of course, this group of hypocrites know well where their bread is buttered. They know well where the votes are and where the votes are not. To react with anything but horror might compromise their chances for reelection. In one case in which I was involved, one of the prosecuting attorneys was demoted because he and colleagues were found to be spending their time on the job gleefully watching pornographic films that had been confiscated in cases in which they had been involved. So much for the hypocrites.

The Young and/or Naive

Another group of people one sees among the validators are the young and naive. Often, they are just out of training and have accepted as valid whatever has been taught to them. Students, in general, are a gullible lot. They generally accept as valid whatever has been taught to them, especially by a person who has a title like *professor*. To get through the "system," they must memorize significant amounts of material and regurgitate it as accurately as possible. Although certainly independent thinking is encouraged by a small percentage of teachers, the vast majority require submissive receptivity and parroting—their professions to the contrary notwithstanding. It is no surprise, then, that independent thinking is squelched in the course of most educational processes, and it should be no surprise, then, that young people hired at low salaries to work for child protection services just don't know how misinformed they are. Any pity I may have for them is more than counterweighed by my indignation over the terrible consequences of their ignorance.

Monetary Gain

A whole power structure has grown up in which an army of prosecutors, detectives, investigators, and others rely on a continual stream of positive findings and convictions if they are to justify their ever-increasing demands for more funds from legislatures. In the private sector, as well, there is money to be made in the field. I have already mentioned the sea of hungry lawyers who are looking for clients and who are happy to take on any kind of litigation, no matter how preposterous. There is also a sea of hungry mental health professionals (psychiatrists, psychologists, social workers, pastoral counselors, nurse practitioners, family therapists, and a whole group of so-called therapists) who are happy to have anyone's business, no matter how preposterous the reason for seeking consultation and treatment. Accordingly, there is big money to be made in the diagnosis and treatment of sex abuse. It is indeed a "growth industry." The validators, then, are only one part of this network in which they all need one another if they are to take their share of the money pie that has been made available by a hysterical society to support the system. Many of the validators fear (with justification) losing their jobs if they conclude that too many of the investigated clients are innocent or the charges unsubstantiated. There are clinics that receive funds only for the treatment of abused children. If an evaluator concludes that the child has not been abused, then the clinic receives no funding for that child's treatment. If the child's family cannot afford to pay for the therapy (the usual case for patients coming to community clinics), then the clinic must either turn away the child or provide treatment for little if any reimbursement. Under such circumstances, it is not surprising that the vast majority of children examined in such clinics are found to have been "abused."

Other Personality Factors

Underwager and Wakefield (1991) describe some of the personality problems that they consider to predispose an individual to believe many of the preposterous statements made by falsely accusing children, thereby causing them to get swept up in the hysteria of the times. One personality factor they describe is discomfort with *cognitive dissonance*. They state:

> People do not like to see or hear things that conflict with their deeply held wishes or beliefs. Interest in supporting information appears to be greater when there is a lower sense of certainty about the correctness of a belief. . . . Some mental health professionals are committed to the proposition that children are to be believed at all costs. If a person has chosen that belief, but is then confronted with a child saying things that are patently false or highly improbable, a state of dissonance is generated. That means the person will reduce the dissonance. (p. 183)

People who have difficulty tolerating such dissonance are likely to selectively shut out material that conflicts with their original beliefs.

Underwager and Wakefield (1991) describe *scapegoatism* as another factor operative for some evaluators. I have already mentioned this factor in hysteria (Gardner, 1993) and validators who have sadistic tendencies (this chapter). For evaluators, a person who sexually abuses a child can be a convenient scapegoat, someone to serve as a target for the examiner's pent-up hostilities. We are living at a time when there has been a shrinkage of potential scapegoats. The authors state:

> For those conversant enough with contemporary attitudes to know that antisemitism, racism, sexual identity prejudices, and any discrimi-

nation is unacceptable, the devil and Satanic devotees are acceptable, indeed a praiseworthy locus for aggression and hatred. It is proper and politically correct to hate the devil. Extremism in the battle of evil is noble. (p. 184)

And the same can be said for punishing those "perverts" who sexually abuse children. Thus we see the overlap between Satanism and sexual molesters. Satanic influences cause them to perpetrate their abominations upon innocent children. The scapegoat allows for hostile expression in two directions simultaneously, namely, Satan and sex perverts.

Intolerance of ambiguity is another personality factor that the authors consider operative. Underwager and Wakefield (1991) state:

> Some people find it difficult to cope with inconsistencies, ambiguities, and unexpected events. Their world needs to be black and white, all good or all bad. (p. 124)

Closely interrelated with this personality pattern is the mechanism of projection, which enables such an individual to project outward onto others thoughts and feelings that would produce intolerable and/or anxiety-provoking ambiguity. The authors also describe other psychopathological processes that may be operative in some of these evaluators.

Of course, there are other kinds of psychopathology that may be present in the kinds of evaluators I describe in this chapter. There are lonely and isolated people who now find meaning in their lives by joining a group dedicated to what is certainly a noble campaign, namely, ridding the world of sexual molesters—people who are so loathsome that they are not even worthy of being considered human beings. Could there be a better cause to which one could devote one's life? Joining with others in the campaign to wipe out sex abuse not only reduces their loneliness but provides them with the ego-enhancement that comes from involvement in such a lofty campaign. And there are people for whom a benevolent relationship is an unknown phenomenon; their only mode of relating is malevolently, and the ongoing battles involved in sex-abuse accusations provide them with such morbid interpersonal gratification. Pent-up rage, which previously could not be easily released, now finds a socially acceptable target.

CONCLUDING COMMENTS

The net result of all of this is that we have here a no-win situation for individuals accused of sex abuse. In the hands of many of these "validators," no one is innocent. Everyone is found to be guilty. Validators operate with impunity. False accusers are protected in most states from lawsuits involving slander and libel. I suspect that these "protective" laws are unconstitutional in that they deprive the accused of the opportunity for direct confrontation with the accuser, a right that is provided by the Sixth Amendment of the U.S. Constitution. In many states the accuser does not even have to mention his (her) name to the reporting authorities and will merely be recorded as "anonymous." Yet an investigation is embarked upon on the basis of the anonymous call, and people have even been jailed as a result of them.

Our founding fathers knew well the terrible indignities and injustices suffered by innocent victims of the European inquisitorial system of adjudication. Hundreds of thousands (and possibly millions) were convicted of crimes they never committed by accusers and witnesses whose identities were unknown to them. It is clear, at least in the realm of child sex-abuse accusations, that we have not advanced beyond those horrible times as far as we would like to think. I know of no falsely accused person who has instituted a lawsuit against a government agency that has utilized such anonymous witnesses as a source of information contributing to the individual's conviction. My hope is that such lawsuits will be instituted and that at least one such case will ultimately come to the attention of the U.S. Supreme Court. The use of anonymous witnesses must be unconstitutional.

Malpractice suits against these overzealous and/or incompetent evaluators have been difficult, especially because most of them practice at the same level as their peers. Generally, the plaintiff in a malpractice suit must establish that the defendant is working at a level below that of peers of comparable training and experience. With so many peers operating at this low level, it is difficult to single out the more egregious examples of stupidity. We would all be better off if there were some well-publicized malpractice suits against such individuals. Such lawsuits might have a sobering effect on the field. Unfortunately, most people who call themselves validators are practicing at the *same* low level of competence (or, more correctly, incompetence) and so do not satisfy an important criterion for malpractice, namely, that the individual's level of practice is far below that which is considered standard for peers at a similar level of training and experience. We are left, then, with a situation in which craziness is considered normality.

As mentioned, therapists who treat children who have been programmed to profess sex abuse when they have not been so abused need to know about the techniques utilized by the programmers. Without such knowledge, they are compromised in their ability to deprogram and otherwise treat these children. I believe that I have provided in this chapter an accurate description of what is taking place in this realm, a description that should prove useful to those who have to "help pick up the pieces" and return these children to their previous levels of functioning.

Last, I wish to repeat that I recognize that there are many evaluators who are extremely skilled and sensitive and who do not manifest the deficiencies described in this chapter. I recognize, as well, that evaluators, like all other people, exhibit a range of expertise from the most incompetent and defective to the most skilled and insightful. I have focused here on the most common deficiencies exhibited by the most seriously impaired evaluators and am fully appreciative that there are many examiners who do not operate at this low level of professional competence. My hope is that readers who react by becoming offended and thereby reject totally all that I say here will reconsider their position and give serious consideration to the possibility that I may be making some important points that may be useful to them. If such readers can overcome this initial rejection of what I say, they might find here some useful principles and techniques.

FIVE

WHAT DOES A PROGRAMMED CHILD LOOK LIKE?

INTRODUCTION

I believe we are now breeding a new type of psychopathology, psychopathology engendered by the aforementioned parade of authorities who are inculcating in children the delusion that they were subjected in early childhood to the abominable act of sexual abuse, a crime that is generally considered one of the most heinous in our society. I believe that I am observing these new types of psychopathology *in statu nascendi*. The symptoms I am observing have usually developed over the few years prior to the time I have evaluated these children. It is too early to say what these children will look like when they are grown up. Obviously, we are not dealing here with one specific "syndrome." It is probable that different types of disorders will emanate from these childhood experiences. Just as childhood sex abuse can potentially bring about a wide variety of disturbances, both sexual and nonsexual, the kinds of indoctrinations I am describing here are also likely to bring about a wide variety of psychiatric disturbances. For each category I describe I will make some projections regarding what I anticipate we will probably be seeing in the future.

The most important determinant as to whether the child will develop the symptoms described below is the intensity of exposure to the programming. Here, too, we have a continuum. At the one end is the child who has been "wound up" to provide a false accusation on one or two occasions and was not then put into "treatment" for having been sexually abused. The accusation has served its purpose: the "hated" perpetrator is removed and all can now go back to "normalcy." Subsequently, the accusation for these children is just a dim memory. They have some faint recollection that x number of years ago there was some "trouble," and they may recall having spoken to a few people, including the police. They do not remember exactly what they said. They are similar to children who have been in a class play, who memorize their lines for the occasion, and then the script evaporates from memory.

I recently had the opportunity to interview some children one year after their "treatment" was discontinued. The termination of therapy had nothing to do with their being "cured." Rather, it related to the fact that the lawsuits had come to an end, the psychologists' testimonies were no longer necessary, and the parents then decided that they could no longer afford treatment. These children had been in "treatment" approximately two-and-a-half years and ranged in age from seven to eight. Interestingly (and gratifyingly), they did not exhibit serious psychological difficulties as a result of their "therapy." From what I could gather, they were presenting their little scenarios to parents and therapists, but otherwise they were not significantly preoccupied with thoughts about their alleged abuses. They had learned that when you go to the therapist's office, you recite the sex-abuse scenario and then go home and go about your business. Because there was no basic sex-abuse experience, there was no real trauma, and there were none of the kinds of preoccupations one sees in a bona fide posttraumatic stress disorder (PTSD) (the diagnosis commonly given to these children by their therapists in rubber-stamp fashion). Accordingly, the sex-abuse scenarios were not deeply embedded in their psychic structures. When I saw them, I had the feeling that their litanies were like well-rehearsed parts in a school play, learned well enough to recite under the proper circumstances, and then forgotten because they were no longer serving any purpose. These children were lucky enough to have been removed from treatment early. There are others, however, who are not so fortunate, whose parents and therapists go on for years convincing them that they were subjected to terrible abominations, entrenching thereby their psychopathological processes.

At the other end of the continuum are those children who are involved in protracted lawsuits and who must repeatedly be reminded of their "traumas." Furthermore, they are in "intensive therapy," the purpose of which is allegedly to cure them of the trauma. In practice, however, they are repeatedly and mercilessly required not only to repeat the alleged traumas but also are encouraged endlessly to bring up into conscious awareness further repressed sexual experiences, both with the identified perpetrator and with others who were not previously recognized as having abused them. The therapy becomes an educational process in which fantasies are turned into delusions. By suggestion and coercion, fantasies originally engendered by the therapist come to be believed. It is these children who develop the symptoms described below. Sometimes, a child who is not in therapy will be given an interview with a therapist prior to a court hearing, deposition, or interview by an examiner such as myself. The purpose here is to help the child remember what had happened in order to ensure that the proper script is presented to the follow-up examiner. Children who have genuinely been abused do not need such "rehearsal sessions." The greater the number of such update interviews, the more the child goes down toward the delusional end of the continuum. I refer to these interviews as "booster shots," and they serve to entrench the child's pathology.

I present here observations of programmed children I have seen since the mid-1980s. I have not conducted any formal follow-up studies. Rather, these are children whom I have seen in association with sex-abuse accusations, especially in the context of lawsuits. These lawsuits tend to drag on for years, during the course of which the children have been subjected to "therapy" of varying lengths. As mentioned, the greater the intensity of the treatment, the greater the likelihood the children will develop the symptoms described here. And, the more protracted the lawsuit, the greater the likelihood children will develop these symptoms because lawsuits typically involve periodic inquiries as well as ongoing preoccupation with the abuse to which the children have allegedly been subjected. The prospect of reaping a fortune down the road is ever in the family's mind and continues to entrench thoughts of the alleged abuses and their presumed effects.

OTHER FOLLOW-UP STUDIES

To the best of my knowledge, there are very few follow-up studies on the effects of this kind of legal process/"therapy" trauma on children. I suspect that one of the reasons for this is that the majority of people who are doing these evaluations are not appreciative of the kinds of trauma to which they are subjecting these children. Obviously, this category of "professionals" is not going to be conducting studies on the untoward effects of their interrogations and "treatment." Those who are appreciative (and our ranks are growing) of the abominations that are being perpetrated upon these innocent children will, I am certain, be conducting such studies in the future. Another reason for the paucity of such studies is the fact that the phenomenon is a relatively recent one, having started in the early 1980s—especially in association with the McMartin case in Manhattan Beach, California. As mentioned, I am convinced that a new type of psychopathology is being developed and that many of the children being subjected to the kinds of "therapy" and interrogations described in this book will be permanently damaged, even to the point of being permanently psychotic. One cannot tamper in this way with the minds of three-year-olds and expect them to be unaffected. One cannot induce significant distortions of reality—over a long period—and expect children so victimized to escape unscathed.

Underwager and Wakefield (1991) provide follow-up data on some of the well-known nursery school and day-care center cases in which orgies of sexual abuse have been alleged. They quote Robson (1991), who states with regard to the Scott County, Minnesota, case:

> More than seven years later, the legacy of Scott County has been one of children crying for their parents in the middle of the night; of divorce and dysfunction among nearly all the families involved; of perhaps permanent emotional damage to the accused and the accusers alike. (p. 50)

Robson further describes subsequent school problems, behavioral difficulties, sexual confusion, and drug and alcohol problems in adolescence. Underwager and Wakefield (1991) describe other cases in which children suffered significant emotional damage after being taken away from their homes and subjected to numerous interrogations in which the interviewers refused to believe their denials.

As is obvious, we are only at the beginning of the process of conducting follow-up studies of children who have been programmed to believe they were sexually abused when they were not. It is too early to make any definitive statements with regard to what will happen to these children. Furthermore, the effects on their sexual lives cannot be separated from the effects of the child abuse prevention programs, especially those that are conducted over many years. Most of the children I have seen were exposed to their "treatment" in the early years of their lives, most often long before the adolescent period. Now, many are entering adolescence, and it is now that we are first starting to see the effects of these earlier indoctrinations, especially the effects on their sexual lives. However, it will be a decade or longer before we will be able to make some definite statements regarding the sexual effects of such "therapy" and interrogation and its attendant programming.

LEGAL PROCESS/"THERAPY" TRAUMA

I use the term *legal process/"therapy" trauma* to refer to the traumatic psychological reactions that children are likely to suffer after being subjected to a series of stressful and coercive interviews in association with a sex-abuse accusation. Usually these interviews (sometimes more properly considered interrogations) are conducted by one or more of the following: the police, detectives, prosecutors, social workers, "validators," child advocates, psychiatrists, psychologists, social workers, "therapists" (often self-styled and unlicensed), lawyers, guardians-ad-litem, judges, and, unfortunately, parents. These interviews are not only conducted in the investigative/evaluative process, but in a type of "therapy" that is often an indoctrinational process under the guise of treatment.

The symptoms so engendered may be similar to, if not identical with, those seen in the PTSD. It is often easy, however, to differentiate between the PTSD that results from sex abuse and that which results from legal process/"therapy" trauma. The former symptoms are usually present, to varying degrees, during the time frame of the abuse and possibly after the time the abuse was discontinued. The latter do not generally appear until *after* the disclosure, when the child becomes subjected to the aforementioned series of interrogations.

Accordingly, the most common symptoms of legal process/"therapy" trauma are similar to, if not identical with, those seen in bona fide sex abuse. It is only by pinpointing the time of onset that one can make the distinction. Furthermore, it is important to note that the same symptoms might have a wide variety of other causes, causes having nothing to do with either sex abuse or legal process/"therapy" trauma. And this is one of the important reasons why there is no such thing as a "sex-abuse syndrome." Some of the more common symptoms of legal process/"therapy" trauma are depression, psychosomatic disorders, regressive behavior, sleep disturbances, antisocial behavior, high levels of tension and anxiety, and school attendance and performance problems. In addition, one may see many symptoms that are seen in the PTSD. However, because the symptoms do not appear until after disclosure, they are not properly considered to be manifestations of sex abuse, but manifestations of legal process/"therapy" trauma. These include preoccupation with the trauma and trauma-specific dreams. One may also see sexual problems, especially because the interviews are often sexualized, especially when anatomical dolls and body charts are used in every session. Such children may exhibit pathological attitudes toward their genitals, shame or guilt over alleged participation in the sexual acts, sexual excitation (including sexual acting out), advanced sexual knowledge for age, and seductive behavior. They may feel stigmatized and suffer with feelings of guilt over the consequences of the divulgence to the accused as well as guilt as a delusion of control. Elsewhere (Gardner, 1995a) I have elaborated on these symptoms and describe techniques for ascertaining whether the symptoms are the result of legal process/"therapy" trauma, sexual abuse, or other sources.

The situation is complicated by the fact that there are other kinds of trauma unrelated to sex abuse and unrelated to legal process/"therapy" that can produce similar symptoms. For example, a child subjected to ongoing divorce litigation, especially a custody dispute, can develop a wide variety of symptoms including those seen in the PTSD. Even children who live in intact homes who are exposed to ongoing parental hostility, neglect, and a chaotic environment can develop PTSD symptoms. Furthermore, there are nonabused children who are subjected to "treatment" for their sexual abuse and/or legal-process interrogations who do not develop PTSD symptoms but do develop other symptoms that do not properly fall under the PTSD rubric. These can include depression, psychosomatic complaints, antisocial acting out, withdrawal, and a variety of other pathological symptoms. In short, detrimental environmental factors can produce a wide variety of symptoms, almost any psychogenic pathological symptom known to those who work therapeutically with children. Accordingly, there is no typical picture and no particular syndrome (a cluster of symptoms that warrant being placed together because of a common specific cause). Rather, there are a wide variety of symptoms that children can develop, and it behooves the examiner to ascertain whether these particular psychogenic symptoms were caused by "therapy" and/or the legal process. Under such circumstances the symptoms can justifiably be considered derivatives of legal process/"therapy" trauma.

FACTORS THAT COMMONLY CONTRIBUTE TO AND INTENSIFY LEGAL PROCESS/"THERAPY" TRAUMA

Removal of the Child and/or Alleged Abuser

When the court concludes that the abuse did indeed take place (whether this is a valid conclusion or not), it is often the case that either the abuser or the child must be taken from the home. This is traumatic enough when the allegation is fabricated; but when it is true, it is not necessarily the only course to take. In spite of the abuse (which may have occurred on only one occasion), the abuser may still be removed from the home or, in certain situations, the child. This is especially the case when the mother is considered unfit and likely to foster or expose the child to further abuses. The disruption of the parent-child bond here may be formidable and the psychological trauma significant, and this is especially the case when the molestation has been mild or there has been no abuse at all.

The Systematic Erosion and Destruction of the Parent-Child Bond

The child may feel guilty over the destruction of the parent's life that was the result of the false allegation. Such parents may become pariahs, and their social and professional lives correspondingly ruined. Some of these children are placed in treatment. The child, then, is being placed in therapy for an experience (or experiences) that never occurred. It is not uncommon for the therapist to work on the assumption that no child ever fabricates sex abuse. Such "treatment," then, cannot but be detrimental. The child may come to actually believe that the abuse took place and suffer with subsequent feelings of guilt and low self-worth. Often the therapist actively fosters expression of hostility and vengeance against the innocent parent, which may result in permanent alienation. In practically every session the child is encouraged to act out hostility toward the father, often with the help of dolls that the child is encouraged to punch, kick, and hit. Nothing good is said about the father. Comfort with normal ambivalence is discouraged. There is progressive programming of the child to believe that the father is the incarnation of all the evil that has ever existed in the history of the world. The destruction of this relationship is tragic for both the child and the father. Even if the father had sexually abused the child, such "treatment" would be inappropriate. The child is taught to be sadistic, to act out hostility without guilt, and this of course contributes to the development of antisocial behavior, and, of course, it creates an iatrogenic disruption of the parent-child bond (Benedek and Schetky, 1987).

"Empowering" Techniques

The child is taught "empowering" techniques, techniques allegedly designed to help the child deal with the father and others who might try to abuse him (her). At the simplest level children are taught to "say no" in situations when abusers approach them. They are taught to run away, to hide, and to appeal for help from a wide variety of authorities. They are also taught that many people may not believe them when they claim that they are in danger of being abused, so they may have to go to a series of authorities before they will receive help. Such "treatment" not only creates the belief in the child that perpetrators are lurking everywhere, but that children should be in a constant state of vigilance in order to protect themselves from sex abusers. This cannot but create unnecessary tensions and anxieties and, in extreme cases, paranoid thinking. Although basically not really capable of fending off sex abusers who would impose themselves, there is another kind of empowering that these children are taught. This second type is not specifically labeled such and is not even recognized by the therapist as an empowering technique. Specifically, the child becomes the center of attention in order to ensure that every verbalization related to sexual abuse is duly recorded. With notebook at hand the parents are ever vigilant for further sexual accusations and will instantaneously record them for posterity. This puts the parents in the child's power. For example, every child has the experience of being told that mother cannot speak with him (her) at that time because she is engaged in a telephone conversation with a friend. All these children need do is state that they have just thought of another sexual encounter they had with the accused and the mother is instantaneously off the phone. All other activities are of lower priority than the child's sex-abuse disclosures. Furthermore, the children may be given presents if they tell an examiner "the truth" and may even extract bribes from parents to provide their sex-abuse scenarios. All this corrupts children and puts them in a position of pathological power.

Courtroom Interrogations

In court the child suffers significant trauma. Most often the child is interviewed by the judge in his (her) chambers. However, on occasion the child is required to testify on the stand in open court. Although the court recognizes that such testimony may be psychologically traumatic, the alleged victim is entitled to face his (her) accuser in an open courtroom, and such testimony is considered one of the rights of the accused under the U.S. Constitution. The alleged perpetrator's attorney is likely to interrogate the child repeatedly, as is the accuser's lawyer. The legal professionals are basically trained in direct and cross-examination techniques. Whereas these may be applicable to the adversary courtroom setting, they are most often psychologically traumatic to children, because they inevitably attempt to zero in and focus on the most sensitive material. Therapists know well that the confrontational approach is often the most anxiety provoking and may be the least efficient method for getting at "the truth." Furthermore, some legal professionals hammer away at, badger, and attempt to wear down the witness to the point where an individual will say anything just to get off the stand. And many such individuals do not consider children exempt from such inquiries.

Or, the court may allow the child to be interviewed in the judge's chambers. However, even here the child is generally quite fearful, because the judge is viewed as an awesome figure of authority. The child's recognition that what he (she) says may ultimately result in the alleged perpetrator being sent to jail adds formidably to the child's tension and anxiety. Feelings of fear, guilt, disloyalty, and low self-worth are inevitable under such circumstances. The child may even believe that he (she) may be sent to jail, especially when the allegation is true. The judge may promise the child that everything said will be held in strict confidence; but this ultimately proves to be a deceit in that the information provided is ultimately communicated to the attorneys and parents who, most often, directly or indirectly, will transmit the divulgence down to the child. The sense of betrayal that results adds to the child's feelings of distrust and betrayal.

COMMON SYMPTOMS CHARACTERISTICALLY SEEN IN PROGRAMMED CHILDREN

Here I describe special symptoms, somewhat different from the more general kinds of symptoms described above, that are seen in children who have been programmed, especially over long periods. It is these symptoms especially that warrant my stating that we are developing a new breed of psychopathology in a new generation of children, a type of psychopathology that did not exist before.

Impaired Reality Testing

A major part of child rearing involves helping children differentiate between fact and fantasy. Children's minds are filled with misrepresentations, misperceptions, and fantasies about the world. It is the role, and even the job, of every parent to continually help correct such distortions. A parent who willfully and knowledgeably teaches a child the opposite of what is the truth is contributing significantly to a compromise in that child's ability to adjust in the real world. Programmed children are being taught to ignore their senses, ignore their perceptions, ignore their memories, and believe that certain events happened to them that did not. Again, there is a continuum from the child in whose mind the engendered fantasy will evaporate to the child in whose mind it will become a fixed delusion.

Let us take, for example, a three-year-old girl who is asked the question: "Did your daddy ever put his penis in your mouth?" The child has never had such an experience; nor has she ever thought about such an encounter, her "polymorphous perversity" notwithstanding. The question per se engenders in her mind a visual image of this kind of encounter with her father. The child answers, "No. Yuch. That's phooey. My daddy wouldn't do such a thing." The examiner may respond, "Are you *sure*?" We see here how the "no" response is not accepted by the overzealous interrogator, whose main purpose is to extract a sex-abuse accusation. In that session the child may continue to deny the experience, or she may acquiesce and say "yes" in order to ingratiate herself to the examiner or avoid his (her) alienation (which she definitely senses, even at age three).

In the next interview, however, with the same or different examiner, the same question is asked. This time the question evokes in the child's mind an image of her father with his penis in her mouth. She does not know, however, whether the image indicates an actual sexual encounter or is merely a repetition of the visual image engendered by the examiner in the previous interview. The mind does not have a little red light that flashes when the visual mental image is false and a little green light that flashes when the visual mental image is true.

The younger the child, the greater the likelihood that she will then say "yes" to this question. She might, in her confusion, say, "I think." The use of this qualification is one of the hallmarks of the programmed child. Children who have actually been abused rarely say, "I think." They *know*. I am not saying that they automatically will describe their encounters to any examiner; I am only saying that they most often know. Nor am I saying that there is no such thing as repression. What I am saying is that such repression of sexual abuse is rare, media publicity about the ubiquity of the repression phenomenon notwithstanding.

I have found the visual memory criterion to be an important one in differentiating between those children who have actually been abused and those who falsely claim sexual abuse. Specifically, those who have actually been abused will generally have some fairly good, if not very accurate, visual memories of their abuses. In contrast, programmed children, especially after there has been a long time gap between the time frame of the programming (which usually begins at the time of the "disclosure") and the time when they are asked to talk about their abuses to an examiner such as myself, may not be able to bring up any visual memory of their abuses. They may claim, however, that they were abused, that they *know* they were abused, but they cannot conjure up any actual memories of their experiences. The child has the delusion, the fixed belief, that the sexual abuses actually occurred, but cannot bring up any visual memory of the abuses. The child will easily be able to bring up other visual memories of the perpetrator in a wide variety of settings, but cannot conjure up a particular visual memory of the abuses—no matter how hard the child tries. Yet, although having no capacity to remember actual events, the child still believes with 100 percent certainty that the abuse occurred. It is as if the child is saying: "I do not remember having been sexually abused, and I cannot actually bring up any visual memories of such abuse, but I know that it happened because so many powerful authorities around me have told me it happened. My parents, the police, the lawyers, the judge, and (in many cases) the jury have all told me that this happened, so it must have happened. He's now in jail; so he must have done it. I am only a child and they are adults. They know better than I." When such children are asked about their abuses, one may get responses like, "My mother told me," "Ask my mother, she knows," "It's all there in those papers that you have on your desk."

There are some children, however, who are falsely accusing yet do have some fragmentary memory of some aspect of the abuse. Most often, these are children who have been in ongoing "treatment," and the inculcation process has extended over a long period, sometimes years. Often the recalled fragments are from the ambient scenarios that one sees in group hysteria. This is what I refer to as the cross-fertilization process in which through the network of parents, therapists, and children, fragments of alleged sexual-abuse encounters become passed around and incorporated into the scenarios of the various children involved. This ambient cross-fertilization process complements that of the therapists and will increase the likelihood of "memories of abuse." For example, in one group-hysteria situation I was involved in, there was an ambient story that the abuses took place in a wigwam. Nobody knew of any wigwams in the area, but this was a general belief (or, more accurately, a delusion) held by all the parents and children in this day-care center. A few years later, a child claimed to me that she had a visual image of the wigwam and "knew" that her abuse took place in the wigwam, but had no other visual images and could give me no further information.

When such programming is completely successful, the child develops a delusion that may be lifelong. These are the children who are likely to have been subjected to the types of "therapy" described above. My prediction is that such children will have difficulties in other areas of reality testing, and some of them will develop paranoid delusions. The fear of strangers, the confusion between reality and unreality, the hypervigilance (see below), and the delusional belief that they have been subjected to an abominable crime lay the foundation for the development of paranoia in the future.

Fears

Programmed children become hypervigilant. The hypervigilance may have appeared prior to the accusation, when they were subjected (I have no hesitation using the word) to the so-called child-abuse prevention programs, which teach children about "good touch" and "bad touch" and how to protect themselves from strangers who may try to sexually abuse them. These programs inculcate into children (who are not confused by them) the notion that sex-abuse perverts are potentially lurking behind every tree in the park and playground and may come out from behind any bush. When one adds to this "foundation" the kinds of programming described above, it is likely that the child will develop a fear of strangers, far above and beyond the usual age-appropriate fear of this kind. Such children want to be sure that the doors and windows of their houses are locked, so that sex-abuse perpetrators cannot enter their homes during the middle of the night.

Programmed children are being continually taught that the world is a dangerous place and that calamity may befall them at any moment. They have had a unique experience, namely, they have had what they thought was a good experience with a certain person (a father, a nursery school teacher, a school bus driver) and then they learn that, without their appreciating it, they had been subjected to terrible crimes and heinous acts. This cannot but produce fears of encounters with other people who, without their knowing it, may perpetrate similar atrocities on them. Separation anxiety is likely to occur. These children appear to be operating on the principle: stay ever close to your mother and father and you will be protected from these dangerous people.

The situation, in a sense, is more anxiety provoking than other sources of fear in which such children may find themselves. Witches look like witches. "Bad guys," at least from the view of the child, are dressed in certain types of apparel. They usually have mean faces and carry guns. And the "good guys" are usually clean shaven and have nice uniforms (like policemen). For these children, people who they thought were "good guys" may actually turn out to be "bad guys." Even their parents were initially deceived and also originally thought that these people were good guys. Their parents, however, their past detection deficiencies notwithstanding, have learned some lessons and are now considered to be the best people to be able to differentiate "safe" from "unsafe" people. One does well, then, to stick closely to them for protection because the world is indeed a dangerous place and one never knows who will turn out to be the bad guys and in what setting the abuses will be perpetrated. Even the protected setting of a nursery school may not be safe enough. These children, then, appear to subscribe to the following dictum: "You do well to hang onto mother's apron strings whenever possible. Do not visit with friends, do not go to day camp, and certainly do not go to sleepaway camp. These are the kinds of places where you can be least certain of protection, the ostensible safety of the environment notwithstanding. You can go to school because the teacher has been clearly designated as a 'good guy.'"

The fear of the alleged perpetrator may generalize to fears of all people of the same sex and similar appearance. Such fears may contribute to dreams and nightmares. However, in the falsely accusing child these dreams and nightmares are not trauma specific, i.e., they do not include direct and readily recognizable elements from the trauma (Terr, 1990). Children who have been genuinely abused are more likely to have dreams in which the perpetrator is easily identified or closely so. Programmed children have more generalized types of nightmares, which are usually not trauma specific. However, in some cases in which the child's delusion has been inculcated deeply enough, the dreams become trauma specific and the delusional perpetrator becomes incorporated into their frightening dreams. The fears engendered in these children are not likely to disappear when they grow older, and this is especially the case if they are subjected to years of the aforementioned type of "therapy." Fears, too, are on a continuum with paranoia. In fear there is an exaggerated reaction to danger. In fear the danger is generally identifiable, and fears are reduced when the patient feels protected. When fears develop into paranoia, protective maneuvers do not work. It is for this reason, also, that I believe that many of these children will ultimately become paranoid.

Antisocial Behavior and Psychopathy

Many of these children are very angry. They have been forced into situations where they have been subjected to numerous interrogations that are confusing and anxiety provoking. They have no choice but to acquiesce. Police and detectives may have threatened them that they will go to jail if they do not tell "the truth." If the reader does not believe that these things are happening right now in the United States, then the reader is delusional. There is much money to be made and power to be enjoyed by a whole parade of prosecutors, police investigators, sex-abuse "experts," "validators," and others in the sex-abuse investigation and prosecution apparatus. The anger engendered by these experiences may be acted out and directed toward safer targets like peers in the neighborhood and classroom teachers. Such children may exhibit a generalized high level of tension and irritability. Under such circumstances they have a low frustration tolerance and even a "low boiling point." It does not take much to bring about outbursts of crying and rage. Such behavior may interfere with peer relationships and school functioning. Often, there is anger at the parents. They, more than anyone else, have usually initiated the course of events that has resulted in the child's being subjected to the series of coercive inquiries. However, anger cannot be directly expressed toward them because they are viewed as the people who are most likely to protect the child from similar such abominations.

In addition, these children have been subjected to experiences that compromise development of conscience. Mention has been made of the girls of Salem who clapped and laughed with joy as they watched their victims being hanged. Typically, the parents and therapists of these children encourage them to act out anger against the alleged perpetrator. In their treatment these children are typically encouraged to hit dolls that represent the accused and to verbalize profanities. I have seen situations in which the children are brought to the courtroom to witness the sentencing. Pictures drawn of the accused in jail are hung up in the therapist's office and at home, much to the admiration of friends and relatives. Therapists consider this healthy "working through." Any feelings of sympathy for the perpetrator (even if guilty) are not expressed. Such impairments in the development of conscience are not generally confined to the accused but tend to spread. They contribute thereby to the development of antisocial behavior and, ultimately, psychopathy.

These children exhibit a somewhat blasé attitude regarding their lying. Most children expect to be confronted with dubiety when they lie, but not these children. The most absurd and preposterous elaborations are often diligently recorded and accepted as valid. Not only does this contribute to the aforementioned impairment in reality testing, but it contributes to impairments in the development of conscience. Most children, when they lie, are confronted by incredulous adults who routinely try to get them to separate truth from fabrication, fact from fantasy. Not these children. Important adults around them accept the bizarre with relish and they transfer this attitude to other examiners. On those occasions when these children are confronted with the absurdity of their comments, they will often come up with yet another lie, so programmed have they been to respond with preposterousness and even fabricated absurdity.

Programmed children are also taught scapegoatism. All of the child's undesirable behaviors that have ever existed are attributed to the alleged perpetrator. Now, according to the parents, everything falls into place. All the behaviors that they previously could not understand are now recognized as having been caused by the sexual abuse. Finding a simple cause for complicated problems is central to scapegoatism. The next step, of course, is to get rid of the scapegoat. Then all will allegedly be right with the world. This factor is especially prominent among adult women who falsely accuse their parents and other elderly people of having sexually abused them in childhood. As mentioned, there is no question that some of these accusations are true; but there is no question, as well, that some are false. It is in the false category that we see the scapegoatism mechanism clearly operative.

When one combines antisocial behavior with deficiencies in conscience development, the foundation for the development of psychopathy is laid. The presence of a lawsuit brings these angry children further down the road to psychopathy. This is most clearly seen in the nursery school and adult-belated-accusation situations. In the nursery school situation, the school is sued for having allowed the alleged perpetrator to subject the children to sexual crimes. In my evaluations of these children, the money issue appears to come up more frequently than in evaluations of other children. I am not presenting this as a strong point because, in our materialistic society, money issues are frequently brought up. In these children, however, the get-rich-quick element is seen more often than in other children. Generally, the parents know well that there is an insurance company from which they hope to extract enormous amounts of money. This teaches children exploitation, which, of course, may contribute to psychopathy. Although I suspect strongly that many of these children will develop psychotic symptoms, especially in the delusional realm, I am not so sure about the psychopathic track down which some of them may go. They are at high risk, however, for the development of this problem and only the future will tell whether this prediction is realized.

Among the falsely accusing adult women, those who are prepsychopathic may go down the track to grosser manifestations of psychopathy. Such lawsuits are generally not instituted when the elderly person has no money. If he has some, or any property of value such as a house, then, with the therapist's support, the lawsuit is instituted. And one of the purposes of the lawsuit is to get money for "treatment." In such situations, I generally see a folie-à-deux relationship in which both paranoid and psychopathic elements are present in both the therapist and the patient. In these cases, it is the patient who is the primary victim. I have seen a few situations in which the accused father was dying of a malignancy or other terminal disease, but this did not result in any hesitancy on the daughter's part to sue him. A more blatant example of psychopathy would be hard to find, even if the father did indeed sexually abuse the woman when he was younger.

Interest in "Mysteries"

Another preliminary finding to come out of my studies of these children has been an interest in mysteries that appears to go beyond its usual frequency. Many children are interested in mystery stories, and this is an age-appropriate interest. However, I believe that more of these children are expressing interest in this form of literature. This is not surprising. There has been, indeed, a great mystery in these children's lives. They thought everything was going well with the alleged perpetrator. They enjoyed being with him and could recount many wonderful experiences with him. Then, sometime later, they suddenly learn that just the opposite was the case, specifically, that although they did not realize it at the time, they were being subjected to terrible and abominable acts, acts too terrible even to describe. Initially, they have no recollection of any of these despicable acts. However, after a series of police interviews and "therapeutic" sessions, they are brought to the point of believing that they must have been abused if so many powerful authorities around them tell them that this was indeed the case. Obviously, this produces confusion, even, I believe, for those who have developed the delusion that the abuse occurred. As mentioned, many of them still have no visual imagery of their alleged experiences. In short, all this is *very mysterious*.

Most often, the interest in mysteries is age-appropriate and typical of what other child their age are involved in, that is, typical detective stories and murder mysteries. An attractive element in such fare is the basic theme that a crime has been committed and it is the primary goal of the investigators to find out exactly what happened. Of course, this scenario exactly parallels these children's situation. One child told me that the reason he likes mysteries so much is that they always end up with people "getting the solution." The child who exhibited this phenomenon most dramatically was the one who told me that when he grew up he wanted to be "a man who tracks down ghosts like the Loch Ness monster." He then elaborated on how he was very interested in the Loch Ness monster because he considered it to be one of the great mysteries of the 20th century. Obviously, this is an unusual career choice and provides confirmation for this initial finding.

With regard to the future, it may very well be that some of these children may actually become mystery story writers. Some might become scientists in order to delve into and learn more about the mysteries of the universe. With regard to the negative effects of this involvement, I have no specific predictions at this point. At least, it is a reflection of confusion and the desire to find concrete absolute solutions to "mysteries" and "unanswered questions."

The Inculcation of Sexual Psychopathology

Such "treatment" also inculcates in children the view that sex is filthy and dangerous. The word *love* hardly appears in such therapy. Certainly there is no love from the father, and if there is any love from the mother, it is the kind that protects the child from danger. The idea that love can be combined with sex is not introduced. Obviously, such indoctrination can have serious effects on the child's future sex life. And the aforementioned programming against the father is likely to be generalized to all men, with the result that there is further interference in the child's capacity to develop a healthy sexual orientation.

Such treatment is generally interminable. The therapist is ever trying to elicit more and more details about the sexual abuses. And these children, in order to ingratiate themselves to their therapists, continue to pour forth with a never-ending stream of abuses that soon reach the level of atrocities. Ultimately, there is no sexual abomination that is not described, and this is especially the case in the nursery school and daycare center situations, where the mass-hysteria element prevails. I am convinced that many of these children are being programmed to become psychotic as a result of this kind of "treatment." And the psychosis so engendered includes bizarre delusions in the sexual realm.

The oldest children that I have thus far seen have been in their early teens, eight years after the time frame of their alleged abuses. Most, however, have been in their preteen years. None of these children had what I considered to be overt sexual problems at the time of my interviews. However, considering their age, this is not surprising. Because they were not actually sexually abused, they did not exhibit the oversexualization often seen by children who were genuinely molested. I believe, however, that there is a high likelihood that these children will develop sexual problems in the future, problems that will probably manifest themselves during the teen/dating period. It would be hard for me to imagine that they would view sex as a pleasurable experience. For many years they have been inculcated with the idea that sex is despicable, sinful, and even a criminal act. In fact, in many of these cases, the alleged perpetrator has been sent to jail, usually for many years. And they themselves were allegedly participants in this noxious act.

The most likely outcome, I suspect, will be sexual inhibition problems. These may take the form of (to use *DSM-IV* diagnoses) Hypoactive Sexual Desire Disorder, Sexual Aversion Disorder, Male Erectile Disorder, Female Orgasmic Disorder, Male Orgasmic Disorder, Premature Ejaculation, Dyspareunia, and Vaginismus. These basic sexual inhibition problems are likely to contribute to the development of broader interpersonal problems that are derivative of the sexual, e.g., fear of dating, perfectionistic attitudes regarding who an acceptable partner will be, fear of commitment to long-term relationships, marital difficulties, and multiple divorces. Of course, these can only be predictions, but I consider there to be a high likelihood that these patterns will emerge.

The Creation of "Professional Victims"

We are living in a time when being a victim enables some people to enjoy an enormous amount of prestige. Professional victims are to be seen everywhere. Anna O., Dora, and Freud's other hysterical patients might today put on "I am a survivor" and "I am a sex-abuse victim" tee shirts and sweatshirts. Group therapy for victims is very much in vogue, and all these victims are clamoring for their rights. Practically every day sex-abuse victims tell their stories on television or describe them in newspaper or magazine articles. Leading celebrities are now "coming out" and divulging their childhood sexual abuses. These people serve as models and facilitate divulgence by others, even by people who have never been abused. These people in high places not only serve as models for others, but provide the promise of notoriety for such disclosures. Being a victim of childhood sexual abuse is very much in vogue.

Children in "treatment" are taught that they are victims of sexual abuse. They become deeply indoctrinated with the notion that they have been victimized, and this cannot but affect their future psychological development. Victims of sex abuse tend to see themselves as victims in other situations. The prophecy may very well be realized, with the result that lifelong patterns of self-destructiveness may become embedded. Such an attitude engenders the notion that they are not responsible for unacceptable, painful, and even terrible things that may happen to them. Rather, they tend to view themselves as the innocent victims of persecutors, and this pattern can contribute to the development of sadomasochistic behavior as well as paranoid thinking.

It is likely that many of the children I have seen will ultimately go down the track to becoming professional victims and will entice others to support their delusion, in addition to those who have supported their delusions earlier in life. *DSM-IV* does not have a diagnostic category of "professional victim." There is no question, however, that it is a widespread phenomenon, with all the hallmarks of psychopathology. Even people who were truly victimized generally appreciate that it is better to "try to forget about it" and go on living, rather than to wallow in self-pity and keep muckraking old injuries and traumas. Such therapy only deepens these beliefs in the brain circuitry and interferes with proper "healing" (to use an in-vogue word, which is a favorite of such victims).

Interestingly, bona fide victims of other calamities do not seem to be joining the parades of professional sex-abuse victims. People who survived childhood physical abuse, emotional abuse, drought, starvation, profound poverty, chronic physical illness, and World War II concentration camps do not seem to feel the need to become professional victims. The sex-abuse "survivors" (both those who were really abused [and they certainly exist] and those who believe they were abused [and were not]) appear to have a special need to band together and to wave the flags of victimization. And all this fuels group and even mass hysteria.

SIX

TREATMENT WITH NONABUSED CHILDREN PROGRAMMED TO BELIEVE THEY WERE SEXUALLY ABUSED

BEFORE THE TREATMENT CAN BEGIN...

There is absolutely no point attempting a therapeutic program with nonabused children who were programmed to believe they were abused if one does not remove the child from the source of the trauma, namely, (1) "treatment" that is actually a programming process and/or (2) exposure to or embroilment in the litigation process. Just as treatment of a child who has been genuinely abused is not possible while the child is still exposed to and possibly involved in sexual abuse with the perpetrator, treatment of a child with legal process/"therapy" trauma is not possible without first removing the child from the detrimental influences of "therapy" and/or the legal process.

REMOVAL OF THE CHILD FROM TREATMENT WITH AN OVERZEALOUS THERAPIST

Before one can treat the child, it is crucial that the youngster be removed from "treatment" with the kind of zealous therapists described throughout this book. If the programming parent has not been convinced that there is no sex abuse, and has become deeply bonded with the aforementioned kind of therapist, it may require a court order to bring about a cessation of that "treatment." Furthermore, it may require a court order to restrain the mother from bringing the child to another "therapist" who will proceed along the lines originated by the first. Unfortunately, there is a sea of zealous therapists who are quite committed to the kinds of therapeutic programs described throughout this book. The likelihood of a reasonable therapeutic program working while the child is in treatment with such zealots is practically zero. I personally would not agree to embark upon a therapeutic program while the child is simultaneously receiving this type of "treatment."

CESSATION OF LITIGATION

Obviously, one is not going to be able to treat a child with legal-process trauma if the child is still subjected to and/or embroiled in litigation. The analogy to the sexually abused child who cannot be treated as long as the abuse is taking place holds here. Litigation, by necessity, requires ongoing exposure to people who are going to keep reminding the child of the sex-abuse allegation. Both the accuser and the accused (each in his/her own way) needs to have the child comment on the abuse in the hope that it will serve his (her) purpose in the litigation. Not only are the parents likely to be continually discussing the sex-abuse issue with the child; the lawyers will discuss it with the child as well. In many cases the child is asked to testify in court, and this is not only psychologically detrimental but entrenches even further the sex-abuse issues in the child's brain circuitry. Furthermore, there are a host of other problems that the child may have, unrelated to those being focused on here, that may derive from exposure to and/or embroilment in child-custody litigation. I have discussed these in detail elsewhere (Gardner, 1986). Under these circumstances treatment is probably futile.

Unfortunately, it may be very difficult to bring about a cessation of litigation. If the accusation has been made in the context of a child-custody dispute, the sex-abuse accusation may have just been a recent spin-off of months and even years of ongoing acrimony. By the time the sex-abuse accusation has surfaced, the rage in both parents may be formidable and the likelihood of their just "turning it off" may be extremely difficult, if not impossible, to accomplish quickly. Their lawyers, however, are certainly going to continue winding them up as long as there is still the possibility of extracting yet a little more money from them.

If the litigation is taking place in the context of a nursery school situation in which the hysteria element is operative, then it is also unlikely that the parents are going to extract themselves. After all, there are megabucks to be made by suing the nursery school for having allowed the "pervert" to become a teacher or caretaker. Similar lawsuits against schools, parishes, ministries, Boy Scout organizations, and anyone else who has backup insurance, is not easily discouraged, considering the amount of money the accusers hope to be awarded down the line. Under such circumstances, however, the parents are not likely to bring the child for treatment of symptoms of programming; rather, they may bring the child for treatment of symptoms of sex abuse. In such cases, my informing the parents that I see no sex abuse invariably results in their finding another therapist who "knows what he (she) is doing."

Accordingly, when the situation is one in which one parent recognizes that programming has taken place, most commonly in the case of a child-custody dispute, and the other denies programming or is unsure, I will make the following statement:

> You have to make an important decision here. As long as you are involved in lawsuits, I am not going to be able to help your child. As long as you are going to subject your child to interrogations by lawyers, child advocates, mental health evaluators, social workers, etc., you are going to continue to traumatize your child and my efforts will prove futile. And, if you are going to subject your child to interviews by judges and/or testimony on witness stands, it is even more likely that your child's symptoms will persist and there is absolutely nothing I will be able to do about it. Accordingly, I will not agree to involve your child in therapy until the litigation is at an end.

I call this the ball-is-in-your-court principle (Gardner, 1992b). In some cases it is within the parents' power to bring about a cessation of litigation; in other cases it is not. In either case, I do not begin treatment until the litigation is genuinely discontinued. Accordingly, it is the child-custody dispute situation that I will be focusing on in this chapter, especially because that is the situation in which the therapist is most likely to have the opportunity for ongoing involvement with the falsely accused father. In those situations in which the perpetrator is not the father (or close relative), then, obviously, work with the perpetrator and the child together is not likely to be done by the same therapist.

SERIOUS CONSIDERATION OF THE NO-TREATMENT OPTION

It is important for the therapist to appreciate that treatment may *not* be necessary. A thorough evaluation must be conducted, not only of the child, but of the mother and father. It is extremely important to define situations in which treatment is warranted and those in which treatment is not warranted. In the service of this goal, it is important to trace in detail the evolution of the sex-abuse accusation—from its very beginning—and to understand point by point the various contributions to the scenarios that subsequently developed. Without this information the therapist is ill equipped to provide therapy for the wide variety of distortions that have been so engendered in the child's mind. In addition, one wants to look for signs of a posttraumatic stress disorder (PTSD). I am not referring here to the PTSD that resulted from the alleged sex abuse (a PTSD that the validators would like to believe exists) but a PTSD that results from the interrogatory processes. Furthermore, one wants to assess for the presence of other psychological problems, problems that might have resulted from other factors unrelated to the legal process/"therapy" trauma. I will not, however, direct my attention to the treatment of these disorders, because they go beyond the purposes of this book. Rather, I will focus specifically on psychological problems that derive from the child's being subjected to a series of interrogations focusing on sex abuse when no such abuse took place.

If one is dealing with a PTSD, it is important to appreciate, as mentioned above, that sometimes *no* treatment at all is warranted. One must respect the natural desensitization processes. The child's preoccupation with the traumatic experiences tends to provide a kind of systematic desensitization to the trauma. It is as if each time the child thinks about the trauma, he (she) becomes more accustomed to it and it becomes less painful. The therapist does not want to muckrake and dredge up this old material that the child is attempting to bury and lay to rest. When I was in medical school we were often taught, "Don't do something. Stand there!" This is an ancient wisdom. We may not be able to make our patients better in many situations, but we certainly shouldn't make them worse. Hippocrates long ago said it in other words: "Above all, do not harm." Hippocrates was referring here to the importance of physicians recognizing that their highest obligation is to be sure that they do not leave their patients worse than they were before the medical treatment.

Accordingly, there are many situations in which I have told the family that they should do nothing at all and just go back to the natural course of living. Sometimes judges react with incredulity to this recommendation. Judges (as well as many other people in this world) seem to have a deep-seated conviction for the value of psychotherapeutic treatment. Generally, they have far more commitment to the therapeutic process than I and consider it to be a far more efficacious modality than I do. It is basically shifting responsibility over to the therapist, who is somehow going to pick up the pieces and presumably make everything all right again. There are other judges who have no real conviction for psychotherapy, but who recognize that it would be very injudicious to publicly profess their dubiety. Often, such referral is merely a way of "washing their hands" of the whole case and moving on to the next one. Accordingly, the idea that things will be "all right again" if one does nothing does not fit in well with the prevailing judicial enthusiasm for psychotherapeutic referral. Most mental health professionals, unfortunately, share judges' views of the value of the therapeutic process. There is a sea of hungry therapists out there and, I am sure, monetary gain plays a role in this commitment to the therapeutic process. My experience has been that the younger therapists have much more conviction for the value of therapy than more seasoned people. Perhaps their optimism is good, but in certain situations it can backfire and do more harm than good, and such is the case for children who are suffering with the effects of a series of sex-abuse interrogations.

Accordingly, when I have concluded that there has been no sex abuse and there has been a minimum of programming, I may see the child once or twice and will often merely recommend a "vacation" of a few months in order to see how the child is doing without treatment. I have no specified time such as one, two, or three months, in that such predictions are ill advised in our field; rather, I merely tell the parents to see how the child is doing without treatment and to look for signs and symptoms of significant difficulty. Of course, they are advised to contact me if they have any questions or concerns about the child's behavior. Obviously, if the child starts to exhibit symptoms that warrant treatment, the child will receive it.

THE CRUCIAL ROLE OF THERAPY WITH ALL FAMILY MEMBERS

It is hoped that the work with the child and both parents can be accomplished under a voluntary arrangement in which both parents agree that one therapist should work with the family. Obviously, this is the most efficacious approach to the treatment of a child who has been subjected to and embroiled in a false sex-abuse accusation. If, however, this cannot be voluntarily accomplished, and it is not likely in the situation where the mother is delusional, then a court order may be the only way to effect such treatment. Generally, such a court order is not likely to have much effect without some threat of sanction if the mother does not comply. These usually fall into the categories of monetary penalties, loss of primary custody, and a jail sentence. The awareness that these may be implemented (and the judge must be serious) can often help such mothers "cooperate" in the therapeutic program. Elsewhere (Gardner, 1992d) I have described in detail such court-ordered therapeutic programs for families of children suffering with a parental alienation syndrome.

INDIVIDUAL WORK WITH THE CHILD

The Importance of the Blank-Screen Approach

Whether the child is being evaluated for treatment or whether the child is in treatment, the therapist does well to be a strong adherent of the "blank-screen" approach. These are children who have been subjected to sexualized interviews and whose view of therapy is that it is a place where one talks about sex. Other things that may have come into the child's mind have been shunted aside in order to achieve the goal of discussing sexual matters. Accordingly, it is crucial that the therapist not repeat the same error and provide specific points of departure for discussion, sexual or otherwise. The best way to find out what's "bugging" the child is to give the child free rein to express whatever is in his (her) mind. Obviously, there is no place in any therapist's room (whether in this situation or any other) for anatomical dolls, body charts, sex-abuse prevention books, leading questions, leading gestures, and leading stimuli. Rather, the traditional playroom equipment will generally suffice, and an atmosphere in which the child is allowed free expression is the one in which the evaluator is going to be in the best position to find out what's going on in the child's mind, especially with regard to whether treatment is indicated.

Dealing with Cognitive Distortions

Preliminary Work with the Mother It is to be hoped that the mother will have been convinced that the sex abuse did not take place. Obviously, if the therapist can accomplish this, then it is going to be much easier to treat the child. If, however, she remains fixed in her belief that the sex abuse occurred and does not believe competent evaluators and a court decision that the sex abuse did not, then the therapy of the child is likely to be compromised. In either case, the therapist does well to communicate to the child exactly what the mother's position is. Accordingly, if the mother has changed her mind, the therapist does well to make comments along these lines:

> Your mother had the wrong idea. She thought that your father had done those bad things to you. You, I, and your father all know that those bad things didn't happen. Your mother used to think they happened. Now she knows that they didn't. She realizes that she made a big mistake. No one is perfect; everyone makes mistakes; and your mother is no exception.

If, however, the mother still believes the sex abuse took place, the therapist must take a different tack:

Although your mother's thinking is okay in many different ways, I believe that her thinking is wrong when she talks about you and your father. She thinks that your father did something to you. *You* know that never happened. *Your father* knows that never happened. And *I* believe it never happened. The *judge* doesn't believe it happened. Yet she doesn't believe all of us. She believes Ms. X. (the "validator"), who also, in my opinion, doesn't think right. I hope someday your mother will change her mind and see things the way they really are.

There are some examiners, I am sure, who would take issue with my approach here, because I am directly criticizing the mother in a very important area. I believe that all competent therapists criticize parents in the course of psychotherapy, whether it be for a false sex-abuse accusation or otherwise. The child does best to grow up in a situation in which he (she) has the most accurate view of the parents, their assets, and their liabilities, and this process should take place whether or not the child is in therapy. It is hoped that therapy facilitates this process and provides the child with more accurate information about the parents than might have been obtained without it. The aforementioned comments, then, are not only made in the service of this general therapeutic principle but, more specifically, in the service of helping the child correct the distortions associated with the false sex-abuse accusation. I am careful, however, to circumscribe the mother's isolated delusion(s) and not expand it into a chronic state of paranoid schizophrenia. I try to help the child appreciate that this is an isolated deficit on the mother's part, and I am careful to point out her positive qualities as well. In the service of this goal, I say something along these lines: "For some reason your mother believes Ms. X. much more than she believes me, Dr. Y., Dr. Z., and the judge." All these people know more about these things than Ms. X. But you and I *know* that these things *never really* happened.

The Correction of Cognitive Distortions For children who do need treatment, an important area to focus on relates to the cognitive distortions that have been introduced in the course of coercive evaluations and presumed "therapy." Children who have been subjected to the aforementioned types of interrogations are likely to have difficulty differentiating between fact and fantasy. They have been led to believe that certain things happened that in fact never occurred. The younger the child, the greater the likelihood these misconceptions will become embedded in the child's psychic structure. Accordingly, it behooves the therapist to find out exactly what these distortions are, and these must be addressed and corrected. This is a crucial part of the treatment of these children because, as mentioned, there is a high risk for the development of psychosis and so everything possible must be done to correct these misconceptions in order to lessen the likelihood that they will become permanently entrenched in the child's mind. We see here, then, an excellent example of a situation in which a cognitive therapeutic approach is warranted. One does well to elicit from such children exactly what they themselves recall regarding the events surrounding the sex-abuse accusation. In a neutral atmosphere, especially an atmosphere in which they are not being asked to "validate" the sex abuse, they are more likely to say what they know is true, namely, that nothing happened.

Many of these children have been brought to the point of believing that they were sexually abused. In such cases it behooves the examiner to communicate to the child that a "big mistake" has been made and that all those people who thought that the father did those things to the child were "wrong." One does well to be specific here and identify the parties who participated in the promulgation of the false sex-abuse accusation. One can say, "Your mother had a wrong idea. She thought that your father touched your wee-wee, but she was wrong." Other comments that can prove useful in the course of such discussions are: "Your father was right all the time when he said nothing happened. He was the one who was telling the truth when he said that he never kissed your pee-pee." "The judge is a very smart man. He spent a lot of time listening to all the people and he decided that nothing happened. He decided that your mother made a mistake. In fact, the whole thing has just been one big mistake." "The police were wrong when they thought that your father did those things to you. They just didn't know what they were talking about. They weren't there, so they don't really know. You were there, and you really know that nothing happened." With regard to the "validators" I make statements along these lines:

> Ms. X. has something wrong with her thinking. She doesn't think straight. She thinks just about every child she sees had something bad happen to the child. That's not so. You know and I know that she wanted

you to say that these bad things *really* happened. She used to get upset with you when you said that *nothing* happened. She would only be pleased with you when you said that bad things happened. Remember how upset she used to be when you said that nothing happened? She used to get out all those funny-looking dolls with all the private parts showing and wanted you to show with the dolls what your daddy did to you. If you said that your daddy didn't do anything to you—which is what really was true—she would get upset with you. And your mother would have been upset too, because she, too, thought that something happened. She also used to teach you that your father was a bad person. She used to tell you to hit that big Bozo doll with your fist and to kick it. I think that was a bad idea. Your father's not a bad guy. He didn't do those things to you. She shouldn't have taught you to be angry at him. I know the judge was angry at her for teaching you these things.

I suspect that some readers will believe that I am "coming down too heavily" on some of the people involved in promulgating the false sex-abuse accusation. They probably believe that I should "soften" somewhat my criticisms of these examiners. One could even argue that I should have more pity than scorn for them. Obviously, my scorn far outweighs any pity I have for these "therapists," primarily because of the terrible damage that they have done and are continuing to do to thousands of children. I am not ashamed of this scorn, however, and I believe that it can play a therapeutic role if judiciously released. It adds conviction to my statements about these examiners' misconceptions, distortions, and even stupidity. It can fuel the enthusiasm with which I approach the treatment of these children. The enhanced credibility of my statements then increases the likelihood that they will have clout with the child and contribute thereby to a correction of the distortions that have been engendered by them.

The examiner does well to bring in the authority of the judge because of the awe that young children generally have of him (her). Quoting the judge can enhance the efficacy of the therapist's messages. However, more important is the relationship that the therapist has with the patient. If it is a good one, then the child will be receptive to this therapeutic "debriefing" program.

The Shibboleth "The Truth" The child may have used the code term *the truth* to refer to the sex-abuse scenario. The therapist does well to help the child appreciate that the real *truth* was not the sex-abuse scenario but the reality of the father-child relationship, especially the reality in which there was no sexual molestation. The child has to be helped not only by words, but by living experience, to appreciate that in this new therapy the search for "the truth" in no way relates to reciting the litany of the sex-abuse scenario. The truth in this new therapy is the *real* truth, not only with regard to the correction of distortions about the alleged sex abuse, but with regard to all other realities in the child's life. Here the child should genuinely validate (and I use the word in the healthiest sense) what he (she) has actually seen. The child should be helped to trust his (her) own observations—at an age-appropriate level of expectation—and then make statements that are commensurate with the observations. In this way the child will be helped to learn what is the real truth in a wide variety of areas having little if anything to do with sexual matters.

Concluding Comments Although one can never be one hundred percent certain that no sex abuse occurred, it is not meaningful for a young child to be told that competent evaluators and the court are "99 percent certain" or that there is "not enough evidence." Rather, the therapist does well to "round things off" and merely state that *"nothing happened"* and "he did *not* do it." Other distortions, as well, may have to be corrected. The child may believe that his (her) genitals have been damaged and this should be discussed, with possible reference to medical examinations by the pediatrician. Correction of other distortions, unrelated to the sex abuse, may be useful. The general approach here is to help the child—at an age-appropriate cognitive level—differentiate fact from fantasy, differentiate what is "real" from what is "make believe." For some children, especially those above the age of five, *The Talking, Feeling, and Doing Game* (Gardner, 1973) may be useful. The vast majority of the cards are reality-oriented and provide the child with catalytic questions and statements that can serve as points of departure for psychotherapeutic interchanges. Some sample questions are: "What is the worst thing that ever happened to you in your whole life?" "Name three things that can make a person sad." "Name three things that can make a person happy." "A girl had something on her mind that she was ashamed to tell her mother. What was it?" "Name three things that can make a person angry."

Obviously, the older the child, the more likely some of the aforementioned messages will "sink in." When we are dealing with three- and four-year-olds, it is not likely that most of them are going to have much of an effect. It is only when we reach the five- and six-year-olds that some of these messages may prove therapeutically efficacious. More important than these messages, however, are the child's actual living experiences, which will serve to prove to the child that the father is not the dangerous individual he was made out to be. The reader is probably familiar with the old Chinese proverb: "A picture is worth a thousand words." I would add to this: "An experience is worth a million pictures." Accordingly, unsupervised visitations, during which the child has natural experiences with the father over time, is probably the best therapeutic approach to the alleviation of the psychological damage done to children subjected to the aforementioned kinds of interrogations.

Dealing with Emotional Problems

Some of the child's emotional problems obviously derive from the cognitive misrepresentations that have been engendered by the zealous interrogators and "validators." It behooves the examiner to learn about the cognitive distortions that form the basis of these abnormal feelings. One does well to delineate these and to use each distortion as a point of departure for conversations in which an attempt is made to correct the misrepresentations. As mentioned, this is a good situation for the utilization of cognitive therapeutic techniques. (It would be an error for the reader to conclude here that I view myself as a "cognitive therapist." I do incorporate the principles of such therapists into my therapeutic program but, as I hope the reader appreciates, it is much broader, because I believe that a pure cognitive therapeutic approach is somewhat oversimplified.)

Pathological Feelings About Sex The child's feelings about sex are likely to have become significantly pathological. Some children who have been subjected to the aforementioned types of evaluations and "treatment" have not experienced any particular sexual feelings. (This is the more common situation.) Accordingly, their accusations have no genuine sexual element with regard to sexual *feelings*. They have been basically reciting scripts, without any appreciation of the sexual-emotional significance of their verbalizations. Others have experienced varying degrees of sexual expression (i.e., varying levels of sexual excitation, masturbation) and know something about sexual pleasure. For these children, however, the sexual feelings were not the result of sexual molestation. Rather, they were children who naturally and normally exhibited sexual feelings at an early age (a not uncommon situation, prevalent myths to the contrary notwithstanding) or have been prematurely sexualized from experiences having nothing to do with sex abuse, e.g., exposure to other children's sexuality and discovery of masturbation as an antianxiety practice or antidepressant. Children in both of these categories are likely to have been taught by "validators" and "therapists" that sex is dirty and dangerous and that people who engage in such activities are somehow seriously defective and perverted.

It is rare for the association between sex and love to be introduced in the course of these children's "therapy." Accordingly, these children have to be helped to view sex in a healthy way and come to see it as a normal desire that grows stronger as one gets older, especially during the teen period. For many children this is purely an intellectual exercise because they don't have the faintest idea what the therapist is talking about. For other children, however, it may have some meaning, and it is for these children that such comments will be most meaningful. Such children have to become comfortable with their masturbatory practices and to learn that, in our society, such activities are generally engaged in privately. They may have interest in normal age-appropriate sexual exploratory play and they must be helped to appreciate that, although such interests are normal, children who engage in such activities may "get into trouble." If, however, in spite of the therapist's mild admonition regarding such behavior, the child is found to be engaged in such activities (an almost universal phenomenon), the parents should be advised to avoid even the mildest kind of disciplinary measures. The child should be told—in a matter-of-fact way—that such behavior is okay and acceptable and that it is not considered proper in public; however, it is certainly acceptable to do it privately. The greater the difficulty the therapist has convincing the parents of these children to utilize this approach, the greater the likelihood the child will suffer with pathological thoughts and feelings about sexuality.

Some of these children's sexual interests involve playing sexual games with other children. (Again, I am referring here to children who have not been sexually abused, but who are exhibiting early sexual interest for the reasons described above.) Such children also have to be told, in an as matter-of-fact a way as possible, that in our society such behavior is not considered acceptable and that those who engage in these activities might "get into trouble." Such children can be told, however, that when they get older they will have more opportunities for such activities. However, this too rarely works well, in that most human beings in this world do not easily accept a waiting period of 10 to 15 years before having an opportunity to enjoy a particular form of gratification, especially one that is very intense. However, the futility of the advice notwithstanding, it is still better to be offered some hope in the future than no hope at all.

Hatred of the Father With regard to the feelings of hatred toward the father that have been engendered in the "treatment," the child has to be helped to appreciate that the father is a loving, affectionate person who is deeply committed to the child (the usual case). However, the treatment of the child in this situation is not for the therapist to provide a total "whitewash" as an antidote to the "backwash" to which the child has been subjected. Rather, the therapist does well to help the child appreciate that the father, like all human beings, is a mixture of qualities that are likable to the child and those that are not. All human relationships are ambivalent, and parent-child relationships are no exception to this principle. The child should be helped to become comfortable with feelings of resentment, when justified, and to deal with them appropriately. Unfortunately, the "validators" think that the appropriate way to deal with anger is to hit and kick a doll and to pour forth profanities at it. They do not appreciate that the appropriate way to express anger is to express directly, in civilized words, exactly what one's resentments are toward the *person* (not the symbol) who is causing the frustration.

Pathological Guilt The child may feel guilty over the grief that the accusation has caused the accused. In such situations the therapist does well to help the child appreciate that he (she) was brainwashed by the mother, validators, and interrogators, and was really helpless to do otherwise, considering the forces to which the child was subjected. The child may feel shame over having been accused of engaging in "bad touches" and "bad acts." The child has to be helped to appreciate that no such activities were engaged in and, therefore, neither guilt nor shame is appropriate. The people who should feel guilt and shame are those who contributed to the promulgation of the false sex-abuse accusation, and these people should be identified to the child.

Psychopathic Behavior If the child's "treatment" has engendered psychopathic attitudes regarding the expression of hostility toward the father, then the therapy must involve attempts to *increase* the child's guilt. This statement may come as a surprise to some therapists who believe that it is improper for therapists to increase guilt under any circumstance. I do not agree with this position. Some people with hypertrophied consciences need relaxation of the internal guilt-evoking mechanisms. There are others, however, who do not have enough guilt, and the therapeutic approach to them is some expansion of their consciences and intensification of their potential to feel guilt. (There are far more psychopathic types in this world than there are people with hypertrophied internalized guilt-evoking mechanisms.) Elsewhere (Gardner, 1994a) I have detailed the approaches I use for the treatment of children with psychopathic behavior.

Feelings of "Empowerment" The therapist must deal with the so-called empowering maneuvers taught by the "validator" therapist. First, the child may have come to believe that sex-abuse perpetrators are ubiquitous and they must ever be vigilant if they are to protect themselves from further abominations. One has to help the child appreciate that sex abuse, although it does occur, does not take place as frequently as the child has been led to believe. The younger the child, the greater the likelihood the therapist will have difficulty getting across this notion. In fact, for children from ages three to four (the most common age level for successful indoctrination), it may be impossible to get across the notion of *relative degrees of frequency*. (Unfortunately, there are many adults who have problems with this concept as well.) The "empowering" maneuvers of saying no, running for help to an authority, etc., have to be addressed one at a time and put in proper perspective. Rather than provide the child with a sense of true empowerment, the empowering maneuvers are likely to have had the opposite effect because the child is really not in a position to implement them. The effect they have is to increase fears and confuse the child regarding what acts to take. This cannot but contribute to feelings of inadequacy (the opposite of empowerment). The child may have come to believe that all male relatives are potential perpetrators, and these distortions must be corrected. Each relative should be discussed and the child helped to appreciate that such an individual is not going to molest her (him).

If the child has been empowered by the accuser in such a way that the accuser has placed herself under the child's domination and "jumped" every time the child claims disclosure of yet another form of sex abuse, this process must be discouraged. The therapist should not be providing such power. This may be very difficult for the child to deal with, especially if such controlling behavior has been the rule over many months or years. The child must be helped to have corrective emotional experiences in which the controlling behavior is not complied with.

DEALING WITH THE FALSELY ACCUSING MOTHER

A mother who promulgates a false sex-abuse accusation generally falls along a continuum, with conscious fabrication at the one end and delusion at the other. Not only does her belief in the sex abuse fall at some point along this continuum, but it may have shifted back and forth throughout the course of the child's interrogations. Sometimes a fabrication progresses to become a delusion, especially when supported by a coterie of "validators," each of whom shares the delusion that the sex abuse did indeed take place. Obviously, the earlier the mother has exposure to competent people who can prevail upon her to reconsider her position, the greater the likelihood of preventing the deterioration of her thinking down the delusional track. Because of the variations among these women, I cannot provide any standard approach to their involvement in the child's treatment. I will, however, comment on dealing with mothers at the two ends of the continuum, namely, the fabricated end and the delusional end.

If the mother is in the delusional category and the delusion is fixed, there may be absolutely nothing the therapist can do to change her mind. If she is in "treatment" with a therapist who shares her delusion, the likelihood of her changing her opinion is reduced to the zero level. Unfortunately, there are many such folie-à-deux therapeutic arrangements, much to the detriment of the children of such mothers. One could argue that a court order that the mother discontinue such treatment would be advisable. Forgetting for the moment the legality of such an order, it is not likely to work. Because there is a sea of such zealous therapists, a court order constraining the mother from involvement with her particular therapist would only result in her involving herself with another of the same ilk. More practical is the court giving serious consideration to a transfer of primary custody to the father. I am not stating that this should automatically be done. What I am suggesting is that the court review the whole picture. If the false sex-abuse accusation is part of a larger package of denigrations, and if the mother is in the severe category of parental alienation syndrome, then transfer of primary custody may be the only way of protecting the child from the mother's campaign of denigration of the father—with the resultant attenuation (even to the point of obliteration) of the child's bond with the father. It is almost impossible to treat a child effectively as long as the child remains in the home of such a mother. No matter how skilled the therapist, no matter how many times a week the child is seen, if the child is subjected to the mother's programming throughout the rest of the week, therapy is going to prove futile.

At the other end of the continuum is the mother who initially fabricated the accusation and knew with certainty that it was false. Also at this end of the continuum are mothers who may have had some concern, who thought there might have been sex abuse, and then were dragged along toward the delusional end by zealous "validators." If one is successful in helping her regain her sanity, to the point where she recognizes that there was no such abuse, then she can be worked with effectively. Such a mother can then be encouraged to tell her child that her accusation was a "big mistake," and she should try to explain to the child how she naively went along with the fanatic and/or naive validators. In such cases she can use the same approaches to the child described above for the therapist, i.e., the various communications in which clarification is provided to the child regarding what actually did happen in his (her) situation. Obviously, the mother's input provides clout to the therapist's clarifications, and when one adds the father's as well, such a program of "debriefing" is likely to be successful.

With regard to the mothers in the middle, that is, between the fabricated and delusional ends of the continuum, the closer the mother is to the fabrication end, the greater the likelihood the therapist will be able to work with her and, conversely, the closer she is to the delusional end, the more hopeless therapy will be.

DEALING WITH THE FALSELY ACCUSED FATHER

As mentioned, the most important part of the therapeutic approach regarding the child's relationship with the father is for the child to have living experiences with the father that are friendly and loving. In the context of such a relationship, there will be no sex abuse and the child is not likely to then continue to fear such activities. The father too should communicate to the child information regarding what the mother's exact status is, i.e., at what point along the aforementioned continuum her position is regarding whether the sex abuse took place. If the mother has recanted, then he should use terms like *mistake* in his communications. If she is at the other end of the continuum, however, he does well to make comments along these lines: "Although your mother has many fine qualities, she has the wrong idea about my having done these bad things to you. She believes Ms. X. (the validator) and some of her friends, who also have the wrong idea. I hope your mother changes her mind. You and I know that these things didn't happen" and, if appropriate, "It was because of these wrong ideas that the judge has decided that you should live with me. That's the only way to protect you from her putting all these wrong ideas in your head."

FAMILY WORK

In addition to individual work with the child and parents, joint conferences can also be useful. If there is still some possibility of improving the relationship between the parents (their marital status notwithstanding), everything should be done to do this. Even though divorced, and even though the grief has been intensified significantly by the false sex-abuse accusation, attempts should still be made to bring about some degree of rapprochement between the parents. Obviously the attempt here is not to bring about a reconciliation of the marriage; rather an attempt should be to bring about an improvement in their relationship for the sake of the child. This is in accordance with the general principle that children of divorce do better if their parents can communicate and cooperate with one another, their animosity notwithstanding. Joint sessions with the father and the child can also help to improve their relationship, especially with regard to the improvement in communication and the correction of distortions. Such meetings also provide the kinds of *living experiences* that can contribute to the reduction of distortions derived from the sex-abuse accusation. Joint interviews with the mother can also be useful. Here the mother can explain her position, especially if she is in the "mistake" category. If in the delusional category, the joint interviews can help the therapist clarify the mother's position and confront the child and mother with the mother's distortions. (I recognize that this approach is not going to be particularly useful for younger children, such as those at the three- to four-year level. I recognize also that the child may thereby be witness to a conflict of opinions and that this may be a detrimental exposure.) My hope is that the negative effects of such exposure will be more than counterbalanced by the therapist having the opportunity to address himself (herself) to the mother's distortions in the presence of the child. This can help the child put them in proper perspective. Again, such discussions are not going to be very meaningful for three- and four-year-old children but may be for older children.

CLINICAL EXAMPLE

Frank's father, Jim, first consulted me when Frank was three-and-a-half. Frank's parents were separated and in the throes of a vicious child-custody dispute. Frank's mother, Betsy, was living with her parents and Frank's father, Jim, was living with his parents and his mother's sister (his aunt, Frank's paternal great-aunt). Jim's reason for consulting me was that he believed that Frank had been sexually abused by his mother, his maternal grandmother, and possibly his maternal grandfather. His reason for believing this was that a few months previously Frank began fondling his paternal grandmother's feet, kissing them, and rubbing her legs. Frank stated that he did this because he wanted to make his grandmother feel good. The grandmother considered this behavior to have sexual implications with the possibility of sexual abuse.

On another occasion, Frank crawled under the table and picked up his grandmother's bathrobe to peer under it. Both she and her husband decided not to say anything and just to watch and see what Frank would do, especially with regard to how far he would proceed. As she sat there, he moved his hand up her leg and actually inserted his finger into her vagina. Both she and the paternal grandfather concluded that this proved their earlier suspicions that Frank had been sexually abused and that the abuser was the mother or one or both of the maternal grandparents. The paternal grandmother also believed that further confirmation of abuse was provided by the fact that in the past, when she wanted to change Frank's diapers, he would get upset, and he often refused to kiss and hug her.

Frank's mother denied ever observing any of the exploratory behaviors in her house, nor had her parents or any of the babysitters. The father and his parents also believed that Frank was sexually abused because his mother "had force breastfed" him at six months and that Frank, on repeated inquiry, had reported that he sleeps in bed with his mother and had been allowed to fondle her breasts. The mother stated that she did indeed breastfeed Frank until nine months and on occasion had trouble getting him to suck, but that she had never coerced him. She also denied that Frank had ever been allowed to fondle her breasts, nor did he even make attempts to do so. Jim also claimed that on *one* occasion he noticed Frank to be wrestling with another child and engaging in movements that he considered similar to those that people utilize when having sexual intercourse.

Investigation by child protection people at that time found no evidence for sexual abuse. This, however, was not their first investigation. Previously, the father had accused the mother of physical abuse because of minor bruises he saw on the child. The mother's explanation always appeared to be credible and child protection service found no evidence of physical abuse. Furthermore, they concluded that there was no evidence that Frank was sexually abused. In their evaluation they found that when he was with his father, Frank would make complaints about his mother's beating him with a stick and stated also that she let him "play with her 'milkies' (breasts)." However, when with his mother, Frank denied that he made these statements.

At the time of my initial consultation I concluded that I was dealing with a false sex-abuse accusation, an accusation programmed by the father, the paternal grandparents, and the paternal great-aunt. The paternal grandmother's behavior—especially her letting this child insert his finger into her vagina—could in itself be considered sexual abuse on her part. At the end of my original consultation, I told the father that I believed that he and his family were inducing this sex-abuse accusation in this child and that Frank was complying with their programming in order to maintain a good relationship with them. It was clear that Jim was dissatisfied with my conclusion.

Jim returned, almost two-and-a-half years later, complaining that there was now even more compelling evidence that Frank was sexually abused by his mother and maternal grandmother. He claimed that the child was now preoccupied with wanting to touch the genitals of his paternal grandmother and that at the time of his overtures he has been saying to her, "It'll make you feel good." Frank further elaborated with statements like, "My mommy touches my wee-wee." When asked why he did not scream, Frank replied, "She put a hankie over my mouth." He also said to his father that his mother "puts her mouth here" (while pointing to his anal area) and he stated, "I make poop in my mommy's mouth and she swallows it." When asked why he didn't tell his mother's parents about this he responded, "I forgot." Frank also said at that time that his mother now puts her finger up his rectum. When asked why he didn't scream out, he again replied that she puts a handkerchief over his mouth. He also stated that he has seen his maternal grandmother, maternal grandfather, and mother all naked together playing with each other's genitals. He stated that he had observed them naked from behind a chair and they did not see him there. Frank stated also that they stopped this fondling when he told them that it was bad and that it was not right. He also described his mother putting her mouth on his penis. All these "disclosures" evolved during the two-and-a-half years between my initial consultation and this update visit. Not surprisingly, the father had repeatedly contacted child protection services, who continually found Frank unconvincing. Jim had also gone to the FBI and the attorneys general of two states (one in the state in which the mother was living and the one in which he was living). At the time of both the earlier and later consultations with this family, the mother refused to accept my invitations to become involved.

Presented here is the transcript of the interview I had with Frank on the occasion of this update interview at around the time of his sixth birthday.

Gardner: Okay, today is the second of May, 1995. Okay, now I want to ask you this. First of all, how old are you?

Patient: Five.

Gardner: You're five years old. I understand that you're going to be six very soon.

Patient: May 5th.

Gardner: May 5th? How many days is that from now?

Patient: One . . . two . . . three.

Gardner: Three days. Right. You're going to be six years old. Okay, now why have you come here? Why are you here today?

Patient: Because my mommy hurts me.

Gardner: Your mommy hurts you?

Patient: Yes.

Gardner: How does she hurt you?

Patient: 'Cause she touches me in my private parts.

TREATMENT WITH NONABUSED CHILDREN

The quickness with which Frank began to speak about his alleged sexual encounters is one of the hallmarks of the false sex-abuse accusation. Furthermore, the transcript cannot convey the calm and matter-of-fact way in which he provided his "disclosures." There was none of the hesitancy and/or embarrassment one generally sees in children who are providing a true sex-abuse accusation.

Gardner: I'm writing this down. "She touches me in my private parts." I see. Now tell me more about that. What does she do exactly?
Patient: She plays with them.
Gardner: She plays with them? When you say "them," what do you mean?
Patient: My private parts. She moves them all around.
Gardner: She moves them around? I see. What room is this that it happens in.
Patient: In Mommy's bedroom.
Gardner: In mommy's bedroom. Is anyone else there?
Patient: No.
Gardner: What else does she do?
Patient: She ties a handkerchief around my mouth.
Gardner: She ties a handkerchief around your mouth. Is that what you said?
Patient: Yes.
Gardner: I see. Why does she do that?
Patient: Because she's bad.
Gardner: Because she's bad.
Patient: And she also does not want me to yell for help.
Gardner: Who could you yell for help to? Who would you yell to?
Patient: A neighbor.

We see here a preposterous element that is one of the hallmarks of the false sex-abuse accusation. At six, Frank does not appreciate that merely tying a handkerchief around his mouth is not likely to prevent screams from being heard by others in the house and possibly in a neighboring house. Because of young children's immature cognitive development, they often do not appreciate the absurdity of some of the elements in their false sex-abuse scenarios.

Gardner: A neighbor. I see. So no one else is in the house when she does that?

Patient: Ma and Pa. [The maternal grandmother and maternal grandfather.]

Gardner: Oh, Ma and Pa are in the house. Is she tying this around your mouth so you won't yell for Ma and Pa? Are you saying that?

Patient: No, Ma and Pa are bad too that they don't want for a neighbor to hear.

Gardner: Ma and pa are your grandma and your grandpa, right?

Patient: Uh-huh.

Gardner: They are your mother's mother and father. But what will happen if they hear?

Patient: They wouldn't do anything because they're bad.

Gardner: They wouldn't do anything.

Patient: Right.

Gardner: I see. I have a handkerchief here. I want you to show me with this handkerchief how she ties it around your mouth.

Patient: (Ties handkerchief around nose and mouth, cowboy style.) When she ties it, it's a little bigger.

Gardner: Tell me again how she does it. It's a bigger handkerchief. It's bigger than that.

Patient: Uh-huh. So it can fit like that.

Gardner: It's like that? Like a cowboy uses? Like a cowboy?

Patient: Uh-huh. But a man's handkerchief.

Gardner: Oh, it's a man's handkerchief. Like that?

Patient: Uh-huh.

Gardner: But it looks like a cowboy, is that it?

Patient: Yes.

Gardner: I see. Now I have a question to ask you.

Patient: What?

Gardner: When you did this, the handkerchief is outside your mouth, right?

Patient: Uh-huh.

Gardner: Is that how it is? The handkerchief is outside your mouth?

Patient: Uh-huh.

Gardner: Does any go inside your mouth?

Patient: No, unless I open my mouth up?

TREATMENT WITH NONABUSED CHILDREN 389

>*Gardner*: But usually it's on the outside, is that it?
>*Patient*: Uh-huh.
>*Gardner*: It's not on the inside.
>*Patient*: No.
>*Gardner*: Now, is that enough for the neighbors not to hear it?
>*Patient*: Yeah.
>*Gardner*: That's enough so the neighbors wouldn't hear it.

We see here compelling confirmation not only of the child's preposterous statement, but of the cognitive immaturity that permits him to make such a statement without embarrassment or recognition of its absurdity.

>*Gardner*: Okay. What does she say when she's touching your private parts?
>*Patient*: She laughs.
>*Gardner*: She just laughs.
>*Patient*: Yeah.
>*Gardner*: But when a person is laughing, the person is usually saying something. What is she saying while she laughs?
>*Patient*: That this time nobody will hear me.
>*Gardner*: That no one will hear you because of the handkerchief around your mouth. Okay. Now, while the handkerchief is around your mouth, what are you trying to do?
>*Patient*: I'm trying to get it off.
>*Gardner*: You're trying to get it off?
>*Patient*: Yes.
>*Gardner*: And why can't you get it off?
>*Patient*: It's too tight.

Another preposterous element in the scenario that lessens its credibility. A six-year-old child can easily pull up or pull down a handkerchief tied cowboy style around his (her) nose and mouth.

>*Gardner*: It's too tight. What else does she say?
>*Patient*: She says that daddy would never know, but daddy does know.
>*Gardner*: She'll say that daddy will never know?

Patient: Yeah, but daddy will know.

Gardner: What else does she say? How will he know?

Patient: From the tape.

Gardner: From the tape. From what tape?

Patient: The tape dad kept. You know from the new tape.

Gardner: You mean he'll know from *this* tape.

Patient: Yeah.

Gardner: But what about from before we made this tape today? How does she say he won't know?

Patient: 'Cause he can't see what's happening.

Gardner: Because he can't see what's happening?

Patient: Yeah.

Gardner: Now, what else does she say?

Patient: She also says that my family up here will never know.

Gardner: Why is that?

Patient: Because they didn't know when it was happening, but they would know now.

Gardner: What else does she say?

Patient: She also says that Ma and Pa know.

Gardner: What else?

Patient: She also says that the neighbors will never know.

Gardner: You said that before. Anything else?

Patient: No. There is one thing else she does. She moves this (pointing to his genitals) around and puts her finger up here (pointing to anal area).

Gardner: She moves what around?

Patient: My wee-wee.

Gardner: She moves your wee-wee around?

Patient: Yes. And she pokes her finger.

Gardner: Let's talk about the front part first. Then we'll go to the back part. What does she move?

Patient: My wee-wee.

Gardner: How does she move it? What is she doing with it? I'm not clear.

Patient: She's moving it like this. (Frank runs his hand once over his genitals from left to right.)

Patient: She moving . . .

Gardner: She's moving it sideways.

Patient: Yeah.

Gardner: Or to the front or what?

Patient: Sideways.

Gardner: Sideways, I see. She moves it with her hand?

Patient: Yeah.

Gardner: And what happens to your wee-wee then, when she does that?

Patient: I don't like it.

Gardner: Why not?

Patient: 'Cause I don't like my wee-wee to be played with.

Gardner: You don't like your wee-wee to be played with. Does anything else happen to your wee-wee?

Patient: No, but something happens to my rear end.

Gardner: Okay, we'll talk about your rear end in just a minute. Does anything else happen to your wee-wee when she plays with it?

Patient: I don't like it.

Gardner: You don't like it. You said before that she hurt you. Does it hurt?

Patient: Yeah.

Gardner: Does it hurt all the time?

Patient: Not all the time. When she doesn't do it, the pain goes away.

Gardner: Okay, when she doesn't do it, the pain goes away. Okay. Now you said something about your rear end?

Patient: Uh-huh.

Gardner: What happens with your rear end?

Patient: She puts one of her fingers up it.

Gardner: Oh, she puts one finger up your rear end.

Patient: Yes.

Gardner: Why does she do that?

Patient: Because she's mean.

Gardner: Anything else?

Patient: 'Cause she doesn't like my daddy.

Gardner: Because she doesn't like your daddy? Why does she do that? Because she doesn't like your daddy, why should she do that to you?

Patient: I don't know.

Gardner: Does she do anything else besides put one finger up your rear end?
Patient: After I fall asleep, she unties the handkerchief.
Gardner: After you fall asleep, she unties the handkerchief.
Patient: Yes.
Gardner: Does she do anything else with your rear end?
Patient: No.
Gardner: Nothing else at all? Your grandma (Frank's paternal grandmother) told me about other things. I'm a little confused. Your grandma said that she does other things with your rear end. Is there anything else she does with your rear end? (I was referring here to the father's report that Frank had told him that the mother kissed Frank's anal area or his allegation that his mother requires Frank to defecate in her mouth.)
Patient: What did she tell you?

Had Frank indeed been subjected to this kind of sexual activity, there is a high likelihood that he would have remembered it clearly and would not have to ask me to refresh his memory. Such forgetfulness is typical of the false sex-abuse accusation. True experiences, especially those associated with high emotion, are very likely to be remembered. As described in Chapter Two, they become deeply embedded in the brain circuitry.

Gardner: No, I want to know what *you* can tell me.
Patient: Well, my cousin George is going to come to you.
Gardner: Your cousin George is going to come to me? Why is he going to come to me?
Patient: To tell you about his mommy?
Gardner: What's this got to do with you and your mommy.
Patient: Well, I was just telling you so you would know.
Gardner: What he does with his mommy?
Patient: No, what she does with him.
Gardner: Oh, this is who? Your cousin George? And how old is George?
Patient: Six.
Gardner: And does your mommy do things with George?
Patient: No, his mommy.
Gardner: His mommy does things with him?

Patient: Yeah.

Gardner: Well, what does his mommy do with him?

Patient: You would have to ask him.

Gardner: I would have to ask him. Well, what's that got to do with you and your mommy?

Patient: I shouldn't have mentioned it.

Gardner: You shouldn't have mentioned it. Okay, I'd like you to go back and tell me the other things that your mommy does with your rear end. What are the other things?

I recognized that Frank was avoiding answering my question regarding what else his mother did to him in the anal area, but I flowed with the digression for a short period because it might have provided me with some information. When I recognized that it was only a diversionary maneuver, I tried to get him back on track.

Patient: She plays with it.

Gardner: She plays with your rear end? With the hole, you mean? Or with the whole rear end? And what does she do with it exactly?

Patient: She moves it around?

Gardner: And what else does she do?

Patient: Well, she stops.

Gardner: Your grandma told me she does *other* things with your rear end and I want to know about those *other* things. What else did you say she does?

Patient: She stops when I'm asleep.

Gardner: No, but your grandma told me that you said that there are other things. Do you know what I'm talking about? What you told your grandma? What are the other things? Do you know what I'm talking about? What are the things you told your grandma that your mommy also does?

Patient: Can you help me remember?

Gardner: To remember? You can't remember? What are the other things?

Patient: I can't think of anything else.

Again, Frank's failure to be able to think of this other thing argues that we are dealing here with a false sex-abuse accusation.

> *Gardner*: You can't think of anything else? What about with doo-doo? Your grandma said that she did something with doo-doo. What's that with your doo-doo?

I was referring here to the paternal grandmother's statement that Frank had told her that his mother makes Frank defecate in her mouth and then she swallows it.

> *Patient*: She waits for it to come out.
> *Gardner*: She waits for it to come out?
> *Patient*: Yes.
> *Gardner*: And then what happens?
> *Patient*: She swallows it.
> *Gardner*: She swallows it?
> *Patient*: Uh-huh.
> *Gardner*: Does that really happen or are you just making that up?
> *Patient*: It really happens.
> *Gardner*: It really happens? How many times did she do that?
> *Patient*: A lot. Most of the time.
> *Gardner*: Why didn't you tell me that before?
> *Patient*: Because she didn't do that before.
> *Gardner*: She didn't do that before what?
> *Patient*: Before both times I come to you.
> *Gardner*: Why didn't you tell me that just now, when I asked you just a few minutes ago? Why didn't you tell me that?
> *Patient*: Because I forgot.

The reader has two choices here. One is to believe that Frank's mother actually asks him to defecate in her mouth and then she swallows his feces. The other is that Frank is creating this scenario, probably as a conscious fabrication. Although there probably are some real people (as opposed to those depicted in the most sordid and perverted pornography) who engage in such a practice, it is reasonable to say that they are so rare that, for all practical purposes, they are nonexistent. And if they do exist, they are probably individuals who are extremely psychotic. There was absolutely no reason to believe that Frank's mother was in this category. Accordingly, I had no problem choosing the latter explanation rather than the former.

Gardner: You said you forgot that. Does she do anything else?

Patient: Well, she does do the same thing with my wee-wee. She waits for it to come out and then she swallows it.

Gardner: She swallows what?

Patient: My wee-wee.

Gardner: She swallows your wee-wee? You mean your urine, your wee-wee, the yellow water that comes out of your pee-pee? She swallows that too?

Patient: Uh-huh.

Gardner: She swallows that. But how does she do that? When you say she swallows your wee-wee, how does she get your wee-wee to swallow it?

Patient: She waits for it to come out.

Gardner: And where does it go? Right into her mouth? But how does that happen?

Patient: She wants it to.

Gardner: Well, where is her mouth when your wee-wee is coming out?

Patient: (Frank points to his genital area.)

Gardner: Oh, it's right there? So she puts her mouth on your wee-wee? I see.

Patient: I'm all done.

Gardner: You're all done? Do you have anything else to tell me?

Patient: No.

Gardner: Did you tell them (the paternal grandparents, paternal aunt, and father) anything about what your mommy does? Anything else? What else does your mommy do, besides with you? Does she do anything else, with anybody else?

Patient: She dances naked.

Gardner: With whom?

Patient: With Ma and Pa (mumbles).

Gardner: With Ma and Pa? And who else?

Patient: And herself.

Gardner: And herself? And where are you when this is happening?

Patient: I'm watching.

Gardner: You're watching? You're standing right there? Do they see you?

Patient: No, I'm hiding.

Gardner: Where are you hiding?
Patient: Behind the chair.
Gardner: You're hiding behind the chair? Do they see you?
Patient: No.
Gardner: They don't see you.
Patient: No.
Gardner: I see. Is this daytime or nighttime?
Patient: Mostly nighttime.
Gardner: It's nighttime. What time at night?
Patient: Eight o'clock.
Gardner: Aren't you supposed to be in bed at eight o'clock?
Patient: Yes.
Gardner: But why aren't you in bed?
Patient: Because I want to give information to you.
Gardner: Why do you want to give me the information?
Patient: So you can help me live with my daddy.
Gardner: Uh-huh. Do you think this will help?
Patient: Yes.

First, we see another preposterous element in this scenario, namely, that the mother and maternal grandparents are dancing around naked and they don't see that Frank is watching them from behind the chair in the same room. We see here further absurd elements that argue strongly that we are dealing here with a false sex-abuse accusation. Furthermore, Frank tells us that he believes that these revelations about his mother and her family will help his father gain custody of him. It was at this point that I had "had enough" and decided that I would embark upon a therapeutic confrontation. The purpose here was not only to gain information about whether this was a true or false accusation (I was convinced that it was false) but, as long I was with Frank, to provide something therapeutic. I did this in part because I recognized the high likelihood that I would not see Frank again because his father, paternal grandparents, and paternal aunt were so convinced that Frank's mother was sexually abusing him in the ways described by the boy that they would not return after being told, once again, that I saw no evidence for bona fide sexual abuse. (And this eventually turned out to be the case, in that I never did see them after this interview.)

Gardner: You see, I don't think it's going to help very much. You know why?

Patient: Why not?

Gardner: Because I don't think any of this is happening. I don't think this is happening. I think you're telling stories. That's what I think. What do you think about that?

Patient: (Sighs.)

Gardner: What do you think? I don't hear you saying anything?

Patient: That is true.

Gardner: That's true? I don't think it's true. I don't think people eat doo-doo. I don't think your mama is eating your doo-doo. I don't think that's happening. What do you say about that? I don't hear your answering? What are you thinking right now?

Patient: I just want to be left alone.

Gardner: You want to be left alone? Why do you want to be left alone?

Patient: Because.

Gardner: You see, I think you're embarrassed now that I know that you're not telling me the truth. I think you're embarrassed, and I think the best thing you can do is to tell the *real* truth. That's what I think. What is the real truth? What's the real truth?

Patient (crying): I want to live with both of them, but I can't decide who I want to live with.

Gardner: So, is it true that you're making up these stories? That's true, you are? Why do you make up these stories?

Patient: Well, I don't know what would happen if I don't.

Gardner: You don't know what would happen if you don't? What do you think these stories are going to do? How is making up these stories going to help you?

Patient: I don't know.

Gardner: How can that help you? It just gets people very upset. How could it help you to make up these stories? How does it help you?

Patient: Last time you didn't think I was making this up.

Gardner: I did or I didn't?

Patient: You didn't.

Gardner: Now, I know. You mean last time you fooled me but this time you didn't? Is that right? But these things didn't really happen, did

398 TREATMENT WITH NONABUSED CHILDREN

they? I know that they didn't really happen. I know that you're making these things up.

By *last time* Frank was referring to the session one week previously when his father, grandmother, and great-aunt returned with him and gave me updated information.

> *Gardner*: Now let me ask you something. I'm going to ask you this question. Did your mommy ever ask you to put your hand inside her private parts?
> *Patient*: (Shakes head negatively.)
> *Gardner*: She didn't. Did you ever try to put your hand in your grandma's private parts?
> *Patient*: (Shakes head negatively.)
> *Gardner*: Did your mommy ever do anything with your private parts?
> *Patient*: (Shakes head negatively.)
> *Gardner*: Did you ever do anything with your mommy's private parts?
> *Patient*: No.
> *Gardner*: Did Ma and Pa ever dance naked around the house?
> *Patient*: No.
> *Gardner*: So why do you tell people these things?
> *Patient*: I don't know.
> *Gardner*: You don't know. So, why tell people these things?
> *Patient*: Because I want to be left alone.
> *Gardner*: Because you want to be left alone? Where did you get these ideas? Where did you learn about these things?
> *Patient*: Oh, no.
> *Gardner*: You must have some idea where you learned about these things.

There are some who hold that false allegations such as these *must* have been programmed into a child's mind. I am not in agreement. I believe that this is certainly a possibility in many cases but, in this case, I believed it was an unlikely one. My main reason for saying this is that the allegations were so absurd and so primitive that it was hard for me to believe that a programmer would actually consider them to have credibility. Those who are going to program children into professing false sex-abuse accusations are generally careful to inculcate credible accusations. They recognize that incredible accusations are not likely to be believed and their purposes for programming, therefore, will be undermined. The question, then, is: *where does this material come from?* I believe the answer is the same one that Freud described, namely, the "polymorphous perversity" of the child. There exists in every human infant's brain a pool of thoughts and feelings concerning the most primitive and bizarre sexual material. It is from this primitive pool that society selects certain behaviors that are permitted and represses those that are not. In Frank's case, I believe that this pool was the source of the material for his false sex-abuse accusations. In fact, I believe that Frank provides an excellent example of this phenomenon. Confirmation of this is provided in his immediate response to my question of where he learned these things:

> *Patient*: I just made them up.
>
> *Gardner*: You just made them up? They *really* come from your own mind? You just made them up.
>
> *Patient* (crying): I want to go downstairs.
>
> *Gardner*: You want to go downstairs? You don't want to talk anymore? Okay, I'll let you go downstairs in just a minute. I want to help you. I want to help you very much. But it's not helping things to make up these stories. Do you want to live more with your father or more with your mother?

There are some examiners, I am certain, who would have "respected" the child at this point and allowed him to go downstairs. They would take the position that one should be very respectful of the child's feelings and not subject the child to too much stress. I am certainly sympathetic to this position. However, there are some who are too respectful in this regard and pull back too quickly when a child exhibits some psychological tension and stress. I try to move ahead a little further and help the child overcome this tension in order to reap the benefits of further therapeutic inquiry. When the child walks out of the room, or the child switches away from a very important subject, therapeutic opportunities may be lost. As the reader can see, Frank's tears here were short-lived and I provided him with the hope of some therapeutic benefit if he would "hang in" just a little longer. And this proved to be the case.

Patient: I don't really know.

Gardner: You don't really know. If your mom and dad were still living together, would you have made up these stories? Did you ever hear anything like this from anybody else?

Patient: (Shakes head negatively.)

Gardner: You just made these things up? So why did you make these things up?

Patient: (Nods positively.) I want my mommy and daddy to live together.

Gardner: That's *never* going to happen again. That's never never going to happen. But I can tell you this. You know what I think is the best thing you can do?

Patient: What?

Gardner: The best thing you can do is to tell everybody that you were making up these stories. You're seeing a doctor. What's his name? A therapist? What's his name?

Patient: Dave Price.

Gardner: His name is Dave Price. Do you tell him these stories? Are you lying to Dave?

Patient: Yes.

Gardner: Why are you lying to Dave?

Patient: I really don't know why. (Patient starts to cry.)

Gardner: I know you're crying. I know it's hard to talk about these things, but it's important that we do. Why are you telling these stories to Dave?

Patient: (Continuing to cry.)

Gardner: Just calm down a little bit. (Therapist waits awhile and patient stops crying.) Okay, now tell me again. Why are you telling Dave these stories? Why aren't you telling Dave the truth?

Patient: Because I don't really know who I want to live with.

Gardner: You want to live half and half. You want to live most with your mother or most with your father?

Patient: I don't know.

Gardner: You don't know. Then why make up these stories? What are they going to do?

Patient: I don't know. Because I want to be left alone.

Gardner: Well, if you tell these stories, everybody's going to do the opposite. Everybody's going to be talking to you a lot. These stories are not going to let you be left alone. When you say these things, everybody pays attention, right?

Patient: (Nods affirmatively.)

Gardner: And they're not going to leave you alone; they're going to talk to you more. When you see Dave again, what are you going to tell him? Next time you see Dave, what are you going to say?

Patient: Can't you say it?

Gardner: Are you ashamed to tell him? You don't want to tell him yourself?

Patient: (Nods head affirmatively.)

Gardner: Now, tell me, do these things really happen? Yes or no?

Patient: (Shakes head negatively.)

Gardner: They really didn't happen. No. So what are you going to tell Dave?

Patient (sobbing): I don't want to . . . (mumbles) . . .

Gardner: You don't want to what?

Patient: Tell anybody.

Gardner: Tell anybody what?

Patient: That I was lying.

Gardner: That you were lying. You don't want to tell anybody. Okay, what about this tape. Do you want anybody to see this tape?

Patient: My dad.

Gardner: You want your daddy to see this tape?

Patient: Uh-huh.

Gardner: Who else?

Patient: My grandma in my daddy's house.

Gardner: Okay, your grandma in your daddy's house. Who else do you want to see this tape?

Patient: (No response.)

Gardner: Okay, what about the family in your mommy's house? Do you want them to see it?

Patient: No.

Gardner: Why not? You don't want the family in your mommy's house to see it?

Patient: No.

Gardner: Why not?

Patient: Because they'll be mad at me.

Gardner: They'll be mad at you. Why will they be mad at you?

Patient: Because they know that they didn't do these things.

Gardner: Because they know that they didn't do these things. Now what will happen if they see this tape in your mommy's house?

Patient: They'll be mad at me.

Gardner: They'll be mad at you. That's right. Yeah. You know what confession means?

Patient: What?

Gardner: Confession means to tell people that you did something bad or wrong and to tell them that you're sorry you did something wrong.

Patient: Can you confess it? Can you tell them?

Gardner: You want *me* to confess for you?

Patient: Yes. I can't really say these things.

Gardner: You can't say these things? You want me to confess for you? If I confess for you, will you promise not to lie again?

Patient: Yes.

Gardner: You promise?

Patient: (Nods affirmatively.)

Gardner: Okay. We'll shake hands on that. (Therapist and patient shake hands.) You promise?

Patient: (Nods affirmatively.)

Gardner: Okay. I'll confess for you.

As is obvious, this was a very difficult session for Frank. However, if therapy is not to be difficult at times, it is not likely to be effective. Although upset, I do not believe that anything traumatic happened here and that the discomforts were well worth the therapeutic advantages. Considering Frank's age, and considering the humiliation he felt, I decided that I would not push him any further with regard to the confession and agreed to take over some of its burden for him.

Patient (sobbing): I don't want anyone to see this tape.

Gardner: You don't want anybody to see this tape. I see. But your family, I made a copy for them. You see I have two over there. (Therapist pointing to videocassette recorders.) I have one copy for myself and I have one copy for your father's family. I think that's a good way so you don't have to face them to confess. I told you I'd confess for you. But the tape can be a confession, can't it?

Patient: Uh-huh. Okay. Show it.

Gardner: Yeah. But you made a promise to me.

Patient: Yeah.

Gardner: That you won't tell any of these stories ever again.

Patient: No, I won't.

Gardner: But I have one more question that is really puzzling to me. I'm very confused about one thing.

Patient: What?

Gardner: You're going to be six years old. When you were about two or three, your grandma, your daddy's mother, says that you were going over to her and you wanted to put your hand between her legs to touch her private parts and you said, "Grandma, I want to make you feel good." Do you remember that? Did that ever happen? And you told your grandma that your mommy does that. That your mommy says that you should do that to her. Did your mommy ever do that and tell you to put your hands in her private parts?

Patient: It was so long ago, I don't really . . .

Gardner: You don't remember. But let's talk about these things a little bit more now. About eating poop. Those stories.

Patient: They're not really real.

Gardner: They're not really real. I know that. But where did you get that idea?

Patient: I thought of it.

Gardner: You thought of it *yourself*. Okay, I just wanted to know. You didn't hear it from anybody else?

Patient: No.

Gardner: Okay, that's interesting.

Patient: I want to live with my mommy and I want to live with my daddy.

Gardner: You want to live with both of them.

Patient: Uh-huh.

Gardner: Well, you *can* live sometimes with your mommy and sometimes with your daddy.

Patient: Okay.

Gardner: And you can live part of the time at each place. Okay, anything you want to say before we stop this tape.

Patient: (Shakes head negatively.)

Gardner: Okay, I want to say something to you. I know that this was very hard for you, you know? And I think you're a *very brave boy* to tell the *real truth*. You hear what I'm saying? You're very brave to tell the truth, but I hope you learn a lesson. What's the lesson to be learned from this?

Patient: Not telling lies.

Gardner: You *don't* tell lies. Lies cause a lot of trouble. Do you think it helps things by telling lies? They just make more trouble. Lies make trouble, and I told you that I can understand that you're embarrassed to tell people, and I'll tell people for you, okay? You want to sit outside while I tell people, or do you want to sit here while I tell people.

Patient: Outside.

Gardner: You want to sit outside. All right, let's say goodbye. Okay, make the promise before you go, on the television. What's the promise on the tape?

Patient: Not tell lies.

Gardner: Why not to lie?

Patient (sobbing): I don't want my daddy to see the tape.

Gardner: You don't want your daddy to see the tape? Why not?

Patient: 'Cause he might do something.

Gardner: He might do something. He'll be mad at you, right? You know something?

Patient: What?

Gardner: He *will* be mad at you. But you know what? He loves you very much, and he'll forgive you. I know it. He will forgive you. I'll ask him not to punish you, okay? I'll ask him not to punish you and I'll ask him to forgive you. If you make a promise that you'll never lie again on something like this, okay?

Patient (sobbing): Yeah.

Gardner: Okay, so I'll show him the tape.

Patient: I don't want him to see the tape.

Gardner: Well, I'll tell you. The thing is I never promised you that I wouldn't show him the tape, and I have to show him the tape, but nothing's going to happen. He's got a copy anyway. I promised him I'd make one for him, too. And it's right over there in the videocassette recorder. (Therapist points to videocassette recorder where the father's tape is.) So I *have* to show it to him.

But he's going to be understanding and I'll tell him and I'm sure he'll promise not to punish you. But he has to see the tape to see what's really going on here. You see, this is the best way for you to confess. We show them [referring to father, paternal grandmother, and paternal great-aunt, who are waiting in the waiting room] the tape and you're confessing on the tape and then you don't have to confess directly, you don't have to tell them directly. They can see the tape and they can see that it wasn't the truth. You see that? That's the best way, so you don't have to be that embarrassed. You understand me? They see the tape and they know that you're telling what the real truth is. Okay?

Patient: (Nods affirmatively.)

Gardner: Anything else you want to say before we stop? Okay, you can sit downstairs, and I'll talk to your mommy and daddy, but I'm going to show them the tape and that'll be your way of telling them that you're sorry. Can you say you're sorry and apologize?

Patient: They can't see it on the tape?

Gardner: Yes, they'll see it on the tape. That's why I want you to say you're sorry and you promise that you'll never do it again.

Patient (sobbing): I'm sorry.

Gardner: And you promise that you'll never do it again?

Patient: I won't do it again.

Gardner: So you want to stop now?

Patient: Yes.

Gardner: I know this is tough for you. Why don't you sit downstairs? You're a brave fellow. Okay, let's have your grandmother and your great-aunt and your father come up now. Let's go down and get them.

[Father, grandmother, and great-aunt enter the consultation room.] I'm making a tape and I'd like you to sit down here. I'll get a couple of chairs. I want our conversation on tape, too. Okay, you're going to see the whole conversation and you'll see what happened. The story that he presents, as I told you at the outset . . . I told you at the outset, before we started, that there was a 95 percent chance that this is a false accusation, and I went through the whole thing. The preposterous elements are the hallmark of the false accusation. You'll see on the tape the handkerchief, it's like cowboy style, that can't stop screaming, you know. As a child he thinks that it can. He puts it around his neck and that presumably is going to stop anyone from hearing his screaming. The hiding around the chair while Grandma and Grandpa and Mommy are dancing naked, and they don't see him—that's preposterous. It's the child's view of the world. The feces eating, the drinking of urine is preposterous. It doesn't happen. Even back-ward psychotics in mental hospitals don't eat their own feces. At the end of the whole story I said to him, "Frank, I don't think you're telling me the truth. This is not true. These stories are not true." He was silent. You'll see this all on the tape, and then he broke down and he admitted that he has been consciously lying, and he knows it. You will see it on the tape. He's lying, and he knows he's lying. I went through the thing with him, and he said that it didn't happen. He's very upset, he's very embarrassed, and he's very fearful that you will punish him for lying.

I asked him *why* he made up these stories. He's afraid that his mother will see the tape and that she'll be angry at him, and he's afraid that you'll be angry at him. Somehow he has the idea that this is some way of dealing, in some vague way, with the marriage and divorce dispute.

I asked him, "Where did you get these ideas?" He said he made them up, that it came from his own mind. I said, "Did you see any of this on television?" No. "Did you hear anything?" Now, this answer that it came from his own mind, as amazing as it may seem to be, is probably true.

Father: I mean, I understand what you're saying and I do agree. Yes, I agree that he could make it up. This is why I've always told you the truth as to what he is saying.

Gardner: In some way, I think the best way I could link it . . . First of all, if you think about it, if you take a child, a newborn baby, a six-month or nine-month-old baby, they touch their feces. They don't know that we in our society consider this dirty, filthy, yuck, you know, you don't touch that. They will put their hands in their mouths after touching feces. You have to teach them that they are not to do that. You wipe it, you flush it down the toilet. You know that it's dirty. This is part of the primitive mind so that it is probably true when he says it came from his own mind. He knows that if he tells you things that Mommy did that are disgusting or bad, that this somehow wins favor with you because of his appreciation of the animosity.

Father: I can acknowledge that, but in no way have I ever told him or ever tried to imply or whatever that these things are acceptable.

Gardner: You don't have to. You don't have to say a word. He knows you're fighting for custody. He knows you don't like one another. He knows that Mom doesn't like Dad and Dad doesn't like Mom. Kids want to ingratiate themselves to adults in authority, especially their parents. They know where their bread is buttered, and they predictably. . . . If the two of you came to me before your separation, as people do, and they consult with me on what the effects of separation will be on their children, I will say to them, "One of the things that will happen is that the mother will say things that are critical of the father and vice versa." And if you're involved in some kind of a dispute, even more so. So you don't have to say a word. You could be a deaf mute. He would do it. Now, Grandma, you look upset as to what I've said.

Grandmother: May I ask you a question?

Gardner: Sure.

Grandmother: And why was he reacting to me in the manner he was? Why was he touching me? Why was he caressing me?

Gardner: Okay, I asked him about that. You'll see it on the tape. He denied that his mother ever let him do that to her. He denied that this ever happened with his mother on the tape and I believe that he's giving a credible retraction. He says he doesn't remember whether this happened. There are two possibilities. He does remember and he's ashamed. When you saw us walking down the stairs, you saw a boy who was mortified, ashamed, and fearful of punishment because of all the trouble that has been caused by this lie. We spoke about confession. We spoke about embarrassment. He promised, you'll see it on the tape, that he would never tell a lie like this again, and he appreciates all the trouble that is caused by lying. And he's afraid for you to see the tape and that you'll be angry at him. I told him, "Your father loves you very much and, although your father may be angry, I am going to ask your father to promise that he won't punish you."

I chose to focus here on the recantation element and not on the grandmother's active contribution to this child's "sex abuse" of her, namely, her allowing this child to explore her genitals without stopping him. She seemed not to appreciate the gravity and even perversity of allowing such exploration and that the vast majority of adults teach children that such curiosity cannot be gratified completely. She basically set this child up for the accusation and the question, "Who taught you how to do that?" could justifiably be answered: (1) My normal primitive sexuality drove me to such curiosity play and fantasies and (2) Your setting me up gave me the idea that I might be able to engage in such exploration without adult intervention.

Father: But I would never do that to him.

Gardner: It fits together. You'll see on the tape, you don't have a child on the tape crying, "It really happened and I'm angry at you, Dr. Gardner, you don't believe me, it really did happen." That's one possibility. When I said that this didn't happen, it was like a test statement thrown out to see what he would do with it. What he did with it was confirmation that it *didn't* happen.

Grandmother: But, Dr. Gardner, do you realize what they were doing to him prior to the time they took him for questioning?

Gardner: What who was doing to him?

Grandmother: The mother and the grandparents.

Gardner: What were they doing?

Grandmother: His reaction toward you when you said, "I don't believe you." This is what he told them, that he had to lie, he made up all these lies about his mother because he wouldn't see his Daddy again.

Father: He wouldn't see Daddy again.

Gardner: We said that. That is part of the cover-up for his. . . . Each side gets a different story. Lies build upon lies. You know how it is. You lie, then there's a second level, third level, cover-up, building up a whole edifice of superimposed lies. So when he's with his mother, he's afraid of his mother. If his mother finds out that he's saying these things about her, he anticipates that she'll be angry. So when with Mother or Mother's delegate, Mother's psychologist, Mother's child protection workers, he says to them, "I told him that story about you doing those things to me. It's not really true. He made me tell it." That's typical of kids. And when he's with his father he tells his father these stories about his mother's sexual molestation in order to ingratiate himself to his father.

Grandmother: But, Dr. Gardner, why was he reacting to me that way and to my sister? Physically, that is not normal.

Gardner: First of all, that he did it, I'm not denying your perception. That he wanted to put his hand in your crotch area and said that he wanted to make you feel good.

Grandmother: Yeah.

Gardner: I don't deny it for one minute. I believe you, and if I didn't believe you, I would tell you that I don't believe you. Why is he doing it? Because I'll tell you. You may find this hard to imagine, but the human animal has sexual drives very early in life, okay? Little children of three, four, five play inquisitive and exploratory games like "You show me yours, and I'll show you mine." That's a standard game among little children, right?

Grandmother: I don't know. I didn't have it, all right?

Gardner: Don't assume that your own experience is like the rest of the world.

Grandmother: Okay.

Gardner: Okay? It is not necessarily the case, okay, and I can tell you that human children have sexual feelings, not as strong as adolescents. I am not saying that they generally are as strong as adults'. Also, there is a wide range in the time when children begin to have strong sexual urges. Some people never have strong sexual urges throughout their whole life. And some people cannot remember a time when they didn't have them. The average person feels a strong onset around the pubertal period and thereafter. But there is a range, okay? We are living in a very highly sexualized environment. This I can say, all these interrogations by all the validators, even me in a way, are entrenching it. But I like to feel that I am putting a stop to the whole thing at this point. I would like to hope that that's the case, at least the sex-abuse thing. So, it comes from the sexualized environment.

More important, the most likely things are most likely. It seems like a stupid statement to make, but it's an ancient wisdom. The most likely thing is that at two or two-and-a-half, whenever he started to exhibit this, he was already having sexual urges, okay? He may have recognized that touching that area is different from scratching your head or your elbow and that it does have the potential for pleasure and that there were sexual urges to Grandmother and he may have said, "This will make you feel good." He himself may have had the same experience. Children his age are certainly capable of giving themselves pleasure by rubbing their genitals. When you reacted with, "Hey, wait a minute, fella, you know that's not proper. That's not acceptable," he does the thing that most children his age do—he blames others: "Don't blame me. My mommy lets me do it or my mommy taught me." That's standard operating procedure for little children. "He made me do it. It's his fault. He likes it." That's the way they talk. You raise children, right? Don't they do that? From everything I know of this case, from everything I've read about the interviews with his mother, she is not a pedophile and she certainly hasn't done all the preposterous things that Frank describes.

Grandmother: Yeah.

Gardner: "She made me do it. She said I should do it. She says it's okay." By saying things like this children thereby justify their own behavior, which you communicate is unacceptable. Isn't it easier to believe this than to believe that she eats her own feces, that she sucks feces out of her own child's anus? Is that something that is easier for you to believe?

Grandmother: No, it wasn't easy, because I've never been in that predicament.

Gardner: Who has?

Grandmother: But I've never been exposed to anything like this.

Gardner: I've been to the back wards of psychiatric hospitals and even there they don't do things like this.

Grandmother: And I don't doubt what you're saying, Dr. Gardner. Please understand. But never having been exposed to this. This is overwhelming.

Gardner: It's less overwhelming than what you are going through where you're not sleeping nights and you're believing every one of these preposterous stories. You see, you should have better judgment in a way. When you think about it, his hiding behind the chair and nobody seeing him while the three people are dancing around the room naked.

Grandmother: I didn't put too much credit in that.

Gardner: Well, the more preposterous elements you have in a story, the less the likelihood of the whole story. If somebody gives you a story with eight lies in it and two things that are true, do you think this guy is telling the truth? Huh? Come on, you don't, obviously, right?

Grandmother: I can't imagine his making all this up.

Gardner: I'm telling you the reasons and the place where it came from, from his own mind. That is the human mind, fueled by sexual urges, and that's the reason I'm taping this part. Now I have a new problem.

You people have a commitment to believing this and I hope that you will hear what I'm saying. I'm giving you an explanation that you are both unreceptive to hearing.

Grandmother: I'm receptive, but you must understand what this is to me. This is overwhelming because I can't imagine a child making all of this up.

Gardner: I'm telling you, I can, easily.

Grandmother: But you've been exposed to it.

Gardner: I've been doing child psychiatry for 35 years. Okay? And I have seen this over and over again. And if you will think back . . . Jim, do you have any siblings?

Grandmother: A brother, my other son.

Gardner: When you have children of one and two, at that period of their lives they are little animals in a way, right? They're animals.

Grandmother: I understand.

Gardner: They are comfortable with the most primitive animal functions. They will touch feces without any problem, right? They'll put it in their mouths without any problem. The good parent says no, you can't do that. That's yucky. That's disgusting. That's not allowed, you know? But, if allowed, they would play in their own urine. . . .

Grandmother: He's a bright boy. Isn't he too intelligent to believe those things at his age?

Gardner: Wait a minute. What does intelligence have to do with it? When he's one, he's still one. Maybe he functions like a one-and-a-half-year old, but he still goes through these stages. He's not born with a 10-year-old concept of the world.

Father: Consistently Frank tells the truth.

Gardner: That may be so in other realms, but this is special. These lies have to do with the child-custody dispute. He's gotten himself into a deep rut here with these lies. He's embarrassed. But you see there's mortification—the cat's out of the bag. And you've got to reassure him that you're not going to punish him. . . .

Grandmother: That's no problem. He doesn't get punished.

Gardner: But the first thing you have to do, before you can forgive him and tell him you love him and reassure him, my job here is to get you off your hysteria. You're on a wave of hysteria. You've been swept up in this hysteria. He told me he was lying to his therapist, Dave, and he was lying to Diane, your therapist, Jim. They were also taken in. You should show this tape to them. They should have seen the preposterousness of this.

Father: Well, what do we do to help him?

Gardner: What should you do to help him?

Grandmother: Apparently, they're not.

Gardner: They're not helping him? Right, because they didn't see through the whole thing.

Grandmother: I'm not talking about the therapists. I'm talking about the mother and her parents.

Gardner: What they're doing I do not know. I don't think they're dancing naked and I don't think he's masturbating his mother, and I don't think she's eating his feces and drinking his urine. I have no reason to believe that they're doing anything in the sexual department.

Grandmother: I don't mean that, Dr. Gardner. I'm talking about you're saying he's lying about this. How could they refuse counseling for him for the help that he needs?

Gardner: What's going on there, I don't know. As you know, they have not responded to my repeated overtures that they involve themselves in my consultations.

Grandmother: Then you ought to meet them. You'd understand why he . . .

Gardner: She will not have any part of me. She's refused all my invitations. Where do we go from here? Before we go to step two, are you willing to let the sex-abuse thing rest?

Grandmother: I have to.

Gardner: No, you don't have to. You can say, Gardner, you don't know what you're talking about. I still believe it.

Grandmother: If there's a little doubt in the back of my mind you must understand. . . .

Gardner: What do you think is the likelihood now, if zero is no sex abuse and 100 is that it actually happened in spite of what I've said, what would you say is the likelihood?

Grandmother: Zero.

Gardner (turning now to great-aunt): What do you say?

Great-Aunt: I say it must be happening or he wouldn't talk like that.

Gardner: Okay, so everything I've said is really a waste of words to you.

Great-Aunt: No, you make sense.

Gardner: But your bottom line is that it must be happening.

Great-Aunt: Because it's him.

Gardner: Because it's him? Okay. (Turning now to father.) Your aunt's response is one that some people have. I could talk myself blue in the face and it doesn't matter. You have to decide whether you want to go along with your aunt's beliefs or what I think is the rational, civilized program.

Great-Aunt: Dr. Gardner, realize that I was so sure that he was telling the truth and all of a sudden to come. . . .

Gardner: The most likely things are the most likely. Try to pull yourself back to reality here. You have been drawn into a kind of crazy world.

Great-Aunt: What I didn't realize was that a child could have a sex drive at that tender age.

Gardner: I'm telling you . . . do you know, you won't believe this. You know they have sonograms now?

Great-Aunt: Yeah.

Gardner: Okay, so you can observe directly. They have sonograms of babies masturbating in utero. Erections in utero.

Great-Aunt: My God.

Gardner: Okay, so when you say, "Where did he get that from? Who'd he learn that from? Where'd he see that, on television?" Okay, erections in utero. Newborn babies can touch themselves, okay?

Great-Aunt: Dr. Gardner, I think you have to appreciate the way I was brought up, the way my sister was, the way Jim was . . . so this is all mindboggling. I know you read about things like this in articles, and say to yourself, no, it couldn't happen to me. You just don't believe it.

Gardner: I'm telling you, the human being is a very sexual animal, and it intensifies at puberty, but that's the reality of the world. And the reality of the world is that your child is probably more sexual than average but he certainly is not in any way perverted. The perversion comes in these lies. That's the perversion. The perversion comes in his saying these bizarre things of what happens between him and his mother. I hope I have provided a very useful therapeutic experience for your son in terms of what I consider the proper therapeutic course, which is the decompression, confession . . .

Father: That's why we're here.

Gardner: The best thing to help him is to obviously talk about this and reassure him that you understand that he's embarrassed. You see what I do on the tape. You can understand that he's embarrassed. The embarrassment comes from the anticipation that significant people are going to react terribly to him for confessing that he had made up these lies about what happened to him and his mother. And he's mortified.

Father: I can understand why he's afraid.

Gardner: Be sympathetic. Reassure him that it was a big mistake. And he has promised on the tape, on a couple of occasions, that he will never lie again about the sex abuse. I would never force him to make a vow never to lie again. But about sex abuse, I have no problem getting him to make a vow that he'll never lie about that again.

Great-Aunt: But, Dr. Gardner, you must understand his reaction toward me. I thought, "My God, what am I doing that makes this child act this way toward me?"

Gardner: I'm telling you that you didn't do anything.

But, as mentioned, the paternal grandmother did do something that did play a role in this problem, namely, allowing this child to explore her vaginal area and put his finger in her vagina.

Great-Aunt: But do you know what a relief it is for me?

Gardner: Okay, fine, I'm glad that I've given you some therapy, too. And we put it on the tape so you can watch it again and hear the messages again. For me the big issue is that. There's an immediate issue of decompressing the whole thing for him. And there is the bigger issue of convincing you people that nothing sexual is happening at his mother's house. Right now, he doesn't want his mother to see this tape. My own inclination is to have everybody who's involved to see the tape. I make no promises. It's best that they all see the tape. The big thing that I see, and this is a message for your ex-wife, Ruth, if she will see this tape and if she will develop a certain amount of conviction or feeling that maybe I can be of some help to her here. The best thing you can do is to show her this tape. You can't let him be the decider. He doesn't want her to see this tape. He's afraid that she'll be very angry and that she'll punish him. I hope she doesn't.

Grandmother: She does, Dr. Gardner.

Gardner: She will punish him?

Grandmother: Oh, God, yes.

Gardner: All I can say is that I don't know the woman and the best thing she can do for her child is to come here with you and try to remove this whole thing from the lawyers, courts, jokers, and a whole parade of people, validators, and child protection services people. There's a civil war between the professionals, and child protection services should come here to try to use my help to resolve this. You have the visitation dispute. You have a communication dispute and it can go on forever. My hope is that if she [the mother] sees the tape, she will have some appreciation that I call the shots as I see them, that I'm really trying to do the best for everybody concerned, and that she will be willing to come here with you. That is my hope.

Grandmother: Dr. Gardner, you'll never get her to agree.

Gardner: It may not be, but at least I can try. If that doesn't work, then the next step is, as I understand it, you're suing for primary custody because of your belief that she is sexually abusing Frank.

Father: Yeah.

Gardner: I'm in a very difficult position to help you there. I haven't seen her, you understand? You'd have to provide very compelling . . . I'm not against going to court and providing support. You say no telephone access, no school access. You describe other exclusionary maneuvers which are clearly negative and which would support your position, but the facts are that she has a very strong positive and that is that she has been the primary caretaker throughout his life, and that weighs heavily in her favor. So, as I see it, these are the steps of how I'm suggesting that you proceed. Number one—you should write these down—you have to work with Frank to reassure and forgive and no punishment. You have to show these tapes to both therapists, Dave and Diane. I hope I will have changed their positions on this. If they are going to say no, this is true, and give all kinds of rationalizations for it, then that's going to put you in a very difficult position. (Therapist turning to father.) If you drop it, will Diane drop it?

Father: I think so. If she wants to talk to you . . .

Gardner: I will be happy to talk to her I can't add anything to what I'm saying on the tape. You know? But the hope is that they will drop it and that they will orient themselves to any kind of work that will assuage his guilt. I believe that no therapy is warranted for this child. I think he should get out of the offices of therapists except for the immediate and final guilt-assuaging forgiveness, reassurance, no punishment stuff like that. I think that you want to get closure here. This is my advice: He should have closure and not be treated at this point. Leave him alone. This is what I see. If there is going to be more lying, then that's a different story. Now, the third thing would be to try to get his mother to see me.

Father: Okay, question. What about the physical abuse marks that have repeatedly shown up?

Gardner: I don't know. I don't know about that. Physical abuse has never been substantiated by outside authorities.

Father: Because right after I kept finding the bruises on him and the hand grips . . .

Gardner: It may be going on, I don't know, but I'm dubious.

Grandmother: What about having the attorney Stanton coming into court and stating that she is a better fit parent than yourself, never having interviewed you, never having spoken to you?

Gardner: Then it's up to your lawyer to discredit him. I made overtures to her. But extend it again. Show her this tape. She'll see me as a human being. Maybe then she'll be more receptive. Okay, look, let's close here.

Father: The other thing that still concerns me is—I can accept when you say what is best for Frank. But again the physical abuse that I had seen; that still concerns me.

Gardner: I think it's best discussed with her, so I would like to reserve that for our meeting. If she turns you down again to see me, after seeing the tape, then let's talk about how to proceed, and we'll have to go into that as one of the arguments.

Father: How do I present the tape—to the attorneys?

Gardner: No, you're a free agent. This is not a totalitarian state. By the way, I want to keep a copy of the tape. I want to ask your permission to have this copy and to use it on rare occasions for teaching purposes. I will not reveal your identity.

Grandmother: Jim, if it can help anybody. . . .

Father: Yeah, what we've gone through . . . I mean this has been incredible.

Gardner: Okay. You make copies of your tape and send her one. Show it to your attorney—whomever you want to show it to. Show it to Diane. Show it to Dave. Have them see the tape. Okay, let's close here. This is the end of the meeting of the second of May, 1995.

Unfortunately, my attempts to impress upon Jim, his mother, and aunt that Frank had not been sexually abused were not ultimately successful. About one month later I spoke with Jim and he told me that he was very disappointed with my findings and was convinced that his former wife was indeed sexually abusing Frank. He provided as confirmation for this Frank's subsequent statements to him, his mother, and his aunt that he had lied to me and that these things had really happened. I learned, however, that this recantation was extracted primarily by his great-aunt, who left my office completely dubious about the validity of my findings and recommendations. We see here the power of hysteria and possibly preparanoid psychopathology. However, I have found the principles presented here useful in selected cases, especially those in which there have not been years of programming of the child and/or the psychopathology of the accusing parents is not deep-seated. The problems with this particular family were worsened by the presence of overzealous therapists who continued to support the accusation, in spite of its preposterousness. Last, throughout the whole course of my contact with this family, not one person pointed out that the paternal grandmother's behavior with this child was bona fide sex abuse, and absolutely no action was taken about this.

☐ SEVEN

CHILD SEX ABUSE AND HYSTERIA
1890s (AUSTRIA)/1990s (U.S.)

*Imagine, if you can, Freud's patients, Anna O., Elizabeth von R., Katharina, and Dora, marching down the street, arm in arm. They are wearing tee shirts or sweatshirts on which is emblazoned "I am a sex-abuse victim" or "I am a sex-abuse survivor." They are waving banners with such slogans as "Believe the children" and "Children never lie." They are proceeding to testify before a public legislative hearing, the purpose of which is to modify statutes of limitations so that adults who belatedly recall that they were sexually abused as children can sue their perpetrators. After providing their testimonies, they will spend the evening in their sex-abuse victims' survivors group. In the next few days, they will have one or two individual sessions with a therapist whose primary purpose is to help them retrieve in ever more specific detail the repressed memories of their childhood sexual encounters with adults. A few days later, they will participate in a marathon weekend for sex-abuse survivors and those who suspect they **might** have been abused as children and hope to bring into conscious awareness their repressed memories of such abuses. In the "healing" process they are encouraged to express pent-up repressed anger against their perpetrators, anger that has long been simmering in the unconscious mind. This is best accomplished by group orgies of beating mats with rubber hoses and chanting barrages of vile profanities directed against the perpetrators.*

If you can envision this scene, then you will have a good idea about the differences between Anna O. and her compatriots and women a century later who profess they were sexually abused as children. They do, however, share one *important element in common, namely, that their sex-abuse accusations against their perpetrators may **either** be true **or** false.*

We are living in dangerous times. Sex-abuse hysteria is omnipresent. Open any newspaper or magazine and the likelihood of seeing an article on sex abuse is extremely high. Hardly a day goes by when there are not at least some television or radio programs devoted to the subject of sex abuse. There is no question that many accusations of child sex abuse are true, and this is especially so in settings such as homes and boarding schools (where the potential abuser has the opportunity for ongoing contact with the children). However, there is no question, as well, that many of the accusations are false, especially in child-custody disputes (where the vengeance element and the opportunity for exclusion of a hated spouse is operative) and day-care centers and nursery schools (where the potential abuser has little opportunity for ongoing contact alone with the child).

The sexual abuse of children, like the abuse of women, is an ancient tradition and has been seen in every society in history. In fact, there is good reason to believe that there is less sexual exploitation of children in Western society (especially because of the proscriptions of the Judeo-Christian ethic) than has existed anywhere in the history of humanity. In recent years, we have become increasingly aware of how widespread sexual abuse of children is in Western society and have come to appreciate that there has been enormous denial of the phenomenon. At the same time, however, we have witnessed an exaggerated reaction to the phenomenon, so much so that the term *hysteria* is often warranted. The hysteria is seen at every level, from the time of the initial suggestion or suspicion to the final sentence meted out to an accused (whether truly guilty of the crime or not). A whole parade of individuals can predictably overreact—an overreaction that beclouds objectivity and lessens significantly the likelihood that a proper assessment will be conducted. I include here parents, police, detectives, prosecutors, psychologists, psychiatrists, social workers, "validators," "child advocates," teachers, school administrators, boards of education, lawyers, judges, juries, and legislators. In this atmosphere constitutional safeguards of due process are ignored, people are jailed on the basis of the babbling of three-year-olds, traditional courtroom procedures designed to protect the defense are no longer followed, and excessively punitive sentences are the rule. I believe that the average murderer in the United States today will be out of jail much sooner than the average person convicted of sex abuse. When it comes to sex abuse, there seems to be an exception to the Eighth-Amendment constitutional safeguard against "cruel and unusual punishment."

Divorced fathers (and even those who are not divorced) have become afraid to bathe and shower their children, or even help them when they go to the bathroom. No sane teacher will spend time alone in a room with a girl. Scoutmasters on overnight hikes are sure to travel two at a time. Many nursery schools have ongoing videotapes, and no one takes a child alone to the bathroom. For at least a quarter of a century now, doctors have been ever-vigilant regarding their patients suing them for malpractice. Now, there is a new danger: accusations of sexual molestation, sexual abuse, and sexual harassment.

HYSTERIA AS A HISTORICAL PHENOMENON

To the best of my knowledge, hysteria was first described by Hippocrates in the fourth century B.C. He observed the condition almost exclusively in women who exhibited crying fits, agitated movements of their bodies, and exhibitionistic displays. He considered the disorder to be the result of the wandering of the uterus, which had somehow gotten loose from its fixations in the pelvic cavity. The word *hysteria* is derived from the Greek word *hystera*, which means uterus. Hysteria, unlike most other psychiatric disorders, has the capacity to spread, resulting in group hysteria and even mass hysteria. Accordingly, a study at any particular level adds to our knowledge of the others. As will be elaborated upon below, my studies of group hysteria have enhanced my knowledge of the individual as well as the mass types.

Group and Mass Hysteria

Group hysteria is an ancient tradition. Human beings are sheeplike, and the desire to "go along with the crowd" is deep-seated and, I suspect, possibly genetically determined. Obviously, it is safer to be one of the "herd" than to be a maverick. If only for the sake of protection from predators, groups are safer than isolated individuals. Those who are different inevitably suffer scorn and rejection. The word *gregarious* is derived from the Latin word *grex*, which means *flock of sheep*. In addition, human beings are amazingly suggestible and can, under proper circumstances, be brought to the point of believing anything, no matter how absurd. And I am not only speaking of children in this regard, but adults as well. Group hysteria is built upon these foundations of gregariousness and suggestibility. Other factors, depending upon the particular needs of those involved in the hysteria, become incorporated. Society must provide acceptable releases for the pent-up hostilities that inevitably result from the predictable frustrations of life. When the group has found a scapegoat for such hostilities, then this element may contribute to the hysteria. Most often the oversimplification element is operative. Life is complex, and most phenomena are multidetermined. Accordingly, simple solutions are much more attractive than complicated ones. When the mob's goal is to remove a particular person or group—and thereby solve all of its problems—the movement becomes particularly attractive. Joining such a movement enhances self-esteem in that one surrounds oneself with others who share—often to a fanatic degree—one's convictions. Feelings of power may also be gratified in that the mob has much more power than any single individual. Although each outbreak has its own special factors, the aforementioned are most often operative.

Some of the more well-known examples: Early in the 13th century, processions of flagellants (people who whipped themselves and others) traveled throughout Europe convinced that their lashings were punishments decreed by God and served, therefore, to assuage the guilt they felt about their sins. Within 20 years these groups spread over Bohemia, Moravia, Poland, and Italy. As late as the 17th century they were still to be found in Russia under the name "the self burners" (Zilboorg and Henry, 1941).

During the Middle Ages we witnessed throughout central Europe waves of dancing hysteria, referred to as St. Vitus's dance. Men and women, usually peasants, would form circles and dance frenetically, as if possessed, until they fell to the ground while foaming at the mouth. The Children's Crusade (Lyons and Petrucelli, 1978) is now generally considered to be another example of mass hysteria. In the second decade of the 13th century, an estimated 30,000 children from all parts of France streamed into Marseilles with the plan of conquering the Holy Land from the Muslims. They fell victim to disreputable merchants who shipped them to slave markets in North Africa. During the same period an estimated 20,000 German children crossed the Alps into various parts of Italy with the hope of reaching the Holy Land via Italian ports on the Mediterranean. Many of these children, like the French group, ultimately ended up as slaves in the Middle East (*Encyclopaedia Britannica*, 1982).

Menninger (1957) describes an epidemic of hysteria that took place in Lancashire, England, in 1787. It all began when a working girl, as a prank, placed a mouse into the bosom of another girl, who was quite fearful of mice. The victim of this prank immediately developed convulsions that lasted 24 hours. This episode served as the nidus of an outbreak of group hysteria that ultimately involved 300 fellow employees. The main symptoms were anxiety, feelings of being strangled, and convulsions. The convulsions lasted from 15 minutes to 24 hours and involved tearing of hair, dashing of the head, and falling against walls and floors. Interestingly, all of the afflicted were cured with an alcoholic beverage and the suggestion that they join in a dance.

Kanner (1935) describes an outbreak that took place in 1892 in Bieberach, Germany, in which 13 girls had attacks that began with headaches and then consisted of dancing movements, hallucinations, delirium, and finally profound sleep. In 1892 in the village of Gross-Tinz in Silesia, a ten-year-old girl exhibited tremors of the hand, which spread over her whole body. Next, several other girls were similarly afflicted. Within a few weeks 20 girls had similar attacks. All this stopped with the summer vacation but, on return to school in the autumn, the wave of hysteria continued, with the girls exhibiting convulsions, astasia-abasia (the psychological inability to stand and/or walk), delirium, *arc de cercle* (psychologically caused bending of the body anteriorally or posteriorally), profuse perspiration, and barking like dogs. Interestingly, only girls were afflicted during this epidemic. Kanner describes other epidemics of hysteria, mainly in Europe.

It is of interest that in the late 19th century, in both the United States and England, we witnessed a period of excessive preoccupation with and Draconian condemnation of childhood masturbation, which had many of the hallmarks of hysteria. Unfortunately, physicians (who should have known better) were actively involved in this campaign of denunciation and attempts to obliterate entirely this loathsome practice. Doctors considered it to be the cause of a wide variety of illnesses, e.g., blindness, insanity, and muscle spasms. Various kinds of restraints were devised to prevent children from engaging in this dangerous practice. Some girls were even subjected to clitorectomies, so dangerous was the practice considered to be. Parents were given a long list of symptoms that were considered to be concomitants or the result of masturbation. Some of the alerting signs were: temper tantrums, bedwetting, sleep disturbances, appetite changes, mood fluctuations, and withdrawal. Obviously, in the hundred years since those sad times, we seem to have gone back full circle. The same list of symptoms that were indicators of masturbation are now considered to be indicators of sex abuse. Legrand et al. (1989) have written a fascinating article describing the similarities between the masturbation hysteria of the late 19th century and the sex-abuse hysteria of the late 20th century, with a comparison of the lists of "indicators."

The Salem witch trials are viewed by many as our country's most famous episode of mass hysteria. Many do not appreciate that the trials lasted less than five months (June 2, 1692–October 29, 1692). During this period 27 people were convicted of witchcraft. Nineteen were hanged (the last hangings took place on September 22, 1692), one man (who refused trial by jury) was executed by being pressed to death with heavy stones (he took two days to die), and four died in prison. On October 26, 1692, the Massachusetts legislature, at the prodding of Reverend Increase Mather (president of Harvard University and United States ambassador to England), dictated to the Salem magistrates that they use much more stringent criteria before judging an individual guilty of witchcraft. On October 29, 1692, Massachusetts Governor Phips dismissed the court. This basically brought an end to the trials. For many years thereafter courts and churches declared days of penance and prayer in apology for the injustices perpetrated upon the accused. In January 1696 12 of the jurors signed a statement of contrition, claiming that they had operated under the influence of the devil. In subsequent years survivors of the accused were granted redress and compensation for their losses. The Salem witch trials are well viewed as the first wave of hysteria that we witnessed in this country.

The Salem witch trial hysteria was not unique to the United States. Actually, belief in witches was pervasive in Europe throughout the Middle Ages, and there have been many episodes of persecution of witches throughout Europe since that time. The Salem witch trial episode can be considered a derivative of the European phenomenon, with additional contributing factors particular to the Massachussetts Colony in the late 17th century. The second great wave of hysteria that we witnessed in the United States was the McCarthy hearings in the early 1950s. In the course of this wave of hysteria, threats of Communist infiltration and takeover of our government were exaggerated enormously, and Draconian punishments were administered to those who had any sympathies for the movement. Even those who had involved themselves in the Communist party only superficially and transiently earlier in life did not escape. Blacklists were drawn up, people were fired from their jobs, and a whole network of investigators and informers served to promulgate the belief in Communism's formidable dangers to the U.S. government. Many of those unfortunate enough to have been subjected to the abominations of McCarthy's committee became social outcasts, and some were even incarcerated. Although thousands certainly suffered during the hysteria of that era, I believe that their numbers are small compared to those whose lives have been destroyed by the sex-abuse hysteria that has been prevalent in the United States since the early 1980s. Accordingly, I believe we are now experiencing the United States' third great wave of hysteria. I believe that more have suffered in its course than all those who suffered in Salem and the McCarthy era combined.

I am certain that the number of people who have died as a result of the current hysteria far exceeds the number who were executed in Salem. These people have not literally been executed, but they have been given psychological death sentences. These people have not been literally hanged or stoned to death, but many have been dealt with the equivalent treatment psychologically. I am convinced that there are hundreds (and possibly thousands) of people who are in jail in the United States today who have been convicted of sex crimes that they never committed. (I am not denying that there are many more incarcerated who actually did indeed commit such crimes.) There are hundreds, I am sure, who have committed suicide because of a false sex-abuse accusation. There are others who have died of heart attacks, strokes, and other diseases caused by the stresses and humiliations of a false sex-abuse accusation. Careers and marriages have been destroyed, reputations ruined, and people are suffering lifelong stigma because of such an accusation.

The event that, to the best of my knowledge, laid the foundation for our current hysteria—which I refer to as sex-abuse hysteria—was the *The Child Abuse Prevention and Treatment Act* (The Mondale Act), which was passed by the United States Congress in 1973. Congress was certainly well intentioned in its desire to protect abused children. However, the results have been disastrous. The law mandated child-abuse reporting laws in all 50 states, laws in which civil and criminal immunity to lawsuits would be provided for anyone reporting the abuse of a child. Furthermore, individuals aware of such crimes—who did not report such abuse—were subject to criminal prosecution. This has resulted in a philosophy of "when in doubt, report." Federal funding was provided for district attorneys to set up special units for the prosecution of child sex abuse, but no funding was provided for defendants. The result has been the development of a nationwide army of zealous prosecutors and a sense of impotence for those (the defendants) who are not wealthy enough to finance their own defense (Clancy and Firpo, 1991). Federal monies were also provided for setting up clinics devoted to the evaluation and treatment of abused children. No funding was made available for children who were found not to be abused or who were found to be used as vehicles for a false sex-abuse accusation.

A cornerstone of our constitutional system is the principle that a man is innocent until proven guilty. This is often stated as the dictum, "Rather 10 (or 100 or 1,000) guilty men go free, than one innocent man be falsely convicted of a crime he did not commit." In the service of this principle, civil courts generally require a *preponderance of evidence* before concluding that the defendant is guilty of the alleged crime. In criminal cases, the requirements are even more stringent in that the jury must conclude *beyond reasonable doubt* that the defendant did indeed commit the crime. These traditional constitutional safeguards are being ignored. Rather, judges now subscribe to the philosophy, "I'd rather be on the safe side" and find defendants guilty with minimal evidence, even "evidence" provided by a three-year-old child who has been relentlessly programmed by her vengeful divorced mother to allege that she was sexually abused by her father. One judge said to me, "If there is a scintilla of evidence that this man sexually abused this child, I will send him to jail for as many years as the law will allow." Although juries in criminal cases have been instructed to subscribe to the beyond-reasonable-doubt principle, the instructions of many judges and the ambient hysteria have encouraged them to ignore this factor in their deliberations. Elsewhere (Gardner, 1991a) I have described in detail the ways in which the current sex-abuse hysteria has been promulgated.

Individual Hysteria

It would be difficult and simplistic to try to apply Hipprocrates' theory that hysteria arises primarily in the uterus to the aforementioned episodes of mass hysteria. Whatever sexual elements may or may not be operative in producing each individual's hysterical reaction, there is no question that a multiplicity of other factors must be operative. The uterine theory, however, has persisted in medicine—down even to the 20th century. Charles Lepois (1563–1633) claimed that the cause of hysteria is not to be sought in the uterus but in the brain (Zilboorg and Henry, 1941). However, this notion was not given general credibility. Although Freud considered repressed sexual factors to be operative in producing hysteria, he did not consider the uterus to be its source, but rather the brain. Interestingly, his colleagues had little conviction for this bizarre idea, especially because they did not believe that the disorder could be found in men. This is particularly surprising because, by that time, the brain was generally considered the seat of mental disease.

In the 1880s, Jean-Martin Charcot described what he considered to be a new neurological disease: "hystero-epilepsy." He considered this to be a disorder that was a combination of hysteria and epilepsy. The symptoms included screaming, crying, convulsions, contortions, fainting, and fluctuating consciousness. His demonstrations of these patients to the professional community at the Salpêtrière Hospital was well known and Freud was one of the enthusiastic attendees. Joseph Babinsky, a skeptical student, claimed that Charcot had invented "hystero-epilepsy" rather than discovered it. He held that these patients' symptoms were the result of the suggestions of Charcot and the attendant staff who were treating them. A hospital decision required hysterics and epileptics to be placed in the same facility and, because the hysterics were very suggestible, they took on the symptoms of the epileptic patients with whom they lived. Babinsky was successful in convincing Charcot that this might have occurred. When patients with hystero-epilepsy were transferred to a separate facility, and when staff members stopped attending directly to the hysterical symptoms but rather addressed themselves to the underlying problems that these patients had in life, the symptoms were either reduced significantly or disappeared entirely (McHugh, 1993).

This link between hysteria and suggestibility is an important one and has been well recognized since. Psychoanalysts are well aware of the seminal studies on hysteria of Freud and Breuer (1895), published in the late 19th and early 20th centuries. Their patients (the most well-known of which are the aforementioned Anna O., Dora, etc.) exhibited a wide variety of symptoms such as convulsive ticks, spastic speech inhibitions, paralysis, crying fits, psychosomatic complaints, neuromuscular complaints, agitation, depression, and even hallucinations. Freud believed that these patients were suffering with sexual inhibitions that were the results of overstringent superegos inhibiting freer expression of their basic libidinal impulses. Many of them described sexual stimulation, overtures, and encounters with their fathers, neighbors, or nearest of kin. Freud subsequently went through a period of disillusionment when he began to doubt the validity of some of the sexual experiences his patients described to him. He resolved this conflict by deciding that his patients' fabrications and/or delusions were also "data" and that their need to create such fantasies was a derivative of their wish to actually have sexual experiences with these individuals.

Subsequently, there has been much debate in psychoanalytic circles over this issue. I myself do not have very much conviction for the inquiry. It is not that I am oblivious to the importance of history. Rather, my disinterest relates to my appreciation that the data that we have available to us is extremely sparse, even though Freud is famous for the meticulousness with which he collected the data he has provided us. The data, however, is 100 years old and there are areas of inquiry that we would investigate today that were not focused on by Freud and Breuer.

Another reason for my lack of commitment to this discussion is that, approximately twice a week, I get letters from people in jail who are claiming that they have been falsely accused of sexual abuse and are pleading for my help. Although some of these individuals may indeed have perpetrated these acts, there are others, I am certain, who are innocent and who are victims of the hysteria of our times. Accordingly, I have devoted my efforts to developing criteria for differentiating between true and false accusations in the hope that I may help these people now and protect other innocent individuals in the future from being similarly incarcerated (Gardner, 1995a).

MY CONCEPT OF HYSTERIA

Introduction

Here I present the results of my own "studies on hysteria," both its manifestations and psychodynamics. The concept of hysteria that I present here is based primarily on the in-depth evaluation of hundreds children and adults involved in sex-abuse accusations over the last 15 years. Most of the "children" were indeed children at the time of my evaluation. Some, however, were adults who claimed that they were sexually abused as children. The evaluated adults included parents and stepparents of the allegedly abused children who were accusers, accused themselves, or provided me with information that helped me ascertain whether the alleged child victim had indeed been sexually abused. Some of the adults were accused grandparents, teachers, clergy, and scoutmasters. These evaluations were conducted primarily over the last 15 years, the period during which we have witnessed our present sex-abuse hysteria. The primary purpose of these evaluations was to ascertain whether the child had been sexually abused. In each of these cases, I made every attempt to interview the accuser, the alleged child victim, and the alleged perpetrator. The conclusions were generally based on the utilization of criteria that I developed for differentiating between true and false accusations. The updated and latest version of these differentiating criteria are described in my book, *Protocols for the Sex-Abuse Evaluation* (Gardner, 1995a).

Interestingly, *DSM-III-R* considered hysteria to be the less desirable term. In fact, it does not recognize a primary diagnosis of hysteria. When somatic elements are operative, the preferred term is *Conversion Disorder* or one may use *Hysterical Neurosis, Conversion Type*. The group of *Dissociative Disorders* may also be referred to as *Hysterical Neurosis, Dissociative Type*. When emotionality and attention-seeking elements are operative, the diagnosis *Histrionic Personality Disorder* is used, without any parenthetic possibility of using the term *hysteria* to apply to this symptom complex.

DSM-IV maintains the *Conversion, Dissociative, and Histrionic Disorders* but has dropped entirely the hysteria equivalent terms. I consider it unfortunate that *DSM-IV* has dropped all reference to hysteria. I have no problem with removing its association with the *Conversion Disorder* because this, by today's standards, is an anachronism. Few believe today that people with psychogenic paralysis are channeling sexual libido into other parts of their body. Nor do I have problems removing the term *hysteria* from the *Dissociative Disorders*, which, today, are being overdiagnosed and are serving to give medical credibility to false accusations of sexual abuse in that the person who has no memory of such abuses is considered to have repressed, dissociated, and depersonalized the experiences (Gardner, 1992a, 1992d). *Histrionic Personality Disorder* provides criteria that are closest to classical hysteria and might justify an alternative hysteria diagnostic label. However, neither *DSM-III-R* nor *DSM-IV* includes the capacity-to-spread factor. I consider this an unfortunate omission.

Manifestations and Psychodynamics

I will use as my starting point the overt manifestations that originally caused Hippocrates to suggest that the agitation he was observing in these screaming women was the result of the roaming around in their bodies of the uterus, which had somehow loosened from its attachments in the pelvis. This is the same behavior that I have observed on numerous occasions in parents (more often mothers than fathers) when they accused someone of having sexually abused their children. In fact, they themselves will often say, "I was hysterical when I first found out about it" or "My wife was in a state of frenzy that lasted at least three days after they told us about it." One mother told me: "When I found out that the bus driver molested that Boy Scout, I called every mother in both the morning and afternoon kindergartens. In my business I need five telephones on my desk. I can make two and sometimes three calls at a time. I have both speaker phones and handsets. I must have made about 70 calls in three hours." (This woman, interestingly, had been a professional actress in her teens and twenties and the "business" she referred to here was a theatrical agency.) Hysteria, as I view it, consists of the following components:

Emotional Outbursts It is this characteristic of hysteria that is most familiar to the general public. And this is the characteristic described by Hippocrates approximately 2,400 years ago. It is also the manifestation focused on in most dictionaries. For example, *The Random House Dictionary* (1987) defines hysteria as "an uncontrollable outburst of emotion or fear, often characterized by irrationality, laughter, weeping, etc." Most individuals get upset at times. Hysterical individuals, however, are more likely to get upset—to the point of exhibiting emotional outbursts—and are likely to manifest such outbursts much more frequently than the average individual.

Overreaction The individual reacts in an exaggerated fashion to events and situations that others would either not respond to at all or respond to with only minimal emotional reaction. In hysteria individuals react with excessive tension, anxiety, and agitation.

Dramatization Hysterical individuals, in association with their overreaction, may become quite dramatic, sometimes akin to a theatrical performance. It is this aspect of hysteria that is referred to as *histrionic* in *DSM-IV* in the diagnosis, *Histrionic Personality Disorder*.

Attention-Getting Behavior Whereas people with other psychiatric symptoms often suffer silently and alone (although they may draw others into their psychopathology), hysterical people typically attract significant attention and attempt to surround themselves with others who will provide them with sympathy and support. This element in hysteria can easily be gratified in the 20th century. Whereas in Freud's time sex abuse, especially by a father, relative, or neighbor, was considered a source of shame, just the opposite appears to be the case in the United States in the last 15 years. By merely picking up the telephone and calling a child protection service, one can call into play an apparatus that will include investigation by "validators," social workers, psychologists, psychiatrists, police, detectives, lawyers, and judges. Another call will bring in the mass media: newspaper and magazine interviews and television appearances. A third call to a lawyer will start things rolling down the track of a lawsuit, with further interviews by lawyers and insurance company people. Another call to a mental health facility will predictably result in "validation" and then "therapy," both individual and group therapy for the abused children, parent group therapy for the parents, and special classes for child "survivors" and their parents. Support groups, political action committees, fund-raising campaigns, weekend marathon experiences, consciousness-raising groups, and victim-survivor groups are ubiquitous. This factor was operative for the accusing children in Salem in that their accusations were made in public situations before magistrates and just about everybody in the community who could get down to the proceedings (Mappan, 1980; Richardson, 1983). But their attention was minuscule compared to what is available today 300 years later.

In short, making a sex-abuse accusation public involves one in a *cause célèbre*. Bringing sex abuse to the attention of the world as a step toward wiping out this abomination engages one in a noble pursuit that is bound to engender the admiration of all.

Assumes Danger When It Does Not Exist In hysteria the individual sees danger in situations in which others do not see danger. In mild cases the hysteria may be reduced and even eliminated by calm discussion and confrontation with reality. In moderate and severe forms of hysteria, confrontation with reality does not dispel the anticipation of harm. Hysteria can progress to a state of delusion, which is not altered by logic and confrontation with reality. Because hysteria can progress to delusion, they are on a continuum. Group pressure, especially, has the effect of moving hysteria down this continuum into the delusional realm.

For example, in sex-abuse hysteria in the context of child-custody disputes, the parents of an accused father, who previously may have been considered to have had a very loving and close relationship with their grandchildren, may come to be viewed as facilitators and even participants in their son's sexual abuse and the children's contacts with them may be cut off entirely by the mother. And the original "proof" of the father's sexual abuse may have been a stain in the crotch area of the child's panties.

The danger element in hysteria has often been intensified by the so-called sexual abuse "validators" who present parents with a long list of the signs and symptoms that are allegedly diagnostic of child sex abuse. These may include just about every behavioral manifestation, normal and abnormal, healthy and pathological, known to the child psychiatrist, e.g., bedwetting, nightmares, mood swings, sibling rivalry, and low self-esteem. Validators may refer to these symptoms as "the sexual abuse syndrome." When looking at such lists, I often think that the subtitle of *DSM-IV* should be: "The Sexual Abuse Syndrome."

Impairment in Judgment States of high emotion compromise judgment. The tensions, anxieties, and overreactions present in hysteria reduce the individual's capacity to think logically and assess situations in a calm and deliberate manner. The impairments in judgment can result in the individual believing the most unlikely, preposterous, and bizarre scenarios and can even contribute to the development of delusional thinking.

Release of Anger Hysteria allows for release of anger in a manner the individual considers to be socially acceptable. The entity that is seen as noxious or dangerous becomes the focus of anger and even rage. The hysteric is essentially saying: "Look how much grief and agitation you have caused me." It is for this reason that scapegoats are often seen in hysteria, especially in group and mass hysteria. Scapegoats not only provide a convenient target for the release of anger but are also used as a simple explanation for all the griefs that have befallen the hysterical person. During the time of the Salem Witch trials, witches were the focus of the anger. The cruelty of children was also well demonstrated then. As the accused witches were hanged, the children literally danced and clapped with joy—with absolutely no sense of guilt or remorse. In the McCarthy hearings, after World War II, Communists were the selected targets of anger. With the breakdown of the Communist empire in the late 1980s, a new scapegoat had to be found for paranoids. One of them is sex abusers. Others (at the time that I write this in the mid-1990s) are space aliens, satanic ritual abusers, and a network of government conspirators planning to invade the homes of individuals and take their guns and other protective equipment. Again, we see how hysteria is on a continuum with paranoia. In hysteria the distorted idea is capable of modification. When the paranoid level is reached, the idea becomes a fixed delusion and cannot be changed by logic.

The Sexual Element Interestingly, I believe that the sexual repression element is still operative in hysteria, although it is handled differently from the way Freud's patients dealt with their sexual thoughts and feelings. Freud's patients lived in a world in which overt expressions of sexuality were not considered acceptable. It may very well be that the amount of premarital and extramarital sex that Victorians engaged in was no more or less than that which people today engage in. However, there is no question that the "official" standards of these two societies are very different, and this must have an effect on the psychological processes of patients living in these two very different eras. Little Hans (Freud, 1909) was warned that if he played with his penis, his parents would take him to the doctor, who would cut it off. (No surprise, then, that Little Hans developed castration anxiety [Gardner, 1972]). A few years ago a mother brought her 14-year-old girl to me for consultation. The youngster was the only one in her group who had not yet started to masturbate and the mother wondered whether there was something wrong with her child. Touching one's own genitals has become a standard part of the repertoire of some rock singers. Every known profanity is now standard fare on television, especially in the context of R-rated movies. These same films, which can be readily viewed by the child by the press of a button of the channel control while Mom is in the kitchen, enable children to view many aspects of heterosexual intercourse.

In spite of these vast differences in the two societies' attitudes toward overt sexual expression, there are still many people in the United States today who are sexually repressed. My experience has been that this is especially likely among people who are extremely religious, e.g., religious fundamentalists. Whereas Freud's patients were dealing with their sexual feelings via repression and somatization, today's hysterics are dealing with their sexuality by repression and projection (externalization). Repression is still operative but projection has replaced somatization. This is one of the reasons why many of the nursery school sex-abuse hysteria cases occur in settings in which there is an affiliated church, often in the strict fundamentalist category. It is as if these parents are saying: "It is not I who harbor within me all these primitive sexual impulses; it is they." Somatization is primarily a personal matter, although the person with somatic symptoms may get a little sympathy from close friends and relatives. Projection, in contrast, is a public matter associated with vociferous condemnation and the need to "take action." Rejecting, punishing, incarcerating, and even destroying those "perverts" serves to lessen the guilt the individual feels over his (her) own unacceptable sexual impulses. And removing them also protects the projecting party from the temptations that might be aroused by contacts with the so-called pervert. This, of course, is the core mechanism in prejudice.

Whereas the sources of sexual suppression and repression in Victorian Vienna were familial and societal, one can only wonder about the sources of sexual repression today, repression that results in the need for projection. I suspect that one source relates to a backlash against the sexual freedom so common in the 1960s and 1970s in association with the so-called sexual revolution. Another factor that I suspect is operative is the AIDS epidemic. I believe that it is no small coincidence that sex-abuse hysteria and the AIDS epidemic both began in the early 1980s. And these elements are part of a broader picture of sexual suppression and repression associated with the rise of religious fundamentalism that we have witnessed in the United States during the last decade. My experiences with families in which sex-abuse hysteria is present have provided me with the opportunity to address myself to the question of hysteria in the *male*. As mentioned, even Freud's colleagues were dubious about his theory because it allowed for the possibility that sexually repressed men might develop similar symptoms. Few if any such males were to be found. This is not surprising because even in the Victorian era young boys and men were still given greater sanction than girls and women to express overtly their sexual feelings. Most of the hysterical men I have seen have been involved in nursery school cases wherein they have been swept up in the hysteria as a manifestation of its capacity to spread. In addition, their hysteria is fueled by the ambient brouhaha seen at meetings and demonstrations in which other nursery school parents are similarly hysterical. Accordingly, they have often involved themselves in a folie-à-deux relationship with their wives who, typically, are the primary agitators in these cases. This element in these men's hysteria, then, has been induced. Some of them are clearly hyperreligious types who project out onto others their own unacceptable sexual impulses. They exhibit the mechanisms of repression, projection, and external condemnation.

Another sexual element in these men's hysteria relates to the unconscious rivalries they have with their potential rivals for their daughters. Freud focused significantly on the boy's sexual attraction to his mother and less on the girl's sexual attraction to her father. He did not give proper attention, I believe, to the complementary attractions of the parents to the children. Of course, Freud's descriptions of patients' fathers who had involved themselves in incestuous relationships with their daughters indicate an appreciation of this phenomenon—but it played a limited role in his broader theories. And even less is said about mothers' sexual attractions to their sons. These parental designs on children are part of the polymorphous perversity of us all and are playing a role in the need of accusing parents to project their pedophilic impulses onto others. The fathers here are basically saying: "It is not I who wants to have sex with my daughter. It is he, that vile pervert." It is this jealous rage that is operative in the traditional warning of such fathers: "I'll kill anyone who even lays a hand on my daughter." And some of these fathers really mean it. Many would actually be willing to accept capital punishment if they had the opportunity to murder the man who sexually abused their daughters. In some of these cases, the "abuse" was no more than "possible" touching of the child's genitals, outside the clothing, without any further sexual involvement. Also, such preoccupations allow for a socially acceptable vehicle for the expression of pent-up anger.

I believe that there are genetic differences, as well, in the somewhat different ways in which men and women today manifest hysteria. Women tend to be more emotional. I suspect there is some genetic loading for this difference, but environmental factors are certainly operative. Accordingly, the histrionic and agitation elements in hysteria are likely to be more apparent in women. In contrast, fathers are more likely to be overtly belligerent and combative. (Here, too, I believe genetic loading plays a role, although environmental factors are certainly operative.) Accordingly, they are more comfortable with the anger-release aspect of hysteria.

Capacity for Spread Whereas other psychiatric symptoms tend to exist in relative isolation and not to spread to other individuals, hysteria is much more analogous to a contagious disease. It is for this reason that *group hysteria* is often seen and sometimes even *mass hysteria*. Although sexual abuse may certainly take place in the day-care center setting, there is no question that many of the day-care center accusations seen in the United States in recent years have no basis in reality and arise in an atmosphere of *group hysteria*. Furthermore, there is compelling evidence that we have been witnessing during the last decade an epidemic of *mass hysteria* in the United States as well as certain Western countries. Because the hysteria involves child sexual abuse, I believe the term *sex-abuse hysteria* is a proper term to describe this phenomenon.

Intensification of Symptoms in the Context of Lawsuits In the context of lawsuits the symptoms of hysteria are likely to become intensified. This is especially the case when the individual has something to gain by such elaboration. Accordingly, in civil lawsuits, when financial remuneration is being sought, the individual—consciously or unconsciously—is likely to expand the symptoms. In criminal lawsuits, wherein the goal is to punish and even incarcerate an alleged perpetrator who is the focus of the hysteria, such elaborations are also predictable.

Lawsuits not only bring about an intensification and elaboration of the symptoms of hysteria, but they also prolong enormously the time over which the pathology becomes imbedded in the psychic structure. Lawsuits require repeated interrogations by lawyers and other mental health professionals. They involve depositions and court appearances (either in the judge's chambers or in open court). The hysterical parents may keep the child in ongoing therapy. Generally, the "therapist" is an individual who does not question for one second the validity of the accusation, who is blind to the fact that she (he) may be witnessing a false accusation and thereby entrenches in the child the notion that he (she) has been subjected to an abominable crime, which may produce lifelong psychiatric disturbance. Placing the child in such "treatment" fattens the purse that will hopefully be acquired at the end of the lawsuit. Such embellishment also has the effect of impressing upon the court the gravity of the psychiatric damage, damage that "requires years of therapy." In fact, one cannot know exactly how long it will take, so traumatized has this child been.

Concluding Comments on My Concept of Hysteria

I recognize that the hysteria I describe here derives from experiences with hysterical people in the context of sex-abuse accusations. I recognize, as well, that my data has been collected in special settings, especially child-custody disputes, nursery school and day-care center group accusations, and belated accusations by adult women. I believe, however, that these experiences have enhanced my understanding of hysteria (especially group hysteria) and such insights should prove useful in other situations in which hysteria is seen, situations in which the sexual element may not be operative.

EIGHT

TREATMENT OF CHILDREN WITH SEX-ABUSE HYSTERIA

INTRODUCTION

In this chapter I focus on children who have not been sexually abused at all; however, they have been swept up in the sex-abuse hysteria of our times. These children fall into two categories. The first are children who have experienced a short, superficial, sexual encounter which, at worst, might have been a prelude to molestation but never got that far. There is hardly a young woman who is not subjected to men who may brush or press against her with sexual intention. I will deal here with hysterical reactions to such universal experiences. One could argue whether this widespread experience can justifiably be labeled *abuse*. However, if courts of law were to consider such encounters to indicate sex abuse on the part of the man, then the vast majority of men in our society would be up on criminal charges, whether the "victim" be a pubertal girl or someone older. When the encounter involves a prepubertal child, courts are generally very receptive to considering such superficial contacts to be a manifestation of a criminal act. Here, too, there are significant cultural differences regarding how the particular society will react to such an encounter. In this chapter I focus on hysterical reactions to such superficial encounters, encounters that are so transient and isolated that no reasonable person would consider the child to have been traumatized, the trauma existing only in the mind of the beholder. In such cases the term *hysteria* is applicable because we see here overreaction, the assumption of danger when it does not exist, high emotional tone, impairment of judgment, and often scapegoatism.

The second category focused on in this chapter includes children (generally prepubertal) who have had no encounters at all with an alleged perpetrator. Accordingly, there is not even an abuser on the scene to accuse of sex abuse. Rather, the child has normal sexual urges and interprets them to indicate depravity and perversity. Prior to the early 1980s (when our present sex-abuse hysteria began), most parents would have considered such sexual urges to be within the normal range of the human repertoire. Now parents swept up in hysteria communicate to the child that these thoughts and feelings are abnormal. Under these circumstances, the child herself exhibits hysterical reactions with associated feelings of self-loathing, self-deprecation, and preoccupation with thoughts of sexual depravity. Under such circumstances the child is likely to develop subsequent sexual problems, especially in the sexual-inhibition realms, because sex then becomes equated with sin and moral turpitude.

For each of these two categories I will detail a clinical vignette that demonstrates well the principles of therapy for these children. In both cases, the therapeutic principles are the same, namely, to reduce the hysteria and to avoid entrenching the hysterical preoccupations.

HYSTERICAL REACTIONS TO ISOLATED, SUPERFICIAL SEXUAL OVERTURES

Carol, age 13, was brought by her parents for consultation because of "sexual molestation." The alleged molestation occurred thirteen months previously while visiting with her girlfriend, Dora, a next-door neighbor. Carol and Dora (then age 12) and two other girls (then age 10) were all sitting on the floor, leaning against Dora's mother's bed, watching television. Dora's uncle, Fred, a man of about 40, came into the room and sat between Carol and Dora, who were sitting in the center of the foursome. In the course of watching television Fred gradually, from behind, reached his hands underneath the blouses of each of the girls sitting beside him. Carol, although minimally developed (she still was when I saw her thirteen months later), had just started to wear a training bra. During the course of approximately five minutes he touched the lateral side of her left breast with his left hand and also licked her right ear intermittently. During this same time, according to Dora's reports, he was engaging in similar activities with her. Although slightly frightened, Carol said nothing. While this was going on Carol was thinking, "Why is he doing this to me?"

About a half-hour later, Fred began to repeat these overtures. This time both girls stopped him and told Dora's mother what had happened. Dora's mother told both girls, firmly and calmly, to stay away from Fred and that she would speak to him on her own. Soon thereafter Carol went home and told her mother what had happened. Her mother stated to me, "I was in shock when I learned what had happened. I told my husband and he wanted to kill Fred."

In subsequent discussions with Dora's mother it was learned that Fred, a married man, was known to be an alcoholic and his wife was aware of the fact that he had a "habit" of fondling young girls. His wife tended to exonerate him with the excuse that he was an alcoholic. Fred denied that he had engaged in any inappropriate behavior with the girls, but did admit that he was in the bedroom with them watching television. (It was difficult for him to deny this because Dora's mother knew that he was in there with the girls, allegedly watching television.) Dora's mother and Fred's wife discussed the question of informing the police and they decided not to do so, especially because neither Dora's mother nor Dora wanted to go to court. All agreed that Fred needed "careful watching" and that he would not be given the opportunity to be in the same room alone with children.

One could argue that the police should have been informed and that these overtures were just that, *overtures* that were the beginning of more serious molestation. I do not deny this. One could argue, as well, that Dora's mother and Fred's wife were contributing to the perpetuation of his improper behavior by protecting him from criminal action, which might very well have been initiated had these overtures been reported to the police. In fact, were I to have been consulted at that point, I would have been required by law to report this overture and would have pointed out to Dora's mother and Fred's wife that they were contributing to the perpetuation and even entrenchment of his problems. At the same time, I would have complimented Dora's mother for her dealing with the situation in a matter-of-fact way and would have pointed out to Carol's mother her overreaction and would have tried to "nip in the bud" the problems that I anticipated would take place if such hysterical overreaction was to continue. But all that never happened because my first contact with this family did not take place until 13 months later. Last, my focus here is not on the issue of the depth of Fred's psychopathology but the actual encounter that he did have with Carol and the hysterical reactions surrounding it.

Two days after Fred's overture, Carol's mother was still extremely upset and crying uncontrollably. She brought Carol to her own therapist, whom she had started to see two years previously, after she had given birth to a stillborn baby. The therapist suggested that Carol write a letter to Fred expressing her anger. With her mother's support, Carol did write such a letter. It was then that Carol began having nightmares in which she reexperienced the sexual events. In each of these dreams, Carol was trying to escape from Fred. It is to be noted that the nightmares did not begin during the days immediately following the sexual overtures; rather, they followed exposure to the mother's ongoing state of agitation and the letter that she wrote approximately one week later.

There is no question that the mother's overreaction and the therapist's advice contributed to Carol's hysteria, one of the manifestations of which was the nightmares. Both the mother and the therapist were keeping the issue alive and not letting memory of the encounter dissipate. Furthermore, the letter-writing recommendation was naive, based as it was on the assumption that expressing anger per se is therapeutic. Although this may certainly be the case at times, especially when such expression may very well improve a situation, in this case it was ill advised. First, as mentioned, it keeps the memories of the event embedded in the brain circuitry and thereby lessens the likelihood of natural dissipation. It also communicates the message that a terrible crime has been committed. This is the opposite of what one wants to do in such cases. One wants to minimize the implications of the encounter and point out that the only thing that actually happened was Fred's superficial contact with a small area on the left side of Carol's breast, *over* her training bra. Furthermore, the likelihood of Fred answering such a letter was very low in that admitting that he made such an overture might subject him to criminal action. Not surprisingly, the letter was never answered.

Within the next few weeks Carol developed eye tics. Over the months these spread to her arms and legs and were still present at the time I saw her in consultation one year after the onset of the eye tics. Because the tics were progressing, her pediatrician was concerned that she might be exhibiting manifestations of a Tourette's disorder and so referred her to a pediatric neurologist. Although he did not consider Tourette's disorder to be likely, he embarked upon a whole series of medications. First, she was placed on Catapress (an antihypertensive agent reputed to reduce tics), which was not helpful. She was then switched to Haldol (a very potent antipsychotic), which did not help either. Then she was switched to Orap (an antipsychotic agent, which is also reported to be useful in the treatment of Tourette's disorder), which produced Parkisonian symptoms—especially tremors. Cogentin was prescribed for this common side effect of antipsychotic medications. When Orap also proved useless for the tics, she was switched to Trilafon (another antipsychotic), which also did not help. Finally, at the time I saw her, she was on Clonopin (an anticonvulsant, reputed to reduce tics), which, again, did not prove efficacious. All medications produced fatigue, dry mouth, and occasional tremors (especially Orap).

As best I could ascertain, all this treatment was symptomatic, and no one considered the possibility that Carol was suffering with hysteria, hysteria generated by her mother's overreaction to the sexual encounter with Fred. I personally believe that the one-year regimen of medications produced some irreversible damage to Carol's brain, although I cannot be certain about this. Obviously, Parkinsonian symptoms are a manifestation of brain cell irritation and possibly injury. Only future research will confirm or refute what I have just said. In any case, Carol has served as a guinea pig for such research. I consider it a sad commentary on the field of biological psychiatry that proper attention is not being given to this widespread misuse of psychotropic medications.

Throughout the ensuing months Carol became progressively more preoccupied with the "sexual molestation" and began experiencing anxiety attacks. She also became depressed and would periodically break into tears. All these symptoms resulted in an impairment in school performance. Accordingly, the mother enlisted the aid of her teachers to provide Carol with reassurance and support, especially during the crying spells that she periodically exhibited, often in front of the class. All this commotion and attention, of course, is typical of the way in which hysteria spreads, and the supporters in school were basically serving as "enablers," thereby intensifying Carol's symptoms. They were providing further support for the mother's belief that Carol had been seriously traumatized.

One month prior to my consultation, at the time of the first anniversary of her molestation, there was a dramatic exacerbation of Carol's symptoms. Specifically, she became progressively more depressed and tense, and her anxiety attacks increased in frequency to two to three times a day. She also became progressively fearful of going to school, so much so that the day of the consultation was the fourth day during which she did not attend at all. Her depression had become so formidable and her crying spells and anxiety attacks so frequent that proper attention to her schoolwork became impossible. Yet, no one identified these blatant symptoms of hysteria. In addition, over the course of the school year she was seeing a school guidance counselor, who was providing her with support and alleged therapy. From what I could learn of this "treatment," the psychologist was providing even further support for the belief that Carol had been seriously traumatized, fueling even further the hysterical symptoms.

On the day prior to my consultation, Carol's mother went to the district attorney to look into the question of pressing criminal charges against Fred. She was told that because Carol was over the age of 11, the decision was hers regarding whether or not to press charges. Carol decided not to do so because she did not wish to face the inevitable court appearance(s) that was entailed. I consider it fortunate for Carol that she did not wish to provide testimony. One could argue that she was thereby providing unjustifiable and unwarranted protection for Fred. This I do not deny. However, with regard to Carol's symptoms, the decision was judicious in that such testimony would have intensified her symptoms, especially because it would have entrenched the notion that she had been subjected to a heinous crime, one for which a person might justifiably be sent to jail. Unfortunately, had this step not been taken prior to my consultation, I would have been required by law to report

Fred's overture to the child protection people, thereby contributing to the intensification of my patient's pathology. Unfortunately, at this time, therapists are not permitted to involve themselves in such considerations.

Interestingly, Dora's parents, after the aforementioned discussions with Fred and his wife, did not pursue the matter further. They decided that the best way to deal with the situation was for the family to go on with the normal routines of life. The parents decided not to discuss the matter further with Dora but to exercise proper precautions regarding Fred's being alone with any young children. They believed that their warning to Fred to stay away would be heeded (which it was, especially because reporting the episode to the police was seriously discussed), and their advice to their daughter not to be alone with Fred would also work (which it did). It was not particularly difficult to implement this program because Fred did not live in Dora's home and the family's contacts with him, even prior to these events, was minimal.

One might view the situation here as a controlled experiment. Both 12-year-old girls were exposed, at the same time, to an identical sexual overture, the only difference being that the perpetrator used his left hand with one girl and his right hand with the other. One set of parents responded hysterically to the overture and the other responded in a far more judicious and nonhysterical fashion. The child of hysterical parents developed hysteria and other concomitant symptoms such as anxiety, anxiety attacks, school phobia, crying spells, depression, tics, and generalized incapacitation. The child of the nonhysterical parents developed no symptoms at all. It has been rare in my experience that I have had the opportunity to be involved in such a "controlled experiment."

In my interview with the parents alone, they informed me that, although Carol began menstruating at age 11, she had not noted significant breast development nor, to the best of the parents' knowledge, had she spoken about any sexual urges. They agreed with me that Carol's question while being molested, "Why is he doing this to me?" indicated that she had no understanding of sexual arousal. Basically, they considered Carol to be quite confused about sex and all that had happened to her since the encounter with Fred. They also informed me that in the third grade Carol had been diagnosed as learning disabled and her IQ was in the low 90s. Although in a regular classroom, she had always received supplemental instruction. Accordingly, it was the teachers in the resource room who were giving her the primary support and extra attention because of the low teacher/student ratio there. In the course of that segment of my interview it was apparent to me that the mother was much more hysterical than the father and cried at many points during the course of my interview.

When I saw Carol alone, projective tests were administered. On the Draw-a-Person Test the first figure she drew was a female. The figure was minuscule and confined to the lower right-hand corner of the 8-1/2 x 11 sheet of paper that she was given. She stated that the girl (Ruth) was 11 years old. Ruth was described as shy and interested in a certain boy (Bob), but she had mixed feelings about his making an overture. A girlfriend of hers (Sarah), unbeknownst to Ruth, asked Bob to ask Ruth to go with him to a dance. Ruth got angry at Sarah for her unrequested intervention, but then was happy also that she had served as an intermediary for her. On the one hand, this is a normal, age-appropriate fantasy. Children of this age typically involve themselves in such "networking." On the other hand, the story might reflect Carol's ambivalence about sexual overtures, a derivative of the hysteria surrounding Carol's experience with Fred. Also of note is the fact that Ruth is 11 years old, two years younger than Carol. On the Draw-a-Person test people commonly depict individuals in their own age bracket. Learning-disabled children, however, often depict children younger than themselves because they feel (often justifiably) that they are functioning at a younger level. The depiction of a younger child might also be a manifestation of Carol's dependency, immaturity, and the desire to regress.

On the Draw-a-Person figure of opposite sex, Carol drew a boy, even smaller than the figure of the girl. This boy (Ted) is nine years old. Ted is harassed by another boy (Jack), who keeps asking him for money. Ted is afraid to say no, and so he gives his money to Jack. All of Ted's friends urge him to assert himself with Jack and to not, by any means, give over the money. Finally, Ted builds up the courage to refuse Jack. As a result, Jack returns the money and stops harassing Ted. We see here, again, the passivity element already depicted in the first Draw-a-Person story. Learning disabled children are often passive. The story deals with conflict over self-assertion. Perhaps this is related to the sexual encounter in which Carol did not assert herself. Carol subsequently learned that she was being exploited and had failed to assert herself properly at the time. In this story she is asserting herself, and it thereby represents a therapeutic advance. However, this fantasy could have other sources, especially the LD source in that children who suffer with this problem are often very passive. Most important, Ted is nine years old, four years Carol's junior. We see here, once again, the immaturity and possibly regressive elements. One cannot say whether these immaturity manifestations relate to Carol's hysteria. Specifically, regression is a common response to trauma. Although the trauma here is not sexual molestation, there is a trauma: the induction of hysteria. Perhaps this kind of a fantasy would have been present anyway in this LD youngster.

Carol was then administered the Draw-a-Family Test. The family she drew consisted of a mother, a father, and a ten-year-old son (Ralph), who was a bully in school. The school personnel received many complaints from parents asking the school to keep Ralph under control. Unfortunately, the school was not successful in suppressing Ralph's antisocial behavior, no matter what methods they tried. Ralph's parents, then, tried to get him psychological help.

Carol denied that anyone picked on her, nor did she have any inclinations to engage in such behavior. I believe the story represents underlying feelings of anger that are pressing for expression, even in an antisocial way. Carol would like to lash out at the world but is keeping everything bottled up. She expresses her anger through this fantasy. Converting herself into a boy provides her with a more common vehicle for such expression and, via the mechanism of displacement, does not have to consider herself responsible for engaging in unacceptable behavior. So great is the need to express such anger that traditional school methods of discipline do not work. The story even ends without a resolution to this problem. Ralph only goes for "psychological help," but nothing is said regarding whether the help is successful. Perhaps Carol's anger relates to her thirteen-month period of hysteria. Perhaps she is angry at her parents for having reacted so hysterically to Fred's sexual encounter. Perhaps the anger relates to the anger generated toward Fred, especially by the therapist who told her to express her anger in a letter to him, an expression that proved futile. Hysteria generates anger. Hysteria allows for a socially acceptable vehicle for anger expression, especially when there is a scapegoat.

Carol was then asked what person she would choose to be if she could not be herself but could choose any person in the whole history of the world, living or dead, past or present, real or from books, famous or not. Carol's first choice: "Janet Jackson, because she's a famous singer and the sister of Michael Jackson." Carol's second choice: "Julia Roberts, the actress, because she's pretty and she's a good actress." Her third choice: "Mariah Carey, the singer, because she's a famous singer." I then asked Carol to select a fourth choice, because her third choice was very similar to her first. Carol's fourth choice: "My girlfriend Dora, because she's sweet and she's hanging out with the guys."

I considered the first three responses to be in the normal range and age appropriate with no particular reference to the sexual encounter and its derivative problems. The fourth response suggests some envy of her girlfriend, Dora, who is now receiving the attention of boys. Carol was not enjoying such attentions at that point. This may be normal envy, unrelated to the experience with Fred. However, considering Carol's depression, withdrawal, and crying spells in the classroom, it is not likely that she would be viewed as desirable for age-appropriate sexual overtures by boys her age.

Carol was then asked what person she would choose *not* to be, just to be sure that she wasn't transformed into someone whom she did not like. Her first choice: "My girlfriend, Janet, because she's got lots of family problems." Carol's second choice: "Me, because I've got lots of problems like tics, since I was molested." Her third choice: "Michael Jackson, because he was convicted [sic] of molesting a boy." The responses here strongly suggest residual reactions to Fred's sexual overtures. Like Janet, Carol has family problems. However, in Carol's case the family problems were self-induced, at least the hysteria element. So great are these problems that she would not want to be herself because she was molested (response #2). We see here an excellent example of hysterical overreaction. The 13 months of hysteria over the five-minute sexual encounter have resulted in such feelings of self-denigration that Carol no longer wants to be herself. This is a common response provided by individuals with feelings of self-loathing. The third choice, Michael Jackson, certainly relates to Fred, whom she would single out as an individual into whom she would not want to be transformed. I am certain that

Carol would have given entirely different responses, responses unrelated to hysteria, had the parents not reacted hysterically to Fred's overture.

I then invited the parents back into the consultation room and told them that I believed that they had overreacted significantly to Fred's sexual overture. I tried to place the encounter with Fred in proper prospective: a five-minute time frame during which there was some physical contact between Fred's left hand and Carol's yet-to-be-developed left breast. I tried to impress upon the parents that their reactions to this encounter were enormously exaggerated and that the numerous psychological problems with which Carol was suffering had possibly one percent to do with this overture and were 99 percent the result of their exaggerated reactions.

Fortunately, I had available the "control case" of Carol's girlfriend Dora, whose mother reacted in a sane fashion and had put the encounter into proper prospective. I pointed out that Dora suffered none of Carol's difficulties during the ensuing 13 months, and Carol's parents appreciated that. I pointed out that they had enlisted a whole parade of people who were fueling the hysteria, including the special ed teachers, the homeroom teacher, the school guidance counselor, the mother's therapist, and the pediatric neurologist—who had prescribed a whole series of medications that were probably adding neurological difficulties to a child whose brain might previously have had some compromises in association with her learning disability.

Carol's father immediately breathed a sigh of relief and said that throughout the whole 13 months he recognized, at some level, that his wife might have been overreacting. As I suspected, the mother was somewhat dubious about what I said. After all, a whole series of "professionals" had been in full agreement with her that something terrible had occurred and I was the only one who thought otherwise. I responded that she would do best not to count noses and merely take a poll in deciding things like this, but to address herself to whose "theory" appeared more reasonable, mine or theirs. Again, I tried to emphasize that the whole event lasted only five minutes and involved only fingertips on a yet-to-be-developed breast. I emphasized Hamlet's wisdom: "There's nothing either good or bad, but thinking makes it so." I pointed out that they had seen terrible danger in a situation in which there was absolutely none, because proper and effective precautions had been taken to prevent any further such encounters by Fred.

I then suggested that the parents call the pediatric neurologist and communicate to him my findings and my belief that Carol should be weaned from all medications. Everyone agreed that after all these months no medication had had any effect on Carol's tics, and they also agreed with me that adding all these medications to a learning-disabled child was not judicious, considering the possibility that some kind of brain cell compromise might be playing a role in her learning disability. I told them that it was not my role to wean her from the medications because I had not prescribed them in the first place.

I advised them to call a moratorium on further discussion of the "molestation" because such discussions could only entrench thoughts of the encounter into Carol's brain circuitry and thereby bring about a perpetuation and even an intensification of her derivative symptoms. I suggested that they allow Carol to talk about her experiences with Fred during the next few days but to inform her, at the same time, that they would soon be refusing to discuss the matter at length.

With regard to therapy, I informed the parents of the dilemma: treating and thereby entrenching the symptoms or not treating and depriving Carol of the benefits that could potentially be derived from psychotherapy. I explained to them the principle of psychological muckraking and told them that I did not wish to involve myself in this because it is generally antitherapeutic. Accordingly, I suggested a follow-up appointment in two weeks in order to then assess the whole situation again and decide what further therapeutic work, if any, would be indicated. The parents asked me if I had communicated any of this to Carol. I told them that I had not and chose not to do so pending their agreement and approval. The father immediately agreed that I should communicate my findings and recommendations to Carol, and the mother reluctantly agreed, also. The mother was able to recognize the judiciousness of what I was saying but could not be expected to change her mind completely after 13 months of hysteria spinning in her own brain circuitry.

Had even one parent refused to permit me to communicate these findings to Carol, I would not have done so against the protestation of the other. Therapeutic recommendations made about a child need the support of both parents if they are to be effective. If only one parent has conviction for the therapeutic program, the child is likely to be placed in the middle of a conflict, like a rope in a tug-of-war. And this cannot but be antitherapeutic. Furthermore, we are living in dangerous times with regard to litigiousness. Malpractice suits are ubiquitous. To implement a therapeutic recommendation against the wishes of even one parent places a therapist at risk for such lawsuits. Accordingly, had only one parent approved of my approach, I would have told them that these were my recommendations and would have brought the matter to a close. My feelings would have been that the child is theirs, and if they wish to deal with her injudiciously and even detrimentally, they are free to do so. My obligation is to *try* to help, not to force my treatment approaches upon anyone.

Accordingly, I called Carol into the consultation room to join her parents and me. I reviewed my findings and recommendations, especially with regard to the family's overreaction. Carol's girlfriend, Dora, served as a convenient example of the proper response to Fred's overtures. Carol, her learning disability notwithstanding, readily appreciated that Dora was not suffering with any of her problems and yet had been subjected to the exact same "molestation." I informed Carol that all her fears, depression, anxiety attacks, and other symptoms were the result of exaggerated reactions to what had happened. I tried to place in proper perspective the actual event of five minutes of superficial contact with the left side of her left breast.

I also told Carol, quite firmly, that she *must* attend school the next day. I impressed upon her that attending school is a law and that not attending school is breaking the law. I informed her that there was absolutely no reason why she shouldn't go to school and that her mother was going to advise the teachers that they are not to give her special attention when she cries about the molestation. I also told Carol that I was recommending that the weekly therapy with the school counselor be discontinued because it was only making Carol worse. It was making her think about the molestation rather than forgetting about it. I told her that I had advised her parents to inform the school guidance counselor that they wanted no further therapeutic sessions and to explain to her the reasons why. I told them that they should not expect her to be in agreement with me, but the important thing was that if they, as the parents, were in agreement with me, they had every right to discontinue the treatment. I told them that I would be pleased to speak with the school guidance counselor if she were interested in talking to me. At that point, the two-hour consultation ended.

Two weeks later Carol returned with her mother. Her father asked the mother to communicate with me that things were now back to normal, that he was very pleased, and that he did not feel the need to attend the session and thereby miss work and lose income. He told his wife to relate to me how grateful he was over Carol's dramatic improvement. Carol stated that she had been upset with me for a day or two following our meeting because so many other people had told her how terrible the experience she had was. However, with the help of her mother and father she came to realize that I was right and that what had occurred was not worth all the grief that everybody was suffering. We see here a good example of how parents can serve as assistant therapists as part of the treatment process and that those therapists who strictly avoid significant contact with parents are compromising their work. Elsewhere (Gardner, 1992b), I have elaborated on this principle in detail.

Carol reported that the day following our consultation, although somewhat fearful, she did go to school and had been attending throughout every day since. During the first day of her return, however, she wanted her mother to stay with her in case she started to cry. Her mother, fortunately, refused to indulge her this and reassured her that there was nothing to cry about. Carol did not cry. We see here how hysteria can spread when those around generate emotion and how it can be decompressed when those around shut off the emotional flow. When the mother returned Carol to school the next morning, she immediately went to Carol's homeroom teacher, as well as the teachers in the resource room, and told them the results of the consultation. They agreed with the mother that what I had to say made sense and they promised that they would not indulge Carol anymore but, instead, would require her to move along, do her work, and not dwell on the sex abuse.

Unfortunately, the guidance counselor (as I might have predicted) was somewhat less receptive to my advice. She insisted that the intensification of Carol's symptoms indicated that more, not less, therapy was warranted. She insisted that the intensification of the symptoms was related to the fact that more abuses had actually occurred and that "more was coming out" and that with increased therapy even more information about the abuses would be likely to emerge. Yet, she had to admit that in her one year of "treatment" nothing more than the lateral breast contact had been disclosed. This is typical of the approach used by overzealous evaluators, which I have discussed at length elsewhere (Gardner, 1991a, 1992a, 1995a). The mother, fortunately, was not convinced by the guidance counselor's arguments and insisted that she not treat Carol anymore. The guidance counselor, reluctantly, submitted to the mother's demand. Actually, the guidance counselor had no choice, in that any parent has the right to prohibit a school guidance counselor from evaluating and/or treating his (her) child.

The mother also called the pediatric neurologist and apprised him of my findings. He, too, was reluctant to wean Carol from medication but had to agree that it had not in any way improved Carol's tics. On the day I saw Carol, two weeks later, the weaning process was two days short of completion.

Interestingly, when I saw Carol two weeks later her depression, ongoing tension, and anxiety attacks were no longer present. In fact, all these symptoms evaporated within three days of my consultation. Furthermore, during the two-week period there was a progressive diminution in Carol's preoccupation with the encounter with Fred—to the point where, at the time of my second meeting, they were rare.

In the course of the second meeting the issue of criminal prosecution of Fred again came up. As mentioned, Carol was already reluctant to press charges, something she was old enough to decide on, because she did not want to go to court. Now she had another and more important reason for not doing so, namely, that going to court would inevitably require her to think more about the molestation and this, she came to appreciate, would make her worse. No one in the family believed now that this was a reasonable price for Carol to pay in order to bring Fred to "justice." Furthermore, the mother had informed me that she had discussed the question of pressing charges with three women friends, all of whom were encouraging her to urge Carol to press charges. All three insisted, "Fred ought to be in jail." However, the mother did not submit to these pressures and recognized that such submission would be psychologically detrimental to her daughter.

I did not know at the time I had set up the second session whether it would be the last. The main determinant as to whether I would see

Carol more was the persistence of symptoms. One should only treat if there *are* symptoms; one cannot treat meaningfully to prevent the onset or recurrence of symptoms. Under such circumstances the therapy becomes sterile and the therapist does not have a meaningful "handle" to use as a point of departure for therapeutic inquiry. There must be pain, there must be discomfort, there must be some kind of an issue that motivates the patient to talk about something related to psychopathology. Furthermore, when one is treating children who have been traumatized, one does not want to muckrake and entrench old preoccupations into the brain circuitry. Because no such symptoms were present, I decided not to set up any further appointments.

The session closed with the mother's telling me that her husband wished her to communicate to me that he was extremely grateful and that it was "the best $250 he had ever spent in his whole life."

HYSTERICAL REACTIONS TO NORMAL SEXUAL URGES

Virginia was referred for treatment at the age of 11 years 2 months with a five-month history of preoccupation and guilt about thoughts that she was "raping" other children. In Virginia's scheme of things, *raping* referred to touching other children's genitals. These fantasies also included other children touching her genitals. The guilt she felt over such thoughts was formidable, so much so that she feared God would put her to death during the night. Accordingly, she suffered with high levels of tension and sleeplessness. One month prior to the initial consultation, while cuddling her one-year-old half-brother, she tickled him on the buttocks and was afraid that she had sexually abused him. Furthermore, on one occasion, while in church, she had the thought that she would like to touch the genitals of a little baby girl. And her guilt over this was enormous.

In the course of my inquiry for background information that might provide insight into Virginia's excessive guilt, I learned that from ages one to six she had spent significant time at the home of her paternal grandmother, during which period she spent many hours watching soap operas. She still had faint memories of these programs, including some of the sexual encounters depicted therein. It was my belief that these programs provided some primitive sexual titillation that may have played some role in Virginia's subsequent symptoms. In addition, it was clear that Virginia was still somewhat "hooked" on soap operas, because after she started school she would watch them whenever she had the opportunity, even though discouraged from doing so by her mother. These had the effect of sexualizing Virginia and contributed, I believed, to her subsequent symptoms.

Virginia's father died when she was four and her mother, Cindy, and stepfather, George, married when she was six-and-a-half. Although Virginia missed her father significantly, George appeared on the scene within a few months after his death and appears to have taken over quite well. I could not see any relationship between the death of her father and the presenting symptoms, although one could certainly argue that there might be some relationship. Children of four often feel responsible for events over which they have no control in actuality. Perhaps excessive guilt related to such feelings about her father's death. However, this must only be a speculation because there was nothing in my consultation to provide verification for this theory. Furthermore, even if this factor were operative, it was certainly a small one compared to the other guilt-evoking experiences she subsequently had, experiences that I could conclude with certainty were playing a role in her exaggerated guilt over normal sexual thoughts and feelings.

From the ages of five to eight, a divorced neighbor took Virginia along with his four-year-old daughter on many trips and excursions. Although Cindy was basically pleased with the arrangement, especially because it provided Virginia with a friend, she was always somewhat suspicious of this man's motivations and, on at least 20 occasions during that period, asked Virginia if the neighbor had ever touched her genitals. Virginia repeatedly denied ever involving herself in such an encounter. However, the question engendered in Virginia's mind a visual image of just such an encounter and I am certain it played a role in bringing about the presenting problems. The question not only engendered a fantasy of a sexual encounter but was associated with warnings that such encounters were bad and sinful, and these indoctrinations could not but produce guilt over sexual feelings in Virginia, guilt that appeared in stronger form during the prepubertal period—in association with the stronger sexual urges that appeared at that time.

At the age of six Virginia and a six-year-old girlfriend danced naked while listening to music on the radio. The two girls made believe that they were stripteasers. When Virginia confessed to her mother that she had involved herself in this game five years previously, Cindy gave Virginia mixed messages. On the one hand, the mother recognized that the game might be considered in the normal range, on the other hand Cindy was excessively condemning of her for having engaged in it. At the time of the initial consultation Virginia felt significant guilt over this game and believed that it was a manifestation of some deep-seated perversion in her and her girlfriend.

Virginia's maternal aunt, Brenda, lived only a few blocks away and was a frequent visitor to the home. Brenda was the mother of three girls—ages one, three, and five—and was literally obsessed with fears that her daughters would be sexually abused. Brenda not only feared that her husband might sexually abuse them but that her father, Virginia's maternal grandfather, might sexually abuse Brenda's children as well. There was hardly a visit to the home in which Brenda did not talk openly about her concerns regarding the sexual abuse of her children. This exposure also played a role in inducing in Virginia fantasies of being sexually molested as well as formidable guilt for having such thoughts. It is important to note that Brenda was also obsessed with watching soap operas, made tapes of those she missed, and watched them with Virginia on many occasions. On occasion, when Cindy learned that Virginia had watched soap operas at Brenda's house, she was critical of Brenda for allowing Virginia to have such exposure.

In addition, at various points in her educational program Virginia had been exposed to sex-abuse prevention programs, which often have the effect of producing unnecessary fears, vigilance, and even sexual titillation in children, the benefits of these programs notwithstanding.

It was clear that Virginia had never been sexually molested and the fantasies she was having were in the normal range for a child her age. However, over many years she had been subjected to a series of guilt-evoking communications from significant figures and was exposed, as

TREATMENT OF SEX-ABUSE HYSTERIA 457

well, to the ambient sex-abuse hysteria that we have been witnessing in the United States since the early 1980s.

The transcript below presents verbatim a two-hour interview. Although originally designed to be a consultation only, it turned out to be a therapeutic experience as well. I had made no promises beforehand to the parents that I would be able to provide therapeutic benefits in just one interview, but if the situation allowed for such therapeutic input I would be pleased to provide it. This family had traveled over 1,500 miles in order to consult with me and so I felt that any attempts on my part to provide additional therapeutic input in the course of the consultation would be especially appreciated. At first I had not planned to videotape the interview. However, after a few minutes it became apparent that videotaping might be useful, especially because I sensed at the outset that I might be able to provide some therapeutic input and that reviewing the tape at home could be therapeutically beneficial for the patient. The tape was set up, then, after about 10 minutes of interviewing, during which Virginia and her parents described the aforementioned presenting problems. In the room at the time of the interview were the mother, the father, and Virginia herself. The parents remained throughout and, as will be seen, intermittently participated.

Gardner: Today is the 11th of December 1993 and we're here with your mom and stepfather and they're sitting there right on the side. You were talking about your thoughts about rape, right.

Patient: (Nods affirmatively.)

Gardner: And you had thoughts about a little girl, and you were telling me that you were having very disturbing thoughts. And I was saying to you—you thought these were criminal and sinful, right?

Patient: (Nods affirmatively.)

Gardner: And I said to you that they're not crimes, there is no crime for having a thought. Nobody's sentenced or put in jail for having a thought, at least not in America in 1993. Most people's religions today do not say that a thought is a sin. And your parents tell me that in your religion a thought is not a sin. What you *do* can be a sin. And I want to tell you a story now that is on this point. It's an old story about a king of Persia. Do you know where Persia is?

Patient: (Nods affirmatively.)

Gardner: It's the present-day country of Iran. Have you ever heard of that?

Patient: (Shakes head negatively.)

Gardner: Iran is a country in the Middle East. Anyway, it's far away. It's near the Holy Land, near Palestine, Israel, Egypt, and that part of the world. Anyway, this king of Persia had heard a lot of things about the prophet Moses. Did you ever hear of Moses from the Bible?

Patient: (Nods affirmatively.)

Gardner: And he heard about what a great prophet Moses was and he heard from far and wide what a good leader of his people he was and how religious and kind and giving and wise he was. So he sent his—these were very olden days, they didn't have photographers or anything—his artists to Moses' country in the Holy Land and he said, "Paint me a picture of Moses so I can show it to my advisors and they can tell me by looking at his face what kind of person he is inside so I can copy him and become a great leader and a wise man like him."

So his artists went to the Holy Land and a very skilled artist painted a picture of Moses and they brought it back to the Persian king. And he sent it to his wise men to look at it and the wise men came back and they said, "We have very bad news for you, King. This man Moses is a fraud. He is despicable. He's dishonest. He's a liar, and he's a thief. He's a pervert; I wouldn't trust him. He is one of the lowest, slimiest worms that ever crawled on the surface of the earth. You can tell that by looking at his face."

Well, the king was very upset. He had heard all these wonderful things about Moses and now his artists brought him back this picture, which they swore was an exact reproduction from the most skilled artist in all of Persia, and his wise men, whom he trusted are telling him, "Don't trust this man, and if you follow him, you'll do terrible things."

So the king decided that he would go to the Holy Land himself to see Moses. And he'd watch Moses and live there with Moses and learn directly for himself what kind of man he was. And before he left for the Holy Land he said to his advisors and artists, "If any of you have deceived me, when I come back whether the artists have not painted properly, or the wise men have not advised me well, I'm going to cut off your heads." In those days they did things like that.

So the king went to the Holy Land and there he lived with Moses for about six months, at the end of which time he said to Moses, "I've watched you and you are without question everything I have heard—that you're a wise man, that you're a great leader of your people, and that you are very kind. You are good, and you are a holy man, and you are a saint-like person. I am very upset with my advisors." And then he told Moses the story of the picture and told him what his advisors have said. And then the king said to Moses, "I'm going to go back to Persia and I'm going to behead those people."

And Moses said, "Don't do that. They're right!"

And the king said, "How could they be right?"

Moses answered, "Your artists painted an accurate picture of me and your wise men have read the picture correctly. I am everything they said I was. Inside my heart, inside my brain, are all of the things they say. I have the most vile, most evil, most terrible murderous thoughts in my brain and in my heart. I have had every one of those thoughts that your wise men have attributed to me. My life is a constant struggle to keep them inside and not act out and do the things that my thoughts and my feelings tell me to do."

What do you think of that story?

Patient: Sounds like me with the thoughts.

Gardner: Right! Sounds like you. So far what you have told me is not different from what other people have. But you seem to be very guilty about those thoughts. Huh? Is that correct?

Patient (nodding affirmatively): Sort of. Yes.

I consider the story to be a powerful one. In fact, it is one of my favorites, not only for use in the therapeutic situation but in understanding myself and others as well. It is an excellent example of how the metaphor can serve as a valuable therapeutic tool. It enrichens the therapeutic package. Were I to have presented the same message with a simple statement, it is not as likely that the message would have sunk in. This is the beauty and the value of the metaphor.

Gardner: I have to learn more about it—how many you have, what kind they are, but I know already that these thoughts are no different than the kinds that everybody has, and *your* problem is that you feel too bad about them. Now I want to hear more about them so I'll be in a better position to understand what those thoughts are. In this way there's a better chance I'll be able to help you. Okay? So tell me, in church you were having these thoughts about a one-year-old baby, about raping a little baby. I'd like you to tell me the picture that you had in your mind.

Patient: She was just standing in front of me. And when I had got home—I had already had the thought in church—and I got home and told my mom about it.

Gardner: You haven't told me what the thought was.

Patient: The thought was taking a little baby and touching her . . . (pause) . . .

Gardner: Touching her what?

Patient: Her private place.

Gardner: Her private place? What do you call that in your house?

Patient: That, private place.

Gardner: There's a name. What name do you call it?

Patient: I know what it is, but I mean . . .

Gardner: Don't you have a name for it? Everything has a name, or most things have names.

Patient: (Turns to mother.)

Mother (to patient): Tell him the word that you know. You can say the word.

Patient: (Patient shakes head negatively.)

Mother: Please, you can say the word.

Gardner: What's the word? You need practice in saying things like that? You must have a word for that in your house.

Patient: We don't really say it, what we just say is that, but . . .

Gardner: You can say it here.

Patient: No, we say "private." That's what we say. We say the "private area" in our house.

Gardner: "The private area." That's the only word you use—just private area?

Patient: Well, yeah, we never say the—but I know what it is.

Gardner: That's all you say, private area.

Mother: I've used the technical, medical name—the physiological name before. (Mother turns to patient.) You can say that word.

Gardner (turning to mother): You think she knows it, but she's ashamed to say it?

Stepfather: Yes.

Gardner: You need practice in overcoming shyness. That's what you need. Your mother says you know the name.

Patient: Well, on a girl or . . .

Gardner: What is it called on a girl?

Patient (putting her head down in her hands): Can I write it or something?

There are some readers, I am certain, who would think that I am pushing this patient too hard. Obviously, she was embarrassed over verbalizing the name for the female genitals, and one could argue that my approach was too coercive. One could also argue that she needed practice (as I had said previously) talking about such matters and that such practice could contribute to the reduction of the guilt, which was clearly a formidable problem for her. We are dealing here with a question of the therapist's judgment. On the one hand, one does not want to push patients so hard that they go into states of panic. On the other hand, one does not want to pull back so far that no anxiety is ever engendered. One must find some middle course. Generally, I proceed to the point where the patient is experiencing tolerable anxiety and/or tension and then will pull back. Although there was some embarrassment here on Virginia's part, she was not at a high level of tension and I therefore proceeded in the hope that my comfort in talking about female genitals would contribute to her comfort via the process of identification. In addition, I was trying to provide her with a corrective emotional experience in which she would come to see that the utterance of this forbidden word did not bring about the terrible consequences she anticipated. Having her parents in the room probably made it easier for her to say the forbidden word because it was her mother, after all, who had taught it to her in the first place.

Gardner: I know the word. I know the word. I can tell you I know the word, but what I want to know is . . . I am asking you to say it for practice because you seem to be shy and one of the treatments for shyness is to force yourself to do the things that you are shy about doing. That helps to overcome shyness.

You see you're here for only one visit. Right?

Patient: (Nods affirmatively.)

Gardner: You've come a long way and we only have a short time together. Right? And what I want to do, besides learning about you, I want to try to give you some advice and some help along the way. So this interview is called a diagnostic-therapeutic interview. That means that the diagnostic part helps me understand what your trouble is and the therapeutic part helps me give you some guidelines for how to help you with your troubles and that's why we're making a tape here, so that you can take it home and watch it when you get home. So I am asking you to try to get some practice in saying that word. See if you can do it. Hmm?

Patient: Right now?

Gardner: Right now. The best time is now.

Patient (in a whisper): It's vagina.

Gardner: Good for you. Congratulations. I'll shake your hand. (Gardner shakes patient's hand.) You said the word *vagina*. Was that so hard?

Patient (wiping tears from her eyes): Yeah.

Gardner: It was. What do you think will happen now that you've said it?

Patient: Nothing.

Gardner: Nothing at all?

Patient: (Shakes head negatively.)

Gardner: So what's so terrible? Did the thunder come? Did lightning flash? Did anybody punish you?

Patient: (Shakes head negatively.)

Gardner: That's a word. That's a standard word in the English language and like all words there are certain times and places to use it. You know? In certain conversations that's the right word to use. In other conversations it's a private matter, it's nobody's business. Right?

Patient: (Nods affirmatively.)

Gardner: Okay. Here in this office this is our business here, you know? Okay, now I want you to go back and I want you to tell me—it's not only important for you to say that word so you have practice in using it, but so I know what you're talking about when you speak.

Okay, so what about this little girl's vagina? What was your thought about this little girl's vagina?

Patient: My thought was to take her, and touch her.

Gardner: And touch her. Now, I'm asking you this question. When you say to touch her, was it with pleasure, or to hurt her, or what?

Patient: I can't answer that. I don't know.

Gardner: Did you want to harm her? Did you want to make her cry?

Patient: No, not really. I don't know what . . . I don't know.

Gardner: Okay. Now. Let me ask you this question. You are now 11 years old. Right?

Patient: (Nods affirmatively.)

Gardner: You were 11 about two months go. Right?

Patient: (Nods affirmatively.)

Gardner: And you are in the fifth grade. Now girls your age, as you know, start to have changes. Right?

Patient: (Nods affirmatively.)

Gardner: Do you know about that?

Patient: (Nods affirmatively.)

Gardner: Did you discuss that with your mom?

Patient: (Nods affirmatively.)

Gardner: Now what kind of changes do girls your age have?

Patient: Their period.

Gardner: Periods! What is a period?

Patient: You bleed.

Gardner: You bleed. Have you started to have your period yet?

Patient: (Shakes head negatively.)

Gardner: How do you feel about periods?

Patient: It doesn't bother me. I don't really think about it.

Gardner: Any girls you know who have started to have their periods?

Patient: Yeah. My best friend did.

Gardner: Oh yeah. How is she doing with that?

Patient: Didn't bother her.

Gardner: Didn't bother her. Okay, that's one change. So you're not upset about that. What other things happen to girls your age. Not necessarily your age, but a little older. What other changes happen?

Patient: I don't know . . . I don't really like saying this, but . . . they get bigger . . .

Gardner: They get bigger in what way?

Patient: Their chest.

Gardner: Their chests get bigger. What is that called?

Patient: Breasts.

Gardner: Their breasts, right. Okay. Has that started happening to you?

Patient: Not really.

Gardner: How do you feel about that change?

Patient: Doesn't bother me.

Gardner: Doesn't bother you. There are three ways of looking at it. Some are very excited and they're very proud and happy. Some are neutral. And some are, "Yuck, no way. I don't want that to happen." Which way are you?

Patient (shrugging): It doesn't bother me.

Gardner: Okay. Any other changes that you know of that happen to people your age?

Patient: I know something happens with hormones, but I don't know anything more about that.

Gardner: Okay. Now one of the things that can happen, not necessarily right now but after you start having your period, certainly, is you can start having babies. I assume you know how that happens. How do babies come?

Patient: The parents have to (whispers) have sex . . .

Gardner: It's hard for me to hear you when you whisper.

Patient (raises voice): The parents have to . . . it doesn't always happen, I guess.

Mother (to patient): Speak up.

Gardner: Have to what? I know this is not easy to talk about, but it's very important for your problem. That I can tell you right now. What do the parents do?

Patient: They have sex.

Gardner: Okay. You say they have sex. What does that mean? What are you picturing in your mind?

Patient (whispers): Oh God. Umm . . .

Gardner: Hmmm?

Patient: They don't . . . have clothes . . .

Gardner: But what did they do?

Patient: They don't have clothes on.

Mother: They don't have clothes on.

Gardner: Yeah, they don't have their clothes on. Then what do they do?

Patient: (Hides her face and cries.)

Obviously, Virginia was very embarrassed at this point. Had I the opportunity to see this patient over a period of time, I certainly would not have pushed this point further at that time. However, I did not have that luxury. Perhaps it would have been easier for her to speak about things had her parents not been in the room. One could argue that I should have asked her at that point if she would have felt more comfortable with her parents outside the room. I cannot deny that this criticism might be valid. At any rate, I decided not to drop the issue at that point, but I certainly was on the verge of doing so. I decided to "hang in" a little longer in the hope that Virginia would overcome her embarrassment and gain the therapeutic benefits of further conversation on this issue. As mentioned, my main purpose here was to make this patient more comfortable about sexual thoughts and feelings and thereby reduce the formidable guilt that she was feeling over such thoughts. And one way of reducing such guilt and shame is to talk about the guilt-evoking issues and having the living experience that others are not going to criticize her, mock her, or react in other ways that she anticipates will be detrimental and ego-debasing. Therapists who say to patients, "There's nothing to feel guilty about when you have such thoughts and feelings," may provide their patients with some therapeutic benefit. However, it is a relatively sterile experience compared to the actual living experience of verbalizing these unacceptable thoughts and observing directly that the anticipated consequences are not forthcoming.

>*Gardner*: You see, I think you need practice talking about that and I know this is embarrassing for you, but it's very good practice for you to help the problem that you have, that I can tell you.
>*Patient*: (Continues to cry.)
>*Mother*: Honey, you have to answer the questions yourself. You're doing good.
>*Stepfather*: You're not going to get into trouble for saying anything.
>*Patient*: I know, but . . .

One can see here how the parents are providing Virginia with support at this point. Had I decided to send them out of the room (an option that clearly has merit), I might have deprived myself of the support that they provided Virginia at this point. Therapy, if it is to be successful, is not smooth, nor is it painless. This does not mean that it must be horrendously painful, only that a certain degree of tolerance of discomfort is necessary if one is to benefit from the therapeutic process.

Mother: You've said these things before in class. You've heard them. You've heard them in class. We've talked.
Patient: I know we've talked.
Mother: Do you know how a baby is born? What has to happen?
Patient: I know, I've just said . . .
Mother: What does sex mean?
Patient: I have a hard time saying it.
Mother: What exactly . . . what has to happen to have a baby?
Patient: Well, she has a tube, and she has an egg, and she ovulates . . . and it's fertilized, and she has a baby.
Mother: How does the egg get fertilized?
Patient: The man . . . puts the . . .
Mother: The egg gets fertilized by the man.
Gardner: Okay, how does he do that? How does that happen?
Patient (crying): I don't know . . .
Gardner: Do you want some Kleenex? Here. How does that happen?
Patient: He . . . sticks . . . his private part . . .
Gardner: His private part. What is that called?
Patient: Penis.
Gardner: Right. He sticks it where?
Patient: Inside of her . . . inside of her vagina.
Gardner: Right. Was that so hard to say?
Patient: No.
Gardner: Did the house catch on fire?
Patient: No.
Gardner: Did lightning come down and strike you?
Patient: No.
Gardner: Is anybody saying you committed a sin or a crime?
Patient: No.
Gardner: If we had a silent movie of this—if we didn't have the sound track—they would think you that you had just confessed to a major crime. That you were just talking about one of the most terrible, sinful acts in the history of the world. Hmmm? Do you see how you're acting that way?

Patient: Yes.
Gardner: You have a very powerful conscience. You're a very guilty person. Hmmm?

At that point, it was clear that Virginia sensed a great feeling of relief. She had described the sexual act and had the living experience that nothing terrible happened after she had done so. I then reinforced her experience, thereby providing both positive reinforcement for what she had done as well as the therapeutic benefit of reducing shame and guilt.

Patient: Well, I was partially raised that way, I mean. . . .
Gardner: You were raised that way?
Patient: Partially, like how to make good grades, I couldn't make bad grades, I can now, and I don't get in trouble, like I did then.
Gardner: Okay, but where does all this guilt come from?
Patient: I don't know, but I always have felt guilty about things.
Gardner: You always have? Like what?
Patient: I don't know. . . . If I did something I made it a lot bigger than it really was.
Gardner: Like what, for instance?

Here, as is my standard pattern, I asked for specific examples. A therapeutic process in which the patient and doctor speak in generalizations only is often sterile and useless. It is only when the generalizations and abstractions are concretized by a specific example that the interchange is likely to be meaningful. The concrete example provides a meaningful point of departure for the interchange. Without such a point of departure the likelihood of deriving therapeutic benefit from an interchange of abstractions is very small.

Patient: I don't . . . (looks to mother) she told me something before. . . .
Mother: Tell him about the incident at school when you wrote the letter "s" and the word "ass."
Patient

to sign my yearbook. Well I didn't even ask, he just took it and signed it and put that I was a bitch, and an asshole, and that's all I think.

Gardner: What grade were you in?

Patient: Fourth grade. But then somebody else had written in my yearbook about "the trees, the grass, and I'm a pain in the ass," but wrote everything but the last letter "s" and I wrote that in, and then I got a referral to the principal for doing that.

Gardner: Okay, and is that why you became so guilty about words and sex and things like that?

Patient (looks to mother): My grandmother . . . died, a couple, a week ago, and I was really, really close to her and I thought that I had caused her to die.

Mother: Her grandmother was on nitroglycerine. She was 79.

Gardner: This is whose mother?

Mother: My deceased husband's mother.

Gardner: Okay.

Mother: She fell and broke her hip. Anyway, she was in the hospital, having had surgery, and she asked Virginia to give her her nitroglycerine and she did. And a week later she died from blood clots after surgery. So she connected it to the time that she gave her . . .

Patient (interrupting): Because they said it could have been something about medication, and too much, and we had gone to my aunt's to ask her about the details and she had said that night, "She'll tell you about the nitroglycerine" about too much or something, and . . .

Gardner: And you think it's somehow your fault.

Patient: (Nods affirmatively.)

I believe that the guilt Virginia described here was in a different category from that which had been focused on thus far in the session. The guilt here is in the category of a delusion of control that often looks like guilt but is not really true guilt. True guilt produces feelings of low self-worth in association with thoughts, feelings, and acts that the individual has learned, generally in childhood from significant figures, is wrong, bad, or sinful. Here, Virginia's feeling that her grandmother's death was her fault related to the need to control what was an uncontrollable event. She created the delusion that if she had somehow done something different with the nitroglycerine, her grandmother would still be alive. This is a common reaction to the death of loved ones but was basically unrelated to the guilt I was focusing on in this session. Elsewhere (Gardner, 1969a, 1969b, 1970) I have described in detail the phenomenon of guilt as a delusion of control. Accordingly, I returned Virginia to the issue of guilt over sexual thoughts and feelings.

Gardner: Okay, look. That is another kind of guilt. It's not the kind of guilt that we're talking about here. Now let's go back to the first thing we were talking about, about this "rape" of this little girl. Okay, let's go back to that. Now as I understand it, we were talking about changes that occur when people are having babies. Now let me ask you this question? What are your thoughts about that particular act in which a man puts his penis in a lady's vagina? What do you think of people doing that? What is your opinion?

Patient: Well, umm, when I was little I used to want to, but I don't anymore, because now I know what it is.

Gardner: Okay, when you were little you used to want to do that?

Patient: Yeah, but I was little—but I didn't really know what it was, but now I do know what it is and I don't want to do that.

When reviewing this transcript I realized that I had made a minor therapeutic error at this point. I should have asked Virginia at that moment about the circumstances under which, as a young child, she wanted to engage in sexual relations. A few minutes later, however, I realized that I had erred here and so I asked the question (see below).

Gardner: Okay, why don't you want to do that now?

Patient: I'm not supposed to until I get older.

Gardner: What is your understanding—and different people have different opinions on this—what is your understanding—you know, how you see yourself—with regard to that particular act? When you say when you're older . . . that could cover a lot of ground.

Patient: When I'm married.

Gardner: When you're married, okay. Besides having babies, do people do that for any other reason?

Patient: Because they love each other.

Gardner: Okay. Because they love each other. Okay. Do they do it for any *other* reason, as you understand it?

Patient: I don't think so.

Gardner: Okay. What are the feelings that people have when they do that? What is your understanding?

Patient: They're happy.

Gardner: Okay. Do they want to do it?

Patient: Most of the time.

Gardner: Is there a strong feeling of wanting to do it?

Patient: I don't know.

Gardner: When you said that you were a little kid you had thoughts of wanting to do that, how old were you then?

Patient: Well, I didn't necessarily have thoughts about wanting to do that—I mean—my mother was always telling me not to watch soap operas and I never will again, because when I was little I always did . . .

Gardner: You watched soap operas?

Patient: Yeah. And I never will again because that's where that came from when I was little, and they'd show stuff like that and I used to want to because I didn't know what was really happening.

Gardner: I see. And then they told you you couldn't watch that stuff?

Patient: Well, I could, but they suggested not. But this is before any of this started.

Gardner: I understand, but maybe that's something that's playing a role in all of this.

Patient: I'm not going to. I haven't watched them . . .

Gardner: You haven't watched them?

Patient: Since my grandmother died I haven't watched them.

Gardner: Okay, but you did watch them for a long time when you were younger?

Patient: I always watched them when I was younger.

Gardner: From what age to what age, would you say?

Patient: From whatever age I was old enough to at least like it till I started school.

Gardner: Okay. So what age did you start school?

Mother: Six.

Gardner: You stopped at six and you started when?

Patient: Well, I didn't stop, whenever I could, I would, but I had school then.

Gardner: When did you start?

Mother: You stayed at your grandmother's from birth to age six.
Patient: I started when I was old enough to watch.
Gardner: Your grandmother used to watch them a lot?
Patient: No, my grandmother didn't watch them. I did. They were sleeping while I was watching.
Gardner: Aren't those soap operas in the middle of the day?
Patient: Yeah.
Gardner: So they were sleeping. The television set was like a babysitter for you?
Patient: Well, maybe I guess you could say that.
Gardner: So you spent many years watching soap operas?
Mother: Grandma would go to the bed and take a nap?
Patient: No, not always. She would either sit on the couch and watch with me or she would sleep on the couch while I was watching them.
Gardner: Okay. And those soap operas used to give you the idea that you would want to do that?
Patient: When I was little, but then I got older and I understood what it really was.
Gardner: Okay, because you could have a baby. Let me ask you this question. Sometimes a person might want to do it just because it might be an interesting thing to do, but sometimes a person might want to do it when they have a very, very strong feeling that they want to do it. Which would you say was true for you? Because there's some feeling in their private places, in their vagina, and their penis where they really feel very strong . . .
Patient (interrupts with surprise): Right now?
Gardner: No, then.
Patient: That's a hard question to answer.
Gardner: I know. Most of the questions I ask are hard questions to answer. I understand that. But they are important questions for me to understand your trouble. So it's a good idea to get clear in your mind things that are happening in your own mind. That's what this is all about.
Patient: What was the question?
Gardner: The question was this. Sometimes a person will say, "That seems like an interesting thing to do," like it might be an interesting book to read or an interesting picture to watch. But there are sometimes you

get a feeling—a very strong feeling—that you would like to do it. It goes beyond.... Let's use this example: You see a food ad. Sometimes you just look at it and you just say nothing. They're advertising apples. *Or* you might say: "I'd really like to have an apple. Wow, am I hungry." You know, you really feel a pang in your stomach. Or you see something on television—a soda or something—an ice cream cone. And you're thinking, "Oh boy, I'm really hungry and I'd really like to have an ice cream cone. Wow, I can just feel it in my mouth now." So there's a very strong craving. Understand? So one is what we call an intellectual experience. It's just interesting, but you don't have a strong craving. The other is you have a strong craving. For something sexual it would be that you feel in your private places—in your vagina, you have a very strong feeling that you want to have something in there. Which would it be for you?

Patient: When I watch TV, and I see something like what you're talking about, because I want to ...

Gardner: Do you have a craving?

Patient: Yeah, a craving.

Gardner: You know what I mean by craving?

Patient: Yeah, you want that ...

Gardner: Craving. Not just that it would be interesting. Now you said you had those cravings when you used to watch those programs.

Patient: No. I'm not saying that.

Mother: She said she had those cravings when she sees *ice cream*, she understands your question related to ...

Obviously, the mother's clarification was important here. The patient was thinking of craving for ice cream and I was thinking of craving for sex. Without clarification here I would really have taken this child down the wrong path. We see here a good example of how parents' participation in a child's therapy can be extremely useful. Elsewhere (Gardner, 1992b), I have described in greater detail the important role of parents in a child's therapy.

Patient (interrupting): I can answer that question, but I can't answer the other one because I really don't want to.

Gardner: Okay. Let me ask you this one in general. Some girls your age have a craving for sex.

Patient: Well, I don't. I don't.

Gardner: What do you think about girls who have a craving for sex?

Patient: They're wrong.

Gardner: If they have the craving, I don't think they're wrong. I think they're normal to have the craving. Okay? That's my opinion. That's normal. In fact, the time will come when you will have a craving. It may not happen now, but there will come a time. Do you understand that?

Patient: (Nods affirmatively.)

Gardner: And if there comes no time in your life that you have a craving, then you will be missing out on something very important for people who have loving relationships. Understand?

Patient: (Nods affirmatively.)

Gardner: Now I believe—let me ask you this question. These thoughts of rape. . . . By the way, I think you're using the wrong word, first of all. I would use the word *touch*. It doesn't sound to me like you're trying to force this child in your mind, in the picture in your brain. Am I correct in saying that there's no forcing?

Patient: (Nods affirmatively.)

Gardner: So that's not the proper word. You're making it like you're forcing a person to do something, and that's not what your picture is in your mind. Hhmmm?

Patient: Well, what do you mean? Say that again.

Gardner: I'm saying that you have a fantasy of touching that little girl in the vagina. That's what I would call it.

Patient: I want to do that then?

Gardner: A fantasy is a thought, and part of you wants to, yeah.

Patient: Well, I don't really feel like I want to . . . I don't really like saying these things, but the other night I was in the bathtub with my little brother, and I don't like to bathe with him, and she (pointing to mother) never makes me bathe with him, but sometimes he'll be getting out, and I'll be getting in, and sometimes I get in before she'll take him out. And he was standing up and he had, I don't know what it was . . .

Mother: His private, his penis touched you.

Patient: No . . .

Mother: Remember that?

Patient: Yeah, it was almost like I wanted to, to touch him . . . it was almost like I wanted to do it.

Gardner: So what?

Patient: That's what, you were saying, "Do I want to?" and I don't really remember feeling that way...

Gardner: What do you think about my saying "So what?" You said you wanted to touch his penis and I said, "So what?" What do you think about that?

Patient: I like it when you say stuff like that. When my mom says it like that I like it because it makes me feel better that I haven't done it.

Gardner: You see, I'm not saying if you actually touched his penis, I would say, "So what?" Do you know what I mean? But to *want* it is normal. Hhmm? You see, your problem is that you think these thoughts make you a low animal, right?

Patient: Right.

Gardner: A real pervert. Do you know what a pervert is?

Patient: A pervert is someone whose mind is always on—sex—and stuff like that.

Gardner: A pervert—it's not so much his mind—but his behavior. He just goes around having sex with everybody under any circumstances, always trying—you know, it's a kind of a low-life life. Do you understand? He's a person who *does* these things. Understand? In our minds, there's a perversion in all of us, you know. All of us in our minds are perverts. We all have thoughts—different people, different kinds of thoughts. What you *do* with the thoughts is a different story. You see I didn't say, "It's okay. Touch your brother's penis." I'm not saying that. I'm saying that to have the thought is normal. Do you believe me?

Patient: (Nods affirmatively.)

Gardner: I'm wondering whether you got a very heavy dose of sex somewhere. Tell me, these thoughts of "rape" that you call it, when did they start?

Patient: That was the first thought.

Gardner: When?

Patient: That one in church, that was my first thought.

Gardner: When was that?

Patient: (Looks to mother.)

Mother: One month ago.

Gardner: Prior to that time you didn't have these thoughts?

Patient: I didn't have the thoughts, no, but I did have incidents...

Gardner: Incidents of what?

Patient: Well, my little cousin—I think my mother told you about this because I was reading the sheet [the mother's list of the patient's problems] she brought to you. I was at his house and we were both laying on the couch and watching TV. My hand was like, under him . . .

Gardner: How old is this little cousin?

Patient: He was five, then.

Gardner: He's five now?

Patient: No, he's six now, but he was five then.

Gardner: Okay, a year ago. Yeah.

Patient: No, it was just in the summer.

Gardner: Last summer, yeah.

Patient: His birthday's in September. And I tickled him on the butt . . . on his seat . . . and he was laughing, and I got on top of him and just . . .

Gardner: You got on top of him and did what?

Patient: I don't really, I thought, the thought went through my mind, and I don't know (looks to mother, and starts to cry). Mom, will you please?

Mother: Tell him what happened, Virginia. You tickled him.

Patient (crying bitterly): Yeah, and the thought went through my mind . . . that . . . sex with him . . . (mumbles) . . .

Gardner (turning to mother): What did she say?

Mother: She tickled him and was on top of him. Then she had the thought that she was going to have sex with him . . .

Patient (crying): I was doing like, and I was like, flat on him, and I was doing like this (makes a rocking motion).

Gardner: Okay. You were rubbing your vulva against him?

Patient: No, not necessarily (looks to mother), it's my whole body was doing like that (gestures in rocking motion).

Mother: She was lying on top of him, and they were wrestling around . . .

Patient: On the couch.

Mother: On the couch. And she ended up on top of him.

Patient: And my whole body was doing that (makes rocking motion with hands again).

Gardner: Okay. And you felt that you could have had sex with him?

Patient: No. The *thought* that went through my mind was that I was going to.

Mother: The *thought* was she was going to have sex with her cousin.

Patient: Yes.

Gardner: Okay. Do you think that that makes you a low-life character?

Patient: (Nods affirmatively.)

Gardner: I have a different opinion on that subject. I'm not saying that you should have sex with your five-year-old cousin. I'm not recommending that for one minute. Okay? Most people would agree that would be a wrong and bad thing to do. But that's different from having the *thought*, you know? Your problem is having great guilt over thoughts. Hhmmm? And I'm wondering where all this guilt came from? Was there anyone in your life who came down heavily on you for these thoughts?

Patient: Well, when I first had them, my mom didn't know what they were about. We didn't know why I was having them.

Gardner: Was last summer the first time you had these sexual thoughts?

Patient: Yes.

Gardner: How often do you have these sexual thoughts?

Patient: I mean they're like constant. They're always on my mind. I wake up at night and I'm thinking about them, and I don't like these, and I've been looking forward to this because—and I think it will—and I thought it was going to help me a lot to get rid of these thoughts.

Gardner: What we're doing right now?

Patient: Yes.

Gardner: Well, I'm not a fairy with a magic wand, you know. Did you think that by this time, already, after three quarters of an hour . . .

Patient (interrupting): No, but I did think that it was going to help me.

Gardner: Do you remember the first thing we spoke about when you came in here? You said you wanted me to help you with your problems and I said, "I'll try." That's the only thing I promise people—I try. Okay? I've never made a promise to anybody when it comes to therapy. Understand? All I can do is *try*. My promise is that I will and I'm trying. Okay? That's the promise. But this I can tell you. An important determinant as to whether I can help is whether a person cooperates. I think you're cooperating pretty well, you know. I think we're talking about some heavy stuff for you that's hard. I understand that. But I can tell you this right now that what I am going to be giving you here is advice for you to carry home and to use over time. You're not going to change. . . . I am not going to evaporate your guilt by any statement I can make. You're going to have to put into practice the things I suggest. Like when I gave you a hard time and said you should say the word *vagina*, I wasn't trying to be cruel to you—in fact, I felt pretty bad that you felt so bad—but I felt it was good experience for you, you know. So that's why I tried to force you to do it.

Now, okay, you're telling me that in the last six months or so you've had a lot of thoughts about sex. Right?

Patient: (Nods affirmatively.)

Gardner: You told me some. You told me about the little baby. You told me about the thoughts about your cousin, about having sex with your cousin . . .

Patient: I've been thinking about these things, I felt nervous about, and I'm thinking of one thing right now, when I was really little I was playing at my friend's house—Christy—and one time we were playing, and she was acting like—we were acting . . .

Gardner: How old were you then?

Patient: I was young. Mom, how old do you think?

Mother: Christy who? What grade were you in?

Patient: I don't know?

Mother: Guess your age. Six, seven?

Patient: I was probably in that area, five, six, or seven.

Gardner: And what happened?

Patient: And we were playing. Do I have to say all this, or can I just the write the whole thing out?

Gardner: You don't have to say anything, but I can tell you this. The more you tell me, the better help I can give you. It's up to you.

Patient: Can I write it down?

Gardner: You want to write it down here? Okay. Write it down (hands pad and pen to patient).

Patient: (Writing.)

Gardner: Okay. Write it down. (Turns to parents.) While she's writing that, what I'm coming to, I see the road I'm going down. I assume you have no personal problems with autoerotic activity?

Mother and Stepfather: (Shake heads negatively.)

Gardner: Okay, fine.

Mother: I don't know where this is coming from.

Gardner: Well, I think some of it—I'm trying to learn more—some of it is normal, age-appropriate estrogen in the blood stream. Has she started to have pubic hair, pubic area changes?

Mother: Yes.

Gardner: You don't get that without high levels of estrogen in the blood stream. And she's getting some level of sexual excitation. At this age it is not uncommon to have it be a broader, rather than purely narrow heterosexual. It's so broad that you can't say there are homosexual tendencies or anything here, it's just, the broader sexual fantasy level, and she probably isn't letting herself have some higher levels of urge. And I think when she asks what she can do, I'm going to explore this area with her on that subject.

Okay, I looked at your notes here on the chart. You mentioned a sex-abuse prevention course program. Okay, let's talk about that. You told me that on the phone. Do you want to talk about that class?

Patient: No, I don't.

Gardner: You don't want to talk about that course?

Mother: That's not integrated in the schools, somehow?

Patient: I take DARE classes. Drug Abuse . . .

Gardner: Okay, we'll talk about that. Are you finished writing that?

Patient: No.

Gardner: Finish writing it and I'm just making a note. We'll go into that. Okay, you told me on the phone about the neighbor man.

Patient: (Finishes writing).

Gardner: Okay, you're finished?

Patient: Yes, but I don't like saying things about this. If you're going to read it out loud I don't want to be in here.

Gardner: You don't want to be in the room while I read it out loud?

Patient: Yeah. Is it okay?

Gardner: Let me just see what it says here. When we use the word "we" here, are you referring to you and your girlfriend?

Patient: Yes.

Gardner: A cousin, a girl?

Patient: A friend.

Gardner: A girlfriend? Your age?

Patient: Yeah, she's two weeks younger than I am.
Gardner: Okay, how many years ago did this occur?
Patient: Um, I don't know.
Gardner: About?
Patient: Probably I was about five or six years old.
Gardner: Five or six years old. Okay, let me read this first.

The patient's note stated:

"We were pretending we were strippers and she put tape (white and wide) over her private areas. I pretended to be a stripper also. Anyway, the tape stuck to her vagina and I offered to help her get it off. Another thing about this—we watched each other while we stripped. We were pretending to strip for men. We did this to music."

Patient: Maybe a little bit older.
Gardner: I can't read this word here—this word—what is that?
Patient: White.
Gardner: And what's this word?
Patient: Wide.
Gardner: Okay. What's this word here?
Patient: Each other.
Gardner: Okay. How many occasions did this take place?
Patient: I think about once, I think. But I went home, one time. Last time I halfway spent the night over there at her house and her brother, her big brother, came over and he was acting like he was going to put toothpaste all over us and stuff like that, and I went home, and that was the last time I ever went to her house.
Gardner: Okay, but this experience you had with this girl occurred on one occasion. Is that correct?
Patient: I think so.
Gardner: Well, do you think that's a normal thing to happen?
Patient: No.
Gardner: Do you want my opinion on the subject?
Patient: Uh hum.
Gardner: I would say that most kids somewhere along their childhood have a few such experiences. What do you think about that?

Patient (whispering): It makes me feel better a little . . .

Gardner: Do you think I'm lying to you just to make you feel better?

Patient: No, 'cause I've heard other people say . . . my mom's told me that other people have these . . . not necessarily these thoughts, but experiences with stuff like that. (Turns to mother.) I don't know, you were saying about people having experiences. . . . She said what you said, basically but different words.

Gardner: Does your mother know about this experience that you wrote down?

Patient: No.

Gardner: What do you think would happen if she knew about it?

Patient: She'd probably say the same thing as you did.

Gardner: And your dad? What would he say?

Patient: Probably . . .

Gardner: Then why didn't you tell them about this?

Patient: 'Cause it's hard for me to.

Gardner: Okay. But just like before, I think you need practice. I could tell—you can say to me, "Don't tell," or you can say, "Will you read it? Will you tell them?" But I think the best thing is if you tell them.

Patient: Me?

Gardner: Yes. I think you need practice. That will help you. You see, you said to me before that you want help with your problems, and I promised to *try* to give you help. If you want help with your problems, then you will tell them about this and get the practice telling, and have the *experience* that they're not going to vomit, they're not going to beat you, they're not going to be astonished, and I bet anything that they're gonna say, honestly, that this was normal and that most kids have things like this happen once in a while.

Patient (motions for Gardner to give back the pad for her to read): Let me see.

Gardner: I think you can tell them.

Mother: This is at Christy's house?

Patient: Yeah. "We were pretending we were strippers and she put tape, white and wide, over her private areas."

Mother: What private areas?

Patient: All of them.

Mother: Okay.

Patient (no longer reading verbatim): And then when she was thinking about taking them off, one of them got stuck and I volunteered to help her get it off. And then. We were watching, though. While she did it, I watched, and while I did it, she watched. And we did it to music, and we were . . . (mumbling) . . . say three-letter words . . . and that's everything.

Mother: You said three-letter words?

Patient: No, I was telling myself, "I have a three-letter word to say, just say it."

Mother: What was the three-letter word?

Patient: Men.

Mother: Men?

Patient: Yeah. We were doing that for . . .

Stepfather: You were *pretending* that there were men there, or *were* there men there?

Patient: Pretending.

Gardner: So you were doing like striptease dances for men, and the tape was like a little striptease . . .

Patient: No, it was just music. It was on the radio.

Gardner: Were you wearing clothes or not?

Patient: At first, yeah, but at the end, you know . . .

Gardner: Okay. It was on a tape. When you said tape, was it a cassette tape . . .

Patient: No. It was a radio, and we flipped the channels to whatever song we wanted.

Gardner: Oh, and you were dancing to the tape on the radio. And you were making believe you were striptease artists and you were making believe that men were there? Okay. Let's see what your mom and your dad have to say about that.

Mother: My thoughts are—to see you crying and getting so upset over saying this—that's normal. That's kids. They're six-year-olds, and she behaves like that, and it's in her behaviors when she's playing around. That is nothing to me.

Gardner (to mother): Let me ask you this. Suppose you came in the room and you saw her . . . this child is a few weeks younger than herself?

Patient: (Nods affirmatively.)

Gardner: The child was a few weeks younger. Okay. I want to ask each of you separately. Let's ask your mom first. You come into the room and you see these kids naked—dancing naked—in front of the radio and making believe that they're strippers. What would you do?

Mother: I'd probably say, "What are you doing?" and then I would know in my head that that is normal behavior and I wouldn't scold at or fuss at her and probably have a talk with her afterwards, that's all . . . about being promiscuous. It's okay to pretend the way she was doing. That's what children do.

Gardner: Would you tell her—would you interrupt the activity at that point?

Mother (pauses to consider): I probably would.

Gardner: Would you tell her to do it again?

Mother: No.

Gardner: Okay. (Turning to patient.) What do you think about your mother's answer?

Patient: I like it . . .

Gardner: Are you surprised?

Patient: No, not really. I had trouble telling her because whenever I first told her she wasn't sure what she had decided—whatever I had had these—that she finally—they thought they'd figured out that I was having these thoughts because of anger. That I was angry about things. And before this she just didn't know what they were, and she got really upset when I would tell her.

Gardner: Okay, she's upset because . . .

Patient: Okay, when I first told her, I had two thoughts first. That one I told you and the one about my little brother. And when I first told her those first two thoughts she didn't know what they were about, and she got really upset with me and she would do things, and she would go, "Oh my God, I don't know what's wrong with you," and "You're scaring me," and she'd just say, "Go to bed" and "Get out of my face" and I got upset when I had those thoughts, I mean when she said that . . .

Gardner: Okay, when she gets upset you think you must really be having some sinful, bad, thoughts, right?

Patient: (Nods affirmatively.)

Gardner: Well, what do you think about how your mother just responded now when she said if she had come into the room and she saw you and this girl doing this that she would basically have said, "Look girls, get dressed," and she would have had a talk with you, and she would have told you not to do it again. What do you think?

Patient: That wouldn't have bothered me, but see then, if she wouldn't—if I told her something like these thoughts that I had, she would have been shocked. She would have been doing like this (patient runs her hands through her hair) and saying, "Oh, my God."

Gardner: She has been?

Patient: She gets angry with me . . .

Gardner: She's shocked, but she doesn't know what it is, but now, I think, she understands better what's going on with you. . .

Patient (interrupting): Yeah, after she found out what was going on, it wasn't like that anymore. Whenever I would tell her something she would get a little angry with me when I first told her about the thoughts, but then she helped me and we talked about things that were bothering me, and I usually felt better.

Gardner: Okay, let's hear from your father now and see what he would do if he came in and saw you and a friend this way.

Stepfather: Under my breath I would probably chuckle a little bit, but I would probably tell her to go and get her clothes on. Word for word I don't know exactly what I would say unless I was in the situation, but I would ask her why she was doing that, and what was going on, I would think. Investigate what they were really up to.

Gardner: Well, the *why* is that it's normal behavior, normal curiosity, normal modeling, mild levels of sexual urge.

Stepfather: Didn't one time at a birthday party, Virginia, summer party you had, didn't one or two of the girls—I think I was watching TV in the living room—and I went to sleep, didn't one or two of them run into the room without a shirt on or something? And what did I do? I said, "You all quit playing around, go back in there and put your shirts back on."

Mother: Alice did.

Stepfather: And that was the extent of that.

Patient: I don't remember that.

Once again we see the value of having the parents in the room. Had they not been there I might have speculated what the parents might have done had they entered the room when the girls were playing this game. I would have had to make many assumptions, however. Having the parents right there to respond immediately provided Virginia with instant feedback that I believe was guilt assuaging. Therapists who do not work closely with parents deprive themselves of such important therapeutic benefits.

>*Gardner*: I'd like to move on. I want to ask you about prevention programs in school. Did you have any sexual abuse prevention programs in school?
>
>*Patient*: No. We have DARE.
>
>*Gardner*: What is DARE?
>
>*Patient*: It's *Drug Abuse Resistance Education*. They had our first lesson and he was explaining to us what we were going to go over, over the year. And he asked, "Okay, what's a bad touch" and "Who should you tell if someone gives you a bad touch" and . . .
>
>*Gardner*: Was that in the DARE program?
>
>*Patient*: Yeah, but it was like a five-minute thing and that was about all we . . .
>
>*Gardner*: That was it—five minutes—that was the whole program? They never mentioned it again?
>
>*Patient*: Well, maybe they mentioned it here and there but I think it was pretty much.
>
>*Gardner*: Have you ever read any books, or seen any videotapes or heard audiotapes on sex-abuse prevention programs?
>
>*Patient*: No, I don't think so.

Sex-abuse prevention programs, especially if they are extensive, can contribute to a variety of sexual problems, one of which is excessive guilt over sexual thoughts and feelings. In this case, however, I believe the exposure was minimal and so the program did not play a significant role in bringing about Virginia's sexual guilt problems. I could only know this, however, after I had made inquiries and obtained details regarding the extent and depth of this often deleterious exposure, the ostensible benefits of the program notwithstanding. Krivacska (1989) has made an important contribution regarding the dangers of these programs.

>*Gardner*: Okay, I'd like to talk about something else. There was a neighbor man who liked you very much till the time you were about five

to the time you were eight. What's that man's name?

Patient: Dennis.

Gardner: Dennis. What can you tell me about Dennis?

Patient: He was a very nice man. He went to—he bought me gifts for Christmas, and he was just really nice to me. He took me places.

Gardner: Did you ever have any problems with him of any kind?

Patient: No. She [referring to her mother] always asked me if he ever touched me or anything like that.

Gardner: How many times did your mom ask you if he ever touched you?

Patient: A bunch.

Gardner: What's a bunch? What's your guess?

Patient: About ten or something like that, maybe less.

The reader does well to note here my insistence upon getting an approximate number. All too often therapists do not take the time to pinpoint and quantify, and this compromises their ability to understand the degree or the extent of a particular phenomenon.

Gardner: What were your reactions to that?

Patient: Well, I would always say no, because she wouldn't let me . . .

Gardner: Was he a married man?

Patient: Yes.

Gardner: Did he have children?

Patient: Well, when I first met him, no, but then his wife had a baby, and when she got older, she was three or four, and he used to take her out in the woods, and they would go see Alex, their friend, and they would bring wood back, and they would go swimming in the woods, and he would take her to the zoo, and Alex's, and places like that.

Gardner: Okay. Your mom asked you about ten times if he ever touched you. Did she specifically say, "In your vagina?"

Patient: No.

Gardner: Did you know what she was talking about?

Patient: Yeah. She just meant did he ever touch you in your private areas and places like that.

Gardner: Okay. Now what were your reactions? What were your thoughts or feelings when she said that?

Patient: Well, sometimes I would get mad because she would never let me go anywhere with him because she was always so worried about me. And sometimes I would get mad and say "No!" and sometimes I'd just say, "No, he never did."

Gardner: All right. (Turning to mother.) How many times in your recollection?

Mother: About 20.

Gardner: Twenty times. You see (speaking to mother), I believe that was a factor. You were giving little drops of guilt and fear. You were inducing a fear and that played a role in the guilt at that time.

Mother: I may add, Dr. Gardner, my sister—whom she's very close to—she's worse about that than I am with her three children. They are like one, two, and five years of age, and she's constantly hounding them, and Virginia hears this.

Stepfather: Her sister's almost obsessed with any kind of fear: going to the mall, getting them lost, somebody kidnapping them, somebody hurting them, harming them, raping them, all these things.

Gardner: And she's (pointing to patient) exposed to this?

Stepfather: Very much so.

Gardner (to mother): What's your sister's first name?

Mother: Brenda.

Gardner: Brenda. (Turning to patient.) What can you tell me about your Aunt Brenda and her talking about sex abuse? What your exposures have been?

Patient: I think, well, not necessarily about sex abuse, but she's *very* overprotective. Her little girl had a diaper rash one time on her vagina. And she came up to her mom one time and she was crying really hard 'cause it hurt and her mom she just got this horrible look on her face, and she got all nervous about it, and she asked her, she said, "Has anybody ever touched you there?" and that was the first thing that came out of her mouth.

Gardner: Okay. How many times have you observed Aunt Brenda to be talking about sex abuse?

Patient: With her kids?

Gardner: Yeah.

Patient: Well, to talking to them—right now, I can remember, I'm thinking about twice right now, but I know it's more than that.

Gardner: So you know it's buzzing around in her head.

TREATMENT OF SEX-ABUSE HYSTERIA 487

Patient: Yeah, because when her little girl, she was hurting somewhere, had a headache or something, and she just turned and looked at her husband with the most frightful face . . .

Gardner: You see, I think that kind of experience with your aunt, as well as with your mother, has played a role in your feeling very guilty about your sexual thoughts and feelings. What do you think about that?

Patient: I don't know if necessarily—she may have asked me a couple of times, but . . .

Gardner: But she [referring to mother] says 20 times she asked if Dennis touched you.

Patient: It wasn't always Dennis, but if anybody ever touched you. Sometimes it would be specifically Dennis.

Gardner: Okay. I think that between your mother and your aunt that they together have been the most important players in producing this guilt in you by making you think that sex is a terrible, bad thing. That's what I think. What do you think?

Patient: Well, I think it probably has helped . . . I don't necessarily think that sex is a terrible bad thing. It can be.

Gardner: But you act as if it's one of the great sins of humanity. That it's one of the great crimes in the history of crimes in this world. When you watch yourself on television you will see someone there who you would think was confessing a murder. Hmm?

Patient (shrugs): Well, I guess so.

Gardner: You see, I think that you have been a victim of a different kind of sex abuse. You've been a victim of your mother and your aunt's hysteria about sexual abuse. We are living in an age that I call sex-abuse hysteria. Everybody is running around scared about sex abuse. There is no question that there is *real* sex abuse. But there is no question that people are going bonkers, people are running around scared about sex abuse, beyond what is the real danger. Like with Dennis, and your aunt who is worried that behind every tree some pervert is going to come out. In every mall someone's going to rape and steal her kid, you know? So I think you are a *victim* of that environment, of your teacher who in your class says, when he's talking about drugs, he throws in sex abuse, which isn't even part of the program. . .

Patient: Well, not really, he was just talking about that in the beginning when he was going over everything . . .

Gardner: Okay, but he selected that from hundreds of other subjects he could have pulled in. He pulled it in. It's not the subject of the course, right? Drug abuse is what you were talking about, right?

Patient: Well . . .

Gardner: He saw fit to add sex abuse when there was nothing to suggest that. Am I right?

Patient: He just said, "What about a bad touch?"

Gardner: Yes, but he selected that from hundreds of other unrelated subjects. Right?

Patient: Yeah.

Gardner: Okay, what's my main point to you?

Patient: That everybody talks and tells everybody about sexual abuse and that's a big cause in this.

Gardner: Causing what?

Patient: That I have these thoughts.

Gardner: No, it's not causing you to have the thoughts. The thoughts are caused by something else we're going to get to in a minute. I think some are caused by the soap operas, but we'll get there in a minute. It's causing you to feel very guilty and feel that sex is a terrible, sinful act. It's making you overreact and go bonkers over normal sexual thoughts. Do you understand my point?

Patient: (Nods affirmatively.)

Gardner: I'd like you to repeat it so that you are clear on what I'm saying.

Patient: You're saying that all this talk to me—my aunt, my mom, and my family—is causing me to be . . . are you saying maybe scared?

Gardner: Scared. Anything else?

Patient: Scared of having these thoughts.

Gardner: And guilty. Aren't you guilty?

Patient: (Nods affirmatively.)

Gardner: You feel bad about yourself. You feel sinful, right?

Patient: I feel different, because none of my friends seem like they're going through anything like this.

Gardner: Well, everybody's different. We're talking about *you* here, now, right? Now let me ask you. Has what I said to you here today made you feel less guilty about your sexual thoughts and feelings?

Patient: (Nods affirmatively.)

Gardner: Are you sure?

Patient: It's helped.

TREATMENT OF SEX-ABUSE HYSTERIA 489

Gardner: See, you can't control the things that spring into your mind. Things pop into everybody's mind.

Patient: Whenever I do something wrong, or think something, I'll tell my mom and she'll either tell me that's okay, or she'll say what are you angry about, or what's bothering you?

Gardner: Your mom *guessed* that it's something to do with anger. Lots of therapists [the patient's mother was a therapist] do that. They guess what's going on in people's minds, and it's a bad idea. I think your mom guessed wrong.

Here I mention the common problem of therapists confronting patients with their speculations regarding what is going on in their patients' minds. Often they do this with an authority that intensifies the gravity of this widespread problem. Virginia's mother not only did this with her patients, but with her child as well. Somehow, she decided that Virginia's central problem had to do with anger and was repeatedly confronting the child with the anger explanation, only to confuse her.

Patient: But when we talk about what angered me or what bothered me, I usually feel a lot better.

Gardner: Okay, but on the subject we're talking about, as I see it, *guilt* is the name of the game here. Guilt is a big thing for you. I saw you crying. I ask you to say the word *vagina*. You'd think I was asking you to take a gun and kill someone. You know? You see how you were overreacting?

Patient: It's just hard for me to say it.

Gardner: I understand that, but that's part of your guilt. Now I would like to talk about what's happened to you. I think that in the last year or so, you, like most girls your age, are starting to have body changes as you start to become a teenager and you grow into adulthood. I understand from your mother that you're starting to get some hair under your armpits, is that right?

Patient: Well, not a lot.

Gardner: Okay, but it's starting to grow there, right? And it's starting to grow on your vulva over your vagina. Is that right?

Patient: (Nods affirmatively.)

Gardner: That's normal. And what I'm saying to you is that when those things start growing, in your bloodstream there's flowing something called estrogen, a sex hormone. Did you ever hear the term *sex hormone*?

Patient: (Shakes head negatively.)

Gardner: It's a chemical. It makes different things happen. It makes you grow faster, taller, so you become a big woman. It makes your breasts start growing. It helps you menstruate. It gives you hair on your vulva, which is outside your vagina, and it also gives you sexual thoughts and feelings. Sometimes the thoughts start before the feelings. That's all normal. In fact, if you didn't start to have all these changes, you'd be in very, very bad shape. And everybody would be very upset, including you, right?

Patient: Well, I don't know.

Gardner: Well, I'm telling you, everybody would be flipping out if you didn't start to grow up. You know, you don't want to remain a baby. You want to become a teenager and an adult, right? And the sex hormones are one of the steps on that path. The sex hormones, that's what they're called. You're getting some of those changes that we just discussed. I think you're getting the thoughts part and you're getting some of the feelings. Like the thought of food, the feeling, the craving. Have you gotten any cravings, yet?

Patient: No, not really.

Gardner: Okay. Well, I think that you will probably start getting cravings soon.

Patient: I might have a couple of years ago, not really had them. When I was little, different boys I liked, and I started liking boys and I used to pretend, to myself you know, that I was . . . having sex with them.

Gardner: Having sex with them. Having their penis in your vagina?

Patient: No, because I didn't know what it was then.

Gardner: Okay, what were you thinking of when you say you were having sex?

All of the patients who have ever worked with me in depth will agree that one of my most common requests is that they be specific and describe exactly what they are talking about. Without a visual image I am hard put to really talk meaningfully about an issue presented to me in the course of treatment. Such requests for specificity can sometimes be irritating, embarrassing, and very difficult for patients—especially those who only speak in generalities. Therapists who do not pin people down and who do not ask for specifics are compromising significantly their therapeutic work.

> *Patient*: (Puts her head on table and doesn't answer.)
> *Gardner*: Another one of my hard questions, but try to answer it.
> *Patient*: Kissing them.
> *Gardner*: Kissing them? That's fine. What else? All these are normal thoughts.
> *Patient*: On top of them . . .
> *Gardner*: Okay. Anything else specifically?
> *Patient*: And the things I've seen. . . the stuff from the soap operas.
> *Gardner*: The stuff from the soap operas? Love things from soap operas? Okay. I think that that wasn't a good thing for you.
> *Patient*: I haven't watched it in . . .
> *Gardner*: I think you got too heavy an exposure of soap operas from your grandma. And that was a bad idea.
> *Patient*: Well, it wasn't really my grandma who made me, she didn't really care about it . . .
> *Gardner*: She should have restricted you. Your grandma shouldn't have let you watch such programs. No way. No how.
> *Patient*: My grandpa didn't let me watch them.
> *Gardner*: He was right. And he should have put his foot down.
> *Patient*: She used to say stuff like—sometimes she would say you *shouldn't* but they never actually said no you *can't*.
> *Gardner* (turning to mother): You didn't even know about this?
> *Patient* (turning to mother): She knew. You knew I watched TV. You knew I watched soap operas every day.
> *Mother*: Yeah. I knew. What I didn't know was the effect it was having on her.
> *Stepfather*: And when I came into the picture, I said no.
> *Patient*: He said I shouldn't watch them either.
> *Gardner*: Yeah. I think that this probably engendered earlier sexual programming. I'm very big on programming, brain circuitry. So the stuff keeps spinning around in your brain, it keeps going, long after, in later years. So the soap opera stuff is still spinning in her brain. And even though you turned off the set, copies have been made, "backups," like computer backups are in her brain, that are probably going to be there

for a long time. She was at a very impressionable age.

Mother: You don't think she should watch soap operas now?

Gardner (to patient): Do you watch them now?

Patient: I haven't watched them much. I can't watch them often because I'm always at school and if I tape them . . .

Gardner: I think it's a matter of dosage. It's still a vicarious gratification. Okay. Anyway, I think you got a heavier dose of sex than the average kid, at an earlier age . . .

Patient: My aunt tapes them. And whenever I go over there she says, "I have a soaps tape," and we usually watch them together.

Gardner: Right now? This is Aunt Brenda?

Patient: She tapes them, because she's not home when they're on.

Gardner (to parents): Well, Brenda's obsessed with sex. Obsessed with condemning it, but obsessed with vicariously gratifying it. (Turning to patient) Now do you watch these with her?

Patient: Sometimes. Like if I'm at their house she'll tape it, and watch it, and then she'll tape over it.

Gardner (to parents): Did you know this?

Mother: I knew it happened occasionally, but . . .

Patient (interrupting): Oh, it's not all the time. When I go over there, when I was home, it was still summertime, and I'd gotten really deep into the soap operas. It was really exciting. Every time I'd go there we would watch.

Gardner: Okay, but do you like watching them with her? That's the question.

Patient: Yeah.

Gardner: You do. You enjoy it.

Patient: I watch them by myself . . . sometimes I enjoy it.

Gardner: Do you have any other interest in sexual things other than soap operas?

Patient: (Shakes head negatively.)

We see here strong confirmation that the excessive exposure to soap operas was generating sexual thoughts in this child, sexual thoughts that might not otherwise have arisen.

Gardner: You don't have any. All right, let me ask you a related question. Do you know what the word *masturbation* means?

Patient: I have no idea.

Gardner: You never heard that word?

Patient: No.

Gardner: Well, what it means is. . . . Did you ever hear of a practice where people play with their own private parts with their hands?

Patient: A practice . . .

Gardner: Where they touch and rub their private parts with their hands.

Patient: Just do it, or for a job?

Gardner: No, not for a job, for their own pleasure. Like when you had the thought of touching the vagina of this one-year-old girl. Right?

Patient: Well, I mean, I do that sometimes.

Gardner: You touch your own private parts.

Patient: Yes.

Gardner: Okay. What do you think about that?

Patient: I had one thought, one time, that that was wrong . . .

Gardner: You thought that that was wrong?

Patient: Yes.

Gardner: Okay. What happened then?

Patient: I just told myself that it wasn't.

Gardner: Who told you that it wasn't, you? Okay. Now everybody does that. Some people do more of that. Some people do less of that, to varying degrees. The question is, do you do it to give yourself pleasure?

Patient: No, I don't think so, no.

Gardner: What do you think about people who do that because it makes them feel very good?

Patient (shrugs): Sure is different. Strange . . .

Gardner: Huh? They're different? They're strange?

Patient: (Nods head affirmatively.)

Gardner: Would you ever want to do that?

Patient (shakes head negatively): Not really.

Gardner: Okay. Well, do you want my opinion on that subject? Why don't you get your mother's opinion on the subject, first.

The reader may note that a typical way in which I introduce an alternative opinion to a patient is to ask them if they want my opinion on that subject. This gets across the message that there are no final answers on most issues that we focus on in psychiatry. However, the patient generally recognizes that my greater experience and knowledge in the realm warrants giving serious consideration to my opinion. I do not present it as gospel from on high, but rather the opinion of a professional who has learned some things about the matter under consideration. I am not falsely humble here; rather, I am merely presenting what I hope will be a more judicious opinion on the subject being discussed. Here, rather than present my opinion first, I decided it would be preferable to have the parents give their opinions on this very touchy subject of masturbation. (I hope the reader will forgive my pun.)

Mother: I think it's normal, and it's pleasurable, and people do it all the time.

Gardner: Ask your father's opinion.

Stepfather: Usually when young people are changing and stuff, the tendency to do that is real common. Real common.

Gardner (to patient): What do you think about that?

Patient: Sort of what I . . . am doing.

Gardner: What?

Patient: 'Cause he said when different things are happening there's a tendency to do it, and that's what I think I do.

Gardner: I think you touch yourself once in a while. Am I right?

Patient: No.

Gardner: You do it for pleasure.

Patient: I don't think so.

Gardner (pointing to parents): They're saying people do it for pleasure.

Patient: I don't know if I do it for pleasure or not. . . . I mean, if you pick up a pen and write, it's not like you are doing it for pleasure, you're just doing it.

Gardner: Okay. I'm saying there are people who do it because they have a very strong desire to do it and they get an enormous amount of pleasure out of doing it.

Patient: I'm not that type.

Gardner: Okay, what do you think of people who do it for reason?

Patient: It depends on their age.

Gardner: Any age. Eleven.

Patient: It's strange and different. That's what I said.

Gardner: Do you think it's wrong?

Patient: Sounds (looks to parents) . . . I don't think so. I don't think . . . is it? I don't know?

Gardner: What does your mom say?

Patient (to mother): You were talking about for pleasure?

Mother: Yes.

Patient (to Gardner): It's not bad then.

Gardner: What did your father say?

Patient: Nothing.

Gardner: I'm sure your father would agree with me on this. See, it's very important what I'm going to tell you now. I said to you before about the normal thoughts and feelings that people have about sex. And I made a clear distinction between having the thought and the desire and doing it. I said to you, "To have the *thought* that you want to have sex with your five-year-old cousin is normal. To do it will cause everybody a lot of trouble." Right?

Patient: (Nods affirmatively.)

Gardner: To want to play a game with your friends, stripping, and dancing to music is normal. To even do it once is normal. But to do it a lot . . . you can get into a lot of trouble. So what do you do with all these thoughts. One thing you do is make yourself feel you're a terrible low worm, right?

Patient: (Nods affirmatively.)

Gardner: I say to you that as you get older, you may have strong feelings to do some of these things. You'll have feelings associated with the thought. Do you follow what I'm saying? Strong desire, like a desire for ice cream. You know? A desire to go to sleep, a desire to eat, you know? A desire to hit someone. Okay? You will have a desire for sex. But you can't have it. A person may not be available. There are a lot of reasons why it's not possible. You're too young, you'll get in trouble, you may get a disease, or you can get pregnant, you know. And what most people do is that they rub themselves and by rubbing themselves it's called masturbation, and then after they release, they get pleasure and their thoughts go away for a while. And things quiet down. And that's what its purpose is.

What did you understand me to just say?

Patient: That some people touch themselves because they want to have sex but they can't so they touch themselves for pleasure.

Gardner: And what happens after they do that?

Patient: Things get better. Bad things, their thoughts and things like that, stop.

Gardner: You call them bad thoughts. I call them normal thoughts.

Patient: Normal thoughts.

Gardner: Normal, sexual thoughts we call them. Do those normal, sexual thoughts then go away forever?

Patient: No, they come back.

Gardner: They come back, right! And they keep coming back. And there's no way to stop them from coming back.

Patient: That's what my mom said, when we were talking when she thought it was anger, and I would tell her the things that bothered me. Usually I would feel better for a couple of days. But then the thoughts started coming back.

Gardner: I don't think it had anything to do with anger.

Patient: When they figured it out, I had told them a lot of stuff that made me mad and I didn't have it for the next day. It didn't even cross my mind.

Gardner: Well, I believe it has more to do with sexual things that we've been talking about. What do you think?

Patient: Probably right.

Gardner: I think this is the track. The right track. Now, my question to you is this. Remember the word I used to talk about touching yourself? What's the word?

Patient: It started with an "m."

Gardner: What's the word?

Patient: I don't remember.

Gardner: I said, it's called *masturbation*. You never heard that word before?

Patient: No.

Gardner: There are some people who think it's a terrible sin or a crime, that it's a very disgusting act. Some people have that opinion. I don't share that opinion. I think it can be very useful. It saves people a lot of trouble in life—both for themselves and for other people. Because then you get the satisfaction without getting into all kinds of trouble. Diseases and pregnancy, and relationships with people who you shouldn't get involved with. You have a desire to have sex with them, but you realize that they're bad-news people. To get involved with them is just going to be a lot of trouble. So it's better to masturbate and get it out of your system. But I'm giving you that for future reference because right now you don't seem to have a desire for that. Right?

Patient: (Nods affirmatively.)

Gardner: But I'm telling you if you do, you may find that that will make you less preoccupied with these sexual thoughts. It's a private, personal thing. It's not something people do in public. You do it in private.

Now let's see what else your mom has said. As I understand, things are going pretty well for you in other ways. Is that correct?

Patient: Yes.

Gardner: Are there any other problems you have that we haven't mentioned today?

Patient: I don't think so.

At that point, having addressed myself to the main problems, and having provided what I believed were important therapeutic communications, I began to explore other areas of possible difficulty. As mentioned, this family traveled over 1,500 miles to see me and I wanted to be as useful as I possibly could be in the limited time I had available for the consultation.

Gardner: Now, let's see. You are in school. You seem to be doing very well. You're in the fifth grade and you're doing seventh-grade reading and seventh-grade spelling. Is that right?

What are you looking at?

Patient: Outside. It looks like it's snowing.

Gardner: Looks like snow? Okay, well maybe.

Patient: I've never seen it. (The patient was born and raised in the southern part of the United States and so snow was really a novelty for her.)

Gardner: You've never seen snow? Well, now's your first chance. People around here won't be too happy about it. Let's go back to the subject, Okay? Seventh-grade reading, seventh-grade spelling, sixth-

grade arithmetic. You're doing pretty well. Your teachers are satisfied? You have good behavior in school?
Patient: Yeah.

School performance, both in the academic and behavioral realms, is a sensitive indicator of psychopathology. In fact, it is one of the most sensitive indicators, and the child who is doing well in school, both in the academic and behavioral realms, is not likely to suffer with significant psychiatric problems. Satisfied that she was doing extremely well in school, I then explored relationships with peers in the neighborhood.

Gardner: No problem. Kids like being with you? You have friends?
Patient: Yeah. I have two best pals. We just kind of split up. . . .

The patient's response indicated she both sought and was sought by peers. Peer relationships are also a sensitive indicator of psychopathology. Children with significant psychiatric problems are not likely to be sought by friends, and they may not seek them either. Accordingly, this proviso of psychopathology was also not satisfied, and so I looked into recreational activities and general functioning at home. When conducting this aspect of the interview, I was using as a guideline the questionnaire that the mother had filled out prior to the consultation. I have found this a very valuable instrument, and it can be extremely useful in the course of inquiry, saving time and expense for the patient and providing me with a very efficient tool for zeroing in on important areas. Elsewhere (Gardner, 1992b) I have described this questionnaire in detail.

Gardner: You take piano. You're interested in piano, movies. You read books. What kinds of books do you like to read?
Patient: See, I've just finished one . . .
Gardner: What's it about?
Patient: Teenagers, it's their life . . .
Gardner: Teenage stories?
Patient: Mystery books, funny books.
Gardner: Now is it correct to say that the suicidal thoughts your mother told me about relate to these things we were talking about?
Patient: Yeah.

Gardner: But you haven't thought suicide about other things, just that?

Patient: No, not really. One day I—it was just part of one of my thoughts but it wasn't about sexual stuff—after I had told my mom about having thoughts about suicide—I only had one—and then it kind of became a bigger topic because she was really upset because she was shocked at what I had said. Then, one time, I had the thought, whenever something was starting to go wrong with her, I was getting in trouble or something and I said, "My life stinks, what's stopping me from . . ."

Gardner: That was just once?

Patient: Yeah.

Gardner: Everybody has that once in a while. The only repeated suicidal thoughts, as I understand it, related to what kinds of thoughts?

Patient: All the sexual thoughts.

Stepfather: I think she felt overpowered by them. And therefore she didn't know how to stop them.

Patient: Like when I picture myself, like the other day I pictured my hair, and it was curly and it was in rings. If it was like empty and it was like free of these thoughts and everything and if it was full it had all these things and my hair was like, dark, dark, brown and it was stuffed with all these thoughts and . . .

Gardner: When you came to see me you wanted to be cured, right?

Patient: Well, I don't think this one time is gonna . . .

Gardner: Do you think I'm going to ever get all these sexual thoughts out of your brain?

Patient: Well at first I did, but I think you're trying to tell me that you're not.

Gardner: And what's going to happen instead?

Patient: I'm going to have to do it.

Gardner: Get the thoughts out of your brain? Is that what I'm saying to you?

Patient: No. I have to tell myself that it is normal and to not get overexcited about it.

Gardner: Right! Because I'm never going to get those thoughts out of your brain. I *wouldn't want* to get those thoughts out of your brain. Because then you'd be a freak. You'd be like no one else around. You don't want to be a freak, do you?

Patient: (Shakes head negatively.)

Gardner: If I had the power to do it, I wouldn't. Those are *normal* thoughts. And someday they will be directed toward someone you love very much. And you will have great joy, if you are healthy and happy with that person. You know? Do you believe that?

Patient: (Nods affirmatively.)

Gardner: It can be. Sex can be a very beautiful and wonderful thing with the right person in the right circumstances. As you get older you will come to appreciate that. But if you have these ideas that it is a sin to have the thoughts, then you're in trouble. So I'm not going to help you with the thoughts popping into your mind. But I did say something—that when they get strong, what can reduce them temporarily? What did I say?

It is most often useful, especially in sessions in which a significant amount of material has been covered, to ask the patient to reiterate the main points. And this is especially important for children who, obviously, are less likely to retain all that the therapist has said. Furthermore, the reiteration is in itself therapeutic, and that is one of the reasons why I am such a strong proponent of videotaping interviews for the patient's home review. Elsewhere (Gardner, 1992b) I have described the value of videotaping interviews in the course of the therapeutic process.

Patient: I can't say that word, umm, "m-a-s..."

Gardner: It's "masturbation." That's the word.

Patient: Yes!

Gardner: That's the word, right? So that can reduce down... and you do that in private. What else can you do about yourself to help you with those thoughts when they come?

Patient: To say that to myself, that they're normal and try to, well, just not think of it as a big, big deal.

Gardner: That's right. Normal—no big deal. So what? Remember that I said that to you before? Remember when you told me that you had a thought about having sex with your cousin I said, "So what?" Remember that?

Patient: (Nods affirmatively.)

Gardner: I wouldn't say that if you *had* sex with your cousin. I wouldn't say that at all. That's different. Thinking and doing are two very different things.

Okay. I would like to know what else anybody here wants to talk about. I've laid here some groundwork, some guidelines, and she has the tape we made here for review. I think she'll need that. Is there anything else that anyone wants to bring up?

Stepfather: Well, the one thing that I discussed with her, she usually talks to her mom about a lot of these things. And I thought it was kind of a guilt thing, but I thought it tracked back to her daddy's death and it all evolved from there.

Gardner: From her father?

Stepfather: Right. Because she couldn't call me daddy, she doesn't want to, and that's okay. But I think she has some feelings there that are not being expressed too well.

Gardner (to patient): Okay, want to say anything about your father?

Patient: I don't know what to say. I don't feel comfortable calling him daddy, for one thing.

Gardner: You don't?

Patient: I don't.

Gardner: What do you call him?

Patient: George. When I first met him, she dated him for about a year, and I called him George. And they got married and it just didn't change.

Gardner: Does he push you to call him "Dad"?

Patient: No. He really wants me to, but . . .

Gardner: But he doesn't bug you or anything, does he?

Patient: Sometimes they do, they try to.

Mother: I don't.

Gardner: The question is, you told me at the beginning that you have no memory of your father, is that correct?

Patient: No. I have some memories of him.

Gardner: What do you remember?

Patient: He was nice. He would go fishing and stuff like that with me. I don't remember this, but I've seen pictures where he would go out in my grandmother's garden and pick watermelons.

Gardner: Did you have a lot of pain after he died? Were you very depressed about it?

Patient: No, 'cause I knew what was happening, but I remember my mother was really upset and we lived in the house in the country and she was—and she was crying really hard and so I went and got my dad's picture and I sat down next to her and I started crying. But I wasn't crying because I was upset. I was crying because she was crying.

Gardner: I don't know whether her father's death has played an important role in this. I don't have that feeling.

Mother: I agree, Dr. Gardner. She's never shown too much confusion or turmoil around his death. I really have often thought it.

Stepfather (to patient): You never had the thought that you caused his death, or . . .

Patient: No, I never thought I caused it. (Turning to Gardner.) But I'm going to tell you something else. They used to tell me to express my anger and that might help. Usually when I get mad at them—sometimes when I get mad at her—I usually express it to him (looking now at stepfather), because he doesn't go crazy when I express it—she does. If I tell him, he either tells me to be quiet, or not to yell, or anything like that.

Gardner: Okay, I don't think that has anything to do with this problem. I'd like to focus on anything else that has to do with this problem.

Mother: I don't think so. I think you've got to the bottom of it.

Stepfather: I think you've nailed it.

Gardner: Yes. The tape is ready to run out, and I would like to just summarize what I think is going on here. It is my opinion that you (looking directly at patient) are basically a healthy person and that the death of your father, although it was painful for you, has not produced significant problems in your life. I think your stepfather, from everything I know, has been lucky for you, and God gave you another father and you've been very lucky to have this man, from everything your mother tells me. And if you don't feel comfortable calling him father, that will be fine. If you do, that will be fine. The important thing is the relationship.

I think that when you were a kid you had excessive exposure to soap operas. Turning you on, somewhat, churning up all kinds of fantasies about that. I think you've had normal sexual experiences in your life thus far. A few incidents of playing strip with another girl, of having some sexual wrestling with your cousin.

I think more recently in the last six months or a year you've started to grow. You're going to have your period soon. You're starting to get development and growing hair under your arms and on your vulva. And you have hormones in your bloodstream and you have sexual thoughts and you feel very guilty about them. And you feel that they are sinful. They're not.

I think your mother and your aunt contributed to that with all this stuff about "Were you touched by anybody?" and your aunt's obsession. And I think your grandma should not have let you watch all those programs to turn you on and produce these interests. I think recollections of that are still spinning around in your brain. Recollections—like a backup disk for a computer—the backup is in your brain. You can get rid of the originals, but the brain is still spinning around.

And now the hormonal flow on top of that is churning it all up. And you've got to remember that these thoughts are normal and that as you grow older and you feel strong desires, you should masturbate in private and that will help reduce the thoughts. And of course once you're older and you start having relationships, and certainly a marriage, and before that that's up to you and your family what you do with the man with whom you have a relationship.

And what I think you should do is call me. I want to hear from you in a week or two. I want to hear what happens. I'm not recommending therapy for you now down there. I think we should try to handle things over the phone. It may be that we don't need any further therapy. It may be that this "diagnostic/therapeutic interview" was enough. If it's not, I think we should try on the phone, and we'll set up telephone times. Feel much better?

Patient: (Nods affirmatively.)

Gardner: Are you sorry I gave you a hard time before?

Patient: (Smiles and is silent.)

Gardner: I gave you a hard time before with those words. Are you sorry? Are you sorry that I was sort of tough on you?

Patient (shakes head negatively): No.

Gardner: You needed that practice to overcome shyness. Okay. We'll end here.

As noted at the beginning of this transcript, the session was conducted on December 11, 1993. Six days later, the mother sent me a Christmas card, dated December 17, 1993, in which she wrote:

Dear Dr. Gardner:

The session with Virginia was most productive and she is free of turmoil, confusion and guilt. My gratitude to you for helping my precious daughter is immeasurable. Also, my consultations have helped me be more effective with my clients—and I always look forward to them. Wishing the best for you and your loved ones.

Sincerely,

Cindy

On March 11, 1994, exactly three months after the consultation, the mother wrote me the following letter:

Dear Dr. Gardner:

Per your request re: my daughter's reaction to our session 12/11/93, here are some results. (1) At Burger King 12/27/93 my husband was speaking to Virginia and me of jealous feelings toward his brother because he had inherited property from their grandfather in California. He also stated he felt guilty for feeling jealous. Virginia responded, "You are just like me, George. You feel one thing and react with guilt. So what you're jealous. Do you hear it thundering? That isn't anything—come on now, get a life." (Recall, "Do you hear it thundering" were your words 12/11/94.)

(2) First week returning to school of 1/94. I asked how she was feeling re: the consultation of Dr. Gardner's. She responded, "Well, let's just say I am not uptight anymore. And he was right. Those thoughts I have aren't going away. But I know they are normal."

(3) On 1/10/94 her report card was issued for 2nd nine weeks of school year, 1993–94. Attached is a copy of her piano report card. See "teacher's comment" highlighted in yellow: "Virginia did a beautiful job on Pachelbel's *Canon*. She seems to have relaxed more and I'm relieved for her sake. We are working on Federation music and will soon be adding our Sonatina selection. Please continue to encourage her to practice. Thanks for your support."

(4) Virginia has been a student whom I thought was too uptight about getting into minor trouble at school, ex: talking. She said to me she did talk during class and was cutting up and she did not get into a whole lot of trouble. She stated, "Things are not as bad as I see them to be. It was fun today to whisper while teacher was talking. It's not so terrible to cut up once in a while."

With warm regards,

Cindy X.

☐ EPILOGUE

WHERE DO WE GO FROM HERE?

In Chapter Seven I commented on the Child Abuse Prevention and Treatment Act (CAPTA) (The Mondale Act), which, to the best of my knowledge, was a pivotal force in bringing about the sex-abuse hysteria that we are witnessing today. Accordingly, if we do not make significant changes in CAPTA, we are not likely to rectify the problems that are at the foundation of the hysteria that is now well into its second decade. These are the changes that I have been recommending during the last few years. These are the changes that must be made if we are to continue to provide abused children with protection and provide the falsely accused of hope of reconsideration of their cases.

    1. **The federal absolute-immunity proviso must be modified**. Absolute immunity, like absolute power, corrupts and fosters irresponsible exploitation. Total immunity encourages frivolous, fabricated, and even malicious accusations. Qualified immunity, like that enjoyed by police officers, is a reasonable replacement. States that maintain the absolute immunity provision should *not* be entitled to federal funding. This change alone would reduce significantly the flood of false referrals being generated at this time.

    Promulgating a false sex-abuse accusation should be considered a criminal act—whether it be deliberate, the result of negligence, or the product of delusion. Malice should not be the sole standard of culpability for this crime because proving malice is extremely difficult. Rather, reporters should be held to an objective, reasonable-person standard, i.e., whether an objective, reasonable person, in the same situation, would consider abuse to have taken place. Failure to prosecute false accusers should deprive the state of federal funding.

2. **The mandated reporting clause must be dropped**. It has resulted in the reporting of frivolous and absurd accusations by two- and three-year-olds, vengeful former spouses, and hysterical parents of nursery school children. Skilled examiners face criminal charges for not reporting these specious accusations to individuals who may be overzealous, inexperienced, even incompetent. Mental health professionals who are licensed by the state to practice should be given the discretion to report. This change also would reduce significantly the flood of false referrals being generated.

3. Evaluators licensed to conduct such examinations should be *required* to interview the accuser, the alleged child victim, *and* extend an invitation to the accused party to be interviewed (accused suspects, of course, must first be informed of their legal rights). The failure to require such provisos should deprive the state of federal funding.

4. States should require that all evaluative interviews be videotaped.

5. Interviews in which suggestive materials are used—specifically anatomically detailed dolls, body charts, and materials depicting explicit sexual organs—should not be admissible in a court of law. There is compelling scientific evidence that such materials so contaminate the interview that they compromise significantly the evaluator's ability to differentiate between a true and false sex-abuse accusation.

6. States in which individuals suspected of child abuse are deprived of constitutional due-process protections should not be provided federal funding.

7. The federal laws now provide funding for child-abuse education and treatment. Such educational programs must be periodically updated

to include new developments, especially in the realm of differentiating between true and false accusations. Professionals involved in child-abuse assessments should be required to attend periodically these course updates. Funding should also be provided for treatment programs for those who are falsely accused and children who have been victimized by being used as vehicles for a false accusation.

8. CAPTA makes funds available for the child's legal representative, the accuser's legal representative, but not for the defendant's legal representative (the public defender). As a result, overburdened public defenders' offices are not capable of providing equal representation for defendants. Prosecutors can generally afford special units devoted to sex abuse; public defenders rarely enjoy this luxury. CAPTA can correct this inequity.

9. Each state must be required to establish an office and procedures to consider applications for postconviction judicial review from anyone convicted of a child-abuse crime. When considering such applications, special attention should be given to: (1) the possibility of violation of the defendant's due-process protections, (2) new scientific developments—especially in such areas as suggestibility, memory, medical findings, and differentiating between true and false accusations—and (3) whether the accuser and/or the alleged child victim have recanted.

The reviewing office should be required to issue a report detailing specifically its reasons for its conclusions regarding the justification for postconviction judicial review. The existence of this office would not preclude a defendant's enjoying traditional postconviction rights and procedures. Federal funding would supplement state funding specifically designated for the implementation of this proposal, especially funding for defendants to engage the services of counsel.

The implementation of these proposals into CAPTA should ensure protection for truly abused children and those alleged perpetrators who may be falsely accused. If these changes are not effected, it is unlikely that the hysteria that is now in its second decade will abate. Unfortunately, at the time that I write this (fall 1995) there is little likelihood that Congress will make the kind of meaningful changes in CAPTA that will reverse the hysteria. Accordingly, we are likely to see a continuation of the kinds of problems described in this book, problems that could be prevented, in part, by proper legislation. It was misguided legislation that was the predominant cause of this hysteria in the first place, and it is only through corrective legislation that the hysteria will be reversed.

REFERENCES

Abel, G. G., Becker, J. V., Cunningham-Rathner, J., Mittelman, M. S., and Rouleau, J. L. (1988), Multiple paraphilic diagnoses among sex offenders. *Bulletin of the American Academy of Psychiatry and the Law*, 16(2):153–168.

The American Psychiatric Association (1952), *Diagnostic and Statistical Manual*. Washington, D.C.: American Psychiatric Association.

The American Psychiatric Association (1968), *Diagnostic and Statistical Manual, Second Edition (DSM-II)*. Washington, D.C.: American Psychiatric Association.

The American Psychiatric Association (1980), *Diagnostic and Statistical Manual, Third Edition (DSM-III)*. Washington, D.C.: American Psychiatric Association.

The American Psychiatric Association (1987), *Diagnostic and Statistical Manual, Third Edition—Revised (DSM-III-R)*. Washington, D.C.: American Psychiatric Association.

The American Psychiatric Association (1994), *Diagnostic and Statistical Manual, Fourth Edition (DSM-IV)*. Washington, D.C.: American Psychiatric Association.

August, R. L. and Forman, B. D. (1989), A comparison of sexually abused and nonsexually abused children's behavioral responses to anatomically correct dolls. *Child Psychiatry and Human Development*, 20(1):39–46.

Ayalon, O. (1984), Sexual exploitation of children: an overview of its scope, impact, and legal ramifications. *FBI Law Enforcement Bulletin*, 2:15–20.

Becker, J. V., Kaplan, M. S., Cunningham-Rathner, J., and Kavoussi, R. (1986), Characteristics of adolescent incest perpetrators: preliminary findings. *Journal of Family Violence*, 1:85–87.

Bell, A. P. and Weinberg, M. S. (1978), *Homosexualities: A Study of Diversity among Men and Women*. New York: Simon & Schuster.

Bell, A. P., Weinberg, M. S., and Hammersmith, S. K. (1981), *Sexual Preference: Its Development in Men and Women*. Bloomington, Indiana: Indiana University Press.

Bellak, L. and Bellak, S. S. (1949), *Children's Apperception Test*. Larchmont, New York: C.P.S. Co.

─────── (1963), *Children's Apperception Test—Supplement*. Larchmont, New York: C.P.S. Co.

Benedek, E. P. and Schetky, D. H. (1987), Problems in validating allegations of sexual abuse, part 2, clinical evaluation. *Journal of the American Academy of Child and Adolescent Psychiatry*, 26(6):916–921.

Bieber, I., Dain, H., Dince, P., Drellich, M., Grand, H., Gundlach, R., Dremer, M., Rifkin, A., Wilbur, C., and Bieber, T. (1962), *Homosexuality: A Psychoanalytic Study of Male Homosexuals*. New York: Basic Books, Inc.

Boat, B. W. and Everson, M. D. (1988), Interviewing young children with anatomical dolls. *Child Welfare*, 67(4):337–351.

Brainerd, C. and Ornstein, P. A. (1991), Children's memory for witnessed events: the developmental backdrop. In *The Suggestibility of Children's Recollections*, ed. J. Doris, pp. 10–20. Washington, D.C.: American Psychological Association.

Browning, D. H. and Boatman, B. (1977), Incest: children at risk. *American Journal of Psychiatry*, 134:69–72.

Bruck, M., Ceci, S. J., Francoeur, E., and Renick, A. (1995), Anatomically detailed dolls do not facilitate preschoolers' reports of a pediatric examination involving genital touching. *Journal of Experimental Psychology: Applied*, 1:95–109.

Caffaro-Rouget, A., Lang, R. A., and Van Santen, V. (1989), The impact of child sexual abuse on victims' adjustment. *Annals of Sex Research*, 2:29–47.

Ceci, S. J. (1991), Some overarching issues in the children's suggestibility debate. In *The Suggestibility of Children's Recollections*, ed. J. Doris, pp. 1–9. Washington, D.C.: American Psychological Association.

_____ (1995), *Jeopardy in the Courtroom*. Washington, D.C.: American Psychological Association.

Clancy, P. E. and Firpo, P. A. (1991), *A System Out of Balance* (videotape). Walnut Creek, California: Clancy, Firpo, and Weisinger (law firm).

Clarke-Stewart, A., Thomson, W. C., and Lepore, S. (1989), Manipulating children's interpretations through interrogation. In *Can children provide accurate eyewitness reports?* G. S. Goodman (chair), symposium conducted at the biennial meeting of the Society for Research in Child Development, Kansas City, Missouri.

Condy, S. R., Templer, D. I., Brown, R., and Veaco, L. (1987), Parameters of sexual contact of boys with women. *Archives of Sexual Behavior*, 16(5):379–394.

Crewdson, J. (1988), *By Silence Betrayed*. Boston: Little, Brown and Co.

Davies, G. (1991), Concluding comments. In *The Suggestibility of Children's Recollections*, ed. J. Doris, pp. 177–187. Washington, D.C.: American Psychological Association.

_____, Stevenson-Robb, Y., and Flin, R. (1988), Tales out of school: children's memory for an unexpected event. In *Practical Aspects of Memory: Current Research and Issues*, ed. M. M. Gruneberg, P. E. Morris, and R. N. Sykes, pp. 122–127. Chichester, England: Wiley.

_____, Tarrant, A., and Flin, R. (1989), Close encounters of a witness kind: children's memory for a simulated health inspection. *British Journal of Psychology*, 80:415–429.

Dawkins, R. (1976), *The Selfish Gene*. London: Oxford University Press.

DeFrancis, V. (1969), *Protecting the child victims of sex crimes committed by adults*. Denver, Colorado: American Humane Association.

Demause, L. (1991), The universality of incest. *Journal of Psychohistory*, 19(2):123–164.

Dent, H. R. (1991), Experimental studies of interviewing child witnesses. In *The Suggestibility of Children's Recollections*, ed. J. Doris, pp. 138–146. Washington, D.C.: American Psychological Association.

D'Udine, B. (1990), The modification of sexual behavior through imprinting: a rodent model. In *Pedophilia: Biosocial Dimensions*, ed. J. R. Feierman, pp. 221–241. New York: Springer-Verlag.

Edgarton, J. E. and Campbell, R. J. (1994), *American Psychiatric Glossary, Seventh Edition.* Washington, D.C.: American Psychiatric Press, Inc.

Eibl-Eibesfeldt, I. (1990), Dominance, submission, and love: sexual pathologies from the perspective of ethology. In *Pedophilia: Biosocial Dimensions*, ed. J. R. Feierman, pp. 150–175. New York: Springer-Verlag.

Encyclopaedia Britannica, Micropedia (1982), Children's Crusade, II:840–841.

Finkelhor, D. (1986), *A Sourcebook on Child Sexual Abuse.* Beverly Hills, California: Sage Publications, Inc.

Flin, R. (1991), A grand memory for forgetting. In *The Suggestibility of Children's Recollections*, ed. J. Doris, pp. 21–23. Washington, D.C.: American Psychological Association.

_____ (1905), Three contributions to the theory of sex: II—infantile sexuality. In *The Basic Writings of Sigmund Freud*, ed. A. A. Brill, pp. 592–593. New York: Random House, Inc. (The Modern Library), 1938.

Freud, S. (1909), Analysis of phobia in a five-year-old boy. *Collected Papers*, vol. 3, pp. 149–289. New York: Basic Books, Inc., 1959.

_____ (1930), *Civilization and Its Discontents.* London: The Hogarth Press, Ltd., 1950.

Freud, S. and Breuer, J. (1895), *Studies on Hysteria.* New York: Basic Books, Inc., 1957.

Friedman, R. C. (1988), *Male Homosexuality: A Contemporary Analytic Perspective.* New Haven, Connecticut: Yale University Press.

Frisbie, L. (1969), *Another Look at Sex Offenders in California.* California Department of Mental Hygiene, Research Monograph No. 12, Sacramento, California.

Frost, M. A. (1986), "Weird science" and child sex abuse cases. *The Champion*, January/February 1986, pp. 17–18.

Gabriel, R. M. (1985), Anatomically correct dolls in the diagnosis of sexual abuse of children. *Journal of the Melanie Klein Society*, 3(2):40–51.

Gardner, R. A. (1968), The mutual storytelling technique: use in alleviating childhood oedipal problems. *Contemporary Psychoanalysis*, 4:161–177.

_____ (1969a), Guilt, Job, and JB. *Medical Opinion and Review*, 5(2):146ff.

_____ (1969b), The guilt reaction of parents of children with severe physical disease. *American Journal of Psychiatry*, 126:636–644.

_____ (1970), The use of guilt as a defense against anxiety. *The Psychoanalytic Review*, 57:124–136.

_____ (1971), *Therapeutic Communication with Children: The Mutual Storytelling Technique.* New York: Jason Aronson, Inc.

_____ (1972), Little Hans—the most famous boy in the child psychotherapy literature. *International Journal of Child Psychotherapy*, 1(4):24–50.

_____ (1973), *The Talking, Feeling, and Doing Game.* Cresskill, New Jersey: Creative Therapeutics, Inc.

_____ (1975), *Psychotherpeutic Approaches to the Resistant Child.* Northvale, New Jersey: Jason Aronson, Inc.

_____ (1976), *Psychotherapy with Children of Divorce.* Northvale, New Jersey: Jason Aronson, Inc.

_____ (1979), *The Parents Book About Divorce* (paperback edition). New York: Bantam Books, Inc.

_____ (1986), *Child Custody Litigation: A Guide for Parents and Mental Health Professionals.* Cresskill, New Jersey: Creative Therapeutics, Inc.

_____ (1987), *The Parental Alienation Syndrome and the Differentiation Between False and Genuine Sex Abuse.* Cresskill, New Jersey: Creative Therapeutics, Inc.

_____ (1988a), *The Storytelling Card Game.* Cresskill, New Jersey: Creative Therapeutics, Inc.

_____ (1988b), *Psychotherapy with Adolescents.* Cresskill, New Jersey: Creative Therapeutics, Inc.

_____ (1991a), *Sex Abuse Hysteria: Salem Witch Trials Revisited.* Cresskill, New Jersey: Creative Therapeutics, Inc.

_____ (1991b), *The Parents Book About Divorce, Second Edition* (hardcover). Cresskill, New Jersey: Creative Therapeutics, Inc.

_____ (1991c), *The Parents Book About Divorce, Second Edition* (paperback). New York: Bantam Books, Inc.

_____ (1992a), *True and False Accusations of Child Sex Abuse.* Cresskill, New Jersey: Creative Therapeutics, Inc.

_____ (1992b), *The Psychotherapeutic Techniques of Richard A. Gardner, Revised Edition.* Cresskill, New Jersey: Creative Therapeutics, Inc.

_____ (1992c), *Self-Esteem: Psychodynamics and Psychotherapy.* Cresskill, New Jersey: Creative Therapeutics, Inc.

_____ (1992d), *The Parental Alienation Syndrome: A Guide for Mental Health and Legal Professionals.* Cresskill, New Jersey: Creative Therapeutics, Inc.

_____ (1993), Child sex abuse and hysteria: 1890s (Austria)/1990s (U.S.). *Bulletin of the American Society of Psychoanalytic Physicians*, 81(2):1–20.

_____ (1994a), *Conduct Disorders of Childhood.* Cresskill, New Jersey: Creative Therapeutics, Inc.

_____ (1994b), Psychotherapy with depressed and suicidal adolescents. In *The Transmission of Depression in Children and Families: Assessment and Intervention*, ed. G. P. Sholevar, pp. 223–258. Northvale, New Jersey: Jason Aronson, Inc.

_____ (1995a), *Protocols for the Sex-Abuse Evaluation.* Cresskill, New Jersey: Creative Therapeutics, Inc.

_____ (1995b), Repression, dissociation, and sex-abuse accusations. *Issues in Child Abuse Accusations*, 7(1):19–29.

Garland, R. J. and Dougher, M. J. (1990), The abused/abuser hypothesis of child sexual abuse: a critical review of theory and research. In *Pedophilia: Biosocial Dimensions*, ed. J. R. Feierman, pp. 488–509. New York: Springer-Verlag.

Gebhard, P. H. and Gagnon, J. H. (1964), Male sex offenses against very young children. *American Journal of Psychiatry*, 121:576–579.

Gibbon, E. (1983), *The History of the Decline and Fall of the Roman Empire.* New York: Modern Library.

Glaser, D. and Collins, C. (1989), The response of young, non-sexually abused children to anatomically correct dolls. *Journal of Child Psychology and Psychiatry*, 30(4):547–560.

Goleman, D. (1988), Lies can point to mental disorders or signal normal growth. *The New York Times*, Science Times, p. C1, May 17, 1988.

Gomes-Schwartz, B., Horowitz, J., and Sauzier, M. (1985), Severity of emotional distress among sexually abused preschool, school age and adolescent children. *Hospital Community Psychiatry*, 36:503–508.

Goodman, G. S. (1991), On stress and accuracy in research on children's testimony. In *The Suggestibility of Children's Recollections*, ed. J. Doris, pp. 77–82. Washington, D.C.: American Psychological Association.

―――― and Clarke-Stewart, A. (1991), Suggestibility in children's testimony: implications for sexual abuse investigations. In *The Suggestibility of Children's Recollections*, ed. J. Doris, pp. 92–105. Washington, D.C.: American Psychological Association.

Goodwin, J. (1987), Developmental impacts of incest. In *Basic Handbook of Child Psychiatry*, ed. J. D. Call, R. L. Cohen, S. I. Harrison, I. N. Berlin, and L. A. Stone, vol. V, pp. 103–111. New York: Basic Books, Inc.

Green, R. (1985), Gender identity in childhood and later sexual orientation: follow-up of 78 males. *American Journal of Psychiatry*, 142(3):339–341.

―――― (1987), *The "Sissy Boy Syndrome" and the Development of Homosexuality*. New Haven, Connecticut: Yale University Press.

Groth, A. N. (1979a), Sexual trauma in the life histories of rapists and child molesters. *Victimology*, 4:10–16.

―――― (1979b), *Men Who Rape*. New York: Plenum Publishing Co.

―――― (1984), *Anatomical Drawings: For Use in the Investigation and Intervention of Child Sex Abuse*. Newton Centre, Massachusetts: Forensic Mental Health Associates.

Hanson, R. K. (1991), Characteristics of sex offenders who were sexually abused as children. *Sex Offenders and Their Victims*, ed. R. Langevin, pp. 78–85. Oakville, Ontario: Juniper Press.

Herdt, G. H. (1981), *Guardians of the Flutes: Idioms of Masculinity*. New York: McGraw-Hill Book Co.

Hess, E. H. (1966), Imprinting. In *Readings for an Introduction to Psychology*, ed. R. A. King, pp. 39–46. New York: McGraw-Hill Book Co.

Hindman, J. (1991), Sexual victim trauma assessment. In *Sex Offenders and Their Victims*, ed. Ron Langevin, pp. 151–165. Oakville, Ontario: Juniper Press.

Jampole, L. and Weber, M. K. (1987), An assessment of the behavior of sexually abused and nonsexually abused children with anatomically correct dolls. *Child Abuse and Neglect*, 11:187–192.

Kahr, B. (1991), The sexual molestation of children: historical perspectives. *Journal of Psychohistory*, 19(2):191–214.

Kanner, L. (1935), *Child Psychiatry, Third Edition.* Springfield, Illinois: Charles C Thomas, Publisher.

Kempe, R. and Kempe, C. H. (1978), *Child Abuse.* Cambridge, Massachussets: Harvard University Press.

King, M. A. and Yuille, J. C. (1987), Suggestibility and the child witness. In *Children's Eyewitness Memory,* ed. S. J. Ceci, M. P. Toglia, and D. F. Ross, pp. 24–35. New York: Springer-Verlag.

Kinsey, A. C., Pomeroy, W. B., Martin, C. E., and Gebhard, P. (1948), *Sexual Behavior in the Human Male.* Philadelphia: W. B. Saunders Co.

Kohut, H. (1977), *The Restoration of the Self.* New York: International Universities Press.

Konker, C. (1992), Rethinking child sexual abuse: an anthropological perspective. *American Journal of Orthopsychiatry,* 62(1):147–153.

Kritzberg, N. I. (1966), A new verbal projective test for the expansion of the projective aspects of the clinical interview. *Acta Paedopsychiatrica,* 33(2):48–62.

Krivacska, J. J. (1989), *Designing Child Sex Abuse Prevention Programs.* Springfield, Illinois: Charles C Thomas, Publisher.

Lang, R. (1994), Personal communication.

Lanning, K. V. (1992), *Investigator's Guide to Allegations of "Ritual" Child Abuse.* Quantico, Virginia: U.S. Dept. of Justice, National Center for the Analysis of Violent Crime.

Leahy, M. M. (1991), Child sexual abuse: origins, dynamics and treatment. *Journal of the American Academy of Psychoanalysis,* 19(3):385–395.

Legrand, R., Wakefield, H., and Underwager, R. (1989), Alleged behavioral indicators of sexual abuse. *Issues in Child Abuse Accusations,* 1(2):1–5.

Levy, D. M. (1939), Release therapy. *American Journal of Orthopsychiatry,* 9(4):713–736.

——— (1940), Psychotherapy and childhood. *The American Journal of Orthopsychiatry.* 10(4):905–910.

Lindberg, M. (1991), An interactive approach to assessing the suggestibility and testimony of eyewitnesses. In *The Suggestibility of Children's Recollections,* ed. J. Doris, pp. 47–55. Washington, D.C.: American Psychological Association.

Livingston, R., Lawson, L., and Jones, J. (1993), Predictors of self-reported psychopathology in children abused repeatedly by a parent. *Journal of the American Academy of Child and Adolescent Psychiatry*, 32(5):948–953.

Loftus, E. F. (1975), Leading questions and the eyewitness report. *Cognitive Psychology*, 7:560–572.

―――― and Davies, G. M. (1984), Distortions in the memory of children. *Journal of Social Issues*, 40:51–67.

――――, Miller, D. G., and Burns, H. J. (1978), Semantic integration of verbal information into a visual memory. *Journal of Experimental Psychology: Human Learning and Memory*, 4:19–31.

―――― and Palmer, J. C. (1974), Reconstruction of automobile destruction: an example of the interaction between language and memory. *Journal of Verbal Learning and Verbal Behavior*, 13:585–589.

――――, Schooler, J., and Wagenaar, W. (1985), The fate of memory: comment on McCloskey and Zaragoza. *Journal of Experimental Psychology: General*, 114:375–380.

Longo, R. E. (1982), Sexual learning and experience among adolescent sexual offenders. *International Journal of Offender Therapy and Comparative Criminology*, 26:235–241.

Lorenz, K. (1937), The nature of instinct. In *Instinctive Behavior: The Development of a Modern Concept*, ed. C. H. Schiller. London: Methuen.

―――― (1950), The comparative method of studying innate behavior patterns. *Symposium of the Society of Experimental Biology*, 4:221–268.

Luria, A. R. (1968), *The Mind of a Mnemonist*. New York: Basic Books, Inc.

Lyons, A. S. and Petrucelli, R. J. (1978), *Medicine: An Illustrated History*. New York: Harry N. Abrams, Inc.

Mappan, M. (1980), *Witches and Historians*. Malabar, Florida: Robert E. Krieger Publishing Co.

McGough, L. S. (1991a), Sexual abuse and suggestibility. In *The Suggestibility of Children's Recollections*, ed. J. Doris, pp. 115–117. Washington, D.C.: American Psychological Association.

_____ (1991b), Assessing the credibility of witnesses' statements. In *The Suggestibility of Children's Recollections*, ed. J. Doris, pp. 165–167. Washington, D.C.: American Psychological Association.

McHugh, P. R. (1993), Multiple personality disorder, *The Harvard Mental Health Letter*, 10(3):4–6.

McIver, W. F. (1986), The case for a therapeutic interview in situations of alleged sexual molestation. *The Champion*, 10(1):11–13.

_____, Wakefield, H., and Underwager, R. (1989), Behavior of abused and nonabused children in interviews with anatomically correct dolls. *Issues in Child Abuse Accusations*, 1(1):39–48.

Medicus, G. and Hopf, S. (1990), The phylogeny of male/female differences in sexual behavior. In *Pedophilia: Biosocial Dimensions*, ed. J. R. Feierman, pp. 122–149. New York: Springer-Verlag.

Menninger, K. A. (1957), *The Human Mind, Third Edition*. New York: Alfred Knopf.

Michael, R. T., Gagnon, J. H., Laumann, E. O., and Kolata, G. (1994), *Sex in America*. Boston, Massachusetts: Little Brown and Co.

Money, J. (1990), Pedophilia: a specific instance of new phylism theory as applied to paraphilic lovemaps. In *Pedophilia: Biosocial Dimensions*, ed. J. R. Feierman, pp. 445–463. New York: Springer-Verlag.

_____ and Russo, A. J. (1979), Homosexual outcome of discordant gender activity role in childhood: longitudinal follow-up. *Journal of Pediatric Psychology*, 4:29–49.

Murray, H. (1936), *The Thematic Apperception Test*. New York: The Psychological Corp.

Myles-Worsley, M., Cromer, C., and Dodd, D. (1986), Children's preschool script reconstruction: reliance on general knowledge as memory fades. *Developmental Psychology*, 22:2–30.

Nakashima, I. and Zakins, G. (1977), Incest: review and clinical experience. *Pediatrics*, 60:696–701.

Overholser, J. C. and Beck, S. (1986), Multimethod assessment of rapists, child molesters, and three control groups on behavioral and psychological measures. *Journal of Consulting and Clinical Psychology*, 54:682–687.

Peters, D. (1991), The influence of stress and arousal on the child witness. In *The Suggestibility of Children's Recollections*, ed. J. Doris, pp. 60–76. Washington, D.C.: American Psychological Association.

Peters, J. J. (1976), Children who are victims of sexual assualt and the psychology of offenders. *American Journal of Psychotherapy*, 30:398–421.

Phongpaichit, P. (1982), *From Peasant Girls to Bangkok Masseuses*. Geneva: International Labor Organization.

Random House Dictionary of the English Language, 2nd Edition (1987), New York: Random House, Inc.

Raskin, D. C. and Esplin, P. W. (1991), Assessment of children's statements of sexual abuse. In *The Suggestibility of Children's Recollections*, ed. J. Doris, pp. 153–164. Washington, D.C.: American Psychological Association.

―――― and Steller, M. (1989), Assessing credibility of allegations of child sexual abuse: polygraph examinations and statement analysis. In *Criminal Behavior and the Justice System*, ed. H. Wegener, F. Loesel, and J. Haisch, pp. 290–302. New York: Springer-Verlag.

Ravitch, D. and Finn, C. E. (1987), *What Do Our 17-Year-Olds Know?* New York: Random House, Inc.

Realmuto, G. M., Jensen, J. B., and Wescoe, S. (1990), Specificity and sensitivity of sexually anatomically correct dolls in substantiating abuse: a pilot study. *Journal of the American Academy of Child and Adolescent Psychiatry*, 29(5):743–746.

Reeves, T. (1981), Loving boys. In *The Age Taboo*, ed. D. Tsang. Boston: Alyson Publications.

Richardson, K. W. (1983), *The Salem Witchcraft Trials*. Salem, Massachusetts: Essex Institute.

Robson, B. (1991), The scars of Scott county. *Minneapolis/St. Paul*, March 1991, p. 48ff.

Rorschach, H. (1921), *The Rorschach Test*. New York: The Psychological Corp.

Saywitz, K. J. (1987), Children's testimony: age-related patterns of memory errors. In *Children's Eyewitness Memory*, ed. S. J. Ceci, M. P. Toglia, and D. F. Ross, pp. 36–52. New York: Springer-Verlag.

―――― , Goodman, G., Nicholas, G., and Moan, S. (1991), Children's memory for genital exam: Implications for child sexual abuse. *Journal of Consulting and Clinical Psychology*, 59:682–691.

Sgroi, S. M., Porter, F. S., and Blick, L. C. (1982), Validation of child sexual abuse. In *Handbook of Clinical Intervention in Child Sexual Abuse*, ed. S. M. Sgroi, pp. 39–79. Lexington, Massachusetts: Lexington Books (D.C. Heath and Co.).

Shanor, K. (1978), *The Shanor Study: The Sexual Sensitivity of the American Male.* New York: Dial Press.

Sigston, A. and White, D. G. (1975), Conformity in children as a function of age level. *British Journal of Social and Clinical Psychology*, 3:388–419.

Silva, D. C. (1990), Pedophilia: an autobiography. In *Pedophilia: Biosocial Dimensions*, ed. J. R. Feierman, pp. 464–487. New York: Springer-Verlag.

Sivan, A. B., Schor, D. P., Koeppl, G. K., and Noble, L. D. (1988), Interaction of normal children with anatomical dolls. *Child Abuse and Neglect*, 12:295–304.

Steinberg, M. (1993), *Interviewer's Guide to the Structured Clinical Interview for DSM-IV Dissociative Disorders.* Washington, D.C.: American Psychiatric Press, Inc.

Steller, M. (1991), Rehabilitation of the child witness. In *The Suggestibility of Children's Recollections*, ed. J. Doris, pp. 106–109. Washington, D.C.: American Psychological Association.

Stoller, R. J. (1975), *Perversion: The Erotic Form of Hatred.* New York: Pantheon.

——— (1979), *Sexual Excitement: Dynamics of Erotic Life.* New York: Pantheon.

——— (1985), *Observing the Exotic Imagination.* New Haven, Connecticut: Yale University Press.

Strassmann, B. I. (1981), Sexual selection, parental care, and concealed ovulation in humans. *Ethology and Sociobiology*, 2:31–40.

Summit, R. C. (1983), The child sexual abuse accommodation syndrome. *Child Abuse and Neglect*, 7:177–193.

——— (1991), *State of Florida vs. Bob Fijnje.* Deposition of *Roland C. Summit*, January 8, 1991. pp. 50–51.

Terr, L. (1990), *Too Scared to Cry.* New York: Basic Books, Inc.

Thompson, W. C., Clarke-Stewart, A., Meyer, J., Pathak, M. K., and Lepore, S. (1991), *Children's susceptibility to suggestive interrogation.* Paper presented at the annual meeting of the American Psychological Association, San Francisco, California.

Toglia, M. P. (1991), Memory impairment—it is more common than you think. In *The Suggestibility of Children's Recollections*, ed. J. Doris, pp. 40–46. Washington, D.C.: American Psychological Association.

Tripp, C. A. (1987), *The Homosexual Matrix*. New York: New American Library.
Tufts' New England Medical Center, Division of Child Psychiatry (1984), *Sexually Exploited Children: Service and Research Project*. Final report for the Office of Juvenile Justice and Delinquency Prevention. Washington, D.C.: U.S. Department of Justice.
Underwager, R. C. and Wakefield, H. (1990), *The Real World of Child Interrogations*. Springfield, Illinois: Charles C Thomas, Publisher.
_____ (1991), Cur allii, prae aliis? (Why some, and not others?) *Issues in Child Abuse Accusations*, 3(3):178–193.
Undeutsch, U. (1989), The development of statement reality analysis. In *Credibility Assessment*, ed. J. C. Yuille, pp. 101–120. Dordrecht, The Netherlands: Kluwer.
Upham, C. W. (1867), *Salem Witchcraft*. Boston: Boston Publishing Co.
Victor, J. S. (1993), *Satanic Panic*. Chicago, Illinois: Open Court.
Wakefield, H. and Underwager, R. (1988), *Accusations of Child Sex Abuse*. Springfield, Illinois: Charles C Thomas, Publisher.
Warren-Leubecker, A. (1991), The influence of stress and arousal on the child witness. In *The Suggestibility of Children's Recollections*, ed. J. Doris, pp. 83–85. Washington, D.C.: American Psychological Association.
Weinberg, K. S. (1962), *Incest Behavior*. New York: Citadel Press.
Wells, G. L. and Loftus, E. F. (1991), Is this child fabricating? Reactions to a new assessment technique. In *The Suggestibility of Children's Recollections*, ed. J. Doris, pp. 168–171. Washington, D.C.: American Psychological Association.
White, S., Strom, G. A., and Santilli, G. (1985), A protocol for interviewing preschoolers with the sexually anatomically correct dolls (unpublished manuscript). Case Western Reserve University School of Medicine, Cleveland, Ohio.
Winnicott, D. W. (1968), The value of the therapeutic consultation. In *Foundations of Child Psychiatry*, ed. E. Miller, pp. 593–608. London: Pergamon Press.
Zaragoza, M. S. (1991), Preschool children's susceptibility to memory impairment. In *The Suggestibility of Children's Recollections*, ed. J. Doris, pp. 27–39. Washington, D.C.: American Psychological Association.

Zilboorg, G. and Henry, G. W. (1941), *A History of Medical Psychology*. New York: W. W. Norton & Co., Inc.

Zuger, B. (1970), Gender role determination. *Psychosomatic Medicine*, 32:449–467.

———— (1976), Monozygotic twins discordant for homosexuality: report of a pair and significance of the phenomenon. *Comprehensive Psychiatry*, 17:661–669.

———— (1984), Early effeminate behavior in boys: outcome and significance for homosexuality. *Journal of Nervous and Mental Disorders*, 172(2):90–97.

AUTHOR INDEX

Abel, G. G. 40,
American Psychiatric Association, The, 17-36, 92, 293, 295, 309, 362-363, 430, 433
August, R. L., 256
Ayalon, O., 44, 46

Beck, S., 44, 48
Becker, J. V., 40, 47
Bell, A. P., 36,
Bellak, L., 253
Bellak, S. S., 253
Benedek, E. P., 350
Bieber, I., 36,
Bieber, T. 36,
Blick, L. C., 129
Boat, B. W., 249,
Boatman, B., 120
Brainerd, C., 214
Breuer, J., 428
Brown, R., 47
Browning, D. H., 120,
Bruck, M., 226, 256, 257
Burns, H. J., 216

Caffaro-Rouget, A., 124
Campbell, R. J., 305, 307-308

Ceci, S. J., 216, 226, 256, 257
Clancy, P. E., 426
Clarke-Stewart, A., 219, 220, 221, 256
Collins, C., 256
Condy, S. R., 47
Crewdson, J., 48
Cromer, C., 214
Cunningham-Rathner, J., 40, 47

D'Udine, B., 45
Dain, H., 36
Davies, G. M., 216, 223, 225
Dawkins, R., 7, 10-11, 12
DeFrancis, V., 119
Demause, L., 37, 44
Dent, H. R., 224
Dince, P., 36
Dodd, D., 214
Dougher, M. J., 43, 45
Drellich, M., 36
Dremer, M., 36

Edgarton, J. E., 305, 307-308
Eibl-Eibesfeldt, I., 46
Encyclopaedia Britannica, Micropedia, 423

526 AUTHOR INDEX

Esplin, P. W., 224
Everson, M. D., 249

Finkelhor, D., 46
Finn, C.E., 319
Firpo, P. A., 426
Flin, R., 216, 223, 225, 319
Forman, B. D., 256
Francoeur, E., 256
Freud, S., 14, 51, 233, 235, 428, 434
Friedman, R. C., 36
Frisbie, L., 47
Frost, M. A., 276

Gabriel, R. M., 256
Gagnon, J. H., 291-292
Gardner, R. A., 59, 67, 71, 78, 84, 87, 91, 94, 96, 99, 100, 101, 110, 111, 113, 118, 119, 136, 138, 150, 151, 156, 157, 162, 175, 193, 232, 233, 238, 242, 249, 252, 261, 257, 267, 288, 293, 294, 304, 311, 338, 348, 366, 367, 370, 375, 379, 426, 429, 430, 434, 453
Garland, R. J., 43, 45
Gebhard, P., 33
Gebhard, P. H., 291-292
Gibbon, E., 51
Glaser, D., 256
Goleman, D., 226
Gomes-Schwartz, B., 120
Goodman G., 257
Goodman, G. S., 218, 219, 220
Goodwin, J., 119, 120
Grand, H., 36
Green, R., 36, 72
Groth, A. N., 43, 47, 271
Gundlach, R., 36

HansHammersmith, S. K., 36
Hanson, R. K., 47

Henry, G. W., 422, 427
Herdt, G. H., 42
Hess, E. H., 57
Hindman, J., 77
Hopf, S., 45
Horowitz, J., 120

Jampole, L., 256
Jensen, J. B., 256
Jones, J., 115, 117, 124

Kahr, B., 37, 38
Kanner, L., 423
Kaplan, M. S., 47
Kavoussi, R., 47
Kempe, C. H., 117, 120
Kempe, R., 117, 120
King, M. A., 225
Kinsey, A. C., 33
Koeppl, G. K., 256
Kohut, H., 48
Kolata, G., 291-292
Konker, C., 38, 39
Kritzberg, N. I., 263
Krivacska, J. J., 484

Lang, R., 48,
Lang, R. A., 128
Lanning, K. V., 334
Laumann, E. O., 291-292
Lawson, L., 115, 117, 124,
Leahy, M. M., 48
Legrand, R., 293, 424
Lepore, S., 220, 256
Levy, D. M., 270
Lindberg, M., 217
Livingston, R., 115, 117, 124,
Loftus, E. F., 216, 225
Longo, R. E., 43
Lorenz, K., 1, 57,
Luria, A. R., 216
Lyons, A. S., 422

AUTHOR INDEX 527

Mappan, M., 230, 232, 244, 432
Martin, C. E., 33
McGough, L. S., 222-223, 224-225
McHugh, P. R., 428
McIver, W. F., 256, 276, 303
Medicus, G., 45
Menninger, K. A., 423
Meyer, J., 256
Michael, R. T., 291-292
Miller, D. G., 216
Mittelman, M. S., 40
Moan, S., 257
Money, J., 36, 45
Murray, H., 248, 251
Myles-Worsley, M., 214

Nakashima, I., 117,
Nicholas, G., 256
Noble, L. D., 256

Ornstein, P. A., 214
Overholser, J. C., 44, 48

Palmer, J. C., 216
Pathak, M. K., 256
Peters, D., 218
Peters, J. J., 44, 48
Petrucelli, R. J., 422
Phongpaichit, P., 42
Pomeroy, W. B., 33
Porter, F. S., 129

Random House Dictionary of the English Language, 2nd Edition, 431
Raskin, D. C., 224
Ravitch, D., 319
Realmuto, G. M., 256
Reeves, T., 42
Renick, A., 256

Richardson, K. W., 432
Rifkin, A., 36
Robson, B., 346
Rorschach, H., 252
Rouleau, J. L., 40
Russo, A. J., 36

Santilli, G., 256, 265
Sauzier, M., 120
Saywitz, K. J., 226, 257
Schetky, D. H., 350
Schooler, J., 216
Schor, D. P., 256
Sgroi, S. M., 129
Shanor, K., 6
Sigston, A., 304-305
Silva, D. C., 49
Sivan, A. B., 256
State of Florida vs. Bob Fijnje, 301
Steinberg, M., 66
Steller, M., 221, 222, 224
Stevenson-Robb, Y., 223, 225
Stoller, R. J., 43
Strassmann, B. I., 45
Strom, G. A., 256, 265,
Summit, R. C., 91, 134, 295-301

Tarrant, A., 225
Templer, D. I., 47
Terr, L., 357
Thompson, W. C., 220, 256
Toglia, M. P., 216
Tripp, C. A., 33
Tufts' New England Medical Center, Division of Child Psychiatry, 119

Underwager, R. C., 249, 256, 293, 338-339, 346, 424
Undeutsch, U., 224
Upham, C. W., 230, 232, 244

Van Santen, V., 128
Veaco, L., 47
Victor, J. S., 334

Wagenaar, W., 216
Wakefield, H., 249, 256, 293, 338-339, 346, 424
Warren-Leubecker, A., 219
Weber, M. K., 256
Weinberg, K. S., 36, 46
Weinberg, M. S., 36
Wells, G. L., 225

Wescoe, S., 256
White, D. G., 304-305
White, S., 256, 265
Wilbur, C., 36
Winnicott, D. W., 268

Yuille, J. C., 225

Zakins, G., 117
Zaragoza, M. S., 217
Zilboorg, G., 422, 427
Zuger, B., 36

SUBJECT INDEX

Abuser
  removal of from home, 349–350
Affect, of child, 305–307
Alcoholics Anonymous, 160–161
Amnesia, 312, *see also* Memory, in children
  as defense mechanism, 216
Anafranil, for obsessive-compulsive disorder, 67
Anatomical dolls, 311, 508
  and blank-screen principle, violation of, 248
  and embedment-in-the-brain circuitry phenomenon, 78
  as leading stimuli, 248–249, 269, 271, 275
    maximally leading, 254–257
  sexual pathology developed in child via use of, 348
Anatomical drawings, as maximally leading stimuli, 254
Anger, *see also* Hostility
  in child over abuse, 43, 114–117, 148
    attention-getting through, 200–209, 242
  in child over divorce, 231–232
  in child programmed to make false sex-abuse accusation, 357–358
  hysteria and release of, 433–434, 447
  in parent making sex-abuse accusation, xviii
  as symptom of sexual abuse, 95
Antidepressant medications, indications for in sexually abused child, 118
Antisocial behavior, 177
  as symptom of hysteria, induction of, 447
  as symptom of legal process/ "therapy" trauma, 348, 349
Anxiety
  in children, 84
Audiotapes, *see also* Videotapes
  affect of child shown by, 307

Ball-is-in-your-court principle, 367
Bedwetting, 84
Behavioral changes as false indicator of sex abuse, 289
Belated accusations of child sex abuse, xix, 359–360

529

SUBJECT INDEX

Belated jumping-on-the-bandwagon phenomenon, xxx
Bipolar disorder, 35
Blank-screen principle, 248, 251, 259, 370–371
Body charts, 271, 348, 508
Brainwashing. *See Programming children to believe they were sexually abused*
Breastfeeding, female pleasure in, 16

Catapress, 443
Child Abuse Prevention and Treatment Act, 426
  recommendations for changes in, 507–510
Child-custody disputes
  effect of on child's treatment, 99, 366
  false sex-abuse accusations in context of, xviii, 348–349
  hysteria in, 432–433
  parental alienation syndrome arising from, 238–244
Child protection services, 246
Child sexual abuse accommodation syndrome
  description of, 295–298
  diagnostic purposes of, risk in utilizing, 298–301
  misuse of, 91–92, 94
Children, *see also False sex-abuse accusations of children; Memory, of children; Programming children; Sexual abuse; Treatment of sexually abused children*
  anger in over sexual abuse, 43, 114–117
  and betrayal, feelings of, 112, 117, 137, 352
  capacity for learning in, 56–57
  cross-fertilization of sex-abuse accusation, and, xix
  females, sexual similarities to, 45

group therapy for, 98–99
guilt, 116–117
  inducing in child, because of false accusation of abuse, 134, 348, 350, 352, 379
  in parental alienation syndrome child, 240
  problems regarding, 95, 106–111, 129
hostility in, 231–233, 242
and hysterical reactions to normal sexual urges, 454–510
imprinting in, 59
legal-process/"therapy" trauma, 346, 347–352
lying in, 227–228, 247, 276–279, 358–359
memory and suggestibility of, 213–227, 286, 509
normal exploratory play in, 42
  clinical example of, 454, 456, 475–484
orgasms, capacity for in, 14–16, 41, 102
protection of from sexual abuse, 97–98, 120–121
removal from home, 97–98, 349–350
self-esteem problems in, 111–113, 352
sexual excitation in, 41, 84, 88–89, 102–105, 138–139, 348
  clinical examples of, 164–168, 168–172
sexuality in, normal, 103–104, 233–238
symptoms of programming in, 294, 343–364
testifying in court, trauma of, 99–100
trauma to, in sexual encounter, 43, 77–78, 81, 122–123
Children's Apperception Test (CAT),

SUBJECT INDEX 531

as maximally leading stimuli, 253–254
Circumcision, sadism in practice of, 39
Clinical examples
 of embedment in the brain circuitry in homosexual male, 72–73
 of embedment in the brain circuitry in pedophile, 74–76
 of embedment in the brain circuitry in sexual trauma, 77
 of hysterical reactions to normal sexual urges, 454–510
 of hysterical reactions to superficial sexual overtures, 440–454
 of obsessive-compulsive disorder, 68–70
 of treatment with programmed child, 384–417
 of treatment with sexually abused children, 164–168, 168–172, 172–176, 176–192, 192–209
Clonopin, 443
Coercion, by overzealous evaluators, 304–305
Cogentin, 443
Cognition
 dissonance in, 338
 distortions of in programmed child, 371–374
Compliance, pathological in sexually abused children, 126–128
Compulsions, as symptoms of sexual abuse, 115
Conditioning techniques, in biased examiners, 302–303
Conscience, impairments in development of child's, 358
Constitutional rights, of accused, 164, 313–314, 315, 340, 508, 509
Coprophilia, 29

Court-orders, for treating children, 85
Credibility
 of children's descriptions of sexual abuse, 283–285
 of children's memories tests for, 224–225
Criteria, for differentiating true from false sex-abuse accusations, xviii
Criteria-based content analysis (CBCA), 224–225
Cross-fertilization, of sex-abuse accusation, xix
Cunnilingus, 15

Danger, assuming existence of in hysteria, 432–433
Darwin, theory of natural selection, 3–4, 8, 12
 mating patterns related to, 4–5
Dawkins
 gene survival and transmission, theory of, 7–12
 human sexual variety, application to, 12–31
Day-care centers. *See Nursery schools*
Delusions, 314
 of control, in sexually abused child, 110
 embedment in the brain circuitry and, 78–79
 and hysteria, 432
 in mothers of programmed children, 372, 380–381
 in programmed child, 345, 359
 of sexual abuse, xvii, 67, 428
  fabrication becoming over time, 228–230, 355
Depression
 in hysterical reaction to superficial sexual overtures, 444
 as symptom of legal process/

Depression *(continued)*
  "therapy" trauma, 348, 349
  as symptom of sexual abuse, 95, 115, 117–119
  betrayal, feeling of and, 117
  guilt as component of, 108–109
  suicidal thoughts and, 117, 118
Desensitization process, 288
  clinical example describing, 177
  definition of, 92
  in posttraumatic stress disorder, 65, 92–94, 95–96, 368–369
  in therapy for sexual abuse, 101–102, 149
Dissociation,
  in child sexual abuse, 66–67, 216
  definition of, 307–308
  maneuver of, by overzealous therapists, 307–311, 312
  in posttraumatic stress disorder, 65–66
Dissociative disorder, and hysteria, 430
Divorce, *see also Child-custody disputes*
  anger in child due to, 231–232
  misuse of child sexual abuse accommodation syndrome related to, 301
DNA
  role in gene survival and transmission, 8–12, 16, 31, 33, 34, 51, 52
Doll play, 270, *see also Anatomical dolls*
Domination, as factor in male pedophilia, 44, 155
Draw-a-family test, 268, 447
Draw-a-person test, 268, 446–447
Drawing, in treatment of sexually abused child, 194–209
Dreams, recurrent of sexual abuse, 93

DSM-IV, 293, 363
  homosexuality referred to in, 17–18, 31–37,
  hysteria as diagnosis in, 430
  paraphilias described in, 17–31
  posttraumatic stress disorder, definition of, 64–65
Dyspareunia, 31

Embedment-in-the-brain-circuitry phenomenon (EBCP), xxi, 55–81
  childhood sexual experiences and, 41, 42, 76–79
Emotions
  deprivation of in childhood, 46–47
  clinical vignette demonstrating, 192–209
  and embedment-in-the-brain-circuitry phenomenon, 55–56
  in hysteria, 431–432, 433
  infectiousness of, 233, 238
  problems regarding in programmed child, 376–380
  and regression, 105, 348, 447
Enemas, 29
Environment
  Darwin's theory of natural selection and, 4
  vs. genetics, 13–14
  pedophilia, as influenced by, 73–76
  role of in depression of sexually abused child, 117
Examiners. *See Overzealous evaluators; Therapists; Validators*
Exhibitionism, 19–20

False sex-abuse accusations of children

cross-fertilization seen in, xix
definition of, xvii–xviii
embedment in the brain circuitry, causes for, 78–79
guilt due to, 134, 348, 352, 379
parental alienation syndrome and, 232, 238–244
preventing, 507–510
psychodynamic factors underlying, 227–245
 attention-getting, 230–231
 keeping-up-with-the-Joneses phenomenon, 228–230
 lying to adults, 227–228
Families
emotional neglect of child in, 46–47
 clinical vignette demonstrating, 192–209
 treatment with, 96–97, 130, 163, 173–176, 370
Fantasies, differentiating from fact, 353
Fantasies, sexual
in children, 235–236, 237
 clinical example illustrating, 454–510
 induced by leading questions in interviews, 266, 353–355
 and embedment in the brain circuitry, 70–79
and paraphilias, 18
Father(s), *see also Treatment of fathers*
as abuser, 144–164
 relationship with child, treatment to improve, 130–132, 382–383
 threats made to child, 127
as accused for sexual abuse of child, 86, 349–350, 382–383
child's hatred of, 378
in parental alienation syndrome, 238–244

Fear, 68
in child making false sex-abuse accusation, 352, 355–357, 362
in child suffering with parental alienation syndrome, 239–240
in sexually abused child, 118, 119–121, 129, 148, 266
retraction of abuse and, 134
Feces, 29
Female(s), *see also Gender; Mother(s)*
mating patterns in, 2–7, 51
Feminism, and sexual abuse accusations, 88, 232, 335
Fetishism, 20–21
transvestic, 25–26, 36
Folie-à-deux relationship
between mother and validator, 334, 381
between parents, 436
between programming parent and child, 244
between therapist and patient, 360
embedment in the brain circuitry and, 79
Foster families, clinical vignette referring to, 192–209
Freud
and causes of hysteria, 427, 429
polymorphous perversity of child theory, 14, 150, 233–234, 237, 247, 436
repression of sexuality in societies, 51, 434–436
Frotteurism, 21–22

Games, contaminating in interviews with children, 268, *see also Storytelling Card Game; Talking, Feeling, and Doing Game*
Gender
differences in,
 domination factor, 44, 155
 and hysteria, 434–437

Gender *(continued)*
    impulsivity, 157–158
    mating patterns and, 2–8
    sexual behavior, atypical and, 19–20, 21, 24–25, 28
Gender identity disorder of childhood, 36
Genetics, *see also DNA*
    vs. environment, 13–14, 30
    male
        dominating characteristics in, 155
        impulsivity in, 157–158
        survival choices influenced by, 3
    role of in sexual behavior
        Darwin's theory of natural selection, 3–4
        Dawkins's theory related to, 12–31
        paraphilias and, 35
Genitals
    feelings about in sexually abused child, 111–112
    pathological attitude toward in programmed child, 348, 375
Group therapy
    for fathers, 146–147, 156
    for mothers, 136
    for sexually abused children, 98–99
Guilt
    definition of, 106
    in child, 116–117, 240
        due to destruction of parent's life in false accusation, 350, 379
        due to hysterical reactions to normal sexual urges, 454–510
    in false sex-abuse accusation, 134, 348, 352, 379
    in father, 151–153, 157
    masochism and, 24
    in mother, 137

obsessive-compulsive disorder and, 68
    clinical example of, 68–70
    retraction of abuse due to, 134
    sexual abuse, related to, 95, 106–111, 129, 266

Haldol, 443
Heterosexuality
    Dawkins's theory and, 12–13
    transvestic fetishism in, 26, 36
Homophobia, 34
Homosexuality
    childhood seduction and onset of, 41
    embedment in the brain circuitry, factors in, 72–73
    gender identity disorder and, 36
    heterosexuality, conversion to, 80
    narcissism in, 48
    as a paraphilia, 17–18, 31–37
    pedophilia and, 35, 158–160
    population control and, 33
    promiscuity and, 33
    transvestic fetishism and, 36
    treatment of, 159
Hospitalization, of sexually abused child, 192–209
Hostility
    in children making false sex-abuse accusation, 231–233, 240
    paraphilias as release for, 30
    in parental alienation syndrome child, 242
    underlying hysteria, 422
    underlying parental alienation syndrome, 238
Human sexual behavior. *See Sexual behavior, human*
Hypersexualization in sexually abused children, 102–105, 138–139, 164–168, 168–172, 192–193
Hypocrisy, in validators, 335–336

Hysteria, 419–438, 447
  causes of, theories on, 427–429
  components of, 431–438
  in DSM-III-R and DSM-IV, 430
  group, 421–427, 437
  historical, 421–425
  lawsuits and, 437–438
  levels of, xxi–xxii,
  in males, 435–437
  mass, 421–427, 437
  masturbation and, 291–293,
    423–424
  in mothers, 135
  sexual abuse, 364, 411,
    child abuse prevention and
      treatment act (CAPTA), role
      of in, 426
    in child-custody disputes, 420
    description of, 420–421
    embedment-in-the-brain
      circuitry phenomenon, in, 78
    group, 420, 437
    in nursery school accusations,
      367, 420, 436
    to sexual overtures, superficial,
      440–454
    in validators, xix

Identification
  with the aggressor
    parental alienation syndrome
      and child's, 241
    pedophilia and, 43–44
  with idealized person, 241–242
Immunity from prosecution proviso,
  in Child Abuse Prevention and
  Treatment Act, 507–508
Imprinting
  in humans, 58–59
  in lower animals, 57–58
  in male homosexuality, 40–42
Impulsivity, in men, 157–158
Inadequacy, feelings of,
  and paraphilias, 30

  in pedophiles, 47, 48–49
Incest, 51, *see also Sexual abuse*
Intelligence, low in pedophiles, 49
Interrogations, courtroom, trauma
  to child in, 351–352

Judges, and conviction for therapy,
  369
Judgment, impairment of in hysteria,
  433

Keeping-up-with-the-Joneses
  phenomenon, 228–230, 267,
  304
Kidney-transplant principle, 130
Klismaphilia, 29

Lawsuits, psychopathy arising in
  children from exposure to,
  359–360
  hysteria in, 437–438
Leading gestures, 250, 256, 266–267
  maximally leading, 271–273
  minimally leading, 268–269
  moderately leading, 269–271
  nonleading, 267–268
Leading questions
  definition of, 257–259
  embedment-in-the-brain circuitry
    and, 78
  maximally leading, 265–266
  minimally leading, 260–262
  moderately leading, 262–264
  nonleading, 259–260
  in programming nonabused
    children to believe they were
    abused
    repetition of, 219, 280–281,
      455–456
    studies on, 216–217
    use of, 249–251, 257–266
Leading stimuli, 248–250
  maximally leading stimuli, 253
  minimally leading stimuli, 252

Leading stimuli *(continued)*
  moderately leading stimuli, 253
  nonleading, 251–252
Learning
  in children, 56–57
  survival value of, 58
Legal-process/"therapy" trauma, 346, 349–352, 365, 368–369
  definition of, 347
  effects of, long-term, 347
  symptoms of, 347–349
Legal-process trauma
  diagnosis of, 84
  symptoms seen in, 84
  treatment of, 366–368
Litigation, 135, *see also Legal-process trauma*
  interfering with child's treatment, 162
    cessation of litigation, 366–368
Lying, in children, 227–228, 247, 276–279, 358–359
  age of child and understanding, 276

Male(s), *see also Gender; Father(s)*
  hysteria in, 435–437
  mating patterns in, 2–7, 24–25, 51, 52
  pedophilia in, 37–50, 74–76
Malpractice suits, against validators, 340
Marriage, troubled history of, 47
Masochism,
  in mothers, 141–142
  in pedophile, 47–49
  sexual, 23–25
Masturbation, 27, 377
  as false indicator of sexual abuse, 290–293
  hysteria regarding, 42h
  as release for sexual excitation in children, 104–105, 138–139, 170, 492–497, 500

sexual problems in mothers, treatment recommendation for, 142–143
social attitudes toward, 104, 234–235
as survival of species mechanism, 52–53
McCarthy hearings, hysteria and, 425
Memory, in children, 213, 286
  age of child and, 215, 219, 220, 223, 225–226
  credibility, 224–225
  motivational element and, 224
  studies on, 214–227, 509
  time interval between event and recall, 224
  visual, as criterion assessing true from false sex abuse accusation, 354–355
Metaphor, use of in therapy, 459
Moralism, in pedophiles, 156–157
Mother(s), 37, 86, *see also Treatment of mother*
  as accuser in false sex-abuse accusation, 314
    therapist's work with, 371–372, 380–382
  compliance in, 127
  contamination of, in interview with child and validator, 274
  delusions in, 372, 380–381
  dependency problems in, 142
  hysteria in, 135
  masochism in, 141–142
  parental alienation syndrome and, preferred parent in, 239–240
  rage in, 135
  relationship with child, treatment to improve, 132–133, 136–140
  relationship with validator, 334, 381
  sexual problems of, 142–143

social isolation of, 142
Multiple personality disorder,
    rareness of, 67
Mutual storytelling technique, as
    minimally leading material, 261

Narcissism, 47–49, 150
Necrophilia, 27
Nightmares, 84, 288–289, 357
    hysteria as causing, 442
Nursery schools
    lawsuits in context of, 367
    sex-abuse accusations made in,
        xviii, 359–360
    disclosures of, 304
    hysteria in, 367, 420, 436
    misuse of child sexual abuse
        accommodation syndrome
        in, 301

Obsessions, 67, 68
Obsessive compulsive disorder, 35
    and embedment-in-the-brain-
        circuitry phenomenon, 67–70
Oedipal fantasies, 237
Orap, 443
Orgasm
    breastfeeding, and potential for, 16
    children's capacity for, 14–16, 41,
        102
    inability to achieve, 31
Overzealous evaluators, see also
    Validators
    education of, 316–324, 508–509
    programming children to believe
        they were sexually abused,
        xvii, 211–342
    belief that children "never lie",
        247–248
    incompetence in, 211–212, 247,
        248
    interviews with child and
        accusing parent only,
        313–314
    leading gestures, leading
        stimuli, and leading
        questions used by, 248–275
    utilization of child sexual abuse
        accommodation syndrome,
        295–302
    removal of child from therapy
        with, 365–366

Pain. See Trauma
Panic attack, 56
Paranoia
    in programmed child, 357, 360
    in validators, 334–335, 360
Paraphilias, 17–31, see also Sexual
    behavior, human
    definition of, 18–19,
    as disease, 35
    environmental vs. genetic
        components of, 30
    homosexuality as, 17–18, 31–37
Parent-child bond, disruption of,
    349–350
Parental alienation syndrome, 232
    psychodynamic factors creating,
        238–244
Parents, see also Father(s);
    Mother(s); Treatment of
    father(s); Treatment of
    mother(s)
    anger, of accusing, xviii
    anger, of sexually abused child
        toward, 114–117, 231–232,
        148
    as assistant therapists, 138, 452,
        465, 472, 483–484
    child's fear of alienating, 239–240
    child's primary psychological bond
        with one of, 239
    emotional neglect of child by,
        clinical vignette, 192–209
    as pedophiles, 43–44, 45,
        144–164, 349–350
    as programmers of false sex-abuse
        accusation in child, 232

Parents *(continued)*
  infectiousness of emotions, 233
  relationship with therapist, 89, 450–451
  as role models, 155, 329
  sexual problems of, 162–163
  therapy with, 114, 162–163
Parkinson's disease, 443
Partialism, 28
Passivity
  in male pedophile, 44–45
  in mothers, 140–142, 188
  in sexually abused child, 127
  in women, 155
Pedophile
  as family member, 43–44, 45, 51, 85, 91, 295–298
  as father, 85, 91, 144–164, 295–298, 349–350
  homosexuality in, 35, 158–160
  masochism in, 47–49
  medication for treating, 163–164
  moralism in, 156–157
  narcissism, 47–49, 150
  relationship with child, clinical example of ongoing possibility for, 176–192
Pedophilia, 22–23, 73–76, 150
  childhood seduction and onset of, 41–42
    identification with the aggressor, 43–44
  definition of, 22
  esteem enhancement in, 45
  emotional deprivation and, 46–47
  exploitation in, 53
  fixated, 40
  historical attitudes towards, 37–40
  in males
    causes of, 37–50
    embedment-in-the-brain circuitry phenomenon in, 74–76
  imprinting factor in, 40–42
  personalities of, 40
  as paraphilia, 35
  procreative purposes of, 23
  religious attitudes toward, 37–38, 39
Peer relationships,
  as indicator of psychopathology, 498
  as indicator treatment of sexual abuse necessary, 96
  passivity in sexually abused child's, 127
Personality traits
  of validators, 338–340
Phobias, as symptoms of sexual abuse, 115
Polymorphous perversity, 14, 150, 233–234, 237, 247, 436
Posttraumatic stress disorder, 344, 349
  definition of, 64–65
  and embedment-in-the-brain-circuitry phenomenon, 64–66
  as healing process, 95–96
  and legal process/"therapy" trauma, 347–348, 368–369
  sexual abuse, symptom of, 92–94, 120
Procreation, *see also Survival of species*
  and paraphilias, 13–14
Progesterone acetate, 163–164
Programming children to believe they were sexually abused, xvii, xxi, 211–342, *see also Leading gestures; Leading questions*
  ascertaining if child can differentiate truth from lies, 276–279
  psychodynamic factors operative in child, 227–245
  techniques used by overzealous

evaluators
- affect of child, termed inappropriate, 305–307
- belief in preposterous descriptions of abuse, 281–283, 417
- coercion, 304–305
- conditioning, 302–303
- "disclosures," use of term, 303–304, 312
- dissociation maneuver, 307–311
- "empowering" child, 350–351, 379–380
- jargon, use of, 312–313
- leading gestures, leading questions and leading stimuli, 247–275
- pathologizing normal behavior, 287–293
- rationalizing as credible the incredible, 283–285
- rehearsal, of sex-abuse material, 311–312
- repeating same question, 219, 280–281
- symptoms created in child via interviews, 294, 343–364
- utilizing other disorders as proof of sex abuse, 293–294
- yes/no questions, utilization of, 2 85–287

Projective tests, 268, 446–447, 448–449
Promiscuity, 6, 33, 52
Prostitution, 42
Prozac, for obsessive–compulsive disorder, 67
Pseudomaturity, in sexually abused child, 128–129
Psychosomatic complaints
- as symptoms of legal process/ "therapy" trauma, 349
- as symptoms of sexual abuse, 120

Questions, of children in interviews
- leading, 78, 216–217, 219, 248–251, 257–266, 353–355
- misleading, 221
- repeating, in programming of children, 219, 280–281, 455–456
- yes/no, 266, 285–287

Rage, 135, 340
Reaction formation, in parental alienation syndrome, 240–241
Recantation of sexual abuse by child, 133–135, 243–244, 295, 297–298, 300, 509
- clinical example of, 402–405, 407
Regression
- as symptom of hysteria trauma, 447
- as symptom of legal process/ "therapy" trauma, 348
- as symptom of sexual abuse, 105
Religion(s)
- moral erosion due to, 329–330
- pedophilia, attitudes toward, 37–38, 420
Repression, 310
- of anger in sexually abused child, 115
- sexual, 51, 434–436
Retraction. *See Recantation*
Role modeling
- of adults, 266–267
- of mothers, 140
- of parents, 155
Romance, sexual fantasies in, 71
Rorschach cards, example of minimally leading stimuli, 252

Sadism
- in false sex-abuse accusation, 232
- in validators, 333–334
Sadism, sexual, 23–25

Sadomasochism, 41
  in mother's relationships with men, 141–142
Salem witch trials, 244, 424–425
Satanic ritual abuse, 334
Scapegoatism
  in false accusation of sexual abuse, 333, 422
  in hysteria, expression of, 447
  as personality factor in validators, 338–339
  in programmed children, 359
School difficulties
  as diagnostic indicator of sexual abuse, 124–126
  depression and, 117
  as indication treatment necessary for sexual abuse, 96
  as symptom of hysteria in clinical example, 440–454
  as symptom of legal process/"therapy" trauma, 348
  as symptom of sexual abuse, 95
Seed-planting phenomenon, 286
Self-assertion
  impairment in male pedophile, 44–45
  impairment in mothers, 140–141
  impairment in sexually abused child, 127–128
Self-esteem, 352
  problems of
    in fathers, 149–151, 155–156
    in sexually abused child, 111–113, 352
Separation anxiety, in programmed child, 356
Sex abuse prevention programs, 247, 456, 478, 484
Sex abuse syndrome
  invalidity of, 84, 295
Sexual abuse, *see also* False sex-abuse accusations of children; Treatment of sexually abused children
  belated accusations of, by adult women, xix, 359–360
  clinical picture indicating, 90–94
  effects of, xvii
  hysteria surrounding, 419–438
  intrafamilial, 51, 85, 91, 295–298
  protections preventing, 97–98, 120–121, 349–350
  reporting of, 89, 441–442, 508
  symptoms seen in, 84, 92–95, 115
  definition of, 439
Sexual behavior, human, *see also Homosexuality*
  children's, normal, 103–104, 233–238
  theory of, 1–54
    genetic components to, 3–4, 12–31
    natural vs. unnatural, 1–2
    variety of, xxi, 17–31
Sexual excitation in children, 41, 84, 88–89, 102–105, 377
  clinical examples of, 164–168, 168–172
  guilt over, in sexually abused child, 108
  masturbation as release for, 104–105, 138–139, 170, 492–497, 500
  in programmed child, 348
Sexual inhibition
  clinical vignette of, 172–176
  as effect of childhood sexual abuse, 121
  as effect of programming children to make false sex-abuse accusation, 362, 440
  in validators, 333
Sexual masochism, 23–25
Sexual problems, 23–25, 30, 31,

121, 142–143, 162–163, 172–176, 361–362, 376–378, 440, 434, 436
Sexual repression, 51, 434–436
Sexual rivalry, in parental alienation syndrome, 243
Sexual sadism, 23–25, 30
Siblings, guilt of sexually abused child and, 109
Sleep disturbances
  as symptom of hysteria, 454
  as symptom of legal process/"therapy" trauma, 348
  as symptom of sexual abuse, 94
Society, values of
  and dominating behavior seen in, 155
  erosion of, 328–330
  mating patterns influenced by, 2–7, 24–25
  pedophilia and, 37–40, 42, 49–50, 150
  sexual abuse
    determination of by, 88, 111, 143, 420, 439
    punishments for, 121
  sexual behaviors judged by, 2, 14, 20, 108
  and sexual play among children, 103–104, 233–238
  sexual repression and, 51
Species survival. *See Survival of the species*
Storytelling Card Game, example of minimally leading stimuli, 252
Stress
  effect on children's memories, 215–216, 218–219
  interviews creating, with validators, 294
Substance abuse, treating in pedophile, 160–162
Suggestibility, in children, 213–227, 509

ages of and response to leading questions and gestures, 256–257
seed-planting and, 286
Suicidal thoughts
  in girl suffering with hysteria, 498–499
  in sexually abused child, 117, 118, 196–207, 209
Survival, of the species, 44, *see also DNA*
  homosexuality and, 32
  learning capacity and, 59
  masturbation and, 52–53
  mating patterns and, 2–7
  paraphilias and, 19–30
Symptoms
  of depression, 95, 115, 117–119
  of hysteria, 440–454, 447
  of legal-process/"therapy" trauma, 348, 349
  of legal process trauma, 84
  of programming in children, 294, 343–364
  of sexual abuse, 84, 92–95, 105, 115, 120, 349

Talking, Feeling, and Doing Game
  minimally leading material in, 261–262
  moderately leading material in, 262
  use of with programmed child, 375–376
  use of with sexually abused child, 208
Telephone scatalogia (obscene telephone call), 27
Television
  sexuality on, 454–455, 470–471, 491–492
  violence on, 329
Thematic Apperception Test (TAT), 248

Thematic Apperception Test *(continued)*
   example of nonleading stimuli, 251–252, 253
Therapists, *see also Overzealous evaluators; Validators*
   child's relationship with, 113–114
   credentials for evaluating and treating sexual abuse, 86–87
   incompetence in, 115, 245–247
   parents, as assistant, 136, 452, 465, 472, 483–484
   parents' relationship with, 89
   psychopathy in, 87–88
   sex of, 114
   training of, 195, 245–247, 508–509
   values of, 111, 157
Therapy, *see also Treatment of children programmed to make sex-abuse accusations; Treatment of fathers; Treatment of mothers*
   when contraindicated for child, 176, 368–370
   joint, with parents of sexually abused child, 162–163
   as educational process in programming child, 345
   embedment in the brain circuitry, for, 79–81
   family, 96–97, 130, 163, 173–176, 370, 384–417
Tics, in patient suffering with hysteria, 443
Transvestic fetishism, 25–26, 36, *see also Fetishism*
Trauma, 345
   blank-screen principle utilized by evaluators to uncover, 248
   in childhood sexual encounter, 43, 77–78, 81, 122–123
   in disruption of parent-child bond, 349–350
   dissociation due to, 308–310
   in hysteria, induction of, 447
   posttraumatic stress disorder and, 93, 95
   due to testifying in court, child's, 99–100
   in therapy with incompetent therapist, 343–346
   legal process/"therapy" and, 346, 347–352
Treatment of children programmed to make sex-abuse accusation, 343–345, 365–417, *see also Therapy*
   blank-screen approach, 370–371
   cognitive distortions, 371–374
   "empowerment" issue, 379–380
   hatred of father, correcting, 378, 382–383
   removal of child from therapy, 365–366
Treatment of children with sex-abuse hysteria, 439–505
   two categories of children in, 439–440
Treatment of father(s), 144–164, *see also Therapy*
   admission/denial of abuse by, 144–146
   controlling tendencies in, 154–156
   group therapy for, 146–147, 156
   guilt, 151–153, 157
   homosexuality in, 158–160
   impulsivity in, 157–158
   isolation, feelings of, 153–154
   joint interviews with child, 148
   moralism in, 156–157
   psychopathy and prognosis for treatment in, 152–153
   relationship with child, improving, 130–132, 147–149
   self-esteem enhancement, 149–151, 155–156

substance abuse, 160–162
Treatment of mother(s), 135–143,
    see also Therapy
  dependency problems, 142
  group therapy for, 136
  hysteria in, 135
  relationship with child, improving,
    132–133, 136–140
  sexual problems, 142–143
Treatment of sexually abused
    children, xxi, 83–210, *see also*
    Therapy
  clinical examples of, 164–168,
    168–172, 172–176, 176–192,
    192–209
  court-ordered, 85
  diagnosis confirmed before, xxi,
    83, 84
  drawing used in, 194–209
  evaluations of
    by previous examiners, 84
  protection of from further abuse,
    120–121, 147
  psychotherapeutic approaches to
    anger problems, 114–117, 148
    betrayal, feelings of, 112, 117,
      137
    compliance, pathological,
      126–128
    confusion, 122–124
    depression, 117–119
    fears, 119–121, 129, 134, 148
    guilt, 106–111, 129, 134
    hypersexualization, 102–105,
      138–139, 164–168,
      168–172, 192–193
    pseudomaturity, 128–129,
      139–140
    regression, 105
    relationship with father,
      130–132, 147–149
    relationship with mother,
      132–133, 136–140

school difficulties, 124–126
self-esteem problems, 111–113
trust, loss of, 113–114
recantation of abuse in, 133–135,
  243–244
technical aspects of, 100–101
Truth
  as code-term for sex abuse,
    279–280, 375
  torture used historically to elicit,
    279

Urophilia, 29–30

Vaginismus, 31
Validators, 326–328, 335–340
  education of, 324–326, 508–509
  history of sexual abuse in,
    330–333
  hysteria in, xix
  incompetence of, 212, 246–247
  paranoia in, 334–335, 360
  programming children to believe
    they were sexually abused,
    xvii, 133, 272–275, 276–316
  sexual inhibitions in, 333
Vengeance
  in accusing parents, xviii
Vibrating-tuning-fork principle, 233
Vibrators, 21, 142–143
Victimization, creating sense of in
    programmed children, 362–364
Videotapes
  affect of child seen in, 307
  depicting child suffering from
    hysteria, 457
  leading gestures of examiners
    revealed by, 255, 272–273,
    275
  use of in family therapy, 173–175,
    404–405, 407
  use of in treating sexually abused
    children, 101

Violence, 329
Voyeurism, 26–27

Withdrawal, as symptom of sexual abuse, 93–94, 349

Yes/No questions, as maximally leading in child interview, 266, 285–287

Zoophilia, 28